DISCOVERING LEVINAS

Emmanuel Levinas is well known to students of twentieth-century continental philosophy, especially French philosophy. But he is largely unknown within the circles
of Anglo-American philosophy. In *Discovering Levinas*, Michael L. Morgan shows
how this thinker faces in novel and provocative ways central philosophical problems of twentieth-century philosophy and religious thought. He tackles this task by
placing Levinas in conversation with philosophers such as Donald Davidson, Stanley Cavell, John McDowell, Onora O'Neill, Charles Taylor, and Cora Diamond.
He also seeks to understand Levinas within philosophical, religious, and political developments in the history of twentieth-century intellectual culture. Morgan
demystifies Levinas by examining in illuminating ways his unfamiliar and surprising
vocabulary, interpreting texts with an eye to clarity, and arguing that Levinas can be
understood as a philosopher of the everyday. Morgan also shows that Levinas's ethics
is not morally and politically irrelevant nor is it excessively narrow and demanding in unacceptable ways. Neither glib dismissal nor fawning acceptance, this book
provides a sympathetic reading that can form a foundation for a responsible critique.

Michael L. Morgan has been a professor at Indiana University for 31 years and,
in 2004, was named a Chancellor's Professor. He has published articles in a
variety of journals, edited several collections, and authored four books, most
recently *Interim Judaism* (2001). He is the coeditor of *The Cambridge Companion
to Modern Jewish Philosophy*.

Discovering Levinas

MICHAEL L. MORGAN

Indiana University

CAMBRIDGE UNIVERSITY PRESS
Cambridge, New York, Melbourne, Madrid, Cape Town, Singapore,
São Paulo, Delhi, Dubai, Tokyo, Mexico City

Cambridge University Press
32 Avenue of the Americas, New York, NY 10013-2473, USA

www.cambridge.org
Information on this title: www.cambridge.org/9780521759687

First published 2007
First paperback edition 2009
Reprinted 2009

A catalog record for this publication is available from the British Library

Library of Congress Cataloging in Publication data

Morgan, Michael L., 1944–
Discovering Levinas / Michael L. Morgan.
p.   cm.
Includes bibliographical references and index.
ISBN-13: 978-0-521-87259-1 (hardback)
ISBN-10: 0-521-87259-6 (hardback)
1. Levinas, Emmanuel.   I. Title.
B2430.L484M67   2007
194 – dc22   2006030993

ISBN 978-0-521-87259-1 Hardback
ISBN 978-0-521-75968-7 Paperback

In Memory of
Emil Ludwig Fackenheim
(1916–2003)

Contents

Preface		*page* xi
Acknowledgments		xix
1	Auschwitz, Politics, and the Twentieth Century	1
	Levinas on Grossman's Life and Fate	1
	Auschwitz and Levinas's Thought	13
	Political Reflections	20
	Zionism, Politics, and Messianism	28
	Responsibility and Forgiveness	32
2	Phenomenology and Transcendental Philosophy	39
	A Preliminary Sketch	39
	Interpreting Levinas's Approach	44
	Transcendental Philosophy	50
	An Objection	56
3	The Ethical Content of the Face-to-Face	61
	The Social, the Face, and the Ethical	62
	The Call of the Face	68
	The Face-to-Face and Acknowledgment	71
	Later Thoughts on Ethics and the Face	80
4	Philosophy, Totality, and the Everyday	85
	Philosophy and the Everyday	85
	Totality and the Infinite	88
	Ethics Beyond Totality	94
	Levinas and Rosenzweig	100
	Totality, Infinity, and Beyond	104

5 Meaning, Culture, and Language   115
   Meaning, Relativism, and the Ethical   115
   Meaning and Language   124
   Ethics and Communication: The Saying and the Said   138

6 Subjectivity and the Self   143
   Modernity and the Self   144
   The Early Stage   149
   Responsibility and Passivity   155
   The Self and Contemporary Philosophy   160
   Levinas and Davidson   163
   Levinas and McDowell   167
   Levinas and Taylor   169

7 God and Philosophy   174
   God and the Philosophical Tradition   175
   Early Works   177
   Later Stage: The Trace and Illeity   183
   Philosophy, God, and Theology   198
   God, Ethics, and Contemporary Philosophy   203

8 Time, Messianism, and Diachrony   208
   Thinking about Time   208
   Early Reflections on Time   210
   Rosenzweig and Levinas on Eschatology   213
   Diachrony and Responsibility   219

9 Ethical Realism and Contemporary Moral Philosophy   228
   Ethics and the Everyday   228
   O'Neill's Ethics and Practical Reason   236
   Levinas and O'Neill   242
   McDowell's Naturalism of Second Nature   247
   Korsgaard and the Perception of Reasons   254
   Levinas's Universalism and Pluralism   259
   Taylor's Ethical Pluralism   263
   What Kind of Moral Thinker Is Levinas?   268
   Cavell's Emersonian Perfectionism   273
   Is Levinas a Moral Perfectionist?   277
   Levinas on Ethics and Politics   283
   Levinas's Single-Mindedness   289

10 Beyond Language and Expressibility   300
   Levinas's Language   301

Levinas and Skepticism: Time and Absolute Diachrony   305
Skepticism in Otherwise Than Being   310
Two Interpretations of Levinas and Skepticism   313
Derrida's Challenge   320
Contemporary Philosophy and the Limits of Thought and Language   323
Frege, Wittgenstein, and Nonsense   328
Ethics and the Limits of Language   332

11 Judaism, Ethics, and Religion   336
Athens and Jerusalem   338
An Austere Humanism   340
Ethics and Prayer   347
The Holocaust and the End of Theodicy   353
Responding to Suffering   366
Revelation in Judaism   370
Ritual and the Law   376
Ethics and Education   379
Reading Jewish Texts   384
Translating the Bible and the Talmud   387
Interpreting Levinas on Interpretation   390
Eschatology, Ethics, and Politics   395
Levinas's Zionism   401
Ethical Messianism   412

Conclusion: Levinas and the Primacy of the Ethical – Kant,
Kierkegaard, and Derrida   415

Appendix: Facing Reasons   421
The Face as a Reason to Act   421
Nagel on Agent-Neutral Reasons   424
Korsgaard's Critique of Nagel   434
Darwall and Intersubjective Value   446
Placing Levinas   448
Levinas and Contemporary Ethics   451
Some Concrete Cases   456
Conclusion   464

Bibliography   467
Index   477

Preface

About six years ago, I began to study Emmanuel Levinas's works seriously. I had tried several times before to read *Totality and Infinity*, unsuccessfully. The work seemed impenetrable, and each time I set out I managed only a few pages before I put the book aside. But in 2000, after Paul Franks and I had finished our translations and editorial work on *Franz Rosenzweig: Philosophical and Theological Writings* and we had agreed to teach a course on Rosenzweig and Levinas, I began to immerse myself in Levinas's works and the secondary literature on him. Paul then left Bloomington to take a position at Notre Dame, and I was scheduled to teach the course on my own. It was quite an experience, an enormous challenge but an exciting one. I found that the students, undergraduates and graduates alike, found something about Levinas gripping, and as I struggled to make sense of him for myself and for them, I also fell under his spell. This book is one outcome of that attempt to explore and decipher Levinas.

I mention these events in part to clarify something about the book. As I have worked on it, I have had several goals in mind, but one persisting reason for writing the book is, in all honesty, to find a way to make clear to myself what Levinas is saying and why it is important. The fact that this book is my extended attempt to say what Levinas means has had a significant effect, I believe, on how it is written. As I study and think about him, my questions about his thinking and his writings continue to increase exponentially, as one might expect, but the ones I have selected to examine and answer here, and how I set out to do so, were very much determined by my own interests, my background as a philosopher, and my personal angle of vision. I have tried to consider many others as the book's audience and to take their needs into consideration, but to a great degree I always remain the book's first reader.

I believe that the great philosophical question of the twentieth century for our culture – perhaps for all cultures – concerns the objectivity of values, in particular moral values. In this respect, the century began in the nineteenth century, at least by the time of Nietzsche, the rise of neo-Kantianism, and the flourishing of high modernism, and it is still with us. Eric Hobsbawm once called the twentieth century the short century, beginning in 1914 and ending in 1989, with the fall of the Soviet Union. But to me the century is a long one, for its central problem emerged before 1900 with the flourishing of the great urban cities of Europe and the crises this phenomenon brought with it, and, as I have said, the problem has not been solved or resolved. And, as one might expect, in many ways the history of Western philosophy during the past century has been the history of attempts to come to grips with this problem – with the threats of nihilism, relativism, and skepticism and the suspicion that groundlessness was the sin of naturalism and the true legacy of the Enlightenment.[1]

This great question and the crisis that has been associated with it crystallized in the Nazi genocide, the death camps, and the events that encircled them, horrific satellites of a totally dark spectacle: World War I, Stalinism, Hiroshima, Cambodia, Bosnia, and Rwanda. It was a century, and it is now a time of cruelty and atrocity beyond our worst nightmares, and there is every reason to see these events as the historical and political expressions of this crisis of objectivity. Facing up to this problem and to these events is a challenge that none of us, philosophers included, can escape. What can be done is a question that has its own abstract and global dimension, but its declension begins with each one of us: What can I do? And for a philosopher, it begins with How do I understand the human condition, and how do I live?[2]

Levinas, once the point and purpose of his thinking began to disclose themselves to me, seemed to speak directly and urgently, dare I say passionately, to these issues. His intellectual world is one that I have some familiarity with, the world of Bergson, Husserl, Heidegger, Blanchot, Derrida, and Marcel. Others whom he discusses and responds to – Rosenzweig and Buber, for example – I have lived with for years. But, as I came to believe, Levinas's thinking has an importance beyond these confines. He is part of a larger conversation. Reading Levinas, I brought with me the tradition of Anglo-American philosophy, as well as my own understanding of the history of Western philosophy. Thinking about Levinas, I also thought about Wittgenstein and readers of him, especially Stanley Cavell, and other philosophers as well: Hilary Putnam, Alasdair MacIntyre, Charles Taylor, and John McDowell. Most – indeed, virtually all – of the secondary literature on Levinas – and it is vast – focuses on the continental partners

---

[1] Alasdair MacIntyre tells this story, in his own way, in *After Virtue*. A classic formulation can be found in Elizabeth Anscombe, "Modern Moral Philosophy." (See Chapter 7, footnote 90 in this book.)

[2] Something like these questions, I believe, are the ones Stanley Cavell associates with "moral or Emersonian perfectionism" and his special brand of romanticism.

in his conversation, and I have not completely neglected them. But I found it important and revealing to bring these other partners to the table, so to speak.

This feature of my own reading has had a special impact on the present book. If I have written it to become clear myself about what Levinas wrote and thought, I also have written it to introduce others to the Levinas I have come to understand. And this is a Levinas who talks with Cavell, Putnam, Taylor, and McDowell, as well as Heidegger and Derrida. At one point in time, this goal of placing Levinas on the map of Anglo-American philosophy seemed paramount to me. Now I realize that it was always important but subsidiary. I realize that if I really wanted to carry out such a task, there might be other ways to do it, ones that pay more systematic and detailed attention to the venue of Anglo-American philosophy and to the categories of work in that territory. In part, that is not my style. I could not simply lay out, in survey fashion, various options, say, in meta-ethics – moral realism, moral particularism, noncognitivism, projectivism, and so forth – and then go about asking how well Levinas fits one category or the other. If that seems like an intriguing enterprise, I invite others to carry it out. Personally, I would find it as difficult to do that and perhaps as unprofitable for me as I would to carry out such a regimented set of comparisons for someone like Cavell.

One of the book's aims, then, is to understand Levinas and his writings by reading those writings carefully, and what this means is that the book contains frequent quotations from those writings with interpretations of them in terms that I hope the Anglo-American reader can grasp. Extensive quotation and discussion of Levinas's own words have seemed necessary; only in this way can the reader actually experience how Levinas speaks and writes, his vocabulary and syntax, his style and tonality. At the same time, this exegetical dimension of the book will, I hope, facilitate the reader's ability to go on and read Levinas on his or her own. For Anglo-American readers, his writings will initially appear to be utterly opaque, almost nonsensical. But my hope is that the persistent reader can overcome these obstacles and find, as I have, something valuable on the other side.

At various moments, moreover, I draw others into the conversation about Levinas's works and the themes he addresses – figures like Franz Rosenzweig, Walter Benjamin, and Emil Fackenheim, on the one hand, and like Stanley Cavell, Donald Davidson, Charles Taylor, John McDowell, Onora O'Neill, and Christine Korsgaard, on the other. Indirectly, in this way I try to place Levinas on several maps at once. One map is that of twentieth-century Anglo-American philosophy – in particular, moral theory. Another is a map of twentieth-century Jewish philosophy, and a third is twentieth-century religious thought. I do all of this in the course of addressing various themes that I think are central to understanding Levinas and that, at the same time, should be of interest to

contemporary philosophers and religious thinkers. Hence, the book is not a
mechanical comparison of Levinas with twentieth-century Anglo-American
philosophy or indeed with any other kind of thinking; it is rather an exploration
of various themes in the course of which Levinas is put into conversation with
others dealing with similar, albeit not identical, issues.

All of this says something about the structure and style of the book, but
it leaves out what is perhaps its central feature. Earlier I said that introducing
Levinas to an Anglo-American philosophical audience has become a secondary
goal for me. The primary one has been to present a way of reading and understanding Levinas that I find attractive and one that places him in excellent
company indeed. There is, I believe, a remarkable affinity between Levinas
and various other philosophers, most notably Stanley Cavell, Charles Taylor,
and John McDowell. All are, to one degree or another, part of the Hegelian and
Heideggerian legacy, a legacy also shared by a host of continental philosophers
and religious thinkers. In Cavell's terms, these are philosophers of the ordinary,
of the lived world of everyday experience, with all its nuances and subtleties,
and yet they focus, too, on the ethical demands that are raised for us as we
live in the world with other people. No one, however, addresses the ethical
dimension of this lived experience as dramatically and urgently as Levinas. No
one locates the original venue of moral normativity, as it were, in the same way
and with the same dedication. No one characterizes the substance of that moral
demandedness so specifically and relates it so fundamentally to the very fact of
human social existence. At least, that is what I try to show. But to do so, I must
show how, for Levinas, what he calls the encounter with the face of the other
person is not a rare episode. Rather, it occurs as a regular, if occluded and compromised, dimension in all of our social lives. It carries with it the purity of a
kind of moral standard, but at the same time it pervades our ordinary daily lives.
The responsibility that we have and that we are, in a sense, eludes us and yet
claims us. For Levinas, the social, the political, and the ethical occur together.
To show this and what it means, as Levinas sees it, are the central tasks of this
book.

The title of this book is *Discovering Levinas*. The word "discover" suggests
an initial encounter or an introduction, and I do think of the book as a way of
introducing Levinas to many who have never read him or who have tried, as
I did, and found him wholly mystifying. I do not think that the book makes
no claims on its readers, but I *do* think of it as introductory in the sense of an
initial encounter. The word "discover" also suggests an act of uncovering or
disclosing something that has been hidden and bringing it to view.[3] I believe

---

[3] This is an act of excavation, as Kevin Houser suggested to me.

that Levinas takes the encounter with the face of the other person, the face-to-face, to be a dimension of all of our social existence that is largely hidden from view and that needs to be uncovered or disclosed. In this sense, discovery is important to Levinas, although it is not a word he himself uses. The book, then, is about furthering Levinas's project by continuing the process of disclosing the dimension of ordinary life on which Levinas focuses, and in so doing it is also about uncovering or disclosing Levinas's thinking, which to a large extent has been hidden for most readers.

Given the analytical scruples of Anglo-American philosophy, it may seem that I do not carry out this project, a kind of translation into other terms, with sufficient detail or nuance. I do not, for example, engage in critical analysis of the analytic philosophers I introduce, and my treatment of Levinas, while it raises a great number of serious problems with his views and his language, is invested in arriving at the most persuasive interpretation of him that I can give. My hope is that the outcome should leave us with a reading of Levinas worth taking seriously and also worth criticizing, but to some it may look highly apologetic. Hence, I agree that others might want to pursue, in much greater detail, many avenues in reading Levinas in a highly analytical spirit. For myself, I will be happy if I have at least whetted their appetites and begun the process, by showing what Levinas is doing and what he means and by making plausible his kinship with various important Anglo-American philosophers and their work.

If there is something concrete and gripping about Levinas's primary insight into the ethical character of human social existence, his writing is highly abstract and arcane. It is filled with neologisms and formulations that have a strange ring in our ears. I feel that one needs to see the concreteness of his thinking, the way that it speaks to our lives. In order to show this and to raise some important questions at the same time, I have chosen to begin the book – as I have begun my courses and my teaching – by introducing Levinas as a reader, specifically as a reader of a fascinating realistic novel about the Battle of Stalingrad. That novel is *Life and Fate*, and in Chapter 1 I discuss the novel and its author, Vasily Grossman, as well as Levinas's infatuation with the book. I then expand the domain of his words by saying something about Levinas's critical comments on the twentieth century as a century of suffering and atrocity. One of the by-products of such a beginning is that we are given a very powerful example of a face-to-face encounter and the response to it, one that we can refer to and consider more carefully later in the book. Another by-product is that Levinas's role as a social and political critic raises early on some important questions about the relationship between ethics or religion, as he calls it, and the domain of moral decision making and political life.

Following the introductory chapter, I try to clarify how one might read Levinas – in particular, the way in which he is and yet is not a phenomenologist. In

the end, I argue that there is in him an important strain of transcendental philosophy. I then turn to the content of Levinas's central claim about the ethical
character of social existence. From there, I discuss a variety of central themes:
the notions of totality and infinity; the relation between various cultures and the
meaning of the ethical; the nature of subjectivity and the self; Levinas's understanding of God; his account of time and history; the kind of ethical understanding Levinas provides when considered alongside certain recent examples
of Anglo-American moral philosophy; the role of skepticism for Levinas and
the sense in which the encounter with the other person occurs beyond the
limits of thought and language; and his understanding of Judaism and its role in
his account of Western culture and philosophy. Finally, in an appendix, I place
Levinas within recent discussions of objectivity, or agent-neutral reasons, in part
to consider, if indirectly, how his understanding of our infinite responsibility
might be distinguished from utilitarianism and in part to clarify the status of his
thinking as a kind of metaphysical foundation for normative moral theory.

It may be that I raise more questions about Levinas than I answer and furthermore that my reading of him raises more questions still. If so, that is all to the
good. If I have succeeded, the reader of this book might look in two directions.
In one direction, the book may intrigue the reader to investigate further a rich
philosophical legacy that is worth further exploration. In another, if the book
is at all right about Levinas, it might lead in another direction: to a recognition
about our responsibilities to others, especially to those suffering and in need,
and then to acts of benevolence in their behalf.

In conclusion, let me repeat two caveats. The first is that some readers may
find me too uncritical of Levinas. The book may appear to defend him too
often and too firmly. As a response to such a concern, I would say two things.
One is that I do raise questions about Levinas's views and claims throughout the book, many of which are major cruxes in any attempt to understand
his views and his work. The book is not simply an uncritical presentation of
what Levinas says; in order to become as clear as we can about what Levinas
means, I use a strategy of challenging what he means and seeking to clarify
his writings to the best of my understanding and ability. But this procedure
may lead some to think that I regularly conclude by agreeing with Levinas,
and this leads to my second response. At some point, I do let things stand,
so to speak – that is, I stop interrogating Levinas and come to places where I
think we have understood what he means and what his reasons are for holding
the views that he does. In general, I do not then register more compelling
reasons to reject his views or find fault with them. In short, more often than
not I do not end on a critical note. This strategy, however, is not to say that
his views are unassailable or that I fully agree with all of them. It is a strategy to bring us to a point where we have understood him sufficiently and

can then continue the process of philosophical conversation and dialogue with his works and his ideas on a sure footing. To arrive at that point for the reader and for myself is one of the goals of this book.

My second caveat concerns the issue of Levinas's philosophical development. This subject has received extensive treatment by commentators and critics of Levinas.[4] Usually, it is framed as a question about his two major books, *Totality and Infinity* and *Otherwise Than Being*, and whether the latter involves a serious modification or even rejection of views stated in the earlier book. Often, too, the question about Levinas's development from the one book to the other invokes the name of Jacques Derrida and asks whether the latter book is a direct response to Derrida's criticisms of Levinas in his famous review of 1963, "Violence and Metaphysics." Sooner or later, virtually everyone writing about Levinas seems to address this cluster of issues. In this book, however, I do not address them directly. Issues about philosophical change and development in an author's corpus ought to be handled with the greatest care and delicacy. I have always found it unlikely that a philosopher – so many great figures come to mind, from Plato and Aristotle to Leibniz, Kant, and Hegel – who wrote a great deal over a period of several decades would never have modified his or her views, altered terminology, come to new commitments, or arrived at new perspectives. My basic assumption about Levinas is a very conservative one. His thinking in the late 1940s and 1950s crystallized in *Totality and Infinity*. As he continued to think about the issues he had raised and his central concepts and terminology – surely, in part, under the influence of Derrida's review – he rethought, revised, and reoriented his thinking, looking at some issues from new perspectives and seeing some issues for the first time and others in different ways from which he had before. But basically, I see this as philosophical growth and development and not as a fundamental reorientation or rejection of earlier views. Hence, there is no chapter in this book about this issue; when a change occurs that I think is important to note, I try to do so and explain what it means and why it occurred. But such attention is paid as we go along, in the context of dealing with a particular theme or idea, and it does not usually lead to extended discussion.

I have one piece of advice about reading the book. I recommend reading Chapters 1–4 consecutively. They indicate why Levinas is important and

---

[4] See John Drabinski, *Sensibility and Singularity*; Robert Bernasconi and Simon Critchley (eds.), *Re-Reading Levinas*; Simon Critchley, *The Ethics of Deconstruction*. The literature on the early and late Levinas is extensive. The issue is also framed as a question about Levinas's use of the phenomenological method and whether that method, if it is in fact used in any strict sense in the earlier work, is also employed in the later book, *Otherwise Than Being*, and thereafter in Levinas's career.

establish the foundations of his views. Even though the remainder of the book is organized in a way that I think is helpful, readers might pick and choose among the remaining chapters, depending upon their interests. For example, Chapter 9 and the Appendix deal with moral philosophy; Chapters 5 and 10 with language; and Chapters 7, 8, and 11 with God, religion, and Judaism.

Acknowledgments

This book owes a great deal to many colleagues and friends. When I decided to invest myself totally in the project of understanding Levinas, I turned to Richard Cohen, who gave me helpful advice. Among other things, it was Richard who recommended that I read Theodore de Boer's excellent essays on Levinas. Bob Gibbs also responded to several queries and offered sage counsel. I then met, first through my reading, then via e-mail, and finally in person, Robert Bernasconi. Robert's generosity has been extraordinary. In response to my requests, he sent copies of essays printed in not easily accessible venues; as a commentator on Levinas, he is without peer. I sometimes think that nothing I could say that is right about Levinas has not already been said and understood by Robert, with great depth and profundity.

Three years ago, Paul Franks, David Finkelstein, and I organized a conference at Indiana University on Levinas and Wittgenstein. The dozen or so participants had an exciting time together. It was an effort to overcome – or better, to ignore – the boundary so often honored between analytic and continental philosophy. My own study of Levinas and reflections about philosophy itself have been enriched by conversations with several who were present – among them Jeff Kosky, Simon Glendenning, David Cerbone, and Gary Gutting – and by reading and discussion with other friends, especially Jim Conant, John McDowell, Chuck Taylor, and Fred Beiser. For several years, Joshua Shaw and I met almost weekly to read Levinas; it is sometimes hard for me to draw the line between my own ideas about issues in Levinas and Joshua's. I also thank Joshua for reading the entire manuscript and making numerous valuable suggestions. On many occasions over the years, my friend Mark Goldman, a physician with a passion for literature and philosophy, has been a great conversation partner on Fackenheim, Rosenzweig, Levinas, and others. He even took on the challenge of reading Cavell, when I touted his importance. For many years, Mira Wasserman and I have met weekly to pore over Levinas's Talmudic lessons and his Jewish essays; her growing involvement with Levinas and his writings has been a joy to behold, and her understanding of Bible, Talmud, and Talmudic commentaries have made her a wonderful partner in study. I have benefited as well from having taught Levinas several times to undergraduates, graduate students, and nonprofessional audiences. Each time, I was surprised and delighted by the intense engagement of so many of these students, whose expressions of puzzlement forced me again and again to find creative ways to clarify Levinas's thinking and whose probing criticisms challenged me to defend it insofar as that was possible. I especially thank Nick Alford for preparing the index.

Philosophically and personally, during the past decade I owe most to three people. Simon Critchley has been a good friend and a wonderful supporter. His philosophical writing on Levinas, Beckett, romanticism, and so much more exemplifies what is best about the philosophical life. During the past few years, since his move to the New School, we have met often in New York City for conversations that always send me off with new insights and nagging questions. Paul Franks and I have spent countless hours together working on Rosenzweig, talking about German Idealism, Jewish philosophy, Cavell, and much else. No one defies the boundary I spoke of – between so-called analytic and continental philosophy – more effectively than Paul, with a philosophical depth and a humanity that are very special indeed. Philosophically, I owe as much to David Finkelstein as to anyone else. While he was my colleague at Indiana, we met weekly for years, talking about his work and mine, sharing virtually everything that we thought about. Our friendship is one of the special joys of my life.

I have been, for my entire career, a historian of philosophy and a Jewish philosopher. I never tried to keep separate these two aspects of myself. Levinas was not a historian of philosophy but rather a philosopher, and he would not, I think, have thought of himself as a Jewish philosopher – he may not even have thought that there is such a thing. But my teacher and my dearest friend, Emil Fackenheim, who passed away while I was writing this book, did think that there was Jewish philosophy, and in his unique way he invested his life and his soul in forging its character with a seriousness of purpose and depth of humanity that are rare. His works testify to this conviction everywhere and to the commitment to go on with our lives in the shadow of a darkness without equal. I never think about Levinas without also thinking about Emil; indeed, dare I say, I never think about anything without thinking about Emil.

Discovering Levinas has meant for me appreciating more fully not only the burdens we all share but also the gifts we receive. My gifts are Debbie, Adam, Sara, Marc, and, most of all, Aud, who more than anyone has shared with me the sorrows and joys that have filled these past few years. I think that she is happy that this book is now completed but happier still, as we both are, with all the good things we enjoy with our daughters and their families. Among those good things are Gabrielle and Sasha, who were thoughtful enough to wait to be born until I was able to make the final revisions on this book.

I

Auschwitz, Politics, and the Twentieth Century

In "Signature," the last piece in *Difficult Freedom*, Emmanuel Levinas (1906–1995) tells us that the list of items in the first paragraph, his biography, "is dominated by the presentiment and the memory of the Nazi horror."[1] Hitler, Auschwitz, and Nazi fascism meant a great deal to Levinas, to his life, of course, to his philosophical thinking, and to his thinking about Judaism. Yet at times, Levinas talks about Nazism – Auschwitz in particular – as part of or characteristic of a larger phenomenon, one that encompasses the horrors of the twentieth century overall – before, during, and after the Holocaust. In this chapter, I will first set out and discuss what Levinas says about this larger phenomenon and later focus on the Holocaust in particular.

Levinas's ethical and philosophical views provide him with a perspective on human living and the everyday world that expresses itself often in his occasional writings, interviews, and more popular essays. A particular focus of this perspective is Auschwitz and twentieth-century life. We have not looked yet at his ethics and philosophy, but we can consider its expression, one of its manifestations, even prior to examining its details, and that is what I will do here, without any preparation or theorizing. What does Levinas say about life in the twentieth century, especially about the "decline of the West" and the crisis of modernity?

LEVINAS ON GROSSMAN'S *LIFE AND FATE*

During the last 15 years of his life, Levinas frequently and passionately cited one work as emblematic of this crisis and his own special response to it. He referred to it at least twice in print, in 1984 and 1986, and also in 1984 in one of his

---

[1] Levinas, *Difficult Freedom* (1963, 1976), 291; cf. Jill Robbins (ed.), *Is It Righteous to Be?*, 39.

annual Talmudic lessons.[2] In interviews in the 1980s, however, he was drawn to it numerous times, almost compulsively. The work is Vasily Grossman's *Life and Fate*, a massive realistic novel about Hitler and Nazism, Stalinism, and the Battle of Stalingrad, but more generally about the crisis of European culture and life. Trained as a mathematician and engineer, Grossman began writing in his twenties and by 1934 had written his first novel and stories that caught the attention of Maxim Gorky. During World War II, while Levinas was in a prisoner-of-war camp, Grossman was a journalist for a Soviet newspaper. He was the first to expose the atrocities of the Nazi death camp at Treblinka. Later, he collaborated in the compilation of *The Black Book*, a collection of documents related to the Nazi death camps.[3] Grossman's writing is realistic, direct, and powerful, and while it has a homiletic and didactic quality at times, it is riveting overall. It is no wonder that Levinas was so impressed by Grossman's magnum opus.

Life and Fate was written in the 1950s, when Grossman was realizing a good deal of public success, albeit in the wake of postwar attacks on him and a formal letter of repentance. Completed in 1960, the novel was promptly rejected for publication as anti-Soviet, and the manuscript was confiscated by the KGB.[4] Depressed and upset, Grossman died of cancer in 1964.[5] *Life and Fate* was eventually published in Russian by a small Swiss press and then translated into French, and German, and finally English in 1987.[6] I imagine that Levinas, who read it in Russian, did so in 1983 or 1984, when he cites it extensively at the end of his Talmudic lesson "Beyond Memory." It begins to appear in his interviews about 1985–86.[7]

The novel is about large events and tiny ones and about people, their sufferings, thoughts, acts, hopes, and anguish. The large event is the German siege of Stalingrad in the fall and winter of 1942–43 and the Soviet victory over Hitler's forces.[8] Robert Chandler, who translated the work into English, captures the themes of this large event nicely:

---

[2] See Levinas, "The Bible and the Greeks" in *In the Time of the Nations*, 135, originally in *Cosmopolitique* 4 (Feb. 1986); "Beyond Memory" in *In the Time of the Nations*, 88–91. This discussion of Tractate *Berachoth* 12b–13a of the Talmud, originally delivered in December 1984, was first published in 1986. See also Levinas, "Peace and Proximity," *Alterity and Transcendence*, 140.

[3] See Ilya Ehrenburg and Vasily Grossman, *The Complete Black Book of Russian Jewry* (originally completed in 1946; published in Vilnius in 1993; translated and edited by David Patterson in 2002).

[4] John Garrard and Carol Garrard, *The Bones of Berdichev*, 260–63.

[5] Garrard and Garrard, *The Bones of Berdichev*, 263–99.

[6] Garrard and Garrard, *The Bones of Berdichev*, 322–23, and Vasily Grossman, *Life and Fate*, 7–11.

[7] *Is It Righteous to Be?*, 79, 80–81, 89–90.

[8] See Garrard and Garrard, *The Bones of Berdichev*, 236–44.

Like *War and Peace*, *Life and Fate* contains many of [Grossman's] own reflections on history and philosophy.... No other writer has so convincingly established the identity of Nazism and Soviet Communism....

The real battle portrayed in the novel is not the clash between the Third Reich and Stalin's Russia, but the clash between Freedom and Totalitarianism. At Stalingrad the Russian people believed they were fighting against Totalitarianism in the name of Freedom.... Grossman movingly describes the development of a genuine spirit of camaraderie and egalitarianism among the defenders of Stalingrad; he also shows how this spirit was stamped out by Party functionaries who saw it as a greater danger than the Germans themselves.[9]

But this is the grand scheme. In addition, the book contains a smaller, more local and particular one. The novel is also about the very precise decisions, challenges, anxieties, and reflections of its actors and actresses, painted in rich, personal touches by a master observer of humanity. Chandler sees this dimension of *Life and Fate* just as clearly:

'The clash between Freedom and Totalitarianism', however, is too grand and abstract a phrase.... The battle Grossman portrays is the battle we must fight each day in order to preserve our humanity, the battle against the power of ideology, against the power of the state, against all the forces that combine to destroy the possibility of kindness and compassion between individuals.... The true victors [in this battle] ... [are all those] whose actions, however historically insignificant, are motivated by the spirit of senseless, irrational kindness. It is these spontaneous, dangerous acts of kindness that Grossman sees as the truest expression of human freedom.[10]

With grand sweep and extraordinary depth and detail, Grossman "has portrayed the life, not of a few individuals, but of an entire age."[11] Here is realism and scope, scrupulously portrayed individuals against the panorama of history, a throwback to the nineteenth century, a novel untouched by the Modernist sensibility of James Joyce, Virginia Woolf, or Robert Musil, a tapestry of lives, psychology, and events as detailed and concrete as it is broad and expansive.

Setting aside personal associations, we can see at a glance what Grossman's novel might have meant to Levinas. It is, in part, about totalitarianism and hence about institutions that seek to surround and dominate everything and everyone. It is also about very concrete events, actions, relationships, and experiences that seem to escape the totality, to grasp what transcends it and yet what enters it as if from the outside – acts of "senseless kindness." *Life and Fate*, moreover, exposes something about Europe and Western history, the immensity of their

---

[9] Grossman, *Life and Fate*, 11–12.
[10] Grossman, *Life and Fate*, 12.
[11] Grossman, *Life and Fate*, 13.

failures and the horrors that have engulfed them in our century. Levinas could
be expected to take this judgment very seriously, with its sense of loss and
despair. But in fact, there is no need to speculate. We are fortunate to have
many interviews in which Levinas calls our attention to Grossman's great work
and to details within it. Let us turn to these themes and details now, in order
to see how and why Levinas read the book.

First, a detail. In the novel, Krymov — an old Bolshevik and once the
husband of a daughter of the main character, Alexandra Shaposhnikova — is
arrested and incarcerated in the Lubyanka prison in Moscow. When Yevgenia
Shaposhnikova, his estranged former wife, hears that Nikolay Krymov has been
imprisoned, interrogated, and tortured, she abandons her love affair with Pyotr
Novikov, a tank commander, and moves to be near the prison. Daily she stands
in long lines to make inquiries or to seek permission to leave a package or a
letter. Levinas recalls Yevgenia's return to her husband as an "act of goodness,
absolutely gratuitous and unforeseen."[12] In addition, he remembers and emphasizes a tiny detail in Grossman's description:

In *Life and Fate* Grossman tells how in Lubyanka in Moscow, before the infamous
gate where one could convey letters or packages to friends and relatives arrested for
"political crimes" or get news of them, people formed a line, each reading on the
nape of the person in front of him the feelings and hopes of his misery.[13]

Levinas calls this scene to mind in the course of explaining what he means by
"the priority of the other person" and specifically what he means when he
refers to meeting the other as "welcoming the face."[14] The face, he says, is not
first of all a collection of features, their shapes and the color of its surface, or
in general an object of perception. It is rather — *first of all and most significantly* —
"expression and appeal," or what he describes as "the nakedness of the other —
destitution and misery beneath the adopted countenance."[15] It is at this point
that Levinas calls upon Grossman's image of "human beings who glue their
eyes to the nape of the neck of the person in front of them and read on that
nape all the anxiety in the world."[16] These are Levinas's words; Grossman had
described the situation this way:

Yevgenia had never realized that the human back could be so expressive, could
so vividly reflect a person's state of mind. People had a particular way of craning

---

[12] *Is It Righteous to Be?*, 89.
[13] *Is It Righteous to Be?*, 208; cf. Levinas, "Peace and Proximity" in *Alterity and Transcendence*, 140.
[14] *Is It Righteous to Be?*, 191–92.
[15] *Is It Righteous to Be?*, 191.
[16] *Is It Righteous to Be?*, 192.

their necks as they came up to the windows; their backs, with their raised, tensed shoulders, seemed to be crying, to be sobbing and screaming.[17]

These words seem to have led Levinas to envision this line of people, to visualize in his mind's eye what it was like to stand in such a line, to focus on the person before you, and to see his or her pain and suffering in the posture of his back or the curve of his neck.[18]

What is it to be presented with another person in this way? What does it mean for our encounter or engagement with another person to be one of being faced with her misery and need first of all and most significantly? Levinas elaborates, in response to Grossman's image:

In the innocence of our daily lives, the face of the other [or the neck or the back] signifies above all a demand. The face requires you, calls you outside. And already there resounds the word from Sinai, "thou shalt not kill," which signifies "you shall defend the life of the other." . . . It is the very articulation of the love of the other. You are indebted to someone from whom you have not borrowed a thing. . . . And *you* are responsible, the only one who could answer, the noninterchangeable, and the unique one. . . . In this relation of the unique to the unique there appears, before the purely formal community of the genus, the original sociality.[19]

For now, I want to ignore Levinas's special vocabulary. What is he saying here? Levinas is drawing on Grossman's image to articulate the very particular experience of being faced with another person's pain and misery and realizing how one must respond to it, out of a sense of obligation, a kind of indebtedness, a sense that one cannot avoid acknowledging that misery, that one must care about it, not ignore it, and hence that one must do something. Levinas seems especially interested in the fact that all of this – the experience of the other's misery and the sense of debt and devotion – is what the other's presence, as a face or neck or back, signifies. This is what this kind of experience means; the meaning combines an exposure, a plea, a demand, and a recognition, all at once. Moreover, this is not what one sees in the features, the pallor, the shape of the other's face or body; it is what the other person means alongside all of this.

This conclusion leads me to another detail in *Life and Fate* that Levinas frequently calls to mind. Like Yevgenia's senseless abandoning of her love affair with Novikov and her allegiance to Krymov, it is what Levinas calls a "scene of goodness in an inhuman world."[20]

---

[17] Grossman, *Life and Fate*, 681–85, esp. 683.
[18] See *Is It Righteous to Be?*, 208.
[19] *Is It Righteous to Be?*, 192.
[20] *Is It Righteous to Be?*, 81.

[T]oward the book's end, when Stalingrad has already been rescued, the German prisoners, including an officer, are cleaning out a basement and removing the decomposing bodies. The officer suffers particularly from this misery. In the crowd, a woman who hates Germans is delighted to see this man more miserable than the others. Then she gives him the last piece of bread she has. This is extraordinary. Even in hatred there exists a mercy stronger than hatred.[21]

If the core meaning of the encounter with another person is a sense of need and demand, the core response to it is an act of goodness or generosity that is beyond explanation, that in fact seems to defy explanation. More than that, as in this case of the woman's act of giving bread to a person whom she hates and whose suffering she seems to be enjoying, there are acts of goodness in a situation that seems to be totally inhumane. Levinas emphasizes that acts like Yevgenia's devotion and the woman's gift are "isolated acts." They are not prepared for and seem to surprise rather than to make sense. And they have no larger effect. They do not change things; the world remains as it was; they are anomalies.

Grossman's description of this episode is more gripping, frightening, and complex than Levinas's memory of it.[22] The scene was tense, as the soldiers removed the bodies from the cellar with the crowd of Russians so hostile and threatening. Then they brought out the dead body of an adolescent girl. The woman ran to the girl's body, straightening out her hair, transfixed by her features. She then stood up and walked toward the officer, picked up a brick on the way, hatred radiating from her, without the guard feeling that he could stop her:

The woman could no longer see anything at all except the face of the German with the handkerchief round his mouth. Not understanding what was happening to her, governed by a power she had just now seemed to control, she felt in the pocket of her jacket for a piece of bread that had been given to her the evening before by a soldier. She held it out to the German officer and said: "There, have something to eat."

Afterwards, she was unable to understand what had happened to her, why she had done this. Her life was to be full of moments of humiliation, helplessness and anger, full of petty cruelties that made her lie awake at night, full of brooding resentment. . . . At one such moment, lying on her bed, full of bitterness, she was to remember that winter morning outside the cellar and think: "I was a fool then, and I'm still a fool now."[23]

Levinas extracts from this episode an act of utterly senseless goodness. Senseless it is: The woman is filled with hatred; she is about to strike the officer, to kill

[21] *Is It Righteous to Be?*, 89; cf. 81.
[22] Grossman, *Life and Fate*, 803–6.
[23] Grossman, *Life and Fate*, 805–6.

him. Instead, she hands him bread to eat. Is it an act of generosity? The bread
was given to her by a soldier; perhaps it represented to her that dead girl and
giving it to the officer was an act of defiance, of repulsion, of hatred? Or was
it more simply a way to avoid killing the officer, a virtually automatic way of
preventing herself from doing what she both wanted to do but also could not
bring herself to do? And yet, it was an act that gave the officer life rather than
taking it from him, one that had no effect on her own miserable and resentful
life, even with regret that she had not struck and killed him. Perhaps, for all its
complexity, the episode has at its core the meaning Levinas found in it: There
was an act of goodness, and it was wholly senseless and isolated. It was an act
of goodness because it gave life to the officer and because she even sacrificed,
it appeared, the little bread she had to do so. And it was done for no other
reason; there was no explanation or justification for it – other than that it was
what it was, an act of grace, of giving, of taking responsibility for the other
person's need and life. And it was rare, isolated in an inhumane world filled
with suffering and misery.

This point brings us to Levinas's other sort of citation of *Life and Fate*. Not
only does he call attention to details or episodes; he also points out what Grossman shows us about the twentieth century and our world. This is a large and
important theme. I want to discuss it in two steps. First, Levinas reflects on the
meaning of Grossman's novel for our understanding of Stalinism, Nazism, and
other totalitarian ideologies in the twentieth century. Second, Levinas refers
to a letter from a strange figure in the novel, an old Tolstoian, that Grossman
presents in what Levinas calls the central chapter of the book.[24] This character, Ikonnikov-Morzh, Levinas takes to represent Grossman's own views, but
whether he does is not as relevant as what these views are, for Levinas clearly
finds them very appealing and even, in a way, identifies with them.[25] "The
essential teaching," Levinas says, "is articulated by a strange, socially marginal
person who has lived through it all. Halfway between simplemindedness and
holiness, between madness and wisdom, he doesn't believe in God anymore,
nor in the Good that would organize an ideology."[26] Ikonnikov, that is, does
not advocate or believe in systems, ideologies, theories, or totalities of any kind.
What he does believe in are unique, discrete acts of goodness or kindness.

Levinas summarizes the main points of Ikonnikov's letter on several occasions.
In the novel, the letter is read by an old Bolshevik, Mikhail Mostovskoy, in a
German concentration camp, alone in his cell, after a lengthy interrogation
during which he had been given "Ikonnikov's scribblings" and was questioned

---

[24] Grossman, *Life and Fate*, Part II, 404–11.
[25] See *Is It Righteous to Be?*, 216–18; cf. 89–90, 120.
[26] *Is It Righteous to Be?*, 120.

about them.[27] Levinas never mentions this context; he only calls attention to what he takes to be Ikonnikov's view of the world and human goodness:

The essential thing in this book is simply what the character Ikonnikov says – "There is neither God nor the Good, but there is goodness" – which is also my thesis. That is all that is left to mankind. . . . He also says: "There are acts of goodness which are absolutely gratuitous, unforeseen."[28]

Levinas gives a fuller account in 1986, when his comments on *Life and Fate* were provoked by the interviewer's question about how upsetting Levinas found the book and a lengthy quotation from the novel:

Grossman's eight hundred pages offer a complete spectacle of desolation and dehumanization. . . . Yet within that decomposition of human relations, within that sociology of misery, goodness persists. In the relation of one man to another, goodness is possible. There is a long monologue where Ikonnikov – the character who expresses the ideas of the author – casts doubt upon all social sermonizing, that is, upon all reasonable organization with an ideology, with plans. . . . Every attempt to organize humanity fails. The only thing that remains undying is the goodness of everyday, ongoing life. Ikonnikov calls that "the little act of goodness." . . . This "little goodness" is the sole positive thing. . . . [I]t is a goodness outside of every system, every religion, every social organization.[29]

In the course of Levinas's comments, the interviewer quoted from the text, but the passage makes little difference; he could have cited almost anything from that chapter.[30] No system houses the Good, nor can any evil harm or destroy what is really good. What Grossman calls "petty, thoughtless kindness," "senseless kindness," "a kindness outside any system of social or religious good" or "stupid kindness" is "what is most truly human in a human being." As Levinas notes, "[I]t is as beautiful and powerless as dew." Such acts are not found within systems, that is, not prescribed or justified by systems; nor can systems engulf or annihilate them. "[H]uman qualities persist even on the edge of the grave, even at the door of the gas chamber." "The power of evil . . . is impotent in the struggle against man."[31]

Levinas finds this letter extraordinarily congenial. He is moved by its optimism, by its commitment to goodness or kindness outside of systems, institutions, ideologies, something about how one acts toward the other person that is beyond theory, rules, and explanation and that is indestructible and permanent,

---

[27] Grossman, *Life and Fate*, Part II, 391–403.
[28] *Is It Righteous to Be?*, 89; cf. 120.
[29] *Is It Righteous to Be?*, 217–18.
[30] The citation is drawn from Grossman, *Life and Fate*, 407–8.
[31] Grossman, *Life and Fate*, 408–10; cf. *Is It Righteous to Be?*, 218.

albeit unique and particular. Furthermore, Levinas agrees that whatever this kindness or goodness is, it occurs in everyday life. It is what the human is all about; it is rare, in one sense, and yet it is fundamental and primary to human life in some sense or other. We can see, then, why it hardly matters for Levinas whether Ikonnikov really speaks for Grossman; what matters is how he seems to speak for Levinas. His is the voice of hope and the humane in the midst of the misery and despair of the twentieth century.

But one cannot and should not forget or mitigate the depth of the despair or the degree of the misery. Grossman does not, nor does Levinas read him that way.[32] Here I come to the last major reason that Levinas cites Grossman: as a true, accurate and compelling witness to the crisis of the modern world in the twentieth century, of which Auschwitz is a part and the principal paradigm. Grossman paints a vast, grim, horrifying panorama of dehumanization and suffering. It is a world in crisis, where the victors and the victims are mirror images of one another, in which indeed there are no victors, only victims.

[Grossman] is witness to the end of a certain Europe, the definitive end of the hope of instituting charity in the guise of a regime, the end of the socialist hope. The end of socialism, in the horror of Stalinism, is the greatest spiritual crisis in modern Europe. Marxism represented a generosity, whatever the way in which one understands the materialist doctrine which is its basis. There is in Marxism the recognition of the other.... But the noble hope consists in healing everything, in installing, beyond the chance of individual charity, a regime without evil. And the regime of charity becomes Stalinism and [complicitous] Hitlerian horror. That's what Grossman shows.... An absolutely overwhelming testimony and a complete despair.[33]

Levinas makes a multiple assessment, that Europe has suffered a spiritual crisis, that it involves the failure of socialism or Marxism and the spiral of socialism into totalitarian violence and atrocity, and finally that this exposes a great truth: "[T]here isn't any solution to the human drama by a change of regime, no system of salvation."[34] Politics must give way to something else, to "ethics without ethical system" or to individual, discrete acts of goodness. This, moreover, is religion – not as it is, institutionalized and organized, but in spirit, as it might be, what "religion" really means. But here Levinas underlines the negative, what twentieth-century life has shown: that one cannot impose, legislate, or systematize goodness and charity. Grossman's novel shows this in its portrait of

[32] Grossman develops his picture of this despair and misery, starkly, in his subsequent novel, *Forever Flowing*.
[33] *Is It Righteous to Be?*, 80–81; cf. 120, 132; see also Levinas, *Proper Names*, 3.
[34] *Is It Righteous to Be?*, 81; cf. 132.

Stalinism and Nazism, which are images of each other.[35] If we rely on systems and ideology, the outcome is totalized domination and violence, despair.

[*Life and Fate*] describes the situation in Europe at the time of Stalin and Hitler. Vassily Grossman represents this society as a completely dehumanized one. There is, of course, the life of the camps; it was the same thing under Hitler and under Stalin. Life seems to be premised upon the total contempt of respect of man, for the human person. Nevertheless, as concerns Stalin, that society came out of the search for a liberated humanity. That Marxism could have turned into Stalinism is the greatest offense to the cause of humanity, for Marxism carried a hope for humanity; this was perhaps one of the greatest psychological shocks for the European of the twentieth century.[36]

Grossman, earlier in his career (1946), gave a very early report of the Nazi death camp at Treblinka and later coedited Russian documents dealing with the Nazi persecutions in Russia, *The Black Book*. But here, in these interviews, Levinas seems to focus his attention on Stalinism as the nemesis of Marxist socialism and the larger implication that even the small, discrete act of goodness that remains is "lost and deformed as soon as it seeks organization and universality and system, as soon as it opts for doctrine, a treatise of politics and theology, a party, a state, and even a church."[37] Hitler, Nazism, and the death camps are not discussed independently or on their own; their significance is swept up by that of Stalinism and its horrors. Levinas sees the twentieth century as a single story, as a failure of "regimes of charity," their transformation into regimes of violence and oppression.[38] This portrait calls to mind an image from Plato's *Republic*: In an unjust polis, the philosopher survives by taking shelter in caves and caverns, hidden from the storms of public life.[39] But Levinas's attack on systems, institutions, regimes, and ideologies is more pointed and much more global.

Levinas's attraction to Grossman's great novel is expressed in his recollection of details and his impressions regarding its large themes. My own reading of *Life and Fate*, underscored by reading his later novel, *Forever Flowing*, suggests that Grossman's great themes were freedom and domination. For Levinas, we might say they were goodness or kindness and domination. Clearly, the novel

---

[35] The opposition to all forms of totalitarianism, particularly to Nazi fascism and Stalinism, recalls similar themes in Hannah Arendt's famous *The Origins of Totalitarianism* (New York: Harcourt, Brace, 1951).

[36] *Is It Righteous to Be?*, 216–17.

[37] *Is It Righteous to Be?*, 206–7.

[38] In *Forever Flowing*, Grossman's indictment is even more powerful and direct; see 176–237; cf. Levinas, *Entre Nous*, 119–20.

[39] See Plato, *Republic*, 496c–e.

represented for Levinas a powerful and even decisive teaching about the human condition: the nemesis of totality in "total domination" and the possibility of salvation only in particular, isolated, "senseless" acts of kindness. In short, the twentieth century – Stalinism, Nazism, the labor and death camps – expose, on the one hand, the depths of need, misery, suffering, and atrocity that mark the encounters of people and, on the other hand, the primordial character of charity and kindness that can arise out of such encounters. They are not the only horrific events of the century – elsewhere, Levinas includes nuclear weapons, terrorism, Cambodia, unemployment, and many other features of the past century – but they are emblematic ones.[40]

I have been looking at Levinas's comments on Grossman's *Life and Fate* for several reasons. For a decade or so, at the end of his life, Levinas cited the novel regularly; it meant a good deal to him. He was upset by it and at the same time elevated by it. I wanted to see if we could determine why he chose to give it such frequent attention, to use it, as it were, as a pedagogical device. We found at least two reasons for Levinas's attraction to the novel. First, he saw examples in Grossman's descriptions of the everyday expression of what he calls the "epiphany of the face of the other" and "responsibility for the other," and he takes Grossman to have given these isolated cases a preeminent status in modern life. Levinas is always looking for examples that illustrate responsibility and goodness as he understands them – acts of recognizing the other person's need and demands and responding with acts of gratuitous giving that are unexplainable, almost dissonant, "senseless" in one sense but ultimately meaningful in another. Second, Levinas sees Grossman as an extraordinarily effective witness to the crisis of the modern world as one of "regimes of goodness" that develop into regimes of "total domination."[41] This reflection on Grossman is part of Levinas's own judgment about the failure of modernity and hence about the failure of politics and the importance of ethics and religion. All of these terms – "politics," "ethics," and "religion" – are terms of art for him, so to use them here is anticipatory at best and hence unclear. Perhaps it would be more accurate to say that Levinas finds Grossman congenial for exposing the failures of politics, ethics, and religion as we have known them and for suggesting how ethics and religion might genuinely be understood and revitalized.

In addition, I believe that by looking at Levinas on *Life and Fate*, we see his philosophical views engaged in a task of literary interpretation and political, historical assessment. This discussion, then, enables us to watch Levinas's

---

[40] For a list of the catastrophes of the twentieth century, see "Peace and Proximity," *Alterity and Transcendence*, 132, 135.
[41] This expression is Arendt's. It is the title of the famous last subsection of *The Origins of Totalitarianism*.

philosophy function for him personally as a lens through which to judge human conduct and the political realities of the twentieth century prior to and during the Second World War. These judgments become a kind of hypothesis. We can now ask if other things that he writes or says confirm this assessment of the crisis of the modern world. Do they provide a perspective from which that assessment would arise? Does such a perspective justify, contribute to, or elicit this assessment and make sense of it? Moreover, we can ask if his remarks about Auschwitz and Nazi totalitarianism fit the pattern of these remarks and if so, in what way.

Furthermore, I wanted to begin our examination of Levinas by looking at how Levinas's philosophy expresses itself in and about the everyday world in which we live. How is it a philosophy about ordinary, everyday life? Recently, philosophers have thought deeply about everyday life, or what some call the ordinary.[42] And not only philosophers: Literary critics, and historians too, have noted how the development in the twentieth century from modernism to post-modernism involves a set of shifts of concern – from high theory to mundane or prosaic expressions of belief, from the old intellectual history to so-called new intellectual history or *Alltagsgeschichte*, from the development and construction of totalizing theories to the examination of fragmentary cultural expressions of people in the everyday, from the rare to the prosaic, from intellectual life to popular culture, from the mind to the body, from the dominantly male to the plurality of gender diversity, from a Eurocentric perspective to anticolonial-ist pluralism, and so forth.[43] One even finds this shift expressed in the general deflationary attitude toward philosophy, associated with Wittgenstein in his later period and more recently with Richard Rorty, Stanley Cavell, and Bernard Williams and also with discussion about the limits of language and thought, the notion of point of view, the examination of skepticism, and much else. Against this background, Levinas appears both novel and old-fashioned, modernist in some ways and postmodernist in others. In order to understand him, I believe that we must consider how his philosophy is engaged with and embedded in the everyday world. By starting with his attraction to Grossman's novel, a vivid and concrete descriptive panorama of people's thoughts and actions in ordi-nary life, albeit in extraordinary circumstances – the momentous days of fall and winter 1942–43 in Stalingrad, Moscow, and elsewhere in Russia – we can watch Levinas as he appropriates and comments on the everyday, or ordinary, world. As we move in later chapters to direct examination and clarification of his philosophy, we should never forget this launching pad. On the one hand, it

---

[42] Most explicitly, the everyday and the return to the ordinary are central themes in the work of Stanley Cavell.
[43] I am thinking especially of Michael Andre Bernstein in *Foregone Conclusions*.

is in an important sense the origins of his thinking. On the other, it will provide vivid examples to which we can return again and again, in order to test our interpretations of his more arcane and technical writings.

AUSCHWITZ AND LEVINAS'S THOUGHT

I want now to turn to Levinas's discussion of Auschwitz. One of the many venues for *Life and Fate* is an unnamed Nazi death camp that is being constructed and used for the first time. Grossman juxtaposes what goes on there – among the events is the thematically important interrogation of Mostovsky and his reading of Ikonnikov's letter – with events in a Siberian labor camp and all of this with Stalingrad and Moscow. As the novel develops, we find it more and more difficult to distinguish how life is lived in them and hence the culture, the mindset of living in these places. But in "Signature" and elsewhere – in terms of Levinas's understanding of antisemitism and persecution and suffering and with regard to his critical approach to Heidegger – the Nazi persecution and extermination of European Jewry, the Holocaust, plays a central role. I want to look at that here; but to the degree that I can, I will defer treatment of the relationship among the Holocaust, Judaism and the Jewish people, Levinas's Zionism, and discussion of responding to the Holocaust, the so-called "end of theodicy," and so forth. Here our questions are: What does the Holocaust mean to Levinas in terms of his historical and political judgments, and how does it fit into his overall understanding of the human condition in the twentieth century? What does Auschwitz tell us about the crisis of the modern world?

Levinas is informed about other treatments of Nazi totalitarianism. In 1985, in a eulogy to his long-time friend Vladimir Jankélévitch, he says:

[N]o one is unaware that he condemned, beyond any possibility of pardon, the crime and the criminals of the Holocaust or Shoah. Jankélévitch never consented to the trivializing of these atrocities committed by Europeans in a Christian Europe, to view them, as sociologists, as a particular case of xenophobia or racism. The horror of the crime committed against the human person and human life was no doubt the essence of what prompted the extreme firmness of Jankélévitch's condemnation.[44]

Not only does this comment seem to reflect Levinas's own accord, it also alludes to the way in which some German historians and scholars were trivializing the Nazi atrocities – perhaps a reference to the *Historikerstreit* and the kinds of criticisms leveled at Martin Broszat, Andreas Hillgruber, and Ernst Nolte – and not them alone. Levinas surely knew Theodor Adorno's comments on Auschwitz and culture, Hannah Arendt's analysis in *The Origins of Totalitarianism* and

[44] Levinas, *Outside the Subject*, 88.

Eichmann in Jerusalem, and the views of French intellectuals Jacques Derrida, Jean-François Lyotard, and especially Maurice Blanchot.[45] Alain Finkelkraut is a secular disciple of Levinas; his *The Imaginary Jew* was published in 1980, and *Remembering in Vain*, on the trial of Klaus Barbie, appeared in 1987. As we shall see in an important essay "Useless Suffering," Levinas refers to and even quotes from Emil Fackenheim's *God's Presence in History*. Overall, then, Levinas could be set within the context of postmodern discussion and critical reflection on the Holocaust and also within theological discussion. But I prefer a more direct route. I would like to look first at his comments about what Auschwitz was and what it meant. Many of these occur in occasional, passing remarks.

In his influential anthology *Face to Face with Levinas*, Richard Cohen includes Richard Kearney's interview with Levinas, first published in 1984. Near the end, Levinas comments on Marxism and socialism as utopian and how Marxism was "utterly compromised by Stalinism."[46] He sees "Marx's critique of Western idealism" as an "ethical conscience . . . demanding that theory be converted into a concrete praxis of concern for the other."[47] Here is the "regime of charity" that Stalinism compromised and abandoned, as we have already seen. But in this remark, Levinas goes on to associate this postwar climate of despair with the student revolts of 1968:

The 1968 Revolt in Paris was a revolt of sadness, because it came after the Khrushchev Report and the exposure of the corruption of the Communist Church. The year of 1968 epitomized the joy of despair, a last grasping at human justice, happiness, and perfection – after the truth had dawned that the communist ideal had degenerated into totalitarian bureaucracy. By 1968 only dispersed groups and rebellious pockets of individuals remained to seek their surrealist forms of salvation, no longer confident of a collective movement of humanity, no longer assured that Marxism could survive the Stalinist catastrophe as the prophetic messenger of history.[48]

There are clear echoes in this text of Levinas's reflections on Grossman – the fall of Marxist socialism into Stalinism with its "totalitarian bureaucracy," the small pockets of group and individual hopes with their "surrealist forms of salvation," the elements of sadness, joy, and despair. But the tie to the events of 1968 has an ominous side: It exposes the conflict between ethics and politics, between

[45] Levinas had known Blanchot since 1926, when the latter first arrived in Strasbourg as a student; they were lifelong friends. Blanchot's *L'Ecriture du désastre* (*The Writing of the Disaster*) appeared in 1980. Maurice Blanchot, *The Writing of Disaster*, Trans. Ann Smock (Lincoln: University of Nebraska Press, 1986).
[46] Richard A. Cohen (ed.), *Face to Face with Levinas*, 33.
[47] Cohen (ed.), *Face to Face with Levinas*, 33; cf. Levinas, *Nine Talmudic Readings*, 97–98.
[48] Cohen (ed.), *Face to Face with Levinas*, 33.

Judaism and politics, when the forces of revolution become political and turn against the Jews as they did in 1933 and then again in 1968.

The 1969 *Colloques des Intellectuels Juifs de Langue Française* had, as its theme, "Youth and Revolution in Jewish Consciousness."[49] In the course of his commentary on *Baba Metsia* 83a–83b, Levinas calls attention to the role of the Jewish people in history and the relation between politics and the Jews:

> But those who shouted, a few months ago, "We are all German Jews" in the streets of Paris were after all not making themselves guilty of petit-bourgeois meanness. German Jews in 1933, foreigners to the course of history and to the world, Jews, in other words, point to that which is most fragile and most persecuted in the world. More persecuted than the proletariat itself, which is exploited but not persecuted. A race cursed, not through its genes, but through its destiny of misfortune, and probably through its books, which call misfortune upon those who are faithful to them and who transmit them outside of any chromosomes.[50]

One of the student leaders of the events of May 1968 was Daniel Cohn-Bendit, son of German Jews who had emigrated to France in 1933. When, on May 22, 1968, Cohn-Bendit was refused permission to reenter France from Germany, student demonstrators took up the chant "We are all German Jews" as an act of solidarity with him and, as Levinas sees it, as an expression of their role as the persecuted.[51] Stalinism, the decline of Marxism, the student revolt of 1968, and Auschwitz crystallize in Levinas's mind with the role of Jews as persecuted victims. The point of these twentieth-century events is to expose the depth of persecution and suffering that modern society and culture has generated and to locate the Jew at the center of the crisis of modernity as the site of this persecution. And what does this persecution mean, in Levinas's terms? On the one hand, of course, persecution is oppression and an agency of atrocity and suffering. But, on the other hand, persecution is what causes or permits this agency, the failure of concern and care. For Levinas, however, the notion of "persecution," as we shall see, is a technical one; to be persecuted is to be confronted by the face of the other person and called to respond. To be persecuted, for Levinas, is "to bear responsibility for everything . . . to be responsible despite oneself. . . ."[52]

---

[49] See *Nine Talmudic Readings*, 94 n. For discussion, see Simon Critchley, "Persecution Before Exploitation: A Non-Jewish Israel" in *Levinas and Politics*, eds. Charmaine Coyle and Simon Critchley, *Parallax* 8:24 (July–Sept. 2002), 71–77.

[50] *Nine Talmudic Readings*, 113.

[51] See *Nine Talmudic Readings*, 119 n. 5. Discussion of the events of 1968 in Paris and elsewhere can be found in Sylvia Harvey, *May '68 and Film Culture*, which also includes a helpful bibliography; Arthur Marwick, *The Sixties*, 615; George Katsiaficas, *The Imagination of the New Left: A Global Analysis of 1968*, 104; Alain Schnapp and Pierre Vidal-Naquet, *The French Student Uprising November, 1967–June 1968*, 211–12.

[52] *Nine Talmudic Readings*, 114–15.

At one level, Levinas aligns Nazism with Stalinism as totalitarian and as dicta-
torships. Both are emblems of overwhelming domination. But at another level,
Nazism and the death camps are distinguished by antisemitism and unbounded
persecution. Auschwitz is about suffering, persecution, and oppression, or,
perhaps more accurately, Auschwitz *is* these things. This is what coordinates
Auschwitz with the Jew and the Jew with Jewish books and their critical teaching. I will return to these specifically Jewish issues at the end of this book, when
we can ask what Levinas takes Judaism to be about in the light of his philosophy
and his ethics. Insofar as Auschwitz is linked with Jews, however, we can see
even now that its meaning concerns persecution and suffering. In the essays
where he deals with Auschwitz explicitly and thematically, it is this association
with suffering that is central.[53]

One of the most comprehensive and thoughtful discussions of Levinas on
the Holocaust with which I am familiar is an essay by Richard Cohen, "What
Good Is the Holocaust? On Suffering and Evil."[54] As Cohen points out, Levinas
examines evil and suffering in four relatively short articles, in which he clarifies
what the Holocaust means and how it is associated with evil and suffering.[55]
Cohen is concerned with the possibility of a post-Holocaust ethics. I will take
up this issue later, together with the more general questions of whether Levinas's
entire philosophical enterprise can be understood as a response to the Holocaust
and what Levinas takes to be an ethically responsible response to Auschwitz.
My present interest is Levinas's assessment of the meaning of Auschwitz within
his overall judgment about the twentieth century and its historical character.
Let me begin by recalling what Cohen says about this matter.

What does Auschwitz indicate about twentieth-century society and culture? Is there something distinctive about the atrocities of Nazi totalitarianism? Is Auschwitz a watershed in history? What characterizes our epoch as
post-Holocaust? Cohen identifies one role that the Holocaust plays, according

---

[53] See Levinas, *Beyond the Verse*, xvi; and "Ethics and Politics" in Seán Hand (ed.), *The Levinas
Reader*, 289–91. In American history, culture, and literature, the role that the Jew and antisemitism plays for Levinas in France, with the memory of the Dreyfus Affair so indelibly
marked in his mind, is played by slavery and the memory of the Civil War and the subsequent
history of racism in the United States. This theme is prominent in Stanley Cavell's reading of
Thoreau and Emerson. For a fascinating discussion comparing philosophy in French and American cultures in Cavell, see James Conant, "Cavell and the Concept of America," in Russell B.
Goodman (ed.), *Contending with Stanley Cavell* (Oxford: Oxford University Press, 2005), 55–81,
esp. 70–71.

[54] Richard A. Cohen, *Ethics, Exegesis and Philosophy*, 266–82. In a later chapter, I will discuss
Levinas on responding to the Holocaust, and there I will discuss Cohen's essay, together with
Richard Bernstein's essay, the discussion by Tamra Wright, and other examinations of Levinas
and Auschwitz.

[55] The four articles are: "Useless Suffering," "Transcendence and Evil," "The Scandal of Evil,"
and "Loving the Torah More Than God." See Chapter 11, footnote 91.

to Levinas, in twentieth-century history and culture: "[F]or Levinas, the 'meaning' – or meaninglessness – of the Holocaust ... is found precisely in the 'end of theodicy.'"[56] The Holocaust has no meaning; its suffering is useless or meaningless. Cohen cites from Levinas's paper "Useless Suffering" to support this claim. This is what Levinas says; my citation is somewhat more extensive than Cohen's:

> Perhaps the most revolutionary fact of our twentieth-century consciousness – but it is also an event in Sacred History – is that of the destruction of all balance between Western thought's explicit and implicit theodicy and the forms that suffering and its evil are taking on in the very unfolding of the century. This is the century that in thirty years has known two world wars, the totalitarianisms of right and left, Hitlerism and Stalinism, Hiroshima, the Gulag, and the genocides of Auschwitz and Cambodia. This is the century that is drawing to a close in the obsessive fear of the return of everything these barbaric names stood for: suffering and evil inflicted deliberately, but in a manner no reason sets limits to, in the exasperation of a reason become political and detached from ethics.
>
> Among these events the Holocaust of the Jewish people under the reign of Hitler seems to me the paradigm of gratuitous human suffering, in which evil appears in its diabolical horror.... The disproportion between suffering and every theodicy was shown at Auschwitz with a glaring, obvious clarity.[57]

I think that this is a crucial text in Levinas's writings concerning the significance of suffering and evil for Western culture and the special role of Auschwitz in the history of evil. Here Levinas points to the incommensurability of suffering and evil in reality – and he names the events and phenomena he has in mind, including the world wars, Stalinism, Hitler, totalitarianisms, genocides, and such – and in thought. Here he points to the challenge Auschwitz makes to our cognitive and systematic capacity to rationalize experience and events, that is, to theodicy. Reason fails to deal with the human reality of suffering and the need for kindness and goodness when it becomes *political* and is *detached from ethics*. Auschwitz is the "paradigm" of this extraordinary suffering and evil; it is the primary location of this failure of politics and of reason, of this "end of theodicy."[58] For Levinas, then, the century is remarkable for its horrors and atrocities, for its suffering and its evil, which are beyond thought. Moreover, Auschwitz is therefore not unique but rather exemplary. It is a paradigmatic, representative manifestation of evil so extreme that it somehow, as we shall see later, destroys all theodicy. At this point, we can take note of this special role,

---

[56] Cohen, *Ethics, Exegesis and Philosophy*, 268–69; cf. *Is It Righteous to Be?*, 40: "And still, today, I tell myself that Auschwitz was committed by the civilization of transcendental idealism."

[57] Levinas, "Useless Suffering" in *Entre Nous*, 97; cf. 161–62 in Cohen's translation of this essay. See Chapter 11, footnote 91.

[58] I shall return to this theme, "the end of theodicy," in Chapter 11.

which we will only be able to understand adequately once we have examined Levinas's ethical metaphysics more fully.

In "Useless Suffering" and in the other essays that Cohen cites, Levinas responds to Emil Fackenheim on the importance of Auschwitz and the obligation to respond to it, and he ties Jewish life to Auschwitz, suffering, and persecution. I will return to these themes in the last chapter. For now, it is sufficient to note Levinas's judgment about twentieth-century culture and the Holocaust. Levinas points to several features of the crisis that we have already seen emerge in his comments on Grossman. First, Western culture and society in the twentieth-century manifest a failure of institutions and theories to realize goodness. It is a failure of social and ideological systems to bring about the good life – to feed the hungry, reduce poverty and homelessness, care for the sick, and provide the resources and opportunities for living a full and healthy life. In fact, these systems become totalitarian, dominating, and evil. Second, it is a failure of politics itself, of organized, bureaucratic strategies to enhance and support human life. Third, it is about the limits of reason, both actively in practical experience and theoretically in our systems of thought, to comprehend human suffering, to make sense of it and hence "domesticate" it. An honest exposure to the real experience of suffering and evil leaves thought impotent and unsatisfied. The "end of theodicy" refers to a condition in which our attempts to understand and explain everything – including suffering, evil, genocide, and such – simply fail; they reach a limit and cannot go beyond it. We become, or should become, humble before such suffering so that the only possible, sensitive response becomes opposition, and any kind of acceptance or complacency becomes impossible, inconceivable.

This kind of opposition to suffering is a dimension of what Levinas here calls "ethics." In *Life and Fate*, Levinas saw isolated acts of senseless kindness; he was stirred by the episode of the Russian woman, filled with anger and hatred, handing the piece of bread to the German officer rather than using the rock in her hand to kill him. Here he calls such an incident to mind when he refers to a reason that should give up being political and reattach itself to ethics. What he suggests is that in the face of useless suffering, we need senseless kindness. In place of politics and ideology, we need humanity, goodness, and ethics. In the place of systems and totalities, we need an acknowledgment and realization of the utterly particular. This would be a "redemption of the everyday," in a sense, not a new version of the old mythologies and metaphysics, but a new version of a new metaphysics and a new philosophy – a metaphysical ethics of a new kind.

Thus far, we have watched Levinas scan some terrain, specifically the political and cultural history of the twentieth century. We have observed him making some large-scale judgments about the "crisis of modernity" in the century.

Levinas is not primarily a political thinker or a political, cultural critic. He does not say a great deal or work out a critique in great detail like the Frankfurt school or like Habermas, Walzer, Rawls, or Taylor. His interests lie elsewhere.[59] Nonetheless, as we have watched him, several points of interest have emerged. We would like Levinas to say more about his doubts about theories, ideologies, and systems. We also would like to hear what he means by ethics and small, isolated acts of kindness and why they are "senseless" and yet have the primacy he seems to assume they have. And if Auschwitz and the other horrors of the century mark the "end of theodicy," is this the end of productive, useful, and meaningful thought about the world and especially about suffering and evil in it? Is this, in a way, the end of religion and perhaps also the end of philosophy? Why was Levinas so moved by the way in which a person's neck and back can express her misery and suffering and by the act of senseless kindness of giving a hated enemy one's last piece of bread? These are questions that need to be answered.

Levinas's comments on *Life and Fate* might tempt us to think that Levinas is unconditionally opposed to ideologies and systems of thought, political and otherwise, and this temptation might be strengthened by treating his reaction to Auschwitz and his conception of the "end of theodicy" as registering a similar indictment. We might be persuaded that Levinas has nothing good to say about traditional systems of thought and the role they have played and continue to play in our lives. Furthermore, his comments on the encounter with the face – the acknowledgment of the other person's suffering and despair – and on the response of gratuitous kindness, uncalled for and remarkable, might lead us to conclude that the occurrence of such acts ought to be the goal of human life, that what we ought to aim at are such discrete episodes of unexpected, almost "irrational" acts of generosity to others. Interpreting Levinas this way is tempting indeed, and many have succumbed to this temptation. Levinas says many things, we shall see, that encourage such a view, and they have led many interpreters to read him as extraordinarily radical and perhaps as a kind of ethical anarchist who opposes systematic thinking, grand theories, general principles, institutions, and organized ways of life in favor of episodic eruptions of ethical purity that are without reason or preparation or purpose beyond themselves. Hence, in addition to the questions I just raised, we are left with this one, which is perhaps the most important of all: Is this radical reading of Levinas as a kind

---

[59] As we shall see, however, his thinking has important implications for political issues and political life. The most comprehensive treatment of the relationship between his thinking and the political domain, in book form, is Howard Caygill's *Levinas and the Political*. Also of importance are the essays by Simon Critchley, Jacques Derrida, Ernesto Laclau, and Richard Rorty in *Deconstruction and Pragmatism*, edited by Chantal Mouffe.

of irrationalist and "moral saint" a compelling one? Is it required by what he says? Does it capture, best of all, the spirit of his teaching?

POLITICAL REFLECTIONS

Among the issues I have raised are several political ones.[60] They concern the failure of politics, a tension between politics and ethics, and the incapacity of politics to institutionalize kindness, goodness, and charity. Levinas does eventually give some analysis of society and politics, how they arise, their character, and such things. Even though he is not a political thinker and his philosophy is primarily ethical and metaphysical, his thinking does have political implications.

In September 1982, during the Lebanon War, the Israeli Defense Forces (IDF) occupied West Beirut to secure stability and protect Lebanese Muslims from the revenge of the Christian soldiers, the Phalangists. During the occupation, the IDF introduced Phalangists into the Palestinian camps of Sabra and Chatila in order to clear out Arab infiltrators, *fedayeen*, who were executing raids into Israel. Over a two-day period, however, the Phalangists massacred hundreds of people in the camps. The IDF made no effort to stop them, and the Menachem Begin government had to take responsibility for the slaughter. Shortly thereafter, Levinas and Alain Finkelkraut were interviewed on French radio to discuss the ethical and political issues raised by the massacre.[61] What did Levinas say about this event?

First, Levinas underscored his sense that in France and Israel there was an immediate, powerful sense of responsibility. Second, this sense of responsibility did not amount to forgetting the Nazi Holocaust; the Holocaust cannot, he said, "justify closing our ears to the voice of men" or absolve us from responsibility. But when attacked, one can and should defend oneself; responsibility for the other does not rule out defense of ourselves and those near to us. That, Levinas said, is politics: "[A]longside ethics, there is a place for politics."[62] But at the same time, once there is politics, ethics is still present; politics does not replace or displace the ethical. In the case of Israel and Zionism, as Levinas put it, we have a

---

[60] Not exclusively, of course. We did see intimations of some important ideas that are peculiarly Levinas's: the face of the other, infinite responsibility, persecution, the limits of thought and language, and the critique of totality. But the failure of Western civilization is marked by the failure of political ideologies and systems, institutions, and bureaucracies and the need for an ethical reorientation.

[61] As one can imagine, Levinas's comments during this interview have been the subject of enormous, conflicting comments and criticisms. We shall return to them later, when we discuss Levinas's Zionism and his understanding of responsibility for one's enemy, in this case the Palestinians; Howard Caygill has a very critical, almost inflammatory account in *Levinas and the Political*.

[62] "Ethics and Politics" in Hand (ed.), *The Levinas Reader*, 291–92.

state, "a political idea which has an ethical justification," to rectify the millennial suffering and persecution of Jews by founding a "political unity with a Jewish majority." The creation of such a state, which reverses the persistent pattern both of causing Jewish suffering and of standing by and allowing it to occur, is therefore a major historical contribution to Western civilization. By reducing widespread suffering, it realizes responsibility toward the Jewish other. The result is a state with all its requisite institutions and capabilities, with an army, and with a mandate to deter aggression against it and to protect itself and its people. This is what politics and political reality require. The Jewish state, which is a political entity, is also, however, ethically grounded in the responsibility to defend the Jewish people, who are its neighbors, so to speak. But this responsibility in reality must be limited, and this is what Sabra and Chatila are about: "an ethical limit to this ethically necessary political existence."[63]

Levinas points out that such a conflict or contradiction, between ethics and politics, is not primarily an issue for philosophy. It is not primarily a matter of some kind of reflective, cognitive engagement. Resolution rather requires "events . . . [and] human lived experience." "In the political and moral ordeal, in the Passion of this war . . . it's there that the relationship between ethics and politics is being decided."[64] At such moments, everyone's responsibility is engaged, and the question of limits is raised in fact; everything is "interrupted" and "disrupted," and everyone's responsibility comes into play. It seems clear that Levinas feels guilt over the massacres at Sabra and Chatila, and yet some may take the comments thus far to represent an avoidance or a failure. But let us give him some time. Here he addresses the larger issue of what is going on, how ethics and politics are doubly related in Israel, with one ethical mandate in fact disrupting and conflicting with another. The state itself is ethically grounded, and its right to protection and to defense is an ethical one. But the massacre is an ethical atrocity. "Ethics will never, in any lasting way, be the good conscience of corrupt politics – the immediate reactions we've witnessed these last few days prove it; and transgression of ethics made 'in the name of ethics' is immediately perceived as a hypocrisy and as a personal offence."[65] The massacres, I think Levinas is saying, are the outcome of "corrupt politics"; they are a "transgression of ethics made 'in the name of ethics.'" Moreover, they cannot be tolerated, and people realize it – Jews included, perhaps Jews most of all, and Israelis, for we see the immediate, profound response: Arguments to the contrary are treated as hypocrisy and offence. What this means, then, is that at moments like Sabra and Chatila, Levinas points out, self-defense takes on a broader character:

[63] "Ethics and Politics" in Hand (ed.), *The Levinas Reader*, 292–93.
[64] "Ethics and Politics" in Hand (ed.), *The Levinas Reader*, 293.
[65] "Ethics and Politics" in Hand (ed.), *The Levinas Reader*, 295.

The state is there to protect not only Jewish bodies but also Jewish souls. Politics without its moral foundation can become corrupt and destructive; it is an offence and is perceived as such.

Levinas's comments do not, of course, clarify what he means by responsibility for the other person and what ethics is. We will begin to examine his account of these matters in the next chapter. What they do, however, is show that for him politics must be justified ethically, and it must answer to ethics. Levinas does not unqualifiedly denigrate the political; he does not argue that we can or should dispense with it. Its tactics, strategies, and regimens are important – and perhaps necessary – in order to implement the ethical goals in social life, in everyday life. But its practices must answer to ethical assessment, and what this amounts to is ethics limiting itself in order to be realized in public life. When sketched very broadly, as we have done, there is nothing especially novel about this relationship between ethics and politics. There is too much we do not yet know about Levinas and his thinking. We do not know yet what kind of justification ethics provides for politics and what that justification is for. Is it a justification for political authority and obligation? for law? for political institutions of particular kinds? What kind of justification is it? We know neither what ethics nor politics means for Levinas. Nor do we know whether their connection is weak or strong. Does politics make room for ethical life, or is it intended as a vehicle for implementing a particular ethical view and way of life? Is Levinas's view of politics similar to a Marxist or socialist view? Or is it liberal and democratic? Can we make sense of it alongside communitarian and republican views or alongside a contractarian account like that of Rawls?

In the 1982 interview, Levinas already suggested that *a* – if not *the* – primary reason for political organization to take shape is defense and protection of people. He admits that this function is not unconditional; it has ethical limits. But it is worth asking what else he says about this function as a justification for the existence of political institutions. Discussing the same theme shortly thereafter (October 1982), Levinas described the "political" situation this way:

If self-defense is a problem, the "executioner" is the one who threatens my neighbor and, in a sense, calls for violence. . . . So the whole problematic of the executioner is opened here; in terms of justice and the defense of the other, my fellow, and not at all in terms of the threat that concerns me. . . . There is a certain measure of violence necessary in terms of justice: but if one speaks of justice, it is necessary to allow judges, it is necessary to allow institutions and the state; to live in a world of citizens, and not only in the order of the Face to Face.

But, on the other hand, it is in terms of the relation to the Face or of me before the other that we can speak of the legitimacy or illegitimacy of the state. A state in which the interpersonal relationship is impossible, in which it is directed in advance by the determinism proper to the state, is a totalitarian state. So there is a limit to the state. Whereas, in Hobbes's vision – in which the state emerges not from the limitation of charity, but from the limitation of violence – one cannot set a limit on the state.[66]

Here Levinas seems to be saying this: Suppose individuals are generous and charitable toward each other. They need each other, and regularly the need is accepted. But in a group of many people, some will not give; they may even threaten. Here we need mechanisms for judging generosity and threat, for protecting people generally from those who threaten them with violence in various ways, and for organizing life to help and protect all. This is what the state is. Only a state that serves these functions, advancing aid and generosity and reducing threats of violence, is legitimate.[67] A state that prohibits such acts of aid and assistance and that militates against acts of kindness is totalitarian.[68] This is Stalinism and Nazi fascism. There is a standard for when a state serves its ethical function and when it does not, a rule against totalitarian domination. Levinas believes that no such limit exists in a Hobbesian account, where there is no ethics, he believes, outside of state power. He is right about this; in Hobbes, ethics only exists within the state and as a function of the power of the sovereign.[69] A Levinasian state, however, aims to protect against violence, to be sure, but it also aims to enhance and support mutual kindness, generosity, and assistance. This is the idea of an "ethical state," which Levinas says is Biblical. "Love must watch over justice," and when it does, "there is a possible harmony between ethics and politics."[70]

For Levinas, then, ethics and politics are complementary. We cannot have the one without the other. "Charity is impossible without justice, and . . . justice is warped without charity."[71] In the actual, everyday world, with many people living alongside each other and engaging with each other, generosity requires judging people's needs, assessing one's own and other people's resources, and determining how to protect people and facilitate mutual assistance. Ethics, that

---

[66] "Philosophy, Justice, and Love" in *Entre Nous*, 105.

[67] We shall see that Levinas also has other reasons for thinking that social and political institutions, practices, and such are necessary; they serve other functions as well. Here he focuses on protection – both within a state, from one another, and externally – from hostile regimes. I take him to be saying here that such protection is sufficient for legitimacy, but in the end it may not be.

[68] See also Levinas, "The Rights of Man and the Rights of the Other" in *Outside the Subject*, 122–23.

[69] Hobbes argues for the existence and role of a very powerful sovereign, but some would argue that the sovereign's power is itself limited by reason. Levinas treats the Hobbesian state as one of competing powers and self-interest; he focuses on the derivative nature of ethics.

[70] "Philosophy, Justice, and Love" in *Entre Nous*, 106, 108, 120.

[71] "Philosophy, Justice, and Love" in *Entre Nous*, 121.

is, requires the state; more broadly, human beings cannot live without principles
and institutions for regulating their interactions. At the same time, political
institutions alone, unburdened by the requirements of generosity and assistance,
can easily run amok and become distorted, even corrupt and oppressive. Politics
needs ethics and is "warped" without it.[72] In fact, insofar as politics and social
organization involve human beings living together, politics cannot exist without
ethics, as we shall see.

I think that it is useful to begin with the idea that for Levinas people live in
social worlds and hence that ethics and politics, love and justice, exist together;
human beings can no more do without the latter than without the former.[73]
In this sense, Levinas takes politics to be natural. Nonetheless, one can see how
his thinking aligns with modern political theorists from Hobbes, Locke, and
Rousseau to Kant and Rawls. For some, the political serves the purposes of
individual virtue; for others, it functions to formulate, publicize, articulate, and
sanction laws that protect individuals from threat, protect rights, or structure
conduct according to principles of justice or enhance autonomy and protect
human dignity. For Levinas, the political is necessary both to protect people from
threat and to facilitate ways in which people assist one another. Polities or states
aim to be "regimes of charity," kindness, or goodness. If some political theories
organize a just and mutually beneficial distribution of goods and emphasize this
goal over policing conflict and aggression, then Levinas's state goes further.[74]
Levinas's ideal is a state governed by the notion of equality as well as justice,
where all are responsible for one another and live that responsibility in limited,
but organized and effective, ways. This is "the political structure of society
under the rule of law, and hence institutions – in which the *for-the-other* of
subjectivity . . . enters with the dignity of the citizen into the perfect reciprocity
of political laws that are essentially egalitarian or held to become so."[75] On
many occasions, Levinas marks off his own view by contrasting it with that of
Hobbes; we have already seen him do this once. It is important, he says, to
know whether the just and egalitarian state arises from the war of all against

---

[72] Cf. "The Rights of Man and the Rights of the Other" in *Outside the Subject*, 116–25; see also
"The Other, Utopia, and Justice" in *Entre Nous*, 229–30; *Is It Righteous to Be?*, 169.

[73] *Is It Righteous to Be?*, 168: "The third party [that is, persons other than any particular one you are
engaged with or related to] isn't there by accident. In a certain sense, all the others are present
in the face of the other." See also *Entre Nous*, 106.

[74] One example of a Jewish philosopher who provides the framework for a political theory that
conceives of the state primarily as an agency for the fair distribution of welfare is Moses
Mendelssohn; see the first part of Moses Mendelssohn, *Jerusalem, or, on Religious Power and
Judaism*, trans. A. Arkush [1838] (Hanover, NH: University Press of New England, 1983), and
my essays on Mendelssohn in *Dilemmas in Modern Jewish Thought* (Bloomington: Indiana University Press, 1992) and in the Routledge *History of Jewish Philosophy*, edited by Dan Frank and
Oliver Leaman (London: Routledge, 1997).

[75] "Peace and Proximity," *Alterity and Transcendence*, 143.

all or from the irreducible responsibility of one for another.[76] Levinas, then, may take politics to be part of the natural human condition, but he is not a naturalist, like Hobbes or Hume. The state is not a construction based on rational calculation and natural desires or preferences that conflict and threaten constant war. Levinas's starting point about human existence is different: It is neither pessimistic nor optimistic in any standard sense. In his own way, Levinas thinks that the state serves the purposes of peace, as Hobbes does, but peace for him is "love," "sociality," and "to attend to the other" and not the lack of conflict or aggression.[77] Ultimately, then, Levinas hopes for a kind of utopia, the ground for which is a permanent, deep feature of all human existence.

Levinas's political thinking is not quietist, but active and utopian. While politics and ethics will always exist together, the ideal should be a "possible harmony between ethics and the State. The just State will come from just persons and saints rather than from propaganda and preaching."[78] There are two themes that are expressed in this acknowledgment of an ethical-political ideal. One is ideology; the other is messianism. Ideology is about the nature of political thinking as totality and system. Messianism is about the movement and aim of history and the need for human action.

In the end, Levinas's opposition to politics as ideology and his advocacy of a kind of messianism may seem to be in conflict. After all, if one is opposed to politics as a total worldview and as dominating and wholly determining, how can one advocate a single, uniform goal for all political life? Even at this stage, having yet to explore Levinas's ethical metaphysics, as Edith Wyschogrod calls it, we should say something about Levinas's commitments to these matters, within the context of his views about Marxism, Stalinism, Hitler, Auschwitz, and the crisis of modern society. We cannot deal with this issue thoroughly here, so any serious, satisfactory account of Levinas's conception of ideology and messianism will have to wait for an examination of his ethics and philosophy. But we can say some preliminary things, especially about his belief in a harmony between ethics and politics, love or peace, and justice. As far as ideology is concerned, it is sufficient to recognize that it is a kind of mystifying rationality and a source of obstacles and illusions.[79] Any conception of history and messianism that Levinas might have surely cannot have this character.

---

[76] "Peace and Proximity," *Alterity and Transcendence*, 144.
[77] *Is It Righteous to Be?*, 113.
[78] *Is It Righteous to Be?*, 181; see also *Entre Nous*, 120–21. Cf. Levinas, "Place and Utopia," in *Difficult Freedom*, 102: "Moral action must not be confused with the tedium of sermons. . . . It is on the basis of this ethical order that these metaphysical abstractions, the toys of our oratory, take on significance and effectiveness."
[79] We shall return later to a discussion of ideology, especially to a discussion of Levinas's essay "Ideology and Idealism" in Hand (ed.), *The Levinas Reader*, 236–48.

Levinas's conception of messianism has one foot in his philosophy and one in his study of Jewish texts. Because I want to defer discussion of Levinas's relationship to Judaism and Jewish thought until a later chapter, let me limit discussion here to what we might call his ethico-political messianism. A good place to begin is his short 1984 paper "Peace and Proximity." In it, Levinas addresses the current crisis of European civilization in a spirit that is largely secular, detached from his Jewish interests. The essay, which cites Grossman's *Life and Fate*, is contemporary with the interviews and texts we have previously looked at. My main focus will be on the way that Levinas understands the "harmony between ethics and politics," a condition in which "love watches over justice."

The problem of Europe, Levinas notes, is that it finds itself in a condition of "peace on the basis of the state," a political peace among independent, national, and competing entities.[80] This kind of peace is tranquility, a cessation of all that has troubled Europe in the twentieth century: "world wars, the genocides of the Holocaust and terrorism; unemployment and continual desperate poverty of the Third World; ruthless doctrines and cruelty of fascism and national socialism, right down to the supreme paradox of the defense of man and his rights being perverted into Stalinism."[81] Part of what is problematic about such a peace, as Levinas sees it, is that it is defined as the terminus of struggle or as the resolution, albeit temporary, of intrinsic competition and conflict among nations and peoples – hence, that it presumes a Hobbesian view of human nature and the human condition, a war of all against all, of international conflict based on acquisitive individualism. Real peace, of course, lies elsewhere, and, as Levinas puts it, people realize it. Or perhaps it would be more accurate to say that this kind of peace as cessation of struggle is insufficient by itself to solve the problems of Western civilization. In addition, such a peace must include a sense of the ethical – that is, within such a peace Europe must find itself with a bad conscience about what it is, with a sense of failure. But the failure is not intellectual; it is an ethical failure that is experienced as "the anguish of committing crimes . . . of the responsibility incumbent upon each one of us in the death and suffering of the other."[82] Levinas calls this "the ethical moment of our European crisis."[83] Real peace, that is, must include an end to struggle and a sense of mutual responsibility.

This is the crisis. The remedy is peace, and peace is tranquility. But what, indeed, does this tranquility amount to? It is not simply the repose of each

---

[80] "Peace and Proximity" in *Alterity and Transcendence*, 131–32.
[81] "Peace and Proximity" in *Alterity and Transcendence*, 132. We have seen this list before, of course.
[82] "Peace and Proximity" in *Alterity and Transcendence*, 135.
[83] Levinas notes that Franz Rosenzweig already attests to this ethical moment in the experience of World War One; see "Peace and Proximity" in *Alterity and Transcendence*, 135–36.

nation or the unity of all into a whole. It is something else, but what? We know that for Levinas each state seeks to protect its citizens from violence, internally and externally, and to facilitate mutual assistance and support – that is, acts of kindness, generosity, and charity. The problem of European civilization is a problem between nations. If the goal of international cooperation and reconciliation is to rid nations of anguish and bad conscience, what is the peace that is being sought? Within a state, individuals need to organize and regulate their responsibility to one another; between states, governments and nations need to organize and regulate their responsibility to one another – to reduce or do away with war, domination, oppression, poverty, and starvation. Levinas calls that "peace" – a real peace; it is "the *fraternal* way of proximity to the other…which would signify precisely the *excess* of sociality over all solitude – excess of sociality and love."[84] This is not a narrowly political peace, not the creation of a new totality, but rather an "ethical peace, a relation to the unassimilable other, the irreducible other, the unique other."[85] Levinas reiterates and elaborates this notion of peace as love with the terminology he employs in his ethical thinking. I want to avoid getting tangled up in that terminology here and simply try to paraphrase what such a peace means to us, a peace that is not a unification, a new totality, merely political, but rather a peace that is responsive to the needs of the other person and our obligation to respect and deal with her. "Peace as awakening to the precariousness of the other," Levinas describes it, calling to the reader's attention Grossman's description of the line of people in the Lubyanka prison in Moscow.[86]

But, Levinas realizes, this notion of peace as love and the unique, particular event of charity and kindness are distant from peace as a social and political reality, the kind of peace that comes when hostilities or wars come to an end. The latter arises as a goal and obligation when justice arises, and this happens when we realize that people live with others in families, communities, and larger groups and that even these groups occur alongside and in interaction with others. We need to grasp who is there, what their needs are, what resources we have; we need to develop institutions and programs to regulate, organize, and facilitate aid and succor. But we must not forget, Levinas notes, what is basic to the state and to social and political institutions and hence to the relationship between states and governments. Here is one place where it is important to remember, Levinas warns, that political institutions arise out of responsibility

---

[84] "Peace and Proximity" in *Alterity and Trancendence*, 137; the language of peace goes back to Levinas, *Totality and Infinity*, 203, 306. In one sense, it is biblical, for Levinas; it is peace of a different order than Hobbesian peace: peace as wholeness, rectification, completion, ultimately a condition where people and nations seek to maximize their acknowledgment and acceptance of others and their responsibility for their needs.

[85] "Peace and Proximity" in *Alterity and Transcendence*, 138.

[86] "Peace and Proximity" in *Alterity and Transcendence*, 140.

and generosity and not out of "a war of all against all . . . so that war does not become the institution of a war with a good conscience in the name of historical necessities." International peace is a kind of cooperation among nations that enhances the opportunities within nations of generosity and goodness. I think that we can infer this conclusion from what Levinas says at the end of "Peace and Proximity." And it is such a state of cooperation, I believe, that is as close as one can expect to reach to the messianic in human history. Surely, there are precise forms of such cooperation that one might advocate as best suited to these ends and precise forms of social, economic, and political life as well. Levinas speaks fondly of Marxism and socialism and of equality and justice as political structures worth endorsing. But here we need go no further in clarifying Levinas's political commentary, nor indeed can we go further, until his ethical metaphysics is in place.[87]

ZIONISM, POLITICS, AND MESSIANISM

There is one question, however, that we might usefully address here, and it concerns Zionism. Often, and with special conviction, Levinas supports and commends Zionism and speaks in behalf of the state of Israel. In our final chapter, we will need to place this advocacy within the context of Levinas's treatment of Judaism and post-Holocaust Jewish life. Here, however, we can ask a preliminary question: How does Levinas understand Zionism as a political view, and how does he approach the state of Israel as a political entity? That is, we should look at what Levinas says about Zionism and the state of Israel as political realities.

Let me begin by considering two of three pieces, collected under the heading "Zionisms," at the end of *Beyond the Verse*. They are "The State of Caesar and the State of David" (1971) and "Politics After!" (1979).[88] In the first essay, Levinas discusses the relation between political power and the divine order. This is a familiar issue. Plato raises it in the *Republic* as the problem of the relationship between philosophical inquiry and political power or, elsewhere, as the relationship between philosophy and rhetoric. Later, in the tradition of moral philosophy, it is located in the discussion of natural law or in theological discourse as the issue of church and state, the City of Man and the City of God. With the rise of modern science, the problem is co-opted by doctrines of legal positivism or views that swallow up ethics into politics, as Hobbes is often thought to have done. Levinas, as we have already seen, not only takes politics

---

[87] For a brief but clear account, see Theodore de Boer, *The Rationality of Transcendence*, 21–24.

[88] The third piece is "Assimilation and New Culture" (1980). *Beyond the Verse*, 196–201.

to be grounded in the ethical, but also believes that it is judged by the ethical. He puts this point as follows:

Although Israel would see itself as descended from an irreducible fraternity, it is aware of the temptation, within itself and around it, of the war which pits everyone against everyone else. . . . the State of Caesar, despite its participation in the pure essence of the State, is also the place of corruption *par excellence* and, perhaps, the ultimate refuge of idolatry.[89]

Now, to believe that politics can be corrupted or tempted to excess requires that politics can be measured by a standard and that it can fail to meet it. Standards can be located in many places; for Levinas, ethics is the standard for the political. Politics must be true to its origins – to its grounds, so to speak – in that responsibility to others is fundamental to human existence.

According to the Talmud, political oppression is what uniquely distinguishes our own epoch from the messianic. The latter is impeded when the State of Caesar becomes an ideal pagan state, "jealous of its sovereignty, the State in search of hegemony, the conquering, imperialist, totalitarian, oppressive State, attached to realist egoism, . . . it is idolatry itself."[90] The messianic state avoids or overcomes this determination and distortion; it is the best human and historical polity we can have. Levinas calls this goal a "monotheistic politics" or a "political doctrine suitable for monotheists."[91] It is, he says, an opportunity for the Jewish state: "At the heart of daily conflicts, the living experience of the government – and even the painful necessities of the occupation – allow lessons as yet untaught to be detected in the ancient Revelation."[92] What might these "new lessons" be? We do not know, of course, until they emerge, but Levinas points in a direction: These lessons will involve a political route that is not devoted solely to the "methods of Caesar," power politics and *realpolitik*, or to a "careless moralism." The new lessons will involve a realization of both ethical responsibility and political power in some kind of cooperation. This is the real aim of Zionism, "beyond the concern to ensure a refuge for those who are persecuted."[93] It is what places Israel in a messianic project in history.

What, then, is the relationship between the divine order and political power? The cooperation of the two in a real, historical, political entity is the challenge that all states face: that all states should seek the blending of political institutions with ethical sensibility. This is messianism; it is the real task of Zionism. It is a

[89] Levinas, "The State of Caesar and the State of David" in *Beyond the Verse*, 183.
[90] "The State of Caesar and the State of David" in *Beyond the Verse*, 184.
[91] "The State of Caesar and the State of David" in *Beyond the Verse*, 186.
[92] "The State of Caesar and the State of David" in *Beyond the Verse*, 187.
[93] "The State of Caesar and the State of David" in *Beyond the Verse*, 187.

kind of political perfectionism. The state is a requisite order for realizing our humanity. And although it can become corrupted, it can also be perfected; and when it is, there is some chance for a life of goodness and mutual assistance for us all.

Opportunities for new lessons – in a situation of conflict and belligerence, of occupation and repression – are still present. In "Politics After!" (1979), Levinas discusses the Arab-Israeli conflict. For Levinas, ethics concerns goodness, generosity, and responsibility; we have seen this again and again, even without having examined Levinas's ethical thinking in detail. In *Life and Fate*, the episode that most powerfully attracted his attention was an act of wholly unexpected, surprising, and even gratuitous kindness toward an enemy. Here, in a political context, where the issue concerns the possibility for an ethical politics and a messianic state, Levinas faces this situation in an especially agonizing form. What can one expect, what one can hope for, in a politics faced with such a conflict?

The conflict between Jews and Arabs in Israel is deep and "dominates all other Jewish-Arab questions." Levinas notes that it "has always been treated in political terms by men of State, public opinion, and intellectuals."[94] But he believes that this is a mistake. His suggestion is that the conflict needs to be understood within the context of the "spatio-temporal, psychological, and moral particularities" of the case.[95] In short, the political by itself distorts or is inadequate. The issue is an ethical one. For Jews, the goal should be "a reconciliation between Jews and Arabs," which is a "fraternal community." Levinas sees Anwar Sadat's trip to Jerusalem on November 19, 1977, and the subsequent peace between Israel and Egypt as a positive step. The character and destiny of the Jewish people and its culture are permeated by the issue of antisemitism and therefore concern ethical matters. Antisemitism is deeper than xenophobia or resentment; it is "the repugnance felt towards the unknown of the other's psyche, . . . the pure proximity of the other man – in other words, social living itself."[96] Antisemitism reveals the rejection of the other person, abandonment of the other, and persecution. Furthermore, Nazism and the cataclysms of the twentieth century expose a world riddled with antisemitism and what it signifies, and in the light of this trauma, Zionism, as a program against antisemitism, is an ambition for a recovery of our moral sensibility. This, Levinas claims, was always the sentiment at the heart of Zionism: "self-assertion [as] responsibility for everyone, . . . both politics and already non-politics."[97]

---

[94] Levinas, "Politics After!" in *Beyond the Verse*, 188.
[95] "Politics After!" in *Beyond the Verse*, 188.
[96] "Politics After!" in *Beyond the Verse*, 190.
[97] "Politics After!" in *Beyond the Verse*, 191. Levinas remarks that Gershom Scholem was one who saw this (192).

That is, Zionism, which has looked narrow, political, nationalist, and particular, is in fact and has always been universal and ethical. This depth and moral character is what sets the stage for properly understanding Sadat's initiative and the Jewish-Arab conflict. That is, Levinas weaves together Nazism, Stalinism, and the crisis of Western culture with antisemitism – he is not the only one to do so, of course; one need only recall Hannah Arendt, Theodor Adorno, and Max Horkheimer – and then portrays Zionism as a movement that developed in opposition to this deep moral failure of responsibility for the other person and indeed to every failure of such responsibility. This tapestry becomes the background for Levinas's assessment of the moral character of the Jewish-Arab conflict and the direction a Jewish-Arab reconciliation should take.

To many, all eyes should be focused on the plight of the Palestinians: "An armed and dominating state, one of the great military powers of the Mediterranean basin, against the unarmed Palestinian people whose existence Israel does not recognize!" But, Levinas asks, "Is that the real state of affairs? In its very real strength, is not Israel the most fragile, the most vulnerable thing in the world, in the midst of its neighbours, undisputed nations, rich in natural allies, and surrounded by their lands?"[98] Surely, it is mystification to treat Israel as a mighty, imperialist power; who is the strong, who the weak? Levinas wonders out loud if Sadat has not seen through these fabrications to the truth in Zionism, its ethical purposes, and understood "the opportunities opened up through friendship with Israel." He wonders if Sadat's trip was not an act beyond all *realpolitik* that found its way to a new venue altogether: the road to peace in the Near East, "if this peace is to be possible at all." Its weakness is its audacity, he says, "the suggestion that peace is a concept which goes beyond purely political thought."[99] This peace is what Levinas referred to earlier as a "fraternal community of Arab and Jew."

Levinas read *Life and Fate* as an indictment of politics and ideology, as totalizing and oppressive, and a eulogy to senseless, isolated, unexplainable acts of kindness. Sadat's visit and its achievement are a similar kind of act. Politically, the visit made no sense; in a situation of war and embattled powers, it stands out as a bold gesture of generosity and hope. Peace is two-fold. There is real peace, and there is political reconciliation. The former is the hope of genuine Zionism, and it should be at the heart of all human aspiration. Sadat's trip seemed an acknowledgment of what real peace requires and that it is at the center of Zionism, when properly understood. In 1982, after the massacres of Sabra and Chatila, as we saw, Levinas did not abandon his allegiance to this kind of peace or retract his belief that it was always the core of Zionism, as he understood it.

[98] "Politics After!" in *Beyond the Verse*, 193.
[99] "Politics After!" in *Beyond the Verse*, 193–95.

For this reason, he could be both affirmative and desperate about Israel's need to live up to her Zionist ideals, to her ethical demand.

RESPONSIBILITY AND FORGIVENESS

There is one final theme that we can deal with now, one that reveals the way in which Levinas's ethical insight reverberates in everyday life and in his assessment of contemporary political affairs. It concerns the responsibility one has toward one's enemies. Two dimensions of this problem naturally confront Levinas: the relationship of Jews to Germans and that of Israelis and Jews to the Arab nations and to the Palestinians. As we shall see even more clearly as we proceed, because each person is responsible for everyone else, one is also responsible for and to one's enemy. But in the everyday world of ordinary life, how does this basic responsibility work out? What does it mean? What role does it play? This is what we want to know at this point in our discussion.

Let me begin by posing the difficulty in the starkest form. In one way, it is a difficulty for us as we try to understand Levinas, and in another it is a difficulty for Levinas to make sense of the relationship between enemies in a world that is deeply grounded in grace and benevolence. We can see how powerful the difficulty is by identifying three points that seem to be in sharp conflict. One is the idea, which we have yet to explore thematically but which has presented itself regularly, that for Levinas goodness is the essence of humanity. Each of us is responsible for and responsible to everyone else in every way, and this seems manifestly to include even those who hate us, assault us, malign us, and inflict pain and suffering upon us. The second point is that there are in everyday life and in politics genuine enemies, even extreme ones, and it seems reasonable at times, if not always, to oppose them when they are a threat, while they are harming us, and even after they have violated us. Everyday life is filled with examples, mundane and not so mundane, but for Levinas it is emblematic to ask: How should one act toward Germans? Indeed, how should one act toward a particular German – say, Hitler himself? And how does one act toward the Arab nations, toward those who hate and attack Jews in Israel and seek the destruction of the Jewish state and the death of Jews, perhaps even the annihilation of the Jewish people? Today, we live in a world of fanaticism and terrorism, of suicide bombings and attacks, of passionate and seemingly irrevocable animosities. How should one act toward those whose fanatical hatred threatens to maim or kill your friends, your family, or yourself? Finally, my third point is to recall the incident described by Grossman of the German-hating woman who for no reason of any kind aborts her attack on him and instead offers the German officer a piece of bread. What are we to make of this act? What about it captures Levinas's moral and humane imagination? Is it that it is an act of kindness, or is it that it is a *wholly inexplicable* act of kindness? What makes this episode exemplary? Of *what* is it exemplary? Are there any recommendations to be made about how to act toward one's enemy – from this case or indeed from any case?

Recall that in 1982, when Levinas and Alain Finkelkraut were interviewed about the events at Sabra and Chatila, he was asked: "Isn't history, isn't politics the very site of the encounter with the 'other,' and for the Israeli, isn't the 'other' above all the Palestinian?"[100] In answering, as I understand him, Levinas rejected the implication of Shlomo Malka, the interviewer, that the "other" is most of all the one who is different from you and opposes you. Rather, he says, "the other is the neighbour," kin or someone who could be. Levinas, I take it, was answering Malka's question as if its point was to ask about Levinas's own position toward the conflict and about his loyalties and responsibilities. In this situation, both the Israeli and the Palestinian are Levinas's others. The one is his neighbor or kin, the other is his neighbor's enemy. If your neighbor treats another neighbor unjustly, then the question is about right and wrong, justice and injustice. Everyone does not, simply in virtue of being an "other," become an enemy. Nor does a friend or kin always remain immune from moral judgment. Ethics reverberates in the political and social domain; in one way, everyone is the "other" and the "neighbor"; in another, you can have friends and enemies, and both can be either right or wrong, depending upon the circumstances. Sheer otherness does not make its demands in an isolated fashion; it does not by itself dictate one's particular response. Nor are there fixed degrees of otherness. Negotiating the vagaries of conflicting demands and responsibilities is what right and wrong, justice and injustice, are all about.

We might reasonably infer, then, that this applies to Germans as well, even during the years of World War II and the Holocaust. After those years, the issue becomes one of forgiveness, one might say. Here the enemy is not just someone in conflict with you over principles or over land and power. Here the enemy is a different sort of person. Jean Améry, in an extraordinary essay, discusses torture and claims that it was the essence of the Nazi Reich.[101] Torture, he says, is an assault on the body that is such that then and forever after the victim loses "trust in the world." He comes away with a sense of no longer being a member of the human, moral community, of being "foreign." Moreover, Améry claims, torture was at the heart of Nazism. They tortured not to get information nor to reduce opposition. They tortured out of a love of torture, out of pure depravity. Nazism hated the word "humanity" like the pious man hates sin.[102] The question – or

---

[100] "Ethics and Politics" in Hand (ed.), *The Levinas Reader*, 294.
[101] Jean Améry, "Torture" in Améry, *At the Mind's Limits* (Bloomington: Indiana University Press, 1980), 21–40.
[102] Jean Améry, "Torture" in *At the Mind's Limits*, 31.

at least one question – for Levinas is: Should one forgive such a Nazi? Should one give him a piece of bread out of principle? And, if one does, should it be for no reason other than that you are human and he is as well?

The theme of the colloquium of French Jewish intellectuals held in October 1963 at which Levinas gave a Talmudic lesson was "Forgiveness." It was meant to include "the question of forgiveness posed by German guilt."[103] Hannah Arendt once described the evils of Auschwitz and the death camps as being beyond the bounds of forgiveness:

In their effort to prove that everything is possible, totalitarian regimes have dis-covered without knowing it that there are crimes which men can neither punish nor forgive. When the impossible was made possible it became the unpunishable, inforgivable absolute evil which could no longer be understood and explained by the evil motives of self-interest, greed, covetousness, resentment, lust for power, and cowardice; and which therefore anger could not revenge, love could not endure, friendship could not forgive.[104]

Arendt is saying that there is something no longer fitting or even possible about asking whether to forgive Germans who express their guilt and seek forgiveness. In fact, they really cannot express guilt and seek forgiveness. There is a difficulty in political and personal life forgiving such Germans as Adolf Eichmann, Heinrich Himmler, and Klaus Barbie.[105] An analogous question arose for Martin Buber when he had to confront whether one could have an I-Thou encounter with Hitler, Heydrich, Himmler, or Goebbels. The issue is not exactly the same, because for Buber it concerns the possibility of a person's life and its meaning arising from a relationship with an enemy and a criminal so extraordinary. Buber wavered on the issue.[106] With respect to Arab-Israeli relations, he was much more convinced and positive, as is well-known.[107] But the challenge to Levinas seems to be more direct and more difficult. It concerns responsibility, kindness, and forgiveness, not reestablishing a relationship and

---

[103] *Nine Talmudic Readings*, 20; cf. 25.

[104] Arendt, *The Origins of Totalitarianism*, 459.

[105] In an interview, when asked about the Klaus Barbie trial and in particular whether Barbie remained an "other" for him, Levinas responded that the trial dealt with "a horror that can never be repaired or forgotten," with events that are "more horrible than any sanction." And then he said, "If someone in his soul and conscience can forgive him, let him do so. I cannot." See Levinas, "On the Utility of Insomnia (Interview with Bertrand Révillon)" in *Unforeseen History*, 129.

[106] Michael L. Morgan, "Martin Buber, Cooperation, and Evil," *Journal of the American Academy of Religion* 58:1 (1990), 99–109.

[107] For an excellent collection of relevant writings, see Paul R. Mendes-Flohr (ed.), *A Land of Two Peoples: Martin Buber on Jews and Arabs* (New York: Oxford University Press, 1983).

some indeterminate directions stemming from it, but rather doing something *for* one's enemy: helping, assisting, accepting, and even forgiving.[108]

In the course of his Talmudic lesson on "forgiveness," Levinas refers to his friend Vladimir Jankélévitch, who had spoken earlier that day. In 1970, Jankélévitch published the essay "The Imprescriptable – to Forgive?" on the character of the Nazi atrocities and the situation regarding forgiveness. Like Arendt, Jankélévitch has profound doubts about the possibility of forgiveness:

This crime contrary to nature, without reason this exorbitant crime is literally a "metaphysical" crime. The criminals are not mere fanatics, nor are they blind doctrinaires or horrible dogmatics: they are, strictly speaking, "monsters." When an act denies the essence of man as man, the prescription which would tend to absolve it in the name of morality, contradicts morality itself. Is it not here contradictory or even absurd to invoke forgiveness?[109]

To Jankélévitch, the Holocaust is beyond our current comprehension; it requires continual examination, exploration, and reflection. It registers in helplessness and powerlessness.[110] It is incomparable and inexplicable. Not a crime like others, how can the perpetrators by charged or pardoned? But all this aside, Jankélévitch argues, there has been no sincere plea for forgiveness. It is a *"fait accompli* abetted by indifference, moral amnesia, and general superficiality." That is, the French have given forgiveness without thought and almost casually; nor have the Germans felt the need to ask for it or have they done so. "Forgiveness! Have they ever asked us for forgiveness? It is only the distress and extreme dereliction of the guilty that could make forgiveness meaningful. But when the culprit is fat, well-fed, prosperous, made rich by the 'economic miracle,' forgiveness becomes a rather sinister joke."[111] At best, he claims, the Germans can be said to *pretend* to ask for forgiveness in the face of such pretense, and he recommends refusing reparations, an act not without significance: "[C]rimes are not convertible into cash. There are no damages that can compensate us for six million victims; there are no reparations for the incomparable."[112] What

---

[108] For a thoughtful reflection on forgetting, forgiveness, and amnesty, concerning the postwar French response to Germans and those who collaborated with the Vichy regime, see Susan Rubin Suleiman, *Crises of Memory and the Second World War* (Harvard University Press, 2006), Ch. 9, especially, on forgiveness in Arendt, Kristeva, Derrida, and Ricoeur, 227–32.

[109] Vladimir Jankélévitch, "The Imprescriptable – to Forgive?," 25 (unpublished trans., from MS); see also his *Forgiveness* (Chicago: University of Chicago Press, 2005).

[110] Jankélévitch, "The Imprescriptable – to Forgive?," 29.

[111] Jankélévitch, "The Imprescribtable – to Forgive?," 47–48, 49, 50.

[112] Jankélévitch, "The Imprescriptable – to Forgive?," 58–59.

there is, Jankélévitch concludes, is an obligation to remember, to not allow the past to be forgotten, to stand as guardians of oblivion.[113]

I think that we can read Levinas's Talmudic lesson in 1963 as a response to Jankélévitch's passionate sentiments about the German crime, his criticisms of French and Germans, and his views on forgiveness. Levinas warns that his lesson does not summarize a general Jewish view on forgiveness. What it permits is the illumination of certain features of forgiveness and the possibility of justice and reconciliation between persons. I do not want to survey Levinas's teaching or even to summarize what might be thought to be his main points. But we can learn something about how complex the situation is from Levinas's perspective by noticing a few especially important points that he makes.

There is a moment in his lesson when Levinas suggests that forgiveness may actually be impossible:

There are two conditions for forgiveness: the good will of the offended party and the full awareness of the offender. But the offender is in essence unaware. The aggressiveness of the offender is perhaps his very unconsciousness. Aggression is the lack of attention *par excellence*. In essence, forgiveness would be impossible.[114]

The emphasis here must be on the word "full." The victim must be willing to forgive but should be willing only if the perpetrator shows, in action and in speech, that he comprehends fully what he has done. But – and this, I take it, is Levinas's point – the aggressive violence of the perpetrator's act shows that the perpetrator is not "fully aware," for if he had been, he would not have performed the act. Hence, essentially and of necessity, forgiveness is impossible. To this argument, which seems fallacious precisely because it fails to acknowledge the importance of time, Jankélévitch adds a key ingredient: The Germans not only were blind to what they were doing – if not in fact fully cognizant in the cases of Hitler, Heidegger, and a host of others – but in addition their descendants in 1965 showed little willingness to acknowledge and admit the crimes of the Nazi years. Levinas's argument may not be valid as a conceptual one, but empirically, in the case of Germans and forgiveness, it is telling indeed.

Levinas follows this argument for the impossibility of forgiveness with a more restricted one for withholding it in a particular case. "One can, if pressed to the limit, forgive the one who has spoken [or acted] unconsciously.... One can forgive many Germans, but there are some Germans it is difficult to forgive. It is difficult to forgive Heidegger."[115] In Heidegger's case – and he was not alone – he spoke and acted knowingly. Notice that Levinas says that here, in

[113] Jankélévitch, "The Imprescribtable – to Forgive?," 62.
[114] *Nine Talmudic Readings*, 25.
[115] *Nine Talmudic Readings*, 25.

the case of those who knew, it is not impossible to forgive, but it is "difficult."
Jankélévitch was much more convinced about this; for him, forgiveness in this
case was more than "difficult"; it was wrong, out of the question. As he put
it, "[A]ll of Germany, its youth, its thinkers, failed to notice that the most
horrific tragedy of history occurred right before their eyes.... They feel no
guilt, they acknowledge no wrong.... Why should we forgive those who show
so little respect for their own infamy?"[116] Neither Levinas nor Jankélévitch
debates Heidegger's involvement, commitment, or failures; they ask: Should he
be forgiven? Levinas says, probably not, if he sought forgiveness or showed signs
of remorse; Jankélévitch, once again so very concrete, says no because he has
shown no regrets, no guilt at all.

In his final set of remarks, Levinas turns to a biblical text and some Talmudic
reflections on it. Levinas asks: If someone has committed an injustice or a
crime and the descendants ask for retaliation or justice, must one forgive the
perpetrator's progeny? Judaism teaches that while one cannot deny the right
of retaliation to others, it might in fact be better for Judaism to deny it to
themselves: "[I]t does not ask it for itself.... [T]o be Israel is to not claim it."
Justice, he says, must be tempered with a kind of goodness, with sensitivity
and compassion, at least for Jews. What exactly does this mean concerning
Jankélévitch's proposals? Is Levinas concurring with the refusal of reparations?
Or is he suggesting an act of generous forgiveness even when it is undeserved?
I am inclined to think the former, that for Jews it is better to forgive as an act
of refusal that shows how deep goodness need be, even to the point of turning
aside justice in its favor.

Forgiveness is about reconciliation between parties whose relationship has
been damaged. I have turned to Levinas's interpretation of the Talmudic text
from Tractate *Yoma* to show how his central insight about the face-to-face
encounter and responsibility applies to concrete ethical situations. Such situations do not call for "saintly" or ethically "extraordinary" acts; they do not
call for us to suspend all thinking or to act for no "reasons" at all. Rather, they
call for careful, responsible reflection on the details of the situation in terms
of a keen attentiveness to ourselves, the other person, and our relationship.
In short, in this text we see Levinas applying his ethical insight in a type of
concrete, everyday situation that we all experience frequently and showing us
what kinds of considerations we ought to examine in the course of determining how to act. Levinas does not recommend suspending such deliberation and
acting with spontaneity and "thoughtlessness." He recommends being sensitive to the nuances of such concrete situations and deliberating in the light of
such considerations and in behalf of action that is thereby recommended by our

[116] Jankélévitch, "The Imprescribtable – to Forgive?," 52.

responsibility to others, in this case to the other person who has injured us. In this way, the face-to-face and responsibility are features of human social relationships in general and not episodes of remarkable conduct.[117]

With this discussion of one's relationship to one's enemy and how one should respond to one's enemy in terms of forgiveness, I bring this chapter to a close. In it, we have observed Levinas considering ethical and political matters in fairly concrete circumstances. His thinking has favored real episodes and the way that individuals, in everyday circumstances, find themselves obligated to act toward others. But he has not shied away from some fairly large-scale judgments about Western and European culture and the crisis of the modern world in the twentieth century. Here, the Holocaust, Auschwitz, and Nazi totalitarianism have played an important but by no means exclusive role. They tell us something about how individuals and groups have come to relate to one another and especially how individuals have been abandoned, injured, and oppressed by one another in extreme ways that indict all of Western culture.

But Levinas's judgments are not *ad hoc* responses to singular events; they are responses that express substantial and deep examined views about the human condition and how we live it. These views Levinas developed in the 1940s and 1950s, and they took expression in *Totality and Infinity* in 1961, were enriched and modulated in *Otherwise Than Being* in 1974 and in *Of God Who Comes to Mind* in 1986, and appeared in numerous essays along the way. Levinas's views have been called an "ethical metaphysics," and there is likely some truth in this expression. In the chapters to come, we will want to see how much truth and what it is.

---

[117] This theme, that the face-to-face encounter is a condition for all human social relationships and not an episodic event, will be developed in Chapter 2.

2

Phenomenology and Transcendental Philosophy

I have made a point of explaining how I approach Levinas in these pages. My goal is to place him and his work within the tradition of Anglo-American philosophy. I will not ignore his relationships to influences such as Bergson, Husserl, Heidegger, Blanchot, Rosenzweig, and others, but if I hope to construct a bridge between Levinas's thinking and a different philosophical tradition, that will involve transporting his work rather than leaving it wholly in its own environment. Thus far, I have tried to observe Levinas doing what a philosopher engaged with ethical, political, and religious matters in the twentieth century might be expected to do: comment on and consider critically the crisis of the century and events within it. Now it is time to turn to Levinas's philosophical thinking and his writings and to ask about the relationship between his philosophy and the assessments and judgments we have seen him making. This will require that we take a brief preliminary look at the content of his "ethical metaphysics" and begin to examine it by asking what Levinas is doing in the course of that thinking, what kind of thinking it is. In the early part of this chapter, then, I will be making a first pass through his thinking, especially in its early development, a project that will unavoidably use terms yet to be clarified as well as paraphrases that may simplify too much and have a certain impropriety and vagueness about them. It will also avoid argumentation, excessive clarification, problems and questions, and all the trappings of careful analysis. That will come later. Before we can try to place Levinas's work in a different world, we must have some picture of what it is like, even in an account with all its flaws and inadequacies.

A PRELIMINARY SKETCH

In order to sketch this picture of Levinas's ethical metaphysics, I begin by drawing on some relatively early works. These include *Time and the Other* (1947)

"Is Ontology Fundamental?" (1951), "The Ego and Totality" (1954), "Philosophy and the Idea of the Infinite" (1957), *Totality and Infinity* (1961), and "Transcendence and Height" (1962). At times, I may use some terminology that Levinas introduced and developed subsequent to this early period; if I do, I will indicate clearly when the terminology is employed. In the late 1960s and throughout the 1970s, Levinas does modify and expand his basic terms, concepts, and metaphors to a certain extent. Some commentators argue that he does more than modify and expand, that he substantially revises, his philosophy; I will say something about that issue later. For the moment, I set it aside and call attention to some important modifications as we go along, in subsequent chapters. But on the basic issue of this chapter, his approach to philosophy and the kind of thinking he is engaged in, I believe that he remains firm. For this reason, I think we are best served by outlining his early account, at least for the moment, in as straightforward a way as possible.

In *Time and the Other* and *Totality and Infinity* Levinas gives an account that appears narrative and genetic; for all its substantive differences, an account like Hobbes's of the establishment of the civil state from an original state of nature might seem to be a reasonable analogue. One might also see similarities with other social-contract theorists, including Rawls. Later, we might want to ask how close the analogy is or how erroneous; for now, it is sufficient to realize that Levinas's account of the origins of society, ethics, and such is not an anomaly, notwithstanding its peculiar features. But just as Hobbes never claimed that the state of nature ever existed in a pure form for all of humankind nor Rawls that anyone actually lived in the "original position," so Levinas's account does not depend upon treating his narrative as a description of the origins and development of actual life. In fact, like these others, Levinas is giving an account of various features of human experience that are manifest in actual life but can be best illuminated by means of a narrative form, of a genetical story. For now, then, we need not be concerned about the narrative shape of the account.

Suppose we begin with a natural world filled with existing things – natural objects such as trees, rocks, mountains, stars, lakes, wind, and rain – and omit any items that are constructed or artificial. Each of these things exists in a certain way, and Levinas tries to say something about this "existing" of things, as it is experienced in our lives, at moments when the particular features of things fade and we are left with a sense of sheer, anonymous existence. At this stage in Levinas's story, of course, we have not yet emerged, so in order to identify this basic *existing*, Levinas looks ahead at experiences of ours that point to it, experiences like fatigue or insomnia. It is brooding and foreboding, like wakefulness to someone who has insomnia and simply cannot sleep; this sheer existence – what Levinas calls *il ya* or *there is* – is inescapable. Imagine

Spinoza's substance in its active sense, as *natura naturans*, but only thought of as manifest at a certain level of complexity, not yet including human beings, who are percipient, cognitive, rational, and reflective. Now, Levinas suggests, let us think of consciousness as "standing out from" this natural existing plenum. "Consciousness is the power to sleep," of tearing itself away or withdrawing from the insomnia attuned to sheer existing and therefore being able to think about itself and its existence, of reflection. What arises with this emergence of consciousness is the "I," or the self.[1]

At this stage, then, we have the I, the particular self, a natural organic being with consciousness, living in the world. Levinas's next step is to consider how this living self responds to or lives in its world, amidst the natural things that surround it. My primary way of living in the world, Levinas calls "enjoyment." "The world is an ensemble of nourishment. . . . To stroll is to enjoy the fresh air, not for health but for the air. . . . It is an ecstatic experience – being outside oneself – but limited by the object."[2] Such enjoyment involves sensation and thought, but it is fuller than mere sensation or thought. It is a kind of involvement with the world, not use but satisfaction, incorporation, and proximity. In a sense, I am at home in the world around me, not unqualifiedly, of course, but sufficiently to appreciate breathing, exploring, viewing, feeling, eating, and enjoying what is there for me.[3]

At first, I am totally invested in myself. Then I turn to the world, to things around me, for enjoyment and nourishment; I sense it, too, and think about it and what it means to me. But I am still alone, as it were. I may now have some perspective on the world and myself in it, but I am alone, and I even tend to lose myself in a universal view of the world.[4] "The world offers the subject participating in existing in the form of enjoyment, and consequently permits it to exist at a distance from itself. The subject is absorbed in the object it absorbs, and nevertheless keeps a distance with regard to that object. . . . It is not just the disappearance of the self, but self-forgetfulness, as a first abnegation."[5] Levinas calls this state, in which "knowledge never encounters anything truly other in the world," "the profound truth of idealism."[6] That is, what we later, philosophically, call idealism, the view that assimilates the world to the self or to a cosmic spirit or mind, is in fact grounded in this fundamental feature of the human condition,

[1] See Levinas, *Time and the Other* (hereafter, TO), Part I, 39–57. For a helpful account, see Michael Purcell, *Levinas and Theology*, 88–94, 95–98, 128–30.
[2] TO, Part II, 63.
[3] Cf. Levinas, *Totality and Infinity* (hereafter, TI), 109–21.
[4] TO, Part III, 67.
[5] TO, Part III, 67.
[6] TO, Part III, 68.

that it includes a "moment" in which the self is alone in the world and even takes the world into itself from a wholly nonparticular point of view.

As I pointed out earlier, Levinas does not mean that as individuals we are ever alone in the world, as if existing in some Eden or state of nature. Nor does he mean that we are ever actually alone. But there are these features in our existence or these dimensions of our inhabiting the world, living within and from it, becoming aware of it, and coming to know it and ourselves in it.[7] What does Levinas mean, however, when he calls our knowledge of this world an "idealism?" For now, it is sufficient to recognize that this claim is associated with Levinas's use of the word "totality" and the ideas of "same" and "other." That is, when I am fully at home in the world and achieve some understanding of it, I grasp it as a totality – as a systematic, orderly whole – from my point of view as a knowing agent, but in terms of general concepts, ideas, principles, and so forth. I organize and order the world and comprehend it; Levinas calls the "I" the "same" and says that in this way the same absorbs the other into itself or forms the other to itself. Particular as my existence is, I think in generalities and commonalities, and I grasp the world by incorporating into these concepts as if into a container. In this sense, all such knowing is a kind of idealism, of taming the world and domesticating it to my capacities and venue, as if my capacities were wholly general and detached and impersonal. I make everything thinkable and knowable by drawing everything within the borders of these conceptual capacities. This achievement of sameness or homogeneity is one outcome of my inhabiting the world.

I skip to Levinas's main idea:[8] This solitude of the I inhabiting the world is shattered or interrupted. The I is not alone; there is an other person whose face I confront and experience. In *Time and the Other*, Levinas puts it this way: "[T]the Other is what I myself am not. The Other is this, not because of the Other's character, or physiognomy, or psychology, but because of the Other's very alterity. The Other is, for example, the weak, the poor, 'the orphan and the widow,' whereas I am the rich or the powerful."[9] In social life, I am always confronted by another particular person, who is near or far, friend or foe, present or absent, but always in the world with me and more importantly over against me or before me. This person is different from me fundamentally – prior to considering her features or character, her height, her complexion, her features, the color of her hair, her humor and mood, whatever. And her difference is

---

[7] TI, 109–74.

[8] In the text, Levinas moves from the same to the other via consideration of suffering, evil, and death; only then does he arrive at the other person, as an unconditionally other that completely negates the self when it is encountered. We shall say more about this later.

[9] TO, 83.

all about what she imposes upon me simply by virtue of being there, before me. What she imposes is dependence and need, integrity and demand. Her presence, before it says anything else to me, says "let me live," "let me be here too," "feed me," "allow me to share the world and be nourished by it too." I am imposed upon, called into question, beseeched, and commanded, and thereby I am responsible, Levinas says. In *Totality and Infinity*, Levinas says: "I must have been in relation with something I do not live from." This relation occurs as an "encounter [with] the indiscrete face of the Other that calls me into question. The Other... paralyzes possession, which he contests by his epiphany in the face.... I welcome the Other who presents himself in my home by opening my home to him."[10] My thinking about the world and understanding it is also, in this way, like my inhabiting and enjoying what nature provides me, interrupted. Something outside or prior to my thinking confronts me: It is the demand and need of another person, of each and every other person. In this way, I am, in a sense, a moral agent before I am a cognitive one; I am responsible before I am an observer or explainer or interpreter. Levinas even associates this "epiphany of the face of the other" or encounter with the other person's need and demand with "language." What he means is that words, communication, and speech all arise out of and are embedded in a prelinguistic relationship between me and a particular other person. This relationship, moreover, has an ethical character; it is a relationship with the other person's "face," not her appearance or mood or whatever; it is with the fragility and dependence of her very being on me.[11]

I have been trying, in these paragraphs, to construct a very spare sketch of Levinas's account of what the human condition is, based on some early texts of his. Let me reiterate: This is merely a very preliminary outline. My intention is a limited one: to provide enough detail to ask these questions: What is the status of this account? In giving it and developing it, what is Levinas doing? Is this a philosophical account? Is it empirical in one way or another? Is it more than empirical? Is it an ethical metaphysics, and what might it mean to say that for Levinas this account frames an "ethics as first philosophy?"[12]

---

[10] TI, 170–71.

[11] TI, 171–74, 197–201, 204–14.

[12] At a crucial moment in TO, a kind of turning point in the development of the work, Levinas stops to make a remark about method that is very revealing. Having developed part of the story that I have outlined, he says, "I have just described a dialectical situation. I am now going to show a concrete situation where this dialectic is accomplished. It is impossible for me to explain this method at length here; I have resorted to it again and again. One sees in any event that it is not phenomenological to the end." Like Hegel's dialectic in *The Phenomenology of Spirit*, Levinas has set out an itinerary or developmental account that reveals the layers or dimensions of human existence and finally arrives at a primordial level. He now proposes to identify and examine in a way like the "phenomenological" a concrete situation that reveals the most fundamental and

INTERPRETING LEVINAS'S APPROACH

Commentators often note that Levinas does not thematically discuss method-ological questions; he even goes so far as to denigrate any overindulgence in such matters. All of this is correct. Levinas may have many reasons for his dis-missal of methodological questions. But there are just as many reasons, if not more, why we need to think about them. If we are to understand his thinking and his writing, we need to understand the precise context or perspective for what he says and does. We need to understand what he is claiming and under what constraints. Even at this stage – before we have examined more fully his views, analyses, arguments, and more – we can see that the observations and assessments Levinas made in the public and political domain ought to be related to the sketch we just gave. But it is not clear how that relationship might or should be conceived. This is the sort of thing we now need to consider. In developing this picture of the human condition, what is Levinas doing and what is its relationship to his comments on our ordinary social and political lives and to our lives themselves?

Levinas may be thought to have answered our concerns explicitly and pre-cisely. In the Preface to *Totality and Infinity*, he says that his method is the "phenomenological method" and that "the way we are describing to work back and remain this side of objective certitude resembles what has come to be called the transcendental method. . . . "[13] Moreover, referring to Husserl, he notes that "intentional analysis is the search for the concrete."[14] He clarifies what this intentional analysis involves: "[N]otions held under the direct gaze of the thought that defines them are nevertheless, unbeknown to this naive thought, revealed to be implanted in horizons unsuspected by thought; these horizons endow them with a meaning." Levinas says that in this way "an objec-tifying thought" overflows with "a forgotten experience from which it lives." This is called a "deduction" – whereby "the formal structure of thought" is broken up "into events which this structure dissimulates, but which sustain it and restore its concrete significance."[15] Here we have an explicit admission that Levinas's method is transcendental phenomenology, or akin to it, and that its goal is to expose forgotten or hidden horizons of meaning that underlie our normal, objective experience of things and our thoughts about them. Would that things were so simple!

---

primordial level in an especially perspicuous way, even though, as he warns, at a certain point it ceases to be phenomenological, strictly speaking. We shall see exactly what he means by this warning in what follows.

[13] TI, 28; cf. 25.

[14] TI, 28.

[15] TI, 28; cf. 44–45. See also *Of God Who Comes to Mind*, 152–65, esp. 15–32.

I do not think that there are any doubts that throughout his career Levinas viewed his thinking as a mode or development of Husserlian phenomenology.[16] Broadly speaking, he saw himself as casting light on a forgotten, hidden, or hitherto unnoticed level of meaning that has a primacy for human (social) living. In a sense, he saw himself as calling attention to a "regime of meaning" that we take for granted, pay insufficient attention to, depend upon, and should attend to more fully in order to become as human as we can become. One way to clarify what his method is and what status his thinking has, what he is doing in thinking as he does, would be to look substantively at his analyses and clarify how they work and what they seem to accomplish. In a sense, the remainder of this book will seek to do that, not always explicitly but at least indirectly. In this chapter, I want to set the stage for any attempt to answer these questions. A standard way of doing this would be to discuss the phenomenological method in Husserl and Heidegger, especially in the light of what Levinas wrote about both, including his Husserl book and his essays on Husserl and on Heidegger. I may say a little about these matters but only a little. Largely, my approach will be a different one, however. First, I want to examine and discuss a distinction that Robert Bernasconi makes concerning interpreters of Levinas and consider its relevance to this issue of method. Then I will discuss the issue of transcendental arguments and transcendental philosophy as it has arisen recently in English-speaking philosophical thinking and ask what its relevance to Levinas might be. Here, one touchstone is transcendental argumentation in Kant and German Idealism; another is its relevance to understanding what philosophy means for Wittgenstein and then, more recently, for figures like Cavell and Rawls. My goal, then, is to sketch portions of a map of some ways that philosophy and transcendental thinking have been understood and to clarify Levinas's thinking by locating him somewhere on that map – or "beyond" it!

I want to begin by discussing observations by two interpreters of Levinas, Robert Bernasconi and Theodore de Boer, but the best place to start is the important paper by Bernasconi on reading *Totality and Infinity* published in 1989. In returning to that work after 25 years, Bernasconi notices that Levinas's face-to-face relation is treated in two ways by interpreters.[17] "Some interpreters understand it as a concrete experience that we can recognize in our lives. Other commentators have understood the face-to-face relation to be the condition

---

[16] For a very interesting and helpful discussion of these issues, see Drabinski, *Sensibility and Singularity*. Drabinski focuses on Levinas's later work *Otherwise Than Being* (hereafter, OB) although he does touch on the earlier writings. There are, as one might expect, numerous treatments of Levinas's debt to Husserl.

[17] The distinction between these two interpretations of the status of the face-to-face relation, as drawn by Bernasconi, is appropriated and employed for their own purposes by Tamra Wright, *The Twilight of Jewish Philosophy*, 16–22, and by Drabinski, *Sensibility and Singularity*, *passim*.

for the possibility of ethics and indeed of all economic existence and knowledge."[18] Bernasconi calls the former an "empirical" reading and the latter a
"transcendental" one, and he remarks that "Levinas himself seems unable to
decide between these rival interpretations."[19] Let me ignore, at least for now,
what Bernasconi does with this distinction, which he says "provide[s] the terms
for almost every introduction to Levinas's thought," and rather consider the
distinction itself, not merely as a device for characterizing differences in interpretation but also as an instrument for investigating what Levinas himself is
doing.

   Is the face-to-face encounter a "concrete experience," or is it a "transcendental condition," or is it neither or both? What would it mean to say that
the face-to-face encounter of the self and the other person, for each and every
other person, is a concrete experience?[20] I think that the point of this question
is to ask whether the event of one person confronting another particular person
in the way Levinas describes as face-to-face occurs or can occur in ordinary,
everyday life. Is it something that happens in the course of life, intentionally
or by happenstance? Can we aim to engage the other this way or aim to create
opportunities for such encounters to occur?

   At first glance, we might be inclined to think that Levinas clearly acknowledges this possibility and might even be thought to idealize such encounters. We
need only recall the two episodes from *Life and Fate* that he cites so frequently:
the act of the Russian woman who hands a piece of bread to the German officer
and Yevgenia's encounter with the necks and backs of those in line in front of
her at the Lubyanka prison. Both seem to be episodes of a particular face-to-
face encounter. Or more accurately, one is an engagement with the face, the
other the kind and generous response to such an engagement. Furthermore,
if human life is meaningful because it is oriented in terms of responsibility to
and for the other, it must be a demand experienced in life that provides that

---

[18] Robert Bernasconi, "Rereading *Totality and Infinity*," in Charles Scott and Arlene Dallery (eds.),
    The Question of the Other, 23.

[19] See Bernasconi, "Rereading *Totality and Infinity*," 23; see also Levinas, *Of God Who Comes to
    Mind*, 86–90, which is a response to an article on the subject of method by Theodore de Boer.
    We shall discuss de Boer below.

[20] I prefer to call this the "episodic" interpretation of the face-to-face rather than the "empirical,"
    or concrete-experience, interpretation. The issue is not whether one self experiences another
    but rather whether the experience of the face of the other is a discrete, identifiable, singular
    event or episode. Does it occur? On this reading, which takes the face-to-face as an analogue
    to episodes like Martin Buber's I-Thou encounters or meetings, Levinas's view seems almost
    quasi-mystical, insofar as the experience or episode has a transcendent quality and is an event
    of a rare and special kind.

orientation. Where, if not from experience, would this sense of responsibility come from?[21]

At the same time, however, it seems utterly impossible that the face-to-face could occur in ordinary life. There are several reasons to be suspicious. First, Levinas says that the encounter with the face is somehow originary and primordial, prior to ontology and being, in his terms an-archic. Ontology is the study of being or the thinking about being, and the domain of being is the world of everyday existence, of objects, life, experience, sensation, thought, and practical affairs. Any theoretical understanding we have is grounded in this world and is about it, in one sense or another. Only in the world of being do objects disclose themselves to us, and only there are they grasped by us. Hence, thought, language, and explanation are exclusive to the world of existing things, as are sensory experience and activity. But if the face is prior to or more original than what exists and presents itself to us, then it cannot be experienced, sensed, analyzed, grasped in concepts, thematized, and so forth. In short, it cannot be encountered in ordinary life; the "epiphany of the face" and the responsibility it calls forth are not episodes that occur. Levinas stretches his terminology in order to emphasize this fact; he denies that the face appears to us or is a phenomenon. Rather, it reveals itself or is an epiphany. It is *like* an appearance but not one. It is preperceptual, prelinguistic, preconceptual, and pretheoretical. Nonetheless, the individual self does engage with or encounter the face of the other person. Given this framework, however, it is hard to believe that this engagement is an everyday event or an ordinary – or even extraordinary – concrete experience.

Second, Levinas calls the epiphany of the face of the other "the infinite" or "exteriority," and he contrasts it with totality, which is the domain circumscribed, encompassed, and to a degree constructed by the self or the agent. In effect, what Levinas means is that the face is outside whatever is the object of our experience and thought. Totality is the domain of reason or mind or culture or theory. Hence, Levinas's point about the face and its presence to us is that it does not reveal itself in the ordinary ways, as an object of normal perception

---

[21] I think that it is unavoidable that in some sense or other the face-to-face does occur as an actually lived experience or, perhaps better, as one dimension of actually lived social experience. Levinas invests himself in examining experiences like insomnia, fatigue, and eros, precisely because they are concrete, ordinary experiences and yet show us to be in touch with what he calls transcendence or the other, in one sense or another. Furthermore, it is precisely such episodes or concrete experiences that he subjects to phenomenological or quasi-phenomenological investigation, in order to expose what is regularly hidden from view. It is very clear, therefore, that the face-to-face is part of our ordinary lives and not some eccentric or anomalous experience, such as a mystical or a ecstatic experience.

or of everyday concepts and thought. To be sure, he says, we do encounter the face – in a sense – and Descartes's claim that we have an idea of the infinite is a groping in the direction of saying this and affirming it, as Levinas sees it. But Descartes does not appreciate either what the infinite is or what it means to have an idea of it, to grasp it. Descartes thinks that the idea of the infinite is an idea like other ideas, at least in many ways, and also an idea of God. Levinas not only reinterprets the sense in which the idea of the infinite is an encounter with God, but also argues that as an idea it is unique, unlike having other ideas. The idea of the infinite just *is* the encounter with the face of the other. Basically, then, if ordinary life occurs within the broad confines of totality, the face cannot be encountered therein or in that way. Descartes's notion of having an idea of the infinite, as Levinas sees it, cannot designate an everyday experience even if it can designate some kind of experience or quasi-experience.

Moreover, for these reasons, Levinas's method cannot be phenomenological, strictly speaking; it can only be like it, one might argue. This is a third reason for doubting that the face-to-face can occur in ordinary life as a discrete episode. As Levinas points out, phenomenology is the study of intentionality, of consciousness as directed at objects, or, perhaps more accurately, at the meaning of objects or of objects as meaning something. It is a descriptive examination of both the subjective and objective dimensions or aspects of things as they appear to us – exactly how this appearing occurs, for various types of intentionality or consciousness, for various types of things, and so forth.[22] Fundamentally, then, phenomenology is the study of appearing, but, as we have seen, Levinas goes to great lengths to distinguish the face from an appearance. Now one reason for this distinction is that the face is hidden or occluded in normal experience. This could mean that the face is a hidden horizon or aspect of an actual perception or experience, analogous to the back side of a cube seen from the front or to other features of Napoleon known only as the general who was defeated at Waterloo. But this interpretation hardly seems radical enough for the status Levinas ascribes to the face. It cannot just be a hidden or undisclosed dimension of an actually perceived person. It is hidden, but it is not contingently hidden; in a sense, the face is necessarily hidden. It does not just happen to be the case that because of circumstances one does not encounter the other person's face where that means perceive the other as a face, as the one who beseeches and demands of me. There is a sense, for Levinas, in which one cannot ever possibly *perceive* the other as a face or as the face of the other person; rather, what one does is encounter the face of the other, and these are very different modes of

---

[22] For a clear and succinct account, see Robert Sokolowski, *Introduction to Phenomenology, passim*; see also Dan Zahavi, *Husserl's Phenomenology* (Stanford, CA: Stanford University Press, 2003).

relation. Or, more precisely, one is a mode of relation; the other is something else, something unique, originary, and determinative.[23]

How can we understand such as encounter? Husserl called the object of the intentionality of consciousness a *"noema"* and the intentional act a *"noesis."*[24] The terminology is confusing and has led to major controversy. Part of the point of exploring the intentionality of consciousness is to appreciate that the self and the world – or better, individual selves and particular things in the world – are not given or do not exist as independent, enclosed, isolated entities, all of whose relations with other things need to be grounded, explained, and justified solely by virtue of attention to features of the isolated, enclosed things to be related. Rather, the doctrine of intentionality claims that selves or persons are embedded primordially in a world of things, persons, and so forth. Selves occur in various forms of a self-world nexus. Phenomenological analysis explores these forms of nexus from both sides and in terms of the features constitutive of each type of nexus: sense perception, enjoyment, work, use, and so forth. From the side of the world in these nexuses, the thing presented in various ways – given its profiles, aspects, and so on – is called a *"noema."* This term has led to several interpretations, but two are especially important. To some, the *noema* is an entity present to consciousness, yet distinguishable from the thing itself. It is a *sense* or *meaning*, grasped by consciousness as a perceptual profile or as a meaning of a concept or word or whatever. To others, the *noema* is the object intended, but precisely as it is intended; it is, in perception, the perceived object precisely as it is perceived, or as it appears from a particular point of view, in certain conditions, and so on.

If, for Levinas, the face reveals itself to the self and the study of the encounter with the face is a kind of or similar to phenomenology, is the face a kind of or like a *noema*? Is it meaning or sense?[25] Or is it the other person when that person

---

[23] See Theodore de Boer, *The Rationality of Transcendence*, 25.

[24] There is an important and fascinating debate about the nature of the Husserlian *noema*. For a discussion, see Sokolowski, *Introduction to Phenomenology* (Cambridge: Cambridge University Press, 1999); the essays by Føllesdal, McIntyre and Smith, and Dreyfus in *Husserl, Intentionality, and Cognitive Science*, ed. by Hubert L. Dreyfus and Harrison Hall (Cambridge, MA: MIT Press, 1982); D. Smith and R. McIntyre, *Husserl and Intentionality* (Boston: Reidel, 1982); Robert Cobb-Stevens, *Husserl and Analytic Philosophy* (Boston: Kluwer, 1990); and Barry Smith and David Woodruff Smith (eds.), *The Cambridge Companion to Husserl* (Cambridge: Cambridge University Press, 1995).

[25] In an important passage, near the end of *Totality and Infinity*, Levinas says, "One of the principal theses of this work is that the noesis-noema structure is not the primordial structure of intentionality...." (294). Throughout the work, of course, Levinas says that the face-to-face is in fact "the primordial structure of intentionality." That is, if we take the notion of intentionality broadly enough, then the face-to-face is a mode of person-other relation that is more basic,

is encountered as a face? When one examines another person in everyday life, engages with that person, and so forth, these events occur within the natural attitude, as Husserl calls it. Examination of the intentionality of consciousness, of the modes of engagement with that person, however, occurs within the phenomenological attitude, in Husserl's terms. This requires a shift of perspective and focus, what he calls "bracketing" or "*epoché*." If encountering the face is to be explored, then, that exploration will have to require a shift of perspective from the everyday to something else. But does this mean that the face-to-face itself cannot occur in the everyday? Surely not. But if the exploration is *like* phenomenological examination but not exactly a case of it, then it might be that neither it nor its exploration is an everyday matter in the usual sense.[26]

TRANSCENDENTAL PHILOSOPHY

We have seen enough to appreciate how difficult it is to say what Levinas's disclosure of the encounter with the face of the other person amounts to. Especially given doubts about its empirical or episodic character, and in particular doubts that it is an extraordinary or anomalous experience, one is tempted to give it a different status altogether. Probably the most powerful case of this kind has been developed by the Dutch commentator Theodore de Boer in the classic essay "An Ethical Transcendental Philosophy."[27] De Boer's basic point is that "Levinas integrates phenomenological ontology into dialogical thought. Only the philosophy of the Other, 'metaphysics,' is able to provide a foundation for this ontology. Dialogue is the transcendental framework for the intentional relation to the world. . . ."[28] Later, he says that "the transcendental condition is not a necessary ontological structure which can be reconstructed from the empirical phenomena; it is an unrecoverable event or ontic incident which intersects the ontological order."[29] Wright, in her book *The Twilight of Jewish Philosophy*,

more determinative than the noesis–noema relation. Insofar as intentionality is a matter of the structure of appearing, however, then strictly speaking the face-to-face is a quasi-intentionality and not literally a mode of intentionality at all. As we shall see, Levinas works hard to use language and yet to stretch it, to clarify the dimension of human existence he is seeking to disclose.

[26] In interviews, Levinas refers to phenomenology as an opening to contexts not present to view and as a search for *mise-en-scène*; see *Is It Righteous To Be?*, 150–51, 159–60, 227. See also "Transcendence and Intelligibility" in *Basic Philosophical Writings*, 158; this essay, first given as a lecture in 1983, was published in 1984.

[27] See Bernasconi's comments in "Rereading *Totality and Infinity*," 26–27, and de Boer's essay, Ch.1 in *The Rationality of Transcendence*, also in Cohen (ed.), *Face to Face with Levinas*. See also Levinas's response in *Of God Who Comes to Mind*, 86–90.

[28] De Boer, *The Rationality of Transcendence*, 2.

[29] De Boer, *The Rationality of Transcendence*, 30.

examines what de Boer says in the light of Levinas's own statements, in order to evaluate de Boer's interpretation. I want to approach de Boer's proposal and Bernasconi's discussion from another direction. I want to examine them in the light of recent treatments in philosophical circles of transcendental arguments and transcendental philosophy. In other words, my interest is to clarify what it would mean if in fact Levinas's philosophical inquiry was in some sense transcendental. In a later chapter, I shall consider the issue of the limits of language and expressibility; for now, I am particularly concerned with the structure and method of Levinas's thought and will take for granted that he has linguistic resources to carry out that method.

Philosophers interested in transcendental arguments often focus, as we might expect, on Kant's use of transcendental methods, especially in the transcendental deduction in the first *Critique*, and on Kant's transcendental views.[30] Contemporary analytic discussion stems from P. F. Strawson's interpretation of Kant and Barry Stroud's criticism of it. The philosophical issues concern the employment of transcendental arguments against skepticism, specifically Kant's use of them against Hume's skepticism. Central issues include the structure of the arguments, their results, their point, and their goals. Against the skeptic, these arguments begin from positions or claims that the skeptic must accept if there is going to be conversation at all, and they proceed to conclusions that refute the skeptic or, more accurately, that lead the skeptic to the abandonment of his skepticism. The skeptic could be denying the existence of the external world, the fact of causality, the existence of other minds, or the objectivity of moral values, among other things. Philosophical discussion predominantly has focused on skepticism about the existence of the external world and about knowledge of that world. These were Kant's concerns in the first *Critique*. There have been controversies about the validity of Kant's arguments and their character and the precise way in which identifying necessary conditions for the possibility of experience, in both broad and narrow senses, foils the skeptic. There has also been a good deal of discussion about what it means to call these conditions "transcendental."

Ostensibly, Levinas's transcendental philosophy, if he has one or if it is helpful to characterize his thinking as transcendental, is more indebted to Husserl than it is to Kant. Still, from about 1906 Husserl himself began to see his

---

[30] Some commentators claim that it was a return to Kant by Husserl around 1906 that facilitated his claims that his own phenomenological method was transcendental in something like the Kantian sense. If Levinas is methodologically indebted to Husserl and Heidegger, and if both are indebted to Kant for their understanding of transcendental argumentation, then there is some reason to turn to recent discussion of Kant and German Idealism and the role and character of transcendental argumentation to clarify what Levinas is doing.

phenomenology as akin to Kant's inquiry and to take it as transcendental in a Kantian sense. It is reasonable to consider the ways that Levinas's thinking might be akin to Kant's as a transcendental enterprise. The latter argues that the categories of the understanding, on the one hand, and space and time, on the other, are necessary conditions for knowledge of the world and for sensory experience of it. Moreover, Kant's transcendental deduction of the categories comes to even deeper conclusions about what makes possible the applicability of these categories and forms of intuition to the sensory manifold in the first place. In a sense, all of Kant's results begin with the self's experience and hence with the I's conscious activity, and its outcomes concern the contributions of the I, the world, and their relationship that make this experience possible. Levinas's commitment to Husserlian intentionality situates him differently. For him, the I and the world begin as interrelated: The self experiences the world in various ways and is situated in the world in many ways, and the world means various things to the self. The question for Levinas is how the manifold interrelations between self and world occur and what makes them possible. How can the face-to-face be an ultimate answer to this question?

For the moment, let me set aside the question of whether Levinas employs or formulates any transcendental arguments per se. Instead, let me ask whether his conclusions about the primordial and determinative character of the face-to-face have transcendental status. How might the encounter with the face be related to everyday experiences or events such that it makes sense to call it a transcendental condition of those experiences or events? Paul Franks calls attention to the fact that some transcendental accounts are regressive, others progressive.[31] That is, in some cases we begin with experience, language, belief, and so on and recover the necessary condition or conditions that make the original phenomenon (experience, language, and so on) possible; such an account is regressive. In other cases, we begin with the necessary condition and proceed to show how the original phenomenon is derived from it; these accounts are progressive. Kant takes the first route; his German Idealist descendants take the latter. Generally, in both cases, the conditioned state or experience is empirical and the condition is nonempirical, or at least nonpsychological.[32] Commentators differ about whether Kant's account is realist or coherentist, about whether his transcendental philosophy grounds experience in facts beyond our normal grasp or whether it demonstrates the internal coherence of our experiences

---

[31] Paul Franks, "Transcendental Arguments, Reason, and Skepticism" in Robert Stern (ed.), *Transcendental Arguments: Problems and Projects*, 116–17 and n. 9.

[32] Ralph C. S. Walker, "Induction and Transcendental Arguments" in Robert Stern (ed.), *Transcendental Arguments*, 20; cf. Robert Stern, "On Kant's Response to Hume" in Stern (ed.), *Transcendental Arguments*, 48.

and beliefs without an external foundation.[33] If Levinas's identification of the face-to-face as basic and determinative is a transcendental outcome, it certainly is in the realist sense; it would be a case of grounding our ordinary experience in a fact that is beyond our normal grasp – beyond the orbit of totality. Quassim Cassam calls one group of transcendental arguments "world-directed": "[T]hey start with the assumption that there is thought or experience of some particular kind, and argue that for thought or experience of this kind to be possible, the world on which these thoughts or experiences occur must be a certain way."[34] Others, he says, are "self-directed": They "tell us something about the cognitive faculties of the thinking and knowing self."[35] Levinas's face-to-face would, in these terms, be both. Hence, it would be a kind of realist condition that is beyond our normal grasp, that tells us how the world is and what the self is and how they are related in order for certain experiences, thoughts, and so on to be possible.

Transcendental grounds are necessary conditions that make certain experiences possible. It is regularly pointed out that transcendental arguments have a close link to skepticism, as I indicated above, but skepticism can be epistemic or other than epistemic.[36] Levinas, we might propose, is primarily or at least initially provoked by moral skepticism or the threat of moral doubt, insecurity, and even nihilism. This sense of worry or threat is part of Levinas's reaction to Heidegger's Nazism and hence a central motivation for Levinas's critique of Heidegger in the years after 1933, continuing through the publication of *Totality and Infinity* in 1961 and even through *Otherwise Than Being* in 1974.[37] The moral skeptic doubts that we live with firm moral beliefs, that we make defensible moral decisions, that morality is a universally grounded mode of life, and that human life is morally meaningful. Levinas, as a defender of the moral and the ethical, begins by setting out how life proceeds, but he must do so in a way that the moral skeptic will accept. He then seeks to show what this life – which is "possible or even actual" – requires in order to occur. As Paul Franks puts it, the transcendental philosopher "has learned from skepticism that there is a pressing question as to *how* this can be the case, and that an answer to the question would provide philosophical insight."[38] To be sure, as Franks subtly

---

[33] See Stern, "On Kant's Response to Hume," in Stern (ed.), *Transcendental Arguments*, Chapter 4, esp. 56–66; and Mark Sacks, "Transcendental Arguments and the Inference to Reality: A Reply to Stern," in Stern (ed.), *Transcendental Arguments*, Chapter 5, 67–82.

[34] Quassim Cassam, "Self-Directed Transcendental Arguments" in Stern (ed.), *Transcendental Arguments*, 83.

[35] Cassam, "Self-Directed Transcendental Arguments," 83.

[36] See Stern (ed.), *Transcendental Arguments, passim*, especially Franks, 113–14.

[37] See also Levinas's short comment on Heidegger's failure, "As If Consenting to Horror," 485–88.

[38] Franks, "Transcendental Arguments, Reason, and Skepticism," 113.

points out, the defender or believer can have many different goals in mind, and to refute the skeptic outright is or might be only one. But the general point is well taken, that transcendental philosophy may begin with skepticism only to work toward an insight that is somehow beyond that philosophy's grasp.

What does that insight provide? Cassam, in discussing "self-directed" transcendental arguments, distinguishes two ways that the necessary conditions contribute to the original experience, beliefs, and so on. I take it that the two are not exclusive; the same outcome could teach more than one lesson. For Cassam, the two ways distinguish types of arguments; for me, they are different purposes that the outcomes can be thought to serve. The first is *regulatory*; the arguments can seek to "uncover" what is necessary, to bring it to our attention.[39] In this way, the transcendental condition that is identified is a philosophical and epistemic outcome; it discloses what is or has been hidden. Second, the argument can also seek to *validate* the experience by showing "that we are justified in operating in the ways we actually operate when thinking about or experiencing the world." Cassam points to how Kant's transcendental deduction of the categories serves this function by showing how our use of concepts in sensory experience is legitimate.[40] Here the outcome or necessary condition serves a *rational* or justificatory role. It shows why we can live as we in fact do live, and the condition is normative, in a sense, insofar as it shows why the possible is possible. I think that it is clear that if Levinas's face-to-face is a kind of necessary condition or ground, or if it is akin to such a ground and plays a transcendental role, it would have a normative or justificatory force. In fact, given its content, as we shall see, it would be not merely a justification for why moral and meaningful human life is possible but also a reason for why a *certain kind of moral life is necessary*. At the same time, in Cassam's terms, the face-to-face would also be *revelatory*, or, perhaps more precisely, the exposure of it would be revelatory, disclosing the face-to-face as the transcendental condition for social life.

Franks also notes, in his discussion of Idealist responses to Kant, that these figures sought "not only a ground of everything, but an absolute unconditioned ground for all grounds."[41] Levinas speaks of the face-to-face as originary, primordial, and an-archic. There is a suggestion here that its status is uncompromised or unconditioned, that it is independent in a sense and underived, whereas all else derives from it, in one way or another, directly or indirectly. I do not want to suggest that Levinas is doing metaphysics in a traditional way, like Hegel, J. G. Fichte, Spinoza, or Aristotle, but there is a sense that nothing, for human existence, is prior to the face of the other person and that eventually

---

[39] Cassam, "Self-Directed Transcendental Arguments," 85–86.
[40] Cassam, "Self-Directed Transcendental Arguments," 86.
[41] Franks, "Transcendental Arguments, Reason, and Skepticism," 116; cf. 122–32.

we need to make sense of this priority, if we are to understand Levinas deeply enough.[42]

There are a number of issues that need to be clarified before we can confidently call Levinas's philosophy transcendental in any useful way. As I have suggested, it is possible to take him to be responding to a kind of moral skepticism. But at this point, this is merely a suggestion that needs to be developed and justified. We should consider whether Levinas's thinking does have this second-person or dialectical quality – that is, whether it carries out its inquiry consistently from this perspective, as if Levinas were engaging in a dialogue with the moral skeptic. This issue is connected, I think, to the question of Levinas's use of the phenomenological method. If his inquiry does involve a phenomenological, or at least quasi-phenomenological, examination of modes of intentionality, then it must take place within the so-called phenomenological attitude, with the natural attitude bracketed or suspended. There is a notorious problem, however, about what motivates this act of suspension and the shift from the natural to the phenomenological attitude, from ordinary experience to philosophical inquiry.[43] This is akin to the problem of what motivates skepticism itself and what in fact motivates philosophy. For Levinas, we might take Heidegger's moral skepticism, as it were, or the threat of such skepticism or nihilism, as Levinas's motive for his own shift of attitude.[44] But once he has shifted his point of view, he would be responding to the skeptic in the skeptic's own terms, and need we believe that the skeptic will follow Levinas in his dialogue with him? This needs to be clarified and our question resolved.

Even if we follow Levinas this far, there is much to be done. If the encounter with the face of the other person is the transcendental ground of what I will call the moral or meaningful human life, how is it identified and what is its relationship to that life? It may reveal how certain features of life are possible and indeed why they occur as actual, but how does it justify them or even require them? Furthermore, is there a sense in which this ground is present in ordinary, everyday experience and enters into it? In what way, if at all, can one consider the

[42] As we shall see, Levinas does see the normativity of the face-to-face as absolute; and while not "grounded" in anything else, it has a characteristic, which he calls "height," that links this absolute normativity with our everyday vocabulary of the divine, "God," and traditional theology, at least in the West. But more of this later.
[43] This problem is regularly discussed in literature on Husserlian phenomenology; the classic treatment is Eugene Fink, "The Phenomenological Philosophy of Edmund Husserl and Contemporary Criticism," translated in R. O. Elveton (ed.), *The Phenomenology of Husserl* (Chicago: Quadrangle Books, 1970), 73–147. For discussion, see Sokolowski, *Introduction to Phenomenology*; Zahavi, *Husserl's Phenomenology*; and Dermot Moran, *Introduction to Phenomenology*.
[44] Later, Levinas treats deconstruction as a form of skepticism and Derrida as a skeptic; for an excellent discussion, see Critchley, *The Ethics of Deconstruction*, 156–69.

ground from within ordinary life? Can the object of phenomenological inquiry be identified, discussed, and understood from within the natural attitude, that is, with the linguistic resources employed in ordinary life and in theorizing about it? Can the infinite be described, discussed, and grasped from within totality and still remain, in a sense, infinite?

I have tried thus far to promote the idea, championed by de Boer and others, that Levinas's inquiry should be understood as a transcendental enterprise of a certain sort. There are reasons, of course, for thinking that it is not only that, an inquiry into the fact that the face-to-face is not an event in everyday experience but rather a dimension of all of social life, but I have paid attention most of all to proposing that it is *at least* such a transcendental philosophy.

AN OBJECTION

There is, however, an objection to this transcendental reading of Levinas that I want to address now. It will lead us to consider another type of reading altogether, albeit one that I shall try to show has transcendental features. The objection is this. Broadly speaking, transcendental arguments aim to derive metaphysical results from psychological premises. Typically, they originate from premises about our ordinary experiences, thought, beliefs, and knowledge, and they terminate by proving the existence of certain features of the world or the self or both, without which the original experiences are not possible. But, the objection goes, even if we can identify what Levinas and his skeptical opponent take those original, ordinary experiences to be, it is surely wrong to take Levinas to have sought or arrived at new metaphysical results. The face of the other person and the responsibility of the self are hardly new entities or new features of the world; they are hardly new constituents of our ontology. They are hidden or forgotten "horizons of meaning" and somehow beyond ontology, being, presence, appearance, and such. They are not new items or features, for they are neither *new* nor *entities* nor *features* at all. Hence, they cannot be transcendental grounds in any meaningful sense. The face and responsibility are the core of Levinas's insight into human existence, but they are hardly transcendental grounds for that existence.

I have been trying to mitigate this kind of objection, but its thrust is potent and direct. It suggests that at best "transcendental philosophy" is a metaphor for what Levinas is doing and, because of its connotations, perhaps a misleading metaphor at that. Like words such as "phenomenological," "analytical," and "synthetic," it is a term used within systems or domains of thought, but Levinas's project decidedly reaches outside such domains. His philosophy is more like Plato and neo-Platonism than it is like Aristotle, scholastic systems, Spinoza, Leibniz, Hegel, and Fichte; it is more like Augustine, F. H. Jacobi,

Søren Kierkegaard, Karl Barth, and Franz Rosenzweig too. It begins within the everyday and then reaches beyond it, but the task is not simply metaphysical or epistemological. It is not aimed at discovery of new entities; it is not aimed at discovery at all. Neither the face of the other person nor our responsibility to and for the other is unknown or absent in the ordinary everyday world. They are present but in a sense hidden or forgotten or, perhaps better, misunderstood and distorted. To learn about them, then, is not a matter of being introduced to new things or being given a new faculty or capacity; it is to see the old from a new perspective, in a new light. It is a bit like Plato's conception of true *paideia* in the *Republic*, a kind of *periagoge*, or conversion, a change of perspective or point of view. What Levinas is doing, one might claim, is to provide a new perspective on the ordinary world as we live in it. He could be said to be opening our eyes to the way we are, in a way that we do not now adequately realize or understand. His philosophy is a new way of our understanding human existence in the world that takes its origin from an appreciation of what kind of beings we are most of all. He does not say that he is the first to see things this way, but he does believe that this understanding, which he thinks is accurate and true, has been occluded, distorted, and obscured and needs to be recovered.

One might still want to call this philosophical approach "transcendental." But there is a difference between a realist and an idealist reading of this transcendental project. Peculiar as it sounds, given Levinas's opposition to the imperialism of totalities and the role of the subject in them, the kind of transcendental project I am describing should be understood idealistically, that is, as a matter of viewing things differently rather than as a matter of discovering new realities or features in the world. To be sure, Levinas wants to introduce or reintroduce us to a way of understanding life in this world, human existence, that we have forgotten or misunderstood. His philosophy is about this world and our lives in it. But it is not a matter of locating entities beyond this world on which it is grounded or which determine it, as much as it is about disclosing features of this world that we do not currently appreciate. When we consider other persons, that is, we use concepts, roles, and rules; we perceive how they look, implicitly grasp similarities and differences, take them into view and react to them in patterns, in terms of common features or distinctive ones, and so forth. However, we do not see their faces. For each face is unique to the particular other; it is sheer plea and command, at once; it beseeches and demands. That is all – until then, in the world, it accumulates its characteristics, features, and so forth. We do grasp the latter; we do not, as Levinas sees it, grasp the former adequately or perhaps at all. Levinas wants to teach us to do so and to show us as well what it means for our lives, for grasping the face of the other is not to take up an epistemic stance but rather to respond to the suffering, need, and destitution that the face expresses to us.

How might the face be taken realistically and how idealistically? Every feature of the other person whom I encounter, every profile, role, and so forth, in the terminology of phenomenology, is a *noema*, the other person precisely as he or she appears to me in a particular mode of intentionality – as an object of seeing, hearing, as a conversation partner, as an object of my action, my affection, my hatred, or whatever. Is the face of the other person a *noema*?[45] Is it a sense or meaning that mediates between my self and the other person? Or, alternatively, is the face of the other present to me as plea and command? The first reading is realist, and it is not Levinas's meaning; the second is idealist, as it were. Levinas's understanding is more like the idealist reading, although not exactly it. The *noema* is the object as it is presented to the self, the thing-qua-x, but it is not the object of a double grasping. The self does not grasp the thing and also its feature or profile, x. It grasps the whole at once, the thing-qua-x. Similarly, when I encounter the face of the other, I do not encounter the other and his face; I encounter the other as face, as plea and command, to be responded to independently of and, as Levinas claims, prior to seeing, describing, and thinking about the other. If the face is a *noema*, then, it is one not present to the self, as the "look" of the other is; nor is it the same *status* as the *noemata* grasped in the remainder of everyday experience.

There are many questions to be asked about Levinas's idea of the face of the other. We have been considering one: What is it? It is, one might say, a hidden or obscured perspective on the other person. But in addition it is a primary or determinative and grounding perspective or profile. It is what the other person means to me first and foremost, more than anything else, before that person means anything else to me. Why is this so? What makes the face more primary than the other person's kinship with me or than her posture or shape or height or complexion? While part of Levinas's project in its transcendental sense, I think, is to expose the face and responsibility, part is to show this priority. How does he accomplish this task? How does he clarify why the face is somehow primordial and fundamental? By showing how the face is beyond totality and ontology, that it comes with a certain force or *gravitas*, and that all human experience derives from it or is grounded in it, whereas it – the need and vulnerability and force of the face – derives from nothing. It simply is in all its brute particularity – as an epiphany or revelation to the self. In later chapters, we will have to see how Levinas accomplishes these tasks.

If Levinas's philosophy is transcendental, then, it is so in a rather distinctive way. Jonathan Lear, in two well-known essays, has argued that Wittgenstein's

---

[45] See Levinas, TI, 294, where Levinas answers this question explicitly with a denial: No, the face is not a *noema*.

project in the *Philosophical Investigations* is a kind of transcendental philosophy.[46]
Is Levinas's transcendental enterprise anything like Wittgenstein's, as Lear
understands it? One of the lessons of this chapter is that Levinas's accomplishment does not fit comfortably into categories that have been proposed for it or
that might seem appropriate for describing it. It is and is not phenomenology;
it is and is not empirical or episodic; it is and is not transcendental. Lear argues
something similar about Wittgenstein. If he is to be regarded as a transcendental philosopher, that notion must be modified from its classical, Kantian sense.
Lear claims that in a suitably extended sense, Wittgenstein's investigation of
rule following in the *Philosophical Investigations* "can plausibly be considered a
transcendental inquiry," for the outcome of this inquiry is a "non-empirical
insight into how we go on."[47] According to Lear, this investigation is transcendental not because it seeks to identify "the necessary structure of the mind,
of the world, or of both," for it "displays no interest in necessary structures"
and looks unabashedly at "ordinary activities like speaking language."[48] What
Lear proposes is a "loosening" of the Kantian definition, so that a "transcendental argument for x is concerned with establishing the legitimacy of x ... by
revealing in its broadest and deepest context what it is to be x," freed of the
skeptical context and of the need to disclose what are strictly speaking necessary conditions.[49] Wittgenstein's attention is on language, psychological states,
rule following, philosophy, and such themes, and especially on how philosophy
obscures rather than clarifies what is going on in language speaking and human
affairs. Moreover, according to Lear, Wittgenstein's inquiry is anthropological
as well as transcendental, empirical and nonempirical at once. It is not necessary
for us to examine here his analysis of Wittgenstein that claims to show this, but
the point is of interest. Is it possible that Levinas also is both an empirical and a
transcendental thinker, but neither in a conventional sense? Levinas's philosophy
is about ordinary life, but it is also about what it is to live that life meaningfully
and morally. Like Wittgenstein and Rosenzweig, Levinas seems to assign to
philosophy a therapeutic role: to cure us and to cure Western philosophy from
mistaken and ultimately destructive ways of understanding and living life in the
world. But to serve this function, Levinas's thinking must be both transcendental

---

[46] Jonathan Lear, "Transcendental Anthropology" in Philip Petit and John McDowell (eds.), *Subject, Thought, and Context*, 267–98, and "The Disappearing 'We,'" in *Proceedings of the Aristotelian
Society* 58 (1984), 219–42. I have been arguing that the face-to-face is, in one sense, an essential
feature of all social existence. For a similar account of Heidegger, see Robert Brandom, *Tales
of the Mighty Dead* (Cambridge, MA: Harvard University Press, 2002), Ch. 11, esp. 328–42.

[47] Lear, "Transcendental Anthropology," 269.

[48] Lear, "Transcendental Anthropology," 270.

[49] Lear, "The Disappearing 'We,'" 222–23.

and empirical. It must be immersed in that life and also reflective about it. I do not believe that Wittgenstein and Levinas carry out their combined projects in the same way, but there are similarities, and Lear's attention to the empirical and nonempirical dimensions of Wittgenstein's approach helps to remind us of them.[50]

Having said this much about method and approach, it is time to consider Levinas's central ethical insight in a substantive way. The questions we have raised and suggestions we have made can only be addressed if we leave our detached view and move into the core of his thinking.

[50] Bob Plant's discussion of Wittgenstein, Levinas, and Derrida, *Wittgenstein and Levinas: Ethical and Religious Thought*, reached me too late to consider here. Indeed, its subtle and complex argument deserves special treatment. To my knowledge, it is the first book-length attempt to think about Wittgenstein and Levinas together, a task that it carries out in a deep and fascinating way.

3

The Ethical Content of the
Face-to-Face

The first things to remember about the face-to-face encounter between the self and the other person are that it is concrete and particular. It is not an idea or concept nor a *type* of action or event. It is a concrete reality, an occurrent event; it occurs. Furthermore, it occurs as utterly particular: The self is a particular person, and the face-of-the-other is a particular revelation of a particular person. What is occluded, hidden, or forgotten in our ordinary lives is not some idea or value; it is this presence of the other's face to me – and my responsibility to and for this person.[1] What we have lost sight of, Levinas says, are this woman's responsibility and this man's suffering. Moreover, this reality or event, which in a sense is beyond our thinking, our concepts, and our rules and prior to them, is determinative and unconditional. It is all plea and command, made again and again, in episode after episode. It is not like the continuing echoes of a single clash that occurred some time in the past; it is more like a pervasive din, always present without an initial crash or origin.

What does the face reveal? Why is its content ethical? How does Levinas clarify and argue for this content? What does the face mean? Is its meaning absolute?

In order to answer these and other questions about the ethical content and the character of the face-to-face encounter, I want to look first at Levinas's writings from 1947 to 1961, from *Time and the Other* to *Totality and Infinity*. Moreover, it will be helpful to compare what Levinas says to an early discussion of Stanley Cavell's that introduces the notion of acknowledgment to characterize the self's relation to the other person. Once Levinas comes to describe this fundamental event in a certain way in these works, he repeats and refines that formulation. If

---

[1] Cohen emphasizes the concreteness, especially in his book *Ethics, Exegesis and Philosophy*; he reminds us again and again that responsibility is not a reflective grasp of the other or an epistemic attitude. It is action; it is doing something.

later he modifies his account, it is a modification of this early description. We
need to have its basic features in hand.

THE SOCIAL, THE FACE, AND THE ETHICAL

We begin with everyday life, a life of people living with one another. Here "the
solitude and fundamental alterity of the other are already veiled by decency."[2]
In the course of ordinary daily experience, we live together, sympathize, and
care about one another. There are social relationships or etiquette and, he says,
a certain kind of reciprocity. "But already, in the very heart of the relationship
with the other that characterizes our social life, alterity appears as a nonreciprocal relationship – that is, as contrasting strongly with contemporaneousness."
There is a dimension of our ordinary social relationships that is nonreciprocal,
and it is always "already there," although hidden from view or, in his words,
"veiled by decency." In life, I join you for a movie; we leave the house together,
go to the theater, purchase tickets, and watch the film together. But more basic
to our experience and our relationship than these features, something not in
sight, is a relationship between us, where you confront me and I am called to
respond, to reject or accept you; this is a relatedness that is "already" present in
the midst of all this. You are other than I; you stand over against me: "The Other
as Other" – in this case you – "is not only an alter ego" – another person different from me who joins me from his own point of view – "the Other is what I
myself am not. The Other is, for example, the weak, the poor, 'the widow and
the orphan,' whereas I am the rich or the powerful." You are exterior, other,
and outside, and your otherness is not a function of or constituted by spatial
difference, nonidentity of features or properties, or anything like such things.
Your otherness is a brute fact; it is wholly made up of your being poor, my being
rich, your need, and my capacity to respond to you and your need.[3] "In civilized

---

[2] TO, 82.

[3] TO, 83–84. Commentators on Levinas have been tempted to look in various directions to
identify antecedents for Levinas's view about the primacy of the call or summons of the other
and to clarify his thinking by comparison with similar accounts. They have turned to Fichte,
Marcel, Sartre, and the Marburg neo-Kantian Hermann Cohen. Cohen is a particularly tempting "source," especially in his late works *Der Begriff der Religion im System der Philosophie* (1915)
and *Religion der Vernunft aus den Quellen des Judentums* (1919). In these later works, the abstract
moral agent is confronted as the suffering and needy individual whose suffering engages the
self as an individual and to whom one shows compassion. For a brief account of the relation
to the other person in these works, see Reiner Munk, "Alterity in Hermann Cohen's Critical
Idealism," *Journal of Jewish Thought and Philosophy* 9 (2000), 251–65, esp. 261–65. For discussion of Levinas and Cohen, see Edith Wyschogrod, "The Moral Self: Emmanuel Levinas and
Hermann Cohen," *Daat* 4 (1980), 35–58.
    See Hermann Cohen, *Religion of Reason out of the Sources of Judaism*, trans. Simon Kaplan
(New York: Ungar, 1972), 18: "If ethics now sees existence afflicted with suffering, then

life there are traces of this relationship with the other" – for example, in sexual difference, what Levinas calls "modesty" and "mystery," and what he also calls "eros," or love.[4] The alterity of the feminine is constituted by this withdrawal and attraction, nothing else. "Love," he says, "is not a possibility, is not due to our initiative, is without reason; it invades and wounds us, and nevertheless the I survives it."[5]

Below the surface of the social, in a sense, hidden from view, is a layer of relationship, a dimension of how we are related to one another, the I and the other person as other, where the otherness is wholly a matter of status, rich and poor, powerful and weak. This is not one person being together with or alongside another; it is something else. Moreover, it is unlike Buber's I-Thou encounter, Levinas says, "where reciprocity remains the tie between two separate freedoms, and the ineluctable character of isolated subjectivity is underestimated.... It is a collectivity that is not a communion. It is the face-to-face without intermediary...."[6] Here, then, is Levinas's starting point, as it were. The self, the I, in normal, everyday life, experiences intimations of otherness, and then in social life I experience "traces" of a primordial relationship between itself and the particular other person. But while those traces include sexuality and love, what is the character of the otherness itself? What metaphors can we use, what further hints, to describe its content? What gives that otherness its dynamic rather than static character, its force? What is its ethical content?

In his important essay of 1951, "Is Ontology Fundamental?," Levinas answers these questions.[7] In this essay, Levinas approaches the relation to the other

---

compassion becomes for it only a signpost for the question: How can suffering be overcome?...This is the turning point at which religion, as it were, emerges from ethics. The observation of another man's suffering is not an inert affect to which I surrender myself, particularly not when I observe it not as a natural or empirical phenomenon, but when I make of it a question mark for my whole orientation in the moral world....It is not a theoretical interest that is aroused in me through this observation. It is the whole meaning of ethics, as the teaching of man and his worth...." Cf. Ch. 8 and 9 and Cohen's account of the emergence of the problem of the fellow man (*Mitmensch*) from the experience of the next man (*Nebenmensch*). In Cohen's terms, the correlation of man and God requires the prior correlation of man and man (see 114). But this all takes place at the level of the abstract individual and not yet at the level of the particular I, which is the domain of religion – of guilt, sin, and atonement. Pierre Bouretz argues for the relationship between Cohen and Levinas in "Messianism and Modern Jewish Philosophy" in Michael L. Morgan and Peter Eli Gordon (eds.), *The Cambridge Companion to Modern Jewish Philosophy* (Cambridge: Cambridge University Press, forthcoming).

4 TO, 84–90.
5 TO, 89.
6 TO, 93–94.
7 See Levinas, "Is Ontology Fundamental?" in Robert Bernasconi, Simon Critchley, and Adriaan Peperzak (eds.), *Basic Philosophical Writings*.

through language, comprehension, and a discussion of Heidegger.[8] "Language is founded on a relation anterior to comprehension," and it is this relation that Levinas seeks to expose. I want to ignore for now the role of language, conversation, and such issues and move to Levinas's description of the encounter in ethical terms, an encounter that Levinas says is prior and irreducible to comprehension.[9] The first thing about this relation between the self and the other person that Levinas says – between each particular self and each and every other person – is that it occurs in the vocative. He calls it "religion," which he associates with imploring and prayer.[10] It is an "event of sociality," and he says that the word "religion" has an "ethical resonance" and "Kantian echoes." For Kant, the highest form of religion is a moral faith intimately tied to human rationality, autonomous selfhood, self-determination, and the moral law. Levinas will differ with Kant dramatically about the core of ethics, its character, the role of autonomy and freedom, and much else, but he agrees with Kant about the centrality of the ethical to human existence.[11] It is this notion of moral religiosity that Levinas has in mind when he calls the basic "event of sociality," of the I encountering the other person, "religion." The term does not refer, of course, to a positive or instituted religion, for it is an event or relation, not a practice or structure of practices. Nor is it a matter of doctrine, of creed, or even of moral theory. What Levinas is referring to with expressions like "religion" is a fact-event, a kind of *Tatsache*, that is the core of both ethics and religion, in what he takes to be their most basic and primordial senses.[12] The hidden,

---

[8] "Is Ontology Fundamental?," 5.

[9] "Is Ontology Fundamental?," 7.

[10] "Is Ontology Fundamental?," 7; cf. Levinas, "Freedom and Command" in Alphonso Lingis (trans.), *Collected Philosophical Papers*, 23; see also TI, 80. Notice that Levinas does not say that the face-to-face is "religious." Rather, he calls it "religion" – that is, the locus of what is genuine and fundamental about religion as it occurs in our ordinary experience.

[11] See "Is Ontology Fundamental?," 10: "[T]hat which we catch sight of seems suggested by the practical philosophy of Kant, to which we feel particularly close." As one might expect, given comments such as this and the centrality of the ethical for Levinas, there has been a great deal of discussion concerning his relation to Kant. A good treatment can be found in Catherine Chalier, *What Ought I to Do? Morality in Kant and Levinas*; see Anthony F. Beavers, "Kant and the Problem of Ethical Metaphysics," and Peter Atterton, "From Transcendental Freedom to the Other: Levinas and Kant," in Melvyn New, with Robert Bernasconi and Richard A. Cohen (eds.), *In Proximity: Emmanuel Levinas and the 18th Century*. See also Conclusion, below.

[12] As Paul Franks has shown, the term *Tatsache* was introduced in the 18th century as a technical term not for a "matter of fact" but more precisely for an "act-event." It was used by Kant to explain the *Factum der Vernunft* (fact of reason) in 1790. Franks emphasizes the active feature of the expression, but because for Levinas the face-to-face is first of all passive, although the subject's posture as responsibility is in a sense an active response, I am not here using it with that same emphasis. See Paul Franks, "Freedom, *Tatsache*, and *Tathandlung* in the Development of Fichte's Jena *Wissenschaftslehre*," *Archiv für Geschichte der Philosophie* 79:3 (1997), 331–44; and

ignored, or forgotten dimension of everyday life, of which we have only traces or hints in that life, is this ethico-religious event which is what constitutes the otherness of the other person for the I. It is an event, a relation, in one sense; in another, it is a dimension or aspect of everyday interpersonal and social life that is hidden from view and that Levinas is opening to our gaze – bringing into the open, as it were. It is an event that constitutes, more precisely, a perspective on – or an aspect of – the ordinary.

The last section of "Is Ontology Fundamental?" is titled "The Ethical Signif-icance of the Other (= the Human Other)."[13] In everyday life, my first-person point of view orients me to the world and to other persons. I name them, classify them, and hence dominate them. They belong to me. This Hobbesian situation is at the core of Levinas's understanding of totality, which we shall dis-cuss in the next chapter. Here the issue I want to focus on is the limited one of how the world, including the other person, fulfills, or at least serves, my needs. Levinas says that the other is possessed: "As consumable, it is nourishment, and in enjoyment, it offers itself, gives itself, belongs to me."[14] These terms come from *Time and the Other*; they will be elaborated on and explored in *Totality and Infinity*. In the ordinary world of everyday life, things are there for me, the I, to use, consume, enjoy, and thereby to become nourished. But, Levinas then says, "[T]he encounter with the other (*autrui*) consists in the fact that despite the extent of my domination and his slavery [that is, despite the extent of the other's enslavement to me], I do not possess him." At a fundamental level, Levinas claims, the other person confronts me with an uncircumscribed, abso-lute choice: either to let her live or to murder her or, in some circumstances, to support her living or to let her die. "The other (*autrui*) is the sole being I can wish to kill." With the other person comes this possibility: to desire its death or to allow it to live. Things – natural sources of nourishment and enjoyment and use, from fruit and vegetables to flowers and sunsets – are there for me, and my first choice, with regard to them, is whether to appropriate them at all, after which I set about determining how. But with persons, a new situation arises.[15] When the other person faces me, *before* I choose to use or dominate her, I must respond to her being a person by allowing her to live or not. She comes on

Franks, *All or Nothing: Systematicity, Transcendental Arguments, and Skepticism in German Idealism* (Cambridge, MA: Harvard University Press, 2005), 278.
[13] "Is Ontology Fundamental?," 9–10.
[14] "Is Ontology Fundamental?," 9.
[15] I am inclined to think that for Levinas, while this "new situation," the fact of the ethical, so to speak, only comes about with the relationship with the other person, it is not confined to that relationship. That is, there is room here to introduce concern for animals as well as for the earth and its resources. These are, however, large and widely contested issues among students and critics of Levinas that I do not discuss in this book.

the scene, comes into my venue, not for me to do something with; she comes with a need to share the world with me. First, she needs my acceptance and risks my rejection. I am tempted, Levinas says: I *can* choose to kill her; I *can* desire her death. But in this *can*, this temptation, this capacity, there is already an acceptance of the other, an acknowledgment of her facing me, needing me, risking me. "At the very moment when my power to kill realizes itself, the other (*autrui*) has escaped me." I have already, at that instant, engaged her, accepted her, or, better, been engaged by her and responded. "The temptation of total negation, measuring the infinity of this attempt and its impossibility – this is the presence of the face. To be in relation with the other (*autrui*) face to face is to be unable to kill."[16] This, Levinas says, is a "depth" rather than a horizon, "a breach in the horizon," if we take horizon to be an expression for unperceived, unattended profiles in everyday life itself, but ones that could be grasped or seen.[17] What does the face, this breach, signify? "In it the infinite resistance of a being to our power affirms itself precisely against the murderous will that it defies; because, completely naked, the face signifies itself."[18] The face does not point beyond itself; it simply is what it is.

Levinas employs the word "face" with the greatest care. The face of the other person is not the appearance of that person; it is not a collection of features given to visual perception. It has no parts, no components. It is basic and, as he says, "self-signifying." The face means what it is: imploring, a plea of the weak to the powerful or the poor to the rich. The face is the way the other person, as the imposing presence I just described, presents herself to me. It is not the object of everyday intentional consciousness but a "breach" in that intentionality. "To comprehension and signification grasped within a horizon [of meanings], we oppose the signifyingness of the face."[19] By "oppose," Levinas means that the special significance of the face of the other challenges the status of everyday meanings and sense; it is more basic than they are, more original, presumed by them as an engagement of the self with the other that lies hidden within every other interpersonal relationship. It is, from the self's side, the responsibility to acknowledge and accept the other that is always already present in ordinary life – preconceptual, prearticulate, prereflective.

Levinas's term "face," then, has something of the nuance of what Bernard Williams called "thick" moral concepts. These concepts do not announce moral

---

[16] "Is Ontology Fundamental?," 9.
[17] "Is Ontology Fundamental?," 10. What Levinas means here is that the face is like a horizon; but because it is deep and primordial and fundamental, in a metaphorical sense, we should think of it as a "depth" rather than strictly speaking a hidden horizon or one that is contingently unattended to.
[18] "Is Ontology Fundamental?," 10.
[19] "Is Ontology Fundamental?," 10.

correctness, as the concepts of right and wrong do, or obligation and permission. Rather, they are such that their descriptive and prescriptive dimensions cannot be separated, even for conceptual purposes; honor, shame, humiliation, and pride are examples.[20] In a similar way, Levinas's term "face" refers to an aspect of one person's being present to another that has its descriptive features, to be sure, but that also has those other features I call "appeal" and "command." That is, in addition to however the other person appears to me, as tall or short, burly or slim, light- or dark-skinned, and so forth – the other person presents a vulnerability and destitution that appeals to or petitions me and at the same time addresses me and makes a demand upon me. This particular young girl, with curly dark hair, smiling, and gangly, whatever else she means to me, also and even "before" in a sense calls out to me, burdens me with responsibility, singles me out for an appeal and a demand. Moreover, there is no way correctly and precisely to sever that appeal and command from the way she looks to me; the appeal and demand is *in* the look, so to speak; it is something that the look means, something primary and fundamental.[21] It is in this way that "face" is like Williams's "thick" moral concepts. It is the way that each of us is a thick moral presence for each and every other person. In later works, Levinas will call my posture toward each person "responsibility," and hence this relatedness, too, can be thought of along the lines of such thick moral concepts. The one caveat we should enter, however, is that, technically speaking, both thin and thick moral concepts, in Levinas's terms, occur within the domains of totality; they occur within everyday life and our theoretical and explanatory articulations of it. Nonetheless, it is helpful to understand what he means by face as having a kinship with thick moral concepts, even if, in general, Levinas is more inclined to talk about the face-to-face and responsibility as the good rather than the right and in later writings avoids calling it "justice," saving that term for political and social rules and programs that are developments of them.

[20] See Bernard Williams, *Ethics and the Limits of Philosophy* (Cambridge, MA: Harvard University Press, 1985), 129, 140, 143–45. Williams's examples are *coward, lie, brutality, gratitude,* and *courage,* among others.

[21] In Charlotte Delbo's imaginative memoir of her time in Auschwitz and release from Ravensbrück, *Auschwitz and After,* in the second book, *Useless Knowledge* (New Haven, CT: Yale University Press, 1995), 204–5, when the liberation of the camps was imminent, the camp organization was deteriorating, and the prisoners clung to life in the midst of the chaotic conditions, Delbo says, "One never met a face that wasn't a question, a face burning with questions: 'Do you think we're going to leave? What's your opinion?'... She was looking at me with supplicating eyes, her voice hardly perceptible, her lips retracted, her pupils enlarged: 'I'm going to die,' her eyes said. 'I'm going to die if I don't leave this place at once.'" Here we have a very vivid portrayal, in the face with the "supplicating eyes," of what Levinas means by the *face;* it was a look of "questioning" that Delbo felt compelled to "answer."

By 1962, when Levinas seeks to summarize the exposition that he gives in the early sections of *Totality and Infinity*, his account of the encounter with the face of the other person has become richer and fuller.[22]

The epiphany of the Absolutely Other is a face by which the Other challenges and commands me through his nakedness, through his destitution. He challenges me from his humility and from his height. . . . The absolutely Other is the human Other (*autrui*). And the putting into question of the Same by the Other is a summons to respond. . . . Hence, to be I signifies not being able to escape responsibility.[23]

The Same is the Self or I; the Other is the other person. The "epiphany" – notice the theological vocabulary that Levinas appropriates – is the event of the other person engaging the I as a face, and the content of that engagement is, from the other person's side, a plea born out of need and destitution and a summons to respond to that plea, and, from the self's side, an unlimited responsibility toward that other person in virtue of that plea and that command. At this level, if we were to speak of it in such terms, the self *is* wholly responsibility, and the other person *is* wholly plea and command. More correctly, perhaps, in everyday life every social interaction, every encounter between one person and another, is always *already* such a nexus of plea, command, and inescapable responsibility *before* it is anything else – which it always is. Only once the self is confronted by a face can it be responsible and must it be responsible – for and to that other person. But if Levinas can say this in 1962, it is because in the intervening decade his reflection on the face and its philosophical articulation has become nuanced and deep. It is worth looking briefly at how this process unfolded.

THE CALL OF THE FACE

We have seen that as early as 1951, Kant was on Levinas's mind. Levinas was attracted to the commitment to the priority of the ethical in Kant's philosophy. Hence, it was natural for him to try to clarify his notion of the ethical character of the face, its ethical meaning, by looking at Kant, or at least at Kantian issues.

---

[22] Why does Levinas use the word "face" to express the way the other person encounters or engages with the self? Negatively, of course, Levinas appropriates a nontechnical word that is not used in traditional epistemological contexts – for example, the word "impression" or "appearance" or "idea." Moreover, the face is a perspective or aspect – for example, the face of a cube or a triangle. Furthermore, the face is characteristic of a living thing, an animal or person, and its bodily presence. The face is the most expressive physical manifestation of such a living being's inner self, its feelings, thoughts, or attitudes. It reveals most vividly its needs, pain, joy, sorrow, or suffering. Above all, in its eyes one sees how the other feels. For such reasons and more, then, Levinas chooses this term to indicate the mode of presence of the other person to the self.

[23] Levinas, "Transcendence and Height" in *Basic Philosophical Writings*, 17.

To a certain degree, he does this in "Freedom and Command" (1953), an essay also written with Plato in mind, especially the priority of the Good in Plato's *Republic*.[24] I will focus only on what the essay says about the ethical content of the face. We should not forget, however, that the essay, if only indirectly, is also a response to Nazi fascism and domination.[25]

Levinas asks, "Does not impersonal discourse presuppose discourse in the sense of this face-to-face situation? In other words, is there not *already* between one will and another a *relationship of command* without tyranny, which is *not yet* an obedience to an impersonal law, but is the *indispensable condition* for the institution of such a law?"[26] Levinas calls this situation or event a "discourse before discourse" and a "relationship between particulars prior to the institution of rational law," a "condition for even the commands of the State" and "the condition for freedom." This is familiar territory. Engagement with the face is, we have seen, a relationship of command, albeit plea and command. It is particular and prior to law, moral and political. It is presumed by all social interaction.

Next, Levinas turns to everyday social interaction in an extreme form: war. War is violence, use, domination; it is – and we have already seen this theme – work, enjoyment, and domination, but here applied to other persons, rather than worldly things. War, however, seeks to violate and dominate what it ignores – it seeks to annihilate an opposing force, but it "does not see the face in the other."[27] Levinas distinguishes the *force* of the other person, its resisting force that lies in its freedom to oppose, from its *face*, which he calls its "pacific opposition." The face is "what resists me by its opposition [i.e., its pacific opposition – plea and destitution] and not what is opposed to me by its resistance."[28] This is an opposition that is prior to its freedom or mine. Levinas uses language he will later refuse himself to describe this opposition: "[I]t opposes itself to me insofar as it turns to me." Moreover, real violence is not war, domination, and so forth; real violence is "ignoring this opposition, ignoring the face of a being, avoiding the gaze," and this means denying its plea to live and to be acknowledged, aided, and sustained, to ignore its suffering, to kill the face and the other, and hence to avoid all responsibility. Here, "pacific opposition" is what earlier, in "Is Ontology Fundamental?," Levinas called the "otherness" of the other person or the other as "negation." It incorporates or is constituted by a command, prior to the commands of moral rules, of law, or of political

[24] Levinas, "Freedom and Command" in *Collected Philosophical Papers*, Ch. 2, 15–23.
[25] See especially "Freedom and Command" in *Collected Philosophical Papers*, 16–17, and the attention to tyranny.
[26] "Freedom and Command" in *Collected Philosophical Papers*, 18, my italics.
[27] "Freedom and Command" in *Collected Philosophical Papers*, 19.
[28] "Freedom and Command" in *Collected Philosophical Papers*, 19.

sovereignty; and the command – "Do not kill me" – is also a plea, something like "Make room for me" or "Feed me" or "Share the world with me" or "Reduce my suffering."

Levinas works at how to formulate the way the face presents itself, its "epiphany." In this essay, he uses the language of expression. "Expression renders present what is communicated and the one who is communicating; they are both in the expression. But that does not mean that expression provides us with knowledge about the other." The other person who is present in expression "appeals" to the self and dominates it. In expression, there is already sociality.[29]

Levinas then turns to another way of clarifying the "originality of the encounter with the face."[30] Thus far, he has emphasized in this essay the dimension of command in the encounter with the face. He has argued that politics requires discourse, and discourse requires the encounter, with its command prior to all command. Levinas now turns to the other dimension of the encounter, its character as plea and the face as expressive of misery and destitution:

The absolute nakedness of a face, the absolutely defenseless face, without covering, clothing or mask, is what opposes my power over it, my violence, and opposes it in an absolute way, with an opposition that is opposition itself. The being that expresses itself, that faces me, says *no* to me by his very expression. . . . [I]t is not the *no* of a hostile force or a threat; it is the impossibility of killing him who presents that face. . . . The face is the fact that a being affects us not in the indicative, but in the imperative.[31]

This face-to-face, then, is a "metaphysical relationship that is ethical," "the ethical impossibility of killing" as the other's resistance to the I.

It is helpful here, as we have regularly done, to consider this passage from the perspective of everyday life, as proposing an insight into an aspect or dimension of ordinary experience that is generally hidden from view. What Levinas is saying, from this point of view, is that in every social encounter, whether violent or benign, the other person stands as other than the self, as a *no* to the I. But, at this basic level, the *no* is not one of hostility or anger or threat. It is, as it were, the *no* of need, of defenselessness, and of dependence: the I has the power of its sheer presence, and the other stands over against it as a plea for acknowledgment, permission, assistance, concern, for a "piece of bread" from the I's mouth.[32]

---

[29] "Freedom and Command" in *Collected Philosophical Papers*, 20–21.

[30] "Freedom and Command" in *Collected Philosophical Papers*, 21.

[31] "Freedom and Command" in *Collected Philosophical Papers*, 21, and see 23 for a summary of the essay.

[32] An obvious comparison with Levinas's face-to-face with the other is the idea of recognition in Fichte and Hegel. Fichte, in his *Foundations of Natural Right*, argues that I must have the concept

Levinas talks of the impossibility of killing.[33] But is this right? Why is it not the case that for the other standing before the I, there is both the possibility and the impossibility of killing the other? The reason, I think, is that even the choice to kill or the act of killing itself *already* in some sense incorporates an acknowledgment, an acceptance, so that one can say that all social encounters, even the most violent and destructive, are acts of responsibility, albeit ones that do not *express* and *develop* that sense of responsibility but rather corrupt and nullify it. In every social interaction, then, there is a plea to be supported in life, and, by its sheer otherness, the other issues a command to be supported. Hence, in every social encounter, each person begins *already* with a responsibility to the other person, which is a standard that is undeniable and demanding to live up to. However the interaction goes, whatever its character or special features, this responsibility is already there; and insofar as it is an ethical matter, an imperative, its directiveness or force permeates the encounter. It is in this sense that sociality is ethical through and through, or from the ground up. Even the most casual meeting, then, includes at its deepest level the command for each party to heed the misery, the plight of the other person and to take responsibility to and for that person. Here is a "metaphysical" layer of human existence at its deepest, that is particular, imperative, and ethical.[34] In this sense, then, murder is impossible.

THE FACE-TO-FACE AND ACKNOWLEDGMENT

Much of this account of the ethical content of the face-to-face remains firmly in Levinas's grasp throughout his career. It is often affirmed in what becomes

of the other in order to have self-consciousness and the grasp of myself as a self. I become a self only insofar as I am summoned to free action by an other, whom I take to be a self in the very act of taking myself to be summoned by it. See J. G. Fichte, *Foundations of Natural Right* (Cambridge: Cambridge University Press, 2000), I, Section 3, 32–37. Paul Franks explains that Fichte takes this process to be the historical genesis of self-consciousness and the notion of the self; the self becomes a self in becoming free, in coming to have the ability to determine myself to comply with the summons of the other or to resist it. See Paul Franks, "The Discovery of the Other: Cavell, Fichte and Skepticism" in Alice Crary and Sanford Shieh (eds.), *Reading Cavell* (New York: Routledge, 2006), 176–77; see also Paul Franks, *All or Nothing: Systematicity, Transcendental Arguments, and Skepticism in German Idealism* (Cambridge, MA: Harvard University Press, 2005), 323–25. Franks points out that Fichte's transcendental project takes the process of the genesis of the self to be historical, unlike Kant, whose transcendental argument is aimed at a justification and not a genetic account of the self's actual emergence. I claim that Levinas's account differs from Fichte's – and from Hegel's later version – in not being historical.

[33] This theme, the impossiblity of murder, is also discussed in an important passage in Levinas, "Is Ontology Fundamental?" in *Basic Philosophical Writings*, 9–10.

[34] For similar accounts, see Levinas, "The Ego and Totality" in *Collected Philosophical Papers*, 39–44; "Philosophy and the Idea of the Infinite" in *Collected Philosophical Papers*, esp. 54–56; and "Ethics as First Philosophy" in *The Levinas Reader*, 82–83.

an almost standard terminology for him – in technical essays on various themes, in occasional writings, and in interviews. What I propose to do here first is to see how it takes shape in *Totality and Infinity*. Then, I want to raise some questions about the account and the very character of the face-to-face as a primordial ethical event or relational experience. Some of these are questions Levinas deals with or tries to deal with. Others he does not – or at least not in ways we might find helpful. In the course of introducing and discussing these problems, I will turn to recent philosophical discussion to help us grapple with his ideas, including, among others, Stanley Cavell's discussion of acknowledgment. Finally, we will take a preliminary look at some later modifications and developments of this account. We should be forewarned, however, that what we have sketched in this chapter is not yet a full account or even a sufficiently developed one. There are terms and features of the face-to-face encounter that Levinas elaborates but that we must temporarily set aside. Some of them we will return to in subsequent chapters – for example, the notion of height; the way in which Levinas understands terms like "God," the "sacred," and "holiness"; and the primordial or originary status of the event. For the moment, however, I want to focus on its ethical character.

The central section of *Totality and Infinity* is Section Three, "Exteriority and the Face," especially "Ethics and the Face." While I will look primarily at this section, I will call attention to phrases and passages elsewhere that tell us important things about the face-to-face encounter as an ethical event, encounter, or experience. To begin with, the "epiphany as a face" is not a form of perception; this phrase does not refer to a way that one person appears to another nor even the way an other person appears to the I. It refers rather to a "putting in question" of the I that "emanates from the other."[35] It is a "moral summons [that] calls into question" the self's powers. That is, as we saw when we surveyed the dialectical story that Levinas gives in *Time and the Other* and that *Totality and Infinity* here elaborates, it is as if the self's power or capacity to work and appropriate worldly things for its enjoyment and nourishment is now challenged by the sheer fact that another person, who also needs those things for his nourishment and enjoyment, presents himself to the I and registers what Levinas here calls a "moral summons," the content of which is to share, to be generous, and most fundamentally to acknowledge and accept that other person.

"The face resists possession, resists my powers. In its epiphany, in expression, the sensible, still graspable, turns into total resistance to the grasp."[36] This resistance, as we have seen, is a resistance to the I's wish to kill, or at least to its power to kill, and it resists that wish or that power with the "primordial

---

[35] TI, 195, 196; cf. 171.
[36] TI, 197.

expression ... 'you shall not commit murder!'"[37] The face does not literally say this, of course; it does not issue an imperative; rather, its presence expresses a summons that we as philosophers can otherwise articulate in these terms. The biblical text, in uttering this commandment as an expression of divine revelation, is giving everyday (and mythical) form to the most fundamental character of social interaction, which is, intrinsically, outside the domain of everyday formulation, as we shall see. In this sense, "the epiphany of the face is ethical." Levinas calls the face, as he had elsewhere, "destitute" and "hungry" and "naked" or "nude" and says that it "arouses" the self's goodness through its plea and command.[38] Moreover, once again calling upon biblical and religious motifs, Levinas says it is an event of "election" or a "call" to serve "the poor, the stranger, the widow, and the orphan."[39] This picturesque, rhetorical language is of course metonymy; the primordial relation to the other via the epiphany of the other's face applies not only to these types of people; in fact, it applies to each and every person, insofar as that person addresses the I out of her weakness, her need, and her intrinsic poverty.

This account, which emerges in *Totality and Infinity*, does have a transcendental character. In this section, Levinas shows how various ordinary experiences and practices presuppose this original, deep level of meaning or hidden dimension. And as we have seen in "Freedom and Command," Levinas has argued that politics involves commanding and that commanding is speech, but speech and discourse presuppose the face-to-face. This line of thought has a heroic quality about it; it is most likely part of Levinas's effort to outdo Heidegger on his own ground and even to overturn him. In recent philosophy, there have been very influential attempts to articulate transcendental arguments for the conditions that make communication possible, but none that would satisfy Levinas more satisfactorily. For they are either idealist or realist in ways that Levinas would surely claim are inadequate or insufficient, more akin to Heidegger's conclusions than to his own.

Exactly how does Levinas attempt to show that discourse and communication are transcendentally grounded in the face-to-face and thereby in the ethical in some sense? In fact, Levinas provides us with an argument that discourse is possible only on the basis of the face-to-face.[40] How does this argument develop, and why – and how – does it result in an ethical foundation or ground for the possibility of language and communication? Levinas's basic argument is rather direct. Language presupposes interlocutors, persons engaged in discourse one

---

[37] TI, 198–99; cf. 178.
[38] TI, 200; cf. 213, 247.
[39] TI, 245–46.
[40] Here I will be looking primarily at "Discourse and Ethics" in TI, Section IB5, 72–77.

with another. Discourse is a "struggle between thinkers" and hence implies "transcendence, radical separation, the strangeness of the interlocutors, the revelation of the other to me."[41] Language and discourse, then, presuppose an encounter between me and the "nudity of the face," which is different from the way a thing is disclosed to me in everyday life.[42] The face is naked, destitute, a plea and a command, that "supplicates and demands, that can supplicate only because it demands . . . which one recognizes in giving . . . the epiphany of the face as face. . . . To recognize the Other is to recognize a hunger. To recognize the Other is to give."[43] It is "calling into question of my joyous possession of the world."[44] Here is the epitome of Levinas's regressive argument, from language to what is its basic condition: Discourse requires two interlocutors in relation to one another; their relation – no matter what else it is – involves the face-to-face encounter, and what that face-to-face reveals is the other's need, plea, and so forth and the self's responsibility. Levinas then adds a progressive argument, which he develops more fully elsewhere, that shows how "this initial dispossession conditions the subsequent generalization of money," the process of generalization, conceptualization, objectivization, and ultimately the realization of "community and universality."[45] Levinas's line of thought begins with this basic event of encounter, plea, command, and generosity and leads through my making of what is mine common, to the universal, to conceptualization, and then to language, community, and thought itself.[46] "Language does not exteriorize a representation pre-existing in me: it puts in common a world hitherto mine."[47] Hence, the face and language are inextricably connected.

This is a very rudimentary sketch of what Levinas says about language and discourse, on the one hand, and the face-to-face encounter, on the other, in *Totality and Infinity*. The gist of his reasoning is that language requires two elements that are both grounded in the face-to-face: first, the otherness or separateness of a dialogical partner or interlocutor, another person to talk with; and second, universality or commonality. For Levinas, there is no private language, and there is no universality not grounded in the encounter with the other's plea and demand in virtue of which I make common what is originally only mine.

Another way to look at this two-dimensional argument, with its regressive and progressive strands, is this. We live in society and communicate with one another, and the latter is possible only because of the former. But what is

[41] TI, 73.
[42] TI, 74–75.
[43] TI, 75.
[44] TI, 76.
[45] TI, 76.
[46] See TI, 100–1, 170–74, 209–12, 296–97.
[47] TI, 174.

it about our sociality that makes communication and discourse possible? It is not simply the normal features of social interaction that we experience and are aware of in ordinary experience. It is not only that we share features or capacities with one another or that we enjoy the same things or feel kinship with some and animosity toward others. All of this may be true, but it is derivative; and while language may enable us to describe these things or capitalize on them, they are not fundamental conditions. What is it then? If language is tied to commonality and universality and only possible in social life, where do these features come from? What is their ground? Levinas's answer is that they derive from a dimension of ordinary life hidden from view but hinted at – the nexus of the other's "supplication and demand" and my responsibility and generosity. Only because of this nexus or event is the world ours and not mine; only because of it is there you and I and not just me. It is by itself not sufficient for language – we do need words, syntax, and so forth – but it is necessary.

One might object that prior to this encounter or event there is an I and then its recognition of the other person. Before the plea is the I and the other, and before responsible generosity is the recognition. Levinas denies both, in a sense. He says explicitly, "To recognize the Other is to recognize a hunger. To recognize the Other is to give."[48] The encounter with the face is not an act of seeing; it is not perceptual or judgmental. What confronts me is the other person's need, misery, destitution, and I do not see them, for I do not see yet at all. I sense and respond. I sense the suffering and give or withhold – that is, I respond, and my sensing, my responding, and my recognizing – acknowledging and accepting – the other are all one. Moreover, in a sense that we shall examine later, at that instant, so to speak, I am all this sensing, this responding, and this recognizing, and that is all I am as a human being; it is the totality of my humanity. In ordinary life, of course, I am much else, and because the encounter with the face occurs, if never purely but only in context, in the everyday, I am always many things in addition to responsible at any given moment. But this is what I am primordially and fundamentally, in a sense before I am anything else. Hence, ethics comes first. My ethical character precedes all else that I am, and ethics is the ground of language and community.[49]

---

[48] TI, 75.

[49] Is Levinas's conception of the primacy of the ethical and the self's relation to the other too simplistic? Does it ignore too much about human interaction by focusing on just one feature of our relation to others, their vulnerability and suffering? I shall consider a criticism along these lines in Chapter 9, but it is interesting to notice that such an objection sounds similar to one that has often been raised against utilitarianism. W. D. Ross, for example, in *The Right and the Good* (Oxford: Clarendon Press; 1930), 19, charges that "[t]he theory of . . . utilitarianism . . . seems to simplify unduly our relations to our fellows. It says, in effect, that the only morally significant relation in which my neighbours stand to me is that of being possible beneficiaries of my action.

Levinas's face-to-face as sensing the other's suffering and destitution, which is distinguishable from perception and knowledge of the other person but always occurs "alongside" our daily experience, should not seem wholly unfamiliar to us. Something like it has played an important role for Stanley Cavell in his reading of the later Wittgenstein and in his own philosophical thinking. I am referring to Cavell's notion of "acknowledgment." This idea arises for Cavell in his thinking about Wittgenstein's reflections on psychological states and about the problem of other minds. It then takes on other roles and a wider scope, eventually playing a central role in Cavell's thinking about skepticism, romanticism, and larger questions about the human condition.[50]

Cavell's early discussion of Wittgenstein on psychological states, other minds, and such themes, although it is obviously aimed at clarifying issues that are not central for Levinas, nonetheless does draw close to Levinasian themes. Just as Levinas, as we shall see, seeks to expose the limits of Western philosophy, Cavell seems to be working his way toward a view of how we live in the world and how we live with other people that breaks sharply with the traditional Cartesian view or any variation of it. He does this by considering skeptical challenges

But they may also stand to me in the relation of promisee to promisor, of creditor to debtor, of wife to husband, of fellow countryman to fellow countryman, and the like; and each of these relations is the foundation of a . . . duty, . . . " quoted by David McNaughton, *Moral Vision*, 177. As we shall see, Levinas does not ignore or reject the moral relevance of such relationships, but he does believe that all supervene on the fundamental social relationship of summons and responsibility, what Ross calls "beneficence." In this respect, there is an affinity between Levinas and utilitarianism, to which I call attention in the Appendix.

[50] Simon Critchley explicitly associates Cavell's conception of acknowledgment with Levinas's notion of justice (in TI) in "Cavell's 'Romanticism' and Cavell's Romanticism," in Russell Goodman (ed.), *Contending with Stanley Cavell*, 50: "[I]n Cavell's terms, tragedy is the dramatization of the failure to acknowledge others. The skeptical teaching of tragedy – and the tragic teaching of skepticism – is the fact that I cannot know the other. . . . [*The Claim of Reason*] closes with the image of Othello and Desdemona dead on their nuptial bed. For Cavell, this image constitutes an emblem for the truth of skepticism. . . . [Othello] could not accept the tragic wisdom of the limitedness of his knowledge of Desdemona and consequently he failed to acknowledge her separateness, her alterity. This is why Othello kills Desdemona" (50). Critchley calls the relationship with the other that Othello fails to engage "what Levinas, and Derrida after him, call justice" (50). We live, in Cavell's terms, between love and avoidance. Tragedy, skepticism, and acknowledgment are the central themes of Part IV of *The Claim of Reason*.

In a discussion of Cavell on the moral of skepticism and moral perfectionism, Hilary Putnam notes that "if Othello's is a pathology, it is an exaggerated form of, so to speak, a *normal* pathology. The point of saying this is not simply to awaken us to the suffering of others, as Levinas does (although I have heard Cavell speak about Levinas with deep respect); it is also to get us to see that an idea of being totally free of skepticism, in this deep sense, is itself a *form* of skepticism" ("Philosophy as the Education of Grownups: Stanley Cavell and Skepticism" in Crary and Shieh (eds.), *Reading Cavell*, 127). I would just like to point out that Levinas would doubtless object to the word "simply" and the suggestion that what Putnam is ascribing to Cavell is not also something that Levinas understands in a very serious way.

to our knowledge of other minds and by glossing that knowledge as a kind of acknowledgment and acceptance of responsibility for the other person.[51] This can be seen clearly in an early essay on these themes. His basic strategy is this: He says that we should distinguish the statements "I know I am in pain" and "I know you are in pain" in the following way. Although they appear to be syntactically similar, the two statements differ significantly. The first claim is really an expression of pain, an exhibiting of me, as suffering, to another, while the second is "a response to this exhibiting; it is an expression of *sympathy*.... But why is sympathy expressed this way? Because your suffering makes a *claim* on me. It is not enough that I *know* (am certain) that you suffer – I must do or reveal something (whatever can be done). In a word, I must *acknowledge* it." To be sure, as Cavell goes on to point out, "the claim of suffering may go unanswered.... The point, however, is that the concept of acknowledgment is evidenced equally by its failure as by its success."[52] Cavell's point, which he gets from his reading of Wittgenstein, is that "pain" language is not about knowledge claims. Its uses both express pain and acknowledge it, and the acknowledgment is a response to a claim made on me, not by the other person's statement or utterance but rather by the other's pain or suffering. As Cavell puts it: When I am presented with that suffering, "I must do or reveal something." I cannot avoid it; whatever I do or say is a response to it. Pain and suffering – and perhaps, or even probably, not them alone – *must be* acknowledged when exhibited.[53]

This bit is important to Cavell, although it is not the end of the matter. It is only part of his discussion of criteria, psychological concepts, other minds, and many other themes. But for my purposes, it is a central passage. Notice some of its features. First, the notion of acknowledging another person's suffering or pain is part of a larger project of clarifying psychological concepts in their first-, second-, and third-person uses. In a sense, then, Cavell begins with an interest in epistemology, language, and cognitive psychology. Second, it applies to a whole variety of such concepts, not just pain and suffering.[54] Third, it will eventually coordinate acknowledging with imagination, in order to tie together the first-person use and the second- and third-person uses.[55] Finally, acknowledgment will eventually become central to Cavell's romantic conception of how we live

[51] See Stanley Cavell, "Knowing and Acknowledging" in Cavell, *Must We Mean What We Say?*, 238–66. The theme is also pervasive in many of Cavell's later works, for example, *The Claim of Reason*.

[52] Cavell, "Knowing and Acknowledging" in *Must We Mean What We Say?*, 263.

[53] See Stephen Mulhall, *Stanley Cavell: Philosophy's Recounting of the Ordinary*, 110–11, 119; see also Cavell, *The Claim of Reason*, 82–85.

[54] See Mulhall, *Stanley Cavell*, 130–38.

[55] See Mulhall, *Stanley Cavell*, 119–22.

in the world and with the world.[56] These features remind us that the relevance of Cavell for understanding Levinas, while limited, is important, and the text we looked at is very helpful. Clearly, for Levinas the suffering of the other person, present to me in her face, is not simply one psychological state among others. It is somehow basic and original, for its everyday occurrences as pain, hunger, or loneliness, for example, are indications or hints of a more basic fact, that the other person's very presence in my world, over against me, is both a plea to share my possessions, my space, and my bread, and a demand that I respond to that plea. In this early essay, Cavell does not see things this way, or at least his purposes in reading Wittgenstein against Descartes and others do not lead him in this direction. His is still a Romantic, subject-oriented conception. What it does capture, nonetheless, is the way in which the other's pain is present and is received, so to speak.[57] That is, once we accept the situation as one of another person's pain or need being exhibited for me or expressed to me, Cavell helps us to see how that exhibition or expression actually constitutes a *claim*: it includes a supplication and a demand that I respond in some way or other. This is what acknowledging the other's pain is: sensing that claim and that demand. Hence, the statements "I know you are in pain" and "I know she is in pain" are not knowledge claims, assertions based on sensory evidence, or anything of this sort. They are acts of sympathy that *express* this acknowledgment; they are public expressions of the face-to-face. If Levinas can show how this encounter is fundamental, Cavell has helped us to see that such an encounter is not strange, extraordinary, or ineffable. Indeed, if Cavell is right, as a category, the face-to-face encounter is exemplified regularly in everyday life. What is remarkable would be how basic the role of suffering is and how regularly our respect or sensitivity to it is occluded or ignored.

In a sense, Cavell's account has the outcome that we are tied into the world and tied together with other people in ways more fundamental than the cognitive, epistemic, and presentational. This is a kind of Heideggerian insight, which Cavell himself acknowledges. It is Husserlian, too, to the degree that Heideggerian *existentale* are modes of intentionality broadly in Husserl's sense.

---

[56] See Mulhall, *Stanley Cavell*, 158–63; see also Stanley Cavell, *In Quest of the Ordinary* (Chicago: University of Chicago Press 1988), *passim*.

[57] Because of the orientation of the philosophical tradition out of which Cavell speaks, the focus, at one level, is on language and the syntactic similarity between the statements "I know I am in pain" and "I know you are in pain." What he proceeds to do, of course, is to show that the two statements serve very different purposes in terms of the interpersonal interaction between parties who utter them. What begins as a narrowly linguistic issue becomes a larger issue about human existence. This larger perspective already emerges in essays such as Cavell, "The Avoidance of Love" on *King Lear* in *Must We Mean What We Say?* and then in Cavell, *The Claim of Reason*, especially Part 4, on tragedy, and Ch. 13, "Between Acknowledgment and Avoidance."

Of course, Levinas would deny that the encounter with the face of the other person is simply a mode of intentionality or even strictly speaking such a mode, but it is quasi-intentional, at least in the sense that it is not a kind of external relation between the other person and the self.[58] This, too, is a feature of Cavell's insight; part of dissolving, not solving, the problem of other minds is to appreciate how fundamentally the I and the other person are tied together. The concepts of expression or exhibition and acknowledgment are intended in part to expose this linkage and to suggest that epistemic "distance" and "detachment," which generate the traditional problem of other minds, are already a mode of that linkage.

What makes the epiphany of the face ethical, then, is that intrinsically it involves a claim — what I have called "plea and command" — on me by the other to respond to the other person's suffering, to her claim upon me and her "election" of me. At times, Levinas puts this in biblical terms: The face says to me, in the imperative, "Thou shalt not kill." But this is no rule or principle in the normal sense; it is nothing general but rather a precise, particular, utterly unique directive. Any rule or principle must come later, so to speak; that is, moral rules and legal principles do occur, but they arise out of the dimension of the face-to-face and are "indebted" to that dimension. What the utterly particular face says to the utterly particular me is "do not kill *me*," "make room for *me*," "help *me*," or "give *me* a share of your bread." It is, as Cavell puts it, a claim or demand, but it is not a rule. That comes only with universality or generality, which we have yet to discuss. What underlies every social relation we have is an utterly unique relation between the other person and me, between each and every other person and me. To be sure, in everyday affairs our relationship is also defined and shaped by a host of rules, regularized patterns, and principles of conduct — social, moral, legal, and otherwise. But it is Levinas's point that all of these "derive" from the encounter with the face, which is particular and determinative.[59] In other words, the priority of the face is not temporal; in a sense, it is incorporated into ordinary life, but only in qualified, obscured, or distorted ways. Neither the face nor the many other ways the other person appears to me occur on their own, in isolation from one another. The other may be my friend, my companion on a trip, an excellent chess player, a lover of Abbas Kiarostami's films, and the claimant of my responsibility, all at once. Some of these relations arise out of conventions, popular culture, common practices,

---

[58] TI, 49: "The 'intentionality' of transcendence is unique in its kind."

[59] Later, we shall discuss this relationship, in part the relationship between ethics in Levinas's deep sense and politics. For the moment, we should note that this account is *not* a genetic account; social relationships with moral and legal rules do not *come from* the face-to-face, but they are "grounded" in it.

and traditional roles, but one relation is constituted by our most fundamental engagement with one another, and that one is Levinas's primary concern.[60]

LATER THOUGHTS ON ETHICS AND THE FACE

We do not yet know why the face has the primacy that it does, why Levinas takes it to be the infinite or transcendent that breaches the totality of our lives and our thinking and what this idea means. Nor do we know in what sense the face has meaning; how it can be approached in language; what gives it the force to make the claim it does; how it gives rise to society, moral rules, and politics; exactly why it is called "religion"; and what Levinas's extensive use of religious and theological vocabulary means. Nor do we understand Levinas's conception of the self and the paradoxical claim that it is originally passive and responsible before it is anything else and that its freedom is derivative and not original. These are among the themes of chapters yet to come. What we do understand is that the epiphany of the face has an ethical content and force. Before we move on, however, I want to consider some of the developments we find in Levinas's later treatment of the face-to-face and terminology he comes to use to designate it. In these later works, Levinas attends more and more to the face-to-face from the point of view of the self or subject. In Chapter 6, we will discuss Levinas's conception of subjectivity and the self, what one might call the "subjective side" of the encounter with the other. Here, even as I turn to Levinas's later writings, I will try to remain focused on the ethical content of the face and its "objective side," that is, the ethical character of the impact of the other on the self.

Regularly, after *Totality and Infinity*, Levinas continues to describe the face and its impact in terms he has already introduced: It puts the self in question or

---

[60] Levinas's understanding of the ethical has some similarities with what is currently called "moral particularism," but it is distinctive. As we shall see, Levinas argues, for example, that each ethical situation has its own features that need to be identified and examined with the greatest care and attention to detail. In the same spirit, David McNaughton points out that the moral particularist holds that "what is required is the correct conception of the particular case in hand, with its unique set of properties. There is thus no substitute for a sensitive and detailed examination of each individual case" (*Moral Vision*, 190). But the particularist associates this attention to detail with a skepticism "about the role of moral principles in moral reasoning. . . . Moral particularism takes the view that moral principles are at best useless, and at worst a hindrance, in trying to find out which is the right action" (*Moral Vision*, 190; cf. Jonathan Dancy, *Ethics Without Principles* [Oxford: Oxford University Press, 2004]). Many commentators read Levinas as endorsing such a view as well, if not an even more radically critical view of moral rules, but I doubt that this is correct, as I shall try to show. Moral rules may not be fundamental in Levinas's eyes, but neither are they useless or necessarily an obstacle to determining what is right or just.

calls it into question; it speaks out of nakedness, destitution, and weakness; it forbids murder; it challenges the self from its humility and height; it summons the self to respond.[61] In interviews, when asked about the face, his responses reflect these same themes.[62] The nudity of the face is a call, an appeal, and also an imperative, he says in 1989.[63] And in his interview with Richard Kearney, published in 1984, he says that "the face is the other who asks me not to let him die alone, as if to do so were to become an accomplice in his death. Thus the face says to me: you shall not kill."[64] Finally, in *Ethics and Infinity* (1982), in his conversations with Philippe Nemo, he describes the face as "exposed, menaced, as if inviting us to an act of violence. At the same time, the face is what forbids us to kill.... The face is what one cannot kill, or at least it is that whose *meaning* consists in saying: 'Thou shalt not kill.'"[65] This account, then, remains a consistent background to Levinas's understanding of the face-to-face. But against that background, there are modifications, new emphases, and new dimensions. These developments are often tied to the use of new terminology. As I indicated, I will restrict present comments to the ethical character of the "objective" side of the encounter with the face, that is, to the ethical import of the face for the self.[66] I will leave discussion of such matters as the religious character of the encounter and its subjective side for later.

In his essay "Substitution" (1968), later modified as the core of *Otherwise Than Being* (1974), we find several new terms associated with the face. The encounter is now called "proximity," and it is characterized as "my relationship with the neighbor" and as "the summoning of myself by the other (*autrui*) . . . a summons of extreme urgency.... The term *obsession* designates this relation which is irreducible to consciousness."[67] On the one hand, Levinas takes the other not to be alien and distant as much as nearby. On the other hand, the emphasis now is on the "urgency" that the face evinces and its alien and yet unavoidable character, which Levinas goes on to describe "as something foreign, as disequilibrium, as delirium, undoing thematization, eluding *principle*,

---

[61] See Levinas, "Phenomenon and Enigma" in *Collected Philosophical Papers*, 69–70; "Transcendence and Height" in *Basic Philosophical Writings*, 16–19; "Meaning and Sense" in *Basic Philosophical Writings*, 54; "Language and Proximity" in *Collected Philosophical Papers*, 120–21; "Transcendence and Evil" in *Collected Philosophical Papers*, 185; "Philosophy, Justice and Love" in *Entre Nous*, 103–5; and "From One to the Other" in *Entre Nous*, 144–46.

[62] See *Is It Righteous To Be?*, 48–49, 114–15, 127–28, 135–36, 144–45, 215.

[63] Levinas, "Being for the Other" in *Is It Righteous To Be?*, 115.

[64] "Dialogue with Emmanuel Levinas" in Cohen (ed.), *Face to Face with Levinas*, 24.

[65] Levinas, *Ethics and Infinity*, 86–87; cf. 85–92.

[66] That is, I will set aside until later discussion of responsibility and the selfhood constituted by it – the subjective side of the face-to-face.

[67] Levinas, "Substitution" in *Basic Philosophical Writings*, 81.

origin, and will."[68] The face not only pleas and commands; it is strange and disorienting; it unsettles – and overwhelms.

Levinas also calls it "an-archic," but not simply as disordering, which involves one order replacing another. The face is "beyond these alternatives." It is somehow independent of order or principle altogether, prior to them, wholly oblique and disruptive. Moreover, because an *arche* is a beginning or starting point, an original principle, the face is something "prior" to beginning and to what, in everyday life or theoretical understanding, is a starting point or founding principle. It is, then, an obsession that is an-archic *persecution*, "a placing in question anterior to questioning, a responsibility beyond the logos of response, as though persecution by the other (*autrui*) were the basis of solidarity with the other (*autrui*)."[69] The face as persecution, moreover, is an *accusation*: "[I]t strips the Ego of its self-conceit and its dominating imperialism."[70] The Ego returns to its true, original self by being accused and hence through its tie to the other person, spontaneity returns to passivity, as it were. "Obsessed with responsibilities, which do not result from decisions taken by a 'freely contemplating' subject, consequently accused of what it never willed or decreed, accused of what it did not do, subjectivity is thrown back on itself – in itself – by a persecuting accusation."[71] The result for the self, engaged by the other via accusation and persecution, is what Levinas calls "substitution" and "being a hostage," "the fact of human fellowship, prior to freedom."[72]

Levinas's new vocabulary is intended in part to show that the encounter with the face of the other person is ethically prior to language, thought, reflection, and the everyday. I will discuss these matters later. For the moment, I want to notice especially the *tonality* of the terminology.[73] Many of the new

---

[68] "Substitution" in *Basic Philosophical Writings*, 81.

[69] "Substitution" in *Basic Philosophical Writings*, 82.

[70] "Substitution" in *Basic Philosophical Writings*, 88.

[71] "Substitution" in *Basic Philosophical Writings*, 88.

[72] "Substitution" in *Basic Philosophical Writings*, 90–91.

[73] Levinas's terminology for the encounter with the other person capitalizes on the richness of the terms, their multiple meanings and suggestiveness. In the case of *hostage*, for example, the other holds the self hostage in the sense that it imposes itself with a kind of force, binds the self, and seeks help in exchange. To hold someone hostage, after all, is to confine that person by force or against his will with an offer of release only in exchange for money or goods of some kind. Levinas says that the other *accuses* the self. An accusation is a charge leveled against someone for a harm or injury committed or for having done something wrong, but the term "accusation" also suggests grammatically the *accusative* case. What is in the accusative is the direct object of the verb and thus is passive. As a final example, the other person *persecutes* the self. To persecute someone is to insult, harm, or inflict a wrong in a continuous or consistent way, over a significant period of time, but more generally it is to dominate or impose oneself on them. We associate persecution, historically, with the mistreatment of minorities of one kind or another, and in Europe the paradigmatic persecution was antisemitism, just as in the United

expressions – obsession, persecution, accusation, hostage – take the earlier themes of calling into question, summoning, and demanding and modulate them into a disturbing, almost assaulting register. From one point of view, the terms call attention to the way that the face-to-face indicts our everyday sense of ourselves, our priorities, and our freedom and pulls us back to our origins – indeed, to a point prior to our origins, against our will, as it were. From another point of view, these terms remind us of what we originally are: accused before we have done anything, obsessed before we have chosen at all and in a sense overcome, persecuted by the demand made of us before we have accepted it. Moreover, the new vocabulary – the terms all virtual metaphors – already marks a shift in Levinas's attention, a development widely appreciated by commentators, from the objective side of the face-to-face, the suffering and misery of the other person, to the subjective side, the kind of self I am as accused by that face. Nonetheless, from either perspective the face is seen as disruptive and demanding, and in this sense Levinas's new expressions only underscore the imperative force of the primordial relationship. Ethics at this level is an assault; we are deluged by responsibility.[74] Whether we think of the disruption caused by the face as original or as a return to origins, it is still unsettling, oblique to the calm confines of cognitive experience and its associated ordinary way of life. As Levinas sees it, human existence does not start out on still waters but rather in a turbulent sea; our humanity emerges for us with the cries of hungry children and the agony of destitute neighbors, floundering and calling for help. At that urgent moment, we are human beings for the first time, so to speak, before we have done a thing.[75]

In Western philosophy, certainly since Hume, the fact-value distinction or the distinction between the descriptive and the prescriptive or normative has

States it has been the racial treatment of African Americans, Indians, and others. Levinas applies these words to the way that the other person is related to the subject, but the connotations he is drawing upon are broader and deeper than some one specific sense.

[74] An entire literature has grown up around the so-called life-saving analogy, utilized in a classic way by Peter Singer in "Famine, Affluence and Morality," *Philosophy and Public Affairs* 1 (1972), 229–43. One development is argument in behalf of a morality of beneficence. An excellent discussion occurs in Garrett Cullity, *The Moral Demands of Affluence*. Cullity characterizes a "failure of *beneficence*" as "the failure to display an adequate practical concern for other people's interests" insofar as "other people's interests in receiving our help give us a clear reason to help them" and "the failure to respond to this reason by going ahead and helping them can be morally wrong" (13; cf. 16). This sounds very much like Levinas. There are affinities between what Levinas has to say and such moral thinking – affinities worth pursuing on another occasion.

[75] We will return to this point: Even though I have used temporal and developmental language, as Levinas often does, I want to emphasize that the face-to-face does not occur "before" the rest of social life. It is a permanent dimension of it, even when it is ignored or hidden from view. As I shall argue later, for Levinas all human life is ethical and political at once. There is no avoiding the face and no avoiding compromising our responsibility to the other person, ever.

played a central role and is contested to this day.[76] To some, a feature of the distinction is the special force of the ethical. Levinas does not use this distinction in any explicit way; it is not a feature of his philosophical vocabulary. To him, it would be a distinction used by philosophers and others within everyday life and our theoretical reflection on it, a characteristic of the domain of being or ontology. But it is illuminating to take his increasingly dramatic and urgent vocabulary for the way the face imposes itself on the self as an expression of his appreciation for how "excessive" and "extraordinary" is the way that the ethical intrudes into our natural lives. Moreover, it is also illuminating to see the relationship with the face as a dimension of human social experience that complements our existence as natural beings and introduces the sense of value and goodness that we believe human life has. Ethics may be elevating and thus one reason for calling it "religion" and later "the holy," but it is also a kind of persecution and accusation. It holds us hostage. Levinas expresses these sentiments about the primacy and yet the difficulty of ethical obligation when he employs such dramatic terms to the way the face of the other confronts the self and calls it into question.

[76] See Hilary Putnam, *The Collapse of the Fact/Value Dichotomy and Other Essays* (Cambridge, MA: Harvard University Press, 2002).

4

Philosophy, Totality, and the Everyday

PHILOSOPHY AND THE EVERYDAY

Most often, when Levinas turns to the encounter with the face of the other in order to shed light on its objective or subjective side, he does so within the context of everyday life and ordinary experience. His accounts are abstract and metaphorical, but they arise out of everyday experiences of misery and suffering, of the orphan, the stranger, the poor, and the widow. Their biblical overtones notwithstanding, such figures are ones whom we meet in ordinary life. As we have pointed out, it is as if he is locating a dimension of experience largely hidden from view, obscured by our habits and ways of conducting affairs or distorted by culturally and historically grounded attitudes, as a reminder of the fundamental meaning of our humanity. The face is both in our lives and somehow not in them; it confronts us in ordinary life and yet also from outside it. The face is not a phenomenon, but rather, as Levinas comes to put it, an *enigma*, or riddle, a challenge to what is customary and accepted, and yet also in some ways a foundation.[1]

Philosophy reaches out and locates the face-to-face and describes and clarifies it, and hence philosophy arises at least in part for moral reasons, because clarification and articulation are needed.[2] But philosophy is located in the everyday and always returns to it. One wonders, however, if and in what sense it really

---

[1] See "Enigma and Phenomenon" in *Basic Philosophical Writings* and "Phenomenon and Enigma" in *Collected Philosophical Papers*.

[2] What philosophy aims at and accomplishes, then, at least in part, is an act of disclosure, of clarification or illumination of what is "dark" or hidden, of articulation – to use an expression that both Charles Taylor and Robert Brandom employ in technical ways; see Taylor, *Sources of the Self* and Brandom, *Articulating Reasons: An Introduction to Inferentialism* (Cambridge, MA: Harvard University Press, 2000), and *Making It Explicit: Reasoning, Representing, and Discursive Commitment* (Cambridge, MA: Harvard University Press, 1998).

leaves it. What philosophy does, as ethical metaphysics, is to see the role of the face-to-face in life and in thought. But in order to do this, does it reach beyond life and beyond thought? In a sense, it does, but in another it does not. In this chapter, we will say something about why and how both are so.

What makes the face primordial? One reason is that it is infinite, and as infinite the face breaches totality, which cannot encompass it. In a sense, then, the face is unconditioned, absolute, unjustified, and given prior to everything else in our lives, our experience, and our thinking. In this chapter, we need to try to clarify these matters. It is a dark saying that the face is the infinite. What does it mean? What did Levinas learn from Franz Rosenzweig, the Weimar Jewish philosopher whom he credits in the Preface to *Totality and Infinity* with having preceded him in opposing "the idea of totality?" Why is the face exteriority, the transcendent, and the other?

From one point of view, this discussion about totality, infinity, ethics, and the face takes the route down from the everyday to its primordial condition or ground. Another route leads up from the face to the everyday world, a world of society, moral system, and politics. If Levinas's ethical metaphysics incorporates a critique of Western society and culture and judgments about episodes of generosity and kindness, then it does so because the face somehow marks our ordinary lives. In the everyday, there are traces of genuine humanity because life and thought, morality and politics, are ultimately grounded in the encounter with the face of the other person. We need to explore this route, too, from the particularity of the face-to-face to the institutions and practices of social life.

One way of distinguishing modernism and postmodernism is to point out how they respond to ordinary, everyday affairs. Modernism is redemptive and elevating. It seeks to transcend the limitations of the everyday through grand action, creativity, and extraordinary religious experience. Modernism is a kind of heroic romanticism. Postmodernism, on the other hand, and some postmoderns who anticipated it − I am thinking of Robert Musil, Siegfried Kracauer, and Walter Benjamin − invoke a redemptive realism and an affirmation of the mundane, the prosaic. One might associate modernism, then, with transcendence and a metaphysical realism of a Platonist kind, an insecurity about the everyday and an elevation of the extraordinary. Postmodernism is, on the other hand, a kind of idealism, confined to our web of beliefs and practices, reverent of revealing more and more of what lies within it. In which camp should we expect to find Levinas? Or perhaps, does he straddle both? Is there a sense in which the face is both a condition for ordinary life and an ideal that ordinary people are called to realize? There are modern philosophers who honor ordinary life and natural existence but seek to find standards of human flourishing within it. Is there a way in which Levinas is both one of their party and also a critic of their inadequacies? Much of this theme will have to wait for a later chapter, but here, in our discussion of Levinas and the everyday, we will take some steps toward clarifying where he stands.

The everyday world, our lives and our thinking, is the domain of totality. What is the infinite, and how does it breach that world? Here I turn to two essays – "Philosophy and the Idea of Infinity" (1957) and "Transcendence and Height" (1962) – and the book *Totality and Infinity* (1961) in order to discuss these issues and answer these questions. The issues are central for Levinas and might be seen as the starting point of his thinking. We may not agree with this priority, but there is no denying their importance, especially in his early period. Among other things, investigating totality and infinity will shed light on Levinas's relation to the Western philosophical tradition as well as to everyday experience, history, epistemology, and metaphysics.

The infinite, exteriority, the transcendent, the Other – these are all expressions for what is outside or what is different, but outside of what? Different from what? And in what way outside or different? Moreover, why is this issue at all significant or perhaps even important? Why does it matter whether there is something outside?

These are not new questions. Plato wondered if there was anything outside the everyday world of sensory experience, the world of nature, notion, and change. Aristotle wondered if there was anything outside the natural world, the world of scientific knowledge, the terrestrial and celestial domains. Plotinus wondered whether there was not a pure unity beyond being. Medieval religious philosophers and theologians – Arabic, Christian, and Jewish – wondered if there was anything outside of the natural order (the ordered world), and modern Cartesian skeptics wondered if there was anything outside the domain of appearances, ideas, or impressions. Kant proposed that outside the domain of sensory experience and scientific knowledge there lies the *thing-in-itself*, and his contemporaries wondered whether this did not conduce to skepticism, leaving the knowable permanently beyond our grasp. Some twentieth-century philosophers and their eighteenth- and nineteenth-century ancestors wondered whether there were minds outside each of our own, and idealists like Berkeley wondered whether there were material things outside minds. Others wondered whether perception requires the presence of some preconceptual given outside the bounds of the "space of reasons" and thought. Against this background, Levinas stands. He does not wonder; he believes that the infinite is outside totality and yet breaches it, like the traditional providential God of Western faiths who exists as transcendent and yet reveals itself, in speech and in act, to human beings within the natural world. But Levinas's infinite is not God, and the infinite's breaking into totality is only metaphorically a revelation or epiphany. What, then, is totality and what the infinite?

In his 1987 Preface to the German edition of *Totality and Infinity*, Levinas comments on the themes of that book:

This book challenges the synthesis of knowledge, the totality of being that is embraced by the *transcendental ego*, presence grasped in the representation and the concept... − inevitable stations of Reason − as the ultimate authorities in deciding what is *meaningful*.... Beyond the *in-itself* and *for-itself* of the disclosed, there is human nakedness, more exterior than the outside of the world − landscapes, things, institutions − the nakedness that cries out its strangeness to the world.... Within the world of appearances, it cries out the shame of its hidden misery....[3]

Levinas's book challenges an old, conventional way of looking at our lives, our world, and our experience. What he challenges about it is not its sufficiency within its own domain; rather, what he challenges is its assumption of its own comprehensiveness. In fact, his charge is that what it omits or ignores is fundamental to everything within it.

According to the view that Levinas opposes, what is meaningful about human life is determined by thought or reason, in a broad sense. That reason is either personal or impersonal, subjective or absolute. It is the individual's rational capacities of synthesis, conceptualization, and organization or those capacities as the ordering principles of the whole of nature; reason is individual and personal or cosmic and unconditional. This tradition of thinking permeates our everyday lives, but its emblem is the tradition of Western philosophy from Parmenides and Plato, through the medievals to Spinoza, Leibniz, Kant, the German Idealists, Husserl, and even, Levinas argues, Heidegger. In this tradition, relative exteriority is eventually assimilated into an ultimate, comprehensive unity or whole. Only occasionally is there a hint of an absolute exteriority, something unqualifiedly outside the domain of reason, albeit not necessarily outside the domain of our actual experience and our actual lives. This domain of reason is what Levinas calls "totality"; it is the "world of appearances," and it is Levinas's claim that an ultimate ground of what is *meaningful* in it comes from the outside, in a sense, from the crying out of the face of suffering, out of its "hidden misery."

TOTALITY AND THE INFINITE

Levinas gives an excellent early account of this kind of totality and the infinity that breaches it in his 1957 essay "Philosophy and the Idea of Infinity."[4] He

---

[3] Levinas, Preface to the German edition of TI, in *Entre Nous*, 198.
[4] There are several translations of this important essay and a detailed commentary by Adriaan Peperzak in his book *To the Other*. I will cite the translation in Levinas, *Collected Philosophical Papers*.

begins by identifying two impulses of Western philosophy and of the aspiration for knowledge, what he calls "heteronomy" and "autonomy." "Heteronomy" refers to the aspiration, especially philosophical, to move from this world to another, from the everyday to the beyond. Heteronomy, then, is characteristic of metaphysics and philosophical theology. Autonomy is the opposite tendency, aimed at "the reduction of the other to the same"; it is the movement of human thought to "domesticate" everything and incorporate it into its own venue — concepts, principles, and theories. Typically, Levinas claims, Western philosophy has inclined toward the side of autonomy, from Ionia to Jena; it has seemed "to exclude the transcendent, encompass every other in the same, and proclaim the philosophical birthright of autonomy."[5]

Levinas uses Plato's terms from the *Sophist* and the *Timaeus*, the "same" and the "other." Basically, the same is the self, mind, thought, and reason; in one sense or another, everything outside the self becomes the same as the self or spirit. The other is everything different or other than the same. Western philosophy's primary impulse is imperialistic, to reduce the other to the same, to think everything, to subject the world to the dominion of reason.

Before we proceed with Levinas's own exposition, it is worth stopping to notice that there are, as we have suggested earlier, two ways of understanding these impulses and their goals. There is what we might call an empirical reading, according to which heteronomy seems involved in a virtually incoherent task, to reach beyond the bounds of thought and consciousness to identify and acknowledge something that may seem to be necessary to make sense of the natural order but that is itself beyond thought and awareness. Levinas pinpoints one such goal as the divine that must be understood as somehow identifiable while being beyond thought, experience, and language. An analogue, in a different context, would be Kant's thing-in-itself or, in more recent epistemology, the target of what Wilfrid Sellars calls the "myth of the given," some kind of preconceptual, brute perceptual sensa or data. All of this, no matter how common in the philosophical tradition, certainly has struck many as smacking of mysticism or obscurantism.

But there is another reading of Levinas's conception of heteronomy and autonomy, what we might call "perspectivalist." According to this view, all that is included in the notion of the same are the typical, regularly accepted, and even mythologized perspectives that we take on things and people in the world. The things called "the other" are not new entities as much as they are or represent unnoticed or repressed perspectives, dimensions, or aspects of the world as we already experience and think about it. The divine, on this reading, represents

---

[5] Levinas, "Philosophy and the Idea of Infinity" in his *Collected Philosophical Papers*, 47–48, esp. 48.

a perspective on nature – say, that it is dependent or ordered, that we might regularly ignore, but that, with greater attention and direction, we might better notice and appreciate. Just as intellectualist approaches to knowledge neglect or distort our emotional lives, for example, recognition of the role of institutions and practices would open up a social perspective that tended to be ignored or reduced to a kind of individual construction. On this account, the other calls upon us to see things we had not seen before, so to speak, although even to speak of "seeing" might at best be a metaphor.[6] Moreover, if the other were treated as something prior or determinative or fundamental, this would mean that the repressed perspective was meaningful in a basic and especially significant way, in a way that is foundational and that shapes other ways we relate to people and things.

It may very well be that Levinas shifts back and forth in his discussion of totality, infinity, and the face, from an empirical reading to a perspectival one. We might compare his practice to Kant's and the shifting in Kant from the transcendental or critical to the empirical or material standpoint. It is healthy, at the very least, to keep in mind that Levinas does not have to be read as an obscurantist or a mystic. He is a philosopher and an ethical thinker and a critic of modern society and culture. And his thinking is ineluctably ordinary and concrete, even where it might seem to be obscure and distractingly abstract.

In Levinas's view, then, Western philosophy is fundamentally egology, as he put, it, attempting unwaveringly to swallow every other into the self, thought, or reason. Hence, in religious terms, it is atheism – or, as we might put it, humanism.[7] This is the dominant pitch of what Rosenzweig called "the old thinking," what both Wittgenstein and Heidegger, each in his own way, charged with distortion and obfuscation.[8] Levinas explicitly acknowledges his debt to Rosenzweig – and indirectly then to Schelling, Kierkegaard, and Nietzsche – and his commitment to expose the shortcomings of this philosophical tradition. But Levinas realizes, or at least claims, that the alternative tendency – toward heteronomy rather than autonomy – is as old and as venerated. It is found, he here notes, in Plato and Descartes at certain crucial moments.[9] He sets about to explore that moment in Descartes' thought; it is a moment he cites regularly to the end of his career.

[6] The other could be diverse, for example, the material and economic character of human experience or the unconscious.
[7] See "Philosophy and the Idea of Infinity" in *Collected Philosophical Papers*, 49–51.
[8] See Hilary Putnam's introduction to Franz Rosenzweig's *Understanding the Sick and the Healthy* (Cambridge, MA: Harvard University Press, 1999).
[9] "Philosophy and the Idea of Infinity" in *Collected Philosophical Papers*, 53. See also on the Platonism of Descartes, Stephen Menn, *Descartes and Augustine* (Cambridge: Cambridge University Press, 1998).

It is indeed a *crucial* moment, for Descartes, for the entire Cartesian project, and for Levinas. It occurs in *Meditation III*. Descartes' reasoning is familiar and famous. In order to prove the veracity of clear and distinct ideas, Descartes seeks to prove the existence of an infinite, perfect, and benevolent God. The argument begins with the premise that I have an idea of an infinite and perfect being. Levinas is interested only in the first premise, what he calls "the *formal design*" of the structure that Descartes' analysis outlines.[10] In the *Meditations*, Descartes argues that in having this idea, in being conscious of an infinite being, we do not create the idea or imagine it. Rather, it must come to us from a source independent of us, and furthermore that the source must have as much "formal reality" as the idea has "objective reality." What this means, roughly speaking, is that the "cause" of the idea's being in the mind must have as high a degree of being as the idea depicts; and because the idea depicts a perfect, infinite being, the cause of the idea must *be* a perfect, infinite being. Levinas focuses his attention on these two features: We grasp the infinite, and this thought comes to us from a source independent of us. This event, then, is *philosophical testimony* to what Levinas had called our heteronomous impulse, to our grasping something that is wholly other.[11]

Levinas proceeds to describe what is involved in this having the idea of the infinite. It is a relationship but not of "a container to a content" or of "a content to a container." It is not like other cases where we have a mental act or representation of an object. Its intentionality is "not comparable with any other," for "it aims at what it cannot embrace." "The alterity of the infinite is not cancelled, is not extinguished in the thought that thinks it." Having the idea, then, is a relationship with an absolute alterity, an exterior or other, "without this exteriority being able to be integrated into the same."[12] Levinas then goes on to ask what this infinite is such that our relationship to it is of this kind.

For Levinas, then, Descartes testifies to there being a nontotalizing relation between the infinite and myself, between the infinite and every self. No standard terminology taken from everyday life or philosophical reflection can describe this relationship literally and adequately. The terms are metaphors, and it is best, perhaps, to use an expression that is not normally a part of epistemological vocabulary and one that marks the fact that the event occurs from the outside, so to speak. Descartes uses his most general, standard expression for a mental grasping, to have an "idea." We might better say that the infinite "engages" the I or, as Levinas puts it, the infinite "calls the I into question."

[10] "Philosophy and the Idea of Infinity" in *Collected Philosophical Papers*, 53.
[11] He cites Plato in the *Republic* and the Idea of the Good as well; "Philosophy and the Idea of Infinity" in *Collected Philosophical Papers*, 53.
[12] "Philosophy and the Idea of Infinity" in *Collected Philosophical Papers*, 54.

We expect that Levinas will go on to identify the infinite as the "face" of the other person that engages me in this way. It is not another thing, wholly different from things in the world. If the intentionality is unique, it is because the engagement by the face gives us a standpoint or perspective on my relation to the other person wholly unlike my normal relations. "The idea of infinity is the social relationship." Levinas calls it the "epiphany" of the face and says that its logos or content is "You shall not kill." It is an engagement that "puts an end to the irresistible imperialism of the same and the I," the resistance to murder. It is the "first given of moral consciousness."[13]

Because this relation is not cognitive, Levinas argues, it has about it a kind of dynamic, driven quality. Hence, Levinas calls it, from the subjective side, "desire," which marks its character as the "propulsion, the inflation, of this going beyond...." It is an "unquenchable" dynamism or aspiration, without satisfaction.[14] The word "desire" is a central one in moral theory and moral psychology; it plays an especially prominent role in the interpretation of Plato, Aristotle, Hellenistic ethics, Hobbes, Hume, Kant, and then in contemporary naturalist moral theory. On the "standard," Humean model of moral psychology, desire provides the causally effective component in moral action, its motivation. The term therefore has a host of implications and is very suggestive.[15] Levinas contrasts it with thought; what he wants to underline is that we do not think or cognitively grasp the face of the other; our relation to it is of a different order. We aspire to it, reach out and respond to it. I am not happy with the language of desire, and there is reason to think that later Levinas has his own doubts about it. Even for him, it is too self-oriented an expression rather than other-oriented. But the crucial points are evident: that the relationship between the self and the other is not cognitive and that its manifestation in everyday life is in the domain of love, eros, concern, generosity, and sensitivity rather than knowing and believing. It is, as it were, a kind of passive striving or aspiring.[16]

The face, then, as the infinite, is an original breach in the self's world, or, alternatively, it is a wholly unique perspective on our relations with other

---

[13] "Philosophy and the Idea of Infinity" in *Collected Philosophical Papers*, 54–56.

[14] "Philosophy and the Idea of Infinity" in *Collected Philosophical Papers*, 56–57. I suspect that Levinas has in mind Plato's notion of *eros*, especially as it occurs in the *Symposium*.

[15] One of the connotations of desire is that having desire is passive, unlike beliefs or judgments, which are active states. Indeed, even rationalist accounts of motivation, which take deliberative judgments or decisions to be motivating, typically take desires to be passive. In this spirit, Levinas's calling the self as responsibility "desire" is quite consistent with the way desire is treated in Western philosophy, at least from Aristotle and the Stoics and perhaps even earlier from Plato and Socrates. On desire, motivation, and internalism, see David McNaughton, *Moral Vision*, and R. Jay Wallace, *Normativity and the Will*.

[16] In *German Idealism: The Struggle Against Subjectivism, 1781–1801*, (Cambridge, MA: Harvard University Press, 2002), Fred Beiser suggests something similar about Fichte.

people, a wholly unique dimension or aspect of these relations.[17] But there is more. It is not just a *different* perspective or dimension; it is a *determinative* one. The relationship with the other is a measure of our injustice, as Levinas puts it, for it "puts into question the naive right of my powers."[18] It is tempting to say that the face's infinity is that it is normative, although, to be precise, *norms* are general rules or principles while the face is a unique presence. It is better to see the face as an imperative entering *into* the *finite* from the outside, from beyond the ordinary or philosophical perspective; in this sense, as revealed by its face, the suffering of the other person is *in* the *finite*. Moreover, when I realize who and what I am in terms of the suffering or need of the other, my response must involve a sense of my own failure in generosity, a sense of *shame*.[19]

Levinas's notion of shame is distinctive, or at least its role is distinctive, unlike the use that someone like Charles Taylor, for example, makes of it. Taylor argues that human beings are distinctive as self-interpreting animals. What this means is that they have attitudes, states, or emotions that incorporate within them a sense of their own character and identity; in this sense, human beings have states that have a special kind of reflexivity. Shame is such an emotion.[20] To feel shame, one must have an understanding of an ideal to which one adheres and a grasp of oneself as failing to fulfill that ideal; moreover, one realizes that the other person is aware of one's failure. The special significance of shame, for Taylor, is that it, like other similar emotional or attitudinal states, reveals something distinctive about human self-understanding and self-interpretation, the acknowledgment of a value or standard to which one holds oneself and that is constitutive of

---

[17] My use of the expressions "aspect" and "dimension" are intended to suggest the Husserlian notion of *noema* or adumbration; as we have seen, Levinas himself takes his method to be one of exposing or disclosing hidden horizons of meaning. Two other terminologies might also be used to suggest the same status. One is Anscombe's discourse treating actions or events "under a description"; the other is Wittgenstein's notion of "seeing-as" or "aspectual seeing." I take it that the point is in this case – where we are dealing with the relationship between a unique person and a unique other – to consider that relationship in terms that do not reify some property or feature but that do draw attention to a nonetheless real constituent of the overall relationship.

[18] "Philosophy and the Idea of Infinity" in *Collected Philosophical Papers*, 57–58. Here I emphasize the sense in which the face discloses a standard for judging the self's responsibility and generosity; later, I will deal with another dimension of its determinativeness – that judgment, language, concepts, discourse, and more, in a sense, are grounded in the face-to-face.

[19] "Philosophy and the Idea of Infinity" in *Collected Philosophical Papers*, 58; see also TI, 83–84. Levinas gives an early account of shame as involving a sense of one's own nakedness to oneself, a kind of self-exposure that is unavoidable, in *On Escape*, 63–65.

[20] Taylor discusses in several places the notion of self-interpretation and the way it is involved in emotions such as shame. See, for example, Charles Taylor, *Human Agency and Language* (Philosophical Papers 1) (Cambridge: Cambridge University Press, 1985), Ch. 2: "Self-Interpreting Animals."

one's sense of identity or selfhood. One dimension of this complex emotion stands out for Levinas: the realization that one's own freedom is "murderous and usurpatory in its exercise."[21] But this most fundamental expression of one's freedom is something one learns about oneself only when engaged by the face of the other person. It is a shame about being free that somehow lies within that very freedom. To be free and expansive, enjoying the world and all it has to offer, may seem enriching and elevating, but with the other present it is also and only then shameful and unsettling. Levinas may agree with Taylor that shame is part of what distinguishes us as human beings, but his reasons differ dramatically.

"Shame," "responsibility," "desire" – all these terms shed the same light on the subjective side of the face-to-face relationship. It is unsatisfied. That is why it is a continual striving – but for what? To relieve the unique other person's suffering, remove her misery, provide aid and support for her. Because the scope is unlimited, I am responsible for everyone and everything, and therefore my responsibility can never be fulfilled. There is always more to do. In this sense, too, the face is infinite, because the desire to give is never satisfied and can never *be* satisfied. Levinas also calls this desire "conscience," for it is a sense of one's own being held to a standard that challenges one fundamentally, a moral standard of giving or generosity. It is a being aware of the imperative that comes with the face. Conscience, as Levinas puts it, lies beyond consciousness.

ETHICS BEYOND TOTALITY

In "Philosophy and the Idea of Infinity," Levinas contrasts his understanding of the face with the dominant impulse of Western philosophy. Paradoxically, he finds in Descartes an especially valuable hint about infinity and the relationship with the other and about this heteronomous tendency. Descartes, after all, is the founder of the modern epistemological turn in Western philosophy and a powerful advocate of the subject-object relation. Yet in him, Levinas finds a clue about our exposure to the other person's face and command and hence about the centrality of responsibility to discursive thought, logic, and so forth. But the main focus of the essay is the way in which Levinas's commitment to the primacy of the ethical stands vis à vis the philosophical tradition. In *Totality and Infinity*, this focus is widened to include a great deal more. But before we turn to that work, I would like to consider an important essay of 1962, "Transcendence and Height," which summarizes the early sections of the book from an epistemological point of view.

---

[21] "Philosophy and the Idea of Infinity" in *Collected Philosophical Papers*, 58.

According to Levinas's own testimony, the way in which Western philosophy has been totalizing and the recognition of its limitations as forms of totality are lessons that Levinas learned from Franz Rosenzweig.[22] With Hegel especially in mind, as Levinas puts it, Rosenzweig delivered a "radical critique of totality."[23] Rosenzweig shows that philosophical systems respond to a desire to know both what exists and why. They tend to be reductionist, on the one hand, and inadequate, on the other. They take God, world, and man and reduce two of them to the third, and they always deal with the general, never with the utterly particular. Hence, Western philosophy fails to respect the differences among God, world, and man and ultimately misses altogether the utterly particular, actual God and the utterly particular, actual I. Rosenzweig, then, finds in the call of that God to that I the ground of meaning for all that lies within the domain of thought, understanding, and action. This is why revelation, for him, is the ground of meaning for human existence in the world. Philosophy, like science, finds the meaning of nature, human beings, and religion in knowledge of the world, the human, and the divine. But for Rosenzweig, the real meaning of my existence in the world is grounded in God's revelation to me, which is an event of love and generosity and not a matter of my knowledge of God or the world or human reason. In a sense, then, for Rosenzweig, knowledge of the everyday and of a scientific kind is useful but limited. Whether it is based on a kind of idealism or realism is another issue; Rosenzweig's point is that knowledge of this sort is limited in what it can show and do. It cannot tell us how to live, what is important in life, or what human beings should value and devote themselves to. Philosophers and scientists may know a great deal, but what they know is not sufficient on which to base a human life.[24]

Viewed this way, Rosenzweig in one sense does not argue for or against epistemological realism or idealism. Both are forms or modes of cognitive life or thought as ordinarily conceived in Western philosophy and culture. His concern is with the limits of both overall; each reduces the other to the same. If we think of knowledge broadly enough, as including knowledge of how we ought to live and what value or meaning human life has for us, then for

---

[22] TI, 28. This acknowledgment is one of those almost "legendary" facts about Levinas's biography that is cited again and again and that is widely discussed, although not always with an accurate appreciation for what Rosenzweig himself thought.

[23] *Ethics and Infinity*, 75–76; see also *Is It Righteous To Be?*, 94, 147; *Beyond the Verse*, 151–52, 155–60; "Franz Rosenzweig" in *Outside the Subject*, 53–59; and "Between Worlds" in *Difficult Freedom*, 187–91.

[24] See Franks and Morgan (eds. & trans.), *Franz Rosenzweig: Philosophical and Theological Writings* (Cambridge, MA: Hackett Publishing, 2000), ch. 4, 8; Rosenzweig, *Understanding the Sick and the Healthy*; Rosenzweig, *God, Man and the World* (Syracuse, NY: Syracuse University Press, 1998).

Rosenzweig the problem with traditional philosophy and science is that they do not know enough. From one point of view, then, Rosenzweig's issue is independent of the debates between epistemological idealism and realism; both are limited forms of Western philosophy. From another point of view, however, Rosenzweig might be seen as a kind of realist, a moral realist or even a kind of epistemological one. That is, on the issue of the knowledge of the meaning of human existence, Rosenzweig believes that only something outside the world of traditional philosophy and science can provide it. It will be interesting and important to determine whether Levinas, in his own way, agrees with Rosenzweig in this regard. That is, do Rosenzweig and Levinas agree about the limitations of Western thought? Do revelation for Rosenzweig and the face for Levinas provide what is needed beyond those limitations, the knowledge of meaningful human life and its ground? "Transcendence and Height" is a good place to look for Levinas's attempt to confront these issues.

Levinas's essay is divided into twelve sections. In sections 1–6, he discusses Western philosophy and its characteristic feature, that as a "search for truth" it involves the attempt to suppress all multiplicity and to assimilate all difference into the Same. Levinas uses the Platonic expression "the Same" to refer to mind, spirit, or reason, to the domain of the self – personal or absolute. Hence, he says, "the great myth of philosophy [is] the myth of a legislative consciousness of things, where difference and identity are reconciled."[25] This myth, he says, "rests upon the totalitarianism or imperialism of the Same." All philosophical thinking is some type of idealism, which extends from metaphysics and epistemology to politics and ethics. Even the traditional distinction between realism and idealism, insofar as it distinguishes types of philosophy, must bow to the *overall idealistic character* of all philosophy. That is, philosophy is rational thought; it is the activity of mind or self seeking to understand everything. Its unqualified hegemony makes it idealist. Everything is encompassed or comprehended by the self, thought, mind, or reason. The real is rational. Even Husserl and Heidegger do not overcome *this* sense of idealism; even realism, in the narrow sense, does not refute idealism, in the broad sense.[26]

Levinas's first conclusion, then, is that all philosophy, whether traditionally metaphysical or epistemological or more contemporary versions of transcendental phenomenology, is idealist and acknowledges nothing transcendent to the philosophizing self, no Other. This conclusion applies to Heidegger, too, and to recent attempts to understand prephilosophical life as it is lived, the so-called *Lebenswelt*. In short, Levinas understands all Western philosophy, whether metaphysical, epistemological, or ontological, to be totalizing or imperialistic

---

[25] Levinas, "Transcendence and Height" in *Basic Philosophical Writings*, 14.
[26] "Transcendence and Height" in *Basic Philosophical Writings*, 14–15.

in this way.[27] This outcome is the "triumph of the Same," of the self, spirit, mind, or reason. Against this background, then, Levinas raises the question of whether there is a realism *beyond* this broad, totalizing idealism – that is, whether there is an Other that the self does not assimilate but that nonetheless *calls the self into question*.[28] In sections 7–12, he introduces this Other as the face of the other person and explores it in ways that we have already discussed.

Levinas makes these points about the engagement with the other person. First, when the Other is wholly other, when it is a human other, it calls the self or the I into question; the other person summons the self to responsibility.[29] Second, the other person is not the object of intentionality, strictly speaking; the self is not conscious of the other person as Other.[30] Third, before the other person, the I "can no longer be powerful"; the I feels shame for its "naive spontaneity" and is unsettled by this shame.[31] Fourth, the I also welcomes the other person, who both "challenges and commands" the I as a face through its "nakedness and destitution."[32] This destitution Levinas calls "humility" and this command "height." Together, they and the face that expresses them "summon

---

[27] It is worth emphasizing two points about this conclusion and the approach in this essay. First, the essay focuses attention on philosophy, but Levinas's point is ultimately a larger, more embracing one: that the same strictures he here applies to the philosophical tradition also apply to science, religion, and everyday life – that is, to all thinking and all living – that are shaped by the same tradition, vocabulary, and modes of thought by the Greeks. Second, as we have claimed earlier, we should not treat this as a conclusion about the limits of philosophical thought as a kind of epistemological or metaphysical claim about the limits of our cognitive abilities or the existence of certain objects. Rather, it is a claim about the way that philosophical concepts, principles, approaches, and practices fail to catch sight of a dimension of what is part of everyday living, in particular everyday social interaction. Levinas's point is that as long as we remain within the philosophical world as we have it, something fundamental and determinative about human existence remains occluded or "hidden" from us.

[28] "Transcendence and Height" in *Basic Philosophical Writings*, 16.

[29] "Transcendence and Height" in *Basic Philosophical Writings*, 16. We have discussed this summons or plea-and-command, which Levinas frames as an imperative, taken from the biblical text "Thou shalt not kill (me)."

[30] "Transcendence and Height" in *Basic Philosophical Writings*, 16. That is, insofar as the other presents herself as face to the self, the self does not "see" the face or observe the other person, but this does not mean, of course, that the I does not see or perceive the other person along with "acknowledging" her, "accepting" her, and giving her a piece of bread to eat.

[31] "Transcendence and Height" in *Basic Philosophical Writings*, 17. That is, the self's freedom and power are compromised, in a sense, prior to their existing at all. Or, we might say that the free and powerful self is always "already" bound to respond to the other when its freedom and its power take shape. In TO and in TI, Levinas tells his dialectical and genetic story about how the self as powerful and capable of enjoying the resources of the world it finds itself inhabiting is confronted by the other person who calls to the self. But, as we have already indicated, the narrative and dialectical character of the story is intended to expose levels or dimensions of human social interaction and not to be taken literally.

[32] "Transcendence and Height" in *Basic Philosophical Writings*, 17.

[the I] to respond."³³ By "destitution," I think, Levinas means both the actual
need or poverty that the other person endures because of particular historical
experiences and that calls out to the I for assistance and, on the other hand,
the very fact of the other person's existence as dependent and as calling for
the I's acknowledgment and acceptance – prior to anything the other person
endures or suffers. Before any more specific needs are to be addressed, there is the
primary issue of "sharing the world with the other." Fifth, the I is not conscious
of its responsibility as a duty; it is "responsibility through and through."³⁴ Later,
especially in *Otherwise Than Being*, Levinas will develop this theme: that in a
deep sense responsibility is not a characteristic of the self, but rather it is what
the self is "before" it is anything else. This responsibility is therefore inescapable;
it is an "election."³⁵ Sixth, this election is an elevation. It does not diminish the
self, but rather, by emptying it of imperialism, egoism, and power, this being
chosen or elected "liberates" the self. "Such an engagement is happy; it is the
austere and noncomplacent happiness that lies in the nobility of an election that
does not know its own happiness. . . . "³⁶ Responsibility is not a burden; it does
not deflate the self. It fulfills it or, perhaps more accurately, it makes it possible
for the self to fulfill itself by responding to, accepting and serving, the other
person. Seventh, in virtue of this engagement or relationship the I is morality.
Through the face, the I is lifted out of nature and consciousness; it is promoted
or elevated and receives height; exercising my responsibility is neither an act of
pity nor of obedience.³⁷ For the same person "*to* whom" I am responsible is the
one "*for* whom" I am responsible; the tie of responsibility is doubly strong.³⁸
The I, then, is elevated and enriched by being infinitely responsible. This is
Levinas's special way of claiming that human life is more than natural existence,
that it is fundamentally social and ethical.

Having described the face-to-face in these terms, Levinas asks about its relation to the idea of the infinite, to metaphysics, to idealism and realism, and
to the philosophical tradition. This grounding moral relation is the idea of the
infinite, but "idea" is not to be taken literally, as an intentional entity or relation.

³³ "Transcendence and Height" in *Basic Philosophical Writings*, 17.
³⁴ "Transcendence and Height" in *Basic Philosophical Writings*, 17; cf. 18.
³⁵ Levinas uses the biblical expression for God's choice of the "children of Israel" as his special
   treasure [*am segulah*]; they are the "chosen" people, "elected" by God. By transference, what in
   Judaism (and of course Calvinism and other forms of Christianity) refers to "divine election"
   becomes at this deep level the way that each other person "elects" each subject.
³⁶ "Transcendence and Height" in *Basic Philosophical Writings*, 18.
³⁷ "Transcendence and Height" in *Basic Philosophical Writings*, 18.
³⁸ As Levinas puts it, the self is responsible for and to the other – for fulfilling the other's needs,
   alleviating the other's suffering, and so on, and to the other for fulfilling them, that is, the self
   is accountable to the other.

In Husserlian terms, "the I *receives* absolutely and learns absolutely . . . a signification that it has not itself given, a signification that precedes any *Sinngebung*."[39]
That is, as Husserl has shown, the sense or meaning of all intentional objects,
their noemata, are constituted by the self, and only insofar as these meanings
are constituted are they objects of consciousness of one kind or another. The
face, however, has meaning prior to all meaning-constitution; its meaning is
given prior to any constitution by the self. Levinas says that intentionality is
overturned by an act that is both submissive and spontaneous; the other has
height and the self has dignity, so that the engagement is both spontaneous and
critical, a kind of double movement of approaching and receiving, producing
"its own critique of reflection" that involves consciousness, judgment, thought,
and eventually philosophy. In this sense, "moral consciousness is primary and
the source of first philosophy."[40]

Levinas contrasts his own view with the hegemony of thought or reason;
he calls the latter "idealism" and his own view a kind of "realism."[41] "Only
the idea of the infinite renders realism" possible. As I have said, this is not
epistemological realism or moral realism as philosophical positions, of course.
It is a realism prior to all philosophy and philosophical positions, prior even
to ontology and to everyday life in its fullness, a realism that does not verify
or justify or explain, but one that makes all else possible for human existence.
Moreover, as he did earlier, Levinas associates this engagement with the infinite
or at least hints of it with Descartes, Plato, and Plotinus, all of whom seemed
to be groping toward a conception of "thinking more than one can think."
For Levinas, this thinking is never mere thinking at all; it is a responding to the
other person by acknowledging, accepting, and aiding that person.

In "Transcendence and Height," Levinas notes how traditional Western philosophy sought to grasp the truth about the everyday world in various ways,
some realist, some idealist, some neither, strictly speaking. Within the tradition,
especially after Descartes, much attention was given to the role of the mind and
reason in determining and verifying that truth. Modern skepticism challenged
belief in the existence of the external world, in the existence of other persons,
and the existence of God and much else. God, the brute given of sensation,
and things in themselves became points of conflict, especially in epistemological
debates about knowledge and its grounds and the limits of what we can know.
But, as Levinas notes, those debates and issues were subsumed in a larger one,
about the character of philosophy itself and the world it sought to encompass and
comprehend. At this level, he claimed, all philosophy *qua* thought was idealist,

---

[39] "Transcendence and Height" in *Basic Philosophical Writings*, 19.
[40] "Transcendence and Height" in *Basic Philosophical Writings*, 20; cf. 20–21.
[41] "Transcendence and Height" in *Basic Philosophical Writings*, 21.

and the question about it was not whether it should accept a thing in itself or a
God but rather whether it was itself as an idealism comprehensive and ground-
less. Was even first philosophy genuinely "first?" His answer in this essay is that
no form of thought is primary for human existence, and this means not only
that philosophy is not the most basic or most elevated human activity but also
that the everyday world as ultimately lived in and grasped in terms of thought or
reason is also not all there is to everyday human life. Indeed, language, thought,
and discourse are not what is most basic and determinative about human life as
social and interpersonal. To say that ethics is more primary than philosophy is
also to say that praxis is more primary than theory and that acting in behalf of
the needs of other persons is more important, more basic, and more the point of
being human than thinking about them or even following rules aimed at them
or their well-being. Caring for you is the most human thing I can do, and a
world in which I act toward you by acknowledging, accepting, and aiding you
is best, enriched by my act and the acts of everyone who acts similarly.

LEVINAS AND ROSENZWEIG

Levinas's account of totality as idealism and the totalized everyday world as
the province of metaphysics, epistemology, phenomenology, and even Heideggerian transcendental ontology looks like Rosenzweig's account of the old
thinking, and Levinas's disclosure of the face of the other person looks similar to Rosenzweig's endorsement of the new thinking and his commitment to
the centrality of revelation. Both may be characterized as realist and even as
ethically realist, if both terms "ethical" and "realist" are understood in suitably
broad ways. One way to tell how close the two are will be to look collectively
at what Levinas says about Rosenzweig on these matters. We shall look at three
of Levinas's essays on Rosenzweig: "'Between Two Worlds' (The Way of Franz
Rosenzweig)" (1959), "Franz Rosenzweig: A Modern Jewish Thinker" (1965),
and "The Philosophy of Franz Rosenzweig" (1982). What does Levinas say
about philosophy, totality, and infinity in Rosenzweig's *Star of Redemption*?[42]

In 1959, in "'Between Two Worlds,'" Levinas associates Rosenzweig's *Star
of Redemption* with the situation that is now called the "end of philosophy."[43]
That situation concerns the relationship between philosophy and life, on the one
hand, and liberation from political systems "that emerge from philosophy," on
the other. It is a time when philosophical totality is experienced as "a totalitarian

[42] As I indicated above, Levinas's debt to Rosenzweig on just this issue – the critique of the
tradition of Western philosophy and so forth as totalizing – has been widely discussed. Of
special interest are the accounts by Cohen, Gibbs, Wright, and Putnam.
[43] "'Between Two Worlds'" in *Difficult Freedom*, 185–90.

tyranny." Such a liberation from philosophy, however, requires philosophy, as Aristotle put it: "[O]ne must philosophize in order not to philosophize." It is a case of philosophy becoming life instead of politics, what Levinas calls "religion." Levinas explains, then, how Rosenzweig delivers a critique of Western philosophy that shows how life – religious life – escapes the totality of comprehensive thought and replaces philosophy with life. The critique challenges the strategy of philosophy to reduce all things to one thing, to force unity on all things by eliding difference. Rosenzweig points to death, the utterly particular experience of the singular individual, as unassimilable and irreducible, and he argues that in view of death and the particularity it brings with it, the philosopher must turn away from homogenizing thought to disclosing experience. The genuine philosophy must describe God, things, and persons just as they are experienced, and ultimately these experiences are linked. "In place of the totalization of elements [God, Man, and World], produced under the synoptic gaze of the philosopher, Rosenzweig uncovers the way in which time itself, and life, are put into motion."[44]

This critique is a revolt against Hegel, as Levinas notes in 1965, but it is also more than that. It is an attempt to bring "philosophy closer to the theological experience and attitude," which "has affinities with the idea, since become familiar to well-established philosophers, of the importance of pre-philosophical experiences for philosophy."[45] This is an important insight; part of Rosenzweig's revolt against the totalizing systems of philosophy is to draw philosophy close to life, to actual human experiences – here, religious ones – by which Levinas means not mystical experience or the content of revelation but "the objective existence of religious communities."[46] Levinas sees Rosenzweig as opposing "an existence frozen into a system" with the experience of the individual, "the inexhaustible newness of life's instants."[47] On the one hand, we find "the man who has become a prisoner of his system"; on the other, "a link between the living instant of human life and a living Eternity," a link found in the experiences and acts of the actual religious life.[48] In these acts and these experiences, the individual's momentary life takes on a certain meaning vis à vis Eternity, the ground of value and purpose, what Taylor calls the source of the good.

Rosenzweig's revolt against Hegel and Western philosophy, his critique of totality, is also, as Levinas describes it in 1982, a "rejection of the primordial

---

[44] "'Between Two Worlds'" in *Difficult Freedom*, 185–89, esp. 188–89; cf. "Franz Rosenzweig: A Modern Jewish Thinker" in *Outside the Subject*, 55–56.
[45] "Franz Rosenzweig: A Modern Jewish Thinker" in *Outside the Subject*, 53.
[46] "Franz Rosenzweig: A Modern Jewish Thinker" in *Outside the Subject*, 53; cf. 54.
[47] "Franz Rosenzweig: A Modern Jewish Thinker" in *Outside the Subject*, 54.
[48] "Franz Rosenzweig: A Modern Jewish Thinker" in *Outside the Subject*, 54.

nature of a certain type of rationality."[49] What Rosenzweig proposes as an alternative to such a reductionist totality is "to grasp religion – Creation, Revelation, and Redemption – as the primordial horizon of all meaning."[50] This Husserlian vocabulary – of a horizon of meaning – draws Rosenzweig into a phenomenological inquiry with transcendental aspirations, one that seeks to disclose a basic, determinative condition or ground of the meaning of the world and history, one *hidden* or *distorted* by totalizing rationality and by philosophy.[51]

Levinas reiterates the fact that although Rosenzweig did not know phenomenology, his thought still "marks the end of a certain idealism." This is the broad idealism we spoke of earlier, the hegemony of thought and reason. But, Levinas notes, this challenge "does not lead back to the facile solutions of naive realism, nor to the objectivism of mathematical structures." It does not, that is, lead either to a kind of traditional realism or to Platonism, for example, along the lines of Cohen and his Marburg disciples. "It ultimately leads to the *human* . . . that is original on the basis of its presence to God, on the basis of the present in Revelation."[52] Here is Rosenzweig's most novel insight, that Husserl's transcendental subject and Heidegger's being-in-the-world do not verify this fact of revelation; rather, they are grounded in it, in "a certain constellation of meaning that appears in Revelation." In this way, because of Revelation, which is the "new horizon of meaning" and is primary and grounding, the *human* precedes all philosophy.[53] "Revelation is . . . an original being-outside-of-self, and, *par excellence*, older, so to speak, than intentionality. . . . Revelation is precisely an entering-into-relation completely different from the one that corresponds to a synthesis. . . ."[54] Whether this idea is really present in Rosenzweig may be controversial; it is surely characteristic of Levinas that there is an original relation with the other that is more primary than all other forms of intentionality and especially more primary than rational thought and its modes of synthesis. For Rosenzweig, that relation is Revelation, the presence of God to the individual.[55] Ultimately, this relation that begins with God's transcendence with respect to nature in Creation and with respect to man in Revelation ends with "the

[49] Levinas, "The Philosophy of Franz Rosenzweig" in *In the Time of the Nations*, 157. This essay originally appeared as Levinas's preface to Stéphane Mosès's *System and Revelation: The Philosophy of Franz Rosenzweig* (Detroit: Wayne State University Press, 1982).

[50] "The Philosophy of Franz Rosenzweig" in *In the Time of the Nations*, 151.

[51] See "The Philosophy of Franz Rosenzweig" in *In the Time of the Nations*, 151; cf. 153 on Husserl, Kierkegaard, and Heidegger. Levinas sees Rosenzweig as a participant in the same "correction" of Western philosophy as these figures.

[52] "The Philosophy of Franz Rosenzweig" in *In the Time of the Nations*, 155–56.

[53] "The Philosophy of Franz Rosenzweig" in *In the Time of the Nations*, 156.

[54] "The Philosophy of Franz Rosenzweig" in *In the Time of the Nations*, 157–58.

[55] See "The Philosophy of Franz Rosenzweig" in *In the Time of the Nations*, 160.

transcendence of man-to-man in Redemption."[56] Here, Levinas even manages to find intimations of the primacy of the face-to-face between persons and responsibility in Rosenzweig's more theistic project.[57]

Levinas's reading of Rosenzweig's critique of and revolt against totality supports our understanding of his own views. Philosophy, politics, and ordinary life – shaped by the Western philosophical tradition – are not false, but they are limited. Looking at human life from their perspective is not sufficient; something primordial and significant is omitted or obscured. For Rosenzweig, it is revelation and its absolute orientation of human life in behalf of human community; for Levinas, it is the infinite desire to aid the other person, to be responsible for and to her. All that totality represents is not, therefore, utterly false, but it is false if that is what one takes to be all there is.

Moreover, Levinas believes that the critique of the *sufficiency* of totality, of philosophy and our various modes of intentionality, leads not to realism or idealism in the typical senses. Overthrowing idealism points to what he calls the *human*. We might call the view he finds in Rosenzweig, so similar to his own view, an "objective humanism." It is *beyond* the epistemological distinction between realism and idealism and even beyond the metaphysical distinction between idealism and naturalism. It is nonreductivist; its locus is an utterly particular event; the character of the event is human and imperative; it yields a new and determinative – Rosenzweig calls it "orienting" – perspective on human life. And the event in all its particularity is *primary* because it cannot be assimilated into any of the systematic totalities of rational thought, and yet all other modes of intentionality of the human as human are derived from it.[58] That the latter is so, we still need to show; for the moment, it is sufficient to note that Levinas believes it is.

---

[56] "The Philosophy of Franz Rosenzweig" in *In the Time of the Nations*, 158.

[57] Cf. "The Philosophy of Franz Rosenzweig" in *In the Time of the Nations*, 158–59. That Rosenzweig's whole approach is theistic, in the sense that for him *Revelation* is the encounter between the divine and the human, is clear to me. This conception of *Revelation* is the one that Rosenzweig inherits from Eugen Rosentock-Huessy and develops in his early writings and then in the *Star of Redemption* (Madison: University of Wisconsin Press, 2005). See Franks and Morgan, *Franz Rosenzweig: Philosophical and Theological Writings* and also the many comments on Rosenzweig in the work of Emil Fackenheim, among other Jewish thinkers of the postwar period. For the past several decades, this reading of Rosenzweig has been controversial; indeed, one regularly finds Levinasian readings of Rosenzweig that take *Revelation* for Rosenzweig to be interpersonal. But this, I believe, is a serious mistake. For Rosenzweig, *Redemption*, or at least human conduct in behalf of it, is interpersonal, an expression of love for the other, but *Revelation* and indeed *Creation* are also relationships between the divine, the human, and the world. For an early example of the Levinasian type of reading, see Robert Gibbs, *Correlations in Rosenzweig and Levinas*.

[58] For discussion of this derivativeness, see later in this chapter and also our discussion of politics and moral theory in Chapter 9.

TOTALITY, INFINITY, AND BEYOND

Totality and Infinity is a large and complex book, and its formulations are often difficult to grasp. By looking at the two essays, one written before the book, one after, we have been able to focus on the main features of Levinas's treatment of philosophy as totality and the role of the infinite in his own account. But now, we should look at *Totality and Infinity* itself to see if anything has been omitted that is important for us to consider.

The general theme of this chapter is the relationship between the self's engagement with the face of the other person and everyday, ordinary social life. Thus far, we have been discussing the concepts of totality and infinity to clarify how the face as the infinite is related to philosophical rationality and the way that everyday life is permeated by and understood through philosophy. In Chapter 2, I sketched Levinas's thinking in *Time and the Other* in preparation for discussing his method. One feature of that account becomes central to his exposition in *Totality and Infinity*; and because of its relevance to the relation of the face to everyday life, we should return to it now. It concerns the order of his exposition and the relation between Levinas's accounts of interiority and exteriority. I do not propose to examine Levinas's very complex, detailed account of interiority; instead, what I want to consider is the structure of the overall argument, specifically how and why it is not genetic or narrative.

Section II of *Totality and Infinity* is called "Interiority and Economy." Basically, this is Levinas's account of the *Lebenswelt*, or life world, or his version of a phenomenology of human *Dasein* as being-in-the-world. Levinas calls it "economy" or "economic existence." At one point, he describes his overall project this way: "[W]e propose to describe, within the unfolding of terrestrial existence, of economic existence (as we shall call it), a relationship with the other that does not result in a divine or human totality, that is not a totalization of history but the idea of infinity" – that is, an engagement with the face of the other person.[59] For the most part, this statement tells us what we already know, but for our purposes the crucial phrase is "to describe, within the unfolding of economic existence." We might paraphrase this claim as meaning that Levinas will be describing how the encounter with the face of the other person occurs or is indicated *within* everyday experience. It does not say that the face-to-face arises out of ordinary life, nor that it takes the self outside of that life. Rather, it says that the face-to-face occurs *within* ordinary life, in some way or other. The idea of the infinite is the engagement with the face; the ordinary world is the domain of totality. The former occurs within the latter, albeit in a unique way. When I meet my friend David, I speak to him; I notice that his hair is curlier

[59] TI, 52; cf. 51.

than usual, that he is wearing a T-shirt, and that he has a new backpack. But at the same time, as it were, and within the orbit of that same meeting – in seeing him and speaking to him – I also acknowledge and accept him; I respond to him and welcome him; I make room for him and give myself to him. Moreover, this acknowledgment, acceptance, and responding is more primary, more fundamental and determinative, than whatever else I do in relating to him. In a sense, the ordinary life I live is grounded in this relation.

In Section II of *Totality and Infinity*, Levinas describes "economic existence" or ordinary life from one perspective, that of the individual's relation to the world. In Section III, "Exteriority and the Face," he describes the ethical, the face, *within* that life – he describes that same life from the perspective of its ethical ground.[60] Put this way, Levinas's project is to show how everyday life has both of these dimensions, what correspond to our natural existence, on the one hand, and our peculiarly human existence, on the other (although this distinction does not match Levinas's exactly). I think that Levinas wants us to see that human existence has both dimensions and that they are interdependent, even though one is still more fundamental or determinative of the meaning and character of our social existence. To see this, let us look at his ideas of enjoyment, nourishment, possession, labor, and gift.

Basically, the presence of the other person asks and demands of me that what I have be shared, that the private be made common, that I make of it a gift. This might lead us to think that the demand and my responsibility to fulfill it are dependent upon my private possessions, my control over things, my power, and ultimately my freedom. Hobbes would say so, and his account of the state of nature and the social contract is organized to show this dependency of social institutions, exchange, and civil norms on basic human powers and liberty and their unlimited character in the state of nature. It is tempting to read Levinas this way, as plotting a line of dependencies, so that his account looks genetic, beginning with a sense of existence as dark, forboding, and

---

[60] Alternatively put, Levinas sees that same life as ethically grounded or determined, or he portrays that life "under the description" of being ethically meaningful or as grounded in interpersonal responsibility. In Kirk Ludwig (ed.), *Donald Davidson* (Cambridge: Cambridge University Press, 2003), in the essay by Alfred R. Mele, "Philosophy of Action," 66–67, there is a discussion of Davidson's thesis that actions can be intentional under one description and unintentional under another description. I think that it is useful to characterize our relationship with others in Levinas in terms of the vocabulary used by Anscombe of "under a description," so that we might say that a relationship with others is a face-to-face under one description and something that supervenes on the face-to-face under another description. This characterization is an alternative vocabulary for articulating the relationship between the face-to-face and other relationships between the I and the other, making the same point as treating the face-to-face as a dimension of our interpersonal relationships or a perspective on them that is most often hidden from view or unattended to.

indeterminate, leading through the emergence of selfhood as self-conscious, its finding its place in the world, enjoying what is available to it, and so on. For Hobbes, however, this kind of story reveals a firm set of dependencies that operate in one direction only. For Levinas, on the other hand, this outcome is not wholly false, but neither is it wholly true. From one point of view, we have needs, seek to satisfy them, acquire nourishment, and so forth. But this is only one dimension of who we are, so to speak; our natural situatedness in the world as a locale for nourishment and enjoyment is one way of understanding or describing our existence. It is, as it were, a picture of us as wholly within totality, as the objects of naturalist explanation, for example, or as the objects of social scientific investigation and comprehension. Yet while totality is not false and systems of thought – philosophical, scientific, moral, political, and religious – do contain some truth, they do so only partially.

What makes some fruit that I have picked enjoyable and nourishing has to do with my needs, my labor, my effort, and my possession and use of it. But the fruit also is or can be a gift, a common benefit, and a shared resource. However, it will only be these things and can only be described in these ways, Levinas says, given the presence to me of the face of the other person, and in view of the other's needs addressed to me and my responsibility to him to confront those needs and satisfy them – to feed the hungry, clothe the naked, and relieve the suffering with which he confronts me. For the fruit to be fully what it can be in the human world, then, I must need or want it, but I also must be faced by your needs. In fact, Levinas wants us to see, the fruit is first and foremost food-to-feed-the-hungry and only secondarily a source of nourishment and enjoyment for me; it is givable to you before it is consumable by me.

Levinas describes this situation in the following terms: The things around us – "good soup," air, light, spectacles, sleep, etc. – are not simply objects that I examine, describe, or analyze. I "live from" them; they nourish me, and I enjoy them. These things "are lived; they feed life."[61] This enjoyment, moreover, is not one psychological state like others; it fuels life and in part constitutes the I as living.[62] What I enjoy nourishes me; things become food, consumable. As Levinas sees it, they are nourishment, and enjoyable first and foremost. But that is not all they are; these objects and states also become available for inspection, description, classification, and more. "The separation accomplished as enjoyment... becomes a consciousness of objects. The things are fixed by the word which gives them, which communicates them and thematizes them.... Over and above enjoyment... a discourse about the world

---

[61] TI, 110–11; cf. 109–21 generally.
[62] TI, 113.

takes form."[63] Within enjoyment subject and object exhibit a separation, and this separation then becomes the framework in which language, discourse, description, perception, and so forth take place. Moreover, as Levinas points out, other activities take place, such as labor, which transforms things, and habitation, which transforms space.[64] The upshot is that this situation makes responding to the face possible, for that response requires giving, a wholly benevolent giving, and it is only because of enjoyment, possession, labor, and habitation that I have something to give.

The transcendence of the face is not enacted outside of the world, as though the economy by which separation is produced remained beneath a sort of beatific contemplation of the Other [person]. . . . The "vision" of the face as face is a certain mode of sojourning in a home, or . . . a certain form of economic life. . . . no face can be approached with empty hands and closed home.

Levinas calls this act of responsibility to the other "hospitality."[65]

Economic existence – everyday life in the world – and responsible hospitality or kindness, then, are two points of view on the same human existence, on social and interpersonal human life. Engaging the face is not an esoteric or ecstatic experience, a "beatific contemplation" or "vision." "The relationship with the Other [person] is not produced outside of the world, but puts in question the world possessed." It is a "primordial dispossession, a donation," and it "institutes a common world." Hence, the two perspectives are interdependent and linked, contemporary, coordinate.[66] Without things to give, hospitality and donation are not possible; and without the engagement with the face of the other, all our possessions are just the objects of our own enjoyment; they are not gifts – or "givables." "This *offering* of the world, this offering of contents which answers to the face of the Other [person] . . . first opens the perspective of the meaningful." Here we have Levinas's own version of the joining of nature and morality, fact and value. "Transcendence is not an optics, but the first ethical gesture,"[67] but neither can occur alone – neither sensibility nor morality. The book's title, after all, is "Totality *and* Infinity," not "Totality *or* Infinity."

We are in a position to say something about an important criticism that is regularly made of Levinas. The criticism is that an ethical relationship with the particular other cannot be expressed in moral rules or political principles. Our

---

[63] TI, 139.

[64] See TI, 146, 150, 152–74.

[65] TI, 172.

[66] See Purcell, *Levinas and Theology*, 101, 162. This point is what Purcell means, I think, when he says, "Responsibility and justice are two sides of the same coin" (162).

[67] TI, 174.

discussion of totality and its relation to infinity, however, provides us with a way of responding to this criticism.[68]

Earlier, I pointed out that there is, in Levinas's philosophy, a way up and a way down, as it were. We have been discussing by and large the way down, what Levinas means by "the idea of infinity" and the way the infinite or the face is a breach in totality, or, in other words, how the infinite occurs in human existence as a hidden dimension or perspective of everyday life and our thinking about it. We have also tried to show how the two are interdependent and how Levinas can be understood as reflecting on two perspectives on the everyday or the ordinary world under two descriptions. To develop that sense of interdependence, however, we need to turn to the "way up" and show how, according to Levinas, the face is the ground of judgment, language, concepts, thought, and eventually moral systems and political values. This is a project for a book, in and of itself, so what I propose is only a schematic account based on a few texts that sketch the basic features of Levinas's view. What we need to see is how Levinas shows universality and commonality to arise out of the utterly particular encounter of the individual and the other and how ethics as a primordial event leads to language, society, and politics.

This account of the emergence of society and politics is crucial for several reasons. First, ontology and all the systems of totality – our theories and our world in the everyday sense – are unavoidable. Levinas takes our task to be the employment of all of this for ethical purposes, to assist the other person, reduce suffering and misery, and act responsibly toward others. "To ensure the survival of the other we must resort to the technico-political systems of means and ends."[69] But this task is plausible only if these *means* are somehow grounded in this end – if, that is, there is a deep connection between them. The account of how the face-to-face leads to society and politics is an important vehicle for understanding this connection.

Second, we do not live in the face-to-face encounter. We live in the world. If everyday life and the face provide different perspectives on the same experience, in a sense, we need to be sure that this distinction does not harbor a rigid, exclusive dualism. Showing how language, society, and politics occur and yet how they are linked to the face-to-face encounter, we see how unified Levinas's understanding of human life really is.

Third, it also, in a sense, clarifies and justifies Levinas's assessment of Western culture, politics, and civilization. The twentieth century has witnessed a kind of degeneration or divorce or infidelity, according to which life has become estranged from its deepest origins and grounds. It might even be viewed as

---

[68] See also, Chapter 9.
[69] Kearney, "Dialogue with Emmanuel Levinas" in Cohen (ed.), *Face to Face with Levinas*, 28.

a kind of Oedipal rebellion, an uprising against parental love in favor of self-righteous conceit. This account will make clear how Levinas's critique works and where its grounds lie.

Before I turn to some key texts in *Totality and Infinity* and *Otherwise Than Being*, it will be helpful to look at some of Levinas's comments in interviews where the issue of society and the political arises. Levinas does seem to be facing a serious set of problems. The face-to-face is uniquely particular, yet society involves rules, principles, institutions, and in general the notion of the universal. How does the universal come from the particular? Furthermore, the self encountering the face seems to be isolated and alone, a pair, yet society is made up of a vast plurality of people, in multiple relationships, institutions, and more. How does Levinas account for the leap from one to the other? Indeed, how does he account for human community at all?

Although we must be cautious about using Levinas's interviews to clarify his ideas, they do contain very lucid, succinct formulations that provide good access to themes addressed more technically in his written works. This is especially the case when Levinas talks about society, politics, and what in his later work he calls "justice." Let me start by recalling something I have emphasized throughout: The encounter with the face is not an experience isolated from everyday life; it is not a mystical or quasi-mystical experience that one has only when separate and detached, in exile from the ordinary. The face-to-face is not like an intuitive grasp of beauty or the good or a visionary, ecstatic experience of God. It is instead one way of being related to another person, a fundamental and determinative way to be sure, but one way along with others. It is, alternatively, one dimension of our interpersonal lives or one perspective on such lives. Hence, it makes no sense to ask where other people come from. The point is that except for extreme and unusual circumstances – that of Robinson Crusoe, for example (before he is joined by Friday) – we normally live among other people, many of them. The issue is not where the others come from; it is what their being in our world, each one *set over against us*, means to us. Levinas makes this point clearly on several occasions. In his 1986 interview with François Poirié, for example, he says, "There is always a third, a fourth, because in fact we are in a multiple society where, on the fundamental relation to the other the whole knowing of justice, which is indispensable, is superimposed."[70] The third and the fourth are people, beyond myself and the other; there are *always* others, and the face-to-face always takes place in a social world where I and the other are related to a host of others, all as selves face-to-face with many

---

[70] *Is It Righteous To Be?*, 54; see also *Entre Nous*, 106–7. In "Peace and Proximity," *Alterity and Transcendence*, 142–43, Levinas speaks of the necessity of reason; he calls the face and peace the "origin, justification, and measure" of the structures of society.

particular others. No single face-to-face is an island; each takes place amidst a vast ocean of others, the entire social world. This social world is "the whole" that is the venue for justice, as we shall see; it is "indispensable" and therefore not only unavoidable, but also the totality of everyday social and political relationships, institutions, and practices that it is our task to employ in behalf of assisting others and reducing their suffering.

Levinas reiterates the same point in 1989:

But we are never, me and the other, alone in the world. There is always a third; the men who surround me. And this third is also my neighbor. Who is nearest to me? Inevitable question of justice which arises from the depth of responsibility for the unique, in which ethics begins in the face of that which is incomparable. Here is the necessity of comparing what is incomparable – of knowing men, . . . transformation of faces into objective and plastic forms. . . . The other is no longer the unique person offering himself to the compassion of my responsibility, but an individual within a logical order or a citizen of a state in which institutions, general laws, and judges are both possible and necessary.[71]

Levinas regularly calls the third the "third party" and takes it to represent the people who make up the social world we live in. Each and every such person, when related to me, presents me with a face and calls forth my responsibility. Moreover, once we turn to these others and ask about our responsibilities, we must compare them, their needs, their suffering, and their relations to us; we develop concepts, principles, and policies, we assess our resources and capabilities, and we evaluate others to see how they fit or suit our norms and resources. The unique other therefore becomes for me a fellow citizen or another moral agent deserving respect or a hungry person or a criminal. In order for our comparisons to occur at all, we develop conceptual resources or adopt ones to facilitate the comparisons; and in order for them to be regular, consistent, and fair, we develop principles of justice to normalize these comparisons. That is, we develop laws and practices according to a sense of fairness and impartiality – that is, for each of us, grounded in our sense of responsibility. Or, alternatively, it is only once we recognize our fundamental responsibility to each and every other person that we see what justice, moral norms, policies, and practices mean to us and to our lives, what their point is. Only people whom we can describe and classify can be evaluated and compared, and once we organize our social world politically this way, we realize that it is as necessary as it is possible to structure our social interactions in some way or other. Ethics is fundamental; politics and political justice are necessary. This comparison of incomparables is what Levinas elsewhere calls "the Greek moment in our civilization . . . [for] the

---

[71] *Is It Righteous To Be?*, 115–16; cf. 193–94, 230, 246.

importance of knowing, the importance of comparing comes from them."[72] As we shall see, the Bible teaches the centrality of the ethical and its primacy; Greek culture and philosophy teach the significance of knowledge, science, and politics.

Levinas often sketches how, in this way, the presence of multiple other persons, the fact of social life, is what gives rise to thought, rationality, judgment, and even philosophy. In 1983, he put it this way: "But I don't live in a world in which there is but one single 'first comer'; there is always a third party in the world: he or she is also my other, my neighbor. Hence, it is important to me to know which of the two takes precedence. . . . Must not human beings, who are incomparable, be compared? . . . Here is the birth of the theoretical; here is the birth of the concern for justice, which is the basis of the theoretical."[73] The word "birth" must be understood with the greatest sensitivity. Theory, for Levinas, involves forming concepts and categories, judgment, comparison, examination, and all that is built on these activities. This is what we associate with thinking, scientific inquiry, and explanation. It is also what we think of as organizational, normative, and functional. Levinas does not mean that all of these activities actually arise out of the face-to-face – in some temporal way; his account may look genetic and developmental, but it is not, as I have indicated on several occasions about many of his accounts. What he means is that thinking, speaking, and so on are social phenomena and must be understood as serving social purposes and ultimately moral ones. Indeed, he seems to be making the strong claim that a society of human beings only has reason to engage in these activities because human life is fundamentally social and ethical. We shall have more to say about this later, but it is certainly part of what Levinas means by the primacy of ethics. Later, in the same 1983 interview, Levinas puts it this way: "[J]ustice itself is born of charity. They can seem alien when they are presented as successive stages; in reality, they are inseparable and simultaneous, unless one is on a desert island, without humanity, without a third."[74] The central point here is that justice and charity or politics and ethics are not "successive stages" in a Hobbesian-like process; they are "inseparable and simultaneous." A nice analogue is the account of the *demiourgos*, or Divine Craftsman, and the formation of the cosmos in Plato's *Timaeus*; even in antiquity, there was a debate about whether Plato intended this account to be genetic and creationist or rather an analytical representation of the rational structure of an eternal

---

[72] *Is It Righteous To Be?*, 133.

[73] "Philosophy, Justice and Love" in *Is It Righteous To Be?*, 165–66; cf. *Entre Nous*, 104.

[74] *Is It Righteous To Be?*, 168–69; cf. 183. One could hardly want a more explicit statement from Levinas that the face-to-face is a relationship between the self and the other that occurs alongside and at the same time as other everyday relationships.

cosmos.[75] Levinas's view is akin to the nonliteral, rational interpretation of Plato's myth.

Finally, Levinas makes one last important point: that while our responsibility is infinite and in itself unbounded, it is justice that limits it, and because of this "I separate myself from the idea of nonresistance to evil."[76] In principle, everyone demands of me; I am responsible to and for everyone all the time in every way. But if a person or group or institution persecutes another, then my responsibility to those who are suffering outweighs any responsibility I have to the persecutor, and I must do what I can to oppose the persecution. Levinas says as much: "If there were no order of Justice, there would be no limit to my responsibility."[77] Indeed, given the encounter with the face of the other person and the existence of justice and the state, there is a kind of mutual limitation. Law, the state, and justice limit my responsibilities by subjecting them to calculation and regimentation, comparing them and determining whom I ought to serve, whom I ought to restrict; at the same time, my responsibility to each and every other person is what "legitimizes" the state and gives it a sense of purpose and value. Infinite responsibility is what gives point to the very existence of states, laws, and political systems; it is their *raison d'être*. "A state in which the interpersonal relationship [i.e., the face-to-face, acts of kindness and benevolence] is impossible, in which it is directed in advance by the determinism proper to the state, is a totalitarian state."[78] In short, a sense of humanity limits the state and determines whether a given state is admirable and perhaps even legitimate. Here, then, we see the ground for Levinas's judgments about Hitler's fascism and Stalinism, which we observed in Chapters 1 and 2.[79]

I have been considering the relationship between the face-to-face and the world as totality – the world of language, thought, judgment, politics, and justice – as Levinas informally discusses this theme in various interviews. It occurs in these interviews in especially clear and vivid ways, I think, but it is a theme that goes back to formulations in *Totality and Infinity* in 1961.[80] There, late in the book, Levinas uses familial, erotic, and gendered language to characterize features of the face-to-face. In introducing the idea of society, he employs the

[75] The debate about how to interpret the *Timaeus* on creation goes back to Aristotle and Xenocrates. For a classic discussion of the issue and whether the dialogue is a myth or not, see Gregory Vlastos, "The Disorderly Motion in the 'Timaeus,'" (orig. 1939) and "Creation in the 'Timaeus': Is It a Fiction?" (orig. 1964), both in R. E. Allen (ed.), *Studies in Plato's Metaphysics*, 379–99 and 401–19, respectively.
[76] See "Philosophy, Justice and Love" in *Entre Nous*, 105.
[77] "Philosophy, Justice and Love" in *Entre Nous*, 105.
[78] "Philosophy, Justice and Love" in *Entre Nous*, 105.
[79] See also "Philosophy, Justice and Love" in *Entre Nous*, 108: "Politics left to itself, has its own determinism. Love must always watch over justice."
[80] See, for example, TI, 213.

term "fraternity." Speaking of the son who is "elected" by his father, who becomes an I as unique for his father, Levinas says, "[B]ecause the son owes his unicity to the paternal election he can be brought up, be commanded, and can obey, and the strange conjuncture of the family is possible." But the child is both unique and not unique; fecundity yields many children, a family.

The I engendered exists at the same time as unique in the world and as brother among brothers. I am I and chosen one, but where can I be chosen, if not from among other chosen ones, among equals?... The human I is posited in fraternity: that all men are brothers is not added to man as a moral conquest, but constitutes his ipseity [i.e., his selfhood].... The relation with the face in fraternity, where in his turn the Other appears in solidarity with all the others, constitutes the social order, the reference of every dialogue to the third party by which the We... encompasses the face to face opposition, opens the erotic upon a social life....[81]

Levinas's language here is more obscure and mannered than we have seen in the later interviews, but he is making the same points that we have seen him make in those interviews: Society comes with the third party, with the plurality of people who live together, each one set over against every other; but each self is the "chosen one" – summoned by the face of the other person – "chosen from among other chosen ones"; in terms of responsibility, all are equal – that is, I am equally responsible for all and each is equally responsible for each and every other; social life is grounded in the face-to-face and also, in a sense, in the basic humanity of all, their equality, that arises out of the face of total responsibility when it occurs in a world of people.[82] Assessing what laws and rules to establish and determining what to do in particular situations, these judgments take place against the background of humanity and equality.

In this chapter, I have been considering what Levinas means by totality, by the critique of totality, and by the way that the face of the other person is the idea of the infinite. I have been especially interested in showing how Levinas's critique of totality is not a disposal of it. For him, human life is a unity of totality and infinity.[83] In the course of my discussion, I have given only occasional attention to the other features of life as totality that arise out of or depend upon society and social relations – thought, conceptualization, and language. I have paid more attention here to ethics, politics, and justice.[84] In Levinas's later work,

[81] TI, 279–80.
[82] See also TI, 214.
[83] The title of Levinas's book is, after all, *Totality and Infinity* and not *Totality or Infinity*, as I have said.
[84] In a later chapter, I shall return to this theme: the relationship between ethics – as the engagement with the face of the other person and as responsibility – and moral and political systems. As I indicated, the question of the relevance of Levinas's insight to moral and political life is a highly contested one.

especially in *Otherwise Than Being*, language becomes an increasingly important subject; we shall consider it more extensively in a later chapter. Suffice it to say for now that the importance of the third party and society does not wane in the later works, for there, too, Levinas notes that "the responsibility for the other... is troubled and becomes a problem when a third party enters."[85] As in earlier work and in the interviews, "enters" is a metaphor; the central point is that living among people requires comparison, judgment, and all the apparatus of conceptualization, theory, and politics. "Proximity [another word for the face-to-face] takes on a new meaning in the space of contiguity [that is, society]."[86]

[85] OB, 157.
[86] OB, 157; cf. 157–61.

5

Meaning, Culture, and Language

In Chapter 2, in our discussion of Levinas's method, we tried to show how Levinas's account of the face is phenomenological and yet not so, how the face both is and is not a Husserlian *noema*.[1] In Chapter 4, we discussed Levinas's notion of totality and how the face and the ethical, as the infinite, lie outside totality. At one level, notions of truth, meaning, and reference occur within the orbit of language, thought, and our theories about them. Insofar as the face and engagement with the suffering and demands of the other person open a different perspective on human existence than that of language and so forth, the notions of "meaning" and "sense" are, strictly speaking, inappropriate. But Levinas does use them to characterize the face, and we ought to examine both how and why, in order to understand better the face-to-face and its role in everyday life.

MEANING, RELATIVISM, AND THE ETHICAL

We eventually must look at Levinas's later work, *Otherwise Than Being*, but before we do there is an important essay of 1964, "Meaning and Sense," that we should discuss.[2] From one point of view, the background for this essay is the problem of relativism and invokes Edmund Husserl, Martin Heidegger, and Maurice Merleau-Ponty. But the theme of meaning and sense is pervasive in

---

[1] Strictly speaking, phenomenology is restricted to the appearances of things that are present and thus to totality. The face reveals itself "outside" totality, as the infinite or the transcendent. We have seen that this means that the face-to-face relationship is a dimension alongside other, everyday relationships between the self and the other person; it is a further, more fundamental, dimension or perspective on that relationship or an alternative and more primary way of "describing" it.

[2] "Meaning and Sense" in *Basic Philosophical Writings*; the essay was composed, from 1961 to 1964; see p. 173, n. 1. It is also reprinted in *Collected Philosophical Papers*, based on the 1972 reprinted version.

twentieth-century philosophy; and as we proceed, it may be useful to draw on a philosophical tradition different from Levinas's – the tradition of Gottlob Frege, Ludwig Wittgenstein, W. V. Quine, Donald Davidson, and others – in order to clarify what the issues are for him and what he is trying to accomplish.[3]

I have argued that Levinas makes it clear that the face-to-face, for all its special significance, is not an esoteric, isolated event, but one that takes place within the social, public world of everyday life. Meaning, then, in the broad sense, is a feature of that life, of the public, communicative sphere where we live. The issue before us is what significance the face-to-face has in relation to the various meanings and modes of meaning that characterize that public and social world. What meaning do these episodes carry for the I who lives them? This is not a question of linguistic meaning, of course, although language and meaning may be relevant to clarifying this kind of significance. Nor is it the meaning of an institution or practice or principle or rule. It is the meaning of a very particular, concrete relation and the mode of selfhood that comes with it. Part of the issue, then, is the formal one of the meaning carried by this *type* of relation or event; part is the material one of the meaning carried by each particular face-to-face episode. All of these points are ones we need to consider, and there may be help available from various philosophical treatments of what meaning is, its origins and grounds, and its significance, especially the pragmatic context relevant to these matters.[4] First, we need to look at Levinas's essay "Meaning and Sense."

This essay – which deals with the general issues of the multiplicity of meanings, cultural relativism, the "death of God," and the return to a kind of Platonism about meaning – will be very important to us in subsequent chapters, when we turn to God and then relativism and realism. For our purposes in this chapter, however, I want to focus on a fundamental aspect of the essay: Levinas's use of the notions of meaning and sense and especially the ways in which these notions are employed in his account of the encounter with the face of the other person.

Levinas begins by clarifying the notion of meaning. He uses as an example a paradigmatic case of perception and considers it according to the method of Husserlian intentional, phenomenological analysis. Levinas rejects an empiricism that treats the given as without meaning, a brute receptivity, and introduces the Husserlian notion of a horizon or world: The object given to consciousness must "first be placed in an illuminated horizon," which is a context, a language

---

[3] For a very provocative and interesting account of how discussion of Quine and Davidson on meaning, and the like can illuminate the work of figures such as Derrida, see Samuel C. Wheeler III, *Deconstruction as Analytic Philosophy* (Stanford: Stanford University Press, 2000).

[4] I think that this theme – the way that Levinas can be understood as a response to problems about grounds of meaning, culture, and language – is central to Bob Plant, *Wittgenstein and Levinas*. If one reads Wittgenstein as a kind of naturalist, given a particular reading of the notion of forms of life, then Levinas can be seen as an alternative to Wittgenstein.

or culture, that is the locus for all the meanings the object has. The horizon or world is a network or field; no object of consciousness is given without such a horizon. All that the object means comes from its location in that world, as it is grasped by the perceiver. "The meaning precedes the data and illuminates them."[5] When Levinas says "[P]ure receptivity, in the sense of a pure sensible without any meaning, would be only a myth or an abstraction," he is, in his own way, formulating the "myth of the given," a Kantian inheritance.[6] In short, words, objects, and acts all are present to consciousness already embedded in worlds or horizons of meaning. All perception is meaningful and perspectival.

Broadly speaking, meaning is born by languages and cultures, and these are constructed. They develop as a result of human activity. People and groups shape these cultures. Levinas calls this "the arranging and assembling, the cultural act, of man.... [M]eaning shines forth in the works of poets and artists."[7] Hence, in order to understand meaning, Levinas says, one does not require a Platonic disengagement from life and history but rather a study of them, and the outcome is not a pure realm of detached meanings. It is the product of many sets of culturally and historically diverse meanings. Furthermore, Platonism is intellectualist, and contemporary philosophy is not. It subordinates "the intellect to expression, ... a coming into contact in a common world, ... the whole concrete density of our corporeal, technical, social, and political existence, ... "[8] The study of meaning is the study of how these various cultural dimensions give rise to a panoply of meanings and how they are grasped, received, dealt with, and exploited in life. All of this yields a "multivocity of meaning" that is disorienting.[9]

[5] "Meaning and Sense" in *Basic Philosophical Writings*, 34–37. For discussion of Husserlian themes, such as horizon of meanings, see Dermot Moran, *Introduction to Phenomenology* (London: Routledge, 2000); and Sokolowski, *Introduction to Phenomenology*.
[6] The most famous critique of this myth is found in Wilfred Sellars's "Empiricism and the Philosophy of Mind" in Wilfred Sellars, *Science, Perception and Reality* (London: Routledge and Kegan Paul, 1963); also see Wilfred Sellars, Robert Brandom, and Richard Rorty, *Empiricism and the Philosophy of Mind* (Cambridge, MA: Harvard University Press, 1997).
[7] "Meaning and Sense" in *Basic Philosophical Writings*, 42.
[8] "Meaning and Sense" in *Basic Philosophical Writings*, 43.
[9] "Meaning and Sense" in *Basic Philosophical Writings*, 44. There are, of course, other famous advocates of the same claim, among them Nietzsche, Foucault, Gadamer, Rorty, Hayden White, and Stanley Fish. These figures are all associated with postmodernism. In an interesting comparison of Alasdair MacIntyre and Jonathan Dancy, David Bakhurst asks if one could turn MacIntyre against Dancy the charge that MacIntyre levels against intuitionism: "that [it is] a graphic illustration of the poverty of ethical thinking after the collapse of the Enlightenment project. The intuitionist responds to our failure to theorize moral judgment by declaring moral judgment largely untheorizable. In this, he simply adopts the problem as his position" (David Bakhurst, "Ethical Particularism in Context" in Hooker and Little (eds.), *Moral Particularism* 167). But in the present context, of course, this is only half true, for the particularist does not lapse into relativism or nihilism: "[P]articularism looks like the uneasy position of someone who has been persuaded that there is no hope for general moral truths and no place for moral theory but who,

In this essay, Levinas largely reserves the term "meaning" for this plurality of cultural, historical, and social values. The word "sense," on the other hand, refers to some single fundamental value.[10] For example, he takes up for consideration that sense or "fixed, privileged meaning," "the sense beneath the meaning," is material or natural needs, and he refutes the possibility of a naturalistic sense in part on the grounds that "every human need is from the first already interpreted culturally."[11] Still, this does not deter him: "Must we not then distinguish the meanings, in their cultural pluralism, from the sense, orientation, and unity of being...?...Do not meanings require a unique sense from which they derive their very signifyingness?"[12] What Levinas is suggesting is that meanings, however plural, only have what meaning they do because of a single, basic "sense that orients them." The loss of this sense is what modern thought refers to with the expression "the death of God."[13]

Throughout his essay, Levinas contrasts meanings as plural with sense as single and unique. Meanings are constructed historically and culturally. Sense is not. Rather, sense is orienting. This is Levinas's favored expression for describing this sense; it is orienting for human life and the construction of cultural meanings. Later, we shall consider how Levinas argues for this sense and for its religious dimension, its association with transcendence and God. For now, I want to consider what he means by "sense as orientation" and how these multiple

unable to embrace the nihilism of academic postmodernism, clings to a residual faith in moral objectivity. As such, it is just another symptom of the postmodern condition" (167). Bakhurst comes to Dancy's defense, however, by claiming that there is something substantial in the notion of properties "mattering" or "having moral salience" or "making a moral difference" (172–73). He begins to sound very close to Levinas when he says the following: "Suffering is enduringly significant because it is something a morally sensitive agent must countenance.... [I]t is an appropriate object of moral concern, a source of moral commitment, and such concerns and commitments are critical to our understanding of ourselves as moral agents" (172–73).

[10] See Drabinski, *Sensibility and Singularity*, 24–28. I do not find that Levinas is consistent about his use of "meaning" and "sense," even in this essay.

[11] "Meaning and Sense" in *Basic Philosophical Writings*, 44–45.

[12] "Meaning and Sense" in *Basic Philosophical Writings*, 46–47; cf. 48.

[13] "Meaning and Sense" in *Basic Philosophical Writings*, 47. In a later essay, "Ideology and Idealism," written in 1972 and published as the first essay in *Of God Who Comes to Mind* (as well as elsewhere), Levinas puts this point as follows: "To the crisis of meaning that is attested by the 'dissemination' of verbal signs which the signified no longer succeeds in dominating, since it would only be its illusion and ideological ruse, there is opposed the meaning prior to 'things said,' repelling words, and incontestable in the nakedness of the face, the proletarian destitution of the other, and in the offense undergone by him" (13). Levinas then takes this lesson to be the teaching of two texts in the Talmud, when read together: "This is probably what was taught by the sages of the Talmud who already knew a time in which language had eroded the significations it was supposed to carry, when they spoke of a world in which prayers cannot pierce the sky, for all the heavenly doors are closed except that through which the tears of the injured pass."

cultural meanings are unified by that sense.[14] Levinas is asking: Is there a point to human existence? Are the disparate activities and practices of human life organized, unified, and oriented in a single way? Is there such a thing as what we commonly call "the meaning of life"?[15] His answer is that there is; it is grounded in the human social relationship that is both the condition of all communication and discourse and the ethical standard for assessing such discourse and the various cultural meanings articulated through it.

As we might expect, Levinas argues that this single orienting sense is the "epiphany" of the face of the other person that "puts me in question, empties me of myself" and that is my Desire for the Other. What does it mean to say that this movement or event is "sense" and that it is an "absolute orientation"? Part of Levinas's answer concerns the role of the face of the other person in communication and discourse. *Communication* via language, cultural acts, and such requires a "hermeneutical structure" or language and an agent or speaker. But it also requires an interlocutor. This is the other as face, "he to whom expression expresses, for whom celebration celebrates." The other whom I face is my primary interlocutor, that is, the other person who puts me in question or engages me as responsible; the other in this sense is the face of misery or suffering, the other in need of my help, my generosity, my acknowledgment.

The Other (*Autrui*) [person] who faces me is not included in the totality of being expressed. He arises behind every assembling of being as he to whom I express what I express. I find myself facing the Other (*Autrui*). He is neither a cultural signification nor a simple given. He is *sense* primordially, for he gives sense to expression itself, for it is only by him that a phenomenon as a meaning is, of itself, introduced into being.[16]

That is, when I talk with someone or act in such a way that she understands and responds to what I am doing, my interlocutor may have various features that I assume, notice, anticipate, and so forth. But, and this is Levinas's point, she is my other, first and foremost, as the other to whom I am responsible, as a face of plea and demand, as the focus of my acknowledgment, acceptance, kindness, assistance, and concern. This dimension, being a face, is not, as he says, "included in the totality of being expressed." It is prior to what is said, presumed by it, what gives it point. Indeed, her face arises "behind" all that I express and all I see, expect, and so forth. In this way, her face is *sense*; without it,

---

[14] See "Meaning and Sense" in *Basic Philosophical Writings*, 48–49.
[15] See "Meaning and Sense" in *Basic Philosophical Writings*, 49; see also p. 51: "To act for remote things at the moment in which Hitlerism triumphed, in the deaf hours of this night without hours – ... is, no doubt, the summit of nobility."
[16] See "Meaning and Sense" in *Basic Philosophical Writings*, 52–57.

without her facing me, there is no meaning, no expression, no communication, cultural or linguistic. Culture requires society.

I do not think that Levinas's point is exactly the same as Wittgenstein's, that meaning is use; nor is it exactly what Grice means when he distinguishes the speaker's meaning and so forth in the pragmatic situation of communication. When I express myself in speech or in a cultural act, there is another person with whom I am engaged, but the person is not simply there. She presents herself to me to be acknowledged, accepted, and welcomed. Levinas means that the other person's presence is first of all a plea and demand for me to care enough about that other to speak to her; it is a face that commands my attention, acceptance, and response – before it is anything else. At a basic level, this is my interlocutor – not, say, my teacher or my friend or a bank teller, but rather a petitioning, commanding face, confronting me. No other meanings – for example, those I seek to express – are possible without this one. If all meanings required such a pragmatic situation, then *formally* there is no meaning without the face of the other.[17] But there is more.

The other person faces me in the world, and yet the face signifies or means what it does independently. and distinctively. This means, first, that I do not encounter the other as face in isolation or detached from everyday life. "The Other [person] is present in a cultural whole and is illuminated by this whole, as a text by its context." The face, in one sense, is one meaning alongside other ones; it is one way of my being with this other person and one meaning that this person has for me. The "world" is a network of meanings or an integrated horizon of meanings.[18] Levinas puts it this way: "[T]he Other is given in the concreteness of the totality in which he is immanent, and which . . . is expressed and disclosed by our cultural initiative, by corporeal, linguistic, or artistic gestures."[19] One meaning, the basic and determinative meaning – the sense – that the other person has for me is as *face*, as the one who summons me, calls me into question, and whom I owe help, goodness, and life itself. The other may be my friend, and the world of our culture and our experiences may give him a set of meanings for me *as* my friend, but in addition, and this is Levinas's second point, he is *face* independently of being anything else.

But the epiphany of the Other (*Autrui*) involves a signifyingness of its own, inde-pendent of this meaning received from the world. The Other comes to us not only out of the context but also without mediation; he signifies by himself. . . . The cul-tural meaning which is revealed – and reveals – as it were *horizontally* . . . is disturbed

---

[17] See "Meaning and Sense" in *Basic Philosophical Writings*, 52.
[18] Or overlapping sets of them – frameworks.
[19] "Meaning and Sense" in *Basic Philosophical Writings*, 52–53.

and jostled by another presence that is abstract (or, more exactly, absolute) and not integrated into the world.[20]

This is the face, whose entry is "not the disclosure of the world" of meaning, but something foreign, strange, unsettling – indeed, orienting. The face depends on nothing.

The face is sense; it also signifies or has a meaning. That meaning, Levinas explores quasi-phenomenologically. The content is what we tried to clarify in Chapter 3. This meaning or what the face signifies is distress and command, vulnerability and destitution as well as a summons or claim. It is the "calling of consciousness into question," a summons to answer and respond.[21] But to signify distress, a command and a summons, is to orient; the face orients the I and, in a way, identifies the I with morality, as Levinas says.[22] It is a prereflective sense or direction of the I, a sense of humility and responsibility, a necessary condition for all other meaning found "at the bottom of the ego [as] an unequivocal sincerity and a servant's humility."[23]

Culture and thought are carried out via reflection, self-examination, expression, and so forth. The primordial responsibility toward the other, however, precedes these meanings and must, as it were, permit these other meanings to take place. The face and responsibility make meanings possible; they give meanings sense.[24] Levinas says this explicitly: "The norms of morality . . . make all meaning, even cultural meaning, possible, and make it possible to judge Cultures."[25] Culture and thought, that is, are features of social life among human beings who live together and interact with one another.

But social and ethical sense also provides a standard for evaluating culture. How is this so? The face is a standard, as Levinas sees it, because the face makes it impossible for the I, the self, to hide in itself; it is a check on idealism. Reflection makes consciousness visible; it is the prelude to critique and self-mastery. The face resists such self-indulgence. It shows that *at bottom* we are a will to others and not a will to power.[26] The face makes possible meanings, because meanings are tied to metaphor and the notion of a genuine *beyond*. Meanings, in the plural, can only exist where idealism is false. Without such a genuine *beyond*, reflection and critique are not possible; without it *judging cultures* would not be possible.

---

[20] "Meaning and Sense" in *Basic Philosophical Writings*, 53.
[21] "Meaning and Sense" in *Basic Philosophical Writings*, 54; cf. 57.
[22] "Meaning and Sense" in *Basic Philosophical Writings*, 55; cf. "Thus in the relationship with a face, in the ethical relationship, there is delineated the straightforwardness of an orientation, or sense" (55).
[23] "Meaning and Sense" in *Basic Philosophical Writings*, 56.
[24] See "Meaning and Sense" in *Basic Philosophical Writings*, 57–59.
[25] "Meaning and Sense" in *Basic Philosophical Writings*, 59.
[26] "Meaning and Sense" in *Basic Philosophical Writings*, 56.

This *judging* not only requires genuine otherness and a nonrelative standard. It requires a standard with content. The face provides that content. It demands, and what it demands is that the subject recognize and act on his responsibilities to each and every other person. "Morality does not belong to Culture: it enables one to judge it. . . . "[27] Levinas, of course, is treating culture as the world of meanings (and values, practices, and so forth) constructed by a community or people historically and hence in a very specific sense. Morality is the demand registered by the face of the other person, the demand for responsibility – for acknowledgment, acceptance, and more. The face and its epiphany, then, make judgment possible by making separation and detached critique possible and by fixing the content of our relationships with others as *oriented* by the other's need for acceptance, assistance, and generosity. This is "to find oneself able to judge civilization on the basis of the ethical"; it is a "return to Platonism" or moral realism "in a new way."[28] In Chapter 1, we saw how Levinas himself engages in this ethical or moral judgment of twentieth-century civilization, especially of Hitler's fascism and Stalinism. The century of atrocities from Sarajevo to Cambodia and Rwanda is to be judged by the standards of justice and responsibility, and when it is, the seriousness of our plight is evident.

The remaining section of "Meaning and Sense" deals with God and the notion of the trace. We shall look at this section later.[29] For now, I want to consider more carefully Levinas's claim that the encounter with the face, its epiphany, signifies or is sense or has meaning. For Levinas, strictly speaking, the face of the other cannot either be or have meaning. If signification is a broad semantic relation that concerns the tie between a word or sentence or object or act, on the one hand, and either what that item or episode means or what it picks out, then items only signify within the scope of our cognitive or practical activities in everyday life. They only signify in the world of things and comprehension of things, ideas, experiences, and such. The notion of an encounter with the face of the other person or its epiphany or engagement with me is intended to point to a relationship or aspect of our interpersonal lives outside those domains. It is not wholly within the domain of consciousness, so to speak; I am related to the face in a different way, a way that our everyday language can only hint at but not express. Therefore, semantic terms like "signification," "meaning," and "sense" are not literally appropriate, or, if

---

[27] "Meaning and Sense" in *Basic Philosophical Writings*, 57.
[28] "Meaning and Sense" in *Basic Philosophical Writings*, 58; there is a nice summary of the point of the essay on p. 59.
[29] "Meaning and Sense" in *Basic Philosophical Writings*, 59–64; see also "The Trace of the Other" and "God and Philosophy," both of which we shall discuss in Chapter 7.

they are, they are false.[30] Nonetheless, they can and must be used – after all, Levinas does so all the time – with an appreciation for this overall caveat: that they are not to be understood literally. Having said this, we can take Levinas to mean something like this: cultural objects and expressions are given a variety of meanings, depending upon the historical background, the situation, the agents, and so forth. A given object means a variety of things. Levinas appropriates Husserlian language and draws on Merleau-Ponty, but the points he assumes are pretty uncontroversial. I think that he uses the notion of sense to refer to the special meaning of whatever gives unity to this multiplicity of meanings, overall, for all cultures, for all human contexts, periods, and groups. Whatever is the *sense* of human cultural experience, then, makes human life meaningful – as a whole, for everyone. "Sense" really means something like "significance" or "the point of it all." Culture only makes sense as the meanings of a social group.

Now, let us turn to the face of the other. Encountering the face is one way we can experience other persons; it is one way of relating to the other person or, perhaps better, one dimension of all our interpersonal relationships. In one sense, then, the face is one way – in fact, the fundamental and determinative way – that other persons have meaning for us. Furthermore, if the face is indeed central to our lives, then the relationship determined by its claim on us provides the sense of human life and culture. It is what gives human social life and culture their point or purpose. It is what makes them significant for us as human beings who live with other human beings.

But to understand the face, we need to articulate not only its *role* as sense but also its meaning-content, as it were – that is, what the epiphany of the face reveals to me. In one way, of course, the face simply reveals itself; it is the face of the other that is manifest to me. But in another sense, in revealing itself, the face reveals something about the other's situation vis à vis me. When I interact with or am related to the other, I may and likely do think all kinds of things about her, look at her in a certain way, expect things, assume things. I may or may not attend to or privilege or respond to her as a face – as vulnerable and summoning me to respond. That is, for Levinas, not only important, it is also orienting. However else I treat her and act should be determined or directed by my acknowledgment of her as a person, in all her need and vulnerability and forcefulness. To fail to do so is to fail to deal with her in the deepest human way. For these reasons, then, the face does have quasi-meaning, or something like

[30] I am thinking here of Donald Davidson's account of metaphors, according to which metaphors are literally false, but because of context and circumstances, seek to get us to see things in a different way. Once that way becomes common and widely accepted, the metaphor in fact becomes literally true. What this signals is a change in the way a community of speakers takes a certain word or expression and uses it. Everyday language, for Davidson, is a reservoir of dead metaphors.

meaning; phrases like "puts me in question," "expresses misery and summons an answer from me," and "calls to me" are like accounts of what words or acts mean within cultures. They are explications or elucidations of the quasi-meaning of the face of the other person, and they help us to see what its special significance is. One can therefore understand what Levinas means when he says that the face is sense and that its meaning is to make me responsible, to confront me with its nakedness, nudity, and destitution and to demand my response, my acknowledgment, and my assistance and generosity.

MEANING AND LANGUAGE

Levinas, in using the language of signification, meaning, and sense, is drawing on a rich tradition. That tradition, for him, included Heidegger, Husserl, Merleau-Ponty, Buber, Rosenzweig, and Bergson. It also includes Hans-Georg Gadamer, Wilhelm Dilthey, Paul Ricoeur, Charles Taylor, neo-Kantians such as Wilhelm Windelband and Heinrich Rickert, and perhaps also Nietzsche and Schopenhauer. Levinas draws on various themes from this tradition, most notably the phenomenological method in Husserl and Heidegger, the extension of the notion of intentionality to affective states, corporeal and noncognitive life, cultural acts, and such, and the notion of horizon and world. What is unique to him is the elucidation of a locus of meaning outside of all this that is somehow present within it and unsettling to it. Moreover, that locus is not an object or act otherwise accessible than by some special intuition or grasp. Rather, the locus is a *dimension* or *aspect* of what is a completely common, normal experience or relationship, indeed of every interpersonal experience or relationship we have, the interaction each of us has with other persons. This locus, as he puts it, is a meaning prior to *Sinngebung*, the giving or constructing of meaning. It is the premeaning of meaning.

Meaning was one of the central topics of philosophical investigation in the twentieth century. As I have indicated, it was central to neo-Kantianism, to thinkers like Dilthey, and to phenomenology. Beginning with Gottlob Frege, it was also central to the tradition of Anglo-American analytic philosophy. Levinas's placing of the face-to-face within the philosophical treatment of meaning is solely indebted to the continental tradition, from phenomenology to hermeneutics to postmodernism. But this does not mean that his thinking has no relevance to other discussions of meaning, especially those that have treated meaning as a feature of human communication and social life.[31] Theories of

---

[31] Philosophers who come to mind are Frege, Wittgenstein, Quine, Donald Davidson, H. P. Grice, and Michael Dummett, among others. A theory of meaning for natural languages was a central theme of Anglo-American philosophy for decades.

meaning can be subjectivist, objective or Platonist, or social-public. They may reify meanings or clarify their role in social practices of communication and action. It is worth asking of Levinas's views: How does language in everyday life have meaning? If the face-to-face is a prelinguistic, preconceptual mode of relationship or dimension of everyday interpersonal life, how is it meaningful? Does it have a kind of meaning, strictly speaking, or is it itself a mode of meaning or significance? Finally, how is the meaning of the face related to linguistic meaning? In part, as a response to the interpretation and critique of Derrida, Levinas does consider some of these issues in his 1974 book *Otherwise Than Being*. But before we turn to it, I would like to look at his 1967 essay "Language and Proximity." As we turn to Levinas on meaning, there is a deep concern that we ought to keep in mind. Many philosophers take meaning to be constituted socially and to occur in the understanding of social agents. If this is so, however, and if linguistic meaning arises out of social situations grounded in the face-to-face, how can we understand the meaning of the face-to-face itself? In terms used earlier, how can the premeaning of meaning itself have meaning?

Levinas begins "Language and Proximity" with the idea that "thought reach[es] the individual only through the detour of the universal."[32] That is, thought is like language; it requires signification. To understand, to claim, to judge – it is all to take this as that, to unify. Whatever is present to consciousness is taken as something, and that something is a universal, a concept, a category. Hence, "every phenomenon is a discourse or a fragment of a discourse."[33] Consciousness, signification, language, and universality go hand in hand. Also part of this package of concepts are identification, knowledge, truth, and communication. One cannot think without universals, and one cannot communicate linguistically without them.

But communication, which is always the attempt to present the truth (at least in one type of linguistic interaction), requires something more, for the truth is always the truth for someone. So, Levinas notes, we need that someone in order to communicate with him; we need a speaker and an interlocutor. But is this interlocutor, this someone, also an object of thought or a kind of knowing? If so, the interlocutor is also a universal or mediated through the universal. Levinas puts the difficulty this way:

[T]he hypothesis that the relationship with an interlocutor would still be a knowing reduces speech to the solitary or impersonal exercise of a thought, whereas already the kerygma [proclamation, summons] which bears its identity is, in addition, a *proximity* between me and the interlocutor, and not our participation in a transparent universality. Whatever be the message transmitted by speech, the speaking is contact.

---

[32] "Language and Proximity" in *Collected Philosophical Papers*, 113.
[33] "Language and Proximity" in *Collected Philosophical Papers*, 112.

One must then admit that there is in speech a relationship with a singularity located outside of the theme of speech, a singularity that is not thematized by the speech but is approached.[34]

Speech, discourse, and communication, that is, *presuppose* a relation between the speaker and the interlocutor, an utterly particular other person, and that relation is preintentional, in Husserl's terms. The other person is not an objective-meaning, the object of the speaker's belief, desire, and so forth, in any ordinary sense. This relation, Levinas, calls "proximity." It is prior to belief, desire, interest, consciousness, memory, and more. Communication requires it, but it is not a mode of communication – that is, it is not itself a mode of everyday communication, even though Levinas does characterize it as a mode of address and as speech. Meaning in the ordinary sense requires this relation, but it is not meaning itself, nor is it meaningful in the same way that the language of communication is meaningful. But it is, we might say, quasi-meaningful. Levinas says, "[P]roximity is *by itself* a signification," but this is signification of a special kind. It "proclaims" something, but not "as something." As Levinas puts it, "the intentional has become ethical," and in a note he elaborates that "ethical" here does not mean "moral" and that it registers the idea that the relation is different from everyday intentional relations: "We call ethical a relationship between terms such as are united neither by a synthesis of the understanding nor by a relationship between subject or object, and yet where the one weighs or concerns or is meaningful to the other, where they are bound up by a plot which knowing can neither exhaust nor unravel."[35] This term "the ethical" refers to a relationship prior to thought, understanding, knowing – indeed, to any conceptualization. It *reverses*, he says, the vector of a subject representing, judging, claiming, or grasping some object as this or as that, which is the character of everyday dealings between subject and object, person and world. Here, on the contrary, there is a "subjectivity that enters *into contact* with a singularity, excluding identification in the ideal, excluding thematization and representation – an absolute singularity, as such unrepresentable. This is the original language, the foundation of the other one." Furthermore, now employing the terminology we have come to expect, Levinas calls the *point* at which the intentional turns into the ethical "the face" and the *contact* with the face "tenderness and responsibility."

I have been paraphrasing a line of thinking from the early sections of Levinas's paper. There are a number of things to be said about that line of thinking. First, Levinas seems to be making a point rather than arguing for one, and that point is

[34] "Language and Proximity" in *Collected Philosophical Papers*, 115.
[35] "Language and Proximity" in *Collected Philosophical Papers*, 116, 116 n. 6.

about thought and language and what, in terms of the relation between speaker and interlocutor, they require. His point is that while all thought and language incorporate concepts or universals, they also require, at a basic level, contact between two utterly particular persons, what he calls "absolute singularity." This contact he calls "proximity." I do not see in the essay any arguments for this point, but it is clearly one main outcome of his presentation. He seems to be assuming that language and thought are grounded in communication and speech between persons, so that the character of thought and language depends upon there being concrete, particular persons engaging one another in a communicative relationship; one speaks to the other. Furthermore, Levinas begins to say something about that contact or proximity: It is a signification; it is the ethical; it occurs via the face of the other person. In short, the relation between communicating persons is not a brute, indescribable, meaningless relation. Rather, it is meaningful precisely because, as a contact between the I and a particular other person, the other person "weighs upon" or "means something to" the I. Once again, Levinas appears to be making this point and not arguing for it.

A second observation is that this point, or at least the first feature of it, sounds familiar, but it does have its own distinctiveness. Philosophers in the twentieth century spent a good deal of time thinking about the ontological status of meanings, whether they are Platonic ideas of a sort or a function of use or rules or socially constructed. Levinas does not seem to be interested here in such matters. But we might take him to be interested in a related issue: how meaning is associated with communication, discourse, and social context. He is not – at least not yet – thinking about how social context gives rise to the meanings of utterances, but he does want us to appreciate that language is a public and interpersonal matter, for thought and language are necessarily associated with communication, and communication requires a speaker and an interlocutor. That is, language is an activity between people, and just as one may never have people who do not or cannot communicate, so one never has communication, discourse, and language without people acting toward others, with people conversing in one way or another. Meaning arises in this setting and is tied to it. This much sounds enough like Wittgenstein, Austin, Searle, Grice, and others to seem unremarkable. But, of course, this is not all that Levinas says.

Levinas also points out that this interpersonal situation in which discourse and communication occur – at its most basic level, so to speak, and prior to any emotional or social character it takes on because of context, and so forth – itself does not have meaning, strictly speaking. It involves persons who are present and *in contact* in all their utter particularity. The meaning of the communicative relationship and the meaning of the content of the speech between the parties, all this occurs later, as it were. Furthermore, this basic relationship, their contact, is constituted as ethical; it is about how the other person, in her particularity, matters to me, is significant for me. Any words that I speak to the other or the other to me, prior to its being meaningful or having content or character, are already a response to the other person, an act of acknowledging that person, accepting her, granting her space and status. In short, the interpersonal situation is prelinguistically not neutral; it already has a kind of content or weight. Not only does language occur in this setting; it even *depends* upon it. It cannot occur without it. What, however, does this mean? What could it mean? Why should conversation depend upon the other person meaning something to me? How can the meaningful depend upon the meaningless?

Levinas does not turn to these questions, at least not directly. Rather, he devotes the remainder of his essay to another task, to clarifying exactly what that contact is between the I and the other – what proximity is. He says: "[C]ontact is tenderness and responsibility," and he proceeds deliberately to explore what these two features are and how they are related.[36] In other words, Levinas takes proximity, as it were, to be a relation or a reality, and he sets about using the phenomenological method, suitably modified, to clarify what that relation involves. Or, more precisely, he takes it to be a relation to the other person that is experienced in a certain way and proceeds to describe how the other person appears to the self within this relation. He seems to think that one needs no argument or account to conclude that this relation *is* required; what one needs is an account of what it is. What does he say, then, about proximity?

"Contact" and "tenderness" are words of a sensory character, particularly of a tactile kind. Levinas begins by talking about "sensibility" or sensory experience. We tend to treat sensation as a kind of theoretical apprehension of an object by a subject. That is, we use the model of sight, and we are inclined to intellectualize the experience. In opposition to this tendency, Levinas – and this is one of his most important criticisms of Husserl and the epistemological tradition, originating with Descartes, that he draws on – wants to call attention to the way our sensory involvement in and with the world is not originally or primarily observational or theoretical. "In sensation," he says, "something *comes to pass* between the feeling and the felt, below the openness of the feeling upon the felt, of consciousness upon a phenomenon."[37] For this reason, seeking to expose this depth of sensory involvement in the world, Levinas focuses on smelling and tasting. Tasting is world-oriented by means of consumption, and Levinas thinks that this attitude of consumption is present in all the senses: "[T]o feel the world is always a way of being nourished by it."[38] This is also,

---

[36] "Language and Proximity" in *Collected Philosophical Papers*, 116.

[37] "Language and Proximity" in *Collected Philosophical Papers*, 117–18.

[38] "Language and Proximity" in *Collected Philosophical Papers*, 118; cf. *Time and the Other* and *Totality and Infinity*, where Levinas elaborates this theme.

as is widely appreciated, not only an anti-Husserlian and anti-Cartesian matter; it is also an anti-Heideggerian one. For Levinas, our sensory involvement in and with the world is a matter of being nourished by it and enjoying it; we are not subjective observers of the world; nor is our involvement with it oppositional or contrary. We welcome and incorporate the world; it feeds and supports us, and our attitude toward it is fulfillment or enjoyment. But these nuances notwithstanding, the central point here is that theoretical detachment, examination, and observation arise out of a more original relationship with the world that is one of consumption and fulfillment.

Levinas then turns to touch. Tactile sensations can become detached, in a sense, and informative, what he calls "doxic." But prior to this, touch is "pure approach" and what he calls, in a typical expression, "a proximity that is not reducible to the experience of proximity," that is, a preexperiential, prethematic, preconceptual contact. This contact, he says, takes form as "caress"; it is a "tenderness." Before we follow Levinas further, we should try to clarify what he is doing here. First, his use of terms like "caress" and "tenderness" is obviously intended to move far from traditional epistemological vocabulary, from words like "sensory quality," "sense data," or "appearance," and to emphasize contiguity, intimacy, involvement, and almost immersion. The terms are the analogues for tactile sensation of the expressions "nourishment" and "consumption" for the gustatory. Second, the terms are clearly erotic and maternal. They suggest a kind of loving drawing-close, an affectionate enclosing, that is easy to associate with a mother's enfolding of an infant, for example, or a lover's gentle stroking of a beloved's body. Third, Levinas seems to elide the boundary between a sensory contact with the world, some object in it, and the contact of one person with another. It is not clear whether he is saying that all sensory observation is grounded or embedded in a special relation of self to world, that is akin to what Heidegger takes being-in-the-world as thrownness to be, or that all sensory observation is grounded in my relation to the other person. In fact, the story is more complicated than either alternative suggests.

In one way, the "caress" and "tenderness" are a vocabulary for describing proximity as the encounter with the face of the other person. "[Tenderness] exists between the face and the nudity of the skin – the one in the context of the other . . . between the pure and the troubled."[39] But Levinas also seems to refer to a sensible proximity: "Sight is, to be sure, an openness and a consciousness, and all sensibility, opening as a consciousness, is called vision; but even in its subordination to cognition sight maintains contact and proximity. The visible caresses the eye."[40] Crudely put, what is it that underlies sensory involvement

---

[39] "Language and Proximity" in *Collected Philosophical Papers*, 118.
[40] "Language and Proximity" in *Collected Philosophical Papers*, 118.

with the world, an encounter of the perceiver with another person or the perceiver's preperceptual contact with what she perceives? Levinas seems to believe
both, but in a special way: underlying our sensory observations and investigation
of things, there is a proximity, a closeness, in which the object means something
to me: "[T]he visible caresses the eye." But this relationship itself derives from
the face-to-face: "[O]ver all things, beginning with the human face and skin,
tenderness spreads." Things mean something to me only because my neighbor
does; things are near to me only because the other person is. Nourishment,
consumption, enjoyment – of things, the world – requires my encounter with
the other person. Levinas calls this proximity an "obsession" and "pure communication" or an "original language," without words or propositions, but an
interpersonal encounter of one with the other.[41] "Matter, which is invested as
a tool, and a tool in the world" – an obvious reference to Heidegger's description of our basic relation to things in the world – "is also, via the human, the
matter that obsesses me with its proximity."[42] Before things are there for my
use, they matter to me; they serve, feed, nourish me, and things matter to me
only because the other person does and because, in a sense, they matter to her.
Thus is tenderness; Levinas now turns to "responsibility."

When I encounter the face, "the neighbor summons me. Obsession is a
responsibility without choice, a communication without phrases or words."[43]
Earlier, we discussed this content of the face-to-face, its character as a plea and a
command, a moment of revealing misery and calling for response. Here, Levinas
emphasizes that it is a communication, but one that is prior to language and, for
me, a responsibility prior to any choice to acknowledge or to accept the other
person. He makes two points: The relationship occurs before my consciousness
of the summons; and it is always past. When I do realize what the other means
and I think about it, the other's face always has already revealed itself. It has no
present, so to speak. Levinas notes that any present awareness I might have of
the other person as proximate, as a face, is a very indirect or "oblique" type of
awareness, because the face is not present as other features are – one's hair color,
one's height, a smile, a frown, one's being a stranger, and so forth. Levinas tries
to point toward this obliqueness by saying that "in representation, [that is, in
awareness or thought or apprehension], presence is already past."[44] That is, the
other's face is "proximate and an absence" at once. He compares this attention or
awareness to a caress that is both an approach and a closeness, hence a proximity

---

[41] "Language and Proximity" in *Collected Philosophical Papers*, 119.
[42] "Language and Proximity" in *Collected Philosophical Papers*, 119.
[43] "Language and Proximity" in *Collected Philosophical Papers*, 120.
[44] "Language and Proximity" in *Collected Philosophical Papers*, 120.

that is not really proximate – yet. Or, alternatively, this absence is a presence of the infinite, but, as we have seen, because the infinite is outside the totality, it is not itself present in life or in thought; it is always beyond, always below, always out of our line of vision. The other person is present as a friend, as angry, as agitated, and more, but all along, at the same time, the other person makes a claim upon me to respond, to acknowledge, accept, and assist. This is the proximity of that person that is also an absence. "It always flees. But it leaves . . . a trace, in which its invisibility is the face of the neighbor."[45] The face presents me with what is always past – a plea and a summons, my responsibility to the other person – both the possibility and the necessity of my responding to the other person's need for me.

Levinas returns to the idea that this contact is a kind of communication prior to words and phrases. It is, he says, a "saying" that "precedes the language that communicates propositions and messages."[46] This is his line of thought: Language involves concepts and universality; universality requires singularity; singularity for human beings only occurs as the proximity of one person to another, the face-to-face. Language and meaning are developments from the foundation of a unique I encountering a unique other, "the enigma of the face." This is what he calls the "saying," which is the ground of all speech, discourse, communication, thought, and conceptualization. Saying, then, is not a speech act, nor a type of speech act; it is not the conversational situation nor the act of speaking. Saying is not what we do with words, the act that we perform in uttering "I promise to meet you at ten o'clock." Or, to be more precise, it is not one among a variety of such acts. Rather saying is the encounter of two utterly unique persons, indeed between every two utterly unique persons. It involves one making a claim of assistance and support on the other and therefore one being totally, unqualifiedly responsible for the other. It is not the act of promising, but it is the act of acknowledging and caring for the other that occurs whenever one makes a promise to another.

Just as this saying is communication prior to words and speech and proximity is prior to consciousness, so responsibility is prior to freedom. We shall return to this claim later, but it is important to realize the context in which Levinas makes it and that it is not intended as an extraordinary or strange one. Freedom, like consciousness, concepts, and belief, is an everyday notion common to all experience, while the face-to-face is a perspective on experience or an aspect of our lives that is not given in ordinary life and that is hidden and not on the line of regular experience. Responsibility does not occur before freedom

---

[45] "Language and Proximity" in *Collected Philosophical Papers*, 121.
[46] "Language and Proximity" in *Collected Philosophical Papers*, 121; cf. 121–23.

in some crude, temporal sense; rather, every free decision and action is always already an act of responsibility toward some person and probably toward many persons. The claim "responsibility... does not refer to my freedom"[47] is not meant to be a paradox; it is meant to convey the thought that the other person makes a claim on me, before I do anything – independently of any deliberation, decision, or action on my part.

Levinas continues to introduce new terms to characterize the face-to-face, terms that register the extremity, the urgency, and the priority of proximity. "Obsession" is one, and from obsession and responsibility without freedom he turns to "hostage" and "accusation." The former terms suggest that the summons and burden are imposed without freedom and that the I is *confined* in place of the other person; the latter suggests that the mere presence of the other person calls one into question, accuses me before I am aware of or have done anything. Fundamentally, I am "obsessed precisely with responsibilities that do not go back to decisions taken by a freely contemplating subject, and thus accused with what [I] never did...."[48] These terms, then, are intended to give us a sense of the overwhelming, constraining character of our responsibility, of its unlawfulness and targetedness. We are its victims, not literally, of course, but in the sense that what we owe to others comes prior to and along with every interaction and every relation we have with them. I become, as Levinas puts it, a "permanent sacrifice [that] substitutes itself for others." Here, with this new term "substitution," Levinas finds the "source of speaking" and the "essence of communication." "Sacrifice" is a religious term, and "substitution" is its secular paraphrase; it is a giving-over and an offering of the self for the other. Somehow – in a way he has not yet clarified – communication between persons depends upon my standing in for others, my being in the other's place.[49] Feelings and attitudes – like pity, compassion, and generosity – Levinas claims, can only arise because primordially I am a hostage. War is not the origin, as Hobbes would have it; "before war there were altars" – that is, the conflict of war requires agents who arise out of encounters of sacrifice. And what holds for war, also holds for society, communication, and language.

Contemporary Anglo-American philosophers do not seem to be worried by the concerns we find in Levinas's essay. He claims that language – and not it alone, of course – is grounded in a contact between the other person and the self. That contact is a quasi-communicative contact; something is conveyed. But the persons and the content are utterly particular. Moreover, this contact is

[47] "Language and Proximity" in *Collected Philosophical Papers*, 123.
[48] "Language and Proximity" in *Collected Philosophical Papers*, 123.
[49] See "Language and Proximity" in *Collected Philosophical Papers*, 124–26.

present, in a sense, in every conversation between persons, although often it is ignored or hidden. Insofar as the other's relation to the self makes speech and ordinary communication possible, we do not yet know how. As I said, however, this does not look like a Levinasian response to Wittgenstein's private-language argument. Levinas's point does not seem to be that language, speech, discourse, and meaning require a social situation, that they are social practices. I think that he takes this for granted; it is not his issue.[50] He begins, as it were, with people in linguistic communities engaging in conversation with one another, speaking to one another, understanding and misunderstanding one another. Ultimately, he says, this practice somehow depends upon and/or arises out of the singular, utterly particular event of one person mattering to another, of you calling me into question. What meaning this relationship has is of a different order than the meaning we associate with language in everyday life. The meanings of our utterances are one thing; the signification or sense or point of this relationship of contact or proximity between us is another. Alternatively, we might say that everyday communication and linguistic acts mean many things, and among them, at a fundamental or fundamentally determinative level, is the fact that each interlocutor puts the other in question, that their conversation, no matter what its semantic or contextual content, is embedded in this relationship of summons and supplication that they bear to one another – not a symmetrical relation but two asymmetrical ones, each one a relation of call and response.

Levinas goes further, especially in *Otherwise Than Being* and various later essays, and shows how everyday social life and language actually *arise out of* this basic relationship.[51] I think that there are two issues here, and it is important to distinguish them. The first is how language arises and what role the face-to-face and responsibility play in the emergence of language. In a sentence, this issue is about language as a system of signs, as having a certain kind of meaning, as serving certain purposes, and it asks what role the ethical encounter as Levinas characterizes it plays in our understanding language as it is. The second issue is different. It is about the relation between language as speech, communication, and conversation, on the one hand, and responsibility and the acknowledgment or acceptance of other persons, as the primordial ground of the ethical, on the other. Language as speech is a certain kind of activity, an interactive activity of exchange, interrogation, rejection, response, and more. How is *this* mode of activity – rather than some other mode – related to the face calling me into question and my being responsible to the other person?

---

[50] Contra Adriaan Peperzak, *Beyond*, 61.
[51] See OB, 153–62: "From the Saying to the Said. . . ." Cf. Peperzak, *Beyond*, Ch. 5.

Let us take the second question first. What does speech as a mode of activity have to do with responsibility? Adriaan Peperzak makes a good suggestion:

Finding myself facing another awakens me to *responsibility*: an infinite responsibility for the Other, who is in need of everything that is necessary for a human life. By addressing myself to another I practice this responsibility, be it reluctantly or not. A total refusal of it would express itself through murder. Total acceptance would coincide with perfect love.[52]

Speaking to the other person, that is, *expresses* my responsibility to her; it is a way that my responsibility reveals itself or manifests itself. Speech lies somewhere between murder and perfect love – not it alone, of course, as a responsible mode of activity, but as one type: everyday, complex, variegated, anything but uniform. Basically, then, when the other person enters my world and I speak to her, whatever else it is, my speech is a form of welcome, of acceptance, of gift, of sharing. When I speak to someone, in a sense prior to anything else, my speaking has this basic dimension of welcoming that other into my space. In Levinas's later terminology, present in every *said* is a *saying*; every act of speaking has an ethical dimension at its ground.

But his point assumes – and this is our first point – that there is language and speech as a distinctive domain of activity, as a way we interact with each other. Is there a sense that responsibility and the face-to-face are implicated in what makes language and speech what they are, in their very character as systems of signs? The issue we just addressed links speech and language with all other interpersonal acts. Levinas refers to many of them – including war, for example – and his point is that all of them are grounded in the face-to-face. Speech and discourse, as an example, require one person addressing another, not simply an other in some role or other or conceived in some way or other, but a unique, particular other. But I am confronted with a unique other only insofar as the other engages me, faces me, calls me into question. Hence, the face-to-face is the ground of speech and all interpersonal relations. And because the face-to-face is responsibility, that responsibility, the necessity of response and the summons to respond generously, is the ground of all speech and all interpersonal relations. It is the ground of all social existence. But that does not tell us what makes language and speech distinctive.

Levinas does not tell a complete story about how the face-to-face gives rise to language. In fact, all he gives are hints of how such a story would go. It is an account, I suspect, that is linked to his story of the emergence of society, morality, justice, and politics. These forms of life – involving groups of people, rules, principles, policies and laws, and modes of organization – all

[52] Peperzak, *Beyond*, 67; cf. 66–68.

involve language, systems of signs used, interpreted and understood by groups of people, large and small. In an earlier chapter, we sketched one aspect of this story – the one that leads from the face-to-face to justice, morality, and politics. Here I want to fill in the linguistic dimension more fully than Levinas does, in order to show that the face-to-face is the substantive, as well as the formal, ground of speech and language.[53] And just as there I argued that the story should not be read as a genuine narrative or as a genetic account but rather should be understood as exposing the fundamental dimension of moral and political life, so here the story should be read as an argument for how the face-to-face and all it signifies is the ground of language and discourse. The central texts will be from "The Ego and Totality" (1954) and *Otherwise Than Being* (1974).

One might be tempted to treat Levinas's claim that language requires an encounter of the speaker with another person as the core of his response to a private-language argument.[54] In fact, I do not think that Levinas ever considers the possibility (or impossibility) of such a language, nor does the face-to-face stand for a linguistic community with at least two members. For Levinas, we live in social groups with languages that we use for communication and other purposes. If the face-to-face is somehow essential to language, it is for some other reason than that it represents sheer plurality or a community of members who speak a shared language. The face-to-face is not the mere social condition that makes language possible; it is not a social fact that is essential to meaningful language.

Another thought is that the face-to-face tells us something about the fundamental function of language, what it is primarily for, what it enables speakers to do. In one sense, this thought is on the right track, although the kind of functionalism it aims at cannot be the kind we find in naturalist, sociobiological, or evolutionary accounts.[55] Still, Levinas does seem to want the face-to-face to show us what the point of language is *fundamentally*, even if, as matters go, it comes to have many other points or functions as well. Moreover, he would like us to believe that somehow language and discourse would be unnecessary and even impossible if it were not for the face-to-face and the special way that particular individuals matter, one to the other.[56] And if philosophers are right who argue that thought and language go hand in hand, then Levinas needs to

---

[53] See Peperzak, *Beyond*, 68, for a brief comment.

[54] As Peperzak does; see *Beyond*, 61.

[55] For example, Dretske, *Explaining Behavior* (Cambridge, MA: MIT Press, 1988); see also Charles Taylor, *Sources of the Self*, and his critique of sociobiology.

[56] For example, Davidson and his account of how meaning arises within a system of triangulation that includes the speaker, the world, and the person with whom the speaker is communicating. I return to Davidson's account shortly.

show why thought as well as language must be grounded in the face-to-face, in the responsibility that one person has for each and every other.

Another way of putting this question is to return to the language of perspectives or aspects that we have used earlier. Levinas takes us to live together in linguistic communities. We inform each other; express our feelings, hopes, and desires; deliberate together; argue; and more. Our relationships with one another can regularly be explicated in terms of the types of discourse we engage in, the ways we talk with one another. But, he says, there is something about our relationships that cannot be expressed in terms of our discourse or communication, and in fact, without it, the basic point of our communicating at all remains obscure. Why bother to seek to talk with one another? Why develop ways of communicating at all? We do not seek to talk with rocks or trees. Why do we do so with people and with other beings, like certain animals? What about other people matters to us in such a way that we respond to them in language and speech?

As I mentioned, the story Levinas tells is not a naturalistic one, at least not in content. Unlike Rousseau, Humboldt, Herder, or Fred Dretske and more recent naturalists, Levinas does not see language as a survival strategy or mechanism. To him, it is not grounded in conflict or aggression. Rather, it is grounded in the need to move from the utterly particular, preconceptual environment of the face-to-face, with its ethical but singular content, to the public, social, and communal world of principles, deliberation, decision, and social policy. Levinas sees a way to tell this story in the 1950s and 1960s and develops it more fully in later years, especially in *Otherwise Than Being*.

Famously, the crucial idea in this account is the entrance of the third party. In our lives, we are never simply alone with one unique other person; there are always others, third parties, in addition to the two of us, and each third party is an I and an other person, to me, to the other person who faces me, and on and on. This means that every interpersonal engagement is only one of multiple ones for each and every I. And for each I, there are also many persons with whom one has no interpersonal contact – distant ones, in addition to those who are proximate and with whom the I has more-direct relationships. What does this situation mean for me? Once we universalize, generalize, and elaborate, it may mean a great number of things, of course, but what does it mean for me as responsible – as the unique locus of any number of summons to respond?

On the one hand, as Levinas sees it, it means that each and every interpersonal relationship in which every I or subject stands to an other person, near or far, is grounded in the ethical demand of the other's presence to the self. No social relationship, direct or indirect, proximate or distant, is simply what it is; it always has an ethical character that it may, by its nature, occlude or express to one degree or another. But the question I am raising is different from this one, about how all social relationships are grounded in the face-to-face. It is about what effect the multiplicity of our social relationships has on the way that the face-to-face is engaged, on how the self responds to the face of the other when we realize that there are always multiple – indeed, infinite – faces that confront it. Here, on the other hand, these infinite other persons face me, and each other person calls me to give up something or everything to serve his needs, to alleviate his misery, and so forth. But clearly, I cannot do so; I cannot give everything to everyone. Each other confronts me solely as need or misery, but I must treat their misery universally, weighing one against the other, assessing the need and my capacity to satisfy it, the circumstances we are in, and so forth. That is, I must judge, compare, and develop devices for doing so, reflect on needs relatively one against the other, and establish for myself, to begin with, some principle or norm or guideline for handling one situation and another and another.[57] This situation, Levinas says, "characterizes the subjective existence capable of discourse *essentially*."[58] He calls this an "impersonal discourse" because the I and the interlocutor are treated as universals, classifiable, conceptualized. The utter uniqueness of the personal is recast in a relationship of roles, types, generalities, and such.[59] The language of the everyday is far from the language of the face-to-face; everyday speech is not pure speech.

In "The I and the Totality," Levinas emphasizes how everyday language obscures pure speech, the language of the I and the other person.[60] He tries to show why the original speech is more elevated, more worthy, and how everyday language fails to express it. "The one to whom I speak stands farther back, behind the concept I communicate to him."[61] "Invocation is prior to commonality."[62] Levinas says that everyday language "threatens and flatters"; it is a form of violence. "The judge speaking to the accused is not yet speaking."[63] But at the same time, he says – although he does not explain – that morality and politics arise out of the face and the presence of the third party and that language and speech, in everyday life, do so as well.

We can surmise how the speculation might go. Language requires concepts and devices for treating people and things in general, devices like pronouns, demonstratives, and such. It needs predicates and words that classify into kinds. Making judgments, comparisons, and so forth are facilitated by techniques

---

[57] OB, 16, 157–61.
[58] "The I and the Totality" in *Entre Nous*, 22; cf. 27.
[59] "The I and the Totality" in *Entre Nous*, 25.
[60] "The I and the Totality" in *Entre Nous*, 30–36.
[61] "The I and the Totality" in *Entre Nous*, 32.
[62] "The I and the Totality" in *Entre Nous*, 33.
[63] "The I and the Totality" in *Entre Nous*, 24, 33.

for doing these things.[64] Social interaction among people makes such devices possible, and these tasks require something like them. The third party, Levinas says, "introduces a contradiction in the saying."[65] It puzzles, confuses, and limits; what it limits is my capacity to respond as I should, as I am called to respond. The presence of the third party is not, of course, the only limitation on my responding; others include my proximity to the other person, my resources, and my recognition of the other's needs. The third party's presence adds to these; I cannot help everyone, certainly not at the same time, in the same way, to the same degree, always. Levinas says that the I needs to assemble, order, thematize, and assess;[66] it cannot simply respond, and basically it needs language, concepts, and thought to do these things. This might be elaborated and made more precise, but we can see how a Levinasian story might go: linking the basic responsibility of the I to the other person with justice, rules, evaluation, and with language and concepts.

ETHICS AND COMMUNICATION: THE SAYING AND THE SAID

What, then, does responsibility mean to thought, language, and speech? Surely, language serves a host of functions and is linked to many purposes and activities. What is the point of showing how it arises out of the face-to-face and the third party? What does the face-to-face and infinite responsibility mean for language, speech, and communication?

Levinas's point about how thought and language are essentially tied to the face-to-face encounter between the self and another person might seem to be saying that thought and language are social in some fundamental sense, and, as I have noted, this kind of proposal might remind us of Wittgenstein and the argument against a private language. But I think that while Levinas might agree that everyday language is, indeed, a social affair, his point is a different and deeper one; it is not about what is required for language to function as communication, but rather about what the point of language and communication are for human social existence. In order to see this, let me compare Levinas's story with a discussion that is in the Wittgenstinian tradition: Donald Davidson's argument for the social character of thought and language.

Davidson's central notion is triangulation; it is the core of what Dagfinn Føllesdal calls his "later theory."[67] Triangulation is "essential to both language

---

[64] For an example of how these functions are served, see Strawson, *Subject and Predicate in Logic and Grammar* (London: Methuen, 1974).

[65] OB, 157.

[66] OB, 157.

[67] Dagfinn Føllesdal, "Triangulation," in Lewis Edwin Hahn (ed.), *The Philosophy of Donald Davidson*, 719–28.

and propositional thought."[68] It is the name for Davidson's argument "to establish the essentially public character of language...that applies not only to speech but also to belief, intention, and the rest of the propositional attitudes,...[ending] with what may be Wittgenstein's conclusion: language is necessarily a social affair."[69] One's first language, that is, cannot be a private language; there must be at least one other person who understands it. Why? The brief answer is that language requires a concept of truth, and truth is an intersubjective matter. One cannot have a concept of truth without there being at least one other person with whom one shares the world and whom one knows shares the world with you. But the brief answer is not sufficient; let us fill in the story a bit.

According to Davidson, language and thought require triangulation. But what is triangulation and why do language and thought require it? The communication situation is one in which two creatures (or persons) interact with each other and with the world they share. Each person interacts with the other person and with the world they share, the physical objects and states of things that they cohabit. One of the persons reacts to something in the world. The other reacts to both the first person's behavior and that object or state of affairs. If we focus on language and speech, the first person hears the second say "There is a table" in the presence of a table. She takes the first person's utterance to be about the table, and we explain her response by taking her to be responding to behavior, the utterance, as caused by the table and perception of it and as an interpretation of "There is a table" to be referring to the table. In this way, language is objective, and language about the world is empirical. It is objective because the statement is true independently of any particular person's uttering it; it is empirical because similar causes lead to similar reactions.[70] When the first person speaks, the other person, the interlocutor, expects the sentence to be true and interprets the utterance based on this expectation and her observation of the causal connection. She takes the first person, the speaker, to have a true belief about what she perceives; she takes the meaning of the utterance to be such that it enables the belief to be true. She takes the utterance to be about the table. By picking out *the* cause of the first person's belief and utterance, he understands what "table" means.

This sketch of Davidson's argument (or account) is incomplete and schematic, and there are a number of obvious gaps that need to be filled in – for example, about how perception serves to locate *the* cause of the utterance of the speaker and what the perception is of.[71] But what we have described is sufficient for

[68] Donald Davidson, "Reply to Føllesdal," in Hahn (ed.), *The Philosophy of Donald Davidson*, 731.

[69] Donald Davidson, "The Second Person," in *Subjective, Intersubjective, and Objective*, 117; cf. 121.

[70] See Davidson, "The Emergence of Thought" in *Subjective, Intersubjective, and Objective*, 108–30.

[71] See Føllesdal and Davidson's reply; see also Davidson, *Subjective, Intersubjective, and Objective*, 129–30.

us to ask: What contribution does the social aspect, the presence of the second person, make to the possibility of language? Why is a second person needed? Why is language impossible unless the self is communicating with a second person?

For Davidson, we need two persons because language requires meaning, meaning requires truth, and truth requires two people communicating one to the other about the world. That is, we need two persons because we need one to speak and the other to interpret the speech behavior of the first. From the speaker's point of view, we also need something to speak about. But in order to locate that something independently of the speaker's belief or utterance, we need another person to react to the world and to the utterance and to seek to interpret the latter, to seek to understand the utterance's meaning. The second person's role, then, is epistemic, in a broad sense. Her goal is to understand what the speaker is saying; without her, the behavior of uttering sounds has no meaning. She is there, present to the speaker, as a partner in conversation, as someone the speaker wants to communicate with, to whom one wants to say something. And from the other person's point of view, the speaker is a communicator, and she wants to understand what is being communicated to her.

Levinas might very well accept the gist of Davidson's argument. He might agree that language and speech are much more complex overall but that to make sense of how language is objective and empirical, Davidson's argument is ingenious and challenging. He might also see the social or interpersonal dimension of the story as having greater depth than Davidson's claim that speech always requires someone who is being addressed as well as a speaker. Still, I think Levinas would take the account to be incomplete or inadequate in the following way. For Davidson, the other person is present to the speaker as a conversation partner, an interpreter, whose whole point for the speaker is to be one to whom something is said that she can understand, be it information, instructions, or whatever. Levinas would agree that in everyday life speakers engage in a host of linguistic activities with others, among which are such acts of communication. But Levinas would say that the basic sense or meaning of the other person's presence before the speaker is deeper than this and thus that the deepest point or significance of the speaker's communication is deeper than any such speech acts. It is ethical. Before the other person is a potential interpreter, in the everyday sense that she is one to whom words are uttered and whose understanding is expected and sought, the other person is a face. Before she is spoken to, she calls the self into question and demands a response; before I speak to her, she calls out to me and demands from me. If I speak, it is already a way of my expressing or realizing my responsibility to her by accepting her, acknowledging her, and by saying that I will share with her. That is, the speaking *is* a responding; before it is a type of speech activity, it is an ethical act, an acceptance that is most basically a *giving*.

Furthermore, this point means that if Davidson is right and the social world, an intersubjective world, is necessary for the concept of truth, for belief, thought, and language, then this world is preceded by the world of nourishment for the particular I, which is yet to be conceptualized, categorized, understood, and shared. There are no private thoughts or private language; in one sense, the world is social and public through and through, not because it is originally conceptualized – a world about which we believe and speak and thus public in this sense – but because it is a world only insofar as it matters to me, it matters to you, and it matters at all precisely because you matter to me. For Levinas, there are, then, preconceptual relationships between unique persons, and there are preconceptual, prearticulated worlds. But in reality, in everyday life these worlds are socially and collectively, so to speak, one conceptualized world, the object of belief and speech and activity. This unity of the world, the world about which the members of a linguistic community have beliefs and about which they speak to one another, has that unity because we are never, in Levinas's terms, without the third party. But with this unity comes the very point of the world and of speech itself, an ethical point, that speakers are acting out their responsibility to other persons in speaking at all.

Davidson argues that language requires two persons; Levinas claims that it requires three. Who is right? One thought is that they can agree, if we see Levinas's point this way. Language has its original role in judgment and comparison. That role only arises once there is a third party. Nonetheless, Davidson shows us that language itself, to be language, only requires two persons. Levinas can agree, that while the reason for language requires three persons, the possibility for language only requires two. But if so, the second person, in Davidson's scenario of two people communicating about a world they share and perceive together, is already detached, independent, and fills a role. The deep character of the relationship is appreciated only when we realize that the second person faces the speaker before the speaker speaks; she summons the speaker, calls him into question. The two-person, face-to-face encounter may not require judgment, comparison, and such, when we take it to be the utterly particular calling into question of the self by the other person. But if we consider Davidson's two-person encounter as a case of what Levinas calls the presence of the third party, then it does require such comparison and judgment. It is wrong to think that for Levinas thought and language require three persons, while for Davidson they require two. Davidson's interactive, communicative encounter is a case of what Levinas means by a social encounter of persons, including the third party or parties. In other words, Levinas knows that two people regularly converse as communication partners, speaking to one another and interpreting what is said. Not all speech is public, involving three or more parties. But until there are three – or only *because* there are three – language has no role to play in society overall, even if the society is only two people. Levinas's deeper point, however, is that already when and only when there are two persons, one summoning and demanding of the other, does the point of speaking reveal its ethical character. It is helpful to recall that just as all human life is social and hides the dimension of the face-to-face and the responsibility it includes, so also does all human life as a life of thinking and speaking reveal the aspect of the third party. We are never without the third party.

This comparison, I think, shows the role of the face-to-face and the third party in the emergence of language. Levinas is not so much concerned with how language works, semantically, how thoughts and words have the meaning they do and play their roles in communication and other speech activities. What concerns him is the moral depth of linguistic practice, of speaking with one another as already – before anything else it seeks to or does accomplish – an ethical act. There is in language a moral depth that is always present and yet is rarely appreciated.

To conclude, let me summarize how the face-to-face has sense and provides the ground of meaning for cultures. On the one hand, it is the presupposition of all language and discourse. Without the face-to-face, language and discourse are unnecessary, and cultures are constituted linguistically. On the other hand, it also is the ethical point of all interpersonal, social existence, including thought and language, so that it contains a standard for assessing the shapes that languages and cultures take as structures of meaning. The meanings of cultures should be measured against how well or how poorly they express human responsibility, benevolence, and justice.

6

Subjectivity and the Self

One of the most bewildering points that Levinas makes concerns subjectivity and the self.[1] He says that primordially the self or person is passive because it is responsible before anything else. First and foremost, I am summoned and called into question. In Kantian terminology, the self is heteronomous before it is autonomous. It is passive before it is active. Subjectivity is accusation, hostage, obsession, and the like. These features are likely to seem so strange that one can hardly grasp what they mean or even what they *might* mean. This chapter is our opportunity to discuss them and to show that they are extreme and provocative but not at all as bizarre and unintelligible as they first appear.

Shortly, we shall have to consider the story of how modern culture, at least from the seventeenth century, has come to enshrine the subject, the individual, the autonomous, free, rational self, as the fountainhead of knowledge, morality, politics, culture, and even religion. Levinas does not ignore or denigrate this self or this conception of the self as the autonomous, rational individual, but he does reconsider its most fundamental dimension, its essential character, and how that dimension reverberates throughout its existential and historical career. To be sure, he believes that this new understanding of the unique individual person as passive and responsible echoes from the ancient past, but in the modern world it is preempted by another view – modern, individualist, and powerful. Levinas's understanding of the self, then, can be understood from both philosophical and historical points of view; we will be served best if we do not ignore either one.

Levinas's thinking about subjectivity goes back to the 1940s and 1950s, but its culmination is the account of responsibility and substitution in *Otherwise Than*

---

[1] In this chapter, I use the words "subject," "self," and "I" interchangeably, as a matter of convenience. Such usage is fairly standard. For Levinas, of course, it is problematic, especially with regard to the word "subject," as we shall see, but I hope the issues are not confused by holding to standard usage.

Being. I shall say something about his early views but focus on his response, in the later work, to the antihumanist critique of the 1960s.[2] By that decade, it is widely appreciated that the concept of the subject is historical, shaped and constructed by philosophers, religious thinkers, novelists, and political theorists, as well as by less theoretical agencies within cultures and societies. The self is not given as a matter of fact; it is constructed. Michel Foucault explored the construction of the idea of the author in ways helpful to any understanding of the modern subject or individual.[3] Authorship is a particular mode of individuality. Levinas's understanding of the subject is embedded in this debate and in the modern tradition, and without a few words about it, his innovation will hardly be intelligible.

MODERNITY AND THE SELF

When philosophers talk about modern views of subjectivity, the self, or the individual, a number of issues are run together. Obviously, these notions are not modern, post-Renaissance inventions. In the philosophical tradition alone, ignoring religious, political, and legal contexts, the idea of the self or the individual person is at least as old as Heraclitus. Soul or *psyche* was a matter of importance and an object of reflection and examination for Socrates, Plato, Aristotle, the Pythagoreans, Anaxagoras, Empedocles, and virtually all of the Hellenistic schools. What happens in the sixteenth and seventeenth centuries, alongside significant political, social, and economic changes, is that the soul, individual person, or self becomes primary in three areas that themselves carry special weight – epistemology and science, religion and morality, and politics – and thus is distinguished by features in virtue of which it achieves its preeminence.

First, the self becomes primary in the domain of science and epistemology. The self is the investigator, the knower, the agent of examination and understanding. The individual person is preeminently a thinking thing, in Descartes's famous words, a *res cogitans*. In these centuries, a shift occurs; more and more responsibility for the scientific knowledge of nature falls upon the potential knower. Doubts about there being such knowledge, skeptical doubts, challenge the self to find secure grounds, and the Cartesian response, via the *cogito* and its sequel, leads to turmoil about how preeminent the thinking self is, what it grasps and how, and what it is capable of knowing outside of its own contents. To be sure, Descartes is indebted to Augustine, Platonism, Montaigne,

[2] See Simon Critchley, *Ethics, Politics, Subjectivity: Essays on Derrida, Levinas and Contemporary French Thought*, 62.
[3] Michel Foucault, "What Is an Author?" in Paul Rabinow (ed.), *The Foucault Reader* (New York: Pantheon, 1984), 101–20.

and others, but his innovation is to have privileged the thinking self as *the* – or at least – *one* starting point for the achievement of natural philosophy. Originally isolated epistemologically in its lonely confinement, the self or mind grasps its own contents incorrigibly and securely; all other knowledge it must struggle to earn through its own efforts. To the privileged examiner, thinker, and knower, the essential characteristic is impeccable self-knowledge,[4] and it is this self-knowledge that provides the foundation on which science as knowledge of nature, other persons, and even God is grounded.

This epistemologically primary self is also ethically and politically primary. In Hobbes, for example, the individual bearer of natural capacities and desires, each person a dire threat to the other, is the vehicle by which social organization, the state, sovereignty, and law come into being, or, if one eschews a genetic reading of Hobbes, this individual, rational and the locus of desire, is the justification for these institutions. In Locke, the equation of right, liberty, and power is fragmented, and rights as moral claims become the central features of individual dignity and the *raison d'être* for the state and political institutions. Science is based on self-knowledge; morality and politics are based on self-control and the capacity to determine one's choices and actions. Thereby, the moral and political agent comes to be characterized as worthy of respect and capable of autonomous choice – in short, it is free and dignified.[5] This is the second, moral-political primacy that the self achieves in the period from the sixteenth to the eighteenth century.

The self's third dimension of preeminence is religious. To be sure, Christianity – and this includes various Protestant sects as well as the Roman Church – treated God as uniquely primary. But it is clear that various developments, even in Lutheranism and the many forms of Calvinism, granted remarkable new roles to the particular individual, the believer, in the arenas of ritual practice, the interpretation of scripture, and the politics of the Church. And as reason and science attracted greater and greater allegiance, rationalist revisions of Christianity – the Romanstrants in the Netherlands and Latitudinarians in England, for example – gave the individual rational believer an increasingly preeminent part to play in the understanding and practice of faith. In place of a selfless submission to divine will, many saw human rationality as God's means for communicating His revelation and as the human way of teaching and expressing one's faith in God.

---

[4] See Alexander Nehamas, Foreword in Alain Renaut, *The Era of the Individual: A Contribution to a History of Subjectivity*, xii. For important discussions of self-knowledge, see Richard Moran, *Authority and Estrangement: An Essay on Self-Knowledge* (Princeton, NJ: Princeton University Press, 2001), and David Finkelstein, *Expression and the Inner* (Cambridge, MA: Harvard University Press, 2003). For an important collection of essays, see Crispin Wright, Barry C. Smith, and Cynthia Macdonald (eds.), *Knowing Our Own Minds* (Oxford: Oxford University Press, 1998).
[5] Cf. Nehamas, Foreword in Renaut, *The Era of the Individual*, xii.

Throughout the nineteenth and early twentieth centuries, these dimensions of the primacy of the self – what came to be called "humanism" – became entrenched. It changed, was reinterpreted and qualified, and yet persisted, to such a degree that it was hardly ever questioned and even more rarely doubted. To be sure, there were challenges to those who installed the self's autonomy as its preeminent feature, to those who enshrined rationality or self-knowledge. But what was largely accepted without debate was the primacy of subjectivity itself as an all-encompassing starting point, ground, and foundation.

This is the conventional story, one often told and widely endorsed. It deserves some qualification, however. The challenge to this humanism and the unconditional primacy of the subject, the individual self, does not have to wait for Heidegger, as is often thought. For example, in a recent, brilliant analysis of the origins of German Idealism, Fred Beiser has argued for an antisubjectivist reading of the early development of that movement.[6] If Beiser is correct, then German Idealism struggled with its Cartesian and Kantian ancestry and was deeply driven by naturalistic, realist impulses. This reading reminds us how powerful, in the nineteenth century, the naturalistic movement became. Indeed, its twentieth-century legacy, philosophically, has been powerful and perhaps even overpowering. One might read the history of twentieth-century Anglo-American or analytic philosophy as a multifaceted struggle over the hegemony of naturalism, a replaying of the conflicts set by philosophers of earlier eras – Descartes, Hobbes, Spinoza, Leibniz, Hume, and Kant preeminent among them. Analytic philosophers regularly debate the distinctiveness of the human; from the philosophy of mind to ethics and epistemology, arguments over Cartesianism and the legacy of Kant and Aristotle are the ways in which the uniqueness and primacy of the subject, the self, or the human are put to the test. One line of defense ties Plato to Descartes and Kant; another links Aristotle with Hegel and even early Heidegger. The standard defense of the triumph of the subjective is hardly as clear and unqualified as some would have it, nor is any tale that omits naturalism, which is, in some of its forms, its most powerful opponent.

Simon Critchley helpfully suggests that Levinas's understanding of subjectivity is not directly a response to the dominant modern tradition. Rather, as he sees it, it is a response to the "post-structuralist and anti-humanist critique of subjectivity," which Luc Ferry and Alain Renaut call *la pensée '68*.[7] What was that critique, and how, for example, did Ferry and Renaut respond to it?

---

[6] Frederick Beiser, *German Idealism* (Cambridge, MA: Harvard University Press, 2003).

[7] Critchley, *Ethics, Politics, Subjectivity*, 62; see also Luc Ferry and Alain Renaut, *French Philosophy in the Sixties: An Essay on Antihumanism* (Amherst: University of Massachusetts Press, 1990) and *Heidegger and Modernity*, trans. Franklin Philip (Chicago: University of Chicago Press, 1990).

Alexander Nehamas gives an excellent, succinct account in his Foreword to Renaut's *The Era of the Individual*.[8] Ferry and Renaut are part of a defense of liberal democracy, and thus of a kind of humanism, against the antihumanist critique, "the thought of '68," which is a legacy of Heidegger and to a certain degree Marx.[9] To them, Heidegger's attack on modernity and democracy is politically and intellectually objectionable. Ferry and Renaut are committed to the protection of rights and opposition to domination and repression. They take the connections between Heidegger's antimodernism and his associations with Nazism to be grim, authoritarian, and reactionary.[10] While they agree with Heidegger about the alienating and oppressive results of technology and mass culture, Ferry and Renaut do not believe that democracy can be similarly indicted. In the modern, technological world, the individual is the center, as the agent of control and manipulation, but also as the victim of her desires and drives. In democratic society, the individual is also at the center, but, for them, it is as the bearer of rights and the autonomous agent of moral and political action.[11] Heidegger's attack on modernity ends up "throwing out the baby with the bath," for while it is linked both to the same metaphysical tradition and deplores its effects on all subject-centered thinking, rationality, and more, it is also in the end itself heir to the metaphysical tradition it attacks, with its cultivation of a poetic language of Being and its distortions of Plato, the pre-Socratics, and figures like Nietzsche – and of course with its allegiance to right-wing fascist politics.[12]

The "thought of '68," inspired by Heidegger, was indebted to thinkers such as Michel Foucault, Jacques Lacan, Jacques Derrida, Pierre Bourdieu, and Louis Pierre Althusser, all of whom saw the individual or human subject as incapable of the self-knowledge and autonomy once ascribed to it, most notably by the Enlightenment.[13] The human subject was not free of social codes, regimes of domination, and broad social and economic forces, even unconscious psychological ones, that exposed subjectivity as a construct, an artifact of impersonal factors. Ferry and Renaut come on the scene as critics of the critics, of their Heideggerian heritage and of their failure to respect the humanity of the subject. Levinas can be read, then, as an alternative critic, not concerned to protect the subject as the locus of rights and dignity, but rather oriented to humanity

---

[8] See Renaut, *The Era of the Individual*, vii–xviii.

[9] Nehamas, Foreword in Renaut, *The Era of the Individual*, vii–viii.

[10] Nehamas, Foreword in Renaut, *The Era of the Individual*, viii.

[11] They owe a significant debt to J. G. Fichte and his *Foundations of Natural Right* (*Grundlage der Naturrechts*) (Cambridge: Cambridge University Press, 2000).

[12] Nehamas, Foreword in Renaut, *The Era of the Individual*, x–xiv.

[13] See Simon Critchley and Peter Dews (eds.), *Deconstructive Subjectivities* (Albany, NY: SUNY Press, 1996), and Eduardo Cadava, Peter Connor, and Jean-Luc Nancy (eds.), *Who Comes after the Subject?* (London: Routledge, 1991).

in a different way. What we need to clarify is the nature of Levinas's alternative humanism.

I suggested earlier that in the analytic tradition, the main challenge to the centrality of the subject has come from a certain form of naturalism.[14] This suggestion should not be misunderstood. It is not my intention to claim that analytic philosophy has not primarily been occupied with human-centered matters. It has. Analytic philosophers have been centrally concerned to explore and understand language, moral conduct, epistemological issues, art, science, and similar human activities, primarily by starting with the subject and the subject-object dualism. My point is rather that certain types of philosophical, reductive naturalism deal with these issues by placing human beings within the order of nature as understood by the natural and social sciences, but fundamentally by biology and physics. In this sense, then, the human subject no longer is treated as unique and privileged but rather as similar to other natural beings and ultimately comprehensible like any other natural being. This perspective on human affairs was canonized in the seventeenth century by Spinoza when, in the preface to Part 3 of the *Ethics*, he pointed out that human emotions should be analyzed and understood just like any other natural phenomena.[15] Materialists like Hobbes were even more thoroughgoing than Spinoza in carrying out this project, in analyzing desire, emotions, deliberation, and indeed all mental events in terms of motion. Such reductive naturalism may still concede the primacy of the human in various ways, but only by stripping it of many of its essential features, most notably (then) free will and immortality. Today, the targets of such naturalistic explanation and the venues of debates over how radical naturalism must be include intentionality and representation, epistemology, consciousness, and morality, among others. As we try to clarify and understand Levinas's conception of subjectivity, then, it will be important to see how his views look alongside both such naturalistic accounts and those of critics of them. Among those whose work will be useful are Davidson, McDowell, and Taylor, but they are only some among many.[16]

I have been trying to place in broad strokes where Levinas stands in twentieth-century views about the self and its roles in our thinking, society, culture, and life overall. In the last century, as I have suggested, the primacy of the subject was challenged from a number of quarters – political, religious, philosophical, and scientific. My emphasis here has been on two philosophical critiques: the

[14] A helpful set of essays is Mario De Caro and David Macarthur (eds.), *Naturalism in Question* (Cambridge, MA: Harvard University Press, 2004).
[15] Baruch (Benedictus) de Spinoza, *Ethics*, Part III, Preface; see also *Spinoza: Complete Works,* trans. Samuel Shirley (Cambridge, MA: Hackett Publishing, 2002), 277–78.
[16] Also Stanley Cavell, P. F. Strawson, Derek Parfit, Fred Dretske, Daniel Dennett, Allan Gibbard, Simon Blackburn, Peter Railton, and Hilary Putnam.

Heideggarian and postmodernist critique and the scientific, naturalist one. These are expressions of totalization in the arena of the individual, ways in which the idealism of totality is compromised in antihumanistic ways or in ways that qualify unconditional anthropocentrism. Levinas, in his unique manner, wants to recover that anthropocentrism. It is tempting to take him to be rejecting anthropocentrism in favor of the primacy of the other. I want to show that this interpretation is a mistake. Levinas's humanism does refer to the role of the face of the other for the subject or self, but it is clearly an effort to rethink anthropocentrism and not to replace it.[17] In the course of this chapter, I shall try to show how this is so.

THE EARLY STAGE

In order to simplify matters, let me look at Levinas's treatment of the self in two stages, first in *Time and the Other*, *Totality and Infinity*, and early essays and then in his more developed views in *Otherwise Than Being*. What are the essential features of human subjectivity? What gives human subjectivity its basic character? What distinguishes the self from other individual entities?

Earlier, we discussed Levinas's genetic account in *Time and the Other* that traces the emergence of the subject, its situation in the world, and its engagement with the human other.[18] I explained that this account should not be interpreted literally, as if the subject actually emerges in stages; rather, it should be read as an examination of those features that distinguish human subjectivity from natural existence. Here we will look at those features in order to give some shape to Levinas's early conception of the self or human existence.[19]

A schematic picture of conceptions of the self in modern Western philosophy will provide us with a map on which to locate Levinas's thinking.[20] In Descartes, the self is the I of the *cogito*; it is essentially a container for ideas or a center of consciousness, and consciousness is an awareness or representation of something. Primarily, the self's consciousness or its ideas are cognitive; the I is an observer and investigator. It is an enclosed mental container that seeks to direct itself to what is outside – the world – in order to see it clearly and understand it; to see it means, of course, first to receive contents that come to it from the world. The self, in this period, then, is predominantly the theoretical subject. In Spinoza

---

[17] Critchley agrees. See his *Ethics, Politics, Subjectivity*, 67. Levinas himself titles one of his collections of essays *Humanism of the Other*; he regularly refers to his view as a form of humanism and to Judaism as an "austere humanism."

[18] See Ch. 2.

[19] Not what makes it an individual, but what makes it *human*.

[20] There are many places to go for such a picture – for example, books by Alain Renaut and David Carr.

and others, this theoretical self is enriched by adding emotional states, desires, and a variety of noncognitive features that link the self to the world and issue in action.[21] And in Hume, the character of the subject is questioned, but still on the basis of the same model, of a theoretical and practical container of ideas or impressions that represent and reach out to a world independent of that self. It is a picture deepened but not basically altered in Kant and the German Idealists who follow him.

With Husserl, this intellectualist picture is modified insofar as intentionality ties consciousness to objects in a variety of ways, but always in an integrated nexus rather than as a relationship between an isolated, enclosed self and an external, separated world. In Heidegger and Wittgenstein, this embeddedness of self in the world is emphasized, and the modes of this embeddedness are practical, emotional, and more, embracing all the ways that human beings exist in the public world. It is at this point that we can locate Levinas. For him, the self is not simply embedded or situated in the world. Nor is its life in the social, public world simply various and multifaceted. For Levinas, each of us is a subject in the world encountered by another person. In his early work, like *Time and the Other*, then, his account of how the subject is in the world *prior* to its encounter with the face of the other person is tailored to expose those features of the self's relation to the world without which the face-to-face encounter could not occur and make sense. As presented in these early accounts, it would seem that the self exists *prior* to the face-to-face; it lives in the world, enjoys its resources, and fulfills itself through work and appropriation. But in another sense, of course, there is no self prior to the encounter with the other. Levinas calls this self "ipseity," but in reality the self never exists as ipseity.[22] The world we live in is social before it is a world at all. But what does this mean? In what sense is the self, as Levinas sees it, an ethical, responsible, and responsive self before it is anything at all? It is time to turn to Levinas's own discussion, to see how he approaches these themes in his own words and to see exactly how he stakes out new territory in this conception of the self.

Levinas gives a summary of the first stages of his account of the self, prior to its encounter with other persons, at the beginning of Part III of *Time and the Other*. "I have dealt," he says, "with the subject alone, alone due to the very fact that it is an existent."[23] Levinas calls this aloneness "solitude" and describes it as "the indissoluble unity between the existent and its work of existing."[24] This

---

[21] This is not to say that Descartes ignored the affective dimensions of subjectivity; they were his focus of attention in the late work, *The Passions of the Soul*. And such states were also of great interest to someone like Hobbes. But for Descartes, the self is primarily a theoretical subject.

[22] See Gibbs, *Correlations in Rosenzweig and Levinas*, 28, 181–182.

[23] TO, 67.

[24] TO, 43.

sounds very obscure indeed, and what follows no less so. This solitude or unity, between a being and what it is for it to be, is overcome, when consciousness arises, and the existent "is put in touch with its existing." The I arises and with it freedom, the freedom of beginning, "starting out from something now." This is "the freedom of the existent in its very grip of existing."[25] The I can now exercise the "work of existing," and this *work* is the subject's "mastery over existing," its "power of beginning, of starting out from itself, starting out from itself neither to act nor to think, but to be."[26]

Let me try to paraphrase Levinas's account to this point. In everyday life, each of us is related to things around us, classified, compared, and contrasted; but at the same time, each of us is fundamentally unique as an existing thing. Levinas calls this existing or being, which each of us manifests or realizes uniquely, prior to the emergence of unique existents from it, the *there-is* [*il y a*].[27] I will here ignore his treatment of it; for us, the important point is that when a person distinguishes itself by taking a grip on his process of existing, Levinas associates this unique event with consciousness and becoming an I or, because he denies that the I is a substance or entity, with becoming a subjective mode of existing. This means that existing for a person occurs as a unique locus for beginning or starting out.[28] Levinas calls this "freedom," prior to free will. It is akin to what Kant calls "spontaneity" or "metaphysical freedom." In our everyday lives, then, we are many things; we act, think, and choose, and what makes this possible for us as the person each of us is is our being an I, which is a center of spontaneous origination. This is, he says, to have "something in its power."[29] It is "first freedom." The basic feature of subjectivity, then, is this metaphysical or existential freedom, the capacity to initiate action, in a broad sense.

The I frees itself from anonymous being and yet becomes bound to itself. It cares about itself; it is "mired in itself." Identity, Levinas says, is a "return to self"; it is "occupied with itself," and the way this occurs is called "materiality." Freed from the anonymity of existing, I am chained to myself and "responsible" for myself, for my body as my way of being in the world. I am "encumbered." "Matter is the misfortune of hypostasis" – of the self or the I – and "everyday

---

[25] TO, 53, 54.

[26] TO, 67.

[27] TO, 46; the *there-is* is the central theme of Levinas's book *Existence and Existents*. As I will discuss in Chapter 7, the *there-is* expresses itself in our everyday lives as the natural dimension of such lives, whereas *illeity*, which manifests itself in religious language about God and theology, expresses itself as the evaluative and ethical dimension of our lives. The *there-is*, then, is *Ur-Natur*, as it were.

[28] One might compare Hannah Arendt on natality. See Margaret Canovan, *Hannah Arendt: A Reinterpretation of Her Political Thought* (Cambridge: Cambridge University Press, 1992), 130–31.

[29] TO, 54.

life is a preoccupation with salvation."[30] Hence, if the self starts out in freedom, it then finds itself in need and with the task of satisfying those needs. Here is its second fundamental feature.

How is the self related to the world? Through its body (broadly speaking), its needs, Levinas says, and then by finding sustenance for that body and satisfying those needs in the world. With an obvious critical nod to Heidegger, he says that "prior to being a system of tools, the world is an ensemble of nourishments."[31] Moreover, living in the world and being nourished by it involve a variety of fulfillments, satisfying our hunger, our sense of smell and touch. All of this Levinas calls "enjoyment,"[32] a posture of assimilating the world and yet remaining separate from it, of being hindered by oneself and fulfilled by the world. It is, he says, "first morality," for while it involves absorbing the world, it also requires a kind of self-abnegation: "[T]he subject is absorbed in the object it absorbs."[33] This is morality as self-forgetfulness.

In Levinas's early work, to this point, the self is characterized as being free, needful, and enjoying the world; it is the locus of self-initiating engagement with a world that it needs and that nourishes it. These three features of human existence, however, are only a kind of preparation for what makes that existence distinctively human. We might say that these dimensions are true of other natural beings and their modes of existing, just as they are true of human beings. Human beings, as natural beings, are not alone in needing the world to live, in being nourished by that world, and being capable of some kind of action in behalf of gaining that nourishment. Of course, that capacity for gaining nourishment is not the same kind of capacity that human beings have, the capacity to initiate, to be an origin, and the satisfaction gained is not enjoyment *per se* but nonetheless a kind of fulfillment. Still, if we take Levinas's account of these three features to be "tailored" to his primary interest, which is the character of human existence, there is a sense in which these three focus on what we might see as the "natural" aspects of human existence and not the distinctively human dimension. They do not, by themselves, shed light on the humanity Levinas is seeking to disclose. So far, in a sense, the I, like other natural beings, is enclosed in the world; it has emerged from a preconceptual and precognitive domain and has settled into everyday life, into the ordinary and natural world, into totality, into a life and a world structured and organized by culture, thought, rules, and principles.

I do not want to belabor Levinas's argument as it proceeds from here, but it is important to appreciate that he does in fact have one. Its basic structure is this:

---

[30] TO, 55–57, 67.

[31] TO, 63.

[32] TO, 63.

[33] TO, 67.

The self and its materiality need the world's nourishment and sustenance, but this – enjoyment – requires appropriation and work. The world, in other words, needs to be "conquered." But work is an expression of effort and brings with it pain, sorrow, and suffering.[34] "In suffering there is the absence of refuge. It is the fact of being directly exposed to being. It is made up of the impossibility of fleeing or retreating ... of being backed up against life and being." Hence, suffering brings with it the "proximity of death."[35] Levinas then argues that death is a mystery; and yet when death is introduced through suffering, the subject experiences passivity; death presents itself as "an event in relation to which the subject is no longer a subject."[36] It is the "end of mastery" and "indicates that we are in relation with something that is absolutely other."[37] Existence is plural. Outside of me and my world is some other, which in this case is the other as a mystery.[38]

To this point, then, Levinas has argued that the self must confront suffering and death and that death brings with it an encounter with the other, alterity, something that transcends the totality of natural, everyday life and theorizing about it.[39] Levinas's next step is to show that the self must encounter not only the *other as mystery* but also the other as other persons. The mysterious death in question here, that first introduces the reality of otherness, so to speak, is my death, and it seems paradoxical to speak of an encounter with it. I may expect it or fear it, but to encounter it seems self-defeating, for death crushes the self and its freedom; it is a negation of the very subject that we might take to be experiencing it. In view of this apparent paradox about the encounter with the other, Levinas thus asks: "How can a being enter into relation with the other without allowing its very self to be crushed by the other?"[40] Is there an other to which the self can be related without being destroyed by it? Levinas's answer to this problem of transcendence is: when the relationship with the other is the

[34] TO, 68.

[35] TO, 68–69.

[36] TO, 70.

[37] TO, 74.

[38] TO, 76. Note that, as Levinas proceeds, the experience that gives us a model of the relation with the other is *erotic*. Death is the mystery that first "introduces" the other and the notion of the other, but it is not the "mode of otherness," so to speak, that proves to be fundamental and determinative. It is not one's own death that matters most to the self but rather the death of the other person.

[39] Later, in "Transcendence and Evil" in Levinas, *Collected Philosophical Papers*, 175–86, and in "Useless Suffering," *Entre Nous*, 91–101, Levinas gives an account of suffering that takes suffering to be an experience of an other. Indeed, even in his early period the *there-is* is already an experience of an other, which occurs in our lives in the experiences of insomnia and nausea. Such a focus on limit-experiences as evidence of access to the other is already found in *On Escape* and *Existence and Existents*.

[40] TO, 77.

"face-to-face," where the face "at once gives and conceals the other."[41] That is, to confront my own death is to encounter negation by the other; to confront the other's death is to encounter an other that threatens me and yet does not negate me but calls me to fulfillment. Here, then, we find a determination or feature of the self that lies in its passivity and yet in which the self is not "crushed" or destroyed.[42] Insofar as the self must confront the other in order to be a self, the other it must confront is the face of the other person that both maintains its otherness and yet imposes itself on the self as other. The self in the face-to-face is wholly passive and yet not negated or destroyed; it is burdened, called into question, and yet summoned.

Levinas, then, has tried to show that work, suffering, and death are not contingent; they are part of human life – undeniably, he argues. Similarly, he must show that the face-to-face is essential to our lives, or, in other words, that interpersonal existence or social life is natural and unremarkable, even if too often we forget its character and its significance for us. Even if we lived a life of total isolation, stranded on a desert island without actual companions, human life is still essentially social.[43] This is what Levinas must show. He puts it this way: "If the relationship with the other involves more than relationships with mystery, it is because one has accosted the other in everyday life where the solitude and fundamental alterity of the other are already veiled by decency."[44] Basically, the other person faces us in everyday life as a free subject with needs. In ordinary experience, "decency" hides the unique character of the other person; I treat her according to rules or expectations, manners, politeness, and so forth. But alongside all of this formality is the brute otherness that she bears to me; and in this unique state of confronting me, she is "the weak, the poor, 'the widow and the orphan', whereas I am the rich or the powerful."[45] In the most primary sense, each and every other person confronts me as one who has-not to one who has.

In *Time and the Other*, Levinas proceeds to clarify this encounter with the face of the other person as an asymmetrical relationship. This clarification takes the form of a quasi-phenomenological account of the erotic relationship.[46] Here

[41] TO, 78–79.

[42] TO, 81–82.

[43] Heidegger makes just this sort of point in his account of *Mitsein* in *Being and Time* (New York: Harper, 1962), Section 26, 156–57. For Heidegger, that is, being-with is an ontological and not an ontic point about human existence. For Levinas, the face-to-face and responsibility are pre ontological.

[44] TO, 82.

[45] TO, 83.

[46] By "quasi-phenomenological," I mean that it is like a phenomenological description even though it is preexperiential and so, technically speaking, an account of a dimension of interpersonal experience that cannot be experienced, that does not "appear" and cannot present itself

he employs and develops a gendered vocabulary: eros, the feminine, modesty, the caress, fecundity, and paternity. It is a vocabulary and an account extensively elaborated in *Totality and Infinity* and widely discussed (and criticized).[47] Given our earlier discussion in Chapter 2, however, we need go no further.[48]

RESPONSIBILITY AND PASSIVITY

I have taken the time to outline and paraphrase Levinas's early conception of subjectivity in order to highlight two problems. Levinas sees the self or the subject as free, needful, and immersed joyfully in the world;[49] he also sees it as passive before the face of the other person. To be sure, the self suffers, anticipates death, and bears children, but these activities and attitudes are in addition to the fundamental ones. There are two central questions, then, that this account must confront and answer. The first is how Levinas's view of the totalized subject, as I shall call it – free, needful, and joyous – should be understood, especially when compared with other contemporary views. The second is how we should understand the passivity of the subject in virtue of the face-to-face and the role of that passivity. In what sense is it a passivity prior to activity and prior to freedom? But before we consider these issues, we should turn to *Otherwise Than Being*, where Levinas's conception of the subject is most fully developed.

In *Time and the Other* and *Totality and Infinity*, Levinas uses a dialectical narrative to display the basic features of subjectivity, as I have just reviewed them, and he then carries out a quasi-phenomenological description of *eros* in order to clarify the face-to-face and the subject's passivity before the other person. In the essay "Substitution" (1968) and then in *Otherwise Than Being* (1974), Levinas focuses on the nature of subjectivity with a new set of terms and new interests, elaborating the earlier view by clarifying and deepening the understanding of the self's passivity, especially as part of a treatment of language. Levinas uses a number of new expressions and develops old ones: "responsibility," "substitution," "obsession," "hostage," "accusation," "persecution," "subjection," "saying,"

---

just as it is. Phenomenological description occurs at the level of what Levinas calls "ontology" or at the level of concrete, everyday experience, whereas the face-to-face "interrupts" ontology and is of a different order or status. But Levinas's description of the erotic experience seeks to use phenomenological method to clarify, articulate, and disclose the features of the face-to-face in a way that is similar to the way that such a method aims at the directly grasped sense or meaning of various modes of everyday experience.

[47] TI, Section IV, 251–85.

[48] It is worthwhile to look at Levinas's discussion of paternity and fecundity, where he answers the question he had raised about enduring the encounter with the other. This would provide the last ingredient in his early conception of subjectivity; see TO, 91. One's child is an other who is independent and yet who commands responsibility and devotion unqualifiedly.

[49] Cf. TI, 110–51.

"proximity," and more. Many of these terms intensify the sense of passivity of the self's relation to the other person and emphasize precisely what seems so paradoxical, that the self is passive, obligated, and burdened, prior to being free and active – that, in a sense, the self is object before it is subject. Before we can consider why Levinas says such things and whether they can be justified, we need to ask what they mean and how they add to our understanding of human social existence.

Subjectivity, the self, or the human individual is beyond freedom; it is "responsibility for the faults or the misfortunes of others" and "cannot have begun in my commitment, in my decision." It is the "null-site" where the Good "has chosen me before I have chosen it."[50] I am commanded to and by the other, who "provokes this responsibility against my will . . . by substituting me for the other as a hostage. . . . I am ordered toward the face of the other."[51] The self, then, is responsibility in response to a trauma, before understanding, "for a debt contracted before any freedom and before any consciousness." Subjectivity is the point where "essence is exceeded by the infinite." Levinas calls this point a "breakup of identity" and a "subjection to everything," a vulnerability. He summarizes these descriptions in a passage that reveals how developed his conception of the human subject has become:

Vulnerability, exposure to outrage, to wounding, passivity more passive than all patience, passivity of the accusative form, trauma of accusation suffered by a hostage to the point of persecution, implicating the identity of the hostage who substitutes himself for the others: all this is the self, a defecting or defeat of the ego's identity.[52]

The central idea here, which we need to examine and clarify, is substitution. Fundamentally, the self should not be characterized as the subject of theory and thought[53] or as the subject of action and *praxis*.[54] The self is not first of all an actor or agent. From the first, the self is animated by responsibility; it is, in Levinas's words, saying and substitution. In *Otherwise Than Being*, Levinas does not ignore the other features of the self: its freedom and uniqueness, needfulness, and enjoyment.[55] He calls this unity the "subjectivity of flesh and blood in matter."[56] But his attention is ultimately on the prior or more fundamental subjectivity that he characterizes as responsibility, saying, and substitution. These other features – freedom, needfulness, and enjoyment, which ground, in a sense,

[50] OB, 8, 10, 57, 102.
[51] OB, 11.
[52] OB, 15; cf. 54.
[53] Cf. OB, 23–26.
[54] Cf. OB, 53.
[55] See OB, 65–81.
[56] OB, 78.

any accounts of the theoretical and practical agent, are not as important to him, for they do not show, as responsibility and substitution do, the purpose of human existence and its essentially social nature.

Having said this much about the subject or subjectivity in *Otherwise Than Being*, I now need to provide some clarification. Commentators regularly cite passages like the ones I have quoted and repeat what Levinas has said, most commonly his unusual vocabulary. But his intent was in part to show the limitations of prior discussions, from Descartes to Heidegger, and to shock his readers into seeing things differently. That can hardly be the goal of commentators. Even the best of these readers formulate important problems about the idea of the subject, only to lapse into citation or paraphrase of Levinas's unusual and surprising expression when it comes to introducing his own thoughts. But this strategy is even less satisfying than providing a traveler with a guidebook and then leaving her at the border of a foreign country without an entry visa.

Many of the terms for this basic level of subjectivity or primary dimension of the self are terms that dramatize the self's passivity vis à vis the face of the other person: The self is accused, obsessed, persecuted, and subjected. The self is made the hostage of the other person; it substitutes for the other person. By itself, such vocabulary is vivid and colorful and seems not to be problematic. We have no trouble understanding what it means to be accused by another person of a fault or injury, to be persecuted by someone who dominates us, and to be subjected to questioning or even demands by one who confronts us. But while Levinas draws on the normal uses of these words, he does so in order to place them in a wholly unique context. For the self that is persecuted has no identity, cannot be said to be, is not conscious or an object of conscious experience, is not a collection of features or properties, is not free to choose or act, and more. In some sense, that is, the self's being persecuted or subjected or accused is primary, first, "an-archic" insofar as it is prior to all beginnings, and so prior to freedom and agency. This vocabulary, then, aside from the drama and intensity it wants to suggest, is intended to point to a truly radical passivity; as Levinas says, it is a passivity that is prior to the passive-active distinction altogether. What, however, does this mean? What could it mean? It is one thing to be persecuted before one has done anything, even to be accused prior to any action, but it is wholly inconceivable how one can be subjected in these ways, from the outside, when one cannot be said to be or to have identity or to be an object of conscious experience. The former conduct might be challenged, as unwarranted or unfair; the latter is intended to precede the very distinction between justified and unjustified persecution or accusation. It is intended to call attention to a fundamental, primary, and unique kind of passivity.

Levinas also says that the subject is substitution, responsibility, and a hostage – all with respect to the other person. If the earlier set of terms looked at the self from the other person's point of view, so to speak, these look at it from the self's own perspective. Of course, Levinas would never put it this way, but it is helpful to notice that he extends his terminology in part to describe the face-to-face and the subject from all possible perspectives. Moreover, he does not say that the self is responsible or substitutes for the other; more precisely, he says that subjectivity – what it means for the self to be a subject – *is responsibility*; it *is substitution*; it *is a hostage*. But in all these cases, the self is these before it acts, before it thinks, before it chooses, before it does anything, and before it is free, that is, before it is capable of originating or initiating anything. Once again, then, we find Levinas saying things that seem to make no sense; he asks us to grasp that the self is capable of and required to respond and that it stands in for the other, before the self is or is free or is capable of acting at all.

Levinas himself appreciates that we might, in fact, be confused by all this. At a crucial point, in the central chapter of *Otherwise Than Being*, he asks: "But how does the passivity of the self become a 'hold on oneself'? If that is not just a play on words, does it not presuppose an activity behind the absolutely anarchical passivity of obsession, a clandestine and dissimulated freedom?" The question has been answered, he says, with the notion of substitution.[57] In the remaining sections of the chapter, he explains how this is so.

What does Levinas mean by this account of subjectivity? How does substitution solve the problem of how passivity can also be a kind of activity – of how it can be prior to both ordinary activity and ordinary passivity and yet be what it is: responsibility?

If we take the notion of priority temporally, we are surely in trouble. Either the notion of passivity and its surrogates are wholly equivocal and mean nothing like what they normally do, in which case responsibility and the like are obscure and mysterious, or we are asked to understand and accept that such a capacity or state is coherent even if without a subject or agent. Suppose, then, that the priority is conceptual. What could this mean? What sense does it make to say that being responsible or accused or obsessed is conceptually prior to being free? I think that we can dispense with these and similar attempts to read Levinas's conception of subjectivity as passivity; all lead to obvious incoherence and impenetrability.

We get closer to Levinas's meaning, as I have suggested, if we think of the self as passivity as a transcendental condition, and this suggestion is akin to thinking about the priority as conceptual, for it directs us to ask: a transcendental condition for what? And how is it such a condition? Indeed, here we seem to be on familiar ground; this reading might be understood as Levinas's version of Husserl's transcendental idealism, with the responsible self replacing Husserl's

[57] OB, 113.

transcendental ego and the Kantian unity of apperception as a transcendental condition of human existence. John Drabinski has suggested such a reading, and it is hinted at in the work of Theodor de Boer.[58] On this reading, the responsible, passive self is the transcendental condition for the possibility of everyday experience, not precisely insofar as it is experience, but rather insofar as it is meaningful, social human existence. As we have seen in Chapter 4, the face-to-face and the responsible self – they are one thing characterized from two perspectives – are what give language, thought, communication, and social life point and purpose. Hence, everyday human life is meaningful and significant as human (and social) only because of the responsible self. The self as responsibility and substitution is the transcendental condition for meaningful human life, for the ordinary and the everyday as the fabric of social, intersubjective, and interactive human experience. Ethics is the metaphysics of meaningful human existence.

This proposal, however, can be developed by realizing, as we have done before, that such a condition is not a postulated entity or a theoretical discovery or construct. Rather it is a *dimension* or *cluster of dimensions* of everyday experience that may rarely – or all too rarely – be in view or that are obscured by contemporary life and culture. Alternatively, we might say that Levinas wants us to see everyday life from a different perspective, one that is determinative of what meaning that life has as social and ethical. On this reading, the transcendental condition of the responsible self is not an *object* of theoretical, philosophical insight; it is a *feature* of our lives that we regularly fail to grasp and therefore a mode of existence that we fail to live or act on. If, on the one hand, we ask about our identities or egos, about our character as cognitive agents, practical actors, and free agents, and what it is for us to be such selves, the answers to these questions can be given by looking at the self or subject in various ways. But if we seek, on the other hand, to understand what the *point* of our theoretical selfhood is or what the *significance* is of our practical agency, the answer to *that* question drives us ultimately to the self's responsibility, to its character as substitution, hostage, and so forth.

If we ask, then, what the agency or selfhood is to which responsibility or substitution is ascribed, the answer is: our normal, everyday selves. The priority of responsibility does not mean we should reject our normal understanding that there must be some person to whom we ascribe responsibility; what it means is that my being responsible is what ultimately gives point to my being me at all. There is no time when I am responsible and not yet an I, although there certainly are times when I am I, in any number of ways, and yet am not responsible or, perhaps better, do not act responsibly.

[58] See Drabinski, *Sensibility and Singularity* and De Boer, *The Rationality of Transcendence*.

When Levinas says that the subject is responsibility before it does anything, then, this should not be read temporally. It is puzzling, but in the end it is not obscure. For what it means is that whenever I am engaged with another person or persons, whatever I am doing, my relationships and my actions are ultimately of significance, in a sense before I am who I am and before my capacity to think or act, precisely because of the capacity I have and the necessity that falls on me to respond to that other person's needs and very existence. I may be blind to this capacity and necessity to respond – my responsibility as responsivity[59] – but it is always there, an aspect of me and my relationship with each and every other person, whether I realize it or not. Hence, in a sense, I am always, in whatever I do, satisfying its directions or failing to do so, unavoidably. I am responsible for and to the other person "before" I am a person, but now we can see that this shocking statement is no contradiction; it is not as paradoxical as it seems. Rather, it is Levinas's attempt to unsettle us into seeing our ordinary, everyday life in a different way.[60]

Different from what? Here it is helpful not to return to the sketch of modern individualism that I gave earlier and the historical context of Levinas's account. We are better served if I call attention to other treatments of the subject or the self in order to clarify Levinas's account and to identify what makes it distinctive. Commentators regularly turn to Heidegger and Derrida, Descartes and Kant for such comparisons, but I shall look elsewhere.

THE SELF AND CONTEMPORARY PHILOSOPHY

Subjectivity and the self in contemporary philosophy are not one problem or issue. Rather, they invoke a whole set of issues and problems, among them the notion of the mind, consciousness, self-identity, self-knowledge, freedom and responsibility, the emotions, and the nature of the first-person point of view. Discussions range over topics in metaphysics, epistemology, language and meaning, ethics, and political philosophy. No one now ignores the fact that human persons have mental and physical dimensions, but philosophers differ dramatically about what the mental is, how it is related to the body, and how the individual should be understood within nature, on the one hand, and within society and culture, on the other. Often philosophers distinguish their views by starting out differently and focusing on one problem or a cluster of them, using this starting point to bring into line a host of other issues. At times, as one scans recent work, the contributions seem incommensurable, or alternatively

---

[59] See Critchley, *Ethics, Politics, Subjectivity*, 62; cf. Martin Buber as well, in "Dialogue" in *Between Man and Man* (New York: Macmillan, 1965), 1–39.

[60] These paragraphs are my reading of OB, 113–18.

a number of ways of classifying them come to mind. I have no interest in a survey or in such classification; what I want to do is to look at a few interesting proposals and contributions that make important claims about what it means to be a human subject or a self and to understand that meaning alongside Levinas's view. Can we see Levinas as engaging in a conversation with contemporary analytic philosophy regarding the nature of subjectivity?

The concept of the subject or person occurs in recent philosophical discourse in a variety of contexts, and it is analyzed and developed for a variety of purposes. The human subject, or the person, means several things. This fact poses a problem for us. Of these conceptions, we can ask: Is this one an attempt to understand the moral self or the agent of action or the epistemological self or the language speaker or the everyday, existential self? Is this conception an attempt to clarify how the person is like or unlike an animal or a computer or a robot? Is it an attempt to identify the scope of moral principles, who is obligated to them or whom they apply to? Is it aimed at defining the subject of rights or the subject of virtues? The subject of consciousness or the scientific investigator or the subject of ordinary beliefs, desires, and other propositional attitudes? Levinas's conception of the responsible self seems to be addressed to an interest in what makes human subjectivity distinctive. Some, but not all, recent analytic discussions deal with the same or a similar question. Certainly, there are features that philosophers have regularly treated as ones that make human existence distinctive – different from that of animals, machines, and gods – and it might be best to look at examples of these, features like freedom, rationality, self-knowledge, self-interpretation, and linguistic ability.

Levinas, at one time or another, discusses all of these features. He certainly is aware that human beings and communities have them and that they are important and perhaps even distinctive. Broadly speaking, however, he thinks that they are characteristic of human life and thought insofar as it is totality, part of a comprehensive natural order, articulated by means of concepts and categories, and understood by theories at different levels and in different ways. What Levinas denies is that any such feature tells the whole story about human subjectivity, and in some of these cases he might believe that a view tells the wrong story. In some cases, that is, Levinas's conception of the responsible self might be compatible with but richer than another account, supplementing it with something that, he believes, is missing. In Chapter 5, I tried to show, for example, that one might take his understanding of the face-to-face as *saying* in this way when set alongside accounts of the public character of thought and language, Davidson's among them. But in other cases, Levinas's conception would find current accounts of distinctively human features, activities, and abilities to be misguided and distorting, in fact false to the human condition. Any account, for example, that wholly ignores the human body and its place in human subjectivity, Levinas would surely find objectionable, as he would any account that ignores or treats reductively cognitive, emotional, and in general mental acts. Nor would he countenance any atomist views, as Taylor calls them.[61] Levinas clearly takes the human subject to be a unity of the mental and the physical and to be essentially immersed in the world, related to it and to other persons like herself. This is clear from *Time and the Other* and *Totality and Infinity* and the dialectical examination of the person as free, needful, and nourished through enjoyment of the world, and as the subject of work, suffering, and death.

For reasons like this, it will be more illuminating to consider Levinas vis à vis those who like him treat the human subject as part of a person-world-social world nexus, those in the Hegelian and Wittgenstinian tradition, or neo-Aristotelians. All are communitarian and historicist, to one degree or another, and the spirit of their work suggests affinities with Hegel and Heidegger; such philosophers include Donald Davidson, John McDowell, and Charles Taylor. This is not to say that these philosophers form a group that can be simply and neatly defined. Among them, they certainly differ in very important ways. It is rather to suggest that we can usefully place Levinas best by considering these figures, given their differences, because in basic terms they and he do share significant similarities. They are certainly not the only analytic philosophers of the self who do so, but they are a good sample.[62]

I shall begin by looking at the conception of the self in Davidson, for whom the ways in which the self, the other person, and the world engage one another are central to his conception of thought, language, and rationality. But Davidson's holism would, I believe, leave out too much for Levinas; the Davidsonian self is naturalistic and rationalist in ways that Levinas could not accept. To reveal at least some of what Davidson does not account for, I turn to McDowell and his "naturalism of second nature" to introduce the contributions of community, culture, and tradition. To see how these features of human situatedness enter into our identity as modern selves, however, and to appreciate the role of history more substantially, it will be helpful to move from McDowell to Taylor, whose conception of human agency invokes background and context from an early stage in Taylor's work and ramifies such conditions in his important book *Sources of the Self*. In the end, however, even Taylor's account, much as it relies upon the role of value and ethics in the constitution of modern identity, differs

---

[61] See Charles Taylor, "Atomism" in *Philosophy and the Human Sciences* (Philosophical Papers 2) (Cambridge: Cambridge University Press, 1985), 187–210; and Onora O'Neill, *Towards Justice and Virtue*, 40–42.

[62] Others who come to mind are Bernard Williams and, more recently, Richard Moran, *Authority and Estrangement: An Essay on Self-Knowledge* (Princeton, NJ: Princeton University Press, 2001).

in significant ways from Levinas's conception of the self. The main purpose of these final sections of this chapter is to show clearly what those differences are.

As we turn to these philosophers and the features they take to be essential to human subjectivity – for example, rationality and freedom, I want to keep in mind that the issue of compatibility or conflict is only one question that is important. Another, which is of paramount importance, is the following: Not only do many of Levinas's formulations seem paradoxical; they also point to problems that are especially highlighted by looking at these other philosophical accounts of the self. For example, if one takes freedom and responsibility to be characteristic of human decision making and action, then how can one be responsible before one is free, before one has even done anything, and before one has any grasp of the other person to whom and for whom one is responsible? How can the other person, as she faces you, mean something to you; how can her suffering and need show itself to you; how can her presence somehow pose a question or make a command – all of this prior to thought, language, and rationality on your part? Such questions concern the very intelligibility of the face-to-face and hence of responsibility, substitution, persecution, and so forth. At the same time, then, they also raise the question of whether Levinas's conception of the human subject as responsibility is possible at all. That is, Levinas's view may challenge some conceptions of the self and claim that they are false, but other philosophical views – even ones seemingly close to his – may pose serious questions about his view and its very coherence and intelligibility.

LEVINAS AND DAVIDSON

About the subject, Davidson is a naturalist and a rationalist. The subject is a part of the natural world that is a network of causal relations of things and events; it is also part of the social world, a set of interactions between the subject and the world, between other subjects and the natural world, and between subjects in the world. But in order to be situated in these ways vis à vis nature and other people, the subject must have beliefs, desires, and linguistic ability. It must be able to communicate with others about the world and in it, but this requires, Davidson argues, rationality – that its beliefs and desires form a coherent whole. Only if the subject is rational can he think and speak, interpret what others say, and communicate with them.[63] As Davidson puts it: "[T]hinking, propositional thinking, is going on, . . . what explains the fact that thoughts are objective, that is, that their truth (generally) is independent of their being believed; and what accounts for the content of these thoughts? The answers to these questions

---

[63] For his summary of Davidson on these themes, see Thomas Nagel, "Davidson's New Cogito" in Hahn (ed.), *The Philosophy of Donald Davidson*, 195–98.

entail, or so I argue, that thoughts would not have objective truth conditions, or the contents they do have, unless they were in the minds of creatures with bodies interacting in a shared environment."[64]

Simon Evnine calls Davidson a "rationalist idealist," because he argues that our mental contents, our beliefs among them, are a whole, a network of states in a pure "normative system: what it is rational to believe, say and do."[65] Persons, then, are rational creatures with bodies embedded in a world, shared with others, who think and speak about that world and act in it.[66] This is Davidson's famous "holism of the mental" combined with his anomalous monism.

Levinas might find a good deal of Davidson's thinking – if strange in formulation and approach – congenial: the embodied character of human existence, the primary role given to language, the importance of social interaction and living in a shared world, the attention to objectivity and the mind-independence of the world, and the way in which human existence is situatedness in a shared world. Levinas might think that Davidson's arguments are less demonstrations of the truth or accuracy of these views than devices for focusing on how thinking and speaking among persons in the world work as reciprocal communication and interpretation between persons. To be sure, Davidson is a naturalist; a crucial place in this theory is given to the causal impact of things on our sensory organs, and Levinas would doubtless wonder if this is not a faulty privileging of scientific assumptions and a distortion in the project of understanding the human, which is an interpretive and descriptive task, requiring phenomenological analysis and elucidation. But, like Levinas, Davidson is no atomist about persons, and he does not treat the mind as a separate substance. He does not limit the human to the cognitive, nor does he work out from subjectivity to objectivity and the social.

In Chapter 5, we claimed that we should interpret Levinas as providing a supplement to a Davidsonian account of language and thought. What, we might ask, is the point of my communicating with others? What is the significance of my thinking at all? And my contention there was that Levinas takes language and communication as manifestations of responsibility to the other person. In other words, by speaking to or listening to him, I am accepting him, taking him seriously, making "room" for him, giving him a place in the world. To communicate at all is *already* to acknowledge and accept the other person and thereby to act out my responsibility to her, to be responsive to and take responsibility for her. Levinas might also agree with Davidson's conception of

[64] Davidson, in "Reply to Thomas Nagel" in *The Philosophy of Donald Davidson*, 207; cf. 231.

[65] Simon Evnine, *Donald Davidson*, 148–49; see Davidson, *Subjective, Intersubjective, and Objective*, 98–99; 123–28.

[66] Of course, not all people are rational to the same degree; see Evnine, *Donald Davidson*, 168–73, 178–79.

the subject as having mental contents – believing, desiring, hoping, choosing – and as ideally rational, embodied, and social. But he would add: In all of this, the subject is already responsible to and for the other person, which makes all the rest of her personhood meaningful and oriented to some point and purpose. We could spell this out in greater detail, but not really add to the basic point: If Davidson has characterized human theoretical and practical life, Levinas adds the dimension that makes it meaningful life.

But could Davidson admit the Levinasian supplement? One difficulty, of course, is Davidson's naturalism. Another is his idealism. A third is the way that Levinas understands responsibility – as a primordial passivity, prior to action, thought, and reason. Let me set aside any problems grounded in Davidson's naturalism as mitigated by his version, which involves the subject's interpretive role, the unity of the mental and the physical, and the integrity of the mental that Davidson allows. As far as his idealism goes, this also can be accommodated, because he has a notion of objectivity and thinks that while the mental is a system, it does relate to something independent of it, something that is other, the world. To be sure, Davidson's theory, for Levinas, would occur within totality; it is reflective, rational, and philosophical. But the central issue is whether it allows, for human existence, an openness to the infinite, to a thought that is more than can be thought. For this is one way that Levinas characterizes the face-to-face and the self's primordial responsibility to and for the other. If responsibility is without agency, without prior action, and so forth, Davidson's view of the person surely makes no room for such a thing. If we take "prior to thought, action, and reason" literally, then Davidson's account should be utterly dissonant with Levinas's chief contention. But we have argued that such a reading is not what Levinas has in mind, and when read as we have claimed, the notion of the responsible self may not be so objectionable. If we set Levinas alongside Davidson, then the person, in everyday life, not only thinks, believes, desires, chooses, and acts; he *also* – *at the very same time* – is responsible to every other person with whom he interacts directly and indirectly, indeed to all other persons, present and future. In choosing to act and to speak, he acts out of that responsibility, immediately when he acts and speaks directly to a particular person and mediately when he interacts with a number of other persons in terms of principles, policies, and institutional arrangements. That is, his actions, as it were, are expressions of that responsibility and either realizations of what he takes that responsibility to mean for him in a given instance or examples of his failure to be attentive to it.

Davidson might very well say that every thought we have, word we speak, and action we perform is an expression of our rationality, to one degree or another. Why, however, would he agree that all of our lives are also expressions of our responsibility to others and that this fact is actually the most fundamental thing about us as human and social beings? Why is it not more fundamental that we are rational beings embedded in a shared natural environment with others like ourselves? What could Levinas propose that might persuade Davidson?

"Rationality" is the term Davidson uses for the holism of the mental. It is one of the ingredients, not of *any* life but of all *human* life.[67] To be embedded in a natural world with other living things is not enough to make us human; one needs to think, believe, and desire in a systematic way. But, in such a shared world, we think and speak with other persons and act in relation to them. This is a fact, a reality. Davidson, no less than Levinas, accepts all of this as a starting point. For Levinas, we approach the natural world with needs – our materiality – and then appropriate it, enjoy it, and live from it. Davidson inquires into what it means for us to perceive, think about, and act in the world, assuming that we do. Levinas asks *how* we do and *why*, what the world means to us. Then, Davidson considers what role our living in the same world with other persons with whom we communicate plays in our understanding what it means for us to think and speak. Levinas asks a different question, one that he takes to be a deeper one: He asks what meaning the other person has for each of us not merely as a partner in communication for the purpose of sharing information and so forth, but also as a being whose existence and well-being challenges each of us and makes a demand upon us. If I choose to speak to that person, in so doing I already – in addition to whatever I convey in words and, Levinas would say, in a sense *prior* to conveying anything – acknowledge him, accept him, and am aware that he is pleading for me to appreciate what he needs and commanding me to respond with some measure of generosity and kindness. In any particular case, when I converse, I have already been addressed with the plea/command: "Pay attention to me – enough attention to acknowledge me and to respond to me by saying something." My conversation, whatever else it is about, *already* says this. Davidson might not agree, indeed he might *very well* not agree. But he could see, I think, Levinas's point, that one has not understood our selfhood *deeply* enough when one has understood that we are rational beings who share a common world with others like ourselves and who think and talk with one another. There is more to being a person, a subject, than this, Levinas wants us to see, and the *more* is fundamental and, as directive and orienting, it is what gives meaning and purpose to the rest. Davidson might respond that he has no interest in clarifying why we live together with others; or he might very well object that any non naturalist answer to such a question about what living socially means is speculative and fanciful. But, I contend,

---

[67] Of course there may be other rational animals, but we can leave that issue aside; see Davidson, "Rational Animals" in *Subjective, Intersubjective, and Objective*, 95–105.

he could and would understand what Levinas is claiming. Levinas's answer to such a demurral would be that there is evidence *in* ordinary, everyday life that this responsibility is present and that it is determinative – what others might call "normative" – for it, evidence that no natural explanation can satisfactorily understand. Perhaps neither would convince the other, but at least this much is likely, that they could understand one another and where they differ and that the difference is important and serious.

There are three major points that would be disturbing to Levinas about Davidson's account. The first is that it is too naturalist in that Davidson takes the basic way that persons are related to the world to be causal. The second is that it is too idealist and hence too totalizing insofar as it takes beliefs, thoughts, and meaning to be organized in systems that are in a certain sense too isolated from the world, not causally but representationally or intentionally. Finally, Levinas would object that Davidson fails to appreciate the moral or ethical dimension of human existence. Levinas would have identified these differences correctly, I think, and they are certainly serious differences between them. If I am right, however, Levinas would not be alone in finding such shortcomings in Davidson. Someone like John McDowell does so as well, and for this reason McDowell might seem a better philosopher to compare with Levinas. His understanding of the way in which the self is embedded in the world and its implications might seem much closer to Levinas, as do his Wittgenstinian leanings toward the primacy of ordinary, everyday experience and his explicit ethical convictions about human life in the world.

LEVINAS AND MCDOWELL

McDowell points out that for Davidson the world has a causal impact on our sensory apparatus and thus on our beliefs, but it plays no role with regard to our reasoning, understanding, and believing.[68] Or at least, it is mysterious how it could. As Davidson puts it, "[N]othing can count as a reason for holding a belief except another belief."[69] But, as McDowell argues, this move isolates mind from world and links them, at the same time, but in different ways, and the result is disastrous for making sense of human experience and of human life. It invokes a dualism of reason and nature that leaves human life unintelligible and that McDowell rejects in favor of an "openness to the world" in which "world and mind are transcendentally made for each other."[70] This is what McDowell

---

[68] John McDowell, *Mind and World* (Cambridge, MA: Harvard University Press, 1994), 139.
[69] Donald Davidson, "A Coherence Theory of Truth and Knowledge" in Davidson, *Subjective, Intersubjective, and Objective*, 137–53.
[70] McDowell, *Mind and World*, 155, 159.

calls a "naturalism of second nature."[71] It is an account of what I have called a mind-world-other-person nexus or, to use Heideggarian terminology, a view of human existence as what we might call "living in the world with others."

In life and the practical sphere generally, this "openness to the world" is part of what distinguishes human from animal life. Here McDowell, calling on Hans-Georg Gadamer and Karl Marx, sounds much like Levinas: "[T]he world is where a human being lives, where she is at home. Contrast the relation of an environment to an animal life. An environment is essentially alien to a creature that lives in it." The human life is free: It is lived in the world; it is not a "coping with an environment."[72] Human subjectivity, then, occurs because there are "animals with the spontaneity of understanding" – free and rational creatures, us. They are responsive to meaning, as McDowell also puts it,[73] and becoming responsive involves learning a language and learning to live in the world,[74] which are the same thing and which mean learning a repository of meaning and becoming "initiated into a tradition" that has been historically accumulated and is available as a way of understanding the world and being in the world.[75] To acquire such a tradition is to acquire a mind, become a person, and take one's place as a human being in the world and in history.

What does being a person mean to us? Is there some special significance to living this way, rather than as a mere animal? I want to save for a later chapter a look at McDowell's ethical thinking, but here we do need to ask him whether human life involves more than thinking, experience, speaking, and understanding. Surely it does, for it incorporates reflection, decision, and action – for reasons. But how? To what purpose? McDowell takes the answers to these questions to be that we are embedded in particular ethical traditions, that we are accessible to rational reflection, and that what happens when we are initiated into a moral stance is what McDowell calls "acquisition of a second nature."[76] In other words, McDowell's meta-ethics carries with it no particular conception of what it is to be a moral self other than being free, rational, historically situated, and reflective. The blending of Aristotle, Hegel, and Wittgenstein that we find in McDowell is free of any substantive ethical ideal and particular values other than these – or at least McDowell does not articulate any such ideal or such values.[77]

[71] McDowell, *Mind and World*, 84–86; cf. 91–95.

[72] McDowell, *Mind and World*, 118.

[73] McDowell, *Mind and World*, 123.

[74] McDowell, *Mind and World*, 125.

[75] McDowell, *Mind and World*, 126.

[76] See John McDowell, "Two Sorts of Naturalism" in *Meaning, Knowledge, and Reality* (Cambridge, MA: Harvard University Press, 1998), 184–197.

[77] One might compare Onora O'Neill on Kant and her criticism of MacIntyre in Chapter 8 of *Constructions of Reason* (Cambridge: Cambridge University Press, 1989).

Bald naturalism – the expression is McDowell's – is far from Levinas. Davidson's version is closer to Levinas and McDowell's naturalism of second nature closer still. But Levinas surely would find McDowell too historical and contextual about the content of one's ethical sensibility. Particular traditions and communities are characterized by ethical sensibility, to be sure, but its content is linked to their particularity. Not so for Levinas, as we know. In this respect, someone like Charles Taylor might be an even better comparison, for his conception of human agency and personhood is firmly historical and communal and yet has real ethical substance.

LEVINAS AND TAYLOR

Taylor's philosophical contributions are extensive.[78] In a later chapter, I shall consider his pluralism and communitarianism, and I shall examine how his historicism is relevant to the problems of relativism and moral objectivity. Here I want to look at his account of human agency, the person, and the self. This means that we need to understand how the self is self-interpreting, what strong evaluation is, and how it is essential to the self; this is "Taylor's idea that the self has an intrinsic moral dimension."[79] Like Levinas, Taylor takes the self or human subject to be embodied, situated in the world, and temporally oriented, with a unity characterized by a narrative organization. But these features are not distinctive of Taylor's account; what is of special interest to us, as we compare him with Levinas, is Taylor's argument that the self is moral through and through. This view is unlike that of McDowell, for whom a moral sensibility is contingent upon the values of the communities and traditions that we inhabit and inherit. It seems akin, however, to Levinas's notion of the primacy of the ethical. But this kinship may only be apparent.

In his book on Taylor, Nicholas Smith gives a nice summary of Taylor's conception of the self. He draws primarily on the essay "What Is Human Agency?" and the discussion of strong evaluation, moral sources, and the good in *Sources of the Self*.[80] For our purposes, we can follow Smith's summary, paying special attention to the role of strong evaluation and the good in Taylor's conception of the self.

Animals have desires and wants. Human agents are like animals in this regard, but in addition they evaluate those desires and wants in at least two ways. On the

---

[78] For a sense of his range, see Nicholas H. Smith, *Charles Taylor: Meaning, Morals and Modernity*.
[79] Smith, *Charles Taylor*, 87; cf. 89–97, 107–19.
[80] See Smith, *Charles Taylor*, Ch. 4, 87–117; cf. Taylor with Korsgaard on "reflective endorsement" in Korsgaard, *The Sources of Normativity* and the discussion of Bernard Williams and *Ethics and the Limits of Philosophy*, Chs. 8 and 9.

one hand, they weigh them against each other or consider if they are compatible and such. This is what Taylor calls "weak evaluation." Human agents also, on the other hand, qualitatively assess these desires and wants in terms of their import or worth to the agent.[81] Taylor calls this second type of evaluation "strong evaluation," and the point of introducing this distinction between weak and strong evaluation is to contrast the different kinds of self or subject that each involves.[82] As Taylor sees it, there is a depth to strong evaluation, an access to something that is a standard of worth or import, that is missing to animals and to weak evaluation as conducted by human agents.[83] In addition, this capacity for strong evaluation includes a taking of responsibility, not only for what we do but also for these evaluations themselves; we endorse them and do not simply carry them out or make them.[84] According to Taylor, we endorse these evaluations and are *responsible for* them insofar as they express or incorporate our sense of who we are as agents. These strong evaluations, that is, articulate our very own self-interpretation that is manifest in and constitutive of our experience, but only unclearly and obscurely.[85] So, strong evaluation invokes the notion of some standard of worth or import that is integral to how the self understands itself and expresses that sense of self in the endorsement that accompanies the evaluation.

Taylor develops these ideas in detail in other essays and in *Sources of the Self*, but for the purposes of our comparison with Levinas, the central idea is that access to a "strong value" or human good is necessary for us to carry out these reflective, deliberative activities. And if such activities and judgments are essential to being a human agent or a person, then access to such values and responsiveness to them is also essential to being such an agent. Moreover, among the classes of such values is one that involves "concern, love, or respect for the 'other human being,'" what we owe to each other.[86] Hence, our lives are sustained in part by our access to this value of concern for others, and thereby we are, fundamentally, "ethically oriented selves."[87] Basically, our lives are "organized by some sense of moral orientation."[88] Alternatively, as Smith puts it, for Taylor "the most fundamental feature of a self is that things matter to it. The self is first

[81] See Charles Taylor, "What Is Human Agency?" in *Human Agency and Language*, 16.
[82] Taylor, "What Is Human Agency?," 23.
[83] Taylor, "What Is Human Agency?," 24–26.
[84] Taylor, "What Is Human Agency?," 28.
[85] Taylor, "What Is Human Agency?," 35–38.
[86] Nicholas Smith, *Charles Taylor*, 91; cf. Nicholas Smith, *Sources of the Self* (Cambridge, MA: Harvard University Press, 1992), 16.
[87] Smith, *Charles Taylor*, 92.
[88] Smith, *Charles Taylor*, 93; cf. 94.

and foremost a being with concerns,"[89] and among those concerns are those for other persons.[90] Smith notes, too, that the inclusion of this concern for others separates Taylor's view from any kind of self-oriented eudaimonism, but perhaps he is too sanguine about the way this view incorporates the exteriority or alterity of the other person, as Levinas sees it.

In order to understand how Taylor's account might be considered in the light of Levinas's priority of responsibility and the face-to-face, we need to clarify what he means by these goods or values and what roles the sources of the good play in Taylor's conception of strong evaluation and so forth. Smith points out, for example, that strong values or goods are not norms or principles; they are "desirable things which are worthy of desire."[91] For Taylor, our identity as selves would be empty without some orientation to these goods; we could not experience things as important for us or take things to matter to us, if we did not have access to these values. Furthermore, these goods need to be grounded in something; Taylor calls such grounds "constitutive goods." They are the ground for the worth of the strong values or life goods we have been discussing, the ones to which strong evaluations refer. They are what makes these goods effective and compelling for us; Taylor also calls them "moral sources" or "sources of the self."[92]

Even at this general level of discussion, we can see that Taylor's account has features that would appeal to Levinas and ones to which he would object. For Levinas, responsibility is the fundamental dimension of all of our relations to other persons; it is how we are precisely because it is the basic way we are toward others. Taylor recognizes no concrete or substantive feature common to every person or subject. To be sure, each of us engages in strong evaluation of our desires, on his account; we are oriented to goods and empowered by moral sources. But no single aspect of our experience shapes all that we are and do. Furthermore, responsibility is no abstraction or value for Levinas; it is the very particular obligation, as it were, to take each and every particular person seriously, to choose and to act always against a "background" of such an obligation to acknowledge, to accept, to sacrifice for, and to aid and support the other person – indeed, each and every other person. In social life, of course, this responsibility manifests itself as goods, values, principles, norms, and so forth. But the self is engaged by the other person first and foremost, and it is this engagement that shapes our sense of obligation and the norms or values that

---

[89] Smith, *Charles Taylor*, 96.
[90] Smith, *Charles Taylor*, 112–13; see comparison with Levinas.
[91] Smith, *Charles Taylor*, 91.
[92] Smith, *Charles Taylor*, 113–16.

occur in daily life as features of our selfhood. Taylor is explicit that his account is an articulation of a Heideggerian conception of the person. Levinas is just as explicit that such a view already assimilates the encounter with the unique other person to abstract, general principles and values. For Levinas, these values are an outcome of being present in society and giving some form or direction to one's basic responsibility. For Taylor, not the face of the other person but rather God or nature or reason grounds the worth or import of these values and principles. Nor do they engage the self from outside ontology and ordinary, everyday life; rather, they are grasped within it.

In the end, things mean something and have import to Taylor's person or self for a variety of possible reasons. For Levinas, all human meaning of this kind is grounded in that single feature of our everyday lives, the way the face of each and every other person speaks to us, calls us into question, and demands of us a response. Before we are anything other than natural beings nourished by the world we live in, we are called to respond to every other person with whom we share the world. Taylor's self or human agent is not free-standing or isolated but rather deeply embedded in the world and open to values and what makes them matter to it. But his pluralism distinguishes him from Levinas, as does the abstractness of his conception of the self. There is more content in Taylor's view than in McDowell's, but his naturalism is at least as enriched by "second nature": culture, tradition, and language. Moreover, the content is no less plural and no less historical, variable, and contextual. And in the end, Taylor's account, like McDowell's, is also too theoretical. He may never deny the particularity or uniqueness of each person, his relations, actions, and life, but the brute particularity of each person vis à vis each other and what that particularity means ethically never enter into Taylor's conception.

Finally, for Taylor, as for Davidson and McDowell, the center of subjectivity is some modes of activity. This much Cartesianism, Kantianism, and modernity in general, all three have in common. All may take the subject to be embedded in the world with others, to one degree or other, in many ways. But, like Husserl and Heidegger after him, there is something privileged about the subject's point of view and the primacy of the subject's posture, capacities, and actions. Levinas does not claim that as selves or subjects we do not occupy a particular, first-person point of view; he does not say that we are not free or spontaneous, nor does he deny that we desire, reflect, deliberate, decide, and act. And much of this picture of human agency and selfhood is distinctive of human beings. What Levinas sees, however, is that all of this picture is insufficient to reach the deepest or most determinative and compelling dimension of human existence insofar as it is social and interpersonal, which it always and essentially is. For that, we need to appreciate that for each of us, what we are is always already *responsive* and *responsible*, under the auspices of each and every other, always already obligated and chosen, our very being called into question and called upon. For Levinas, we are social before we are singular.

When, in ordinary, everyday life, we meet someone, say hello, ask something of her, or respond to a question or an imperative, our freedom – to listen, to speak, to interpret, and to act – is always "preceded" by this responsibility so that the freedom itself and all it gives rise to are, in a sense, constitutive of acting on that responsibility and so should be, in our eyes, bound by its dictates. Whatever we do, then, we do under the umbrella of responsibility; it is unavoidably an act of responsibility, whatever else it might also be. In this respect, then, Levinas's conception of the deepest stratum of our subjectivity or selfhood is anterior to our first-person point of view, our freedom to choose, and what Taylor calls our "ethic of authenticity," of being true to oneself. The self is intrinsically social and ethical, and the ethical dimension, its normativity or force, derives from the other person's claim on the self. It is in this respect that Levinas takes the self to be substitution, accusation, traumatized, a hostage, and hence passive. There is no paradox here, no contradiction. What Levinas calls to our attention is how different in outcome would be such a dramatic alteration in our perspective on selfhood and subjectivity.

7

God and Philosophy

Our appreciation of what philosophy is at any given historical moment, how it is understood by its practitioners and derided by its critics, is helped by examining its relationships with what is commonly called theology and religion. The stories of the relation between philosophy, religion, and theology are complex and lengthy. Frankly, the more we understand of these stories, the better would be our grasp of Levinas's references to religion and God and his penchant for using theological and religious expressions to refer to the face and the ethical.[1] Both features are present early in Levinas's works. Long before *Totality and Infinity*, he could say, "The absolute which supports justice is the absolute status of the interlocutor. His modality of being and of manifesting himself consist in turning his face to me, in being a face.... This is not at all a theological thesis; yet God could not be God without first having been this interlocutor."[2] These words come from 1954; even then, Levinas struggled to articulate how his insight about the central importance of the face-to-face and responsibility is related to God and religion. His views, I believe, certainly changed and developed, but at the same time they retained a common core. In this chapter, I want to look at what he says about God, how he should be understood, and why he says it. In view of recent, renewed philosophical interest in God, theology, and religion, these matters – so important to Levinas – are also important to us.[3]

---

[1] An excellent treatment of these themes can be found in Jeffrey L. Kosky, *Levinas and the Philosophy of Religion*; see also the essays in Jeffrey Bloechl (ed.), *The Face of the Other and the Trace of God*, and Bloechl, *Liturgy of the Neighbor: Emmanuel Levinas and the Religion of Responsibility* (Pittsburgh: Duquesne University Press, 2000). See also the books by Wyschogrod, Gibbs, Cohen, Wright, Purcell, and Peperzak.

[2] Levinas, "The Ego and the Totality" in *Collected Philosophical Papers*, 33.

[3] For a recent account, see Michael Purcell, *Levinas and Theology*.

GOD AND THE PHILOSOPHICAL TRADITION

In his *Theological-Political Treatise*, Spinoza explains that the word "miracle" is used to refer to events or facts that we have yet to understand.[4] One might extrapolate: God or the divine or the transcendent refers to a cause or agency for events and facts that we cannot (yet) explain satisfactorily based on our everyday (and then scientific) understanding of how and why things occur in the natural world. There is an element of truth in this account; it is certainly not true of all theological belief at all times and in all places, but in the West it is partially true that as science and the social sciences grew and developed, many found their belief in and commitment to God or divinity waning, especially their belief in divine providence or in divine agency directly operative in nature and history. The history of Western philosophy, to a degree, reflects these changes. One can take Aristotle's treatment of the divine in *Metaphysics Lambda* and in *Physics Theta*, for example, as part of a strategy to make room for natural explanation, to maintain a link to transcendence, and to tie the two together. Many of Aristotle's heirs in the Middle Ages and the early modern period appropriated his model and adapted it to changes in science.[5] Moreover, when the need for God or the divine in theoretical matters waned and then disappeared completely, philosophers could either find another role still necessary or dispense with theology altogether. Kant and Hegel, for example, took the former route, albeit in very different ways, as did Kierkegaard, while, one could argue, the "masters of suspicion" – Marx, Nietzsche, and Freud – famously took the latter route.

Philosophy in the twentieth century moved away from religion and the theological and then, more recently, has made room for movements to return to them.[6] Early twentieth-century responses to historicism and the relativism that was associated with certain accounts of the social sciences included philosophical ones that navigated from religion, or near to it, such as some versions of

---

[4] Spinoza, *Theological-Political Treatise*, 2nd ed. (Hackett, 2001), Ch. 5.
[5] If we are liberal about whom we consider such heirs of Aristotle, we could include among them Descartes, Hobbes, and Spinoza to Locke, Leibniz, and Newton.
[6] I am thinking of the critique of religion, theology, and metaphysics that we associate with logical positivism and scientistic forms of analytic philosophy, largely naturalist of one kind or another, perhaps best exemplified by A. J. Ayer's *Language, Truth, and Logic* (New York: Dover Publications, 1952). Then, in the postwar period we have the return to an interest in the philosophy of religion and philosophical theology – early in figures like Antony Flew, Alasdair MacIntyre, and Basil Mitchell, more recently in philosophers like Alvin Plantinga, Nicholas Wolterstorff, William Rowe, and Richard Swinburne. All of this activity occurred within the Anglo-American, so-called analytic circle; a quite different but significant shift occurred in the world of continental philosophy with figures such as Derrida, Henry, Marion, and Levinas himself. See Kevin Hart, *The Trespass of the Sign: Deconstruction, Theology, and Philosophy*.

neo-Kantianism, *Lebensphilosophie*, and even phenomenological developments like those of Karl Jaspers and Rudolf Bultmann. Some might even argue that the early Wittgenstein left room for religious and theological experience,[7] and if one considers figures like Karl Barth, Rudolph Bultmann, Paul Tillich, Martin Buber, Franz Rosenzweig, Georg Lukács, and Walter Benjamin philosophical, then the age of high modernism can be read as a moment of special rapport between philosophy and religious impulses. In one way or another, all of these figures found in God or transcendence a ground of meaning in and for human life. But with the rise of logical positivism and its influence in England and the United States, religion was marginalized and largely excluded from serious philosophical discussion until late in the twentieth century. In the 1950s and subsequent decades, with the influence of the later Wittgenstein and ordinary-language philosophy, various religious phenomena were sanitized and examined, especially issues of language and the proofs for God's existence; but outside of this almost "experimental" approach to the rationality of religious belief, such matters were of only incidental philosophical interest. In the late decades of the century, this began to change, and even in the circles of Anglo-American philosophy, there has been a revival of sorts in which religion and theology have become interesting in new ways. Levinas might best be viewed, in this venue, as contributing to this revival or at least, once he is accessible and made available, as a potentially significant and interesting contributor.

Part of the story to be told about Levinas and his role is that he is responding to Nietzsche's slogan "the death of God" and to the challenge put to twentieth-century philosophy to address the question of the meaningfulness of human existence and the challenge to the sources and foundations of value articulated by Nietzsche and others. This kind of story is so well known, it is hardly necessary to retell it.[8] The point is that if Levinas increasingly seeks to clarify the character of religion and the role of God, the sacred, and holiness in human existence, the avenue he chooses is largely an ethical one. In this sense, Levinas is structurally like Kant insofar as Kant, too, once he had banished God and religion from the domain of science and the life of theory and explanation, sought to recover them by showing how moral agency required a belief in God and a revised interpretation of religion as a moral faith. There is indeed something like this going on in Levinas: that God is, in some sense, present in the face of the other person does have something to do with the ethical, and to say that this is not a theological thesis is to deny that God has a theoretical or cognitive role to play. But as it is, this is much too simple and inaccurate to

---

[7] An influential contribution is Fergus Kerr, *Theology after Wittgenstein* (Oxford Blackwell, 1986).
[8] For a recent telling, see Julian Young, *The Death of God and the Meaning of Life* (London: Routledge, 2003).

be helpful. We need first to look much more carefully at what Levinas says and then to place him within recent philosophical discussion of the grounds and sources of normativity in ethics. This metaethical setting may not turn out to be the only venue for understanding what Levinas says about God and religion; it may not even turn out to be the best venue. But it is a natural starting place, especially, I think, given his proximity to someone like Charles Taylor, who himself increasingly has shown an affinity for religious sources of the good.[9]

EARLY WORKS

As we approach Levinas's works, our goal will be his 1975 essay "God and Philosophy," which later (1986) became the centerpiece of his book *Of God Who Comes to Mind*. But there are earlier steps: his treatment of God and the sacred in *Totality and Infinity*, in essays of the sixties, and importantly in *Otherwise Than Being*.[10] Throughout these works, Levinas's views become richer and fuller; his desire – is it a need? – to come to grips with the role of religion and our theological ideas and language becomes more and more intense, even relentless. Religion and the sacred provide a vocabulary for the ethical that he finds seductive and compelling. And yet, in these works Levinas stays within the bounds of philosophical analysis and exploration. These are not confessional discussions, and the outcomes are not parochial. They are meant to expose a dimension of his view of human existence as yet unexplored and in need of illumination. We will have to see what he achieves in employing religious vocabulary as he takes on this task.

As we begin to look at Levinas's writings, we should keep in mind some features of his thinking that we have already seen in operation and their relevance to the issue at hand. For Levinas, traditional theological beliefs and language occur within the domain of totality. They employ concepts and discursive argument, make general claims, and so forth. Theology is theoretical, and it is continuous, to one degree or other, with philosophy, metaphysics, and science, as well as with ethical theory and even political thought. In addition, religious practices, texts, and religious life in general occur within the ordinary, everyday experience of many people. Whatever the explicit intentions and attitudes of religious practitioners, religious life can be and has been examined by the social sciences

---

[9] In addition to *Sources of the Self*, one should now look at *Varieties of Religion Today*, *Modern Social Imaginaries*, and *A Catholic Modernity?*

[10] There are also his Jewish writings, collected in *Difficult Freedom*, *Beyond the Verse*, and *In the Midst of the Nations*, as well as his Talmudic commentaries. But these are not explicitly philosophical works, do not employ philosophical analysis and clarification, and do not yield philosophical results. We discuss these writings in Chapter 11.

and given explanations rooted in psychology, sociology, and even economics. Theology and religion, then, are manifest in historical life and contemporary experience, and existing accounts of religion and theology examine the meaning of their beliefs and practices in scientific terms.

Religious life may be taken to reflect or express beliefs about God and the world, to express attitudes and feelings, or to indicate principles of behavior and hopes for the future. With respect to God, then, theological statements may be understood to be descriptive of God, and religious statements may be interpreted as petitions or eulogies or reprimands. Distinctively and as we might expect, Levinas, we shall see, associates our language and practices concerning the sacred and the divine with the primary ethical dimension of our lives, as he has characterized it. With respect to the idea of God that we think about and the word "God" that we use in our ordinary lives, what is the relationship between these thoughts and utterances and the ethical relation? In everyday thinking and speech and in theoretical experience – from ontology and metaphysics to theology and the sciences – words mean what they do and refer to things in ways that philosophers have examined and debated. But the face of the other person, while it may shed light on our lives and have significance, is not connected directly to thought and speech as everyday experience is. What Levinas needs to do, then, if he takes the face-to-face and the presence of the other person to have a primary and elevated status for us, is to clarify how it, as a dimension of our everyday lives, albeit often hidden from view or occluded, is related to the way we think and talk about God in those lives.

It cannot be the case that the word "God" simply refers to the face of the other person or to the other person herself. In a sense, that face is "unreferable" and "meaningless." But if "God" does not describe or point to something *in* the ethical relation, how is it related to that relation, if it is at all? Levinas begins, one might say, with an insight from F. W. J. Schelling, Søren Kierkegaard, Martin Buber, and Franz Rosenzweig, among others: that God in reality is never captured by thought or concepts; no matter how complete and articulate the system of thought, it can never comprehend God. The unique fact of God always remains outside of that system. Nonetheless, that reality is one we, as unique individuals, can encounter. As Buber puts it, God is the Eternal Thou, the Divine Presence, one who can only be addressed and never expressed.[11] We can speak to God but never about God. In his own way, Levinas begins with this thought only to push it further: If this is so, then at its own level, theological thinking should not be interpreted as descriptive; it is not that it is

---

[11] See Martin Buber, *I and Thou* (New York: Scribner, 1970), *passim*. Levinas would not articulate the relation to the divine this way, as we shall see, but there is a sense that his understanding of our relation to transcendence does have an origin common to this tradition.

descriptive and false but rather that it should be understood to have a different kind of significance altogether.

Moreover, we need to ask: When we address God, what are we doing? We are not escaping the everyday world in order to engage in an extraordinary encounter with an otherworldly being. But if not, what, then, does it mean to say that I am addressing God? What kind of an experience am I having? If the idea of God signals our acknowledgment of transcendence and if to grasp that idea is not part of a descriptive or referential act, then what does it mean to acknowledge transcendence in our lives, to receive the call of the genuinely other?[12]

If we imagine Levinas raising these questions for himself, we can see how his thinking about God might have struggled to attain some kind of clarity. For these lines of thinking suggest that the idea of God and theological language overall are associated with what is deepest and most significant for our lives as human lives, for what he calls the ethical and also the religious.[13] In a sense, God is very close to us, indeed, and yet exceedingly difficult to grasp. Levinas's lifelong wrestling with "God" and the idea of God shows how firm is his commitment to both the proximity and the distance of the idea. As we read what he says, we want to understand the steps that he takes as he seeks greater and greater precision and clarity about God and the ethical, at the same time that he revises and deepens his approach to the ethical itself.

There is one relationship between God and the ethical that Levinas will have to reject, and that is a divine voluntarism that takes God to be the source of moral rules or principles. Levinas may not be disturbed by narratives of divine command or theological reflections about God as a God of revealed laws, as long as these forms of discourse are not interpreted descriptively, literally, or theoretically. He may find such narratives or statements or theories valuable, if properly understood, or he may find them disturbing and confusing. What he cannot do is to attach such a notion, of God as a moral commander, to his understanding of the ethical dimension that is the orienting feature of human experience. Levinas realizes that in our lives people hold moral views; they accept moral principles and respect them; some may even have well-developed moral theories. Moreover, God may be thought to play some moral role in such theories, or God may be replaced by natural sentiments or rational agency. But everyday moralizing and moral theorizing, even theological moral thinking,

---

[12] It is a central theme of Samuel Moyn's *Origins of the Other: Emmanuel Levinas Between Revelation and Ethics* that Levinas is importantly indebted to religious debates of the Weimar period, especially to figures like Barth, Rosenzweig, and others on the notion of revelation.

[13] See Levinas, "Transcendence and Height" in *Basic Philosophical Writings*, 29–30 (the discussion after the talk, which occurred in 1962).

are one thing; the encounter with the face of the other person and the burden of responsibility that accompanies that encounter are another. God cannot enter Levinas's thinking as a divine commander, no more than he could enter Kant's moral thinking in that role. The thought of a commanding God may be important, but like any thought of God, it would be one thought too many.

In 1954, Levinas said that God has something to do with the encounter with the other, but this is no theological thesis, even if it is true that "God could not be God without first having been this interlocutor."[14] This suggests that Levinas, at one stage in his career, identified God with the other person; however, I am inclined not to take this sentence literally, but rather to see it as a rhetorical device to exaggerate what seems paradoxical: that God must be something else before being God – indeed, that God must be *human* before He is God. To understand what this means, however, we are better served by turning to some pages on the sacred in *Totality and Infinity*.

Levinas's affection for apparent paradox is evident when he says, "To relate to the absolute as an atheist is to welcome the absolute purified of the violence of the sacred."[15] It is a strange thing to say, that one draws near to God, the absolute, only when one becomes an atheist.[16] Theism and the domain of the sacred are the province of everyday religious life and traditional Western theology. What Levinas will advocate is a new sense of religion and of God, where the weight falls on the face-to-face and its ethical character. This is one meaning of atheism, an acknowledgment of God that is not, strictly speaking, theistic, an acknowledgment of God that is not a belief in the existence of a transcendent God. The theistic God is a "myth," Levinas says, whereas the God who "speaks" to us does so through the other person, the *real* transcendent, who engages me as the stranger, the widow, and the orphan, out of her destitution and yet, as he puts it, with her "eminence, height, and lordship."[17] The idea of infinity, transcendence, and the face of the other are "the dawn of a humanity without myths."

In these pages, then, Levinas rearticulates what occurs in the encounter with the face, but this time in theological language: revelation, epiphany, and the comprehension of God. The encounter with the face is the relation with God. "There can be no 'knowledge' of God separated from the relationship with man."[18] But what does this mean? Is God the human other? Or is God somehow associated with the "height" of the face? And if so, what does *this* mean? How are we to understand such a reformulation of the face-to-face in religious language?

[14] "The Ego and the Totality" in *Collected Philosophical Papers*, 33.
[15] TI, 77.
[16] Cf. Richard Cohen, *Elevations: The Height of the Good in Rosenzweig and Levinas*, 180–82.
[17] TI, 76–78.
[18] TI, 78.

First, Levinas tells us that "[T]he Other is ... indispensable for my relation with God. He does not play the role of a mediator. The Other is not the incarnation of God, but precisely by his face, in which he is disincarnate, is the manifestation of the height in which God is revealed."[19] The relation with God, then, only makes sense insofar as the self is engaged by the other, but that other – the other person – is not a "mediator" between the self and God, as in Christianity; nor is the other identical to God. Rather, the face reveals a *height* that is the locus of the divine revelation. In a moment, we will have to ask what "height" means, but even without an interpretation, we can say this much. "Theological concepts," Levinas says, possess the "signification they admit of" only in virtue of "our relations with men." And these relations, between "the being here below" and "transcendent being" – that is, the face of the other person – he calls "religion."[20]

In *Totality and Infinity*, then, God, as a theological concept, is a myth, which means that it does not refer to a real being but rather expresses something – a relationship or a feature of a relationship – that is, given its honorific and elevated tonality, especially significant for human existence. Moreover, divine revelation is not the epiphany of the face of the other, nor is it mediated by the other, as if God were a distant being, beyond direct encounter. For Levinas, God is *revealed in the height of the face*. God is not the face or its height, but the language of God – of the divine, the sacred, and the holy – is a theological way of expressing that height, of calling attention to it and acknowledging it. But what does "height" – itself a metaphorical expression – signify? Adriaan Peperzak notes that "height," as a metaphor, underscores the asymmetrical character of the face-to-face; the other addresses the self, supplicates, and commands; the self is passive to all of this, but especially to the command. The self is called upon to respond and, in a sense, made to respond.[21]

Richard Cohen, commenting on this sentence in *Totality and Infinity*, emphasizes that the divine is *a* dimension or that height is *the* dimension of the divine, and he identifies this dimension as "a *moral* dimension, the dimension of moral height, goodness."[22] He also associates the notion of height with the *asymmetry* of the relation between the self and the other. Cohen's best formulation is this: "By 'height' Levinas means the *moral* force encountered in the *other's* face *as the subject's* obligation to and responsibility for that other person."[23] If Cohen is right, then for Levinas in *Totality and Infinity* God is not the other but rather the moral force in virtue of which the other commands the self, the fact that

[19] TI, 78–79.
[20] TI, 80; cf. 81.
[21] Peperzak, *Beyond*, 125, 133, 137, 208.
[22] Cohen, *Elevations*, 183; cf. 183–88.
[23] Cohen, *Elevations*, 185.

the face engages the self's responsibility and calls for goodness rather than, say, presents itself as a certain kind of person, with a precise role, or calls for a judgment of aesthetic commendation, or is wholly petitionary.

But even this seems to outstrip Levinas's cautious formulations and transgresses what is possible, as he sees it. The problem comes from asking in too literal a sense what the word "God" refers to.[24] Levinas's starting point is to acknowledge the widespread use of religious language and theological concepts, and his most decisive claim – like Buber's, Tillich's, and others' – is that such language is not descriptive; the term "God" does not pick out any reality or fact. But as a myth, it does perform some functions; it is, after all, a linguistic expression, and its use is a matter of linguistic behavior. It expresses human aspirations, obligations, attitudes, or hopes. It is a response to some dimension or aspect of human experience, and it is Levinas's view that there are more and less accurate accounts of what that dimension is and hence more or less genuine ways of responding to it. Generally speaking, he contends that such concepts as "divine revelation" or "relationship with God" are responses to the moral determination that, he claims, is central to human life. Cohen is right to associate the height of the other's face with this moral determination or force; he is wrong, however, to think that this is God. For what this might lead one to think is that God reveals Himself to us in the moral force of the other's face. But this is to distort Levinas's thinking dramatically. It is more correct to say that in uttering statements about God's revealing Himself, if we accept Levinas's view that our lives are significant first and foremost as responsive to the needs and the suffering of others, our utterances are in part a response, as an acknowledgment, to that insight. To say "God reveals Himself to me" is one way of expressing one's acknowledgment of the primacy of the ethical and our responsibility to and for others. To say that human beings are created "in the image of God" is to say that human beings present themselves to us, each to each, as valuable, worthy of care and generosity and help. The language of God and the divine image are not about God and His image; they express the sense of value, significance, and worth others have for us. In *Totality and Infinity*, I believe, this is the significance of Levinas's appropriation of religious and theological language.[25]

---

[24] There is a very good discussion of this issue in Wright, *The Twilight of Jewish Philosophy*, 71–73.
[25] In "A Religion for Adults" in *Difficult Freedom*, Levinas makes this point and clarifies it with a reference to Maimonides's treatment of divine attributes: "The moral relation therefore reunites both self-consciousness and consciousness of God. Ethics is not the corollary of the vision of God, it is that very vision. Ethics is an optic, such that everything I know of God and everything I can hear of His word and reasonably say to Him must find an ethical expression. In the Holy Ark from which the voice of God is heard by Moses, there are only the tablets of the Law. The knowledge of God which we can have and which is expressed, according to Maimonides, in the form of negative attributes, receives a positive meaning from the moral 'God is merciful,'

Furthermore, theological language expresses one's recognition of a particular aspect of the ethical relationship and responsibility, what Levinas calls "height." The metaphor points to a number of features of the encounter with the face of the other: that the other person stands at a distance, that it addresses the self from above or from a higher status, that the other has a priority or eminence and is elevated with respect to the self, that the other has authority over the self and perhaps power over it as well, that they are not equals in every way, and that they are related asymmetrically in at least one manner. All of this and more perhaps is contained in the metaphor, and I am inclined to think that Levinas wants us to think of the metaphor broadly and suggestively, rather than narrowly. Just as face is novel as a philosophical term, so is height, and its association with divinity and the sacred is meant to call attention to the traditional nomenclature of divinity as royal and paternal and yet to represent a declension away from that terminology, both like it and unlike it, just as face is like appearance and yet unlike it. The primordial or originary encounter with the other person presents us with a face that means something other than and more than how the other person looks; so the height of the face presents us with a status that is other than and more than the status of God as King or as Father. The face has an authority beyond all authority, more basic than the difference between authority and its lack, for it is authority that both pleads and commands. It singles us out and calls us into question at once and so "speaks to us" or "addresses us" from a height that is as low as it is high, so to speak. The suggestiveness of the metaphor of height, like so much of Levinas's vocabulary, is meant to perplex and to redirect our thinking and attention; it is not meant to clarify and make precise what begins as vague and unclear but rather to change our perspective altogether.

LATER STAGE: THE TRACE AND *ILLEITY*

In *Otherwise Than Being* and in the important essay "God and Philosophy," Levinas develops his understanding of the relationship between the ethical relationships of the face-to-face and theological language.[26] He discontinues the use of "height" as the chief metaphor that points to the locus of their relationship. But does his thinking change in significant ways? Does he continue to understand religious language as an expression of the moral responsibility that orients human life?

As we have seen, Levinas elaborates a large, new terminology to explore the conception of the face of the other person: "hostage," "obsession," "proximity,"

---

which means: 'Be merciful like Him.' The attributes of God are given not in the indicative, but in the imperative.... To know God is to know what must be done" (17).

[26] See Wright, *The Twilight of Jewish Philosophy*, 80–94; Cohen, *Elevations*, 190–94.

"accusation," "persecution," "substitution," and more. Two terms that he uses seem linked in his mind with theological language, "trace" and "glory."[27] In *Otherwise Than Being*, he says that "a face is not an appearance or sign of some reality ... a face does not function in proximity as a sign of a hidden God who would impose the neighbor on me."[28] Levinas wants us to realize what theoretical thinking and reason – "representation and thematization" – do to the face, how they can lead us astray by asking the wrong questions and by giving us the wrong idea about what the face means. Such thinking transforms "the trace into a *sign* of a departure." It turns the *trace* into a *sign*, the face of the other person into a representation of the divine or a mediator between us and a hidden God. By *thinking about* the face, rather than responding to it as destitute and commanding, we "open the dangerous way in which the pious thought, or one concerned with order, hastily deduces the existence of God."[29] Levinas sees traditional arguments for God's existence as mistaken routes or responses to the event that registers as a religious one. The way to respond to the face authentically is with responsibility, not by thinking, deducing a divine commander or a first cause. The terms "trace" and "glory" must carry new senses.[30] In everyday terms, a trace is a clue to something other than itself, like a footprint in the sand, which signifies the foot that made the imprint and has since passed by. But here the "trace is of itself," and "glory" is not the splendor of a hidden source but the "glory of the infinite," a self-exposure of the transcendent.[31] All of this terminology is meant to warn us against using social interaction as the beginning of reflection on God's existence. Levinas notes that ignoring the face and turning to such questions is one sense of Nietzsche's slogan "the death of God"; it is also a sense of the affirmation "the life of God."[32] Both are conditions to be avoided.

Levinas returns to the theme of the "glory of the infinite" in a later chapter of *Otherwise Than Being* and there adds importantly to his account of the

---

[27] As we shall see, the word "glory" has a specifically biblical resonance for Levinas. The Hebrew word "*kavod*" means "glory," "honor," or "splendor."

[28] OB, 93–94.

[29] OB, 93.

[30] OB, 94.

[31] I will return to the notion of a *trace* later in this chapter and then again in the next chapter. Levinas first introduces it in his essay "The Trace of the Other" (1963) in Mark C. Taylor, *Deconstruction in Context* (Chicago: University of Chicago Press, 1986) and then employs it in OB. Like much of Levinas's innovative vocabulary, "trace" is suggestive. It refers to something left behind and is both like and unlike evidence, a clue, a remnant, or a remainder. In addition to the sense of being left behind or of being passed on, "trace" also implies the notion of a copy that outlines an original, a tracing of it; it also points in the direction of a notion of remainder, of something that is part of an original, small and fragmentary.

[32] OB, 94–97.

theological response.[33] The *glory* of the infinite is the self's giving to the other and its dedication to the other. It is that dimension of our speech and our action toward the other that makes of it a responsible donation; Levinas calls it "sincerity,"[34] and he proceeds to connect glory and sincerity with language, witness, and prophecy, and in this context he explores more fully what God means in human experience. In the course of several pages, Levinas makes a number of observations and claims that extend what he has already said. We have seen that he takes theological discourse concerning God's existence to fail to illuminate what "God" and the idea of God mean for human existence, and in early work we saw God associated with the moral character of the face as supplication and especially as command – indeed, with a plea that commands and a command that pleads. But God is no hidden commander; indeed, theological language responds to the ethical character of the face and is one expression of our awareness of it and its primacy. Presumably, the introduction of the notion of sincerity and its association with language, witness, and prophecy extend the lines already proposed by these ethical associations of theological discourse.

"The glory of the infinite" is another expression for the face-to-face and the self's responsibility. Levinas makes this claim in a number of ways – for example, "the saying prior to anything said bears witness to glory." He suggests that in this relation lies a hint of the uniqueness of the I and its character as "elected," its passivity to the other. But "glory" connotes preeminence and status, like the shining rays of the sun – as the term "height" did in *Totality and Infinity*; it suggests the command of the other, the call to responsibility, and testifies to the other's status for me, as the locus of my selfhood and my obligation to be responsive to each and every other and responsible to and for them.

"Witness" is both a religious expression and a term of art. A witness testifies to the truth of some statement, conjecture, belief, program, or claim; the witness experienced an event or action and describes how it appeared to him and how he takes it to have been, what the facts are. He says: This is how the event appeared to me, this is how I saw it; I was there; something happened, and this is how I recall it. To say that the face-to-face is a witness, then, is to use the term metaphorically and not literally. The self's readiness to respond to the face and obligation to respond to the other – what Levinas calls, with a biblical allusion, the "Here I am" [*hineni*] – is not a witness to an event; it is, Levinas says, "a witness of the Infinite."[35] He emphasizes that this witness is not cognitive,

---

[33] OB, 140–52.

[34] OB, 142–44.

[35] OB, 146. The testimony here, the witness, is not to what happened. Notice that Levinas does not say "a witness *to* the Infinite," but rather "a witness *of* the Infinite," that is, of the impact of the Infinite. It is not descriptive. It is an expression of one's availability and more, one's

phenomenological, experiential, and epistemic. It is not evidence for a truth. "The Infinite does not appear to him that bears witness to it."[36] The self's readiness to respond, its acceptance of what the other's face means to it, is not a response to a visual or sensory impression; it is not testimony to the other's face, nor is it itself a clue, a hint, or a trace of such an impression. "On the contrary witness belongs to the glory of the Infinite. It is by the voice of the witness that the glory of the Infinite is glorified."[37] Levinas puts the point in another way: "The glory of the Infinite is glorified in this responsibility."[38] The face-to-face has, as it were, two sides: It is the face of the other person petitioning and commanding, and it is the self readied to respond, acknowledging the face, and accepting the other person. This latter is responsibility – or the commitment to respond, the capacity to respond, and the act of responding. The face "shines" for the self – as glory; the self's acceptance points to that glory, the face's significance for the self, precisely insofar as that readiness to act, commitment to act, and action are indeed responsibility to others and responses to their plea and their command. But the two sides are one; hence, the glory of the infinite is what it is, glorified, in the witness of the self, which is the self's responsibility to what "shines forth for it from the other person's face." One relationship, one event, as it were, but two sides.

Levinas then points out that this "witness" is the way the engagement of the infinite – the encounter with the face – "passes its command,"[39] and he then,

---

willingness or even eagerness to be available. The biblical reference is virtually explicit, to Abraham's response to God's call in Genesis 22, when he is awakened during the night to the call "Abraham, Abraham" and responds with "*Hineni*," "Here I am," not to identify or locate himself – after all, God certainly knows who he is and where – but to signify his availability and readiness to heed God's command, here to take Isaac to Mt. Moriah for the sacrifice, even prior to knowing what the content of that command is. Later in Genesis 22, when the divine messenger calls to Abraham again, Abraham answers in the same way: *Hineni*. Like the famous response of the people to God at Mt. Sinai – *na-aseh v'nishma* ("We will do, and we will hear"), where the readiness precedes the very hearing and then interpreting and understanding of the *mitzvot* ("commandments") – here, Abraham's response indicates a readiness to respond and obey prior to any cognitive act: hearing, understanding, and deliberation. Levinas discusses these issues in his Talmudic commentary, "The Temptation of Temptation," in *Nine Talmudic Readings*; for discussion of *hineni*, see Hilary Putnam's brief comment in "Levinas and Judaism" in Critchley and Bernasconi (eds.), *The Cambridge Companion to Levinas*, 38. See also the excellent essay by Lawrence Kaplan, "Israel under the Mountain: Emmanuel Levinas on Freedom and Constraint in the Revelation of the Torah," *Modern Judaism* 18 (1998), 35–46, in which Kaplan examines Levinas's Talmudic commentary in relation to traditional Jewish interpretations and commentaries.

[36] OB, 146.

[37] OB, 146.

[38] OB, 144.

[39] OB, 147.

in a few pages, moves from "witness" to the notion of *illeity* to religion and prophecy and finally to an important conclusion about theological language:

I can indeed state the meaning borne witness to as a said. It is an extraordinary word, the only one that does not extinguish or absorb its saying, but it cannot remain a simple word. The word God is an overwhelming semantic event that subdues the subversion worked by *illeity*. The glory of the Infinite shuts itself up in a word and becomes a Being.[40]

This word – "God" – should be taken in a very broad sense. It includes the cultural elaboration of theological language and religious expression, in technical theology, in prayer, and beyond. Levinas realizes that such elaboration is "inevitable." In its own way, all language has this religious dimension; it is determined by "inspiration or prophecy,"[41] that is, by witness to the responsibility of the self. Levinas calls it "a possibility both of ideology and of sacred delirium."[42] In short, the word "God" and theological language, indeed all language, contains, obscures, and even distorts the face-to-face and the human responsibility for the other person, which is the ground of meaningful social and human existence and yet is ever present, ineluctable in human experience. In new ways, then, Levinas seems to be reiterating what he has said before.

But the centrality of the notion of responsibility is new to *Otherwise Than Being*, and Levinas ties it to a new elaboration of his earlier affinity for the vocabulary of religion – to notions of witness, trace, and then eventually prophecy.[43] The term *"illeity"* and the notion of "that-ness" seem crucial to this train of thought, but the neologism is obscure indeed. What does it mean? How is it related to glory and witness, on the one hand, and to the word "God," on the other? How does Levinas's thought move from witness and glory to *illeity*, prophecy, and God?

Let me begin with the neologism *"illeity,"* which Levinas used in "Meaning and Sense" (1964) and in "Enigma and Phenomena" (1965), drawing on the earlier essay "The Trace of the Other" (1963).[44] In the years after the publication

---

[40] OB, 151.

[41] OB, 151–52.

[42] OB, 152.

[43] I am ignoring the important way in which God, *illeity*, and diachrony figure in Levinas's claim that in a certain sense the saying and the said occur together. This is central to my belief that for Levinas the ethical or responsibility, as the encounter with the face of the other person, is the very basis of social existence and thus occurs in ordinary life and is continuous with everyday morality and political life. It is also, I believe, the core of his response to Derrida in OB.

[44] It is generally believed by many commentators that in the years following the publication of *Totality and Infinity* Levinas's thinking is directed in part by issues provoked by Derrida's long, influential review of that book: "Violence and Metaphysics." This is an issue that I largely

of *Totality and Infinity*, Levinas seems to have thought hard about the relationship between ethics and religion, between the face of the other person and God. It is a line of thinking that begins in these essays, continues in *Otherwise Than Being*, and culminates for all practical purposes in "God and Philosophy" (1975; 1986). The key terms that mark this route, I think, are "trace" and "*illeity*," and I want to begin with the latter. We have seen that "trace," "glory," and "witness" are all terms that in ordinary discourse point beyond themselves to something not present but somehow called to our attention through what is in fact present. Levinas tries to pry the terms away from this referential dimension or role and yet at the same time to draw attention to the sense that the present is not really present at all. By employing this religious or theological vocabulary, then, if the moral force of the face is what conveys the face *as* a command, one might assume that what is not present and yet is present, as a trace, is God or an epiphany of God. But Levinas wants to steer us away from such a conclusion, and the term "*illeity*" is part of his warning, an indirect but recognizable directive to avoid the belief that God is a being who authorizes through command the obligation to care for the suffering of others.

Levinas draws on his essay "The Trace of the Other" in the last section of "Meaning and Sense," which is titled "The Trace." As we have seen, in this early paper Levinas describes the face-to-face and its significance as a "return to Platonism in a new way."[45] This remark is illuminating, for throughout the essay Levinas keeps both Platonism and neo-Platonism in mind. The question of its last section, "The Trace," is whether the absolute or the One, from which the face comes, is not another philosophical idea or principle. In other words, perhaps there is no transcendence here at all; the One, or God, is just another element in the idealist system. To avoid this, Levinas must clarify how the face does not point beyond itself to something transcendent or absolute that it signifies. In a sense, there is nothing beyond the face. And yet for the face to carry the force it does, there must be such a beyond or absolute ground; either each face must be such a ground or must point beyond itself to a ground.[46] Perhaps, Levinas suggests, Plato and Plotinus can help us to see how to solve this problem, how to see the Good, or the One, as a ground and also as genuinely transcendent, beyond Being.[47]

---

ignore in this book. Among the best comments on the Derridian influence can be found in several essays by Robert Bernasconi and in the work of Simon Critchley.

[45] "Meaning and Sense" in *Basic Philosophical Writings*, 58.

[46] See, "Meaning and Sense" in *Basic Philosophical Writings*, 59.

[47] For Levinas, Plato and Plotinus are like Descartes in this respect, that is, in identifying a genuine infinite or transcendent, which is beyond being and yet to which we have access; cf. "Meaning and Sense," 59. The notion that I use here, of a ground, is of course a metaphor, in a sense, for the relation between what is genuinely transcendent and what is within the circle of being

The face of the other person, Levinas says, "proceeds from the absolutely Absent," but its relationship "*does not indicate, does not reveal*, this *Absent*; and yet the *Absent* has a meaning in the face."[48] The language of relationship is no more apposite here than it is for the link between the self and the face, but it may be unavoidable. The face is not a thing or an appearance of a thing, the Absent not an entity, and the relationship is not one of signifying, referring, pointing, revealing, or representing, in one direction, nor is it one of explaining, justifying, or demonstrating, in the other. For the Absent is no "world behind our world."[49] Levinas uses the word "trace" for this relationship; "the beyond from which the face comes signifies as a trace. The face is in the trace of the utterly bygone, utterly past Absent." We will discuss the temporal aspect of this relationship in the next chapter, the sense in which the face itself is a past that is never present and the Absent or *illeity* an utterly bygone past. Here I want to ask what this Absent or beyond *means* for the face. What function does the Absent or *illeity* serve? What does it do? And particularly what is its ethical role? Levinas approaches these questions in stages.

First, Levinas gives it a name. Because it is not encountered, nor does it encounter the self, it is neither in the first nor the second person. This *beyond* is neither I nor you. It is there, in the third person: something distant, separate, and always so. Not I or you, it is *that*. It can never be a *you*; it is always detached, out of the line of meeting; it is what Levinas calls "*illeity*" ("that-ness" or "he-ness").[50] Second, the relationship with the face as it proceeds from *illeity* is ethical; it is a relationship that bears on responsibility and obligation. *Illeity* is the otherness of the other that is present in that other as a trace. But because that other person, as other, is the stranger, the widow, and the orphan, whose otherness from me pleads for help and commands aid, its otherness is constitutive of its ethical force, its obligating me to respond to it, its compellingness and *gravitas*, as it were. In this sense, then, as a trace – as in the everyday phenomenon of traces – *illeity* "disturbs the order of the world." A trace is what is left by what seeks to escape but fails; it "obliges."[51] Finally, Levinas calls *illeity*, with its "height," "divinity," and he quotes Plotinus's account of the One when he says "the trace of the One gives birth to essence, and being is only the trace of the One."[52] As

---

is not, strictly speaking, one of ground to grounded, or *explanans* to *explanandum*, but rather a relation analogous to such relationships at best.

[48] "Meaning and Sense" in *Basic Philosophical Writings*, 60.

[49] "Meaning and Sense" in *Basic Philosophical Writings*, 60.

[50] "Meaning and Sense" in *Basic Philosophical Writings*, 61; cf. 64.

[51] This point is underscored in "Enigma and Phenomenon" in *Basic Philosophical Writings*, 75–77.

[52] "Meaning and Sense" in *Basic Philosophical Writings*, 63; see also Plotinus, *Enneads*, trans. A. H. Armstrong (Cambridge, MA: Harvard University Press, 1984), vol. 5, p. 5.

a footprint in the sand is a trace of a step that has passed by and is gone, so *illeity*, or divinity, is in the face of the other person as a trace of what is forever absent – and never present. The divine is only present in the face; it is never present in itself, and it is the *obliging character* of the face that is this trace of divinity.[53]

Clearly, the main point of Levinas's analysis and account in "The Trace of the Other" is that *illeity* is not an entity and its trace in the face not a sign. In addition to relying upon Plotinus to help him make these points, Levinas also calls upon a contrast with Buber and Marcel, who prefer the Thou to the It. Levinas's face is not exactly a Thou, and certainly *illeity* is no It. Levinas also turns to the biblical text. He interprets "being in the image of God" as meaning "to find oneself in his trace." The trace of God is in the face of the other person; hence, to find oneself, to find who one is, is to respond to that face. Then, Levinas turns to Exodus 33: The God who has passed by is forever absent, never present.[54] He always has passed by and the trace God leaves behind is in the face of the other person. To draw close to God, then, is to respond to the face of the other person. This is the meaning of human existence. Levinas calls it "the illuminated site of being [that] is but the passage of God."[55] When we speak of encountering God or of God revealing Himself to me, this is an expression of my desire to respond to the other person with kindness and generosity, my sense of being called by the other and being obligated to her. Indeed, doing the latter is the only way one can experience the former. One cannot know God or encounter God directly; all religious experience is ethical action.[56]

In *Otherwise Than Being*, Levinas makes the same point: "The Infinite passes in saying."[57] In the face-to-face and responsibility, God has passed by, and His trace remains. Insofar as "saying" or the encounter with the face of the other

[53] In contemporary analytic meta-ethics, this weight might be called "normative force," although the notion of a norm or rule would not apply to Levinas's conception of the ethical character of the face; it would, however, apply to the principles that one finds in moral theories and that are employed in everyday moral reasoning in various ways. As we shall see shortly, Levinas, in discussing these matters, also calls attention to Moses' encounter with God in Exodus 33. It is interesting to compare Levinas's interpretation of this passage with Buber's in *Moses* (New York: Harper, 1958).

[54] Exodus 33:18–23:

And [Moses] said: "Show me, I pray Thee, Thy glory." And He said: "I will make all My goodness pass before thee, and will proclaim the name of the Lord before thee; and I will be gracious to whom I will be gracious, and will show mercy on whom I will show mercy." And He said: "Thou canst not see My face, for man shall not see Me and live." And the Lord said: "Behold, there is a place by Me, and thou shalt stand upon the rock. And it shall come to pass, while My glory passeth by, that I will put thee in a cleft of the rock, and will cover thee with My hand until I have passed by. And I will take away My hand, and thou shalt see My back; but My face shall not be seen."

[55] "Enigma and Phenomenon" in *Basic Philosophical Writings*, 77.
[56] See OB, 147.
[57] OB, 147.

person is witness, it testifies to this fact, as it were; the glory of the face occurs as the self's responsibility, and this is witness – to the face, to God, to itself. God is present only in His glory; He shines forth. And His glory is always reflected, as it were, in the face. And the face is always how I encounter the other and my responsibility to and for her. Hence, my responsibility is witness. But to witness is not to talk about or refer to or represent; it is to be responsible, to receive the order from the other, to accept it, and to obey it.[58]

Here in *Otherwise Than Being*, then, as in his earlier works, Levinas claims that the face-to-face is the way God is present or effective in human existence, although words like "present" and "effective" are themselves only to be taken figuratively. We have claimed, however, that this is not intended as an extraordinary, isolated event, as if the encounter with the other person is Levinas's substitute for religious or mystical experience or indeed a leap of faith. Rather, we have argued that Levinas takes all human existence to be social and interpersonal and that his examination of the face-to-face is meant to call attention to that dimension of social existence that gives point and purpose to human life. Here, in *Otherwise Than Being*, he elaborates the link between society (and justice) and the face-to-face in the light of his discussion of God, the trace, and *illeity*.[59] We have already had occasion to discuss some of these issues; here we want to focus on this last set of themes – how God, the trace, and *illeity* figure into his account. What role does God play in the way that responsibility is related to social justice? If, in his earlier works, God as *illeity* was present in the face as a trace and as its ethical force, does this role still dominate this later treatment? Does God have any different or special role to play in social justice, above and beyond His role in the self's responsibility?

I think that these questions confuse Levinas's approach and his goals. He is not seeking to find the way that God as *illeity* contributes uniquely or directly to social justice. Rather, his task should be conceived differently. We find ourselves, in everyday life, in society, engaged in institutions, policies, and roles. Our lives are just or seek to be. And religious vocabulary is regularly used by some to articulate our goals, for justice and peace, for religion is a significant aspect of our lives and has been historically. If, as Levinas has argued, theological language expresses our sense of personal responsibility for each unique other, how then can it also express our commitments to justice and peace? Why do we say that God commands us to seek peace and to pursue justice, to create and sustain just institutions, to feed the hungry, clothe the naked, and care for the stranger, the widow, and the orphan? How is God associated with social and political goals, if indeed His infinite, absolute absence is present as the trace in the face of the

---

[58] OB, 149.
[59] OB, 140–62.

poor and destitute other? This, I think, is Levinas's question: What justifies our *extending* theological vocabulary into the domain of social and political life?

Levinas distinguishes the "third-person" character of *illeity* from the "third party" that is the source of society, justice, language, and more: "This 'thirdness' [of *illeity*] is different from that of the third man; it is the third party that interrupts the face to face of a welcome of the other man, interrupts the proximity or approach of the neighbor; it is the third man with which justice begins."[60] What exactly does Levinas mean? First, that God as *illeity* is present in the face, but that the third party has a different relation to the face of the other. In society, God is related to the other but not as a third party; God is the other's ethical force. The third party is other to my other; there is a third, a fourth, and more; society is complex and multiple, and our lives are unavoidably social. God as *illeity* is other, but not as an other. Second, God is what calls to me from the face, whereas the third party compels me to stand back and to judge and assess how I am to execute my responsibility to all others. The third party pushes me to judgment, deliberation, and the formulation of principles and rules. God pushes me to responsibility prior to any of these. Finally, God is the author of responsibility and a kind of identity through substitution for the other; "God" is the term that comes to our lips when we seek to express the weight or burden that we feel toward the other. It is the term that in ordinary parlance we use when the authority of moral responsibility comes to mind, while the third party is the author of justice through detachment and evaluation and separation.

But while the third party or third man brings on justice and is not identical to the third-person character of *illeity*, the two are related. For in every social interaction, which is potentially or actually just, responsibility is felt. The face of my neighbor orders me; "the order [is] in my response itself," and *illeity* is "this way for the order to come from I know not where." "It is the coming of the order to which I am subjected before hearing it."[61] Moreover, all this is present in society and gives society the urgency of justice and hence its purpose, its significance. Levinas calls this social condition and striving for justice "a betrayal of my anarchic relation with *illeity*" that is also "a new relationship with it." That is, God is involved in my being "a member of society," but this involvement is a betrayal of and also the establishment of a new relationship with God as *illeity*.[62] I think that it is clear what Levinas means. There is a sense in which the reciprocal relationships of social life "betray" [or compromise] the utter particularity of the face-to-face and its asymmetry. The infinite responsibility to the other person is now qualified, restricted, and directed; it enters into a

---

[60] OB, 150; cf. 156–62.
[61] OB, 150.
[62] OB, 158.

kind of calculation and a distribution process. We have moved from personal
kindness to a welfare system, as it were. Moreover, we shift from being wholly
passive – accused and traumatized – to active. Hence, the purity and infinitude
of our original responsibility is "betrayed." But at the same time that this shift
is a betrayal of God, of the divine trace in this particular face, it is also true that
"it is only thanks to God that, as a subject incomparable with the other, I am
approached as an other by the others." That is, I am only put in a position,
with everyone else, of developing institutions and principles of justice – as Rawls
argues, for example – insofar as I am encountered by others, and this means if
God is present in the other's face. It is only because the other is valuable to me
by being someone I care about and sense a need to help that I then – in the
social situation with many others, indeed vast numbers – feel bound to set about
developing principles, institutions, and policies concerning just and benevolent
distributions. As Levinas puts it, "[T]he reciprocal relationship binds me to the
other man in the trace of transcendence, in *illeity*. The passing of God . . . in
precisely the reverting to the incomparable subject into a member of society."
Society and the responsibility that underlies it, so to speak, both are grounded
in the ethical force of God.[63]

We can conceive of that force and its relation to *illeity* in the following way.
In traditional theology and philosophical thinking about God, God is conceived
as infinite, omnipotent, and overwhelming. Such thinking can seem to be
confronted with a paradox about how the human can confront the divine, the
finite the infinite, and still survive, indeed about how the finite can encounter
the divine and respond to it. The reason for the paradox is that if divine power
is unlimited and infinite, it leaves no room for finite freedom, and yet the
latter exists. A traditional response is that in the very encounter the divine
exhibits its infinite power both by commanding and by conferring upon the
human the freedom to respond to the command. On the one hand, then, in
order to cope with the relation to the infinite God, traditional religion must
somehow reconcile divine power and human freedom or, on the other, God
would be taken to withdraw completely from such relationships and become a
hidden God, *deus absconditus*. But Levinas sees things differently. It is as if there
are moments in human existence when the divine encounters the human and
yet "departs" at the same instant, and in departing, the divine leaves behind a
"trace" of itself. That trace resides in the face of the other person to whom we
are related; it is a trace of a divine presence that is in fact a divine absence, an
illeity, and its effect is to leave behind a residue of its overwhelming power, of
its infinity, a residue that is manifest in the other person's face, her vulnerability
that in virtue of being the site of the divine trace is also her demandingness.

---

[63] OB, 158; for Levinas's fullest account of society and justice, see 158–62.

It is God's "having passed by via the other's face" that gives the other person's presence to me its obligatoriness, its ethical force. And with that, together with the fact that the divine is not present other than in this way, the self is free to respond in one way or another. In this sense, as Levinas says, "I am obliged without this obligation having begun in me, as though an order slipped into my consciousness like a thief, smuggled itself in...." (*Otherwise Than Being*, 13).

Levinas takes it that the normative force of the ethical resides in the way the other person, in all his or her particularity, is present to me and calls to me. Here, in his account of *illeity*, he depicts what lies behind that force, so to speak, where it comes from, what grounds it. After all, it cannot come from the other person, who is just another person like me. It must come from transcendence, not a transcendence that is present but rather a transcendence that always "has passed by" and leaves its residue or "trace" – the way that the other person's very existence matters to me, concerns me, obligates me. Later in *Otherwise Than Being*, Levinas says that "the Infinite orders to me the neighbor as a face.... This way for the order to come from I know not where, this coming that is not a recalling, ... we have called *illeity*. It is the coming of the order to which I am subjected before hearing it, or which I hear in my own saying. It is an august command, but one that does not constrain or dominate...." (150) This latter – this elevated order that does not overwhelm – I have said is the residue left behind by an awesome transcendence (divine omnipotence) that has passed by, so to speak. It is the normative force left behind in the face of the other person who confronts me; it is what makes that face not only vulnerable to me but also binding for me. Indeed, there is *no other way* that ethics could be binding for Levinas.

Otherwise Than Being elaborates and develops what we found earlier in *Totality and Infinity* and the essays written shortly after it. Levinas adds a rich temporal analysis that we will look at in the next chapter and the role of theological language for expressing the meaning of social and political justice. But *illeity* remains the term he uses for pointing to the trace of divinity in the face, its ethical force or ethical character, as I have called it.[64] In a sense, *illeity* is what accounts for the normativity, the compellingness, or the obligatoriness – what in ordinary terms we might call the authority – that is present in the other person's face. It is what makes it the case that when we encounter the other person, it is with this sense of moral burden, of having to respond to her and to do so with care and concern. He adds explicit comments on God and politics, not because God contributes *directly* to political justice but rather because he wants to show how the political and social are grounded in responsibility and the

---

[64] Cohen uses the phrase "*moral* force" in *Elevations*, 185.

face-to-face and hence how theological language is appropriate to both. This discussion is Levinas's opportunity to comment on the relationship between church and state or better on the relationship between religion and politics; it is his way of engaging with the Hegelian commitment to the primacy of the state and the objection of those who take religious institutions to be the primary vehicle of history. In his own way, Levinas returns to the Kantian synthesis of the religious, the ethical, and the political. We might put it this way: We can now understand why God wants us not only to love one another, to be kind and generous, every one of us to each other, but also to make the world just.[65] We can appreciate why religious Jews, for example, acknowledge God and God's role in social and political affairs as well as in personal ones, but, on Levinas's view, only if they take the religious to be the locus of the ethical.

How can Levinas distinguish between *il y a*, the "there is," and *illeity*? Levinas's notion of *il y a* is also a difficult one. He first wrote about it while in a POW camp during the early 1940s in an article that after the war became the core of *Existence and Existents*.[66] The there-is is the impersonal, anonymous space that is present prior to any individuality or emergence of distinctive beings. It is prior to the distinction between being and nothingness and prior to particular subjects, and it is present even after death. As Nathan Kleinberg puts it, "Therefore, Heidegger's description of anxiety in the face of death is a misconception. Individual beings encounter anxiety, but after death they are returned to the realm of anonymous being, which does not. Therefore, the cause of anxiety, according to Levinas, is not the finitude of death, which is the limit of our self, but instead the infinity of anonymous being that continues long after we have shed our mortal coil. . . . The question for Levinas is: 'Anxiety before Being – the horror of Being – is this not more original than anxiety before death?' (*Existence and Existents*, 20)."[67] As Levinas would later recall, in the interviews published as *Ethics and Infinity*, "In *De l'Existence à l'Existant*, I analyzed other modalities of Being, taken in its verbal sense: fatigue, indolence, effort. In these phenomena I showed a dread before Being, an impotent recoil, an evasion and, consequently, there too, the shadow of the *il y a*."[68]

The strategies of Western philosophy, the discovery and elevation of the self or the subject, are intended to cope with this anxiety, but they fail. For even

[65] See Wright, *The Twilight of Jewish Philosophy*, 89–93, on theological language in OB. My account has similarities but also significant differences.

[66] For a helpful discussion to which I am indebted, see Ethan Kleinberg, *Generation Existential: Heidegger's Philosophy in France, 1927–1961*, 247–56; see also, on Maurice Blanchot, 215–19.

[67] Kleinberg, *Generation Existential*, 251. Kleinberg cites Simon Critchley, "*Il y a* – A Dying Stronger than Death (Blanchot with Levinas)," *Oxford Literary Review*, 15:1–2 (1993), 81–131; a later version can be found in Simon Critchley, *Very Little . . . Almost Nothing*, Lecture I, 31–83.

[68] *Ethics and Infinity*, 51; quoted by Kleinberg, *Generation Existential*, 252.

death does not provide an escape from being engulfed in this anonymity. The primacy of the subject and the emphasis on individuality and authenticity are camouflages that do not succeed. At death we lose our individuality, but there is no avoiding the sea of being that awaits us.

The *il y a* is beyond representation and articulation, but it does manifest itself, I think, in our understanding of the world in which we live and our lives in it. Let me propose that we treat Nature as the chief manifestation in our thinking and our lives of the *il y a*. Hence, the impersonal, anonymous character of the *il y a* can be taken to manifest itself in the way Nature is conceived by traditional naturalists; I am thinking of Hobbes, for example, or Spinoza. The latter may believe that understanding how we as human beings are merely natural beings and hence how our lives should be understood within the processes of Nature will bring us peace of mind and tranquility and even a kind of immortality of the soul, but Levinas wants us to believe that this sense of being immersed wholly in Nature and yet of being unable to escape it in fact brings anxiety of a deep kind.[69] Our emphasis on our individual distinctiveness and the virtues of the self is a strategy to avoid the dread of being swallowed up by Nature, by the threat of insignificance. And this gives rise to the question, then: Is there a way of confronting those anxieties, those fears?

Levinas's answer, I believe, arises with his understanding of our encounter with the other person. If the *il y a* is manifest in our lives and thinking as Nature and the threats posed by a thoroughgoing naturalism, then our way of coping with it comes with the introduction of value and meaning, with a sense of our own freedom and worth. But from where does that sense come? In a world of facts, so to speak, where do values arise? Levinas's answer is that value arises for each of us in our encounters with other persons. Our distinctiveness is given value by being engaged by others. It is not our own needs and concern for our own finitude that makes our lives worthwhile; it is the needs and finitude of the other person.

But why is this so? Why is the other person's suffering and pain, the other person's vulnerability and destitution, not just an object of reaction for us? Why do we not simply recoil from such suffering? Why does it confer worth on our lives? Levinas's answer is *illeity*.

If *il y a* manifests itself in our lives and thinking as Nature, then *illeity* manifests itself in our lives and our thinking as God. Moreover, if naturalism threatens us with our being engulfed by natural processes and simply an insignificant constituent of the natural order, then God threatens us with the complete

---

[69] There is an analogue in Bernard Williams's famous paper "The Makropulos Case: Reflections on the Tedium of Immortality" in Williams, *Problems of the Self* (Cambridge: Cambridge University Press, 1973).

domination of the "Wholly-Other," to use Barth's expression. That is, divine power and omnipotence threaten to overwhelm us, to subordinate us unqualifiedly. But while *illeity* may find its way into our thinking and practices by our concept of God and our language about God, *in fact* it finds its way into our lives quite differently. It never confronts us in its overwhelming presence. Here, I am confident, Levinas is attuned to the biblical text, especially to Exodus and God's warning to Moses that no one can see God's face and live. Rather, God will pass by and Moses will see his back, his glory (Exodus 33: 18–23). That is, *illeity* is only evident in our lives as a trace or residue, as having passed by, and the locus of that having-passed-by and of that trace is the face of the other person. It is that residue of God's overwhelming power that gives the face of destitution and need its imperative character, its normativity, so to speak. Or, to put it otherwise, the force or import of the ethical is a residue of God's infinite power, or omnipotence. The other's face, as we have said, confronts us with a plea and a command; the plea comes from the other's natural state, his needs and pain, while the command comes from the fact that he is the venue of the trace of the divine's having passed by, of infinite power.[70] Less than such a passing-by and leaving-a-trace would not be sufficient to provide the moral force; more than them would destroy our freedom and capacity to exercise our moral responsibility.

Il y a and *illeity*, then, are what stand behind the fact-value distinction, so to speak. Too much of one would mean a thoroughgoing naturalism; too much of the other would mean absolute subordination to God. Neither is acceptable. Human existence occurs neither in a world of facts nor a world of values *simpliciter* but rather in a world in which the two interpenetrate and suffuse one another. That interpenetration occurs in human social life, our lives with one another.

What this shows, moreover, is exactly how Levinas thinks God and *illeity* are associated with height and the authority of the face. It is tempting, as I have claimed, to treat *illeity* as what grounds the authority of the face of the other person, but until now it has been unclear how that it so. This account of the distinction between *il y a* and *illeity* helps us to see how the two differ and how they cooperate; it also helps us to see where the normativity of the face comes from. It is the way that infinite divine power manifests itself in our lives. In Kantian terms, it is that residue or trace that accounts for the primacy of the ethical or moral value.

How does this groundedness of moral obligation express itself in religious life and language? It is revealed in the language of divine command. That is, what

---

[70] In short, Levinas has found a rather extraordinary way to ground our sense of ethical obligation in God without taking it to be a set of divine commands.

Levinas shows us is that the trace or residue of the absolute absence of *illeity* occurs, in the terminology of Judaism especially, as the vocabulary of God's commands, what in Hebrew are called *mitzvot*. In other words, the Bible's terminology of God's commanding Moses and the Israelites to perform laws and statutes is one way that religious sensibility indicates its appreciation of the *moral force* that manifests itself in the face of other persons, in their pain and suffering, in their expression of need. Such moral force is *in* the face but only insofar as that face itself is the trace of an unbounded, overwhelming power that no individual could confront and survive.[71]

PHILOSOPHY, GOD, AND THEOLOGY

Levinas's thinking about "God" and the idea of God culminates in the essay "God and Philosophy." Perhaps the first thing that the reader notices about this essay is that it is explicitly about the concept of God in the tradition of Western philosophy. We have seen that this is not the central focus of Levinas's earlier thinking about "God" and the concept of God. Thus far, his attention has been broader, in a sense. He has wondered what the meaning of "God" is when it is used by religious practitioners or by theologians or in theological texts, even liturgical ones. Moreover, Levinas has exploited the tone and texture of religious and theological vocabulary for his own philosophical purposes.

In this essay, however, he wants to understand how philosophy has incorporated the concept of God and how it should do so. In such a context, then, he asks "[I]f God can be exposed in a rational discourse which would be neither ontology nor faith," and he points out that this will require doubting "the formal opposition . . . between the God of Abraham, Isaac, and Jacob . . . and the god of philosophers" for example, the god of natural theology. I think that what he has said in the works we have already examined indicates clearly why this pair of opposites really does not "constitute an alternative,"[72] that is, an exhaustive set of alternatives. Indeed, his answer will be yes; there is a "rational discourse" other than ontological and other than theistic or fideistic for articulating the concept of God. When we use theological language, we do so when we feel moved to call attention to the fundamental character of our responsibility for and to others and especially to the way that the other's face appeals to us and commands us, the way in which it impresses us ethically. The other's face is

---

[71] See Purcell, *Levinas and Theology*, 43–44. Purcell takes the divine absence to permit human responsibility. His reading strikes me as similar to the view that divine omnipotence must withhold itself in order to permit human freedom.

[72] "God and Philosophy" in *Basic Philosophical Writings*, 131; cf. Cohen, *Elevations*, 176–79. The essay "God and Philosophy" appears in several places, including *Of God Who Comes to Mind*, *Collected Philosophical Papers*, and *A Levinas Reader*.

both a gift and a burden; we should experience it as calling us to respond with generosity and concern. "God" is the word we use, in certain religious and theological contexts, to express and call attention to this twin fact. We do not ever encounter, experience, or think directly of God. We experience the face as appealing to us and commanding us; this twin fact is "the trace" of something never present but effective only here, in the face. That is *illeity*, and, in a sense, it is what is divine; it is the "holy" or "holiness." It is what "God" means. Clearly, this is neither the God of natural theology nor the object of religious experience, of faith. In Levinas's thinking, it *is* nothing, an absence, not part of our ordinary, everyday experience or our conceptual schemes or our theories. It does not designate any thing, but it is meaningful nonetheless.

In order to answer the question of how God can figure in philosophy but not as a theme, topic, or concept, Levinas returns to his familiar appreciation of Descartes and the way, in *Meditation* III, that the *I* acknowledges its grasp of the "idea of the infinite," its having the idea of God as perfect and infinite.[73] Levinas calls this act of grasping the idea of the infinite "a passivity more passive still than any passivity"; it is "an idea signifying with a signifyingness prior to presence ... prior to every origin in consciousness and thus an-archical," that is, without an origin or beginning, "accessible in its trace." It is a "trauma of awakening," a calling to attention, a disturbance, and "a demand."[74] This terminology and these claims are familiar territory. But there is a distinctiveness about Levinas's emphasis. Here he does not simply note Descartes' clue to our relationship with what is transcendent to consciousness or beyond our thought, but he also underlines the fact that Descartes associates this transcendence with God. Levinas then explores the experience phenomenologically, to show how it is an awakening, a putting into question, a dazzling, and thereby a desire. But it is a desire unlike others; it is beyond satisfaction; he calls it a desire for the Good. But what does this mean, and why does he speak of the Good?[75]

What is Levinas doing here? In one sense, with his most mature vocabulary for the face-to-face, Levinas is associating God with that encounter. But he is in fact doing more than associate the two. He is exploring the face-to-face in order to *expose* where God fits into the experience, what about that experience and relationship it is that the word "God" expresses, why we in fact should, in thinking about God, realize that the human context or space that is the venue for God, as it were, is the face of the other person and our responsibility for and to the other. How does Levinas accomplish this task? The gist of Levinas's answer occurs in section 14 of the essay.

---

[73] "God and Philosophy" in *Basic Philosophical Writings*, 135–37.
[74] "God and Philosophy" in *Basic Philosophical Writings*, 137.
[75] "God and Philosophy" in *Basic Philosophical Writings*, 139–40.

Being in touch with the genuinely transcendent, with the infinite that is beyond totality, beyond being and essence, beyond thought and comprehension, is to have a desire that reaches out to something that is beyond being thought, being desired in ordinary ways, and so forth. In this desire, this craving or love or striving for the transcendent, the desirable must be both near and far. Levinas calls this "Holy." He also calls it the "Good." My life has the meaning it does because I encounter other persons as needing me and calling me to aid and support them; I want to respond to them, and in my wanting and responding, goodness and sanctity enter my life. Hence, what makes my desire possible is near insofar as it *orders me*, but it is far or "different" insofar as it orders me to what is undesirable: the other. This double-aspect relationship is proximity, "a responsibility for the neighbor," pure election or pure *supporting*.[76]

Levinas asks us to think of our everyday life as a kind of sleep or delirium. This is the life of ordinary experience, relationships, language, thought, and desire. Suppose one of our social encounters with a friend, a mere acquaintance, or a stranger, normal in every way, suddenly shakes us; something in the look, the eyes, or even the nape of the neck of the other, disturbs us – we are awakened to a sense of responsibility, to a sense of obligation to reach out, to extend a hand, to give a piece of bread, to share even our last morsel. This encounter is what Levinas calls "being accused by the other" or "being hostage for the other" – awakening or being sobered up – being in the grip of the Good.[77] In the midst of ordinary experience, our life takes on an ethical character, an ethical orientation or definition. In this way, the Infinite or God "refer[s] . . . to the nondescribable proximity of others"; the term for the Infinite or God as it performs this act of awakening the self to its responsibility in the face of the other person is "*illeity*."

Levinas's description is obscure. He says that the supremely desirable turns us to the nondesirable. That is, we desire the Good; the Good calls forth our love for it, but then it turns our love from the Good and "orient[s] it toward the other, and only thus toward the Good." The Good calls forth desire for it from us, but it remains separate or "holy" by directing us to help the other person. It remains thereby "a third person, the *he* in the depth of the You." God arises for us in the other person and directs us toward the other. But in this movement, God is "neither an object nor an interlocutor" but rather "absolute remoteness," which "turns into my responsibility." God is not the other but "other than the other" and "prior to the ethical bond with the other."[78] That is, the other's face engages me – petitioning and commanding – and I experience that other

[76] "God and Philosophy" in *Basic Philosophical Writings*, 140.
[77] "God and Philosophy" in *Basic Philosophical Writings*, 140.
[78] "God and Philosophy" in *Basic Philosophical Writings*, 141.

person, indeed each and every other person, as worthy of my acceptance and concern; *illeity* is essential to this call to me, this weight that falls on me. But how?

In a footnote, Levinas compares the dialectic whereby the Good or God calls us and then turns us to the other person to a similar dialectic in Franz Rosenzweig's *Star of Redemption*: "Franz Rosenzweig interprets the *response* given by man to the love with which God loves him as the movement unto the neighbor."[79] In Rosenzweig, this response is redemptive, and it is a response to revelation. One might read the dialectic, as it applies to both Levinas and Rosenzweig, this way: God reveals to us that human life is meaningful and valuable; this is His gift to us, and it inspires us to act on it and moves us to gratitude, which we do by extending ourselves to others. We aid their lives the way God has aided ours; we sacrifice for them out of love and generosity. We respond to God's love for us by sharing our love with others. This, for Levinas, is responsibility and substitution. Viewed from one angle, this picture shows us drawn to, burdened by, and devoted to the other person: our neighbor. We respond to the face through responsibility for and to the other; we value the other as needful of our concern and care. The revelation, for Rosenzweig, is God's loving gift to us of a meaningful human existence. The revelation, for Levinas, is in the face of the other person and thus is always a trace of what is holy, absolutely absent, and separate, *he* and never *you*. This is why encountering God is being responsible for and to my neighbor and why the Good is God or what we call "God."[80] In Rosenzweig, revelation and redemption are distinguishable ways that the subject experiences the world, God, and others, and their structure is revealed in a narrative account that tracks the experience of the one and then the other. For Levinas, revelation is the background for redemption, as it were. That is, responsibility arises as a call from the face, which is moved to affect the self by revelation, that is, by its sanctity or holiness or ethical force.

Levinas continues, as he had done in *Otherwise Than Being*, by tying this face-to-face encounter to witnessing and testimony via *saying*. Everyday language – the *said* – is preceded by what he calls "saying," this "testimony of responsibility."[81] His point is that discourse and speech are not only linguistic acts, of course, but also acts of assistance and benevolence: They act out the obedience to the other, to the command of the face that is given its force through

---

[79] "God and Philosophy" in *Basic Philosophical Writings*, 190 n. 21; the reference is to Franz Rosenzweig, *Stern der Erlösung* (Frankfurt am Main: Suhrkamp, 1988), 174–228, or "Birth of the Soul" in *Star of Redemption*, trans. Barbara E. Galli (Madison: University of Wisconsin Press, 2005), 156–204.

[80] See "God and Philosophy" in *Basic Philosophical Writings*, 141–46.

[81] "God and Philosophy" in *Basic Philosophical Writings*, 145.

illeity. In speaking to another, I acknowledge and accept her. Hence, saying or obedience is witness to God, as we discussed above. Readiness to respond, the biblical "here I am" (*hineni*), is an expression of this witness, this *saying* that is prior to the *said*; it is the basic expression in religious language for the presence of God in human life:

[T]he sentence in which God gets mixed in with words is not "I believe in God." The religious discourse that precedes all religious discourse is not dialogue. It is the "here I am" said to a neighbor to whom I am given over, by which I announce peace, that is, my responsibility for the other.[82]

Not surprisingly, then, this utterance, the paradigmatic one, is characteristic of the prophets and of prophetic inspiration. Famously, it is Abraham's expression but also that of Isaiah, for example, who confronts God with his readiness and in so doing, Levinas tells us, responds to the other with willing acceptance and care. "Prophesying is pure testimony, pure because prior to all disclosure; it is subjection to an order before understanding the order."[83] This is not about "religious experience," Levinas reminds us; it is about philosophy grounded in prophecy, a kind of Platonism, and a reenchantment of human life through a revelation of the importance of the other person to it.

Levinas had a lifelong investment in reflection about theological language and religious life. "God and Philosophy" is the culmination of that effort. But while it integrates discussion of God and especially theological language with his later terminology for the face-to-face – substitution, hostage, holiness, enigma, proximity, accusation, glory, and more – it primarily elaborates earlier insights. In ordinary discourse, we associate "God" with various features, with status of a preeminent kind, with power, transcendence, and such. Levinas locates or exposes these features in responsibility and the face-to-face. In this way, he argues that our use of divinity and the associated vocabulary of divinity arises out of and expresses the ethical engagement that manifests them. Terms like "holiness" and "glory" and "sanctity" are ones we associate with what is ultimate, preeminent, overwhelming, and dominant; to assign them to the locus of the ethical in our lives is to say that the aura of religion and theology is in fact projected by what is the deepest ground of our ethical sensibility. We may find the details of Levinas's quasi-phenomenological account unpersuasive or even question begging. But the account is not beside the point. Put in simple terms, it is his attempt to show the way in which our social situation, which is grounded in a sense of obligation and responsibility toward the other person, is orienting and determinative. The face of the other is an ethical matter and not

---

[82] "God and Philosophy" in *Basic Philosophical Writings*, 146.
[83] "God and Philosophy" in *Basic Philosophical Writings*, 146–47.

an epistemological one, and it is the ground of what gives human existence its point and purpose. Philosophy does not show us what human existence is, but rather it directs us to live it and exposes what desire or intensity should drive that life. Ordinary life is complex. Its religious features have a special role to play only if they are properly understood. Philosophy has tended to intellectualize them. Levinas seeks to correct this distortion, to show that religion, like life, is essentially ethics.

As we have seen, a key term in Levinas's account, perhaps *the* key term, is "*illeity*." There is a tendency for commentators to treat it as any other name or designation and to look for its referent. But this is a mistake; the term does not denote. It does signify something by helping us to appreciate that the face does not supplicate and command in virtue of its own features, shape, skin color, expression, and so forth; the face calls me into question insofar as it is a trace of a distant thing that is no thing, of an absolute absence. That absence, as present in the face, so to speak, is *illeity*. It is not a thing or entity or object nor literally a manifestation of one. It is not a you or Thou. In a sense, it *is not*. But without *illeity*, the face cannot mean what it does to me. It is what accounts for the particularity and transcendence of the face and for the infinity of my responsibility, for *illeity* is why the face carries weight with me and demands of me – why it matters to me. It is *that* about the face of the stranger, the widow or the orphan *that* calls, cries out to me, singles me out, and registers with me as binding. Hence, the word "God" comes to my lips when I realize that I am responsible, when I appreciate my social condition and take it seriously.

The other central term for Levinas is the word "trace" and what it implies, that the face-to-face is diachrony, as he puts it. But this brings us to an aspect of Levinas's thinking that is difficult and challenging, his treatment of time. It is the subject of our next chapter.

GOD, ETHICS, AND CONTEMPORARY PHILOSOPHY

Before we turn to time and temporality, however, it is worth showing that Levinas's attention to theology and religion is not unique among recent philosophers, something that could not be said of English-speaking philosophers in quite the same way even two or three decades ago. In contemporary philosophy, a return to discussion of God and religious life, after the banishment effected by logical positivism and its legacy, can be found in more than one venue. One such tendency is a new version of natural or rational theology that begins from a commitment to naturalism or a modified naturalism and finds ways to secure religious commitments, using a good deal of logical and linguistic apparatus, within the compass of analytic metaphysics, epistemology,

and philosophy of mind.[84] Another tendency, neo-Thomist of a sort, is associated with Alasdair MacIntyre and developments in moral philosophy. The most
interesting reappropriation of religious themes, however, part of a large-scale
rethinking of secularism and liberalism, is that of Charles Taylor in *Sources of the
Self* and in later publications.[85] It is worth taking a moment to consider Taylor's
motives and his strategy in order to shed additional light on what Levinas has
and has not accomplished.

Taylor's discussion of God and religion can be understood as part of his
examination of the "malaise of modernity," as he calls it, and the deficiencies
of contemporary secularism.[86] We need not review the overall plot of Taylor's
critique; a sketch will suffice. Modern societies, as Nicholas Smith puts it,
"breed alienation, unease and discontent."[87] They are committed to freedom
and reason and yet realize these values only inadequately, in ways that lead to
oppression, frustration, and distress. Still, the modern identity does have positive
features, and one of these is "the idea that the moral life should be directed
toward alleviating the suffering of the whole of humankind and implementing
a system of universal justice."[88] It was thought that privilege and class should
give way to a welfare state, under the guise of what Taylor calls "providential
deism," with God as the moral source that empowers the commitment to use
instrumental reason to cultivate virtue for human purposes.[89] But eventually,
God as the moral source gave way to self-determined, free action, and Taylor
argues that this replacement of a religious moral source with a secular one fails
to realize the *goods* aimed at – including benevolence and justice.[90] What occurs
in modernity, then, is a dissonance between the goods that are supremely valued
and the moral sources that underwrite and empower those goods.

One feature of Taylor's solution to this crisis is theistic; it involves discovering
ways to accomplish access to "the divine affirmation of the human."[91] Briefly,
Taylor argues that we continue to affirm the goods of justice, benevolence, and

---

[84] E.g., in the work of Alvin Plantinga and Nicholas Wolterstorff, among others.

[85] Charles Taylor, *Varieties of Religion Today* and *A Catholic Modernity?*

[86] See Smith, *Charles Taylor*, 199–236. In addition to Taylor's *Sources of the Self*, see also James L. Heft
(ed.), *A Catholic Modernity?: Charles Taylor's Marianist Award Lecture*, with Responses . . . (Oxford:
Oxford University Press, 1999); Charles Taylor, *Varieties of Religion Today: William James Revisited*
and *Modern Social Imaginaries*.

[87] Smith, *Charles Taylor*, 199.

[88] Smith, *Charles Taylor*, 205–6; see especially *Sources of the Self*, 266–74.

[89] Smith, *Charles Taylor*, 209–10.

[90] See especially Smith, *Charles Taylor*, 210–14. See also Alasdair MacIntyre, *After Virtue* (South
Bend, IN: University of Notre Dame Press, 1981), and the classic account in Elizabeth
Anscombe, "Modern Moral Philosophy" in Anscombe, *Collected Philosophical Papers*, vol. 3
(Minneapolis: University of Minnesota Press, 981), 26–42.

[91] Taylor, *Sources of the Self*, 516, 521; see also Smith, *Charles Taylor*, 222–23, 228–31.

the reduction of suffering. To do so, however, requires an "unconditional love"; the demands are extraordinary and beyond our secular resources. As Taylor puts it, "the question which arises from all this is whether we are not living beyond our moral means in continuing allegiance to our standards of justice and benevolence."[92] Only if we are overwhelmed with an unconditional love for the beneficiaries of our actions can we feel obligated to benevolence and empowered to carry it out.[93] This state, of being overwhelmed by an unconditional love, is what theism provides: an openness to a transcendent source that empowers that love through love of us.[94]

Although set within the context of Taylor's own receptivity to a kind of Augustinianism, this recommendation in behalf of a theism capable of grounding an unconditional love for others sounds very familiar to any reader of Franz Rosenzweig. For this reason, too, it should sound familiar to us, as we try to understand Levinas's discussion of theological language and the concept of God. Taylor and Levinas do approach their discussion of God from different points of view. Levinas, as I have urged, begins with theological language, religious practice, texts, and so forth and asks what this complex means; the language of "God" comes to mind, as he puts it, insofar as we are human beings as responsible selves obligated to other persons unconditionally and when we are aware of this responsibility and seek to express it. Taylor, on the other hand, begins by articulating our modern identity and a central moral dimension of it, only then to claim that our commitments to justice and benevolence and to reducing suffering are insecure and ungrounded. Theism emerges for him as the most plausible and compelling way to ground and empower the attitude necessary to hold that moral commitment; when secularism fails to find such a ground after its assault on traditional theological beliefs, Taylor encourages a recovery of a form of religious affirmation. In a sense, then, Taylor argues for a recovery of a kind of theism, as a connectedness to God and affirmation of certain religious beliefs. Levinas does something quite different, as we have seen.

Still, Taylor and Levinas bear some significant resemblance. Both are convinced that our human commitment to benevolence and justice is central to our modern sensibility. About this, Levinas is probably more extreme, for this commitment is not merely modern for him, nor is it fundamentally a commitment. Rather, it is the orienting dimension of all human experience and social life. Moreover, both are sure that this commitment or orienting attitude

---

[92] Taylor, *Sources of the Self*, 517.

[93] Smith, *Charles Taylor*, 229–31; cf. Heft (ed.), *A Catholic Modernity?*, 33; cf. Smith, *Charles Taylor*, 231–33.

[94] Taylor associates this, I believe, with Augustine and the Augustinian tradition; one thinks of figures like Karl Barth. In Jewish thought, figures like Franz Rosenzweig and later Abraham Joshua Heschel, Joseph Soloveitchik, and Michael Wyschogrod come to mind.

is somehow related to the divine. In Taylor, the relationship is more traditional and conventional; to be sure, God is no commander, but divine love is an act of grace, and it empowers our love for others. For Levinas, God's role in our ethical character is more difficult to locate and less traditional. Levinas is no theist, certainly not a traditional one; God is no lover. Indeed, our sense of benevolence and generosity, our responsibility, is given in the face of the other who is destitute and commanding at once, and this impact of the face is the *trace* of a distant, absolutely absent God. This God or *illeity* is beyond existence or nonexistence, which is not to place it in a different metaphysical space as much as it is to refashion its "venue" as ethical through and through. It is not love that empowers but suffering and need that demand; from the first, we are obligated and burdened, not beneficiaries of a loving grace as much as traumatized by the face of the needful and suffering other person. In content, then, Levinas's turn to religion is more gripping and extraordinary than Taylor's recovery of a traditional Augustinianism. While it seeks to understand why we use theological language and engage in religious practices, it also takes the locus of the sacred to be outside traditional ontology or metaphysics, to be located instead in the central ethical commitment of our lives as social beings.

So even in their similarities, Taylor and Levinas differ. One serves to underwrite our beliefs and commitments by turning to God; the other claims that these views are already rooted in our unconditional responsibility, which has in turn a "divine" character. Much of what distinguishes Taylor and Levinas is captured in the difference between Taylor's turn to love and Levinas's appreciation for responsibility, accusation, and trauma. For both, there is the grace of Goodness, but it is a Goodness with distinctively different faces.[95]

As with Taylor, then, the context in which God and religion arise for Levinas is ethical, and even more precisely it concerns our interest in justice and benevolence. Taylor's account is historical; he develops what is in effect an argument for a kind of theism, based on the need for an ontological commitment to support our moral convictions. He wants us to realize that we are rightly committed to reducing suffering; opposing cruelty, neglect, and assault; and acting in behalf of benevolence and justice. Levinas, of course, is not about arguing for a theological or religious belief of any kind; his goal is to shed light on what role theological discourse plays in our lives and where God fits into philosophy, as he conceives it. But for all their differences, Taylor and Levinas share a good

---

[95] I borrow the phrase "the grace of Goodness" from Georg Lukács's essay "On Poverty of Spirit (Von der Armut am Geiste): A Conversation and a Letter," *Philosophical Forum* 3:3 (Spring–Summer 1972). For discussion, see Michael Morgan, *Interim Judaism: Jewish Thought in a Century of Crisis* (Bloomington: Indiana University Press, 2001), and, on the early Lukács, the works cited there on p.126, n. 10.

deal as well, not the least of which is a desire to respond to the "malaise of modernity" and the crisis of twentieth-century culture. Both sense deeply the need for obligations toward others, to oppose fascism and oppression, suffering and injustice, and both realize that these obligations must be grounded and our commitments empowered in some way. For both, finally, God somehow figures into that grounding.

The purity and unusual character of Levinas's conception of the preeminence of the ethical and its location in the face of the other person as the *trace* of the divine are distinctive of his response to the crisis of modernity. One expression of that purity is Levinas's way of understanding time and the temporal relationship between the face and the divine, as well as between the face and our ordinary lives. But Levinas's treatment of time, which I turn to now, is as difficult as it is important.

8

Time, Messianism, and Diachrony

Levinas's interest in time, temporality, and history was lifelong. He wrote about these themes early and throughout his career. They are among the most difficult aspects of his thought to grasp; yet they are central to his philosophy. Especially given his orientation to these issues – against the background of European philosophical and theological treatments of time, history, messianism, and death, what he says may sound strange to the ears of Anglo-American philosophers. But these are important matters. In this chapter, I will situate his treatment in the context of thinking about time in the period from the turn of the century through Weimar, follow the basic stages of his views about time, and then place the latter in the context of contemporary philosophical discussion. Without understanding Levinas's discussion of time, we would fail to appreciate fully what he says about ethics, religion, and politics.

THINKING ABOUT TIME

It is helpful to see the interest in time at the turn of the century as part of the debate concerning the *Naturwissenschaften* and the *Geisteswissenschaften*. In this context, time entered into questions of scientific method, the nature of philosophy, history and historical method, and ethics, especially relativism and historicism. In his own way, Levinas reflects on issues in several of these areas; his thinking is part of the revival of Kantian philosophy. It is post-Kantian insofar as the debate itself was, and it is indebted especially to Bergson, Husserl, Heidegger, and Rosenzweig.[1]

---

[1] For an overview of the historical and cultural role of changing views of time at the turn of the century, see Stephen Kern, *The Culture of Time and Space, 1880–1918* (Cambridge, MA: Harvard University Press, 1983). Mary Ann Doane reflects on the relationships among time, photography, and early cinema in *The Emergence of Cinematic Time: Modernity, Contingency, the Archive* (Cambridge, MA: Harvard University Press, 2002).

The natural sciences examine and attempt to explain empirical phenomena, and they do so from a detached, impersonal perspective. Their objects are viewed from the outside, as it were, and their interactions are comprehended according to causal laws, laws of probability, or mathematically formulated relationships. The social or cultural sciences analyze and examine human actions and interactions. Hence, as Wilhelm Dilthey and others would argue – including philosophers like Wilhelm Windelband and Heinrich Rickert of the Southwest, or Baden, school of neo-Kantianism – they treat human beings as agents who from their individual and collective point of view value objects, institutions, and actions, who communicate linguistically in speech and writing, and for whom acts and such mean something. There is a continuity, that is, between the way human beings as agents, thinkers, and speakers are studied by the cultural sciences and the way they live in the world. Human beings live as subjects with values and as both providers and consumers of meaning; insofar as they are biological or physical entities governed by natural laws and understood like any natural entity, they are not subjects but rather objects. As subjects, they are centers of significance and experiencing selves.

Experience, however, has its own temporal character: It flows into the future and recedes into the past. It goes on. To be sure, there is the time that exists objectively, that is divided into past, present, and future, and that is measurable, an analogue of spatial, linear magnitude. There is, that is, time chopped into bits – years and months, weeks and days, hours, minutes, and seconds – astronomical time, clock time, public time. But this is not our sense of temporal passing, of flowing experience, what Bergson, in a famous expression called "duration." When, in 1981, Levinas was asked to clarify Bergson's "principal contribution to philosophy," he answered: "The theory of duration. The destruction of the primacy of clock time; the idea that the time of physics is merely derived. . . . [Bergson] liberated philosophy from the prestigious model of scientific time."[2] And with this liberation, Levinas points out, comes a dispelling of the fear of mechanism or fatalism, of lack of purpose, of living without hope and future – a lived future. It is no wonder that Levinas would consider Bergson's *Time and Free Will* to be one of the four or five finest books in the history of philosophy.[3]

When history and the other cultural or social sciences study human beings, then, they (should) study agents who experience their lives temporally in this first-person or subjective sense and for whom the world and everything in it

[2] *Ethics and Infinity*, 27. Henri Bergson introduces the idea of duration in Chapter 2 of *Time and Free Will: An Essay on the Immediate Data of Consciousness* (New York: Harper, 1960; originally in English, 1910; originally 1888).
[3] *Ethics and Infinity*, 37–38.

mean something. In the language of turn-of-the-century neo-Kantianism and much of the German philosophy of the day, human agents take the world and its contents, including items, facts, actions, and institutions, to have worth or value. Historically, these insights flowed into various philosophical streams and into the study of knowledge, experience, metaphysics, social and psychological phenomena, and more. In their own ways, Dilthey and Bergson are lone voices, but alongside them there emerged schools and traditions that adopted and modified their insights – *Lebensphilosophie*, Southwest neo-Kantianism, and Husserlian phenomenology among them.[4] One of the outcomes of these developments was a tendency toward relativism and historicism; another was the movement to a philosophical anthropology grounded in the subjectivity of human existence and its temporality, its embodiment, and historical situatedness. There were some who took routes along this way that led to hermeneutical accounts of human existence and to the brink of relativism; others stayed with the temporality of human experience but sought some kind of unconditional orientation for human life, for ethics and existence, by linking time to "eternity," as it was often called. It was left to Levinas – and perhaps not to him alone – to find that unconditional orientation in a strange transcendence that is both immanent to human life and transcendent as well, or, perhaps more accurately, that is beyond immanence and transcendence.

One dimension of Levinas's account of time, then, is an attempt to follow Bergson – and Husserl and others – away from the forlornness of scientific time to a commitment to subjective temporal experience, only to realize its risks and to find in the relationship with the other person a way out of relativism. Another dimension involves a new account of the subjective temporal experience. As we trace the development of his discussion of time, we need to keep our attention on both dimensions of his thought.

EARLY REFLECTIONS ON TIME

The earliest version of Levinas's philosophy, as we have seen, is *Time and the Other*, the very title of which signals that time figured centrally in Levinas's thinking from the outset. It continued to do so throughout his career. There are obvious reasons for this centrality, among them his indebtedness to Bergson, Husserl, and Heidegger, all of whom focused attention on our experience of time and on the fundamental temporality of human experience and existence.

---

[4] To a certain degree, as well, the perspective of the engaged, historically and culturally embedded agent was taken up by students of society and the founders of modern sociology, from Georg Simmel to Max Weber. See Wolf Lepenies, *Between Literature and Science: The Rise of Sociology* (Cambridge: Cambridge University Press, 1988).

But Levinas adds something important: an account of why the encounter with the face of the other person is associated with our experience of time and how it gives to our temporal existence its human significance. This insight is already present in his account of time and death in *Time and the Other*.

The path to time leads through suffering. Levinas introduces suffering and death in Part III of *Time and the Other*. Suffering, he explains, is pain and hence an engagement with one's own existing, as a physical being, that is beyond escaping. It is "the impossibility of fleeing or retreating" from being, "the fact of being backed up against life and being" and "the impossibility of nothingness."[5] At the same time, suffering points to death and even hints at death as an unknown, a mystery. Death presents itself as something that we cannot master, in the face of which we are utterly passive. It is, Levinas says, the "limit of idealism."[6] If suffering is the impossibility of nothingness, then death is the impossibility of possibility. With it, he says, I am confronted by what is wholly beyond my experience and beyond me, even though it happens to me. Calling upon Epicurus, Levinas notes the temporal character of death: Because death is beyond experience, it is never a present.[7] Our relationship with death is a "unique relationship with the future." Levinas uses a language of agency and control to clarify what is not present in the relationship with death. There is no "mastery," "heroism," or freedom. With suffering and therefore with the hint of death, my activity becomes passivity, and I lose my capacity to grasp, master, and control.

In *Time and the Other*, Levinas draws several conclusions from this account of death. First, the approach of death is an end of activity and mastery. Second, this means that death is "the impossibility of having a project."[8] Third, "the approach of death indicates that we are in relation with something that is absolutely other"; it is absolute alterity, for it is outside experience and marks the "impossibility of possibility," not an anticipation of nothingness but the presence of what is outside of experience. Fourth, this means that "existence" is plural; there is, in my very being, an other as well as myself, and yet this other is a mystery to me. Death presents me with what is other-than-me, even if that other, in this case, is a negation of me. Levinas then proposes that *eros*, in life, is a "prototype" in life of this relationship with the other as death. That is, if death presents me with an other but an other that is beyond me or negates me, *eros*, or love, presents me with an other that is beyond me but does not negate me and does so *in life* and not *beyond life*. Finally – and this is the central point for us here – this analysis

[5] TO, 69.
[6] TO, 70–71.
[7] TO, 71.
[8] TO, 74.

of death shows us that the future, as ungraspable, is the other. What Husserl calls the "protention" of the future in the present and what Bergson notes is our present anticipation of the future are *not* the future; they are "the present of the future and not the authentic future."[9]

What does Levinas mean when he associates the future and otherness? Clearly, he means more than the obvious point that in the present we experience the future as an anticipation or as a projection, that is, that in the present we experience a flowing into what is not-yet but that we expect will-be. How is our relationship to the future to be understood in relation to the relationship to the other? To begin, Levinas claims that there is an other, unlike death, that we are related to that does not crush us or destroy us but rather in a sense affirms us. Levinas takes the face-to-face encounter with such an other, the other person, to be this relationship. So the question becomes: How is our relation to the future associated with our relation to the other person in the face-to-face? I can make some sense of the idea that for me death is the future, but what sense is there to say that the face of the other person is the future? Frankly, this new proposal seems to be nonsense.

I think that Levinas gives us some clues regarding his meaning. He says, "It seems to me impossible to speak of time in a subject alone, or to speak of a purely personal duration."[10] This doubt is expressed immediately after Levinas concludes that the "relationship with the other" is the "relationship with the future." Here he seems to be claiming that in idealism there is no genuine sense of temporality, and, in the second clause above, he denies that "a purely personal duration," or what Bergson thought of as subjective time, is really time. Indeed, insofar as objective, measurable time is also conceived as a human structure, even it is not really time. Somehow, real time requires transcendence, something genuinely other, and death will not do. Levinas actually says precisely this: "The future that death gives the future of the event, is not yet time."[11] What is it, then, that ties the future to the present in a way that constitutes real time? This relationship is accomplished, he says, "in the face-to-face with the other." As he puts it in the last sentence of Part III, "the condition of time lies in the relationship between humans or in history."[12]

We can make sense of these statements by contrasting Levinas's view with two others, what I have called earlier objective and subjective time. These can be taken to be two ways that we conceive of temporality or two ways that we experience time. According to the objective view, time is measured change,

[9] TO, 75–76.
[10] TO, 77.
[11] TO, 79.
[12] TO, 79.

and it is experienced in terms of the categories of past, present, and future that are imposed by our cognitive capacities and measured by objective means – for example, astronomical events or clocks. According to the subjective view, time is the flow of our experiences that are experienced by me from my I's point of view as here and now, with a sense of flowing from what has been in view and what will be, as anticipated, expected, and projected. In this sense, the past is before what I now experience, and the future is after or what is yet-to-be. In one way, then, time is objective, and in another it is subjective. We might call the first "natural" time, or time as science understands it and how we understand it – measured and in measurable units – in everyday life. The second is personal time, from each of our personal, or first-person, perspectives. Now, to be sure, Levinas does not deny that in our lives we experience temporality in both of these ways. He acknowledges the special significance of Bergson's distinction between the two ways of understanding time and accepts it, to a degree. What he does deny, however, is that the distinction captures everything that is important about our experience of time.

Indeed, this distinction does not capture what Levinas thinks is the deepest and most profound dimension of our temporal existence. It is not enough to experience time in these ways, nor is it enough to live with the sense that time and history are going nowhere and have no purpose or that their only purpose is what each of us gives to them. In other words, Levinas's concern with time is that it is meaningful in a way we do not usually realize. Bald naturalism and subjective relativism or idealism do not tell the whole story about time. Our temporal experiences mean more than either the objective view or the subjective view suggests, and it is the ethical character of our social existence that gives them their meaning. Moreover, to turn our attention to the meaningfulness or significance of our existence as temporal is not to change the subject. For our experience of time, as flowing or as measurable and an object of calculation, is shaped as well by our sense of its being the modality in which our living occurs.

ROSENZWEIG AND LEVINAS ON ESCHATOLOGY

Franz Rosenzweig has a similar concern about time and history. What he thinks is provided by revelation and what he conceives as a link to eternity, Levinas thinks is provided by the encounter with the face of the other person. Both believe that time and history only have an absolute direction and significance if our lives are tied to transcendence. In his famous letter to Rudolf Ehrenberg in 1917, Rosenzweig attributes the idea that "revelation is orientation" to Eugen Rosenstock. He says "in 'natural' space and in natural time the middle is the point where I simply *am* . . . ; in the revealed space-time world the middle is an immovably fixed point, which I do not displace if I change or move myself."[13] For Rosenzweig, revelation is the divine command to redeem the world through love; for Levinas, a similar sense of obligation to accept and help others and to alleviate their suffering is the content of the face-to-face. Just as revelation, then, gives time and history an absolute structure and direction – and a determinate future and goal – so the face-to-face does. Or, in other words, for Levinas our experience of time takes on meaning and purpose only when understood in terms of the face-to-face with the other person, when understood as the temporal setting of social existence in its deepest sense.

For Rosenzweig, revelation is the event of divine grace, of the divine coming to manifest itself to the human in an act of love that is also an act of command; God says to each person that his life is valuable and with purpose. In other terms, as an act that orients or places each person in a certain position, posture, or attitude, revelation calls the human to a life of love and concern that seeks the creation of genuine community and solidarity with others. Levinas also believes that revelation is an event that places each of us in a certain position, posture, or attitude prior to anything that we do or any act we perform; for Levinas, too, revelation is an event of election or summons and command, and for him the call is to create communities of love and concern. But the difference between them is about the setting for that call, that summons, and the way in which that revelation or election occurs. As we have seen, for Levinas the location of revelation is the *face* of the other person. The needfulness, the destitution, the suffering of the other person – these call to each of us and place us under a burden and under the umbrella of an expectation for the future, for every future, that we respond and realize that each act we perform is a response to others and that prior to every decision and every act, we are so bound. Like Rosenzweig, then, without revelation, time and history have no meaning, and that meaning is in one sense a gift and in another sense a duty.

It is for this reason that Levinas can appropriate the religious vocabulary of messianism and eschatology for the face-to-face and its relation to history.[14] Of course, what it means for him differs from what it does in traditional religious thinking, both Jewish and Christian. But to understand that meaning, we need to look at *Totality and Infinity*.

Levinas does not delay introducing the notion of eschatology in *Totality and Infinity*; it occurs in the Preface. The early pages of the Preface use a language

[13] Franks and Morgan (trans. and eds.), *Franz Rosenzweig: Philosophical and Theological Writings*, 49–50; cf. 63–65.
[14] See TI, 22–26, and the Talmudic readings on Messianism in *Difficult Freedom*. See also Robert Bernasconi, "Different Styles of Eschatology: Derrida's Take on Levinas's Political Messianism."

of war, politics, morality, eschatology, and violence. Levinas also introduces here the terminology of totality and infinity or transcendence that is central to the book. *Prima facie*, this seems obscure and confusing. Why begin a book about metaphysics and ethics by talking about war and violence? And what does eschatology, doctrines or beliefs about the end of history and the end of time have to do with any of these matters?

The early pages of *Totality and Infinity* anticipate what Levinas will discuss more fully later. For now, let me consider first the relation of war, totality, and politics. Then I will turn to the expressions "eschatology" and "prophetic eschatology." To begin with, war, Levinas says, threatens morality. "The state of war suspends morality." If politics refers to the rational strategies for foreseeing war and winning it, then, like war, "politics is opposed to morality" as well.[15] Of course, Levinas is being literal here, but he is also anticipating larger issues, for he takes war to be a feature of what he calls "totality." War is everything that forces people to play roles and to betray themselves through institutions, practices, and public life. It is whatever impedes our being ourselves uniquely by forcing us into roles and types. Morality, on the other hand, is our expression of our unique selfhood and thus something that system cannot capture. Yet, we live in both worlds, in a sense, in the world of politics and war and in the world of morality, but only if we are attentive to morality, and this means to peace, as Levinas calls it.[16] "The moral consciousness can sustain the mocking gaze of the political man only if the certitude of peace dominates the evidence of war."[17]

From one point of view, then, war and politics are opposed to peace and morality. A life lived in society, without any appreciation for our obligation to others in all its depth and pervasiveness, is war or susceptible to war. The antidote is to be aware of peace and strive for it, to seek to realize it. Levinas then glosses this picture with a religious terminology: What needs to be done is to graft "the eschatology of messianic peace" onto the "ontology of war." That is, war is the ultimate form of totalizing thinking and ways of life, of idealism, and Heidegger's ontology is its most recent avatar. We need more than the threat of war so central to ontology; we need to live according to the goal of messianic peace; instead of ontology, we need to orient our lives by eschatology, that is, a sense of purpose, obligation, and direction. Levinas calls this "prophetic eschatology" or "eschatology" by itself. But it is not an old-fashioned, traditional eschatology; it does not provide a goal or orientation *within* ontology and history. What it does provide – through its link with the

---

[15] TI, 21.
[16] For peace and the face, see "Peace and Proximity" in *Alterity and Transcendence*, 139–41.
[17] TI, 22.

infinite, the other – is a significance *for* our lives and hence *for* history. Prophetic eschatology tells us that our lives are invested with goodness insofar as they are ruled by a sense of compassion and concern for others.

This kind of messianic eschatology, then, is not a doctrine about the end of history; it is unlike views about even the wars that some think will occur at history's culmination. "The eschatological, as the 'beyond' of history, draws beings out of the jurisdiction of history and the future; it arouses them in and calls them forth to their full responsibility."[18] That is, it is outside the wars of history's end, outside of politics and such. "It restores to each instant its full signification in that very instant." As Levinas puts it, this is not a last judgment but rather "the judgment of all the instants in time."[19] In other words, history or time is lived day to day. Religions – some sacred in spirit, some secular – confer purpose on the years, months, days, and hours through the expectations of an end to historical development. Not so for true eschatology, which is not about an end of days. It is not about a conclusion or resolution of history as a measurable sequence of temporal units; it is about living every instant with a sense of what one owes to each and every other person, and therefore about living each moment, with suffering and need and with a devotion to alleviating the one and caring for the other. Life becomes meaningful not because of what will ultimately occur but because of how we live and act at each and every moment.[20]

Later, in *Totality and Infinity*, Levinas elaborates these themes by developing the account of *Time and the Other*.[21] I do not think that it is necessary to survey the details of these pages, but it is worth noting some points that underscore what we have been saying. First, Levinas calls "time" a "space" that is opened up when, through our acts and experiences, death is "postponed."[22] It is in "this space of time" that a "meaningful life" is "enacted," not in virtue of a "measure of eternity," but rather through the relation with the other person.[23] Religion would typically associate this shaping of a meaningful life with eschatology; earlier, Levinas reinterpreted the term to suit him, but ultimately, I think, he eschews it for the expression "messianism."[24] But the central idea is that this meaningful life is *not* something realized only after history, time, and human experience have run their course. Rather, it involves a "perpetual duty of vigilance and effort that can never slumber, . . . the incessant watching over

[18] TI, 23.

[19] TI, 23.

[20] See TI, 22–26.

[21] See especially TI, 220–47, 281–85.

[22] Cf. TI, 236–39.

[23] TI, 232.

[24] See TI, 285; see Kearney interview in Cohen (ed.), *Face to Face with Levinas*, 30–31.

the other."[25] Eschatology or messianism is a matter of living every moment of life in a certain way, with compassion and concern for others.

Clearly, Levinas has a very episodic view about what makes human life meaningful. His conception is distinctive in this respect. For Rosenzweig, for example, as for traditional eschatologies that view history as a kind of *Heils-geschichte*, it is primarily the totality of history – or the sum total of all human experience and action – that has meaning, and this meaning is developmental.[26] The significance of the linear route comes with its ultimate resolution, its goal, or *telos*. Given such a picture, individual, discrete actions or events are significant as means to that end or as stages along the way to it. Levinas's view differs. To him, such a view totalizes human experience; either it conceives of all of each person's life as a whole, or more often it conceives of all human experience or history as a whole, and then takes discrete actions as instrumental and derivative. But for Levinas, the significance of our lives arises for us as particular, unique individuals, and that particularity is tied to our responsibility in each and every situation, with respect to each and every other person. Hence, human life is meaningful insofar as each of us responds out of kindness and generosity at each and every instant. It is for this reason that I said Levinas's view is episodic. The very temporality of each experience we have is conferred by its relationship to the messianic, by its potential for itself being messianic. Like Walter Benjamin, but in a quite different spirit and with a different sense, Levinas would say that "every second of time [is] the strait gate through which the Messiah might come."[27] Not life as a whole or history as a whole is meaningful; rather it is each instant, one by one.[28]

This way of living meaningfully is about living with a sense of responsibility to and for others. One religious expression for this way of living is to say that one lives under "the judgment of God." That is, if we think of history as having some standard or being measured by some ideals or principles, this expression

---

[25] Kearney interview in Cohen (ed.), *Face to Face with Levinas*, 30.

[26] A classic discussion of such philosophies of history can be found in Karl Löwith, *Meaning in History* (Chicago: University of Chicago Press, 1970).

[27] Cf. Walter Benjamin, "Theses on the Philosophy of History" in Benjamin, *Illuminations* (New York: Harcourt, Brace & World, 1968), 266, and "On the Concept of History" in *Walter Benjamin: Selected Writings, vol. 4: 1938–1940* (Cambridge, MA: Harvard University Press, 2003), 397: "For every second was the small gateway in time through which the Messiah might come." Also, "The historian [of the new kind] establishes a conception of the present as now-time [*Jetztzeit*] shot through with splinters of messianic time." These texts and Benjamin's late reflections on history have been the subject of extensive discussion. Cf. Michael Morgan, *Interim Judaism*, 104–8.

[28] See Levinas, *Difficult Freedom*, 89–90: "Messianism is therefore not the certainty of the coming of a man who stops History. It is my power to bear the suffering of all. It is the *moment* when I recognize this power and my universal responsibility" (italics mine).

means that the real standard for understanding and assessing what goes on in history is not *in* history; it must be somehow a measure for history and not a mere apology. Levinas says that this standard of judgment is "the invisible [that] must manifest it if history is to lose its right to the last word, necessarily unjust for the subjectivity, inevitably cruel." Ultimately, then, this standard is what in religious terms is called "the judgment of God." It "is produced as judgment itself when it looks at me and accuses me in the face of the other – whose very epiphany is brought about by this offense suffered, by this status of being stranger, widow, and orphan. The will is under the judgment of God when its fear of death is inverted into fear of committing murder."[29] This marks a crucial shift, from a view of human existence as living toward death to a view that sees it as living for the other person at every moment or, to put it otherwise, as living against the other's death at every moment. It marks a shift from living for oneself to living for the other person, from struggling with one's own finitude to being burdened by the threat of the other person's finitude, from self-concern to concern for others.

Moreover, Levinas sees added significance in the notion of *judgment*. It signifies that history and time are being measured and that they have meaning in virtue of that process of measurement and of aspiring to realize an ideal. But there is more to the idea of our being judged. "Judgment is pronounced upon me in the measure that it summons me to respond. Truth takes form in this response to a summons."[30] The expression "judgment of God," then, means that what gives human experience, time, and history their significance is the fact that each and every person is under this judgment; each is summoned, called, elected. This is justice (in *Totality and Infinity*; later, justice only arises with the social and the third party) and goodness; it is a summons "to go beyond the straight line of the law," to become a unique I.[31] It is to "dread murder more than death"; it is a "deepening of the inner life."[32] This understanding of the judgment of God is not eschatological in the ordinary sense; it looks forward to no peculiar perfect age, no end of history. It transforms the ordinary and the everyday and renders us subjects or agents of a different kind.[33] This "judgment of God" confirms me as it judges me; I am who I am insofar as I am being judged and called to responsibility.

In view of these reflections in *Totality and Infinity* that we have been discussing, then, one might think of Levinas's early thoughts about time and

---

[29] TI, 243–44, esp. 244.
[30] TI, 244.
[31] TI, 245.
[32] TI, 246; this means to live "beyond the judgment of history" and under the judgment of truth.
[33] TI, 246.

historical experience as his account of how we should understand the way we experience the future. Such experience is not an anticipation of death, nor simply a projection or imaginative expectation based on current experiences – "protention" in Husserl's vocabulary. When Levinas tells us that we should fear murder more than death, he is not recommending that we replace one mode of anticipation or expectation with another. Rather, he is asking us to reconceive dramatically our sense of what is ultimate about the self and what its deepest concern ought to be, what makes human life valuable and significant. Our experience of the future, then, is not a hope for a perfect age for us individually or collectively. Rather, the future is about what we should do in the present and for the future; it involves what is expected of us, demanded of us, and what we should expect of ourselves. In this way, the central issue about the future is what it does for the present as meaningful life and how it does it.

DIACHRONY AND RESPONSIBILITY

If Levinas's early concern with time and temporality is about the future, in his later work he turns to the past and how our experience of the past is significant for the present. In fact, he comes more and more to reflect on time – in *Otherwise Than Being* and later essays, such as "God and Philosophy" and "Diachrony and Representation."[34] And at least part of the reason for this preoccupation concerns the face-to-face itself and the role of God and the way in which their relationship articulates how our sense of the past is determinative for the present.[35]

Probably Levinas's most advanced statement of these later interests and what he means by focusing on the diachrony of the face-to-face, and what that means, is the essay "Diachrony and Representation." It is also explicitly about cognition, concepts, and philosophy; in a sense, the essay does for the issue of diachrony and time what "God and Philosophy" (1975) did for God and theological language. So let us turn to this late essay first, and, if necessary, we can fill in any gaps between it and *Totality and Infinity* thereafter.

In an interview in 1983, Levinas summarizes what this essay seeks to accomplish:

[T]here is the time that one can understand in terms of presence and the present, and in which the past is only a retained present and the future a present to come. Representation would be the fundamental modality of mental life. But starting from

---

[34] See *Entre Nous*, 159–77; see also *Is It Righteous to Be?*, 176, 268–69; and "Transcendence and Intelligibility" in *Basic Philosophical Writings*.

[35] See *Is It Righteous to Be?*, 204–10, and *Entre Nous*, 232–33; see also the courses found in *God, Death, and Time*.

the ethical relation with the other, I glimpse a temporality in which the dimensions of the past and the future have their own signification. In my responsibility for the other, the past of the other, which has never been my present, "concerns me": it is not a re-presentation for me. The past of the other and, somehow, the history of humanity in which I have never participated, in which I have never been present, are my past. As for the future – it is not my anticipation of a present which is already waiting for me, . . . "as if it had already arrived." . . . The future is the time of prophecy, which is also an imperative, a moral order, herald of an inspiration. . . . [36]

Here Levinas points to his plan in "Diachrony and Representation." Even for someone like Husserl, our internal time consciousness involves a present that contains, as it were, a present experience of a past that was once present and a present experience of a future that is yet to be present. In short, our retentions and protentions – and then our memories and our anticipations, hopes, and expectations – are derivative of present experience, which is shaped by the subject and which tolerates no genuine transcendence or what Levinas also calls "exteriority." What Levinas calls to our attention is a sense of the past and a sense of the future that are radically different. These are a real past and a real future, that are not just recalled or projected or expected *presents*. The past and the future are not, as it were, states of affairs or facts. The past "concerns me," and the future is an "imperative." But in order to see what this means, we need to turn to the essay of 1985.

In 1988, in an interview, when asked about the "major preoccupation" in his current work, Levinas said that the "essential theme" in his research is "the deformalization of the notion of time."[37] He gives a nice, if brief, sketch of the problem of time, as he sees it, and the roles played by Kant, Hegel, Husserl, Heidegger, and Rosenzweig in dealing with it. Basically, as Levinas sees it, Kant, Hegel, and Husserl all saw time as the form of human experience, but none felt that time requires as a *condition* any "meaningful content somehow prior to form."[38] In other words, the flowing of the past and imminence of the future are not seen as "attached" to a "privileged empirical situation" that gives these temporal experiences meaning. Certainly, we might think, Kant and Hegel had philosophies of history, and they saw human experience as oriented to goals, individual but more importantly social and collective. But neither they nor Husserl understood actual temporal experience as itself oriented in terms of specific features of our human existence, past and future. Levinas takes Heidegger and Rosenzweig to have added just this, and that accounts for their novelty.

[36] *Is It Righteous to Be?*, 176.
[37] Levinas, "The Other, Utopia, and Justice" in *Entre Nous*, 232.
[38] "The Other, Utopia, and Justice" in *Entre Nous*, 232.

In Heidegger's case, he asks: What are "the situations or circumstances" characteristic of human existence that are associated with the experience of past, present, and future? Schematically, Levinas describes Heidegger's answers: *Experiencing the past* involves "the fact of being, without having chosen to do so"; and "of dealing with possibles *always already* begun"; *experiencing the present* involves "the face of control over things" and "being near them"; and *experiencing the future* involves "the fact of existing-toward-death."[39]

Rosenzweig, on Levinas's reading, sought to answer the same question, to add content to the formal character of temporal experience. To him, our experience of the past refers to "the religious consciousness of creation"; our experience of the present refers to our "listening to and receiving revelation"; and our experience of the future refers to our "hope of redemption." The three religious ideas become "conditions of temporality itself."[40] Each of these ideas, we realize, concerns the human situation vis à vis God or transcendence as an orienting ground beyond our metaphysics and beyond our conceptual schemes. Hence, for Rosenzweig, the very temporality of human existence and human experience is somehow tied to our relationship with God, to revelation in the broad sense of our relationship to God. What are *immanent centers* of meaning for Heidegger become *transcendent centers* for Rosenzweig. Levinas's own contribution, in a way, is to realize how immanent that transcendence really is.

There is of course much more we could say about Heidegger, Rosenzweig, and their predecessors. Temporality is not just a matter of our experience of time for them. It is, for Heidegger and Rosenzweig at least, a central feature – perhaps *the* central feature – of the existence of human beings. Their very existence or being is temporal, and hence, as tied to their relation to the world, to customs, traditions, and death, it is meaningful or not, or, to use Heidegger's terms, authentic or inauthentic. Levinas's argument that human existence occurs in relation to an immemorial past of ethical responsibility to the other person and in anticipation of a realization of that responsibility is his attempt to advance beyond both Heidegger and Rosenzweig and to give a more accurate account of what constitutes authentic, meaningful human existence in which the social and ethical are primary.

It is now time to turn to Levinas's essay "Diachrony and Representation" (1985). Suppose you and I are having a conversation. As we speak to one another, we may express beliefs and attitudes, share information, and do much

---

[39] *Entre Nous*, 232–33; cf. Robert J. Dostal, "Time and Phenomenology in Husserl and Heidegger," in Charles Guignon (ed.), *The Cambridge Companion to Heidegger*, 141–69; and Richard Polt, *Heidegger: An Introduction*, 96–109.
[40] *Entre Nous*, 233.

else. Levinas asks whether, in such an encounter, what is *said* is primary. Is it
"the unique, original, and ultimate rationality of thought and discourse?... Is
language meaningful only in its *said*, in its propositions in the indicative, ... in
the theoretical content of affirmed or virtual judgments, in pure communication
of information ... ?"[41] In an earlier chapter, we looked at Levinas's answer and
what it means, that what is more deeply meaningful than this discourse as
content is the *saying*, the responsibility to the other person that underlies it
and that it actually enacts. That is, what is most deeply meaningful and what
gives such conversation its point and purpose as a social encounter is the fact
that in conversing each of us acknowledges and accepts the other, is responsive
to the other, and is responding to the other's call or summons. Here, Levinas
adds the notion of temporality. The conversation as communication of content
takes place now, in the present, but is this mode of temporal activity – the
present – "the primordial intrigue of time"? Is there not a temporality associated
with the "from-me-to-the-other," of the face-to-face, that is deeper and more
determinative of such social engagements?[42]

Levinas characterizes the temporality of our conversation, of your remarks
and mine, given their content, our thinking, hearing, speaking, and responding, as "synchronous."[43] Occurring in the present, they occur together, at the
same time, at least roughly so, and they are grasped, when we think about
them, together, as located within a temporal whole. But if all of this is experienced roughly as synchronous, the *saying* – each of our responsibility to the
other – is experienced, as it were, as *always already given*; "the face of the other
obligat[es] the *I*, which, from the first – without deliberation – is responsive
to the other.... [T]he response of responsibility ... already lies dormant in a
salutation, in the *hello*, in the *goodbye*."[44] This *already* indicates that the relation
between our conversation, which is a social act and which occurs in the everyday, and this original responsibility is not synchronous; they do not, as it were,
occur at the same time. They are, as Levinas says, diachronous. Justice, society,
and more – these place "the nakedness of the face" in the world, "destitution,
passivity, and pure vulnerability," and yet it is always past, always already how I

[41] Levinas, "Diachrony and Representation" in *Entre Nous*, 164.
[42] "Diachrony and Representation" in *Entre Nous*, 164–65.
[43] More accurately, each act, such as this conversation, is synchronous and diachronous, both
relatively – that is, the act occurs at the same time as certain other events and actions and at a
different time from certain other events and actions. Our conversation, for example, occurs at
the same time as a meeting of the city planning commission and as a coffee break for workers
at a local office; it even can be said to occur at the same time as the other event-descriptions
under which it falls – for example, its being a discussion of a joint philosophical project. It also
occurs at a different time from my eating lunch today at my favorite restaurant with my wife.
[44] "Diachrony and Representation" in *Entre Nous*, 166.

and you are related.[45] At any moment, whenever and however any two of us are related and act toward one another, it has always already been the case that we are responsible to and for one another; each of us – prior to saying anything, deciding to do or doing anything – is under the summons from the other and is called to respond to the other. We always *already have been* responsible; we *never are coming to be* responsible. Levinas calls responsibility "the secret of sociality"; it is "a voice that commands: an order addressed to me, not to remain indifferent to that death, not to let the other die alone."[46]

Thus, as Levinas sees it, the temporality or temporal modality that is primary to human existence as social existence is that of *the past*. It is a diachronous past, an always-past. But what does this mean? Two events are synchronous when they occur at the same time, or together, and thus when they occur both as past and present. Two events are diachronous when they occur along a temporal spectrum, when there is a temporal continuity between them. A particular event that occurs in the world and as an event in time is synchronous with some other event or events and diachronous with other events. Empirically, every event is both synchronous and diachronous relative to some other events. But responsibility, as a kind of state or attitude of the self toward each and every other person, is *only diachronous*. There are no other events or states or whatever with which it is synchronous. It is thoroughly, unqualifiedly, and absolutely diachronous. As an attitude or posture or state of the self toward the other person, it is always diachronous with respect to all properties, beliefs, states, actions, and attitudes of that self.

For Levinas, then, my existing now has a dimension that points to the past, but the past in question was never a present, so that the diachronous link between that past and my present existence is unique. It is not retentive, nor is it memory or the past-relatedness of a reference or symbol or piece of evidence or indication.[47] In a section of the essay called "Immemorial Past," Levinas calls this dimension "the ethical anteriority of responsibility." This is the face-to-face and my always already being responsible; in terms of its temporal relation to my present existence, it is "a past irreducible to a hypothetical present that it once was."[48] Levinas uses the expression "throws back toward" to describe how I am with respect to this responsibility and obligation. That is, at any moment, I experience what I do, converse, act in subjective and objective time; I recall earlier actions, anticipate what I will do, and so forth. But if I am aware of and appreciate my responsibility to others, I realize that the impact of the

[45] "Diachrony and Representation" in *Entre Nous*, 166–68.
[46] "Diachrony and Representation" in *Entre Nous*, 169.
[47] *Entre Nous*, 71: "a past that is articulated . . . without recourse to memory."
[48] *Entre Nous*, 170.

other person's needs and the obligation I bear have always been with me; I enter every moment with them; unlike the lived past, they do not fade; and unlike the objective past, they never were a present themselves, so that I could say, "Before this, I was not responsible and now I am." Of responsibility, I never recognized it for the first time or accepted it; it was never in my power or control. It came upon me, or, from my present point of view, I was "thrown back toward" what matters for me and commands me. This responsibility, then, in relation to what I am now and what I do, is an "immemorial past."[49] All the actions that I take now or at any time − noticing, accepting, rejecting, choosing, deliberating − whenever I engage in them, I do so as *already* responsible; my obligations toward others comes with me. There is no action that makes me responsible. I always already am responsible. That is diachrony, pure and unqualified, not relative and conditional. However "old" is any act, responsibility is "older."[50]

This is the "past" of human existence; there is also a "future." What Levinas says in these later works builds on the account we gave earlier. We live out of the past and into the future, what Levinas calls a "pure future."[51] I live with an obligation to the other that signifies "*after and despite my death*," calling attention to "a meaningful order signifying beyond this death . . . an obligation that death does not absolve. . . .[52] This is the content of a future that is beyond any yet-to-be, beyond "my anticipations or pro-tentions." Moreover, as in infinite obligation that is not limited even by my death, this is an *imperative* that "concerns me," matters to me. Levinas notes that as an order or imperative, with no limit to its realizability, what comes to my mind is the expression "word of God" and the entire theological vocabulary of revelation. He calls this future orientation of responsibility an imperative to be fulfilled, "the fall of God into meaning." "Time," he says, "[is] the to-God of theology."[53] The significance of our sense of the future is captured in our *obligation* to care for the other, our responsibility for the other's death, for a future that is beyond me.[54] Dying may mark the end of my life, but the meaning of my existence reaches beyond my death. Just as my natural existence is future oriented toward my death and thus is in the grip of my own finitude, so my meaningful social existence is future oriented toward the death of the other by means of the imperative to me to prevent it, an infinite and unfulfillable imperative that nonetheless has me in its grip.[55]

---

[49] *Entre Nous*, 171, 172; cf. OB, 10, 30–31, 52; and *Basic Philosophical Writings*, 116–19.

[50] Note Levinas's use of "already" in *Entre Nous*, 172.

[51] *Entre Nous*, 172–74.

[52] *Entre Nous*, 172–73.

[53] *Entre Nous*, 173.

[54] *Entre Nous*, 174; cf. 174–175.

[55] There is a provocative comparison to be made here with Kant's argument in the second *Critique* for the postulate of the immortality of the soul and the hope for the realization of ethics in a purely good will.

In the past, the meaning of my existence recovers a responsibility that is original, and in the future it grasps a *commanding* that grounds it and expects its realization but is more than I can ever accomplish.[56] These orientations are not historical time, objective time, or even Husserlian experienced time; they are diachrony, the absolute difference between what gives my existence meaning and that existence, and at the same time the interpenetration of my existence by this temporality. Levinas draws closer and closer to religious vocabulary to express the way these modes of temporality characterize our lives. He calls it "holiness"[57] and calls reflection on it "a theology without theodicy" and a "difficult piety . . . of the twentieth century, after the horrors of its genocides and its Holocaust." It is the "deformalization of time,"[58] for here time is conceived as more than the form of our experience; it also is its ethical and religious content.

This account of responsibility as diachrony mirrors the account of the idea of the infinite and the transcendence of totality. In our everyday lives, as we experience people and things, as we live and act, our living does have temporal features. We experience others at certain times; we make plans to meet; we spend hours together; we celebrate anniversaries. Also, we see, hear, walk, talk, and work, recalling the past, remembering episodes, anticipating a vacation, looking forward to seeing a film, hoping for a brighter day. And at each moment, our experience and actions flow into the past and future like a stream – as Bergson, James, and Husserl have shown us. But – and this is Levinas's central theme – the temporal dimensions of our lives include other ones that are unlike a measured or dated past or a remembered one and that differ radically from a date set for a fixed time in the future or a hoped-for future. Our lives recall a past that was never present and anticipate a future that will never occur. They are pure past and pure future – purely diachronous, never contemporaneous with any present. In other words, they disclose to us what it means for us to have everyday presents, pasts, and futures. They disclose *why it matters to us* that our existence is temporally arranged, why recollection and anticipation have point and purpose. Living in the world with other persons, living historically and temporally, means what it does to us because of our obligations to serve the needs of others. When we respond to these obligations, individually in episodes of kindness and concern and collectively in practices of justice and generosity, we give our personal and collective temporal and historical lives what meaning they have. One can live in history and in time without attention to such responsibility, but when we do, we allow life and history to be hollow and mechanical.

[56] *Entre Nous*, 175.
[57] *Entre Nous*, 175.
[58] *Entre Nous*, 176–77.

As we have examined some of the things Levinas says about time, it has become clear that he is not concerned with time as an objective feature of our public lives. He is not concerned with past, present, and future as modes of time or years, months, days, and hours as units of time, or even with before, now, and after, as perspectives on time. Nor is he interested in developing a phenomenology of time consciousness or correcting Husserl's efforts along these lines. He is responding to Heidegger's account of the temporal modalities of human existing, which are about the ways we are involved in all that is given to us, all that we currently are doing, and all that we expect in the future.[59] In a sense, for Levinas our sense of the past is *deeper* than our awareness of being situated amidst things – resources and traditions already there when we come on the scene – and our sense of the future is *deeper* than the realization of our finitude and our anticipation of our own death. Authenticity, for Levinas, is more than resolute decision; it involves acknowledging and acting upon our sense of obligation toward every other person. In the end, then, Levinas's interest in time and history is about the meaningfulness of human existence, individually and collectively. The temporality of our existence and of how we live, act, and work is tied to what makes that living, acting, and working meaningful for us as human beings, and that amounts to having a sense of generosity and devotion to others.

A crucial expression, I believe, that helps us understand Levinas's point here is the expression "always already." This is my terminology and not his – although one does find him using something like it on occasion. But I think it can help us to see why he thinks our sense of our unique past is what is determinative for us and why that past is a "past that was never present." As I have tried to emphasize, responsibility is past in a way unlike any state or feature or fact is past, present, or future. At any given moment in our interaction with others, we find ourselves in a situation already there. In a theater, watching a film, I realize that prior to my entrance the theater was there – the chairs, the screen, the walls, and so on were there. But everything was, at one time or another, for us or for someone else, something new, created or shaped or built in the present and bequeathed to the future. There was always for these things – the theater, the chairs, the film – a time when they were not. Even the persons with whom I sit and talk and laugh and cry were, at one time or another, born, the objects of adoration, love, nurturing, and more. But as we have seen, for every particular person to whom we are related in this present, not only was she already there but also our turning to her, our acknowledging her, our responding to her presence or look, or her saying "hello" was, in a sense, already there. There

---

[59] See Polt, *Heidegger*, 96–98.

is, however, a difference in these cases of *being-already-there*. The difference is that she was once in the present for others and for me, but my responsibility to and for her was never in the present, in the sense that there was a time when it first came into being. This means that I never chose it, created it, or acquired it – originally; it *always was already there*. And this is true for every relationship between persons; this responsibility comes first, so to speak. It is that dimension of or perspective on our relationship that I easily forget or that is hidden from me but that is *always already there*. In my social existence, your death is more orienting for me now than my own death is – or, as Levinas puts it, I should fear murder more than death, and the future that matters most to me is yours, not mine.

Moreover, to return to the themes with which we began this chapter, this prominence of the past, when I am aware of it, can give my life meaning and can give history meaning, not by promising a final end to history or a personal salvation but rather by determining how I live and act and thereby giving my acts and experiences their deepest significance. This is no traditional eschatology and no traditional, speculative philosophy of history. But it is a vision of peace and justice, of kindness and generosity.[60] It is a messianism of the moment in which you and I are the agents of its realization.

---

[60] See Bernasconi, "Different Styles of Eschatology."

9

Ethical Realism and Contemporary Moral Philosophy

ETHICS AND THE EVERYDAY

There are many questions that arise when we ask ourselves what Levinas's philosophy has to do with ethics. In Chapter 3, we considered the content of the face-to-face, and we saw that it is a dimension of everyday social interaction that involves the brute particularity of the I and the other person insofar as the other person calls the I into question and demands that the I take responsibility for him and be responsive to him. This relationship, then, is a plea for goodness and justice and a demand for kindness and generosity. When, as Levinas puts it, the other calls out to me, "Thou shalt not murder" – which means acknowledge me, accept me, help me to live, and respond to my needs – this sounds ethical, and Zygmunt Bauman, in his book *Postmodern Ethics*, associated it with the central theme of Knud Løgstrup's book *The Ethical Demand*. But what does it mean to call the face-to-face "ethical," and what does Levinas mean by saying that ethics is first philosophy? In what sense is this central aspect or dimension of human existence "ethical?"[1]

Furthermore, the face-to-face is not a theory. If it is associated with ethics, what does it have to do with ethical or moral theory? Is it akin to or associated with some meta-ethical theory, say, moral realism of one kind or another? Some moral theories take moral value to reside in natural features of human life or to be associated with human rationality. Is Levinas's thinking similar to any of these theories?[2] And how is the face-to-face related, if it is at all, to normative theories

---

[1] Strictly speaking, Levinas does not say that the face is ethical. He says that responsibility *is ethics*, that being called into question by the other's face *is ethics*. As we have seen, he also calls it religion and later holiness, glory, substitution, trauma, enigma, and a host of other things.

[2] R. Jay Wallace, in a response to Korsgaard on the relationship between normativity and the will, distinguishes three types of moral realism about the source of the normative force of moral principles. According to Wallace, realist approaches have this in common, that "their normative

228

like Rawlsian constructivism or Kantian ethics or any kind of utilitarianism or consequentialism?[3] These questions and others like them have been raised by several commentators, often as features of a criticism of Levinas: that his ethical commitments surprisingly do not, or perhaps cannot, result in ethical directions of any concrete and precise kind.[4]

---

force is taken to be prior to and independent of our particular decisions about what to do" ("Normativity and the Will," in *Normativity and the Will*, 71, cf. 72). One approach, which Wallace claims is rarely if ever held by realists but is often ascribed to them by antirealists, he calls "objectual" insofar as it holds "that the furniture of the world includes . . . an array of concrete normative entities or values, conceived as particulars of some kind or another" akin to the concrete objects that are objects of sensory experience (72). The second approach, which he associates with Richard Boyd, David Brink, and Peter Railton, he calls "factive," because it takes moral discourse – say, about what is right or wrong – to be answerable not to objects in the world but rather to "a set of distinctive facts about what is the case" that are related to that discourse in terms of some kind of "explanatory significance" and that make sense of that discourse about whether or not individuals have reason to act in the way involved. The third approach, which Wallace himself endorses and which he associates with Thomas Nagel, Derek Parfit, Joseph Raz, and T. M. Scanlon, he calls "normative moral realism." This approach takes the reality relevant to normative force to be factive, but it holds that the facts must be relevant to the agent's moral deliberations and thus must count for what makes a course of action right or wrong as a reason for doing it. This is still a form of realism, Wallace argues, because "it holds that when we project ourselves into the practical point of view, and set our minds to the question of what we ought to do, our deliberation is an attempt to get clear about an objective and appropriately independent fact of the matter, namely what an agent in our deliberative situation has most reason to do" (73).

    Wallace's scheme is a useful one for us to keep in mind as we place Levinas in conversation with various philosophers in the analytic tradition. Unlike Korsgaard, who argues for a kind of constructivism as an alternative to realism, and surely unlike people like David Gauthier and Simon Blackburn, Levinas appears to take the needs, pain, and suffering of persons to be a "reality" that brings with it – *qua* face, a claim on every self – moral force, prior to and independently of our explicit awareness of it. But if so, what kind of reality does that need and suffering have? Or ought not Levinas be considered a moral realist in any of these three senses, strictly speaking?

3 Levinas's view can sound especially like utilitarianism: An infinite responsibility to alleviate suffering and such can sound like a primary obligation to maximize the good by reducing pain and increasing pleasure. Alternatively, Levinas sounds very much like what some have called "beneficence theory," which is especially concerned with feeding the hungry and in general reducing suffering. A recent account is Garrett Cullity, *The Moral Demands of Affluence*; the tradition includes Shelly Kagan, *The Limits of Morality* (Oxford: Oxford University Press, 1991); Peter Unger, *Living High and Letting Die: Our Illusion of Innocence* (Oxford: Oxford University Press, 1996); Liam Murphy, *Moral Demands in Nonideal Theory* (Oxford: Oxford University Press, 2003); Tim Mulgan, *The Demands of Consequentialism* (Oxford: Oxford University Press, 2002); and perhaps earliest, Peter Singer, "Famine, Affluence, and Morality," *Philosophy and Public Affairs* 1 (1972), 229–43.

4 See Simon Critchley, in the Introduction to Critchley and Bernasconi (eds.), *The Cambridge Companion to Levinas* and in *The Ethics of Deconstruction*. See also Putnam in *The Cambridge Companion to Levinas*. See also Steven Hendley, *From Communicative Action to the Face of the Other: Levinas and Habermas on Language, Obligation, and Community*.

Some consider Levinas's ethical insight to be a reply or antidote to views that might be understood as antirealist, relativist, or pragmatic.[5] Is this plausible, to take his obligation to responsibility as an objective ground of morality, somehow independent of individual agents, cultures, and so forth?[6] And is his view a kind of moral universalism, akin to Kantian ethics, and in that way insensitive to the arguments of communitarians and neo-Hegelians like Michael Sandel, Charles Taylor, Michael Walzer, and even John McDowell?

Levinas's philosophy is steeped in his moral reaction to Heidegger's Nazism, and it emerged as a critique of Heidegger's account of human existence in *Being and Time*. It is a virtual commonplace to take him to be responding to the way in which Heidegger's conception of authenticity is not immune to fascism.[7] Is this right? Does he see the responsibility to the other's suffering as a response to a philosophical view, such as Heidegger's? Is his thinking a response to Stalinism, as a distortion and corruption of Marxism, and to Hitler's fascism? This is suggested by the points we reviewed in Chapter 1, but is it an accurate way of understanding Levinas's work? Or is it something else?

Finally, is there a way that we can understand Levinas's account of the responsible self, its relation to normative moral theory, and its implications for political life and political thought? Is this self a standard by which moral and political systems should be evaluated? Or is its relation to them to be understood differently?[8] In many parts of the world, the separation between ethical conduct and moral principles, on the one hand, and political life, war, violence, oppression, and revolution, on the other, barely exists. In *Totality and Infinity*, as we have seen, Levinas uses a dramatic and intense vocabulary of war, violence, and peace, alongside traditional philosophical expressions and even religious ones, and one outcome of such usage, one might argue, is to elide any seeming boundaries between the theoretical and the practical or existential in human existence. It would be surprising if the central feature of his metaphysics were not implicated in moral and political life in important ways, but it may not be easy to see exactly how this is so.

In earlier chapters, I discussed texts that served as especially helpful places to examine what Levinas had to say about meaning, subjectivity, God, or time. Here, however, the themes we need to address pervade all his major works, his essays, and his interviews. The burden of our task is not so much to interpret

[5] I am thinking particularly of Derrida, but Rorty comes to mind as well.
[6] The issue was raised above; see Chapter 5.
[7] See Kearney, "Dialogue with Emmanuel Levinas," reprinted in Cohen (ed.), *Face to Face with Levinas*, 20–21, 26; see also *Is It Righteous to Be?*, 186. The point is made frequently by commentators.
[8] Kearney, "Dialogue with Emmanuel Levinas," in Cohen (ed.), *Face to Face with Levinas*, 29–30.

a text here or there as it is to shed light on what he is really saying virtually everywhere.

Before we turn to the questions we have raised, let me recall some episodes that we discussed in Chapter 1 and summarize what Levinas says about ethics and politics in various interviews and informal writings. In such places, he is engaged in the ethical life – as a commentator, as a critic of moral and political conduct, as a moral judge, and as an observer of moral and political phenomena. Whatever answers we give to the questions we have raised about the status of his ethical thinking and its purposes ought to make sense in the light of his more concrete ethical judgments and conduct.

Certainly among the most noteworthy features of Levinas's interviews of the 1980s are his admiration for Grossman's *Life and Fate*, especially his insight about the moral center of that book. In his 1986 interview with François Poirié, he remarks that Grossman's novel chronicles the "end of the socialist hope" as "the greatest spiritual crisis in modern Europe." Why? Because "Marxism represented generosity" and "the recognition of the other," which finds its nemesis in "Stalinism and Hitlerian horror." So a political ideology can indeed express or represent the deep human impulse to accommodate and care for others; but in our time, he believes, that ideology was destroyed. Grossman, however, also shows that in the midst of that destruction there can remain "goodness without regime, . . . goodness [that] appears in certain isolated acts," such as the remarkable event, which we discussed in Chapter 1, of the Russian woman gratuitously and surprisingly handing the German lieutenant a piece of bread. This, Levinas says, is "an act of goodness exterior to all system." Where there is "no system of salvation, [t]he only thing that remains is individual goodness," and Levinas associates this vision with his own book *Totality and Infinity* and what he calls in the interview "ethics without ethical system." Grossman's book, he notes, is sprinkled with such episodes.[9]

We cannot push these remarks too far, of course; they occur in interviews and do not constitute by themselves a doctrine or theory. But they do suggest several points to keep in mind. First, both political ideologies, regimes or systems, on the one hand, and individual acts, on the other, can express or represent responsibility to the other person with varying intensities and to different degrees. Second, Stalinism and Hitlerian fascism exemplified a historical epoch or world in which this political-ethical ideal was wholly subverted by extraordinary cruelty, oppression, inhumanity, and violence against persons. Third, goodness or ethical value can be realized in discrete, spontaneous human acts, even in a situation of overall cruelty and suffering. This reflection of Levinas, then, can serve as a kind of emblem of the reality of goodness and the modes

---

[9] *Is It Righteous to Be?*, 81; cf. 197, 202–3.

of the ethical in a Europe under siege. Here we can see, for example, how one might even be responsible for one's enemy and how one might act out that responsibility,[10] and we can see how ethics as a moral or political system might be conceived as separate from and yet related to ethics as act. Levinas even hints at how a political theory like Marxism might represent or express responsibility to the other by articulating "the noble hope consist[ing] in healing everything, in installing, beyond the chance of individual charity, a regime ... of charity."[11] Finally, Levinas seems to admit that there can be both ethics with system – moral or political – and ethics without system and that while the latter is fundamental and determinative, the former is neither avoidable nor always corrupt and inadequate.

Levinas portrays the state and much else as emerging from the face-to-face; his account in *Otherwise Than Being* is presented genetically, as I have shown.[12] Its point, however, is not genetic or narrative but rather quasi-transcendental. In interviews, he insists on the fact that politics, the state, and social institutions are necessary. Life cannot do without them; "we are never, me and the other, alone in the world. There is always a third; the men who surround me."[13] Levinas repeats the point regularly; "the State, general laws are necessary. Institutions are necessary to carry out decisions. Every work of politics and justice is necessary." The face-to-face, then, proximity as responsibility, is part of our political and social life; it is determinative of its *mise-en-scène*, as he likes to put it; it is presupposed by politics, law, and institutions.[14] Indeed, on at least two occasions Levinas uses just this word, "presupposed," claiming that politics and "all human relationships" presuppose the face-to-face.[15]

These comments underscore two points that I have made about Levinas in earlier chapters. The first is that we should understand Levinas as presenting a philosophy of the everyday whose primary concern is to identify and clarify a dimension of our ordinary social life, with all of its interpersonal encounters, institutions, and such, and not as someone who is advocating some extraordinary experience that ought to replace in some way the everyday. The second point is that this dimension or perspective is, in some sense, a necessary condition for all of our social and political lives, for language, thought, law, and everything else in our social and political lives. Our lives are a network of people and

---

[10] Cf. *Is It Righteous to Be?*, 208.
[11] *Is It Righteous to Be?*, 81; cf. 216–21.
[12] OB, 157–62.
[13] *Is It Righteous to Be?*, 115; cf. 100, 205–7, 223; see 230.
[14] *Is It Righteous to Be?*, 108.
[15] See *Is It Righteous to Be?*, 108, and *Ethics and Infinity*, 89. In a discussion of Martin Buber, Levinas says that society (the face-to-face) is not a successor to politics but a "moment" of it; see "Utopia and Society," *Alterity and Transcendence*, especially 115–16.

relationships grounded in interpersonal responsibility, rarely acknowledged with clarity, sometimes facilitated but often occluded, of the humanity of others and our obligations to accept, help, and alleviate their suffering. If these two points are confirmed by these interviews, we can see that the face-to-face is not intended to replace moral theories or normative principles. Rather, moral theories should be attentive to this dimension of the face-to-face and express it. There is also a sense in which they require it and are grounded in it. We might say that it provides a standard for evaluating them and that they should make every effort to live up to this standard, although often such theories do not.[16] The face-to-face is an "ethical measure of a necessary politics" and of moral theories as well; in Levinas's words, charity and kindness are the judge of justice.[17]

Levinas is an ethical universalist in the sense that he takes all human existence, for each and every one of us, to be grounded in the face-to-face. We are all responsible selves before we are anything else. In this respect, historical period and cultural differences build on the same foundation. In another way, however, it is tempting to treat his ethical view as radically particularized, because the I and the other are both utterly unique and particular and because paradigmatic acts of kindness and generosity are unique, situated historical events. Indeed, one might read him as a critic of moral theories that are based on rules or norms precisely because they formally impede or distort the practice of discrete, spontaneous acts of kindness in favor of moral regimentation or standardization.[18] On the one hand, Kantians as diverse as John Rawls, Jürgen Habermas, Christine Korsgaard, and Onora O'Neill might all find Levinas's universality of scope appealing but take his favoring of particular acts over rules, institutions, and policies to be completely mistaken. Postmodernists like Zygmunt Bauman, on the other hand, and moral particularists like Jonathan Dancy would react to his ethics in a contrary way for precisely opposite reasons, that while Levinas is sensitive to the unique particularity of each I and each other, he is committed to a single moral standard for all. Moreover, the reaction of communitarians and pluralists, feminists among them, might favor the situated character of our obligation to

---

[16] *Is It Righteous to Be?*, 235: "What is essential in the ethical is often lost in the moralism which has been reduced to an ensemble of particular obligations."

[17] *Is It Righteous to Be?*, 100, 223.

[18] For this kind of criticism, see Zymunt Bauman, *Postmodern Ethics*. For an excellent collection of papers that deal with moral particularism and the critique of generalism and the priority of principles or rules in ethics, see Hooker and Little (eds.), *Moral Particularism*. Many philosophers have been called moral particularists – Jonathan Dancy, John McDowell, David Wiggins, and David McNaughton, for example – but not all reject the role of moral rules or principles altogether. For one who does, see Jonathan Dancy, *Ethics Without Principles* (Oxford: Oxford University Press, 2006). For all his "particularism," Levinas certainly need not and, I think, would not.

responsibility but despair of the universalism that lies behind it. But all such criticism ultimately would focus on Levinas's universalism; hence, it makes a difference what kind of universalist Levinas is and what form the various criticisms of his universalism might take.

Because Levinas is not engaged with ethics in ways that analytic philosophers typically are, it is difficult to place him and to grasp the various strands of his philosophical and ethical thinking. One thing to keep in mind is that Levinas is not engaged in ethical theory as we understand it, nor is it the aim of his philosophical thinking to construct a moral theory. When he says that ethics is first philosophy, he does not mean that ethical theory or a system of ethics is his metaphysics. What plays the *role* of metaphysics or first philosophy – and the allusions to Aristotle and to Descartes are certainly intentional – is not a theory at all. It is ethical life, human existence lived in terms of an ethical orientation that is fundamental to all human existence. Just as metaphysics was the study of basic principles for Aristotle and the basic and most universal modes of being and substance and just as it became, for Descartes, an account of indubitable knowledge on which science could be built, so, for Levinas, ethics is the most original, determining way of living human life. It is what precedes everything else, in a sense, what orients us in the world and with other people prior to anything else – any thought, any thinking, any feeling. It is our original attitude or posture toward the world and others. To be sure, he is interested in how that ethics is realized in social and political life; what rules and policies express it; when it is neglected, ignored, distorted, and even suppressed; and how twentieth-century culture has virtually destroyed it. But his focus is always on that lived sense of obligation, that orientation to others, that posture or dimension or relationship.

Moreover, there is a sense in which Levinas is anti-intellectualist about ethics and morality, although his doubts about moral philosophy are not exactly those of someone like Bernard Williams, as we shall see. He is no naturalist, although he does have respect for our desires and needs. Nor is he a rationalist exactly, even if he does associate responsibility with freedom and reason. The aim of philosophy – and not philosophy alone – is not to make us better thinkers or to understand better, at least not for its own sake. It is to get us to live better lives, to act with greater generosity and goodness, to be a better parent, a better friend, a better lover, a better statesman, a better teacher – all by acting toward others with more responsibility and concern than we do. Our goal should be to see, and to act because we see, that caring for others is the whole point of our lives at all; it is to respond to the "secret tears" of the other.[19]

---

[19] "Transcendence and Height" in *Basic Philosophical Writings*, 23.

Levinas often says that in everyday life we must make choices about how to act, who most deserves our time, effort, and resources, and what principles best balance and guide what we ought to do and what we can do. Moral decisions, moral systems, and laws are about such situations, but all, if they are to be genuine and effective, must express and respond to what is fundamental and orienting for human life. In short, the best moral and legal systems must be true to who we are, in a deep sense. Historical and political contexts will differ, as will types of society and culture, but the obligation to be responsible to and for the other person, to be ready and willing to assist and share and serve, this remains constant. Both this obligation and moral and political principles are necessary, even at times when the former is virtually hidden from sight and when the latter are wholly oppressive – the twentieth century with the preeminence of imperialism, totalitarian regimes, global economic domination, and much else being Levinas's prime examples. Levinas does not himself engage in ethical system building. What we find in John Rawls, Onora O'Neill, Alan Gibbard, Alan Gewirth, and others is a different task from the one he takes on. But this should not be understood, as someone like Bauman does, to indicate a blanket criticism of all such systems on his part. Levinas's reverence for Grossman's picture of a world of episodic goodness or kindness amidst the ruins of Stalinism and Hitler's fascism is not an unqualified rejection of all moral principles. To be sure, it does represent deep reservations about such systems and about ideologies and any comprehensive theories when owed absolute and fanatical allegiance and pursued with unqualified zeal. But while Levinas may recognize the necessity of "totality" and yet is certainly not an apologist for totalizing schemes or institutions, his views about moral and political theories and systems are carefully calibrated. His comments about Grossman's *Life and Fate* are a judgment about what kind of hope can still exist in a world where political and moral systems and ideologies have been totally corrupted. This judgment is not opposition to all universal rules and all moral foundations. Levinas certainly despairs of moralism and excessive moral rigidity, but one should not infer a denial of all morality, of all conventional political institutions, or of all legal systems.

This chapter is structured in a wholly different way than others in this book. I do not analyze Levinas's works or even regularly cite them. In it, I assume that we have clarified sufficiently the basic themes of his thinking and can now go on to place him in conversation with some examples of Anglo-American moral philosophy. To carry out this task, however, I do not conduct a survey of various categories of moral theory and assess where Levinas is best suited to fit; rather, I raise questions about Levinas and place him in conversation with particular philosophers whose work might illuminate his thinking, and I do so in such a way that the chapter follows a dialectical course, beginning with his Kantian affinities, moving to issues in moral epistemology, and eventually arriving at the question what kind of moral thinker Levinas is, the implications of his work for moral theory and politics, and the question of what we might call his "ethical fanaticism." In this chapter, then, moments in Anglo-American moral philosophy become opportunities for further clarifying Levinas's contribution.

O'NEILL'S ETHICS AND PRACTICAL REASON

There has been a good deal written about Levinas and Kant, what they share and how they differ.[20] It will be worthwhile, then, to look at recent versions of Kantian moral thinking, to see what Levinas might think of them. Here I suggest a brief consideration of the work of Onora O'Neill.

O'Neill's book *Towards Justice and Virtue* nicely sums up her Kantian version of a rationalist moral theory.[21] O'Neill's project is to develop a moral theory that joins our concern for justice with our concern for virtue. It also seeks to show how careful we should be about thinking of the one as exclusively universalist and the other as exclusively particularist. O'Neill's theory is based on an account of practical reasoning and in particular on the idea that because practical reasoning is employed to justify a decision to act or to establish a policy, it aims to persuade others or to defend a proposal against the objections of others. Therefore, practical reasoning rests on a "minimal . . . but authoritative demand: others cannot be given reasons for adopting principles which they cannot adopt."[22] Practical reasoning, that is, must be directed to others who can understand and follow the principles of action that are under consideration. The idea is that practical reason is about principles that are followable, and its scope and character derive from this fact.[23]

From this (rather lean) foundation, O'Neill develops an account of the scope and content of moral obligations that is fairly robust. Practical and moral reasoning is a social activity concerning decisions, actions, policies, and kinds of life. This is the assumption that grounds O'Neill's thinking. It requires that we think about the conversational or communicative features of that social activity and especially the abilities of the interlocutor, whom we are trying to convince to accept a principle and hence to take seriously a type of action. On the surface, this strategy looks like it might be appealing to Levinas. It recognizes the other person and even gives the other a kind of priority in our moral thinking.

---

[20] See especially Chatherine Chalier, *What Ought I to Do?: Morality in Kant and Levinas* (Ithaca, NY: Cornell University Press, 2002).

[21] O'Neill, *Towards Justice and Virtue*; see also *Bounds of Justice* and her earlier *Constructions of Reason*. I do not want to consider O'Neill's system overall but only features of it that might help us to understand Levinas better.

[22] O'Neill, *Towards Justice and Virtue*, 3; cf. 51–59.

[23] O'Neill, *Towards Justice and Virtue*, 52.

O'Neill is interested in principles and obligations, but she sees them as closely connected to our respect for the other person as an interlocutor and a fellow member of one community or another. In some cases, we live in the same world, accept the same traditions, and have the same commitments. In other cases, we share little but seek a cooperative resolution, even though we live in different political or cultural worlds.[24] Moral principles, then, are determined by reasonable expectations about the other person, and this looks like something with which Levinas might agree. But we should not be too hasty in drawing this conclusion. Apparent similarities between O'Neill and Levinas may hide deeper differences.

There are two questions that we should ask concerning Levinas and O'Neill. The first is this: Insofar as O'Neill frames her account of practical and moral reasoning in terms of the social character of such reasoning, has she correctly identified the dimension of that social character that is most plausible and also most relevant ethically for the exposition of moral principles? Second, from Levinas's point of view, does O'Neill's focus on the followability of moral principles yield a set of moral obligations concerning justice and virtue that Levinas would agree accurately reflects the most fundamental ethical relationship we have with one another? It is clear that Levinas would answer no to the first question, and we need to see why and what it means for him to differ with O'Neill about this. On the other hand, Levinas does not give us much to go on concerning the second question, because he says so little about how the face-to-face and responsibility are related to justice and the principles of justice, but still there are things we can say, given O'Neill's own detailed accounts of ethical obligations.

The first question we raised could be addressed to Hobbes and Locke as well as to Rawls, Scanlon, O'Neill and many others as well. Suppose, for example, that Levinas were presented with Rawls's famous account of deliberations in the Original Position. While the account is constructivist and is intended to produce principles of justice for society, it starts with a rather naturalist account of individual needs, desires, and capacities. The situation, however, is a social one; individuals deliberate in the company of others, together with these others, and in terms of others, in order to arrive at principles that all can accept. Rawls stipulates what these individuals possess, are aware of, desire, and so forth. He then argues why they can be expected to choose the two principles of justice as he formulates them. Levinas, I think, would agree that principles of justice do arise for a group of individuals in a social situation where they have to deal with and live with each other. For Rawls, what drives their deliberations is their

---

[24] O'Neill, *Towards Justice and Virtue*, 53–55; cf. 52–59. O'Neill also uses social assumptions to clarify the scope of ethical principles; see 101–21.

rational assessment of what each other will do based on expectations about their rationality and desires. Levinas realizes that people can and do deliberate rationally about what to do and what principles to hold. But for Levinas, the very sociality of the situation – the state of each individual as confronted by another person who petitions to be allowed to live, to be helped, assisted, served, and also, by her presence, even demands to be accepted and responded to – is primary to how each person understands what he or she does, what he or she ought to do, and what should be most important to all of them in their social lives. There is a sense of dependency and obligation, what Levinas calls "responsibility," that ought to be determinative of each individual's life. If Rawls is right and they do negotiate about what justice requires as a social policy, Levinas would contend that they do so because each individual appreciates the burden of responsibility and what it requires and takes such negotiation and deliberation to express it faithfully. In short, the very point of individuals joining together to arrive at principles of justice is to respond to others out of responsibility, and the more they realize this fact, the more influenced those very principles will be by their sense of obligation to others.[25]

If we turn to O'Neill, the Levinasian response would be similar. She takes as central the fact that practical and moral reasoning concern principles that are followable by those to whom that reasoning is addressed. Levinas might ask: But what is going on when we reason with each other about principles? Is such a conversation not already an expression of our responsibility for each other and, in its own way, an acceptance of the other's very existence and a shouldering of some of the burden for it? In trying to persuade the other person to accept a certain principle, am I not, in so doing, taking her life to be worthwhile to me and to be in some way my own responsibility? And, Levinas would say, is that responsibility and my shouldering it not the ground of my ethical stance toward her, prior to the fact that she is one to whom I am speaking and who I think could follow the principle in question? That is, Levinas might argue, my responsibility in a sense precedes and gives point to my seeking to persuade her and hence the assumption that she could follow the principle I am defending. If we were to ask: Why bother to seek to persuade her of this principle, one answer would be: because she could perform it and it would be just or generous or whatever to do so; another more basic answer would be: because I care for her sufficiently to think it good for her to accept it and act on it.

---

[25] I am indebted to Joshua Shaw, who pointed out in his dissertation on Levinas's ethics and politics that Eva Kittay's critique of Rawls in defense of special dependencies would alter the character of the principles of justice, that the participants arrive at. My point is that even if Levinas would accept the principles of justice, as valuable as they are, he would point out that Rawls gives no satisfactory account of the point of human social existence itself, without which the collective deliberations in the "Original Position" have no purpose.

Of course, O'Neill might respond, what Levinas says might be true but not relevant to her project, which is to show how the activity of practical reasoning, when understood properly, carries enough weight to generate various ethical principles concerning justice, generosity, and more. What might a Levinasian rejoinder to this charge look like? According to O'Neill, practical reasoning is about principles of action, and "principles do not dominate or determine those who act on them or live by them: rather agents refer to or rely on principles in selecting and steering their activities."[26] Levinas would agree about the need for principles and how I might rely on them, as long as we are talking about practical and moral reasoning in social situations where I seek to act responsibly toward others and need to assess how I might act when there are many other persons to whom and for whom I am responsible. O'Neill considers what kind of principles these are and what their content would be.

In characterizing them as obligations, she argues that some have corresponding rights, while some do not. This is an important distinction and one, I think, that Levinas would find very attractive. O'Neill notes that contemporary treatments of justice regularly begin with an account of rights, because they take just institutions and laws to be organized to protect rights. For her, however, the central moral notion is that of obligation. She comments that starting with rights does not ignore obligations "since any principle that defines a right always by implication defines some obligation."[27] But it is not true, she argues, that all obligations have corresponding rights in just the same way. In the case of universal rights, such as liberty rights to free speech, access to public places, and privacy, the rights entail obligations for all others in the same domain not to interfere.[28] O'Neill argues that other universal rights, however, such as rights to goods and services or so-called "welfare rights," are not exactly the same. Without institutional arrangements to assign "agents to recipients," there are no rights to be claimed or waived.[29] If there is no institution, there are no rights. From this asymmetry, O'Neill concludes that the perspective of obligations is not equivalent to that of rights and the perspective of recipience not equivalent to the perspective of agency – even in the domain of justice.

These distinctions – between the perspective of agency and that of recipience and between obligations with and without rights – are even more important outside the domain of justice.[30] O'Neill is especially interested in obligations without corresponding rights. Some are tied to particular roles – for example, the trustworthiness of a lawyer or a doctor. Others are universal, among them

---

[26] O'Neill, *Towards Justice and Virtue*, 123.
[27] O'Neill, *Towards Justice and Virtue*, 128.
[28] O'Neill, *Towards Justice and Virtue*, 129.
[29] O'Neill, *Towards Justice and Virtue*, 131 and esp. 132–34.
[30] O'Neill, *Towards Justice and Virtue*, 136–41 and Ch. 7.

honesty, courage, and beneficence. O'Neill points out that these obligations, which articulate types of actions that express virtues or character, are what were called, in the eighteenth century especially, "imperfect obligations."[31] One example she gives is helpfulness: "[T]he virtue of helpfulness would be manifest in a life informed by a principle of helping where one can and where it is needed, although, by hypothesis, in this case nobody would have a right to specific sorts of help from specified others."[32] Many of these imperfect obligations are expressive of generosity, helpfulness, charity, and kindness toward others. If one favors rights and the perspective of recipience, such obligations either do not arise or are treated as supererogatory. O'Neill calls this a "demotion" of these obligations and argues against such demotion.[33]

In the final two chapters of her book, O'Neill shows how the feature of practical reasoning she calls "followability"[34] yields obligations in four categories: universal and special obligations, some perfect and some imperfect. Her account, she points out, is constructivist; it generates principles of justice and of virtue that include the rejection of avoidable injury; being tolerant, truthful, and honest; and providing selective care and assistance.[35] Specifically, the obligations of virtue involve rejecting "indifference to others" through acts of loyalty, social reform, direct assistance to those in need, and preservation of resources.[36] The ones O'Neill focuses on, she calls "social virtues"; the principles or obligations that express these virtues are precisely those that are related most closely to what Levinas calls responsibility. We ought to be especially interested in how O'Neill characterizes these obligations and defends them.

O'Neill provides a general argument that obligations of justice are insufficient. Principles of justice involve rejecting various forms of injury, especially systematic and gratuitous injury. Justice "is most effectively expressed through specific institutions that limit risks of injury, so helping to secure and maintain basic capacities and capabilities for action for all."[37] If we live among others, that is, we need just institutions and rules of justice to provide a degree of security for all. But given the ways we are vulnerable and in need, in order to maintain our "capacities and capabilities for action," it seems arbitrary that such principles would be sufficient to direct our actions "towards others to whom we are

---

[31] O'Neill, *Towards Justice and Virtue*, 139 n. 14, 145, 147, 148–51; cf. O'Neill, *Bounds of Justice*, 107.
[32] O'Neill, *Towards Justice and Virtue*, 139.
[33] O'Neill, *Towards Justice and Virtue*, 143–45.
[34] As I indicated, for O'Neill practical reasoning occurs in conversations, where one wants to persuade another or others, and thus practical reasons must be intelligible and capable of being followed.
[35] O'Neill, *Towards Justice and Virtue*, 167–78.
[36] See O'Neill, *Towards Justice and Virtue*, 205; cf. 187–89.
[37] O'Neill, *Towards Justice and Virtue*, 191.

connected."[38] Some of our vulnerabilities, deficiencies, and needs are natural to us at certain stages of life, but others of various kinds arise as circumstances change.[39] Just as we can justify rejecting principles of injuring others, so we can justify principles of rejecting principles of "indifference to and neglect of others,"[40] and a whole variety of principles for social virtues can then be derived from "the fact that agents have reason to reject principles of indifference or neglect."[41] The basic idea behind this justification is that "no vulnerable agent can coherently accept that indifference and neglect should be universalized, for if they were nobody could rely on others' help; joint projects would tend to fail; vulnerable characters would be undermined; capacities and capabilities that need assistance and nurturing would not emerge. . . ." Hence, people with "plans and projects," with some interest in how their lives should go and who "intend to continue living and acting" must hope to rely on others and agree to principles that endorse such assistance and support, rather than indifference and neglect.

O'Neill argues, then, that indifference to and neglect of others must be rejected as policies. There must be ethical obligations to assist and care for others, to alleviate suffering and satisfy needs, and to support the projects and plans of others. Articulating them, however, demands accommodations.[42] "Since nobody can provide help or care for all others, or even for some others at every time, the rejection of indifference and neglect cannot be expressed in action for all others."[43] The point is that we must avoid *systematic* indifference to others and do *something* for *some* others; this kind of selectivity is necessary. As O'Neill puts it, principles of social virtue cannot require "generalized or maximal benevolence or beneficence, . . . but only *selective* and *feasible* help, care, love, generosity, support or solidarity."[44] Nonetheless, "trivial and sporadic" help is also unsatisfactory insofar as such acts are insufficient to express real rejection of indifference and to supply sufficient aid. What is needed to be effective are "patterns of action."[45] Finally, it is not objectionable that these principles may direct assistance or help only for some. O'Neill asks: "Can selective helpfulness or care that addresses the expectations or needs of some, but wholly neglects those of others, be all that social virtues demand?", And her answer is that some accommodation is unavoidable: "[N]o degree of cultivation of social virtues

[38] O'Neill, *Towards Justice and Virtue*, 191.
[39] O'Neill, *Towards Justice and Virtue*, 192.
[40] O'Neill, *Towards Justice and Virtue*, 193: using a universalizability argument.
[41] O'Neill, *Towards Justice and Virtue*, 193.
[42] O'Neill, *Towards Justice and Virtue*, 195–200.
[43] O'Neill, *Towards Justice and Virtue*, 195.
[44] O'Neill, *Towards Justice and Virtue*, 195.
[45] O'Neill, *Towards Justice and Virtue*, 195–96.

can avoid some indifference and some neglect both to those near and dear and to those in distant or present need."[46] Limitations in resources, capacity, and distance, as well as other factors, make this obvious. The hungry, the oppressed, and those in urgent danger – no one can have an obligation, O'Neill says, "to help all the needy of the earth, . . . to rescue all those in danger."[47] Something must be left to choice and circumstance, and this is no flaw in our ethical principles.[48] If one can only save one person of two, then one expresses help and concern by so doing; if one can save both, then one should do that, although one shows no more fully or clearly one's sense of concern and responsibility to others.

This sketch gives us the framework of O'Neill's ethical system. It is grounded explicitly in our nature as beings that engage in practical reasoning, but it also assumes that we do so together with other persons and that each of us does so in the course of lives for which we have plans and projects. The principles of both justice and social virtue that constitute the ethical requirements for such practical agents are, in a sense, instrumental. They organize a society in which such agents will develop the capacities and have the capabilities to act effectively and live fully and rationally. The principles of justice concern harm and injury; those of social virtue concern assistance and care and the avoidance of indifference and neglect. At least with regard to the latter, Levinas might be thought to sympathize and to find much that is appealing. But it is worth taking a closer look, both to get clearer on Levinas's views and his project and to see how it compares with O'Neill's.

LEVINAS AND O'NEILL

One common criticism of Levinas is that his insight about responsibility, which he calls ethics and religion, is never shown to be sufficient to result in precise moral obligations.[49] Clearly, Levinas does not so much as nod in the direction of such a derivation, certainly not in a systematic way. But it is one thing for him to have attended to other issues and left such developments to others; it is another to oppose such a project altogether. O'Neill carries out her program of construction on the basis of some fundamental claims about human beings as rational agents. Like Levinas, she takes the human situation to be a social one in which people confront each other and have to deal with each other. But from this basis, she constructs a program for determining precise moral principles. Is

---

[46] O'Neill, *Towards Justice and Virtue*, 198.
[47] O'Neill, *Towards Justice and Virtue*, 199.
[48] O'Neill, *Towards Justice and Virtue*, 201.
[49] See Simon Critchley, Introduction in *The Cambridge Companion to Levinas*, 27–28.

Levinas opposed to such programs? Would he find O'Neill's work attractive or disturbing? Is her project compatible with Levinas's insight?

Levinas does not develop a system of ethical principles in the way that O'Neill begins to do and that others such as Rawls and Habermas seek to do.[50] But is this because he opposes systems of moral and political, legal principles? One way of looking at Levinas might be this: Nazi fascism and Stalinism were the ultimate realization of totalizing policies. Levinas's emphasis on transcendence, infinity, and the ethics of responsibility is opposed to such totalizing tendencies, both in philosophy and in politics. Hence, he rejects moral and political systems – as ideologies – that are one expression of such thinking, for they seek to derive universal moral principles naturalistically or from reason. While some reject the formulation of rules or norms as impediments to freedom and obstacles to human spontaneity, Levinas has another reason: Such rules or norms distort the very particular, uniquely effective impact of the face of the other person on each and every one of us. Ultimately, then, this argument might go, Levinas is a situational ethical thinker, who rejects moral systems as well as political ones as the best expression of our ethical nature. Ethics is fundamentally intuitive, situational, and responsive.

I think that this interpretation of Levinas is a tempting one. It seems to suit his critique of totalitarianism, modern culture, and cold war politics; it also can appeal to examples of ethical acts, like the extraordinary acts of kindness that Levinas cites from Grossman's *Life and Fate*, and to the utterly particular character of the face-to-face. But it would make Levinas's ethical views fundamentally iconoclastic and irrational and would ignore the way that Levinas argues that justice and the state derive from proximity and the face-to-face.[51]

In the section of *Otherwise Than Being* where Levinas explores the derivation of the *said* from the *saying*, he points out that systems of justice and principles arise out of proximity and the self's responsibility.[52] Here he says that we are never without the third party: "[T]he other is from the first the brother of all the other men."[53] I have emphasized this claim and its presence in Levinas; we are never without the third party, for social life is always constituted of multiple selves in conversation. Moreover, the social situation requires that we assess our responsibilities in terms of the many claims on us, our resources, and all of the constraints placed on us in particular circumstances. He calls the third party

---

[50] Also, Alan Gewirth, Joel Feinberg, Tom Scanlon, Bernard Gert, Peter Singer, Alan Gibbard, and Simon Blackburn.

[51] For an excellent survey of how ethics is related to the state for Levinas, see Caygill, *Levinas and the Political*.

[52] OB, 156–61.

[53] OB, 158; 159: "the others concern me from the first." On the third party, see also *Entre Nous*, 195–96, 228–31, esp. 229.

a "limit of responsibility," because if fundamentally the responsibility of each individual is infinite, for it is to and for everyone in every respect and to an unlimited degree, then the presence of multiple individuals forces each of us to limit our assistance and generosity. Levinas uses terms like "comparison," "assembling," "order," "measure," and "weighing" to express what *justice* in society requires in order to set these limits of responsibility and obligation. He calls this "the order of justice [that] moderat[es] or measur[es] the substitution of me for the other, and giv[es] the self over to calculus."[54]

At the same time that he claims that rules, norms, and systems are necessary, however, Levinas argues that they must be grounded in proximity, in this sense of concern we ought to have for others. Others do not "obsess" me or call for my acceptance and assistance merely as "examples of the same genus," but rather "fraternity precedes the commonness of a genus."[55] The ethical and legal principles that are necessary for social and political life are not basic; they derive from the very character of interactive, interpersonal encounters, from the infinite responsibility that each of us has for every other person in every way, in particular and from the outset, so to speak. This is what Levinas means, I think, when he warns against thinking that "justice is . . . a legality regulating human masses" and reminds us that "the law is in the midst of proximity," for "nothing is outside the control of the responsibility of the one for the other." Rules or norms do not come first, as it were; they are derived from a deeper ground.[56]

Furthermore, justice or this system of principles does not "degrade" or "diminish" our responsibility or "neutralize the glory of the Infinite."[57] In fact, the two go hand in hand. Levinas notices features of the social situation that O'Neill also highlights. For example, even though we formulate rules and principles and make decisions in situations where our concern for others cannot but be limited, our system of justice must be grounded in a fundamental equality: All others demand our attention, whether near or far, even if the "weight" of these demands differs. Levinas even notes that this gives us a "surplus of duties over rights," but it is a surplus derived from the face-to-face and the other's demand upon me.[58]

For Levinas, then, a system of moral rules or systems of such rules are necessary for social life. They do not degrade or diminish the self's responsibility. They certainly circumscribe its infinite character, but that character is never realized and is never realizable in any perfect way. In fact, these rules and

[54] OB, 158–59; cf. 157ff., esp. 161.
[55] OB, 159.
[56] OB, 159.
[57] OB, 159.
[58] OB, 159.

systems express that responsibility and even, he argues, should be derived from it, rather than from other foundations. He says explicitly that "it is then not without importance to know if the egalitarian and just state in which man is fulfilled . . . proceeds from a war of all against all, or from the irreducible responsibility of the one for all. . . . " I take it that for Levinas the same judgment applies to systems of moral principles as well as to legal and political systems. It makes a difference whether they derive their character and authority from some naturalistic account of human beings as rational, self-interested agents, from an account of them as socially deliberating partners, or from a conception of persons as practical reasoners. I think that what Levinas means is that to lose sight of the fact that equality and justice, moral and political systems of the best sort, are grounded in our original responsibility to others is to lose sight of what such systems mean, what their purpose is and ought to be, and thus what justifies them. All such systems are accommodations, but not fundamentally of our freedom or our desires or our interests. They are not intended to facilitate our survival or our happiness. Rather, if Levinas is right, such rules and systems help us to regulate and organize our assistance to others, to facilitate our concern with their health and their lives. They are strategies for dealing with our limitations in a structured, organized way, not because *we* may need assistance but because *all others do* – from each and every one of us. For reasons like this, then, it makes a difference whether we ground our moral systems, like Hobbes and others – even like David Gauthier and Rawls, in self-interest or, like Kant, O'Neill, and Korsgaard, in our rationality. Even if some of these strategies seem to ground the force of such norms or principles in a concern for common humanity, they do so only insofar as that humanity is expressed in rationality or in some such common feature of human beings. For Levinas, in a sense, that does not reach far enough, for it begins by classifying persons in terms of certain capacities and abilities and does not yet engage the face of each other person as a revelation of need, suffering, and a command for acceptance and help – a particular, unique revelation and command to a particular I. This engagement is a call that grips me prior to any description or categorization of the other as a human or rational being.[59]

This reading of Levinas suggests that he would find much that is appealing in O'Neill's moral thinking. Both her principles of justice and of social virtue would be expressive of proximity and responsibility, in his eyes, and he would certainly appreciate her realization that generosity and assistance and the rejection of indifference and neglect are important and yet in practice must be limited and qualified. And he would appreciate, I think, that she is aware of human vulnerability, even if she does not, of course, appreciate its extent and its extreme character. But, as we might have expected from the start, Levinas would prefer

---

[59] For an excellent description of OB, 156–62, see Simon Critchley, *The Ethics of Deconstruction*, 220–41.

to show how these principles are grounded in our responsibility to and for others rather than in our commitment to the desiderata of practical reason.[60] To be sure, O'Neill – like Kant, Habermas, and Korsgaard – offers a better alternative than Hobbes, Gauthier, and other naturalists, who derive peace from an original type of war rather than giving peace the primacy it deserves. I do not think that Levinas denigrates reason, but he certainly reframes the context in which it functions and the goals that it serves. And ultimately, he believes that for all its importance in our lives, reason, in a sense, serves higher purposes when it functions well and is capable of being used to realize great horrors when it does not.[61]

By looking at Levinas and O'Neill, we can see that there might be a sense in which Levinas, like O'Neill, is both a universalist and a realist about ethics, morality, and politics. That is, responsibility for the other person is a determinative or orienting aspect of all human social life; generosity and help for the other are required of us all. Furthermore, this responsibility is a real feature of our relationship to others. It is not a matter of our self-interested desires or needs, but it is nonetheless natural to human existence insofar as it is a social existence of individuals engaging one another. Moreover, the responsibility that arises out of the encounter with the other's face is intrinsically ethical and normative; it is in and of itself good and demanding or obligatory. Indeed, Levinas does not want us to think that its goodness is something added to its character, but rather that its character as obligatory care and assistance *is* its goodness. Levinas would find John Mackie's famous argument from queerness a very strange bit of reasoning, precisely because it takes goodness and rightness to be separate from the features of an act or practice or state.[62] For Levinas, there is no such separation between the way a person appears to us and the meaning that person has for us, between the facts and the value ascribed to them; this is part of what the notion of the face is intended to mean.

Levinas leads us to believe, moreover, that responsibility is both the ground from which moral principles and political institutions are derived and the standard for judging such rules and institutions. The verb "desire," that is, does not mean "wholly determine." Responsibility for others in a social world requires judgment, decision, language, thought, and much else. But insofar as all of this occurs in situations of different kinds with a variety of features and

---

[60] See also Critchley's response to Axel Honneth on Hans-Georg Gadamer in *The Ethics of Deconstruction*, 268–69, 273–76.

[61] As a critic of modern culture and society, instrumental reason, rampant technology, and totalitarianism, Levinas shares a broad view of twentieth-century civilization with thinkers as diverse as Heidegger, Arendt, Strauss, Adorno, Horkheimer, and others.

[62] See J. L. Mackie, *Ethics: Inventing Right and Wrong* (Harmondsworth, England: Penguin, 1977), 31–42.

conditions, these rules, theories, institutions, and practices turn out differently. Responsibility is necessary and sufficient for some kind of political structure, but by itself it does not determine how many kinds and what they look like in detail. Hence, given the historical and cultural context, these diverse cases can always be measured against the standard that grounds them – that is their origin, so to speak. Levinas certainly favored democracies and socialisms over totalitarian regimes and doubtless over despotisms, and he found more to reject in Nazi Germany and Stalinist Russia than in postwar states, simply as a matter of degree. And he did at times think well enough of the state of Israel and the kibbutz movement to eulogize them.[63] Insofar as moral systems and political-legal ones are necessary accommodations to our social existence, they can function more or less well by being more or less expressive of our basic responsibility, by directing its implementation more or less justly and extensively, and by doing more or less to encourage and enhance its realization in our lives. The test for all of this is how well individuals are cared for in these regimes, how much suffering these constitutions tolerate or produce, and how they deal with poverty, hunger, and homelessness.

If Levinas's ethical insight has these functions, then he seems to be an ethical realist, who is committed to a kind of moral truth. On his view, each of us ought to be able to identify, deliberate about, and accomplish to some degree what is morally right. That is, one ought to be able to understand what generosity and kindness require of us and to do it, at least in some way and to some effective degree.[64] But it is clear that for Levinas this process of identifying and understanding our responsibility and what it requires by engaging the face of the other and responding to it is a process of "sensibility" and not of rational, conceptual judgment. At least at one level, the face-to-face is preconceptual and precognitive; grasping the face is more akin to sensation or intuition than it is to thought. Unlike O'Neill, then, Levinas takes the ground for identifying how we ought to act ultimately to lie not in reason and interpersonal persuasion; rather, it has a different character. At this point, Levinas's view begins to look like a form of ethical intuitionism, and there are many who would find this objectionable and a serious problem for his "ethical metaphysics."

McDOWELL'S NATURALISM OF SECOND NATURE

When I confront another person, I see many things: the color of her eyes, as well as their expression, her complexion, her posture and physical demeanor,

---

[63] There are many articles and short pieces to cite here; see also Caygill, *Levinas and the Political*, *passim*.

[64] See above, note 2.

who she is, her hair. What makes it possible, what equips me, to see her face –
her need, her dependency, her destitution, her suffering, her command to
me that I respond and assist, care for, and accept her?[65] Among recent moral
philosophers, David Wiggins and John McDowell have been called "sensibility"
theorists because of how they understand the way that we grasp moral truths.[66]
It may help us to understand what Levinas has in mind if we were to look at
McDowell's views, for example, to clarify how he deals with this issue in moral
epistemology.[67]

McDowell has given a very restrained and cautious account of what he
has tried to achieve in his writings on ethics: "[T]o counter bad reasons for
supposing that the idea of truth – getting things right – is unavailable in the
context of ethical thinking, [let me provide] a limited and piecemeal defense of
the thesis that truth is indeed achievable in ethics."[68] One of the outcomes of this
defense is the belief that "people who care about morality do not have a problem
distinguishing 'moral' facts from other states of affairs in the world."[69] Doing so,
for McDowell, may very well and often does involve rational deliberation, or at
least improving one's moral character involves such deliberation and reflection.
And then, equipped with or being of such character, one can pick out what is
right to do, choose what is good in a situation, or at least try to do these things
and hopefully succeed. For McDowell, then, there is some reason to think that
people with moral character, cultivated through education and training, can see
what morality requires, as it were.[70]

65 See Chalier, *What Ought I to Do?*, 93.
66 In addition to Wiggins and McDowell, one might look also at Rosalind Hursthouse, Sabina
Lovibund, David McNaughton, and even older so-called intuitionists – for example, W. D.
Ross. See also Russ Shafer-Landau, *Moral Realism: A Defence* (Oxford: Oxford University
Press, 2005); Robert Audi, *Kantian Intuitionism* (Oxford: Oxford University Press, 2004); and
the helpful anthology, Philip Stratton-Lake (ed.), *Ethical Intuitionism: Re-evaluations* (Oxford:
Oxford University Press, 2002). I choose McDowell to discuss here rather than a representative
of more traditional forms of ethical intuitionism because his special brand of moral thinking,
with its sources in Aristotle and Wittgenstein, has affinities with Levinas that are missed in more
traditional accounts.
67 We have already seen that there is something to recommend looking at Levinas alongside
McDowell. The latter's naturalism may seem a drawback, but in fact, given its nature, I am not
reluctant. There is a Wittgensteinian element in McDowell, as in Cavell, that is akin enough to
the Heideggerian side of Levinas to warrant looking at them together.
68 John McDowell's response, in Nicholas Smith (ed.), *Reading McDowell*, 300.
69 John McDowell's response, in Nicholas Smith (ed.), *Reading McDowell*, 302.
70 McDowell's response, in Nicholas Smith (ed.), *Reading McDowell*, 300–3. Sabina Lovibond
summarizes McDowell's account in "Are Moral Requirements Hypothetical Imperatives?" in
Ethical Formation, this way: "[T]he virtuous person has a *distinctive way of seeing* situations,
persons, courses of action, or anything else that we regard as a logically appropriate object of
moral evaluation. This way of seeing is *objective* in that those who become party to it are thereby
alerted to genuine features of the world. And it is *practical* in that, for the virtuous, to draw

His disclaimers notwithstanding, there is some reason to call this a kind of moral or ethical realism.[71] McDowell's angle on such realism is not metaphysical but rather from the agent's point of view. Two doors to his view are his understanding of Aristotle's virtue of character in terms of the notion of second nature and his Wittgensteinian treatment of rule following.

What enables us to see what is the morally right thing to do? McDowell refers to the notion of second nature as he sees it implicit in Aristotle's account of how we acquire virtue of character, which embodies *phronesis*, or practical wisdom.[72] To acquire such wisdom is a matter of "the moulding of motivational and evaluative propensities," and this, McDowell points out, is "an aspect of one's nature as it has become" – a natural process of maturation and "moral education."[73] This education enables us "to step back from any motivational impulse one finds oneself subject to, and question its rational credentials."[74] In short, moral education is one way that we "open [our] eyes to reasons for acting," and McDowell emphasizes that we do this from the vantage point of the "ways of thinking one acquired in ethical upbringing." This kind of reflection is a "communal activity" in one way or another, but it regularly involves an evaluation of natural impulses regarding their rational credentials, whether they are reasons for acting or not. As a form of "ethical realism," this view finds more in the world than natural properties studied by the sciences, and the more is what our practical, moral virtue – as a cultural product of an "inherited ethical outlook" – makes available to us.[75] McDowell picturesquely calls people like this, following Philippa Foot, "volunteers in the army of duty." "Reason reveals the dictates of virtue to them as genuine requirements on a rational will," and the reason that does this is "their acquired second nature," which is a set of abilities "opened up to them by their ethical upbringing."[76] To be sure, reason does not dictate to them from the outside; it guides them from the inside, so to speak. But what this means is that we grasp what is right to do from the vantage point of the rational moral person we have come to be through training and

---

attention to such a feature of a situation . . . may be to give a nonelliptical explanation of why something has to be done – an explanation that does not need to be filled out by appealing to any independent desire of the agent" (13).

[71] See McDowell, *Mind, Value and Reality, passim.*

[72] McDowell, "Two Sorts of Naturalism" in *Mind, Value and Reality*, 184.

[73] McDowell, "Two Sorts of Naturalism" in *Mind, Value and Reality*, 185, 188. The importance of such education to the cultivation of moral character and thus moral sensibility is developed by Lovibund in *Ethical Formation*; see also Rosalind Hursthouse, *On Virtue Ethics*, and Stephen D. Hudson, *Human Character and Morality.*

[74] McDowell, "Two Sorts of Naturalism" in *Mind, Value and Reality*, 188.

[75] McDowell, "Two Sorts of Naturalism" in *Mind, Value and Reality*, 192, 194.

[76] McDowell, "Two Sorts of Naturalism" in *Mind, Value and Reality*, 196–97.

education. In a sense, we just see what is right, but the seeing is rational and shaped by our upbringing and training.

This intriguing blend of Aristotle and Kant provides one route to McDowell's belief that we grasp moral truths. Another route arises from his discussion of Wittgenstein on rule following as part of an account of virtue and reason.[77] In a classic paper, McDowell characterizes virtues as requiring a "reliable sensitivity to a certain sort of requirement that situations impose on behaviour." Such a sensitivity, which McDowell takes to be a kind of knowledge, is a "sort of perceptual capacity."[78] He argues further that such reliable sensitivities are what virtue is, that they always result in "right conduct," and that virtue in general is "a single complex sensitivity" to recognize what situations require.[79] For McDowell, then, there is moral knowledge, and it gives us reason to act; moreover, it is a matter of seeing what a situation requires, and it is a kind of perception. But in addition, McDowell argues that this knowledge is not codifiable in rules; one cannot set out what virtue requires in a set of principles, norms, or rules. Aristotle is clear about this, and McDowell calls on Wittgenstein on rule following to clarify how this is so.

Levinas, too, is cautious about rules – especially moral rules, law, and social institutions – that organize and regulate our lives.[80] McDowell's reasons for doubt, however, are not focused on the risk of excess or the dangers of corruption – that is, on political matters, but rather on theoretical issues about the very character of rule following and the nature of meaning.[81] On the one hand, McDowell's concerns about the role of rules in morality – which do attract O'Neill's attention precisely because her own moral system focuses on rules and obligations[82] – do not apply to Levinas. His conception of the ethical center of our lives is not a matter of rules; and while he does recognize the need for such rules and institutions, it is at the political level. On the other hand, however, Levinas does seem to make room for moral systems that occur somewhere between the central ethical relation and legal, social, and political

---

[77] See McDowell, "Virtue and Reason" in *Mind, Value and Reality*, 50–73.
[78] McDowell, "Virtue and Reason" in *Mind, Value and Reality*, 51. R. Jay Wallace, in a critical response to McDowell, argues that this sensitivity akin to a perceptual capacity should be understood not on the model of intuition but rather on the model of connoisseurship; see "Virtue, Reason, and Principle" in *Normativity and the Will: Selected Essays on Moral Psychology and Practical Reason* (Oxford: Oxford University Press, 2006), 241–62, esp. 253ff.
[79] McDowell, "Virtue and Reason" in *Mind, Value and Reality*, 52, 53.
[80] See Caygill, *Levinas and the Political*, 151–58, esp. 156–58.
[81] For a good collection of papers, see Alexander Miller and Crispin Wright, *Rule-Following and Meaning*.
[82] O'Neill, *Towards Justice and Virtue*, 77–89. For a defense of McDowell and a critique of O'Neill's attack, see Jay Garfield, "Particularity and Principle: The Structure of Moral Knowledge," in Hooker and Little (eds.), *Moral Particularism*, 185–92.

norms and regulations. The issue is the character of these rules or moral principles, how they are related to our ethical sensibility. O'Neill takes them to have
a kind of primacy, independence, and basic character. For Levinas, they clearly
are derivative. For this reason, it is worth looking at what McDowell has to say
about moral rules. It is also useful in order to clarify whether McDowell's use of
Wittgenstein on rule following will help us to understand what the perception
or sensibility is like that McDowell associates with moral virtue.

In discussing Wittgenstein's famous comments on rule following and understanding how we "go on," in *Philosophical Investigations*, section 185,[83] McDowell
quotes Stanley Cavell's comments on "the competent use of words":

We learn and teach words in certain contexts, and then we are expected, and
expect others, to be able to project them into further contexts. Nothing insures
that this projection will take place (in particular, not the grasping of universals
nor the grasping of books of rules), just as nothing insures that we will make, and
understand, the same projections. That on the whole we do is a matter of our sharing
routes of interest and feeling, modes of response, senses of humor and significance
and of fulfillment, of what is outrageous, of what is similar to what else, what a
rebuke, what forgiveness, of when an utterance is an assertion, when an appeal,
when an explanation – all the whirl of organism Wittgenstein calls "forms of life."
Human speech and activity, sanity and community, rest upon nothing more, but
nothing less than this. It is a vision as simple as it is difficult, and as difficult as it is
(and because it is) terrifying.[84]

What is it that keeps communication on track? "Nothing but shared forms of
life." But, McDowell points out, we worry that this is too little, that it is weak
and not objective. So we recommend "our grasp of rules." But this will not
do, for it presumes that there is something objective about following the rules
that will guarantee our keeping on track, and the truth is that grasping and
following the rules is itself embedded in a form of life, initiation into which
enables us to follow the rules and go on.[85] All of this, McDowell then argues,
applies to "a virtuous person's reliably right judgments as to what he should do
on particular occasions."[86] In particular circumstances, such a person realizes

---

[83] See Wittgenstein, *Philosophical Investigations* (New York: MacMillan, 1968), Sections 185–241, as
well as other texts. For a helpful overview of the discussion of Wittgenstein on rule following,
see Paul A. Boghossian, "The Rule-Following Considerations," *Mind* 98, 392 (Oct. 1989),
507–49. In general, see the essays in Miller and Wright (eds.), *Rule-Following and Meaning*. See
also, Gary Ebbs, *Rule-Following and Reason* (Cambridge, MA: Harvard Univresity Press, 2001)
and bibliography.

[84] McDowell, "Virtue and Reason" in *Mind, Value and Reality*, 60; see also Cavell, "The Availability
of Wittgenstein's Later Philosophy" in *Must We Mean What We Say?*, 52.

[85] McDowell, "Virtue and Reason" in *Mind, Value and Reality*, 61–65.

[86] McDowell, "Virtue and Reason" in *Mind, Value and Reality*, 65.

how one should live and selects and acts on certain concerns rather than others. This involves seeing one fact as more relevant than another and therefore as more pertinent or more important for his deciding what to do.[87] Hence, the virtuous person perceives the situation in a certain way and sees what the right thing is for him to do.[88] For McDowell, then, as for Aristotle (on his reading), one cannot codify in rules what is the morally right thing to do in any given situation; ethics is about deciding and acting based on how we, once we are educated and trained, see the situation.[89]

O'Neill suggests that McDowell takes rules to offer no guidance at all, and this applies to moral rules and obligations, as well as other kinds.[90] In following rules, "we assume a background of life and experience, of response and of reaction, which forms a precondition for theory and practice, for judgment and communication."[91] But, she argues, this is not the whole story: "[R]ule-following is a commonplace activity, and (far from being a myth) is integral to most forms of social life and activity. . . . [T]he presuppositions [of rule-following] are widely met, and rule-following flourishes." The central point is that these rules are not objective and independent of us; we construct them and use them in order to organize, coordinate, and direct behavior, ours and others.[92] They do not *make us* act in certain ways, but we formulate them as ways we agree that we should act.

I do not want to enter this debate about rules and render a judgment and raise objections about whether O'Neill has accurately understood McDowell's argument.[93] His point, I think, is that moral virtue as a kind of knowledge (and as a kind of perception) is like our understanding of language: It amounts to a set of abilities that we acquire by being educated into a certain way of life, a social and cultural world. I do not believe that McDowell thinks rules are either inappropriate or impossible or dysfunctional as a feature of moral deliberation and decision making. But clearly, for him, such rules or principles are not the centerpiece of moral character and conduct. They have no intrinsic

---

[87] McDowell, "Virtue and Reason" in *Mind, Value and Reality*, 67–69.
[88] McDowell, "Virtue and Reason" in *Mind, Value and Reality*, 71.
[89] For O'Neill's account, see *Towards Justice and Virtue*, 79.
[90] O'Neill, *Towards Justice and Virtue*, 83–89. I do not think that this claim about McDowell is correct. If it were, then McDowell would have to say that dictionaries and lexicons offer no guidance in any context, but surely he admits that rules of a linguistic kind can be helpful in certain cases and are widely used. Similarly, moral rules and principles are used and can be helpful, even if they cannot be taken to be morally authoritative and necessary for moral virtue and moral insight – in all situations or even as a standard of moral virtue.
[91] O'Neill, *Towards Justice and Virtue*, 84.
[92] O'Neill, *Towards Justice and Virtue*, 84–85.
[93] Garfield argues effectively that O'Neill has misunderstood both McDowell and Wittgenstein and that both should not be taken to reject rules or principles altogether. I agree on both counts.

force, nor are they authoritative by themselves. What is central is a kind of moral perception that enables us to see what is important in a situation and determine what is the right thing to do.

For Levinas, responsibility is sensibility, for it is a responsiveness to the face of the other person, which is prior to and different from a perceptual experience of the other person. It is presensible sensibility. Technically, such an engagement with the face, which is wholly passive, is preconceptual and prearticulate. What I grasp in the face, what accuses me or traumatizes me, is its pain, its suffering, and its dependency, and what arises for me is responsibility to and for it, which is then the self's primary mode of sensibility – being ready to respond in behalf of the other's need. As we have seen, moral and legal principles and even rights of a sort are introduced in order to organize our responses in society when there are many other persons in situations of varying nuance and complexity and given our own limitations.[94] But the face-to-face and my responsibility are prior to these rules, and in this respect Levinas's thinking bears a structural similarity to McDowell's. Moreover, each takes ethics to originate, in a sense, in our being directly aware of what is right for us to do. That original awareness or recognition, however, is very precisely focused, for Levinas, on "seeing" what the face means and requires, as we know, that even to call it a kind of seeing or perception is not accurate. Still, although the responsible self is wholly passive and in a way that is prior to all receptivity and spontaneity, what this means is that the utterly particular relation of the I and the other makes a claim on the I that is prior to general rules or any categorization as such.

Moreover, the self's ability to see what it is obligated to do in the face of the other is more basic than any cultural or social world that it occupies. It derives from the brute fact of being faced by another person, prior to any "form of life" with all its familiarities, practices, and such. Indeed, for Levinas such forms of life are based, in a sense, on the particular engagements of selves and others and the reality of pluralities of them.

Levinas does share some features with McDowell, but they differ in at least one important way.[95] They share a kind of ethical realism and the idea that we can "perceive" moral truths, although that perception involves rational deliberation for McDowell and is a quasi-phenomenological seeing for Levinas. But the priority and character of that truth and the grasp of it for Levinas show how far they are from one another. The moral perception that McDowell identifies is, in the end, much more epistemic than it is for Levinas, for whom the seeing of the face is not so much a cognitive act as it is an awareness of the other's

---

[94] See Caygill, *Levinas and the Political*, and essays in *Alterity and Trascendence* and *Outside the Subject*.
[95] See Axel Honneth in Nicholas Smith (ed.), *Reading McDowell: On Mind and World* (New York: Routledge, 2002), on the comparison with perception.

need and a responsiveness to it, all at once, a reaching out to help that is an understanding of the other's need and a grasp of a responsibility that is an act in behalf of the other.

KORSGAARD AND THE PERCEPTION OF REASONS

I suggested that it might be useful to look at McDowell because moral virtue, for him, is a perceptual capacity of a sort. Christine Korsgaard does not agree, but in the course of discussing what morality and moral normativity are, she claims that "pain is the perception of a reason" and that reasons are associated with obligations.[96] We might think that Korsgaard enables us to understand how we can perceive obligations, and that might help us to interpret how Levinas thinks we can grasp directly our responsibility in the face of the other person. It will turn out that we are wrong about this, but it is useful to see how and why.

In Lectures 3 and 4 of *The Sources of Normativity*, Korsgaard sketches a Kantian-style account of normativity. Lower animals perceive the world and have desires; we do as well, but we also reflect on our perceptions, desires, and beliefs and consider which of our desires and impulses, for example, is a reason for us to have a particular belief or to act in a certain way. "Reason" is an honorific term that we confer when our reflective assessment succeeds in locating what it seeks, and what it seeks is an action that is expressive of who we are, of our *identity*. When we locate such a reason and see that its action is expressive of who we are, we take the reason to be what obligates us to act that way.[97] Moreover, if that *identity* is our identity as rational human beings, then these obligations are *moral* obligations. Morality rests on our sense that our humanity and rationality are valuable; what makes morality special, Korsgaard says, is that it springs from our identity as rational human agents, which has a preeminence with regard to all our other contingent, specific identities – for example, as men or women, Americans or Chinese or Brazilian, Jews or Christians or Muslims, lawyers or doctors or computer programmers, mothers or fathers, friends or enemies, and children or adults.[98]

With this account of moral obligation in hand, Korsgaard turns to two possible objections: that valuing our own humanity does not involve valuing that of others and that we also need to be concerned with other animals.[99] For our purposes, I want to focus attention on our social nature and the role it plays in her response to both concerns. When Korsgaard turns to the question of

[96] Korsgaard, *The Sources of Normativity*, 149; cf. 100–3.
[97] Korsgaard, *The Sources of Normativity*, 93–113.
[98] Korsgaard, *The Sources of Normativity*, 113–30, esp. 125.
[99] See Korsgaard, *The Sources of Normativity*, 131, and Lecture 4.

altruism, or our obligation to others, she disposes with attempts to build on self-interest or even private reasons and focuses on clarifying our social nature and its "depth," as she calls it.[100] She calls on Wittgenstein's argument against a private language and builds a corresponding argument against private reasons. In the course of that argument, Korsgaard introduces a distinction that is very intriguing for considering the ethical character of the face of the other person in Levinas.

Korsgaard presents us with a social situation in which one person is present to another. Her description has the other person order me to do something, but later she widens the scope of the situation by drawing the conclusion: "I am merely describing a deep psychological fact – that human beings are very susceptible to one another's pressure. We tend to cave in to the demands of others. But nothing I have said so far shows that we really have to treat the demands of others as *reasons*."[101] Social encounters, as Erving Goffman classically showed, need not be verbal and articulate in order to make demands.[102] Korsgaard's phrase "susceptible to one another's pressure" does not restrict the pressure to verbal pressure or orders; the pressure could just as well come from a person's presence, the posture of her body, or the look on her face that puts that pressure on me. The point is that it is there, and it is perceived. In responding to you, I "am not able to help it," as Korsgaard puts it, and that is because I sense a "necessity" that is "normative and compulsive," that is, I sense an *obligation*. These are Korsgaard's words, not mine, and they are chosen to express how she understands our reaction to the pressure of another's presence: It involves taking that presence as obligatory, and that means as a reason for me to respond and to act.[103] There is more to Korsgaard's argument that "we really have to treat the demands of others as *reasons*," but for now it is sufficient to notice her conclusion, that in a social situation, the pressure that each puts on the other is a rational demand; it is an obligation.

But this is not yet a moral obligation, Korsgaard claims, and this is the distinction to which I want to call attention. That is, for her, something other than this pressure of obligation accounts for the fact that one person's reasons *morally* obligate another. Korsgaard draws on an argument from Thomas Nagel to show what this something is.[104] He imagines that two strangers confront each other, one tormenting the other, and the victim tells his tormentor to

---

[100] Korsgaard, *The Sources of Normativity*, 132–36.
[101] Korsgaard, *The Sources of Normativity*, 141.
[102] Erving Goffman, *The Presentation of Self in Everyday Life* (Garden City, NY: Doubleday Anchor, 1959).
[103] Korsgaard, *The Sources of Normativity*, 139–42; esp. 139.
[104] Korsgaard, *The Sources of Normativity*, 142–43; see also Thomas Nagel, *The Possibility of Altruism*.

stop, pleading with him to consider how he would like it if he were a victim of such torment. Korsgaard observes that the victim has obligated his tormentor to stop by "forcing" him to value the victim's humanity and requiring him to respect it.[105] What occurs is that the agent is called on to acknowledge that he and his victim are human beings alike, that they share that humanity. They speak and listen, understand and acknowledge each other as human beings. "We can think and reason together," and therefore, as human beings, we are "social animals in a deep way."[106] As Korsgaard puts it, "[T]he space of linguistic consciousness – the space in which meanings and reasons exist – is a space that we occupy together."[107] Moral obligations, then, arise for us once we recognize the human in each other and value that humanity in us both. Your humanity, as what we all share, makes your suffering or pain a reason for me to stop tormenting you.

We might summarize this line of thinking by noticing that for Korsgaard the other's pain, by itself, does not obligate me morally to relieve it. In addition, I need to be aware that we think and reason together as human beings and that it is your pain as a human being's pain that obligates me to relieve it. Once more, then, we see that for Korsgaard moral obligation is tied to our humanity or human identity as reasoning beings. What is normative or obligating is, in a sense, the need to express my humanity in action and to respect that of others. I am obligated to relieve the other's suffering or pain *because* she is someone human like myself, and her humanity is valuable in and of itself, to support and protect, just as mine is. But, as Korsgaard realizes, pain and suffering are not restricted to human beings. If pain is "intrinsically normative," then the pain of other animals ought to obligate me as well, even if they are not valuable as rational human animals. Korsgaard's examination of this objection leads her to clarify her naturalism and to show how far she wants to go in "humanizing" animal activity.[108]

Certainly, Levinas would want to raise questions about Korsgaard's naturalism, but even prior to that he should have doubts about her emphasis on "reflective endorsement," as she calls it, and the primacy of reasons in her account of obligation and moral obligation. But her argument does raise the question for Levinas of why the pain, suffering, and demand of the face of the human other carries the weight it does. What distinguishes it as the ground of ethical responsibility? I think that Korsgaard's analysis of the role of the value of rational humanity, which is at the center of her account of moral normativity

[105] Korsgaard, *The Sources of Normativity*, 142–43.
[106] Korsgaard, *The Sources of Normativity*, 144–45.
[107] Korsgaard, *The Sources of Normativity*, 145.
[108] Korsgaard, *The Sources of Normativity*, 145–60.

and of our obligations to others, is, at best, derivative. But it is not clear how the face can impose itself on us independently of any recognition of the humanity of the other or independently of some recognition of its identity. We may have allowed Levinas too much or perhaps failed to understand him deeply enough. Furthermore, Levinas takes responsibility to be sensibility, whereas for Korsgaard moral obligation is arrived at by rational reflection and deliberation. One wonders if there is any room in Korsgaard's account for a grasping of obligation that is akin to perception, and this is where pain comes in, where she says that "pain is the perception of a reason." What does this mean, and could we also say that being obligated by another person's pain is also the perception of a reason?

Drawing on Wittgenstein, Korsgaard claims that even if we agree that pain is a kind of sensation, the "painfulness of pain" – what we might call the central point of being in pain – is that, whatever these sensations are like, we are inclined to fight them and rid ourselves of them.[109] Pain, as she now glosses this point, is the perception we have of our bodies' condition that gives us a reason to change that condition.[110] Now turn to pity or sympathy: Why is pity for another a reason for you to help him? Surely not because you are feeling distress or discomfort in yourself; rather, it is because your pity is "the perception of *another's* pain, and so the perception that there is a reason to change *his* condition."[111] This is how pain is a perception of a reason for the being in pain and for another who feels pity or sympathy to that being for its pain. Furthermore, because some nonhuman animals can feel pain, they perceive a reason for themselves to change their condition and to relieve it. And if we pity them, we also perceive a reason to assist in relieving it. Pain is the way a being perceives what is threatening its identity and so makes that being aware of or inclines it to what it should do to maintain that identity. As Korsgaard describes it, the animal does not know that it has a reason, but it does perceive it. Hence, obligation for human beings is what pain is for nonhuman animals, "a rejection of a threat to [one's] identity."[112] What pain and hunger do for animals, moral obligations do for human beings.

From this point, where Korsgaard wants us to see rationality and morality as natural devices for preserving our humanity, akin to pain and hunger in animals, it is a quick step to her saying that just as we cannot fail to respond to a person's calls for help, so we cannot fail to respond to an animal's cries of pain and suffering.[113] We share our humanity with other persons and our nature of

---

[109] Korsgaard, *The Sources of Normativity*, 147–48.
[110] Korsgaard, *The Sources of Normativity*, 148 and n. 19.
[111] Korsgaard, *The Sources of Normativity*, 149.
[112] Korsgaard, *The Sources of Normativity*, 150.
[113] Korsgaard, *The Sources of Normativity*, 153.

animality with other animals; *their* pain can obligate *us*.[114] When we pity them or see them in pain, our perception of their being in pain obligates us, insofar as we share with them an animal's identity and we are rational beings who are aware of obligations that make demands of us.

All of this account surely encourages the thought that Korsgaard is a moral realist of a kind. For morality and moral obligation are fixtures of our rational nature as human beings. We are as much moral beings as we are rational ones, and rationality is central to our nature. Furthermore, what we ought to do is articulated in reasons and obligations, the types of decisions and actions that are expressive of that rational humanity in us and in all persons. Moreover, to extend our obligations to animals, Korsgaard finds in them *states* – pain, hunger, suffering – that function as these do for us and yet that in us are subordinate to our more articulate, rational ability to grasp reasons for choice and action. Still, this means that we also feel pain and pity. Before we think about our own pain and how to relieve it, then, we are inclined to remove it, and also, before we reflect on it, when another human being cries in pain or presents us with a face of suffering, hunger, or despair, we are inclined to relieve its suffering. We see in her eyes or the posture of her neck or head the pain and the call to us for help, a kind word, and a hand extended in assistance. For Korsgaard, this kind of basic pity only becomes effective when we deliberate and reflect, when it becomes a reason for us to act, and when it becomes an obligation to help.

What would Levinas say about all this? For Levinas, we might imagine, several things are true. First, this attitude to the other's need and pain is fundamental and already ethically determinative. Second, the other does not yet have to say anything or even feel pain or suffering; its very existence calls out to us and elicits our response and even demands it. Third, this relationship is not general; it is particular, prior to any reasoning, conceptualizing, reflective interpretation or assessment. Fourth, while each case is particular, this "pity" in response to the other person's "pain" is universal; it is a feature of all social existence. Whenever there are two persons, I and you, it is there. And finally, because it is prior to any conceptualization or reflection, one can easily see that the other person need not be a human being. Any animal can have a face, as long as it can be in need and call out to us.

We can summarize in the following way the conversation between Levinas and the philosophers we have discussed thus far in this chapter. Korsgaard's moral realism is a kind of foundationalism, rationalism, and naturalism; it uses the notion of having reasons and of our idea of rational humanity as a ground for

---

[114] Korsgaard, *The Sources of Normativity*, 153. See also Korsgaard, "Fellow Creatures: Kantian Ethics and Our Duties to Animals," *Tanner Lectures on Human Values*, 24 (Feb. 6, 2004), 79–110.

moral norms and obligations. O'Neill is very Kantian, too, but her emphasis
on reasons, practical reasoning, and sociability does not take this decidedly
naturalist turn. McDowell is indebted not only to Kant and Aristotle but also to
Wittgenstein. While an ethical realist, his naturalism is, as he calls it, a naturalism
of second nature – constructivist, cultural, communal. Without Aristotelian
metaphysics and science, McDowell's view loses one kind of foundation, and
his use of Wittgensteinian forms of life seems to open the door to a plurality
of moral outlooks and systems of value, as long as they are compatible with
the role of reason, rational deliberation, and such. With these three outcomes
in mind, it is tempting to see Levinas as stepping beyond all such attempts to
understand ethics and the moral life and to read his central insight as realist,
foundationalist, and intuitionist, but of a very distinctive kind and in a stronger
sense than any of these philosophers.[115] If such is the case, however, his insight,
for all its privileging of alterity and the other person, brings with it a serious set
of concerns about pluralism and difference, and these concerns demand some
attention.

LEVINAS'S UNIVERSALISM AND PLURALISM

There is a peculiar problem about this view of Levinas, however, and it concerns the character or depth of what we might call Levinas's pluralism. On the
one hand, everything starts with the other person, and as a result one would
expect a rich appreciation of concrete others: other cultures, ways of life, and
so forth. On the other hand, Levinas's ethics of care and responsibility is a kind
of universalism, and it is not clear how receptive it can be to a rich pluralism.
This is a point that Howard Caygill worries about in *Levinas and the Political*,
especially concerning Levinas's attitude toward the Palestinians and the State of
Israel in the period after the Six Day War through the massacres in Sabra and
Chatila in 1982.[116] But it is not solely a problem about his particular political
responses. It is about what responsibility really means for our sense of particular

---

[115] This is not to say that he showed much explicit concern with moral relativism, although one
might take his worries regarding *totality* in all its dimensions and expressions to be akin to a fear
of relativism, conceived as one outcome of subjective domination. Moreover, his gradually
deepening reflections on God and on the face-to-face and responsibility as the locale of glory,
height, and holiness might lead us to take his emphasis on transcendence and infinity as a
claim about the inadequacy of any morality or politics built solely on rationality or nature.
These interests suggest that Levinas does have powerful concerns about moral relativism,
skepticism, and nihilism. There surely is something right in such intuitions about his work
and his central project, and his political critique of Nazi fascism, Stalinism, and the West does
serve to underline the point.

[116] Caygill, *Levinas and the Political*, Ch. 5.

loyalties and identities and what special relationships, solidarity, and affiliation mean for that responsibility.

For some years now, a debate has raged about what Levinas offers, in terms of an ethical ground, as a corrective to certain possible excesses of deconstruction. One stimulus for the debate is Simon Critchley's book *The Ethics of Deconstruction* and subsequent discussion regarding Derrida, Levinas, and Habermas about ethics, rationality, pluralism, politics, justice, and such matters. Participants, in addition to Critchley, include Axel Honneth, Richard Rorty, Drucilla Cornell, and Derrida himself. I do not want to trace the course of this debate, interesting and important as it is, but it will be useful to call attention to a few central issues raised in it.

Can one talk about an ethics of deconstruction? Is Derrida committed to justice in some fundamental way? Critchley has argued that there *is* indeed an ethical opening in deconstruction or an ethical dimension but only if "ethics" is treated in Levinas's sense and involves an ethical demand, as Levinas understands it. This conversation, then, raises the question: If one is committed to a plurality of worldviews or interpretive frameworks, is there no room for a basic, orienting ethical demand, or does Levinas provide such a ground? Or is there no escape from these frameworks? Is every text, every community's life, every form of life, ethically speaking, as good as any other, for the people who understand it, read it, and live according to it? It certainly appears that calling upon Levinas to complement Derrida is an attempt to provide a determinative ethical quality for any such pluralist program or position. If so, how does it claim to provide that foundation?[117]

This is one set of questions that certainly is of interest. A second concerns *the precise way* the ethical demand or moment is related to the rest of our lives, especially our political and institutional lives. This is an issue that has arisen in debates over the ways that Derrida and Habermas might be seen as closer than one might have thought.[118] The question is how ethics, in Levinas's sense, is related to politics, and the suggestion is that it cannot be foundationally related to it. Political decisions must be situated and particular, based on a responsiveness to the ethical demand of justice, but they are not *derivable* from it. Only in this way can ethics be nonfoundational enough to protect the freedom of politics and politics be nonarbitrary enough to be ethical and just.[119] This way of formulating the issue raises the question, more broadly, of whether Levinas

---

[117] See Critchley, *The Ethics of Deconstruction*, especially Appendix 1 to the 1999 edition, 248–66.

[118] Critchley, *The Ethics of Deconstruction*, Appendix 2, 267–80; "Remarks on Derrida and Habermas," *Constellations* 7:4 (Dec. 2000), 455–66; and "Metaphysics in the Dark," *Political Theory* 26:6.

[119] Critchley, "Remarks on Derrida and Habermas," *Constellations*, 455–66.

might be conceived as providing an ethical starting point for a whole variety of forms of moral and political life. Can one accept the priority of the ethical in Levinas's sense and still be a pluralist? Is it more accurate to call the engagement with the face of the other directive and orienting rather than foundational and grounding? Or is it the case that the face-to-face is of no public, political, or social importance at all – what Richard Rorty calls a "mere nuisance?"[120] Is it, in other words, at best a matter of private conduct and irrelevant to public, political decision making?

As I have claimed, it is tempting to treat Levinas as a foundationalist who, like Aristotle, Hobbes, Descartes, Spinoza, or Fichte, has found a basis on which to build his philosophical system or who at least points in that direction. To be sure, on the one hand Levinas consistently criticizes totalizing thinking and political regimes dominated by a commitment to totality – or system, but, on the other hand, the infinite or the transcendent might be viewed as his "replacement" for the Cartesian "*sum*," or "I exist," on which all knowledge and understanding can be built. Although he does not put it this way explicitly, Levinas might be thought to replace Descartes' "I exist" with the biblical "*hineni*," which means "Here I am" in the sense of "I am ready" ("I am at your service, I am available) as an act of unreserved offering of oneself.[121] Or, in a way he does put it, "Here I am" does replace the Cartesian "I think" or the Kantian transcendental unity of apperception.[122] All of this, which is regularly discussed by commentators, might lead us to think that moral systems and politics, obligations and rules, can be derived from or at least constructed on this foundation. But we should not leap too hastily to such a conclusion.[123]

What we need to appreciate is the way that the self's responsibility to the other is not a foundation for systematic moral or legal thinking, but neither is it wholly private and completely detached from public life.[124] Levinas uses the biblical expression *hineni* (here I am), alluding to Abraham's response to God in Genesis 22 and Isaiah's in Isaiah 6:8, for a number of reasons, but none of them is to fix a systematic foundation for ethics or politics. Levinas wants us to see the connections between how the biblical author portrays a person's readiness to respond to a divine call by acknowledging it and one's availability and willingness to act and Levinas's own understanding of how, prior to all thought, deliberation, and even choice, the self responds to the other person's

---

[120] Richard Rorty, *Achieving Our Country* (Cambridge, MA: Harvard University Press, 1998), 96–97, quoted in Critchley, "Metaphysics in the Dark," *Political Theory*, 806.

[121] See Hilary Putnam, "Levinas and Judaism" in Critchley and Bernasconi (eds.), *The Cambridge Companion to Levinas*, 38–39, based on OB, 146.

[122] Levinas, "God and Philosophy," in *Basic Philosophical Writings*, 140, 144, 146.

[123] See Critchley, *The Ethics of Deconstruction*, 219–36 and 268–69.

[124] See Critchley, *The Ethics of Deconstruction*, 268–69.

presence as need with a recognition and acceptance of what that presence means. Levinas juxtaposes the ideas of unconditional giving of oneself to God and of responding to the other person with care and assistance. The "here I am" is how I see the other's face; I do not affirm my existence, articulate my feelings, or describe my thoughts or plans. I accept the other and extend myself to her first, and whatever then happens is, in its own way, based on that acceptance, although it is not derived from it or constructed on the basis of it. What it can be is made to fit the spirit of it, as it were.

Moreover, these are not temporally arrayed stages in a process. They occur at once. On occasion, I – like Abraham and Isaiah – may acknowledge first and then deliberate, question, and more. But more often, I talk with others, make plans, meet, engage in activities together, and in the conduct of these activities and experiences I acknowledge and accept my responsibility to and for the other. What I do or say is my way of sharing myself and the world with another – in addition to being the action or utterance it is. Furthermore, while in one sense all action or speech is responsive to the other, in another sense, some is more attuned to the significance of that responsiveness and some is less attuned to it. Responsibility is unavoidable and necessary, but there are degrees of it.

Beginning with this understanding of "here I am," Levinas discusses how it, moral experience, and political life are all dimensions of life that can go well or poorly. Rorty is wrong about Levinas: In public life, infinite responsibility is anything but a nuisance. Indeed, it is the point of it all. The responsibility of the self, that is, is the primary significance of all interpersonal experience; and by realizing this, we understand what the point is of our social lives. If, then, we consider our practices, principles, and policies in the light of this responsibility, we ask ourselves whether and to what degree they live up to its standard, as it were. One can easily imagine, then, that a variety of ways of organizing our lives might satisfy this way of understanding them. Many sets of social practices, political organizations, legal systems, and such will be just, to one degree or another; some succeed very well, and some do not succeed and are paradigms of injustice and oppression and domination, even violence and horror. For Levinas, Hitlerism and Stalinism are the central historical examples that he always has in mind – emblems of extraordinary suffering and human abandonment. Justice is not, for Levinas, a foundational principle for deriving a set of practices, policies, or institutions, as it is for Rawls. As an obligation to assist, support, and care for others, our primary relation allows for degrees of generosity, of respect, of benefaction, and for various sorts of institutional arrangements and sets of principles for organizing both individual and collective actions toward others. In this way, Levinas is not a relativist, for whom any group's practices and policies are acceptable, but he is a pluralist, for whom many sets will be satisfactory, to one degree or another. He is not Rorty, whose only constraints are pragmatic and intuitive.

TAYLOR'S ETHICAL PLURALISM

Among moral philosophers, Charles Taylor is perhaps the one whose thinking is, in this regard, closest to Levinas's. What I have in mind is the multicultural side of Taylor and then only its structural, not its substantive, character, for Taylor is far more historical than Levinas and much more focused on the freedom and identity of the subject or agent. But in other ways, his pluralism is similar to Levinas's. Let me try to explain how, in order to clarify the special way that universalism and pluralism intersect for Levinas.[125]

Taylor believes that there is an intrinsically moral dimension to our selfhood. This moral dimension involves the fact that our sense of identity requires, Taylor argues, an orientation to the good; it is in terms of some conception of the good that people, actions, institutions, practices, and all such things *matter* to us or that we value them. In this very basic way, we live in a kind of moral space, and practical reason is the way we navigate ourselves in it. Taylor calls "moral sources" those factors that motivate and justify our particular moral commitments in this moral space.[126] Levinas also takes our selfhood to be intrinsically moral or ethical, although of course his account of why and how this is so differs from Taylor's. Moreover, like Taylor, he takes "moral sources" very seriously. But if for Levinas these sources and the moral dimension of our selfhood occur with the other's needfulness, her poverty and suffering, and the language of religion, what does Taylor say about the content of the moral dimension of our selfhood? Is it wholly open to circumstance, context, and one's social-cultural world? Or is it more universally defined, and if so, how?

Like Korsgaard, Taylor takes us to be reflective beings, who can focus attention on our desires and impulses in order to evaluate them. For Taylor, we evaluate these desires and impulses and articulate their value to us in terms of some conception of the good that we have. This conception of the good is part of who we think we are and who we want to be; that is, it is part of our identity. This, too, is like Korsgaard. In Taylor's case, it is important to realize that such reflection or evaluation "makes explicit the sense of worth the evaluator

---

[125] In Rorty's terms, the question is whether Levinas is a liberal ironist. See Critchley, *The Ethics of Deconstruction*, 274.
[126] For convenience, I follow the account in Nicholas Smith, *Charles Taylor*, 88–89.

has in his pre-reflective life."[127] My question is: Is this largely or purely a formal matter? Or, as in Korsgaard, does such "strong evaluation" or "reflective
endorsement" carry with it a moral content?

Taylor describes what he calls "three axes of moral thinking," which sounds
like it means "all moral thinking" or "moral thinking in general."[128] In fact,
Taylor says that "something like them probably . . . exists in every culture."[129]
So the three are common features of whatever goes by the name of moral
thinking. They are: "our sense of respect for and obligations to others"; "our
understandings of what makes a full life"; and some sense of our dignity.[130]
He claims that the modern world is particularly disturbed by the second axis
and the whole issue of meaningfulness and the option that life is empty and
without significance. But overall, Taylor believes that all cultures do have moral
commitments about all three matters: obligations to other persons, self-respect,
and the meaning of life. This historical or descriptive claim is grounded in
Taylor's account of selfhood as an involvement with reflective assessment and
some sense of the good. These three axes are important components of our
moral lives *because* we are moral beings of the kind we are. For this latter claim,
Taylor presents an intriguing transcendental argument.[131]

At this stage, Taylor's account appears to treat the meaningfulness of human
life, regard for others, and a sense of dignity (or self-respect) as equally important
for morality and all three as derivative from our moral rationality, or what we
might call the way we as rational beings are related to some conception of
the good. Until we look at his transcendental argument for tying together our
identity and the good, we have every reason to treat rational evaluation as the
basis of these axes, and if so, Taylor's similarity to Korsgaard is all the more
telling. Both, of course, acknowledge the importance of our desires, impulses,
and emotions, but what grounds morality is reason, in one sense or another.
Levinas does not denigrate reason, but he does want to place it properly in
human experience and, as Theodor Adorno, Max Horkheimer, and so many
others warn, not allow it unqualified dominion over our lives. Levinas might
be similar to Taylor and Korsgaard in this regard, but it is not exactly clear
what that similarity might come to. It will help to look more closely at Taylor;
perhaps his transcendental argument will clarify the role rationality ultimately
plays for him. In some ways, reason certainly seems to be constitutive of our

---

[127] Nicholas Smith, *Charles Taylor*, 91; cf. Charles Taylor, "What Is Human Agency?" in *Human
Agency and Language* (Philosophical Papers 1) (Cambridge. Cambridge University Press, 1985),
and Taylor, *Sources of the Self* (Cambridge, MA: Harvard University Press, 1989), Ch. 2.

[128] Taylor, *Sources of the Self*, 14–16.

[129] Taylor, *Sources of the Self*, 16.

[130] Cf. Smith, *Charles Taylor*, 91–92.

[131] Smith, *Charles Taylor*, 92–97; cf. *Sources of the Self*, 32–36.

lives as moral beings, but the question is how important a role it plays, for our moral character involves more than our rationality and does not seem to be grounded solely in it.

Taylor's transcendental argument has a formal character. If our lives were not organized by the good as a "standard of coherence," we would "suffer a painful and frightening emptiness" and fail to live as "healthy functioning" agents. Clearly, this kind of healthy agency is what we ought to seek to accomplish in our lives. Therefore, some moral orientation is needed for psychic wholeness of any kind, and human agency requires such wholeness, some sense of our own identity.[132] The issue of a sense of coherence or wholeness to one's life is, as Taylor argues, a historical one arising from trends from the sixteenth and seventeenth centuries to the present. But it is also a general one about what is essential to human agency *per se* and social communication and interaction.

As Nicholas Smith puts it, the sense of "moral" here is very expansive and broad. What is essentially moral about the self and agency may not be that "all human agents must be concerned with the welfare of others," but rather that "human agency involves some grasp, however inchoate or inarticulate, of the contrast between mere life and good life."[133] Hence, what is crucial, for Taylor, is some good that one can articulate as part of the process of reflectively considering what to choose and how to act. What is essential, at one level, is our capacity to reflect and evaluate; at another, it is that there be such a value for us in terms of which we can engage in this evaluation. That value and our commitment to it make things matter to us; they give desires, actions, and resources the worth they have for us. Smith points out that this tells against any narrow intellectualism, although rationality must at least be available for the human agent, in order to carry out the reflective consideration and assessment. Furthermore, many values can play this role; there are many possible goods.

In fact, however, Taylor claims that we grasp our identity as a unity, although its components derive from various sources. Each of us regularly is faced with a variety of goods, and part of our task is to deal with incommensurabilities among them, often by forming some kind of hierarchy of them. But the most highly ranked goods, what Taylor calls "hypergoods," can conflict with each other or force us to sacrifice other goods.[134] Moreover, different individuals can have disagreements over hypergoods, or conflict can occur between members of diverse cultures or peoples.[135] Taylor, that is, admits the possibility of

---

[132] Smith, *Charles Taylor*, 93; *Sources of the Self*, 27–29, is the most important text in Taylor, where he sets out this transcendental argument.
[133] Smith, *Charles Taylor*, 94, 95 ("non-monadistic, expansive understanding of the good").
[134] Smith, *Charles Taylor*, 103–4; *Sources of the Self*, 62–75.
[135] Smith, *Charles Taylor*, 104.

genuine conflict in such cases and certainly genuine conversation, and he clarifies how practical deliberation and debate proceed. How such reasoning might go, as Taylor sees it, depends upon the goods in question and how they stand up under questioning and so forth, not upon certain principles about procedures or the character of rational argument.[136] In short, Taylor tries to keep his account of human agency as neutral as possible among various moral orientations in order to allow a variety of goods and hypergoods to play roles in human selfhood. Although his account has a rational character and does seem somewhat Aristotelian in character, it leaves open the possibility of many values and conceptions of the good life. Presumably, however, no good could be determinative or primary for the self, on Taylor's account, if it were incompatible with those features of agency that are essential: a sense of the wholeness of the self, a sense of one's own capacity to choose and act, a capacity for rational reflection or strong evaluation, and a sense of self-respect or dignity. Whatever pluralism Taylor permits, historically speaking, is surely restricted when legitimacy comes into play.[137]

Taylor's comprehensive picture starts with the notion of human agency, and this looks like something to which Levinas would certainly object. Smith argues that Taylor can appropriate the Levinasian insight to fend off the objection that his account is too eudaimonistic, too focused on the self's well-being and insufficiently responsive to the welfare of others.[138] But is this really Levinas's point? Where, if at all, might Levinas's face-to-face and responsibility fit into Taylor's picture? Smith's proposal is that Taylor might treat "concern for the other person as a hypergood."[139] If so, such concern would override self-interest and many "life-goods," as he calls them. In Smith's words, responsibility for the other is, on the one hand, "integrated into the structure of selfhood" or "the highest vocation of human subjectivity" and, on the other hand, responsive to the needs of the other.[140]

Smith, however, has failed to understand Levinas fully or correctly, and in so doing he has mistaken the point where Levinas's insight might contribute to Taylor's understanding of the human and the ethical. Smith makes it sound as if the problem is how to find a place for exteriority or the other in ethics, without stepping outside ontology. Certainly, this is not Levinas's problem or

---

[136] See *Sources of the Self*, 60–62, 71–75.
[137] Legitimacy at least in the sense of acceptability *to us*, given our situation and perspective.
[138] Smith, *Charles Taylor*, 112–13.
[139] Smith, *Charles Taylor*, 112.
[140] Smith, *Charles Taylor*, 112–13, refers to an article of his own and to Paul Ricoeur, *Oneself as Another* (Chicago: University of Chicago Press, 1992). Cf. Richard Cohen, "Ricoeur and the Lure of Self-Esteem" in *Ethics, Exegesis and Philosophy*, 283–325, and Cohen (ed.), *Ricoeur as Another: The Ethics of Subjectivity* (Albany, NY: SUNY Press, 2002).

one he would accept; the other, originally, comes to one from the outside, as it were, and what this means is that the dimension he calls the "face" is present to the self in a way anterior to, more primary than, all those dimensions of the other person that are understood or grasped in everyday, social scientific, ethical, or political terms. That is not an artifice or a construction; it is the most original feature of social existence. All social interaction – conversation, debate, or agency of all kinds – is already this engagement, whatever other content or character it also has. In Taylor's terms, Levinas might say that crucial to all action is that it *already involves* the recognition of what this engagement, this relation to the other's face, means – its point or purpose. One might very well treat obligation to others, as a principle, among one's goods or even as a hypergood. It may be best to do so. But what makes it good is that it expresses in public and generally what each encounter or interpersonal engagement *already* means fundamentally and particularly. We are a responsible self *before* we are agents, deliberators, evaluators, and free, so to speak. Or, alternatively, we are all that we are – with our sense of identity, value, and purpose – only as we are *already* and more primarily responsible for and to each and every other person, who suffers, calls to us, demands of us.

Smith suggests that we fit concern for others – à la Levinas – into an open-ended slot in Taylor's largely formal account–that is, as one good among many, or even as one hypergood among several. But Levinas's point is that benevolence and justice, as general and public principles, are rooted in something deeper or more determinative. Regard for others is not, therefore, one option among many, in this deep sense; to ignore or reject it is to be blind to what I am as a social individual. It is not to take a position in a disagreement about goods or hypergoods. Levinas's sense of the ethical at this level can be realized in principles and practices of various kinds, insofar as they realize or express it to one degree or another. For him, the ethical functions in something like the way rationality, the good, and our sense of identity function for Taylor.

Taylor not only makes room for a plurality of goods and for the incommensurability of such goods when endorsed by difficult cultures; he also explores in detail how such goods are figured into conceptions of identity and how practical reasoning works in conversations or debates between members of such different cultures. He does a great deal more than examine how such goods figure in practical reasoning and human agency. Levinas does more as well, more than identify the engagement with the face of the other, but he does not examine our modern Western identity or elaborate the moral and political implications of it in the way, for example, we find it in philosophers such as John Rawls, Jürgen Habermas, Adam Gewirth, O'Nora O'Neill, Peter Singer, Joseph Raz, Ronald Dworkin, and Tom Scanlon. Levinas, as an ethical thinker, seems to be doing something else. His intent is different; he means something different by "ethics." Richard Rorty is dismissive of this sense, when Simon Critchley calls attention to it.[141] Rorty takes ethics to be the project of looking for principles to use in making decisions in certain kinds of situations, where the alternatives are what we would take to be moral ones.[142] He finds what Levinas does irrelevant to this project and thus not ethical, in any recognizable or helpful sense of the term. But Rorty is mistaken, as Taylor no doubt would agree. But if Levinas is doing something different and yet its focus is the ethical, what kind of an ethical thinker is he?

WHAT KIND OF MORAL THINKER IS LEVINAS?

In a later essay, Critchley asks: "[I]s ethics the right word to describe the experience that [Levinas] is trying to express?"[143] Critchley then follows Hilary Putnam in appropriating a distinction from Stanley Cavell, between "two species of moral philosophers: legislators and moral perfectionists"[144] and in referring to Levinas as a "moral perfectionist."

Putnam takes "moral perfectionists" to be one of two "species of moral philosophers."[145] The other species is "legislators," who provide "detailed moral and political rules." This is Putnam's category, not Cavell's, but, according to Putnam, Cavell singles out "moral perfectionists" as those philosophers who do not reject what the legislators seek to accomplish but rather "believe there is a need for something *prior* to principles or a constitution, without which the best principles and the best constitution would be worthless."[146] As Putnam reads

[141] Richard Rorty, "Response to Simon Critchley" in Mouffe (ed.), *Deconstruction and Pragmatism*, 41; see Critchley, "Derrida . . . " in Mouffe (ed.), *Deconstruction and Pragmatism*, 32.

[142] Rorty, "Response to Simon Critchley" in *Deconstruction and Pragmatism*, 41.

[143] Critchley, Introduction in Critchley and Bernasconi (eds.), *The Cambridge Companion to Levinas*, 27.

[144] Critchley, Introduction in Critchley and Bernasconi (eds.), *The Cambridge Companion to Levinas*, 27; cf. Stanley Cavell, *Conditions Handsome and Unhandsome*; Putnam, "Levinas and Judaism" in Critchley and Bernasconi (eds.), *The Cambridge Companion to Levinas*, 36–37. The expression "moral perfectionism" or "Emersonian perfectionism" refers to the central theme of courses that Cavell taught over many years, at Harvard and elsewhere. In *Cities of Words*, which is a version of these courses, Cavell explores these themes in a number of philosophers and in a variety of films. It is also associated with the role of modernism and romanticism in Cavell. For interesting discussion, see the essays in Russell B. Goodman (ed.), *Contending with Cavell*. See also Richard Eldridge, "Cavell on American Philosophy and the Idea of America" in Eldridge (ed.), *Stanley Cavell*, 175, 183–85; and William Rothman, "Cavell on Film, Television, and Opera" in Eldridge (ed.), *Stanley Cavell*, 221–30, especially Rothman's comments on Cavell's readings of Ibsen's *A Doll House* and the film genres that Cavell calls the "comedies of remarriage" and the "melodramas of the unknown woman."

[145] Putnam, "Levinas and Judaism" in Critchley and Bernasconi (eds.), *The Cambridge Companion to Levinas*, 36.

[146] Putnam, "Levinas and Judaism" in Critchley and Bernasconi (eds.), *The Cambridge Companion to Levinas*, 36.

Cavell, however, perfectionism is not really a species of moral philosophy as much as a "dimension" of moral systems and systematic moral thinking. It has to do with that aspect of moral systems without which their real value cannot be understood. Putnam also calls this dimension a "moment in ethics" and notes that figures like Kant and Mill clearly engage in both.[147] The systematic articulation of rules and principles occurs, Putnam says, at a later "stage" of ethical thinking. Moreover, the perfectionist moment or dimension concerns the question about what kind of life one ought to live or what kind of self one should aspire to be. The perfectionist identifies a very demanding standard for one's life but one that provides a way of understanding why the rules or principles mean what they do.

Critchley takes Putnam to be following Cavell in distinguishing legislators from moral perfectionists as "two species of moral philosophers."[148] He identifies Rawls and Habermas as legislators and Levinas and Cavell as moral perfectionists, for whom "ethics has to be based on some form of basic existential commitment or demand that goes beyond the theoretical strictures of any account of justice or any socially instituted ethical code."[149] One point of moral perfectionism is to show how ethical theory "expresses" this basic demand so that the theory does not "simply spin in a void." It also explains the motivation for acting on the ethical theory.

Although Critchley and Putnam approach Levinas from different directions, both seek some way of understanding the sense in which Levinas's insight is an ethical one. For Critchley, one might say, ethical theory occurs within the domain of totality; hence, he wants to find some way of characterizing as ethical an insight that is grounded in our experience of transcendence. Putnam realizes that like Heidegger, Buber, Rosenzweig, and Levinas are not doing moral thinking in the ways Hobbes, Locke, Hume, Kant, and Mill do it, and yet he wants to see their thinking as relevant to ethics. Both find Cavell's attention to moral perfectionism attractive, but his understanding of it, as one might expect, is far different from and more nuanced than theirs.

Cavell takes himself to be considering ethical issues in a very broad sense, as issues about humanity, our need for self-examination and development, the character and diversity of human relationships, and the space of the human in democratic politics. Cavell finds these themes in Emerson, Wittgenstein, Kierkegaard, Kant, and a host of other thinkers and writers, as well as in literature

---

[147] Putnam, "Levinas and Judaism" in Critchley and Bernasconi (eds.), *The Cambridge Companion to Levinas*, 37, 58 n. 8.

[148] Critchley, Introduction in Critchley and Bernasconi (eds.), *The Cambridge Companion to Levinas*, 27.

[149] Critchley, Introduction in Critchley and Bernasconi (eds.), *The Cambridge Companion to Levinas*, 28.

and Hollywood films of certain genres – screwball comedies, melodramas, and more. But he is not engaged in categorizing moral theories or in doing systematic moral philosophy. Rather, in a way, he takes his own thinking and that of Emerson and others to be anterior, or prior, to such systematic work; certainly, it is vastly different from it. As Cavell himself puts it, there is a "conversation of justice" among some people in public places, and what he is interested in are the conditions under which people participate in such a conversation.[150] What does the situation have to be like, and what does the self have to be like, for "a conversation of justice" to take place?

Perfectionism in ethics and political thinking is not one thing but rather a cluster of things, related in different ways, some in very indirect ways. Cavell's use of the word "perfectionism" and various forms of it is, as one might expect of him, very idiosyncratic and ellusive.[151] I think it will be useful to step back first and say a few words about different ways the term "perfectionism" is used. One reason for our considering Cavell's perfectionism at all is to see if it really does help us to clarify the sense in which Levinas's central insight is an ethical one and also perhaps what the claim "ethics is first philosophy" means. But another reason is that it may help us to understand how the face-to-face and the responsible self are related to moral principles and political, legal systems. Let me begin, then, by considering how perfectionism is discussed in contemporary political theory.

In liberal political theory, some kind of neutrality is regularly advocated. That is, it is argued that "the state should remain *neutral* toward citizens' own conceptions of the good life."[152] There are many reasons for this kind of position and many ways of clarifying its point. In one sense, neutrality involves taking the freedom and autonomy of citizens as a primary value and thus protecting it to the fullest degree compatible with stability and security for all. It also is about respecting the individual and protecting her rights, all that is closely associated with who she is insofar as she is like others, a human being deserving of such respect. Neutrality is also about the distinction between public interests and private ones.

Moreover, neutralism often appropriates, in modern liberal states, what it can from older views, many religious, that call individuals to live certain kinds of lives: sacred or holy, loyal, committed to group practices and tradition, and

---

[150] See Cavell, *Conditions Handsome and Unhandsome*, xviii–xxxviii, 101–26, esp. 102, 103–5, 106–8.
[151] Cavell is very clear that by "Emersonian perfectionism" he does not mean *perfectibility*; see *Conditions Handsome and Unhandsome*, 3–4.
[152] John Christman, *Social and Political Philosophy* (London: Routledge, 2002), 98; see also Sher, *Beyond Neutrality*.

so forth. It is the view that such individual or communal identities and the ideals of selfhood they endorse are important, but also that their importance may not be shared by all in a particular society. While tolerance of or even respect for such conceptions needs to be safeguarded, the need to do so for all requires a set of rules and practices that favors none of them, if that kind of detachment can be achieved. Everyone has certain requirements that must be satisfied to work at realizing these ideals, and political institutions should do their best to provide what is needed without intruding on these particular efforts to accomplish these distinctive identities. There are complicated issues of scope involved in defending and attacking neutralism, but for our purposes the central point is that it is an issue about how political and legal institutions should be related to individual and group conceptions of what the best kind of human life should be like and to their efforts to live such lives.[153]

The distinction between political neutralism and *political perfectionism*, then, concerns whether one advocates a kind of continuity or discontinuity between ethical/religious self-identity and political institutions.[154] *Moral perfectionism*, on the other hand, is one way of understanding the idea of the best life. Typically, moral perfectionists articulate some set of skills, abilities, or features that human beings generally ought to develop and realize. In Aristotelian moral theory, for example, these abilities are rational and concern virtues of character and the development of practical intelligence – *phronesis*. Moral perfectionists, of course, can be pluralist, as Charles Taylor is. The basic idea is the same, that some ideal way of life is taken to involve perfecting one, or more regularly, a set of abilities and excellences. Indeed, the Romantics can be understood as perfectionists for whom artistic creativity is an expression for such a set of skills. For religious perfectionists, the ideal is often conceived as divinely revealed and mandated; true piety is dictated by it. It is not uncommon, moreover, to find moral perfectionist strains in moral theories that seem organized around rule-governed behavior and obligations – for example, Kantian and Millian moral philosophy.[155] In a sense, then, moral perfectionism – or religious perfectionism – is not a distinct type of moral theory. Rather, it is one way of characterizing an ethical or religious conception about how to live, focusing on how individuals should model their lives. Clearly, then, the model or paradigm can be conceived in various ways: a tight-knit unity or a loosely connected set of features, as dictated by an authoritative source or conceived as a natural, teleological

---

[153] See Christman, *Social and Political Philosophy*, 98–103, and Sher, *Beyond Neutrality*.
[154] On perfectionism, see Christman, *Social and Political Philosophy*, 103–11.
[155] See Christman, *Social and Political Philosophy*, 108–11; Putnam, "Levinas and Judaism" in Critchley and Bernasconi (eds.), *The Cambridge Companion to Levinas*, 58 n. 8; and Cavell, *Conditions Handsome and Unhandsome*, 19–20, for example.

goal, and so forth. In a liberal society, there is no one, precise form that moral perfectionism or religious perfectionism must take, nor is there one content that all do or should have. Or is there?

Famously, it has been argued that liberal political theory and neutralism must be grounded, to one degree or another, in its own form of perfectionism and hence that it is not really, ultimately neutral. That is, some believe that liberalism is a bogus neutralism. I do not want to enter this fascinating, dense thicket here, but it does raise the question about whether there is, in a sense, a *level* of moral perfectionism that is prior to the particular conceptions of the good and that provides a standard for assessing which ones are compatible with the liberal political framework and which are not. In Rawls's case, for example, citizens, although they may have different conceptions of what is involved in living the good life, must be committed to the principles of justice and equality, according to which political institutions are constructed. They must share, that is, a lean conception of justice, and such a conception is itself a standard for determining which identities are suited to the liberal state and which are not.[156] In this direction, then, there may lie a distinction between *operative* moral perfectionisms, which are discontinuous with the liberal state and its rules and institutions, and *justifying* moral perfectionism, which is continuous with that state and in fact with all the particular identities compatible with it.

This sketch should give us a feel for the various ways in which the expressions "perfectionism" and "moral perfectionism" have been used. As we turn to Cavell's Carus Lectures, however, we will see that his own uses of these expressions do not easily fit into this terrain. Cavell's explicit goal is to reflect upon what he calls "Emersonian perfectionism," which he associates with figures like Emerson, Thoreau, Wittgenstein, Nietzsche, and Heidegger, not as a theory they hold or position they occupy but rather as "something like a dimension or tradition of the moral life that . . . concerns what used to be called the state of one's soul" and concerns, but not exclusively, "the possibility or necessity of transforming . . . oneself and . . . one's society."[157] Emphatically, he cautions that perfectionism is not a theory but a dimension or moment of any moral thinking. But if so, is it a kind of thinking or an approach to thinking about

---

[156] See Christman, *Social and Political Philosophy*, 111–17; Sher, *Beyond Neutrality*, 26–29; Joseph Raz, *The Morality of Freedom*, Ch. 5; John Rawls, *A Theory of Justice*, Section 50, 325–32.

[157] Cavell, *Conditions Handsome and Unhandsome*, 2; quoted by Putnam, "Levinas and Judaism" in Critchley and Bernasconi (eds.), *The Cambridge Companion to Levinas*, p. 58, n. 6 cf. 4, 18, 31 (perfectionist moment), 46, 62. Cavell explicitly refuses to give a definition of this "Emersonian or moral perfectionism" and gives a list of figures who express it, in one way or another, a list that runs to nearly two pages. See also Timothy Gould, *Hearing Things: Voice and Method in the Writing of Stanley Cavell* (Chicago: University of Chicago Press, 1998), 208–14; Alice Crary, "Austin and the Ethics of Discourse" in Alice Crary and Sanford Shieh (eds.), *Reading Cavell*, 58–60.

moral matters? Does it have any generic content? Is it always thinking about certain sorts of matters? Does it have a normal style? A consistent subject? Does it reflect a persistent tendency or attitude or set of interests?

CAVELL'S EMERSONIAN PERFECTIONISM

In the course of his reflections, Cavell refers to perfectionisms, in the plural, to false perfectionisms, to modest and extreme versions,[158] but most often to the kind he calls "Emersonian" or "moral."[159] As I indicated, he locates the latter type, which he finds congenial and provocative, in Emerson, Heidegger, Wittgenstein, in the films he calls "comedies of remarriage" and "melodramas of the unknown woman," in Ibsen's *A Doll House*, and in Heinrich von Kleist's *The Marquise of O_____.*[160] Let me explain, if only (at first) by citation and paraphrase, what Cavell says "Emersonian perfectionism" deals with and what it accomplishes. If I am right, the interesting question about Levinas is not simply, whether he is a perfectionist, in some sense or other, but rather, is he an *Emersonian* or *moral perfectionist?*

Emersonian perfectionism is not a teleological doctrine, akin to Aristotelian moral theory; Cavell is explicit about this.[161] It has no precise conception of what constitutes the good life, what sort of life one ought to aim at living; it finds us at odds with ourselves and invokes the process of finding our way back to what we have lost. It is, then, thinking about how an ethical agent sees himself in a transformed or altered way,[162] in such a way, Cavell says, that it is about one's freedom, one's capacity to enter into conversation with others, into social life and political life, and to think and speak with others about justice.[163] It is not about "favoring" one way of life over another but about entering into a society that welcomes discussion of justice and is involved in "measuring the degree of one's life's . . . departures from compliance with those principles [of justice]."[164] Such perfectionism is a dimension that "any theory of the moral life may wish to accommodate,"[165] insofar as it sees as valuable the process of one's becoming clear to oneself, understanding where one stands. For it is about

---

[158] Cavell, *Conditions Handsome and Unhandsome*, 48–49. One can also find the terminology pervasive in Cavell's recent book on his oft-taught course on moral perfectionism, *Cities of Words*. The expression also occurs elsewhere in his works.

[159] Cavell, *Conditions Handsome and Unhandsome*, 46–63, esp. 48.

[160] Cavell, *Conditions Handsome and Unhandsome*, Ch. 1, 3; see also Preface, Acknowledgments, and Introduction.

[161] Cavell, *Conditions Handsome and Unhandsome*, xviii.

[162] Cavell, *Conditions Handsome and Unhandsome*, xviii–xix.

[163] Cavell, *Conditions Handsome and Unhandsome*, xxii, 48, 102–4.

[164] Cavell, *Conditions Handsome and Unhandsome*, xxiv–xxv, xxvii.

[165] Cavell, *Conditions Handsome and Unhandsome*, xxxi.

"searching for direction" in one's life, as if one has lost one's way and is looking for some light to find the way.[166] This activity involves readying oneself to enter a "conversation of justice" insofar as it includes others and conversation with them.[167] There is an element in it of being true to oneself and hence of having some sense of one's self's unity and at the same time one's social life with others.[168]

Cavell believes that this sort of perfectionism is anything but elitist. In fact, it is not only compatible with democracy, but essential to the idea that democracy engages in a criticism from within, for the self capable of engaging in such criticism, willing and interested, is such a perfectionist self.[169] It is reflected in texts about seeking one's "unattained but attainable self," as Emerson puts it.[170]

Why call this "perfectionism?" Cavell takes Emerson to be struggling against moralisms that "fixate" on some ideal.[171] Emersonian perfectionism is not about such false enterprises. It is about *changing* oneself in such a way that one can engage with others in the social world and in a "conversation of justice."[172] Hence, it is about education. There are false and true perfectionisms. Cavell sees "false or debased perfectionisms" everywhere in our society.[173] The true one, Emersonian perfectionism, first comes to be ashamed of how life is going and how our society leads us, and readies our selves to find direction and a new sense of how our lives with others ought to go. He calls this effort "releasing the good,"[174] which involves our learning how to respond to the failures of democratic life. Cavell also associates this effort with "Wittgenstein's picture of thinking [as] . . . one of moving from being lost to oneself to finding one's way, a circumstance of spiritual disorder, a defeat not to be solved but to be undone."[175] Perfectionism is about perfecting but not about attaining perfection.

Part of what provoked Cavell's thoughts in *Conditions Handsome and Unhandsome*, he tells us, was a careful reading of Rawls's *A Theory of Justice*. Rawls permits us to see, Cavell says, "how the justice of justice can be assessed," and

---

[166] Cavell, *Conditions Handsome and Unhandsome*, xxxii.

[167] Cavell, *Conditions Handsome and Unhandsome*, 104.

[168] Cavell, *Conditions Handsome and Unhandsome*, xxxiv–xxxv; cf. 1–2. Broadly speaking, then, moral perfectionism is an "ethic of authenticity," in Taylor's sense of the expression. It is also akin to the Socratic notion of *therapeia tes psyches* (caring for the soul), as it is discussed by Pierre Hadot.

[169] Cavell, *Conditions Handsome and Unhandsome*, 3.

[170] Cavell, *Conditions Handsome and Unhandsome*, 8 ("History," para. 5).

[171] Cavell, *Conditions Handsome and Unhandsome*, 13–14, 56.

[172] Cavell, *Conditions Handsome and Unhandsome*, 125.

[173] Cavell, *Conditions Handsome and Unhandsome*, 16, 46, 123.

[174] Cavell, *Conditions Handsome and Unhandsome*, 18.

[175] Cavell, *Conditions Handsome and Unhandsome*, 21, 61–63, Ch. 2; freed from the old philosophy – to the ordinary.

Cavell's task, as he sees it, is to show how Emersonian perfectionism discloses something else, in addition to a theory of justice and its institutional test, for carrying out such assessment; that is "the idea of the cultivation of a new mode of human being" that is essential to sharing a just life with others.[176] This new human life involves freedom and autonomy as essential to a democratic and just life.[177] Here the issue is about the paradox of consent and authority in democratic, just polities; but for Cavell, Rawls's thinking hides a deeper layer. Cavell sees Emersonian perfectionism, at this point, as an encounter with Rousseau and Kant and as "questioning what or who the self is that commands and obeys itself and what an obedience consists in that is inseparable from mastery."[178] It seeks to clarify how I join others in society in such a way that the moral life is possible and with it the political life and conversation about justice.[179]

In sketching some of Cavell's interests in his reflections on Emersonian or moral perfectionism, I have tried to identify some central issues and to do so in Cavell's own words. I think we can draw some tentative conclusions. In general, there are many kinds of perfectionism, but what Cavell is primarily thinking about is a way of understanding the self's character insofar as it is eager to find itself, is capable of entering into social relations with others and conversing with them about how to live together, what obscures or distorts their capacity to do so, what justice would require of them, and so forth. In terms of our earlier look at various types of perfectionism, Emersonian or moral perfectionism is neither political nor substantive; nor is it even justifying, as a common set of moral commitments that all participants in a democratic state share. It is a way of looking at moral life and moral thinking that discloses what selfhood requires of us in order for any kind of moral and political life to go on, insofar as it involves conversation about justice and how we ought to live together. In this sense, Cavell's thinking here is about the transcendental conditions of moral and political selfhood, considered historically – that is, insofar as the selves in question are ours, living as we do, in liberal democracies, in the twentieth century, and so forth. In order for us to think about justice, to assess what justice requires, to determine what life would have to be like, and how it would have to change to suit our convictions about justice, we have to prepare ourselves to become and to be the kind of selves that can discuss these matters with others with whom we live.

Moreover, moral perfectionism is not simply a theory or dimension of moral thinking; it is also a dimension of moral life, of life itself, about how we as selves

---

[176] Cavell, *Conditions Handsome and Unhandsome*, 25, 106.
[177] Cavell, *Conditions Handsome and Unhandsome*, 28, 56.
[178] Cavell, *Conditions Handsome and Unhandsome*, 31, 118.
[179] Cavell, *Conditions Handsome and Unhandsome*, 117, 124.

need to change and what we need to be like in order to become persons who can engage in this kind of just, democratic, and liberal state as genuine participants. The goodness of this kind of state and the goodness of this kind of citizenship and humanity go hand in hand. As Cavell notes, Plato already saw, albeit with a different set of political convictions, that political organization and individual personality suit each other in this way.[180] There is in addition a dimension of moral perfectionist thinking that treats the educational question of how to learn to become this kind of self, which means, among other things, how to learn to see what distorts who we are, what prevents genuine conversation, and so on. This kind of perfectionism also points to what we need to understand about others and ourselves, about language, and indeed about whatever we need to grasp if we are going to be real participants in public discourse about justice.

For Cavell, then, moral or Emersonian perfectionism has no clear, precisely defined and articulated, uniform ideal that it advocates and aims to realize.[181] Elaborating its features is a piecemeal, contextual, and exploratory business, and what we arrive at may seem very formal and abstract in one sense, very imprecise and fragmentary in another – without the clarity and precision one would like perhaps and surely without the kind one might expect from contemporary analytic moral philosophy. In fact, such elaboration must be done by examples – literary and cinematic best of all.[182]

Cavell sees this project as one that Rawls's moral and political theory provokes but also ignores. Rawls shows how we can arrive at principles to assess the justice

---

[180] Cavell, *Conditions Handsome and Unhandsome*, 6–7; see also his *Cities of Words*, Ch. 17.

[181] Emersonian perfectionism emerges in Cavell's thinking, but its sources can already be found in a work such as *The Claim of Reason*. In his review of that work, Richard Rorty associates its brand of antifoundationalism in ethics with the work of Iris Murdoch: "Part III [of *The Claim of Reason*], all by itself, is one of the best books on moral philosophy that has appeared in recent years. It ranks with Iris Murdoch's *Sovereignty of Good* as a criticism of the notion that moral philosophy must be a search for yet more 'absolute simples' – self-evident principles, basic values" (Rorty, "Cavell on Skepticism" in Russell Goodman (ed.), *Contending with Stanley Cavell*, 17 (originally in *Review of Metaphysics* 34 (1980–81)). Rorty quotes Cavell on moral rules: "The appeal [by philosophers to rules in theorizing about morality] is to explain why such an action as promising is *binding* upon us. But if you *need* an explanation for that, . . . then the appeal to rules comes too late. For rules are themselves binding only subject to our commitment" (*The Claim of Reason*, 307). When Rorty's review first appeared, not long after the publication of *Philosophy and the Mirror of Nature*, Rorty certainly had his own reasons for enlisting Cavell among the ranks of so-called antifoundationalists.

[182] The best places to see Cavell carry out this project, I believe, are his books on two "genres" of classic Hollywood films: *Pursuits of Happiness* and *Contesting Tears*. The first deals with what Cavell calls "comedies of remarriage" and the second with "melodramas of the unknown woman." In both, the primary subject of Emersonian perfectionist education and personal development is a woman.

of political institutions, but he does not worry about the question, What do we have to be like in order to arrive at, converse about, and apply these principles? As Cavell sees his work, Rawls does not dig deeply enough into the turf of human existence and social life. Emerson, Heidegger, and Wittgenstein do – or at least they show *what* should be done and *how*, on particular issues, it should be done. Does the free, autonomous self provide any standard by which the justice of political and social life should be judged? That is, are Rawls's principles of justice derived from a conception of the self that Cavell would endorse? Or does Cavell's Emersonian self have enough precision and definition to serve as a test for principles of justice and their application? I do not find any easy answers to these questions in Cavell. Indeed, the moral character of the Emersonian self is itself not easy to define.

It no doubt is unfair to Cavell to distinguish too sharply between the content and the form of what he calls moral perfectionism. Nonetheless, it is helpful to do so. Formally, it seeks to disclose the existential conditions for the self's participation in moral and social life and in a "conversation of justice" about that life. Substantially, it shows that such a self must be free and autonomous, receptive to change and to seeing itself as lost and in need of a new direction, capable of unburdened thinking and discourse with others, and eager to understand what justice requires for life and with those others. This substantive picture, perhaps, would constrain the principles of justice and their application. No political or moral system that ignored or defied it would be acceptable.[183] In order to be acceptable, it would at least have to respect citizens as free, autonomous agents, committed to living together in a just way, cognizant of the threats to autonomy and justice in modern culture, and willing and eager to change themselves to be better citizens and better people.[184] These are the formal and substantive features of the perfectionism that Putnam, and then Critchley, use to clarify the Levinasian insight.

IS LEVINAS A MORAL PERFECTIONIST?

If this is Cavell's "moral perfectionism," is Levinas a perfectionist? Does his central insight about the responsibility of the self have a perfectionist character?

---

[183] This sounds like the perfectionist side of Habermas or O'Neill.

[184] In "Austin and the Ethics of Discourse" in Alice Crary and Sanford Shieh (eds.), *Reading Cavell*, 57–60, Alice Crary describes attention to "the perfectionist dimension of the moral life" as talking about "the possibility of further perfection or cultivation of the self" (58). This perfection or cultivation involves "emotional and cognitive growth," "moral development," and "self-cultivation." For Cavell, "perfectionism" then does not refer to realizing a precise ideal but rather the process of cultivating or "perfecting" one's self as a self in conversation with others.

Does his thinking occur in the perfectionist dimension of moral thinking and moral life?

It is tempting to argue that since Cavell's moral perfectionism is somehow anterior to Rawls's constructivism, is not the same kind of moral thinking as utilitarianism or Kantian deontology, and is not as elitist as Nietzsche or as determinate as Aristotelian perfectionism, and because Levinas's ethical insight also differs from all these types of moral thinking, the two are obviously similar in significant ways. Hence, it is tempting to think that Levinas is a moral perfectionist in the same way Cavell's Emersonian perfectionism is. Using the distinction I made earlier between the formal and substantive features of Cavell's perfectionism, one might claim that Levinas is perfectionist in a formal sense, but the content of his perfectionism is distinctive. Just as Cavell says that "Moral Perfectionism is a dimension of any moral theory," so we could argue that Levinas's face-to-face is a dimension of all human existence, of all social and moral life. In this way, then, we could support Putnam and Critchley up to a point, and we could also support Critchley's contention that if Derrida's notion of justice is indebted to Levinas, then there is a sense in which Derridean deconstruction is an ethical view, contra Rorty, whose understanding of ethics would be judged too narrow indeed, so narrow that with Levinas and Derrida it would exclude Cavell as well from the party of ethical thinkers.

Appealing as this strategy might be, we should be cautious to employ it. If Levinas is a moral perfectionist, it is not clear that he is an Emersonian or Cavellian one. Levinas does say that human existence is ethical in a very primordial and determinative way and that to miss seeing this is to fail to understand human life correctly and to fail to *live* it correctly. It may be that the demand for generosity, kindness, and concern is quite open-ended and that its satisfaction in particular encounters or in general principles and policies can take many forms. But it is still in the end a demand for responsibility to and for others. In one way, such responsibility is a condition for thought, discourse, and social conduct, but in another it is a standard for directing and assessing how we live. For Levinas, human life ought to have a very precise character. Cavell might be taken to be saying that justice and a "conversation of justice" can occur only where free, autonomous persons can talk with each other. Emersonian perfectionism is about realizing such conditions by educating and transforming oneself and by others doing so as well. Levinas believes that all social life can only occur when persons interact with each other and are responsible to and for each other, whether they realize this or not. But when we do realize how this dimension is hidden, occluded, or distorted by society and culture, we come to see who we really are, and this means what we ought to do, how we ought to live, individually and generally. But the ideal of generosity and concern for others is not only a condition for social life; it is a substantive ideal for all individual and social life. It circumscribes or defines what life ought to be like, far more precisely than Cavell's moral perfectionism does.

In this respect, I think, Levinas is more akin to Nietzsche, whom Cavell criticizes as elitist and not democratic.[185] My claim for such kinship may sound very odd, because Nietzsche seems to be advocating the maximization of excellence over any concern with the well-being of others, something that Levinas takes as somehow fundamental.[186] And I would agree fully that the Emersonian and Cavellian attention to democracy, justice, and suffering is something that Levinas would find appealing. But Cavell's perfectionism operates explicitly at a different level than these interests, while Levinas's does not. If Levinas is a perfectionist, sensitivity for the other's suffering precedes all else; justice is, in a sense, primary, and it is determinative in one way or another for all of life – moral and political.

Cavell calls Emersonian perfectionism a "training for democracy" and then clarifies this phrase: "I understand the training and character and friendship Emerson requires for democracy as *preparation to withstand* not its rigors but *its failures,* character to keep the democratic hope alive *in the face of disappointment with it.*"[187] That is, what Emerson teaches, as Cavell affirms it, is an education in what the self must be like to cope with cultural and social distortion or defects, what have been called "conformity" or "philistinism" or "imprisonment" or "alienation" or "exile."[188] It is not an education in an ideal human life, what he calls "extreme" perfectionism; Cavell doubts such a reading of Nietzsche and of Emerson, for example.[189] "There is [no] separate class of great men ... for whose good ... the rest of society is to live." There are no higher selves or great human beings. Earlier, I think, Cavell calls this a "false or debased Perfectionism" or "a form of moralism that fixates on the presence of ideals in one's culture and promotes them"[190] and takes Emerson as decidedly an opponent of it – and with Emerson, Nietzsche, too. My claim is that Levinas, like Nietzsche, does take the perfect self to be ideal and exemplary, at once a condition for social life and also an ideal for it – even if the ideal is equally accessible – or better, inaccessible – to all.[191] Nietzsche's ideal, to be sure, differs dramatically

---

[185] See Cavell, *Conditions Handsome and Unhandsome,* 1, 49–54; on 56, Cavell affirms Nietzsche.

[186] See Cavell, *Conditions Handsome and Unhandsome,* 49, where he calls attention to this feature of Nietzsche's thinking.

[187] Cavell, *Conditions Handsome and Unhandsome,* 56.

[188] See Cavell, *Cities of Words,* 251, where he gives a brief list of such defects or deficiencies and associates the various expressions with Emerson, Nietzsche, Pascal, Hume, Rousseau, Kierkegaard, Marx, Heidegger, and Wittgenstein.

[189] Cavell, *Conditions Handsome and Unhandsome,* 49.

[190] Cavell, *Conditions Handsome and Unhandsome,* 13.

[191] In this sense, that justice is, for Levinas, both a condition for all social life and an ideal for the best life, I take Levinas to be in the spirit of Plato, for whom, one might argue, the Forms

from Levinas's, but they share a common role, and yet Cavell argues vigorously against such a reading of Nietzsche as a form of moralism. Would he also argue in the same way against such a reading of Levinas, even if his responsible self is deeply concerned with the sufferings and injustices of others?

One way to tell would be to see how close Nietzsche and Levinas are, and for this a look at "Schopenhauer As Educator" is helpful. Rawls, at the outset of section 50 of *A Theory of Justice*, distinguishes between two forms of perfectionism, basically where there is one ideal or standard or a cluster of them.[192] There are, furthermore, two versions of the single-standard form, a strict and a moderate version. Nietzsche, he says, is characteristic of the strict version, Aristotle of the more moderate one. For Nietzsche, Rawls says, "the principle of perfection . . . is the sole principle of a teleological theory directing society to arrange institutions and to define the duties and obligations of individuals so as to maximize the achievement of human excellence in art, science, and culture."[193] As evidence for interpreting Nietzsche as claiming that we and society should strive to produce great individuals and work for the good of these highest exemplars, he cites a text from section 6 of "Schopenhauer As Educator."[194] This strict version of perfectionism is something that Rawls rejects, as Cavell says, because it is "inherently undemocratic, or elitist."[195] Cavell treats Rawls's rejection as a "misreading, or over-fixed reading, of a set of Nietzschean sentences," and he takes these Nietzschean sentences as a "virtual transcription of Emersonian passages," which he seeks to reclaim and to read in a different, certainly democratic spirit.[196]

What we have here is a straightforward reading of Nietzsche by Rawls and a "defensive" alternative reading by Cavell. To anticipate, if Cavell is right, then Emerson and Nietzsche advocate a renewed self equipped to participate in a democratic conversation about justice, focused on selfhood as free and capable of public discourse; if Rawls is right, then Nietzsche seeks the education of an exemplary, ideal self, a great person, a philosopher or genius, whose flourishing ought to be the goal of society. Of these two kinds of perfectionism, then,

---

in general and the Form of Justice in particular are both universals and thus conditions for the order of nature and society and also ideals or standards for human life, both personal and political. Many would argue that metaphysically these two functions of the Forms, as universals and as *paradeigmata* or standards, fall apart and that it is one of the purposes of the famous Third Man Argument to show that this is so, but it is perhaps more exciting to take Plato as recognizing these twin functions of the Forms as important and ultimately compatible.

[192] Rawls, *A Theory of Justice*, 325.
[193] Rawls, *A Theory of Justice*, 325.
[194] See Friedrich Nietzsche, "Schopenhauer as Educator" in *Untimely Meditations*, 161–62.
[195] See Cavell, *Conditions Handsome and Unhandsome*, xxiii–xxiv, 3–4.
[196] Cavell, *Conditions Handsome and Unhandsome*, 4; see also 49–53.

which – if either – does Levinas exemplify? Is it possible that there is something of both in Levinas?

I have tried to say something about Cavell's formal or transcendental reading of Nietzsche's perfectionism as one might find it expressed in "Schopenhauer As Educator." It is, I think, an interpretation hard to defend. Nietzsche's monograph is about the cultivation of the unique selfhood of the artist, his freedom, his creativity.[197] The self's creativity and deepest capacities are hidden, obscured by conventional culture; only a genuine educator can assist the liberation of the self.[198] Such an educator, a true philosopher, is also an example for the self of how to liberate its selfhood, express it, and live it.[199] He can give us "a picture of life as a whole" so that you can "learn from it the meaning of your own life."[200] This model responds to our deepest desire and striving: "the longing of man to be *reborn* as saint and genius," to be great by "being free and entirely himself."[201] Nietzsche calls this the cultivation and education of "the Schopenhauerian image of man" and refers to such a life as "heroic."[202] He summarizes the goal of this education in a passage that occurs on the page prior to the one Rawls quotes: "[T]he fundamental idea of culture...sets for each one of us but one task: *to promote the production of the philosopher, the artist and the saint within us and without us and thereby to work at the perfecting of nature.*"[203] These are the ideals, the figures of individual great men, that all society should aim to produce. They are maximally free, in the sense of creative and self-expressive, free of external limitations, free of ignorance, social constraints, illusions, and such. Nietzsche's naturalism manifests itself here, and his sense of freedom, like that of Hobbes and Spinoza, is a state of natural power or capacity unrestricted, uncoerced, unbounded by external powers, forces, and influences. Nietzsche calls this goal, each individual's for himself and for society, "the supreme goal, the production of the genius," and it is clear that each of us naturally strives to realize it in ourselves and should see society and culture as facilitating it as well.[204]

Any reading that takes this perfectionism as transcendental and democratic in tone or spirit is surely strained. Nietzsche makes it clear that he wants us to follow nature and that only social convention and cultural resistance discourages our so doing: "[O]ne would like to apply to society and its goals

[197] Nietzsche, "Schopenhauer as Educator" in *Untimely Meditations*, 127–29, 143, 159.
[198] Nietzsche, "Schopenhauer as Educator" in *Untimely Meditations*, 129–30, 145, 146, 147–55.
[199] Nietzsche, "Schopenhauer as Educator" in *Untimely Meditations*, 136.
[200] Nietzsche, "Schopenhauer as Educator" in *Untimely Meditations*, 141.
[201] Nietzsche, "Schopenhauer as Educator" in *Untimely Meditations*, 142, 145.
[202] Nietzsche, "Schopenhauer as Educator" in *Untimely Meditations*, 152–55.
[203] Nietzsche, "Schopenhauer as Educator" in *Untimely Meditations*, 160.
[204] Nietzsche, "Schopenhauer as Educator" in *Untimely Meditations*, 164, 174, 181, 182.

something that can be learned from observation of any species of the animal or plant world: that its only concern is the individual higher exemplar, the more uncommon, more powerful, more complex, more fruitful."[205] Similarly, according to natural evolution and its goals, "mankind ought to seek out and create the favorable conditions under which those great redemptive men can come into existence."[206] Nietzsche criticizes our habit of thinking that the only way for our individual lives to receive the highest value or greatest significance is for them to contribute to the betterment of all or most.

Nietzsche's point is not bizarre. He asks us to consider the ends – the goal – that our lives serve, our lives overall. That is, if my life is significant only because of what it contributes to some future lives, is it more correct to think that my life becomes more significant by contributing to the happiness of all or the happiness of the majority or plurality or by contributing to the excellence of a few great exemplars? Nietzsche argues that one is genuinely committed to culture, in fact, only if one takes its goal to produce perfect, ideal persons – no matter how few. Social-political life is like any evolutionary process; success is measured by longevity, which is a function not of sheer numbers but rather of maximally perfect specimens.[207]

This naturalism is far from Levinas. If he does take the responsible self, obligated to care for others, responsive to the face of suffering and need, to be a feature or dimension of all social existence and a standard for ethical and political institutions, rules, and practices, it is a far cry from Nietzsche's conception of the genius or great individual as creative and self-expressive, in some narrow egoistic sense. Levinas's conception is, to be sure, transcendental as a condition of all social life and thus of conversation, moral discussion, and political practices. But it is also an ideal or standard of care for the other, of self-sacrifice in behalf of other persons. It is a self that is free only as responsive to the other; otherwise, it is not free at all. One might put it this way: For Nietzsche, freedom *from* external compulsion is primary; for Levinas, freedom *for* the other person is secondary, and freedom *from* the other is myopic and a distortion.

Is Levinas, then, as Putnam and Critchley suggest, a perfectionist, in Cavell's sense of the term? One answer is obvious: Strictly speaking, Levinas is no Emersonian perfectionist. His ideal self is more than formal, more than transcendental – more than striving for self-identity and committed to conversation with others, more than free and creative. She is obligated, bound, and devoted to the care for the other person. She is more than *capable* of participating in the conversation of justice; she is also *obligated* to do so and, in a sense, her

---

[205] Nietzsche, "Schopenhauer as Educator" in *Untimely Meditations*, 162.
[206] Nietzsche, "Schopenhauer as Educator" in *Untimely Meditations*, 162.
[207] Nietzsche, "Schopenhauer as Educator" in *Untimely Meditations*, 161–64.

freedom, rationality, and linguistic ability are derivative. They only arise in that conversation and because of her fundamental obligation or the demand placed on her by the other. For Cavell and for Emersonian perfectionism, the striving of the self for itself is fundamental and the conversation with others concerning justice and such is contributory; for Levinas, the shaping of the self arises only in terms of one's relationships with others in a social world, and the significance of those relationships is fundamentally a matter of responsibility, of the self's being called and singled out by the other, indeed by every other. Life matters to each of us only because the other person matters to us.

LEVINAS ON ETHICS AND POLITICS

Levinas, then, is not Rawls or Habermas, but neither is he Cavell – exactly, as an ethical thinker.[208] But this is not to say, as Rorty has, that Levinas – like Derrida – is not an ethical or political thinker at all.[209] One way to clarify the public and political implications of Levinas's thinking is to look briefly at several essays in which he discusses Hobbes, Kant, the rights of man or natural rights, and what he calls "rights of the other." There are three essays, written in the 1980s, that discuss these matters and shed light on the political implications of his ethical insight.[210]

The language of "rights" is central to liberal political theory. In some cases, rights are coordinated with obligations; the possessor of a particular right has a claim against some specific agent or class of agents to perform or not perform certain specified actions. In such cases, rights are precisely described and defined. In other cases, people have rights that are open in important respects: They apply to certain possessions or objects but extend to an indeterminate audience or population. Some argue that rights have no corresponding obligations; in certain cases, too, there are obligations with no determinate audience and no corresponding rights. In "The Prohibition Against Representation and 'The Rights of Man'"(1981), Levinas argues that the biblical prohibition against representation should be understood as calling attention to the fact of totality

---

[208] Nonetheless, Levinas is closest, I believe, to Cavell. One can see their similarity best by looking at Cavell's understanding of the truth or moral of skepticism and Levinas's attention to the face-to-face and the way that responsibility calls for acknowledgment of the other person, acceptance of him, and more. Like Cavell, Levinas can be understood as calling to our attention that human relationships are much more than cognitive.

[209] See Rorty, *Deconstruction and Pragmatism*, 41.

[210] Levinas, "The Prohibition Against Representation and 'The Rights of Man,'" and "The Rights of the Other Man" in *Alterity and Transcendence*; and "The Rights of Man and the Rights of the Other" in *Outside the Subject*; see also Howard Caygill, *Levinas and the Political*, 151–58.

and the engagement with transcendence and how it is in the latter that the notion of "right" first arises. In short, "rights" attach to the other who makes demands of me and needs me *before* they attach to me, to the subject. In social existence and social life, the other person has rights with respect to me before I have rights toward her. The phrase "right of man" or "human right" is not, that is, basically a feature of individualism.

One helpful way of reading this essay is as a plea for a biblical view of rights over a Hobbesian one, and because the Hobbesian one – which is also Grotian – is appropriated by Locke, Samuel von Pufendorf, and Kant, for example, this essay stakes out Levinas's challenge to this entire tradition of rights and the discourse of rights.[211] In this tradition, rights are tied to the conception of the individual self as the building block of social and political life, a conception grounded in the atomism and dynamics of the New Science, in the thinking of Galileo, Boyle, and Newton.[212] Levinas proposes an alternative *origin* for the idea of *right*. It is not brought to an artificial social situation; it is intrinsic to a natural social condition, in which particular persons interact with one another. Furthermore, his *conception* of *rights* must differ as well; it must start not with what are later, in the eighteenth century, called "perfect rights," the transgression of which are injustices or harms, and then be extended to so-called imperfect rights, which we would call "needs" or "interests." Rather, Levinas's rights begin with imperfect ones and extend to perfect rights, only when they become institutionalized and normative.[213] While this context, however, is not explicit in the early essay, it becomes explicit in the later ones.

Levinas begins "The Rights of Man and the Rights of Others" (1985) by pointing out that what we call human rights – to respect, life, liberty, and equality before the law – are based on a prior, original sense of right.[214] Human rights are fundamental to law and *a priori*, but, he asks, might they be grounded in some prior *authority*? Something about the unique particularity of each person confronting the other person involves that authority.[215] It does not, Levinas says, come from God; it is not grounded in Revelation.[216] The authority of human rights, then, arises from a right that is particular and human. It is, he

[211] For important historical discussion of the rights tradition, see James Tully, *A Discourse on Property* (Cambridge: Cambridge University Press, 1983), and Richard Tuck, *Natural Rights Theories* (Cambridge: Cambridge University Press, 1979). See also Levinas, "The Rights of Man and the Rights of the Other" in *Outside the Subject*, 120.
[212] For a classic statement of this view, see J. W. N. Watkins, *Hobbes's System of Ideas* (London: Hutchinson University Library, 1965).
[213] For O'Neill, as we saw, both perfect and imperfect duties – and rights – arise out of the requirements of ethical conversation between agents.
[214] "The Rights of Man and the Rights of the Other" in *Outside the Subject*, 116.
[215] "The Rights of Man and the Rights of the Other" in *Outside the Subject*, 117.
[216] "The Rights of Man and the Rights of the Other" in *Outside the Subject*, 117–18.

will show us, the right of the other – with respect to the self but of the other as other.

Levinas turns to what he calls the "respecting of a right," which requires, he says, human freedom, something that is not unproblematic given the causal character of natural events and the realities of political oppression. To respect rights, one has to have resources and the social and political freedom to do so. Levinas notes that after general human rights there is a whole series of special rights underwritten by law: the right to health, work, rest, and so forth.[217] But with advancements in technology and science, not only are there expanded resources for meeting needs and for the determination of precise rights; there also comes the possibility of a "new determinism" – of "mechanization and enslavement" in totalitarian regimes.[218]

There is no reason to think that my rights and the rights of the other person will not conflict. Even justice involves "a certain limitation of rights and free will."[219] That is, justice is the administration of principles to coordinate freedom and the rights of the other. Levinas notes that the uniqueness of the self involves what might be called, in Kantian terms, "an uncoercible spontaneity, which bears witness both to the multiplicity of humans and the uniqueness of persons."[220] Here is the freedom of the responsible self in the face of the other's suffering and need. Justice involves what Levinas elsewhere calls the "third party" – "comparison . . . on the famous scales of justice, and thus to calculation," and then eventually "politics, . . . its strategies and clever dealings."[221] Levinas suggests, too, that the need for politics may devolve into a "totalitarian state" and the "repression and mockery" of the very rights for whose administration the state was first called into being.[222] Human rights, then, are grounded in the rights of the other and point to legal rights, justice, and politics, which runs the risk of totalitarian oppression and denial of just those rights that gave rise to the state. Political life may be a response to human rights, but it is no guarantee that such rights are respected. Levinas explicitly calls attention to the way that responsibility and care are the standard for political life:

. . . the defense of the rights of man corresponds to a vocation *outside* the state, disposing, in a political society, of a kind of extra-territoriality, like that of prophecy in the face of the political powers of the Old Testament, a vigilance totally different from political intelligence.[223]

---

[217] "The Rights of Man and the Rights of the Other" in *Outside the Subject*, 120.
[218] "The Rights of Man and the Rights of the Other" in *Outside the Subject*, 121.
[219] "The Rights of Man and the Rights of the Other" in *Outside the Subject*, 122.
[220] "The Rights of Man and the Rights of the Other" in *Outside the Subject*, 122.
[221] "The Rights of Man and the Rights of the Other" in *Outside the Subject*, 122, 123.
[222] "The Rights of Man and the Rights of the Other" in *Outside the Subject*, 123.
[223] "The Rights of Man and the Rights of the Other" in *Outside the Subject*, 123.

The liberal state, he says, has the "capacity to guarantee" this kind of goodness or benevolence toward others. He calls this capacity "the conjunction of politics and ethics."[224] For Levinas, then, it is through politics and its institutions that rights and justice come to be organized for social life. He says that human rights are grounded in "a vocation *outside* the state," that is, their basis is the unique encounter of each person with the other's face and suffering, the duty that provides the standpoint or "vigilance" for judging how well the state succeeds. When he says that "the liberal state" has the "capacity to guarantee" justice and benevolence, he does not mean that it always succeeds. It has the "capacity" insofar as it *seeks* to respect rights that are ultimately grounded in the other's right to assistance, aid, and welfare and that are to be respected. Its degree of success is a historical, contingent matter.

In order to see the state as founded to organize and realize justice in society, however, we cannot accept the Hobbesian view of political authority and sovereignty. Levinas alludes to Hobbes when he says that justice, and therefore human rights, "requires a different 'authority' than that of the harmonious relations established between wills that are initially opposed and opposable."[225] What Levinas means, of course, is that the face-to-face that founds the possibility of and need for the state and political justice is a condition of *attraction* whereby the other person needs me and I respond to that need with kindness and generosity. Levinas calls this a "prior peace" and associates it with "love," or what he calls here "proximity," "myself *for* the other," and "original sociality-goodness."[226] For Hobbes, individuals in the state of nature, potential threats to one another, seek peace. But this is a constructed or derivative peace, the goal of rational deliberation and something yet to exist. For Levinas, the fundamental character of the social relationship, of the other calling to the self and demanding its aid and support, is already a kind of peace. Society is based on love and concern, not power and conflict.

In a way, Levinas is more akin to Rousseau than he is to Hobbes – or to Rawls, for that matter. The natural state, which for him is preconceptual or presystematic, of course, is one of need and sympathy – of a kind. Social structure and political institutions arise to organize and facilitate benevolence, to regulate the negotiations of imperfect rights and perfect rights. The state originally is a mechanism for welfare distribution and, insofar as there are human rights and rights determined by law in order to implement them, only subsequently

---

[224] "The Rights of Man and the Rights of the Other" in *Outside the Subject*, 123.
[225] "The Rights of Man and the Rights of the Other" in *Outside the Subject*, 123.
[226] "The Rights of Man and the Rights of the Other" in *Outside the Subject*, 123–24, for the allusion to Hobbes. See also "Philosophy and the Idea of the Infinite" in *Collected Philosophical Papers*, 57.

a system of protections.[227] It is liberal but perhaps also, ideally, socialist rather than capitalist. As Levinas puts it at the end of the essay, it is a state in which "fraternity" is more primary than "freedom." As we would expect, for Levinas it is responsibility, not freedom, that is basic. The self's freedom is derivative. Its "freedom and rights" first arise in its responsibility and only thereafter in its "opposition to the freedom and rights of the other person."[228] Another way of putting Levinas's point is to say that the self is first and foremost social and only derivatively separated and isolated. Its initial freedom is its responsiveness to the call of the other person; its subsequent freedom, its self-interest and self-involvement, comes later and with it human rights and the need for just institutions to protect them.

In "The Rights of the Other Man" (1989), Levinas focuses on the paradoxical way in which freedom gives rise to law and the state, to protect itself, but only it would seem by sacrificing itself. Clearly, Levinas thinks that understanding how these human rights are *grounded* in the rights of the other person will help to understand and dissolve the paradox.

Human rights are natural, not granted by tradition or some prior authority; they are *a priori* and equal. Once framed by law, they are all versions of a right to free will[229] – in different forms, the right to work, to live, to well-being, and even, perhaps, the right to holidays and the benefits of Social Security. But, Levinas considers, if we have a whole collection of people with the right to free will, surely they would limit and violate each other's rights. Indeed, this picture looks suspiciously like Hobbes's state of nature: "the war of each against all, based on the Rights of Man."[230] This is precisely how Hobbes derives his conception of the natural state, based on natural right, which he defines as natural liberty or natural power. Conflict, mistrust, and fear are the outcomes, unless as rational agents all people limit their freedom freely in order to secure peace. Levinas elides Hobbes and Kant: Peace between free wills is possible if all subordinate themselves to the "rationality of the universal" or respect for the other.

But, at this moment Levinas asks the *central question*: Why would the free will do this? Why subjugate itself to the "freedom of the neighbor" and sacrifice its own right to free will? In Kant's terms, why would a free will choose to

---

[227] This conception of the state as an agency for regulating benevolence and therefore as a welfare distribution agency is also found in Moses Mendelssohn's political philosophy. See Part I of Mendelssohn's *Jerusalem* (Hanover, NH: The University Press of New England, 1983) and the essay by Levinas on Mendelssohn, "Moses Mendelssohn's Thought," in *In the Time of the Nations*.

[228] "The Rights of Man and the Rights of the Other" in *Outside the Subject*, 125.

[229] "The Rights of the Other Man" in *Alterity and Transcendence*, 145–46.

[230] "The Rights of the Other Man" in *Alterity and Transcendence*, 147.

subordinate itself to reason? In Hobbes's terms, why would a naturally free agent give up all of its freedom – or power – to the rationality of an omnipotent sovereign?[231] Levinas's answer is that the self would do this only of it *already* cared more for the other person than for itself, or, in other words, if the right of the other preceded the rights of man. He makes the point in Kantian terms: Such practical reason or a good will is possible only if "*good will were will*, not just out of respect for the universality of a maxim of action, but out of the feeling of goodness" – "an attachment to the other in his alterity to the point of granting him a priority over oneself."[232] This is the meaning, Levinas says, of the *novelty* of the Rights of Man, that they are "originally the rights of the other man." In our political lives, that is, as we relate to others in society and to the laws and political institutions with which we live, the rights we have under these laws and that obligate others and ourselves are grounded in our acceptance of limitations on our freedoms. We respect other citizens's rights, however, because their rights – their needs and their significance for us – are original and basic. We *respect* them legally because we *respect* them humanly. Our own rights, natural and equal, link this *double respect*, which related us all the time in liberal democracies. In a sense, neither exists without the other: We respect others under the law only because we respect them fundamentally, and when we respect them fundamentally – care about them and take responsibility for them – we do so in societies of law and political institutions. And we respect them fundamentally – that is, only in a state in which laws articulate human rights and express our respect for other's rights *directed toward* each and every one of us.

These essays, then, as Howard Caygill puts it nicely, "[S]eparate rights discourse from its roots in individualism, without, however, lapsing into the fraternal politics of communitarianism" and "amount to a vindication of the universal mission of prophetic politics."[233] They are especially significant as evidence that Levinas took ethics and politics to be continuous. The very particular ethical character of our relationship to each and every other, the face-to-face dimension of all social existence, can register in a precise legal and political environment and must register in some such environment; the face-to-face does not occur alone or isolated from society. The right of the other, moreover, should shape the political institutions that organize our rights in a liberal society. These rights and the political system that frames and protects them are grounded in

---

[231] Strictly speaking, not really *all* of its freedom, insofar as it retains the right of self-defense and the freedom to act on it; see Hobbes, *Leviathan* Pt. II: *Of Commonwealth*, ed. Edwin Curley (Cambridge, MA: Hackett Publishing, 1994), Ch. 21: "Of the Liberty of Subjects," 136–45.

[232] Levinas, "The Rights of the Other Man," in *Alterity and Transcendence*, 149.

[233] Caygill, *Levinas and the Political*, 151–52.

the "feeling of goodness" that is basic to our relation to the other. Levinas leaves no doubt about his convictions regarding the best political life, just as he is sensitive to the risks of politics and the possibility of totalitarianism and technological oppression.[234] Politics can always be corrupted, but it is unavoidable. The ethics of goodness and generosity must ground it, justify it, and be a permanent conscience warning against its violation.

LEVINAS'S SINGLE-MINDEDNESS

As I conclude this chapter on Levinas as an ethical and political thinker, I want to turn to one last criticism. It is easy to think that Levinas has set the bar for a good human life very high, perhaps even too high, and that this is a double fault. On the one hand, his sense of ethical demand may be too demanding for normal persons, or even for extraordinary persons, to accomplish on a regular basis.[235] On the other hand, it may be that his commitment to the priority of the ethical is too narrow or exclusive, allowing little or no room for other valuable human experiences and activities. Is Levinas as narrow and elitist as he seems? Is his central theme an important corrective that has become overwhelming and indefensible?

Here I want to consider this second problem. Does Levinas require such a single-minded emphasis on responsibility – assistance, generosity, and kindness – and an obligation to the other person that it leads to the following objection:

---

[234] "The Rights of the Other" in *Outside the Subject*, 118–21; Caygill, *Levinas and the Political*, 153–56.

[235] In *Moral Demands in Nonideal Theory*, Liam Murphy calls this – with reference to a universal obligation to beneficence – the problem of over-demandingness. Levinas's claim that our responsibility to other persons is infinite certainly sounds excessive. The charge of being too demanding is often leveled against consequentialism. As Stephen Darwall puts it, "[C]ritics sometimes argue that consequentialism is too 'demanding,' since it holds that agents act wrongly when they fail to do all they can to respond to unmet needs even at levels of sacrifice substantially beyond what commonsense morality would require" ("How Should Ethics Relate to [the Rest of] Philosophy? Moore's Legacy," in Terry Horgan and Mark Timmons (eds.), *Metaethics after Moore* (Oxford: Oxford University Press, 2006), 33). Darwall seems to be taking "over-demandingness" to mean that consequentialism results in every action one takes being wrong, but this strikes me as a conclusion from an overly strict requirement that certainly needs to be clarified. One has to ask in what way consequentialism would be too demanding. R. Jay Wallace remarks that direct utilitarianism is taken by some to be "demanding in a way that would systematically thwart the project of integrative eudaimonistic reflection," that is, "the demands of living an individual human life" ("Reason and Responsibility" in *Normativity and the Will*, 141), which is a way of being too demanding that shades into the second criticism mentioned above and the one that I focus on in the text. Meeting the charge of over-demandingness is a main theme of Garrett Cullity, *The Moral Demands of Affluence*, esp. Ch. 5–10.

Does this conception, "utopian and, for an I, inhuman" not go too far? Does it leave room for the importance of other human activities and values? Does it not drain our lives of many things that could and do make them truly human? This is Hilary Putnam's criticism: "[T]o be *only* ethical, even if one be ethical to the point of martyrdom, is to live a one-sided life." Or more accurately, Putnam asks whether Levinas considers ethics too narrowly – perhaps "the ethical life has more than one *sine qua non*."[236]

In making this criticism, Putnam calls attention to Aristotle, but one might also refer to diverse philosophers, from Kierkegaard and Nietzsche to Heidegger and Buber, from Bernard Williams to Charles Taylor. All allow for authentic human lives filled with various activities; none restrict authenticity to ethics alone or restrict ethics as Levinas seems to do. In Heidegger's terms, authenticity concerns living a human life that is genuine and fulfilled, and there are many ways to do so, many activities that enrich us and make our lives worthwhile, as long as they are expressions of resolve and self-determination and self-realization.[237]

These problems are all associated with the singleness of Levinas's ethical focus. But let us be careful. The ethical, for Levinas, is also the religious; he calls it "holiness" and uses a host of religious terms in referring to it.[238] It is the orienting character of human existence that makes that existence ultimately worthwhile and meaningful. But does Levinas mean that activities other than acts of kindness and generosity are not valuable? Or that they are less valuable? Or only valuable insofar as they are associated in some way with the ethical? What would Levinas say about self-love or duties to oneself? To a life devoted to art? To one devoted to art at the expense of others, the love of others or concern for them and their well-being?

Insofar as responsibility is the religious, should we not consider it as Kierkegaard or Buber does the relationship with God or the divine or transcendent? For all their differences, both treat that relationship as the overarching and determinative framework in which life ought to take place. It is the overall engagement, like a marriage of lover and beloved or an abiding relationship of friends, that gives meaning and purpose to a host of diverse activities and practices lived by both parties together and many lived by each on his or her own. Marriage does not mean that neither party can any longer do something alone or that only activities directly contributing to the bond between the partners are

---

[236] Putnam, "Levinas and Judaism" in *The Cambridge Companion to Levinas*, 55–57, esp. 56, 57.

[237] See Taylor, *The Ethics of Authenticity*, and Charles Guignon, *On Being Authentic* (London: Routledge, 2004).

[238] See, for example, Levinas, *Is It Righteous To Be?*, 47, 49, 51, 59, 109, 111, 113, 191, 204, 235–36; "God and Philosophy" in *Basic Philosophical Writings, passim*; and OB, *passim*.

significant. It calls for certain types of actions of joint agency or based on mutual concern, but it also alters the character of many actions performed by the partners privately or relatively independently. Other actions remain untouched, to be sure, but this makes room for mutual actions, personal actions given special character by the marriage, and relatively independent conduct. Why should we not think of Levinas's face-to-face along these lines?

Putnam's objection has its analogue in the objection, often made of moral systems, that they cannot adequately make sense of our obligations to others.[239] This is a criticism regularly leveled at Socratic eudaimonism, for example, and also against Platonic ethics.[240] Indeed, it is frequently made against all attempts to link private interests with altruistic ones. Putnam's objection, at least in part, runs in the reverse direction: If our primary obligation is to others and the obligation is unlimited, then what room is there for obligations to oneself? Can one argue from social responsibility to self-love and self-concern? It would seem that the best Levinas could do is to argue that we ought to be concerned with ourselves and our well-being only because others must be or because others have an interest in us and our resources, but this type of reflected concern seems odd, if not totally bizarre and even a distortion. H. A. Prichard once argued that one can never escape self-interest, and any moral theory based on it must be a mistake precisely because it fails to reach the moral at all. We might argue, against Levinas, that his account is also mistaken, but for the reverse reason: that it can never reach the self in all its richness and diversity. To say that we are valuable to ourselves only because we are valuable to others is counterintuitive and incoherent.

The marriage metaphor suggests that Levinas's notion of the priority of the other person might not be read exclusively.[241] Concern for the other does not exclude concern for oneself; it is our primary obligation but not our sole obligation. In a sense, who I am involves the other alongside and yet prior to my own self-concerns. For Levinas, to put it in terms of our metaphor, what makes each life significant and gives it point is the marriage or the marriages in which it occurs; and furthermore, there is no individual life or self without such marriages. Human existence is social through and through, and its sociality

---

[239] See Susan Wolf, "Moral Saints," 138.

[240] See, in a very large literature, T. H. Irwin, *Plato's Moral Theory* (Oxford: Oxford University Press, 1977), and *Plato's Ethics* (Oxford: Oxford University Press, 1995); see also Richard Kraut, *Socrates and the State* (Princeton, NJ: Princeton University Press, 1984), and *The Cambridge Companion to Plato* (Cambridge: Cambridge University Press, 1992).

[241] Those familiar with the work of Stanley Cavell will recall how important the relationship of marriage is to Cavell's work on Emersonian perfectionism, especially to his understanding of those Hollywood films of the 1930s and 1940s that he calls "comedies of remarriage." See his *Pursuits of Happiness* and recently *Cities of Words*.

gives value to its independence. Levinas is certainly not denying that we are free, expressive, creative, inclined to enjoyment, to work, to fulfill our desires for beauty and a sense of awe, and for a sense of self-worth and self-esteem. None of this, however, is primary to who we are, how our lives ought to go, what point they have for us, and why certain actions and objects matter to us. They fit in, but they should not predominate. They do not orient our lives and give them authenticity, so to speak. They are not a wasteful use of time or effort, but a life lived only in their terms is deficient in a very serious way.

As I indicated, Putnam may be asking whether Levinas's focus on ethics is not too single-minded and exclusive or, alternatively, whether his conception of ethics as responsibility is not too narrow – even as an ethical or moral view. There are, of course, different ways of responding to the two criticisms. If one were persuaded that a full human life might very well – and perhaps should – contain more than one ethical character and morally right form of conduct, then one might try to show that Levinas does indeed permit or even endorse such diversity. On the other hand, one might try to show that ethics, when properly understood, is not only necessary but also sufficient for human fulfillment and that Levinas does understand ethics in a suitable way to be sufficient for such a life. I can see these two strategies merging, moreover, and depending upon how Levinas's conception of the ethical should be understood. If one does take that conception to be a very rich one, it might not matter, then, whether its sufficiency is direct or indirect or, to put the matter in other words, whether the best human life incorporates only ethics or a good deal more than ethics.

Simon Critchley asks whether Levinas is talking about ethics when he discusses the responsibility of the self in the face of the other. In order to mark off the special character of the self's responsibility, John Llewellyn calls it "proto-ethics," and Robert Bernasconi refers to it as an "ethics of suspicion."[242] As we have seen, Putnam associates it with what Stanley Cavell calls "ethical or Emersonian perfectionism." Levinas calls it "religion" and "glory," as well as "substitution," "hostage," "trauma," and "persecution." It is the need and demand for response – acknowledgment, acceptance, generosity, and more – as well as responsibility to and for the other. So, if it is a primary or fundamental ethical obligation or demand, it is so in a very unusual way. How should we understand its role, its character, and its ethical nature?

We have shown that Levinas takes politics as a necessary feature of our social lives and that a liberal politics that organizes and protects human rights and a host of legal rights is characteristic of the best possible state. Such rights are

---

[242] See Critchley, *The Ethics of Deconstruction*, 256–57.

grounded in and expressions of the rights of the other person, but they are individual *rights* and hence concern people's needs and interests, what citizens find valuable and enriching.[243] Why worry about the provenance or character of such a liberal state and the protection of citizens's rights, if the good life had no significant value for these citizens? Levinas seems to hold that ethics and politics contribute to the well-being of others and of each and every self as well. They are both about seeing to it that nourishment, clothing, and enjoyments of various kinds are distributed to all members of society. Care and respect for all others demand an overriding commitment to acting responsibly toward them; politics is the set of practices, policies, and institutions that enact this commitment for given particular societies, but the demand to do so "precedes" the political even while it always occurs along with it.

Understanding Levinas this way, however, seems to run headlong into Putnam's kind of objection. Should all our lives, social and political as they are, be guided by a single, comprehensive, determinative commitment: to care for others? Moreover, as we have noted, is this not a form of moral fanaticism or moral sainthood? And if so, is such a life not unappealing and even undesirable?

The objection can be elaborated this way. There is no question that Levinas appreciates how limited embodied, social, historical existence is. He says explicitly that our practices, institutions, and principles provide mechanisms for dealing with the needs of others beyond our capabilities to satisfy them and given their infinite scope for each and every one of us. This limitation has various sources: either because we do not have the resources or because the persons and their needs are too many, offering competing demands, or are too diverse – or more. The fact of human existence, then, makes it impossible for any one of us – indeed, for any group of us – to satisfy completely our responsibilities or responsivity. Still, this could mean that we are always morally deficient, lacking to one degree or another, and that we should aim at moral perfection, even if it is unattainable or impossible. Recognizing our finitude, we may nonetheless need to strive to do what we can and achieve what we are able to achieve for others. Minimally, each of us should accept the existence of others – the fact of our sociality – and each of us should be bound to the command addressed by every other person to each of us, "Thou shalt not murder." Levinas seems to leave no room for acts above the call of duty, supererogatory acts; the bar is far too high for that. Whatever we do for others is necessary, in a sense. Moreover, Levinas seems to leave no room for life spent on other things: art, music, sports, hobbies, and so forth. Such activities take time, effort, and resources away from doing good for others, from benefactions and aid to the poor and hungry. Or so it would seem.

---

[243] This way of putting the point was suggested to me by Joshua Shaw in conversation.

But this outcome is excessive and involves, I believe, a misreading of Levinas. The key to resolving this problem is to appreciate that for Levinas the ethical is the social, that the primacy of the ethical goes hand in hand with the unavoidability of the political and the public, and that all we do, then, occurs within a complex, infinitely ramified setting of social relationship so that every action we perform is in one way or another, directly or indirectly, an enactment of responsibility – of acceptance and assistance to the others that constitute the social world in which we live. This is the crux of the solution. Let me now seek to clarify it.

For Levinas, responsibility is infinite. This means that it is always, in social life, compromised, but it is also always expressed. Duties are always in conflict; our responsibilities reach beyond those whom we know or can serve and assist and beyond the resources we have or could ever have. As Derrida puts it, responsibility, to be real responsibility, must be infinite or unlimited and hence always in need of moral and political compromises.[244] Only because responsibility cannot be bounded or precisely defined are there "moral and political problems." Human existence is like this; it is why we have politics and live in history, Derrida says.[245] Moral conscience calls for our realizing this and doing what we can – individually and collectively; it requires living just and caring lives and creating a just political environment. Does it mean, however, that we cannot enjoy anything – an ample, well-prepared meal, a work of art, a movie, or a concert? To do so, of course, is to compromise our responsibility and to qualify our acting on it. But we always do this. What we need to consider is whether the circumstances dictate that this compromise is intolerable or acceptable, whether it is important in some compelling way or not, whether it is unusual and a consciously chosen alternative or part of a pattern of acts of mine that regularly ignore the needs and suffering of others. In short, every act we perform is in some way a compromise or attenuation of our responsibility as well as an expression of it; what distinguishes one from the other is our reflective assessment of the act and its role for us and for our lives, as part of the overall fabric of our lives. We make judgments about what to do, what policies to establish, what our commitments are. This is not extraordinary; it is a permanent feature of our lives insofar as they are embodied, social, finite, and yet demanding in an unlimited way. The issue is not whether we should enjoy our lives, but rather whether we believe that enjoyment is all we care about

[244] See Conclusion, below.
[245] Derrida, "Remarks on Deconstruction and Pragmatism" in Simon Critchley, Jacques Derrida, Ernesto Laclau, and Richard Rorty, *Deconstruction and Pragmatism*, ed. Chantal Mouffe (London: Routledge, 1996), 86–87.

or whether enjoyment (pleasure, self-satisfaction) is what gives our lives their value and point.

But Levinas does not simply urge us to accept the inevitable; there is more to be said about the significance of the variety of our lives. Some of us are creative, some musically talented, some painters or poets. These activities call attention to various features of human existence, the world, and life. Some performances are elevating, some thrilling, some soothing, others exciting. We react in these ways to what we see and hear and do; we may feel intense enjoyment or anxiety or regret. All of this matters to us and to others. Levinas realizes this and sees it as unavoidable. What *is* avoidable is a kind of forgetfulness of what is determinative and basic, in a sense, about social life, that there is no limit to what we owe others, no limit to what need and suffering call on us to give up, to do, and to share, and that all we do is social. Whatever it is that we do, no matter how personal in orientation or how much pleasure it gives us, it is done among others, involving acknowledging and accepting them – with them in mind, so to speak. The issue, then, is one of orientation and overall direction. There is no goal here that can be met only if we try single-mindedly enough. What there is is a consideration, an obligation that is always present alongside all other obligations, interests, and values, and one that calls out for primacy. Depending upon the circumstances, it succeeds to one degree or another, never wholly, always in a limited way.

It is very one-sided to look at art, music, poetry, and such activities as exclusively self-satisfying and self-serving. They are, after all, in their very creation, a gift to others, a communication and a sharing, an act of the self for others.[246] At one level, then, artistic creation, performance, and production respond to and for others. I think that Levinas's thinking about paternity moves in this direction. The artist, like the teacher, is akin to the parent. Children, students, and audience are all others who call out and receive, who need and demand, and in all such cases the self is responsible – capable of response and acknowledgment and obligated to do so. We must feed the hungry and clothe the naked, but then we can and should sing, paint, and write poetry. These, too, are acts of responding and reaching out to others, acts of generosity and concern for others.

If this is one response to Putnam's criticism, there is another. It may be that his criticism and the concern it represents are misplaced. It may be, that is, that worries about the narrowness or exclusivity of Levinas's ethical ideal do not arise for him. Let me explain.

---

[246] Jill Robbins argues that for Levinas art that is ethical, that makes an ethical difference, is not aesthetic; see *Altered Reading*, 134–54.

Of a moral theorist, one might ask: Why give special preeminence to ethics? Why is ethics of such singular importance to human existence? Furthermore, why advocate an ethical theory with such a demanding ideal? Why elevate the saint such that most people must be satisfied with sin?[247] Are there not many activities worthy of our interest and attention, in addition to moral activity? And should not ethical goals be attainable? Is not any ethical theory that is worth our endorsement required to answer such questions? One might think so: Aristotle needs to account for "external goods," Plato for art and poetry, and so forth. But does Levinas face the same requirement? He realizes that the demands of responsibility are infinite and that there are few saints.[248] He admires them, but few of us attain their status. But what does this fact mean? What sort of problem for Levinas is this? Indeed, is it a problem at all?

Putnam calls Levinas an "ethical perfectionist," and we have considered what this might mean. But one thing we should keep in mind is that it cannot mean that Levinas is an ethical theorist. He is a phenomenologist of human existence; his goal is to disclose a frequently ignored and largely occluded dimension of social existence. That dimension concerns responsibility as a blending of obligation and responsivity. If Levinas is right, social life has this dimension; each of us is infinitely responsible to and for each and every other person. That is a *fact* about social existence, indeed *the most basic fact* about it, and it is a fact that unites call and response, which makes it deontological and responsive at once. What it means, in other words, is that an *ought* precedes every experience we have, every decision, act, and so forth. This fact may be – and is, if it is so – very demanding. But it is a fact that is not revealed by or articulated through theory. It is exposed by a certain kind of thinking, to be sure, and by art and literature, through ritual and study, but that thinking is not theoretical in the sense of a proposal or a claim or a hypothesis. We can ask if a life that is attentive to it would have a certain shape or would look at art or leisure in a certain way, and so forth. We can even appreciate that activities not guided directly or addressed directly to the self's responsibility are inevitable, worthwhile, and sometimes fulfilling. What we cannot do is say that Levinas's theory is unattractive or unappealing because it is too exclusive or because its moral expectations are not realistic enough. Existence is what it is; social life is social life. Levinas says that it means most of all that each of us must respond to the utter particularity of each other person because that particular person, indeed every particular person, makes a claim on me and calls me into question, requires me to acknowledge and

---

[247] Does this make Levinas's ethical ideal akin to the doctrine of original sin, but without the promise of redemption from it?

[248] See *Is It Righteous to Be?*, 183.

accept her. If he is right, we are. We can take it seriously, find it rewarding, or proceed in denial. To refuse to accept what Levinas says as a theory is one form of denial; it is not to refute what he says but to misconstrue it and avoid our social responsibility in so doing. Putnam's concern is not an objection to a theory; it is a concern about our lives, for Levinas's point is not about ethical theories, but rather about life insofar as it is ethical or religious or valuable and significant for us.

In a famous paper, Susan Wolf argues that "moral perfection, in the sense of moral saintliness, does not constitute a model of personal well-being toward which it would be particularly rational or good or desirable for a human being to strive."[249] She is very clear that the issue, for her, is about "moral theory" and its character, its rationality and suitability for normal people, that is, its salience for our everyday moral intuitions. Wolf distinguishes between "Loving Saints," who serve the welfare of others as a primary motive, and "Rational Saints," who act in this way out of duty.[250] To all appearances, of course, both act the same way, leading lives, she claims, that "may seem to be . . . strangely barren."[251] She argues that to commonsense moral thinking and theories, such as utilitarianism and Kantianism, the ideal of the moral saint is unappealing. What this means is that the moral point of view needs to be considered as one option alongside another that she calls the "point of view of individual perfection," "from which we consider what kinds of lives are good lives, and what kinds of persons it would be good for ourselves and others to be."[252] From this point of view, we would not claim that it is always the best thing to act morally or to be moral. Wolf's point is that the preeminence of morality is not to be taken for granted: She calls into question "the assumption that it is always better to be morally better."

This sounds like a claim that Levinas would find hard to accept, but I am not sure that in fact he would not agree with the spirit of it, for two reasons. One reason concerns the role of the face-to-face and responsibility in human social life, as Levinas sees it. To be sure, this dimension is always present in all social interactions and relationships, but it is never purely present. It is always qualified or attenuated. In a sense, Levinas might say that all social interactions are, whatever else they are, also ethical − acts or expressions of responsibility and justice. It is not always better to be maximally moral, but it is always necessary to be moral or ethical, to one degree or another.

---

[249] Wolf, "Moral Saints," in Kruschwitz and Robert C. Roberts (eds.), *The Virtues*, 137–52; reprinted from *Journal of Philosophy* 79:8 (Aug. 1982), 419–39.

[250] Wolf, "Moral Saints" in *The Virtues*, 138.

[251] Wolf, "Moral Saints" in *The Virtues*, 139.

[252] Wolf, "Moral Saints" in *The Virtues*, 150.

Levinas's second reason for not rejecting Wolf's point might be that it is not, on her own terms, a dismissal of ethics as much as a reconfiguring of its place in our lives. Moral theories tend to treat our values "on the model of a hierarchical system with morality at the top."[253] Wolf rejects such a model. Morality is not "a universal medium into which all other values must be translated"; nor is it "an ever-present filter through which all other values must pass." Both options presuppose that morality is at the top of a hierarchical system, but there is no such system and no such top. But this denial no more implies that ethics or morality is unimportant than it forbids ethics from being the most important value for "evaluating and improving ourselves and our world." Even if it is such a value, however, it is one alongside others. To be sure, Levinas does think that all other values and their realizations are *also* moral, precisely insofar as they are social and involve a network of acceptance and responses to the needs of others. But like Wolf, I think, he does not see morality as the preeminent value in a hierarchy. Rather, ethics or religion is a pervasive feature of all values and all social existence.

Where Levinas would disagree with Wolf, however, has to do with the very character of morality and its relation to theory. As I said earlier, for Levinas the issue is not what a moral theory would hold or require. I do not think that he would find moral sainthood as restrictive and barren as Wolf does. But for him, it is not an ideal to be evaluated against our moral theories or by rational considerations. Morality as responsibility pervades our existence.[254] It sits alongside other human activities and ideals and is compromised in social life, even though it is centrally important. Theory does not tell us this; life does.

Putnam, then, charges Levinas incorrectly. Levinas may sometimes – even regularly – sound obsessed with the moral. Twentieth-century history and culture and his worries about both certainly incline him to worry, if not despair. His highly rhetorical vocabulary and sense of urgency bespeak such worries. But in principle, this is not an exclusivist obsession or a form of moral or

---

[253] Wolf, "Moral Saints" in *The Virtues*, 151.

[254] Can one criticize Levinas for not appreciating that an acceptable moral theory must allow for supererogation as distinct from morally acceptable conduct? That is, because Levinas seems to require everyone to be a moral saint, there seems to be no room in his thinking for a distinction between what is one's duty and what is beyond the call of duty. Discussion of this issue in recent literature goes back to J. O. Urmson's "Saints and Heroes", in A. I. Melden (ed.), *Essays in Moral Philosophy* (Seattle: University of Washington Press, 1958), 198–216. For discussion, see Jonathan Dancy, *Moral Reasons*, 127–43. This problem, however, insofar as it is a problem about moral theories, is a problem at the level of "ontology" for Levinas – that is, at the level of everyday judgment and conduct and theory – and not a problem about the face-to-face as a "social fact" about all human existence. Levinas makes it clear that our decisions, conduct, and policies satisfy the demands of responsibility to different degrees, but they never do so perfectly or without qualification.

moralistic fanaticism. Its aim is to recall attention to an abiding feature of our lives that has been regularly ignored, distorted, and obscured, that demands of us care and responsiveness to the hunger, destitution, and suffering of others, but that is also more prosaically a matter of our basic acceptance of others as coinhabitants of our social world. For him, the level of the need is sufficient to warrant the focus and tenacity of his concern, as we showed in Chapter 1. Ethics does not eliminate or seek to eliminate the rest of human life; it does, however, seek to place it in its context in the good, as our determinative and unavoidable concern.

10

Beyond Language and Expressibility

Levinas uses the term "totality" to refer to a number of features of Western life and culture. It is the world that we, as thinkers and agents, live in and the sum of our ways of understanding, explaining, and organizing that world, culturally and intellectually. Central to totality, then, are the principles and concepts that we use to carry out these projects. In short, totality is the sum of thought and language as well as the world shaped by them.

"Infinity" and "transcendence" refer to what lie outside totality, in a sense, and yet those factors or actualities with which we, within totality, still engage. We have discussed the face, as the central fact of transcendence, and others, like *illeity*, the "there is," and suffering, are central features of human existence, as Levinas sees it.

But if language is a function of totality, if our everyday discourse and our theoretical languages are part of our everyday lives, how can we speak about such factors as the face and *illeity*? Do they not lie beyond the limits of language and discourse, beyond expressibility? Levinas employs a large vocabulary to designate the face-to-face encounter, a vocabulary that develops and changes during his career – terms such as "epiphany," "proximity," "enigma," "trauma," "persecution," and "accusation," but how are these terms being used? Are they purely metaphorical? Is transcendence only graspable indirectly? Is the face ineffable? What kind of philosophy can deal with such transcendence, with what lies beyond language and indeed beyond thought?[1]

In his famous essay on *Totality and Infinity*, "Violence and Metaphysics," Derrida explores the tension between Levinas's claim that the face lies beyond being and totality and hence beyond language and the fact that he nonetheless

---

[1] There are two questions that should be distinguished: (1) whether the face-to-face cannot be thought and expressed because we do not now have the cognitive and linguistic resources to do so, and (2) whether it cannot be thought or expressed in principle.

speaks about it and discusses it. It is widely held that *Otherwise Than Being* was written, at least in part, as a response to Derrida and to such criticism about language and expressibility. It is especially the distinction between *saying* and the *said* that is thought to be the core of that response. But if it is, how is it a response? How – if at all – does the distinction clarify or show how the face is associated with language?

These themes are the subject of this chapter. Levinas's relation to Derrida has not only been the subject of extensive discussion; it has also shaped much of the interpretation of Levinas. My goal is different. It is twofold: to clarify how Levinas uses language philosophically in order to expose and characterize the face-to-face encounter; and second, to demystify the sense in which the face-to-face is itself beyond thought and language.[2]

LEVINAS'S LANGUAGE

As we have learned, Levinas approaches the issue of the face and its relation to thinking and speaking, from his early writings on, as a matter of experiencing what is beyond being and beyond totality. "Our relation with the other person ... overflows comprehension ... because in our relation with the other, he does not affect us in terms of a concept."[3] But this, as we have so often pointed out, does not refer to an isolated *relation* or *experience*. As Levinas puts it, even in this very early essay, being summoned by the other and comprehending the other do not occur one after another; "the two relations are intertwined."[4] Here Levinas calls this "relation" of being summoned, the "face-to-face," "language," or "speech" and claims that it is the "condition of any conscious grasp." This speech is a matter of interpersonal conversation, of address and response in the second person. It is a "calling to" that is intertwined with "calling" or "describing." In speaking to the other as clerk or as friend or as client, I speak to him, and he speaks to me.[5] This is sociality or religion that occurs with and yet is not derived from ontology. "What is named is at the same time that which is called."

Earlier, we saw that this relation or engagement with the face of the other person has significance, its own kind of meaning.[6] Here we see that it is "part" of all social intercourse and is, in Levinas's early writings, characterized as speech

---

[2] Also, another goal is to demystify what Levinas means by the language he uses for *illeity*, the "there is," suffering, and other such features of our existence.
[3] "Is Ontology Fundamental?" in *Basic Philosophical Writings*, 6.
[4] "Is Ontology Fundamental?" in *Basic Philosophical Writings*, 6.
[5] "Is Ontology Fundamental?" in *Basic Philosophical Writings*, 7.
[6] See "Meaning and Sense" in *Basic Philosophical Writings*. See also Ch. 5.

302   Beyond Language and Expressibility

or language.[7] But in this regard, language is second-person address or dialogue; it is not descriptive. The everyday second-person encounter, *even when* it is conversation or face-to-face intercourse, includes both a conceptual or descriptive feature and another feature, that the other faces me and calls me into question.

Language, in these uses, is not our concern here. What we want to understand is not how language works in ordinary, everyday speech or in theoretical discussion. Nor are we interested here in the sense in which the face-to-face is itself linguistic, a relation of second-person address in which the other person summons, commands, and calls upon me. These are substantive roles of language. Rather, our concern is in the way Levinas uses language philosophically in order to designate and call attention to the face-to-face relation, the way the face of the other reveals suffering, pain, need, and demand to the self, and also in order to characterize the "there is" and "*illeity*" that similarly are manifest from their transcendental origin, like a divine revelation or epiphany. Once the face – and for now, let us focus on it – is described, does it not cease to be face? Is face not given only outside of concepts words, principles, and categories? To use Buber's language, is it the case that the face is only addressed and never expressed?

"Face," of course is, in one sense, a philosophical term of art. On the one hand, in everyday social interaction persons confront each other in many ways and for many purposes. We observe each other's postures; we hear what we say; we see our faces and our facial expressions. But, on the other hand, "face," "enigma," "proximity," and so forth designate, for the phenomenological philosopher, how the relation to the other person, in its primary and determinative dimension, occurs. These terms here reach out and point to an aspect of everyday social relationships that is always present even when hidden or ignored and yet is in a sense also extraordinary and surprising, even transcendent. What we want to ask is how these terms do their work, insofar as, strictly speaking, the person *qua* face is beyond thought, concepts, and expressibility. How does the philosopher use language to speak the unspeakable?

In *The Rationality of Transcendence*, Theodore de Boer takes up this problem, especially in the essay "The Rationality of the Philosophy of Levinas."[8] De Boer discusses in these pages Levinas's method, in particular the way that Levinas uses language to explore and illuminate the experience of the face, the self's relation to the other person as a transcendent fact. Insofar as the other person

---

[7] "Dialogue" refers to an encounter between persons that is in the second person; at other times, it is itself a linguistic encounter, a conversation, while at other times it is an interpersonal relationship without words – for example, two persons dancing together or playing chess or wrestling one another.

[8] Theodore de Boer, *The Rationality of Transcendence*, 56–82, esp. 64–73.

confronts or engages the self, it does so outside the linguistic conventions and discourse of everyday life and theoretical vocabulary. Levinas is keenly aware that the other person is present or revealed in a way other than as an appearance or as thematized or conceptualized in descriptions, accounts, or explanations. Moreover, in Levinas's "ethical metaphysics," the terms he uses for the way the other is present – "face," "enigma," "accusation," and so forth – are not intended to provide his readers with descriptions or identifying characterizations. Rather, they are intended to direct attention to an aspect of everyday social interaction regularly ignored and to evoke respect, concern, and devotion due it.[9] Intentionally, the terms Levinas uses are not those philosophers use for the object of experience, nor are they even terms regularly used by philosophers at all, whether in epistemological contexts or non-epistemological ones. They are dramatic terms with striking nuances, evocative and compelling, rhetorically equivocal and intended to surprise and confuse. Using them is more like attempting to cultivate interest and reverence than it is like classifying, informing, or describing and conveying information. Levinas seeks to evoke surprise and intrigue, not to convey comprehension and clarification. But at the same time, he does want us to understand what he is calling us to appreciate and respect. The terms he uses are drawn from everyday life and given a surprising role in a locale unlike their normal one, and his goal is intellectual only to the degree that it is ethical and cognitive all at once.

De Boer sees some of this. He points out that increasingly, in his later work, Levinas uses two linguistic techniques: *iteration* and *exaltation*. The first is a "rhetorical duplication" – for example, when he says that the primordial relation "means a meaning" or "expresses an expression." The effect he seeks is to encourage us to think at a more basic, determinative level; the experience of the face of the other person does have meaning and is an expression – but not in the ordinary, everyday sense. The second technique, exaltation, is Levinas's strategy of pushing us to think of excellence, perfection, or the superlative by exaggerating the normal. Levinas often says that he loves emphasis and hyperbole.[10] Perhaps the most characteristic expression of this type occurs when Levinas describes the self as substitution as "more passive than any passivity."[11] Phrases like this recall the strategies of neo-Platonism and, among medievals, of the *via negativa*: God described as being that is beyond being and not-being or wise beyond wisdom or ignorance.

[9] They testify, witness, call attention to, point toward something that lies hidden in much of ordinary experience.
[10] See Levinas, "Questions and Answers" in *Of God Who Comes to Mind*, 86–90, esp. 89–90. In this conversation with de Boer, Levinas calls "exasperation" "a method of philosophy."
[11] See de Boer, *The Rationality of Transcendence*, 66–67; cf. Levinas, OB, 115.

Along with such devices, Levinas uses terms such as "obsession," "hostage," and "trauma" that are clearly metaphors intended to call attention to features of the face-to-face, not literally true but rhetorically, figuratively surprising and disturbing. Regularly, such terms are meant as alternatives to standard philosophical vocabulary. Just as "face" is meant to suggest a mode of presence that is particular, demonstrative, and petitionary, as distinct from the merely presentational character of an appearance or impression, so "substitution" and "hostage" are meant to suggest the self's being burdened, called, bound, and being responsible for representing the other, in a way that mere identity or surrogacy does not. These suggestive associations, moreover, incline away from the intellectualism of traditional terminology and the visual, presentational tone of conventional language; they also incline away from the utilitarian character of language, as Heidegger saw it, the language of use, equipment, and of being ready to be used. The terms and metaphors Levinas employs, in contrast, suggest being bound, being under a burden of need and urgency, and being called or summoned in an ultimate way, associated with divine command: from "obsession" and "hostage" to "accusation," "glory," and "election."

As de Boer sees, however, all such talk of using terms nonliterally, of employing figures like repetition and exaggeration or hyperbole, will not answer the real question of expressibility and its limits. This is how de Boer reads Derrida's challenge in "Violence and Metaphysics," that "as soon as it speaks, philosophy is also a *Dit*, something said, a formulation in language. . . . It seems, then, that metaphysics is necessarily reduced to phenomenology (ontology)." In Derrida's terms, Levinas's philosophy suffers from an "inner antinomy. It would discuss a realm beyond being in a language which can be used to describe being only."[12] In short, Levinas can never leave the domain of totality, of thought and language. Or, to put it differently, the relation between persons can take place only within totality; nothing transcendent can be thought or spoken of. If philosophy speaks, it speaks within totality, and if Levinas claims for philosophy a speech about the face, then that, too, occurs within totality. We cannot stand where we stand and reach beyond in thought or speech.

Clearly, Levinas recognizes this challenge as a serious one; it is one reason for his having written *Otherwise Than Being*.[13] He calls it a "methodological problem" and a seeming "betrayal" – "whether the pre-original element of saying . . . can be led to betray itself by showing itself in a theme . . . and whether this betrayal can be reduced."[14] "The very task of philosophy," he says, "becomes

[12] See de Boer, *The Rationality of Transcendence*, 67–71, for de Boer's statement of the problem.
[13] See OB, 5–7, esp. 7; see also 165–71.
[14] OB, 7.

possible [in this] indiscretion with regard to the unsayable."[15] That is, in order for there to be philosophy, it must go beyond ontology and expose the face, the infinite, to clarify it and its significance. But by doing this, philosophy in a sense incorporates the face into its structure, its categories, and its domain. It "thematizes" the face, thereby neutralizing its otherness, its transcendence. It expresses the inexpressible, says the unsayable, and hence betrays itself and fails to grasp the face in its alterity. In Derrida's terms, all metaphysics is violent; there is no humility and deference in it.[16] Levinas appreciates that his philosophical work threatens either to compromise the very character of the face of the other as other or to compromise philosophy and the possibility of disclosing the face in the course of philosophical discourse.

LEVINAS AND SKEPTICISM: TIME AND ABSOLUTE DIACHRONY

De Boer points out that Levinas, in *Otherwise Than Being*, appeals to the role of skepticism in Western philosophy in order to respond to Derrida's criticism.[17] There has been extensive discussion of Levinas's strategy here, and it is important for us to reconsider and clarify exactly what Levinas says.[18] For it is skepticism that reveals the absolute diachrony that is unique to the saying and the said, totality and infinity, everyday experience and the face-to-face.

I want to back into Levinas's use of skepticism, as it were, by discussing first a short essay, first published in 1980 and later included as the final chapter in *Of God Who Comes to Mind* in 1986. It is called "Manner of Speaking," and it deals with philosophy, language, and knowledge.[19] Expressly, as Levinas puts it, the essay is about "the contradiction of principle" involved in "theoretically" asserting the "independence of ethical intelligibility relative to thought and to being."[20]

Philosophy claims knowledge of what is and how it is; this even applies, Levinas says, when Plato discusses the One in the first hypothesis in the second part of the *Parmenides* and seeks to "demonstrate" the separation of "the One and . . . being." "The classical refutation of skepticism," he says, is a "model" of this demonstration insofar as, like it, "the refutation . . . has never

[15] OB, 7.

[16] De Boer, *The Rationality of Transcendence*, 68. He compares it to Wittgenstein in the *Tractatus*, 69.

[17] De Boer, *The Rationality of Transcendence*, 71–73, 81–82; see also OB, 7, 153–62.

[18] For an excellent discussion, see Critchley, *The Ethics of Deconstruction*, 156–69.

[19] On skepticism and its persistence, see also Levinas, "Humanism and An-archy" in *Collected Philosophical Papers*, 128.

[20] "Manner of Speaking" in *Of God Who Comes to Mind*, 178.

prevented the return and the renewal of skeptical discourse, nor its pretension to a philosophical dignity."[21] Negation or refutation *does not prevent* the return of thought and the negation of the negation, that is the affirmation of a further, more serious truth. The "classical refutation of skepticism," then, is a *model* of a similar but *deeper* return central to philosophy itself.[22] Levinas offers a comparison: Just as "the indicative proposition . . . might carry and embody the *question* as a derived modality of the assertion [that is, the interrogative mode derives from the indicative]," so the philosopher can consider the *question* and "search for its proper, original meaning," all the way back to its ethical ground. It is no mere *metaphor*, Levinas points out, that "rationality might call itself *justification* and not always demonstration [that is, the ground of rationality is ethical], or that intelligibility refers to justice."[23] As he puts it, "philosophy can hear these reasons [that is justice] behind the ontological forms that reflection reveals to it." This is the "enigma of philosophy" and its "permanent crisis." The "ontological" content of philosophy, that is, wants both to unsay itself and to be said.[24]

I have let Levinas speak in his own terms here, the terms of Heideggerian ontology and of Husserlian phenomenology. From his account, we can extract the following. First, Levinas is concerned with philosophy and how it conducts itself. Hence, the essay is about philosophical understanding and a certain tension within it, what he calls its "enigma" or "permanent crisis," that it has a certain cognitive character – the face-to-face and responsibility – and yet seeks to go beyond it, that it speaks both sense and nonsense and does so intentionally and in full view.[25] Second, the "classical refutation of skepticism" is a *model* of how this enigma or tension reveals itself. Skepticism is a philosophical stance regarding the knowledge philosophy seeks; it claims that such knowledge is impossible and thus is or proposes a "negation of truth." The refutation is the well-known claim that skepticism is self-refuting; it charges that the skeptic claims to *know* that *knowledge is impossible*. This refutation, however, "has never prevented" the return or persistence of the skeptical stance, the inclination to doubt the possibility of knowledge. The refutation seems true but is ineffective. Levinas asks why, and he answers: For the same reason that *the charge* **that genuine philosophy cannot assert that the ethical is independent of the real, that responsibility is separate from everyday life**, *is ineffective.*[26]

[21] "Manner of Speaking" in *Of God Who Comes to Mind*, 178.

[22] "Manner of Speaking" in *Of God Who Comes to Mind*, 179.

[23] "Manner of Speaking" in *Of God Who Comes to Mind*, 180.

[24] "Manner of Speaking" in *Of God Who Comes to Mind*, 180.

[25] See OB, 137.

[26] This criticism or charge against philosophy, that it cannot do what it claims to do, is how Levinas reads the Derridian objection, as I see it. Levinas's response is to show why the criticism seems true but is ineffective and thus why philosophy goes on nonetheless, just as skepticism goes on even given the apparent truth of the refutation of it.

Philosophy aims at justification, even while it claims knowledge. That is, while it presents itself as *knowing* human existence, philosophy in fact *justifies* it – that is, discloses its ethical ground. But, we ask, what is the *reason* behind skepticism's capacity to return, which means philosophy's capacity to withstand the attack on it? What is the *reason* behind philosophy's capacity to describe human existence and at the same time to justify it by referring to the face-to-face?

These are the questions that Levinas should answer in the crucial passages in *Otherwise Than Being*.[27] How is it possible for skepticism to go on, to return, in spite of the refutation of it? How is Levinas's philosophy possible, in spite of objections that it is in tension with itself? In a vocabulary that Levinas employs in the later essay, he says that philosophy works by a process of "alternation." Philosophical thinking, he says, "comes and goes between [the] two possibilities" of letting us see hidden meaning and freeing itself of the forms it uses to do so.[28] In *Otherwise Than Being*, Levinas calls this "an alternating which we find in the refutation and rebirth of skepticism"[29] and uses it to clarify how I can be understood as a unique I and also "in the concept" or as "an ego belonging to the concept of ego." As a unique I, he says, I am summoned, accused, obsessed, even as I am understood as a case of a universal – that is, as an ordinary person with various features and characteristics.

But to say that thinking alternates is not to clarify how such alternation is possible, and the crucial notions for explaining that possibility are "trace" and "diachrony."[30] "The order that orders me to the other does not show itself to me, save through the trace of its reclusion, as a face of a neighbor. There is a trace of a withdrawal which no actuality has preceded. . . . "[31] As philosophy alternates, that is, it moves back and forth from grasping the I as characterized as self, as father, as teacher, and so forth and grasping the I as always, at every moment, always already responsible, singled out, called, summoned, accused, and utterly unique. Whatever is understood to be my social relation to my neighbor – as brother, father, friend, colleague, and so forth – I am always already called and commanded to respond to her, her needs, and her suffering. Levinas calls this summons "glory" – one among his array of terms from religion and theology, terms that suggest elevation and ultimate worth – and says that it "could not appear, for appearing and presence would belie it by circumscribing it as a theme." Rather, "it comes from a past more distant than that which is within the reach of memory . . . from a past that has never been represented,

---

[27] OB, 7; 131–71, esp. 165–71.
[28] "Manner of Speaking" in *Of God Who Comes to Mind*, 180.
[29] OB, 139.
[30] See OB, 7, 140.
[31] OB, 140.

has never been present.... "[32] It is "older than every beginning" and prior to every present. It is permanently past, never synchronous with any present, *forever diachronous* – at every present instant unconditionally past, as we have seen. This is the sense of "always already," a phrase that we discussed earlier. Whatever my public, articulable relation to the other person, I am always also already responsible for her – responding, acknowledging or denying, accepting or avoiding her.

Why is it, however, that philosophical reflection on and exposure of the face, obsession, substitution, accusation, and so forth do not "reduce difference"?[33] Why is the other not qualifiedly different? Levinas claims that "what shows itself thematically in the synchrony of the said in fact lets itself be unsaid as a difference of what cannot be assembled.... The very exhibition of the difference goes diachronically from the said to the unsaid."[34] But this is just to say that the saying and the said, the face-to-face and all social relations, are *different* in some fundamental way. But how? Philosophy must somehow clarify this difference. Levinas takes philosophy to expose the apparent contradiction by "*reflection* on the condition of the statement that states this signification," that is, by thinking about the condition of the attempt to describe the face-to-face in words. Levinas proceeds to clarify what this "reflection on conditions" means:

[I]n this reflection, that is, only after the event, contradiction appears: it does not break out between two simultaneous statements, but *between a statement and its conditions, as though they were in the same time.* The statement of the beyond being, of the name of God, does not allow itself to be walled up in the conditions of its enunciation. It benefits from an *ambiguity* or an *enigma*, which is ... the effect ... of an extreme proximity of the neighbor, where the Infinite comes to pass" (my italics).[35]

What philosophy reveals, then, in its reflection on its own claims about the face-to-face and human existence, is the *condition*, different from those claims, that makes them possible. Similarly, in Kant space and time, the categories of the understanding, and the transcendental unity of apperception are the outcomes of transcendental argumentation and the objects of transcendental idealism; they are transcendentally ideal but not experientially real. In Levinas, this condition is a relation that seems contemporaneous with the state described by the philosophical claim itself, but in fact it occurs in a past never present, as what always is already so. Hence, philosophy carries out its business and, in its

[32] OB, 144.
[33] OB, 154–55.
[34] OB, 155.
[35] OB, 156.

own way, shows by misdirection what it purports to be describing but cannot succeed in so doing. The two poles of the seeming contradiction appear to be contemporaneous, but they are not so. One is present, the other past; indeed, whenever the one is present, the other is past. The condition – the justification, the face-to-face and responsibility – is *always past* and was never present.

Up to a point, then, this is Levinas's answer about how philosophy is possible without contradiction, without speaking nonsense. Philosophy is reflection after the fact of philosophy; it brings to attention what is "always already" so, the condition of its own statements or assertions.[36] Philosophy points in one direction while hinting in another. But if this dissolves the problem of philosophy, it does so only once philosophy is on the scene. However, Levinas asks why the problem ever arises: He asks, Why even talk about the face-to-face? Why invite contradiction? Why philosophy?[37]

The key to Levinas's answer is the permanent compromising of responsibility that he calls "justice" and that is generated by the presence of the third party. Social life and the demands of justice, that is, require comparison and system, thinking and evaluation. Levinas calls this a "betrayal of my anarchic relation with *illeity*, but also a new relationship with it."[38] Philosophy is an eventual outcome of this situation, of human social existence.[39] The special role of philosophy is to clarify how everyday social life "betrays" its deep dimension of responsibility and concern for others; philosophy's role is to expose the difference, the dissonance between ordinary life and its ethical foundation, so to speak.

Levinas argues this way. My "responsibility for others," Levinas says, in social life "bears witness to . . . this anarchic hither side" and is the locale for scientific, social scientific, and philosophical discourse.[40] Philosophy, he argues, comes with the issues and problems raised by justice – measurement, comparison, and assessment.[41] In social life, to use Levinas's terminology, "infinity or the transcendent" occurs always as a "trace" of a "past that was never present," and philosophical reflection is a constituent of social life as well as an examination of it. He calls this face, as *trace* of the other and its authority or *illeity*, "enigma," "ambivalence," and "ambiguity." Basically, it is "nonthematizable" and "ineffable," even though it is asserted and discussed, which Levinas calls a "betrayal which philosophy is called upon to reduce." That is, philosophy arises in order to speak about this trace and to show that it is diachronous with the said, with

[36] See OB, 7, where Levinas calls this a "secret diachrony."
[37] OB, 157.
[38] OB, 158.
[39] OB, 157–65.
[40] OB, 160.
[41] OB, 161.

social life, language, discourse, and so forth. It is the "wisdom of love at the service of love." Philosophy reflects on and exposes to view the difference of the face-to-face from everyday life and its role in that life; it "justifies and criticizes the laws of being and of the city."[42]

Philosophy arises in social life as a way to "justify" how human existence goes and how we live together. It also calls to our attention the standards for our evaluation and critique of social and political life. In these ways, philosophy is valuable and even, in a sense, necessary. In order to do its work, however, philosophy must analyze and clarify how life goes and also bring to light what everyday life tends to hide. Its crucial insight is that life and responsibility occur together and yet are different; they "assemble" but do not occur at the same time. In this respect, philosophy recognizes something that skepticism also recognizes, what Levinas calls the diachrony of the saying and the said. Just as skepticism raises its doubts, is subject to refutation, and yet returns, so philosophy justifies and criticizes social life, is attacked for speaking the unspeakable, and yet recovers by showing that the standard of justice is not an attempt to realize justice but a demand to do so.

SKEPTICISM IN *OTHERWISE THAN BEING*

In the final section of Chapter 5 of *Otherwise Than Being*, titled "Skepticism and Reason," Levinas explains how these conclusions are got. First, Levinas characterizes systematic, conscious thought as reason; he associates it with the tasks of uniting terms, of representation, and of spontaneity. But, he says, one can and must ask if the beginning is absolute, if there is not in a sense an "anarchy," a nonorigin, more ancient than every beginning. Reason asks about the limits of system. Being together with my neighbor, talking or acting, is there not, even prior to our "community," a proximity? "The unity of the human race is in fact posterior to fraternity."[43] Strictly speaking, as Levinas emphasizes, this proximity or fraternity is "indescribable, . . . unconvertible into a history, irreducible to the simultaneousness of writing. . . ."[44] But philosophy does designate this fraternity as a feature of my social life that always has been fixed, a responsibility that I have already, no matter what else I am doing or saying. Levinas calls this proximity a "pre-original reason that does not proceed from any initiative of the subject, an anarchic reason."[45] It is not absorbed into system, into the "reason characteristic of justice, the state, thematization, synchronization,

---

[42] OB, 165.
[43] OB, 166.
[44] OB, 166.
[45] OB, 166.

representation.... "[46] Philosophy works, as he says, by "alternation" and "diachrony," just as does *skepticism* and the *refutation of skepticism*. Here Levinas describes "the return of skepticism" and its refutation as a "temporality." He puts it this way: "Skepticism, which traverses the rationality or logic of knowledge, is a refusal to synchronize the implicit affirmation contained in saying and the negation which this affirmation states in the said."[47] Philosophical reflection exposes this contradiction as only apparent, as mistaken; skepticism is "insensitive" to the refutation of it, for skepticism, like philosophy – or better, *as philosophy*, realizes that the affirmation and the negation – its own affirmation that knowledge is impossible – do not *occur in the same time*, as it were. "It is as though skepticism were sensitive to the difference between my exposure without reserve to the other, which is saying, and the exposition or statement of the said in its equilibrium and justice."

Here Levinas takes a new and important step. Skepticism and its refutation are *not simply a model* for how philosophy must conduct itself. They are more important than a model or analogy; "philosophy is not separable from skepticism." Philosophy does have the last word, he says, but only because skepticism always returns. The real truth of skepticism is what it, *as philosophy*, reveals: the difference between the saying and the said. "This return of the diachrony refusing the present makes up the invincible force of skepticism."[48] That is, the invincibility of skepticism, its immunity to refutation, shows what philosophy seeks to expose, for that invincibility, which is actual, is only possible if the very challenge to philosophy is an act in response to a summons always already present when the challenge is made. Hence, as Levinas elliptically puts it, "language is already skepticism."[49] Speech or discourse, claiming to totalize, belies that claim by disclosing what founds it; just as skepticism does in its return after refutation, in its refusal to go away, and its resiliency. System already involves "repression"; "structures ... are not the ultimate framework of meaning."[50] Rationality and logic are, at bottom, politics.

On the one hand, then, Levinas takes skepticism to be a *model* or *analogy* for how philosophy reveals the difference between the saying and the said, between responsibility and the face and the ordinary world of which it is the condition

---

[46] OB, 167.
[47] OB, 167. In this sentence, "traverse" means to oppose or deny or reject; skepticism is the denial of the possibility of rational knowledge. But, in denying knowledge in its explicit assertion or claim, skepticism, philosophy shows, refuses to or is unable to "synchronize" the affirmation that the ethical expresses and the negation that the claim makes – that is, it looks like it is treating them as simultaneous, but in fact it shows that they are not simultaneous.
[48] OB, 168–69, 171.
[49] OB, 170.
[50] OB, 170, 171.

and standard. It is in this way that Levinas claims that philosophy is not nonsense. For its use of language to describe the face-to-face and to characterize its role, even if itself meaningless within the compass of everyday language and thought, does go on, and its going on is only possible if it is meaningful, if the relation it designates is a condition for the very possibility of its asserting anything at all. On the other hand, skepticism in all its tenacity is *more than a model*. It is how a philosophical reflection on social life and its groundedness in the face-to-face is carried out. It is that mode of philosophy that reveals the truth of philosophy, its love of justice, its striving for justification for social life. Skepticism is at once the denial of philosophy and its *most essential expression*.

How should we understand this final claim: that skepticism – the return or invincibility of skepticism – is the most essential expression of philosophy, and hence that "language is already skepticism"? One key is Levinas's statement that in skepticism the affirmation and the negation *do not occur in the same time*. In one sense, this is false. If the skeptic says "knowledge is impossible," his claiming to know and what he claims to know are said at the same time. Furthermore, if skepticism is philosophy and language is skepticism, then it is not the claiming to know and what the skeptic claims to know that are at issue. It is something deeper. These two may generate the contradiction that the refutation has in mind, but it is not the duality that skepticism takes note of, reveals, and sees as "diachronous" and hence not really contradictory. This latter, deeper duality is between the saying and the said – between the claiming that knowledge is impossible, made to the believer or interlocutor, and the face-to-face, which occurs as well. Or, to put it otherwise, the duality to which skepticism – and philosophy and language – calls attention is between the act of challenging the believer's, and everyone's, claim to knowledge and the responsibility to the believer that is involved in the response to the believer's summons or command. These differ as act-descriptions; they characterize different relations. But they occur together, at the same time. Why does Levinas say that they do not? Why are they, in his terminology, diachronous? Because, as he sees it, he does not say that they are not synchronous. Rather than say that both act-descriptions are true simultaneously, we are more correct to say that in registering doubt *to* the believer, the skeptic is always already responsible to him. That is, whatever he does will constitute, prior to his deliberation or choice, an acknowledgment and acceptance of the believer. The act-descriptions may be synchronous, but the skeptic's being responsible is not. At the time of any and every skeptical challenge, the skeptic always already is responsible. The command-summons always already has occurred; it never *occurs* then and there, but rather it is always the case that it *has occurred*, as it were. It is a relation that *always already has existed*. In this sense, it is a *condition* of the skeptical encounter that is never synchronous with it.

Levinas's language here and elsewhere, as we discussed in Chapter 2, suggests that he took his method to be phenomenological, insofar as it is akin to an intentional analysis that reveals a horizon of meaning hidden from view, and transcendental, in that this horizon of meaning – the face – is a condition for the possibility of all social interaction. This condition, however, is not a feature or property of the self *per se*; it is rather the outcome of the self's being called into question by each other person. It is, as he puts it, a responsibility that is the outcome of an event that never occurred, a unique interpersonal encounter that is reiterated infinitely. What distinguishes it, however, is that the event never *occurs*; it *always already has occurred*, as it were. That is, because it is a condition for each and every episode of social interaction or social relation, no matter whether proximate or distal, it is a *permanent* condition; but as the outcome of an event of address or encounter, it can be said to be permanent only by saying that it always has already occurred, and this is what Levinas means when he calls it a "past that was never present" or the memory of an immemorial present. Skepticism and the refutation of skepticism bring this difference to light, and in doing so they constitute a paradigm of philosophical disclosure.

Language does this too. Hence, in a way, "skepticism is already language." In philosophy, then, language about the face-to-face discloses, in its performance, the face-to-face, not by description but by calling to mind the way skepticism returns and the reason it does so. Moreover, the terms it uses – "face," "trauma," "obsession," "enigma," "accusation," and more – call attention to the way the encounter with the other is not intellectual but akin to the practical, the imperative, and the petitionary. There is always a gap between the meaning of such terms and the face-to-face that is revealed or disclosed, between the description and the pointing, and language acknowledges that gap and even emphasizes it. Talking about the face of the other philosophically is both impossible and necessary.

TWO INTERPRETATIONS OF LEVINAS AND SKEPTICISM

Two very prominent commentators have read Levinas's appropriation of skepticism and the problem of language and expressibility somewhat differently than I have. It is worth looking at their accounts. The first is Theodore de Boer in *The Rationality of Transcendence*; the second is Robert Bernasconi in "Skepticism in the Face of Philosophy."[51]

De Boer asks: "How does philosophy [for Levinas] save itself from this precarious position, in which it tries to express the inexpressible?" How can it

---

[51] De Boer, *The Rationality of Transcendence*, Ch. 3, esp. 70–82; Bernasconi, "Skepticism in the Face of Philosophy" in *Re-reading Levinas*, 149–61.

"thematize being" and "at the same time . . . raise our gaze 'beyond being'?" How can it be both a saying of the said and an unsaying of it?[52] According to de Boer, Levinas defends this double operation of philosophy in *Otherwise Than Being* by appealing to skepticism, which keeps returning, even after it has been refuted. The skepticism debate tells us how philosophy can function. "Philosophy lures skepticism into the trap of self-refutation," but in fact it also traps skepticism's assumption that its claiming and the claim itself do not take place at the same time, Levinas argues. "The skeptic speaks, as it were, in two tenses," and "the same is true of philosophy."[53] De Boer takes Levinas to be alluding to Husserl's comments on skepticism in the *Logical Investigations* and the distinction between "the performative act of assertion and the asserted content."[54] There is a temporal difference between the act of assertion and the asserted content, which is the same temporal difference as that between the saying and the said that philosophy reveals. Philosophy capitalizes on this same "diachrony" that skepticism employs. De Boer calls the conflict in skepticism a "pragmatic paradox" and asks whether Levinas's philosophy can be saved by the comparison with the return of skepticism. His answer: No.[55] Why?

To be precise, de Boer says that his "initial" answer is that the reference to skepticism does not solve Levinas's problem about philosophy because while it calls attention to the distinction between the speech-act of asserting and the asserted content, this is not the distinction Levinas needs between the speaking self and its responsibility. This distinction marks a deeper "diachrony," de Boer says, than skepticism reveals and than philosophy seems to be able to reach.[56]

This response is de Boer's initial "no." But, he argues, Levinas does not stop here. He suggests that philosophy – ontology – already includes "breaks" or "gaps" that point beyond itself to the reader, whose experience is already, through experience, attuned to follow the clues, to look "outside." Expressions like "heteronomy of freedom" point beyond traditional philosophy and everyday life to something already experienced but thus far not identified or designated. When or if we take these metaphysical statements literally or conventionally, we "misunderstand." They are intended to point to gaps or lacks in traditional Western language and conceptions. De Boer claims that Levinas's metaphysics is a response to a lived sense of "unrest and longing," which "manifest themselves in the very heart of *theoria* and *praxis*." This is what is meant by following, or tracking, the said to the saying or the unsaid to the

[52] De Boer, *The Rationality of Transcendence*, 70.
[53] De Boer, *The Rationality of Transcendence*, 71.
[54] De Boer, *The Rationality of Transcendence*, 72.
[55] That is, the "initial" answer is No. See de Boer, *The Rationality of Transcendence*, 73.
[56] De Boer, *The Rationality of Transcendence*, 73.

face-to-face.[57] De Boer takes this to be accomplished through language or better, what Levinas calls "an abuse of language" or "the pain of expression." "Language," de Boer says, "is pressed to yield a new or forgotten meaning,"[58] and the language involved is ethical and religious, terms such as "hospitality," "goodness," "justice," "responsibility," "witness," "prophecy," and "inspiration." Hence, Levinas seeks to "give expression to a pre-philosophical experience of existence."[59] Based on this reading of Levinas's exaggerated use of language and his ethico-religious terminology, which call attention to what is revealed in prephilosophical experience, de Boer proposes "another interpretation of the skepticism argument," whereby we take "the return to saying as a return to a 'pre-historcian ontificating' saying," that is, the return of skepticism shows that there is a dimension of experience, the face-to-face and infinite responsibility, hidden from all language and yet primary to it. Skepticism shows us that *"more can be said than that which is."*[60]

This is one conclusion that I came to earlier by reading "Skepticism and Reason" in *Otherwise Than Being*. The return of skepticism – its resiliency and invincibility – reveals more than the distinction between the act of assertion and the asserted content. It reveals also the distinction between both of these and the face-to-face as a condition and determining dimension of all social interaction. But I went further. For de Boer, skepticism remains a model – for Levinas's ways of using language philosophically to designate the face-to-face. On my reading, Levinas argues that philosophy is necessary, that skepticism is necessary or essential to philosophy, and that language is itself skepticism. It is not *like* skepticism; it is a form of it. In what sense? Insofar as language applied to the face-to-face *and* even in everyday life *always* discloses the said and points to the saying; it says and unsays at once. In this way, language *is* skepticism.[61]

---

[57] De Boer, *The Rationality of Transcendence*, 75–77, esp. 76.

[58] De Boer, *The Rationality of Transcendence*, 77.

[59] De Boer, *The Rationality of Transcendence*, 79; cf. 37 n. 17.

[60] De Boer, *The Rationality of Transcendence*, 82.

[61] I think that Stanley Cavell means something like this when he talks about the truth or moral of skepticism. He also says something similar about film, especially those films he calls "comedies of remarriage." For Cavell, viewed from one angle, knowing and describing and asserting that the world is so and so or that people are such and such is already to acknowledge them. What Levinas adds, if we view it this way, is that acknowledging the other person is always "called for" or "summoned," as it were. Cavell wants to say, I think, that philosophy is not capable on its own – or perhaps at all – to show or depict this acknowledging, but certain types of film can do so. This is part of what he means, I believe, when he says that features of these comedies of remarriage are a "framing of the problem of other minds." Such film is philosophy. In a passage that I am not sure I understand completely and that I might be reading too much through the lens of the issues discussed here, Cavell describes this problem of other minds in the following way: "The existence of others is something of which we are unconscious, a piece of knowledge we repress, about which we draw a blank. This does violence to others, it

The problem we have been discussing is what Robert Bernasconi, in "Skepticism in the Face of Philosophy," calls "the second reason for Levinas's interest in skepticism."[62] As Bernasconi puts it, Levinas sees a parallel between the philosophical refutation of skepticism and the objection raised against his own philosophy that it contradicts itself when it purports to express in language what lies beyond the limits of expressibility. Bernasconi also underlines the fact that "Levinas is giving skepticism and its refutation the status of a metaphor or 'model.' He is not himself adopting a skeptical position."[63] True, in one sense. In another, however, as Bernasconi even suggests, "skepticism both is and is not philosophy";[64] skepticism may challenge philosophy, but it is also a permanent possibility of it. Wherever there is a commitment to gain knowledge, the possibility of doubt lurks as well.

Bernasconi, like de Boer, takes to be superficial the distinction between the act of asserting and the asserted content. Rather, by "disdain" for its refutation, skepticism shows something deeper: It plays by philosophy's rules and yet contests them – at once. Bernaconi quotes Levinas as saying that "it is *as though* skepticism were *sensitive* to *the difference*" between the face-to-face and everyday talk,[65] but he denies that here Levinas finds in skepticism a "recognition of the difference between the saying and the said."[66] Bernasconi takes the sensitivity to the difference to be based on skepticism's "inability to apply its denial of truth to its own claims . . . as if its saying did not occur 'at the same time' as its said." In this way, skepticism contests the comprehensiveness of Western philosophy.[67]

It will be helpful to stop here and clarify Bernasconi's reading. When skepticism challenges philosophy, it claims that knowledge is impossible. The philosopher, in his refutation, then responds that the skeptic is both claiming to know

---

separates their bodies from their souls, makes monsters of them; and presumably we do it because we feel that others are doing this violence to us. The release from this circle of vengeance is something I call acknowledgment. The form the man attempts to give acknowledgment is to tell their story. The film can be said to describe the failure of this attempt as a last attempt to substitute knowledge for acknowledgment, privacy for community, to transcend the barrier without transgressing it." Cavell calls this process an attempt to create "a little community of love . . . [that] is an emblem of the promise human society contains room for both, that the game is worth the candle. You cannot wait for the perfected community to be presented." Certain films disclose this process and hence, for Cavell, function the way that Levinas says skepticism, philosophy, and language do. I have quoted from Cavell, *Pursuits of Happiness*, 109. See also Cavell, *Philosophy the Day after Tomorrow*, Ch. 6, "What Is the Scandal of Skepticism?," 132–54.
[62] Bernasconi, "Skepticism in the Face of Philosophy" in *Re-reading Levinas*, 149.
[63] Bernasconi, "Skepticism in the Face of Philosophy" in *Re-reading Levinas*, 150.
[64] Bernasconi, "Skepticism in the Face of Philosophy" in *Re-reading Levinas*, 151.
[65] OB, 168 (italics mine).
[66] Bernasconi, "Skepticism in the Face of Philosophy" in *Re-reading Levinas*, 151.
[67] I am not here interested in the whole of Bernasconi's intriguing paper, only in its early pages: "Skepticism in the Face of Philosophy" in *Re-reading Levinas*, 149–53.

and ruling out or denying knowledge. How does the skeptic continue? One view is this: The skeptic denies the refutation by pointing to the distinction between his asserting and what he has asserted and by claiming that they occur at different times. The latter does not contradict the former. But the problem here is that the assertion or doubt is general and timeless; hence, it does not matter that the act of asserting occurs at a particular time. The refutation goes through; the rejoinder fails. For this reason, we should try another interpretation of the skeptic's response. The skeptic does not comprehend the refutation; the latter tells the skeptic to apply his universal doubt to his own act of assertion, but the skeptic fails to do this or fails to understand how he can. Bernasconi says that the skeptic is unable to apply his denial or doubt to his own assertion. Why? For Bernasconi, I think, the reason is that there is a temporal similarity between this situation and that of all language and hence of philosophy too. Just as ordinary discourse attests to the self's responsibility, which always already has been established and thus is unqualifiedly diachronic, a past that was never present, so the skeptic's asserting is always already past when he asserts that knowledge is impossible. On any occasion when the skeptic utters that statement, it already has been uttered. He cannot, that is, attend to it by uttering it and attend to it as being uttered by him then at the same time.[68]

I am not convinced that Bernasconi's suggestion about why skepticism cannot *follow* or *grasp* the refutation is correct. Let me come back to that. But on the other hand, I am sure that he is right that Levinas's point is that in skepticism's response is revealed or disclosed the face-to-face and the distinction between the saying and the said. However, he insists that in this respect skepticism is a model for language and for philosophy, both of which also disclose this difference.[69] Levinas certainly is not supporting skepticism in the narrow sense: as a position of doubt about knowledge. Bernasconi emphasizes this. But he is urging the ubiquity of skepticism and what is central to it and thus one thing that it shares with language and with philosophy. Insofar as all disclose the unsayable, the face, all are the same, which is why he can say that language is skepticism and not just like it. I think that Bernasconi sees this identification and takes it seriously.[70]

This cannot be a correct reading of Bernasconi, however. I have claimed that Bernasconi takes skepticism to be a model for language and philosophy, that its "inability to apply its denial of truth to its own claims" is like the way language and philosophy disclose the face-to-face and responsibility. But Bernasconi says

[68] Cf. Richard Moran, *Authority and Estrangement: An Essay on Self-Knowledge* (Princeton, NJ: Princeton University Press, 2001). Is the attending to it externally even attending to the same thing he is doing in uttering it?

[69] See Bernasconi, "Skepticism in the Face of Philosophy" in *Re-reading Levinas*, 152.

[70] Bernasconi, "Skepticism in the Face of Philosophy" in *Re-reading Levinas*, 152–53.

that language and philosophy, and "not only skepticism," are "sensitive to the interval between the saying and the said." Skepticism challenges truth, just as Levinas says philosophy should do, by "subordinating truth to ethics."[71] This is why I said that all three share something deep. But if so, how is skepticism's inability also a *sensitivity* to the difference between itself and its responsibility? How is *that* difference disclosed in skepticism and to the skeptic?

The key to Bernasconi's reading is this: The skeptic's rejoinder is not to deny the refutation, nor is it to fail to grasp it. It is to return even though he cannot reply.[72] "In spite of losing the argument skepticism returns unabashed," and this is possible only if there is a "secret diachrony" that enables the skeptic to escape the contradiction.[73] That is, the skeptic *concedes* the argument and yet goes on as a skeptic. This is a fact. Yet because no articulable distinction enables this fact, it must be one that cannot be articulated or thematized. Explicitly, Bernasconi points out, Levinas finds no "recognition of the difference" in skepticism; his point is that in order to accept the refutation and still return, it must thereby be showing that it is sensitive to such a difference. Bernasconi never precisely explains what about the skeptic's thinking underlies this sensitivity. In the end, he believes that Levinas does not either. He affirms the sensitivity, and that is that. Skepticism's *tenacity* or its *bold resiliency*, then, shows how one can talk about the inexpressible without falling into contradiction.

As I remarked earlier, I wonder if we can do better. Can we try to clarify how and why the skeptic accepts the refutation, which claims that he is self-refuting, and yet goes on nonetheless, and especially *how* that sequence involves, even if not consciously for him, the face-to-face, the sense in which the epistemological exchange has a primary ethical dimension? Here is one attempt. The refutation of skepticism depends upon skepticism; to accept the refutation and cease to be a skeptic negates the refutation in succumbing to it. To continue to live, then, is to act in its behalf, to respond to it by "feeding it out of one's own mouth." It is an act of generosity. Indeed, the other demands but also petitions; the skeptic's articulate challenge is like a master's command that a slave commit suicide. To do so would be to negate the master's status. The invincibility of skepticism keeps alive its refutation.

This proposal strikes me as too narrow, perhaps, although I think that it inclines in the right direction. Levinas notes that "if, after the innumerable 'irrefutable' refutations which logical thought sets against it, skepticism has the

---

[71] Bernasconi, "Skepticism in the Face of Philosophy" in *Re-reading Levinas*, 152.

[72] The skeptic continues to return, even though he has no reason to do so. Bernasconi takes this to be a historical fact, which Levinas thinks can be explained or clarified only by referring to a difference that is unacknowledged by the skeptic and unknown to him.

[73] Bernasconi, "Skepticism in the Face of Philosophy" in *Re-reading Levinas*, 150; cf. Levinas OB, 7.

gall to return . . . , it is because . . . a secret diachrony commands this ambiguous or enigmatic way of speaking. . . . "[74] Later, at the end of his consideration of skepticism and reason, he notes that the "periodic rebirth of skepticism" shows that the contradiction in its refutation "does not strangle the speaker."[75] No matter how many times the philosopher refutes the skeptic by charging him with self-refutation, still the skeptic speaks and registers doubt about philosophy and knowledge. The skeptic continues the conversation.[76] For Levinas, we know, the "secret diachrony that commands" is the face of the other before whom we are always already at any time responsible to and for the other. If the skeptic, then, hears the refutation of the other person, the philosopher, and yet rejects or ignores it and "has the gall to return," he does so in response to that command. He continues to speak and, in so doing, responds to the other out of generosity and concern. He shows, thereby, that to respect the other person or character of philosophy in one sense requires of him that he disrespect it in another. If he simply accepted the refutation and remained silent, then he would (perhaps) have shown a different sort of respect and a different sort of disrespect, a sort not as deep, Levinas believes, as what he does show.

Let me compare the skeptic's return with the gratuitous act of kindness shown by the bereaved Russian woman toward the German officer, as Grossman describes it in *Life and Fate*. We cannot explain why she did not kill the officer out of rage and vengeance but rather offered him a piece of bread. In a sense, the act is inexplicable, but in another sense it reveals what Levinas calls here "a secret diachrony." It is understandable, then, but surprising or even stunning. Similarly, the skeptic's return is inexplicable or surprising. In one sense, insofar as the skeptic is a philosopher, we expect him to yield to a compelling argument. That he does not, that he continues to speak, is stunning. Why? Because we do not expect him to make metaphysics defer to ethics, and yet he does. It is best not to try too hard to "clarify" the skeptic's motives toward the philosopher other than to recognize that there would be no motive at all if it were not for the responsibility he senses toward him and that his "going on with him" discloses.

These thoughts encourage us to revise our earlier interpretation. The skepticism that reveals the face and this "secret diachrony" is the invincible, returning, persevering skepticism. It is just the skepticism that seems in one way to be philosophy no longer. Yet, I think, Levinas's point is that in an important sense

---

[74] OB, 7.

[75] OB, 171.

[76] How? Does he hear the refutation, so that even in refuting the skeptic, the refuter acknowledges him? Or does he respond by doubting the refutation? Or does he ignore the refutation and go on with his own doubts about knowledge and philosophy? All of these? Or something other than these?

all language, all philosophy, indeed all social interaction, is like that skepticism. It always has that hidden dimension, that "secret diachrony." Philosophy's use of language to designate the face-to-face is, in a way, simply an exaggerated case of every use of language, including ordinary, everyday discourse. It is just that the apparent ignoring of a contradiction, like skepticism's ignoring of the refutation of it, makes vivid the responsibility that the act reveals, or what he calls the difference between the saying and the said. When an act of ours looks altogether surprising and inexplicable in these settings, it has a great or special capacity to show us what grounds it, but in that respect such acts are not unique. The face, responsibility, and so forth are dimensions of all social life. Levinas's point here is that not all actions or discourse are equally stunning as vehicles to get us to appreciate this fact.

One way of reading the challenge to Levinas about philosophy, language, and the face-to-face is that philosophy never ultimately "reaches out to" the face. By designating it, the inexpressible is expressed or is left untouched. Philosophy ends up confined to totality in either case. Nonsense is either sense or nonsense. On my reading, however, attention to the refutation of skepticism and to the "return of skepticism," its invincibility or resiliency, shows that philosophy, language, and indeed all social life are not so confined. The face is disclosed by language, by everyday language, by philosophical discourse, and certainly by designating the face with terms like "hostage," "obsession," and "accusation." Levinas does not tell us how this occurs and in fact cannot tell us that. What he can show is that it must occur and does. That is the point of phenomena like the emphatic return of skepticism.[77] The domain of the inexpressible, the saying that is unsayable and so is not said, is unavoidable, a dimension of all social interaction and of all human life. We can ignore it or confuse it, but we cannot be rid of it. Levinas's philosophy invests everything in the otherness of the other that is beyond language, thought, and being; it is wholly taken up with saying the unsayable and the saying that is unsayable.

DERRIDA'S CHALLENGE

Suppose that Levinas's discussion of skepticism, then, is an attempt to show that we can, we must, and we do live with the inexpressibility of the face of the other person and that it is a response to Derrida. It is also the case that Derrida acknowledges a debt to Levinas, especially to his notion of the trace,

---

[77] In Cavell's terms, this is the truth or moral of "skepticism after the refutation of skepticism," to point out the relatedness of the self and the world, the self and other persons, that is not captured by cognitive considerations alone – that is, by the quest for truth. There is something beyond ontology, and it is ethics.

which, Derrida claims, is unthinkable and unsayable.[78] Bernasconi has written about Derrida's debt to Levinas. Analytic philosophers have found it useful to compare Derrida with Gotlob Frege and Wittgenstein on these matters, and looking at Bernasconi will prepare us to consider their discussion and the light it sheds on our understanding of Levinas.[79] The issues concern the limits of thought and expressibility and the nature of nonsense.

Let me make two asides before I turn to Bernasconi's essay. The first is about Levinas. There is a tendency to assimilate Levinas's face of the other person to the very notion of otherness itself or at least to think that for Levinas the face of the other person *is* the other. In our terms, this is to say that all social life involves a dimension of one unique person's being engaged by another unique person via a supplication, a call, a summons, and a command. But it is clear that one of Levinas's earliest convictions, part of his critique of Heidegger in the 1940s, is that each existing thing exists against the background of an inarticulable other, and indeed that each human being lives with respect to various others. In *Existence and Existents* and in *Time and the Other*, preeminently, Levinas calls attention to various experiences – limit experiences like insomnia, fatigue, and nausea – each of which points beyond itself to a dim, inarticulable, often foreboding backdrop, not an object of experience but rather a source for it, in a sense. What he calls the "there is" is such a source or backdrop, as are death and suffering. The other person, prior to or more primary than its presence as describable, experiencable, and so forth, is such an other. In Blanchot's phrase, this is a "knowledge of the unknown."[80] Hence, for Levinas, there are many domains that language points to but cannot grasp or designate. The face – as enigma, hostage, trauma, persecution, and the like – is the central one, but it is not exclusively inexpressible.

The second point I want to make is about Levinas's method and transcendental conditions in the Kantian sense.[81] We will come back to this point later, but it is worth mentioning here. One philosophical strategy for talking about what is outside everyday experience and discourse is to do so as part of a transcendental account of the conditions that make everyday experience possible but that are themselves ungraspable by such experience. If there is a sense in which the encounter with the face of the other can be understood as a transcendental condition for the possibility of social life, discourse, ethics, and so forth, then

---

[78] Bernasconi, "The Trace of Levinas in Derrida" in Wood and Bernasconi (eds.), *Derrida and Différance*, 13–29; see also Bernasconi, "The Silent Anarchic World of the Evil Genius" in *The Collegium Phaenomenologicum*, 257–72.

[79] See Simon Glendinning (ed.), *Arguing with Derrida* (Oxford: Blackwell, 2001).

[80] See Maurice Blanchot, *The Infinite Conversation* (Minneapolis: University of Minnesota Press, 1993), Ch. 5, "Knowledge of the Unknown," 49–58.

[81] See A. W. Moore, *Points of View*.

there is also a sense in which the face lies outside the bounds of language – that is, ordinary language. This is a path to clarifying the limits of language in Levinas that we ought later to consider. In Kantian terms, this would mean that the face is transcendentally ideal but not empirically real, so to speak. For the moment, however, let us turn to Bernasconi on Levinas and Derrida.

Ostensibly, Bernasconi's essay seeks to clarify if Derrida's positive acknowledgment of Levinas's notion of "the trace of the Other" in his lecture in 1968 "*La différance*" indicated a change in his attitude toward the inexpressibility of the face and a past never present, as spelled out in "Violence and Metaphysics" (1964).[82] The central issues of the essay concern the relation of the trace to ontology and language. I am less interested in the historical question Bernasconi sets for himself or even the question of Derrida's reading of Levinas and Heidegger than I am in what it means to treat the trace, and thus the face of the other person, as ineffable.[83] In the course of his analysis, Bernasconi notes Derrida's interest in "how Levinas seems to embrace the unthinkable"[84] and yet wonders whether this means "giving up philosophizing." As Bernasconi puts it, Derrida appears to take Levinas as "held to the tradition he seeks to escape" – that is, the grand metaphysical tradition of Parmenides, Hegel, and others; he seems to want to go beyond totality and yet is bound to it.[85] This is not contradictory; it is, Bernasconi claims, part of Derrida's view that Levinas seeks to point beyond philosophy, but only from within, by locating himself at the point where the dichotomy "inside-outside" no longer applies, is no longer exclusive.[86] Part of Derrida's change of attitude may be that he comes to think that Levinas is himself attentive to this special self-location – or at least that Derrida himself is more keenly aware of it.[87] In "Violence and Metaphysics," Derrida warns the reader against treating his comments as a critique. Rather, they are a reflection on the "meaning of a necessity: the necessity of lodging oneself within traditional conceptuality in order to destroy it."[88]

Let us move now to the notion of the "trace," of what Levinas says is the "presence of whoever, strictly speaking, has never been there; of someone who

[82] Bernasconi, "The Trace of Levinas in Derrida," in Wood and Bernasconi (eds.), *Derrida and Différance*, 13–14.

[83] As we have noted, Levinas introduces the notion of the trace in "The Trace of the Other" and in "Meaning and Sense" in *Collected Philosophical Papers*.

[84] Bernasconi, "The Trace of Levinas in Derrida" in *Derrida and Différance*, 16.

[85] Bernasconi, "The Trace of Levinas in Derrida" in *Derrida and Différance*, 16–17.

[86] Bernasconi, "The Trace of Levinas in Derrida" in *Derrida and Différance*, 17–18.

[87] Bernasconi, "The Trace of Levinas in Derrida" in *Derrida and Différance*, 18–19.

[88] Bernasconi, "The Trace of Levinas in Derrida" in *Derrida and Différance*, 19, quoting "Violence and Metaphysics," in *Writing and Difference*, 111.

is always past."[89] Bernasconi argues that the notion of trace is introduced as part of an attack on Heidegger and his "metaphysics of presence" but is present in *Totality and Infinity* in the idea that all language presupposes the face and the command "Thou shalt not kill."[90] Derrida sees the trace as present in contemporary philosophy and even earlier, at critical moments, in Western philosophy, when metaphysics *articulates* "from within the traces of the *before*, the *after*, and the *outside* of metaphysics."[91] For him, of course, the trace is not of the other, of the face and ultimately of *illeity*, but rather of a text; Bernasconi points this out.[92] And he draws the conclusion that for this reason Levinas would take Derrida to be insufficiently radical and bound to totality.[93]

A central point for us, then, is Bernasconi's convincing argument that Derrida is *not criticizing* Levinas when he says that Levinas uses language to designate the ineffable, that Levinas stays within the tradition of philosophy and metaphysics while pointing beyond it. This is to be located at the point where philosophy breaks up, in a sense. It is the point where the limits of philosophy are exposed – but only to philosophy.[94] This location is very important to Derrida, of course, as it is to Stanley Cavell, Richard Rorty, and Bernard Williams and to recent interpreters of Wittgenstein, especially those who emphasize, like Putnam, the therapeutic character of philosophy. It is the point where philosophy articulates the limits of expressibility by saying what cannot be said. Derrida finds Levinas, like himself, at that point, but it is a place of risk and uncertainty for him, while for Levinas it is a place where responsibility is exposed as original, fundamental, and determinative for human existence.

CONTEMPORARY PHILOSOPHY AND THE LIMITS OF THOUGHT AND LANGUAGE

For our purposes, the issue here is whether one can, within philosophy or every-day life, speak the ineffable or say the unsayable. Twentieth-century philosophers, addressing such a question, have turned to Kant, Wittgenstein, J. L. Austin, and Cavell and argued that all of them have sought to expose features of

---

[89] Bernasconi, "The Trace of Levinas in Derrida" in *Derrida and Différance*, 19, quoting "The Trace of the Other," 45.

[90] Bernasconi, "The Trace of Levinas in Derrida" in *Derrida and Différance*, 20–21.

[91] Bernasconi, "The Trace of Levinas in Derrida" in *Derrida and Différance*, 23, quoting Derrida, *Speech and Phenomena* (Evanston, IL: Northwestern University Press, 1973), 127 n. 14.

[92] Bernasconi, "The Trace of Levinas in Derrida" in *Derrida and Différance*, 24.

[93] Bernasconi, "The Trace of Levinas in Derrida" in *Derrida and Différance*, 25–26; cf. Levinas, OB, 44.

[94] See Bernard Williams, *Ethics and the Limits of Philosophy* (Cambridge, MA: Harvard University Press, 1985).

human experience – thought and speech – that cannot be described in thought and speech precisely because they are conditions for them and not facts represented in them. Among these contemporary philosophers are A. W. Moore in his book *Points of View*, Graham Priest in *Beyond the Limits of Thought*, and the participants in a conference, sponsored by the journal *Ratio* in Reading in 1999, on Anglo-American philosophy and Derrida.[95] Is Levinas's philosophical effort to say the "unsaid" comparable to Derrida's treatment of "*la différance*," and, as these philosophers have argued, to Kant, Wittgenstein, and Austin? Let me look first at the proceedings of the 1999 conference "Arguing with Derrida," in which these issues about language and expressibility are addressed.[96] My strategy is to show how contemporary philosophers – here, A. W. Moore and Abraham Priest, for example – use a certain reading of Frege and Wittgenstein to interpret Derrida. Then I will introduce a recent alternative reading of Wittgenstein on nonsense in order to locate the most fruitful way of reading Levinas on the inexpressibility of transcendence.

At the conference on Derrida, the discussion of nonsense and ineffability begins with A. W. Moore's presentation. Moore seeks to locate "some important points of contact between conceptual philosophy [his term for analytic philosophy] and the work of Derrida."[97] He begins by reminding us of Frege's point, developed by Wittgenstein, that language sometimes misses thought in the sense that language is used to call attention to something it cannot characterize and that the reader will have to concede this, "to begrudge a pinch of salt."[98] Wittgenstein says the same of his *Tractatus*, that it is an attempt to say what cannot be said, that it is nonsense, and that the reader should throw away what he says – doctrines and theories – once they have been used, like a ladder once climbed. Moore uses these materials to construct an argument either that conceptual philosophy is not really philosophy, because what it says about the "ineffable unity – of language, of reality, and of language with reality" – is nonsense, or that it is very impoverished philosophy.[99]

Here is where Moore finds a kinship with Derrida, particularly in his essay "La Différance."[100] In this essay, Moore claims, Derrida is "directing our attention to... something that is in some important sense ineffable" insofar as it

[95] A. W. Moore, *Points of View*; Graham Priest, *Beyond the Limits of Thought*.
[96] Simon Glendinning (ed.), *Arguing with Derrida*.
[97] A. W. Moore, "Arguing with Derrida" in Glendinning (ed.), *Arguing with Derrida*, 60.
[98] Moore, "Arguing with Derrida" in Glendinning (ed.), *Arguing with Derrida*, 62; referring to Frege, "On Concept and Object," in P. T. Geach, *Translations from the Philosophical Writings of G. Frege* (Oxford: Blackwell, 1952), 54.
[99] Moore, "Arguing with Derrida" in Glendinning (ed.), *Arguing with Derrida*, 63.
[100] Moore, "Arguing with Derrida" in Glendinning (ed.), *Arguing with Derrida*, 63. On 63 n. 12, Moore refers to Graham Priest, *Beyond the Limits of Thought*, Part 4, esp. Ch. 12 and 14.

"resists expression by any *customary* linguistic means," that is, "resists expression by means of the affirmation of truths."[101] In the text Moore discusses, Derrida calls this something "*différance*" and also "trace" – of what can never be presented and that itself can never by presented. This something cannot be named, then, or described or identified. As Moore notes, calling on Geoffrey Bennington's commentary, *différance* is not a concept or an object; it is the condition of names and concepts.

Moore does not explore what Derrida takes *différance* to be about. He is interested in its form, not its content, as it were. He wants to notice, that is, that just as Frege and Wittgenstein acknowledge and even focus on the ineffable as somehow fundamental, so does Derrida.[102] In one sense, we cannot think about or describe *différance*; in another sense, we can speak about it so that the reader's attention can be directed to it. And this use of language can be performed as part of an attempt – we might call it "transcendental" – to locate, identify, put us in mind of the conditions of language and thought about the world. Moore's own view is that philosophy's real business is to identify and affirm truths; some things are ineffable, he agrees, but philosophy's primary interests should be to determine those truths that apply to the ineffable and to go on from there.[103] That is, Moore takes there to be ineffable knowledge, which cannot be put in propositional form but which can be put to use, so to speak. He never explains, even during the discussion after his talk, what knowledge is associated with insight into *différance*, but he does say that wherever there is ineffable knowledge, it does mean something to one who has it, because it concerns how he or she goes about doing things – like thinking, speaking, and acting.[104] What I think Moore has in mind is that in addition to the things we need to believe or know or want in order to go about living our lives, there are things we need to know about in order to be persons at all. This latter repertoire is ineffable knowledge or at least incorporates elements of ineffable knowledge. *Différance* is or might be part of that repertoire, as might the face of the other, he would say.

Graham Priest's book *Beyond the Limits of Thought* is about the limits of thought or conceptual limits in Western philosophy. In the cases that interest him, "there is a totality (of all things expressible, describable, etc.) and an appropriate operation that generates an object that is both within and without the totality." He calls these situations, respectively, "closure" and "transcendence."[105] In Chapters 12 and 14, he discusses this framework in Frege

[101] Moore, "Arguing with Derrida" in Glendinning (ed.), *Arguing with Derrida*, 63–64.
[102] See Moore, "Arguing with Derrida" in Glendinning (ed.), *Arguing with Derrida*, 65.
[103] Moore, "Arguing with Derrida" in Glendinning (ed.), *Arguing with Derrida*, 68.
[104] Moore, "Arguing with Derrida" in Glendinning (ed.), *Arguing with Derrida*, 69–82.
[105] Priest, *Beyond the Limits of Thought*, 4.

and Wittgenstein and then in Derrida.[106] Like Moore, Priest rehearses Frege's problem with the notorious example "the concept *horse*": "Frege needs to be able to talk about concepts in order to express his own theory. Yet he cannot do so (meaningfully) by his own theory."[107] Hence, the outcome is that "much, including his own theory, [is] beyond the limit of the expressible."[108] Wittgenstein extends the point, to show that language has a limit, with what lies beyond it being "nonsense."[109] What language cannot point to or describe, then, is nonsense (*Unsinn*); it is, Priest claims, the logical form of sentences that represents the structure or form of facts. It is shown, however, even when it cannot be said or expressed.[110] Priest explicitly compares these structural facts, which Wittgenstein discusses and yet which he claims can be shown but not said, with the *objects* (*sic*) of Kant's transcendental idealism – that is, with Kantian noumena.[111] Wittgenstein sees the problem and "faces it squarely," even solves it (Priest's words) in *Tractatus* 6.54, when he says that his propositions serve as "elucidations" that the understanding reader should recognize as "nonsensical," a ladder once used but then to be thrown away.[112] Priest, however, denies that this is a solution: Wittgenstein's sentences either are nonsense or can be understood, but not both.[113]

Moore's diagnosis of Frege and the early Wittgenstein shares a good deal with Priest's, and both follow a standard pattern. Let us follow Priest, then, as he uses these results to understand Derrida. Priest takes Derrida to be concerned with the indeterminacy of meaning or sense[114] and to raise the question: If meaning is not grounded in a "semantic correlate" such as a Platonic form, Aristotelian essence, or Lockean concept, how is meaning determined or fixed?[115] His answer is that all there is are texts; nothing outside of them can fix meaning. All that exists are the "differences and deferrals" among texts, a phenomenon that Derrida calls "*différance*."[116] It is a phenomenon grounded in the fact that texts and words can mean different things in different contexts, a fact that Derrida

---

[106] Prior to these chapters, Priest discusses these issues in Plato and neo-Platonism, Aristotle, Anselm, Kant, Hegel, and others. He also discusses Quine and Davidson.

[107] Priest, *Beyond the Limits of Thought*, 200.

[108] Priest, *Beyond the Limits of Thought*, 200.

[109] Priest, *Beyond the Limits of Thought*, 200–1.

[110] Priest, *Beyond the Limits of Thought*, 201.

[111] Priest, *Beyond the Limits of Thought*, 210.

[112] Priest, *Beyond the Limits of Thought*, 210.

[113] See Priest, *Beyond the Limits of Thought*, 211–13, for a summary.

[114] Priest compares Derrida to the later Wittgenstein and to Quine and Davidson; see Priest, *Beyond the Limits of Thought*, 235–45. For a very interesting discussion of Derrida and Davidson, see Samuel C. Wheeler, *Deconstruction as Analytic Philosophy* (Stanford, CA: Stanford University Press, 2000).

[115] Priest, *Beyond the Limits of Thought*, 236.

[116] Priest, *Beyond the Limits of Thought*, 238.

calls "interability."[117] In Derrida's account, then, *différance* "is the structure that gives rise to meaning; it is the precondition of any meaning at all," and yet "it itself is beyond expression."[118] Derrida sees this about *différance*, but goes on nonetheless to speak about what cannot be said, using techniques, such as erasure, to indicate how the structure itself is both present and absent, is indeed beyond presence and absence.

It is clear that in his account of Derrida, Priest gives us a picture not unlike Moore's. He is more specific about what it is that *différance* contributes to human experience. He places it and Derrida generally within a discussion of meaning, in particular linguistic meaning. The issue he raises is how Derrida can speak about what is a condition of all speech, when that condition is not an entity or fact but a feature of the system of language that in fact defies any ground of meaning in behalf of a situation of fluidity, change, and indeterminacy. Moore's treatment is less specific, broader, and aimed at language and thought overall. But the final point is the same, that *différance*, like Fregean concepts and Wittgensteinian logical form, cannot be spoken of, designated, or described. They can be elucidated or shown perhaps, but not *named*. Speaking about the ineffable is a kind of nonsense, but it is a nonsense that does some work nonetheless; it is not pointless nonsense.

As Wittgenstein says and some commentators emphasize, the nonsense in his *Tractatus* is a "liberating" or "redeeming" nonsense, and what it redeems us from is confusion, perplexity generated by our philosophical tendencies.[119] In order to clarify this role, however, we need to appreciate that Wittgenstein means something very precise by "nonsense" and that recent commentators have not agreed about what that is. What does Wittgenstein mean by "nonsense" in the *Tractatus*? What is the task of philosophy, and how does it function? What does Wittgenstein mean when he notes that what cannot be said nonetheless can be shown? It is tempting to take these matters and apply them to Derrida and perhaps to Levinas. But until we are clear about them and how commentators take them, the temptation must be deferred.

Even at this point, however, it is worth noting a doubt that one might register. Levinas himself, in clarifying the experience of the face of the other and the experience of all others, turns to analogues in Western philosophy: Plato, Plotinus, but most of all Descartes. He wants us to realize that his reference to an experience of what lies outside of nature and even outside of being is not unique. Others have recognized the significance of similar experiences, ones that reach out to God conceived as beyond being and as infinite. The linguistic

[117] Priest, *Beyond the Limits of Thought*, 237, 240.
[118] Priest, *Beyond the Limits of Thought*, 241; cf. Jacques Derrida, "*Différance*" in *Margins of Philosophy* (Chicago: University of Chicago Press, 1982), 76.
[119] See Matthew B. Ostrow, *Wittgenstein's Tractatus*, 16–17 and *passim*.

side of such acts of reaching out involves problems about religious language, divine attributes, and even negative theology. Levinas does not exploit this side of the issue to any great extent, but it obviously exists. One might wonder why I am not emphasizing this aspect of the linguistic problem: how are we to understand Levinas's talk about and terminology for the face of the other. Why am I focusing instead on a kind of Kantian strand in twentieth-century philosophy that deals with conditions for thought and speech and the way philosophers talk about them?

There are a few reasons for this emphasis. First, if there is a connection between the face, as a condition for social experience and more, and Derrida's *différance* as a condition for all signification, language, and such, then focusing on the other as a transcendental condition for thought, speech, and social life seems like the appropriate strategy to take. That is, there may be a theological or religious dimension to Levinas's thought, but the Kantian background is also very important.[120] Second, God can be seen, in traditional natural theology, as a transcendent condition for nature's existing as it does. Much of traditional metaphysics, as systematic, can be viewed as setting out conditions for nature and cosmology. Levinas, however, is no systematic metaphysician. Rather, he is in the tradition of Kant, Husserl, and Heidegger. He is concerned to identify, in part, what makes human experience, thought, speech, and action possible. Hence, it seems legitimate to turn to Wittgenstein and readings of him, to his views on philosophy and what it does for us, for clarification about Levinas's philosophical thinking about the face. Finally, if there has been any recent attempt by Anglo-American philosophers to clarify Derrida on these issues, it has been through a comparison with Wittgenstein and his legacy.[121] It makes sense to turn to that discussion, then, to place Levinas, whose connection with Derrida is evident – even if it is controversial – and whose affinity with Wittgenstein has not gone unnoticed.[122]

FREGE, WITTGENSTEIN, AND NONSENSE

Let me return now to Frege and Wittgenstein and especially to the distinction between saying and showing in the *Tractatus* and how it is used, by philosophers like Moore, to understand the ineffability of *différance*. Interpreting Frege and Wittgenstein on these matters is certainly controversial, and I am not interested so much in the accuracy of interpretations of them as I am in the light such

---

[120] See Kevin Hart, *The Trespass of the Sign*, 189–94.
[121] I include Wheeler's *Deconstruction as Analytic Philosophy*, which deals explicitly with Derrida and Davidson, as an important contribution to this attempt.
[122] See Bob Plant, *Wittgenstein and Levinas*.

interpretations shed on Levinas. Moore and Priest, in this regard, as readers of Frege and Wittgenstein and interpreters of Derrida, are helpful, for their reading is a rather orthodox one, like Peter Hacker's reading of Wittgenstein.[123] In discussing this style of reading, Cora Diamond, in a famous paper, calls it "chickening out." Her interpretation of the *Tractatus* focuses on Wittgenstein's conception of philosophy, what role nonsense plays in it, and what nonsense means.

Diamond draws together four features of the *Tractatus*: Wittgenstein's distinction between what can be said and what can only be shown; Wittgenstein's denial that he is putting forward philosophical doctrines; his claim in *Tractatus* 6.54 that whoever understands him "eventually recognizes [his propositions] as nonsensical"; and the claim, also in 6.54, that the comprehending reader, when he has done this, using them as steps "to climb up beyond them," "must throw away the ladder after he has climbed up it."[124] Roughly speaking, the orthodox or standard view, which Diamond calls "chickening out," only pretends to throw away the ladder.[125] It reads Wittgenstein as holding the view that *there is something* called "the logical form of reality," which incorporates certain *features of reality* and which cannot be expressed in words, although it can be shown or, as Diamond says, gestured at. That is, chickening out – by an interpreter of Wittgenstein or by Wittgenstein himself – would be to believe that reality has certain features that cannot be described in language or thought about directly in inquiry and examination, but that we do have access to, via some indirect methods. To purify philosophy is to turn it from describing such features to doing what is appropriate to showing it, presumably by articulating the ideal, logical structure of language. She calls this "pretending" to throw the ladder away, because in a sense it is to stand on it and to commit to the existence of certain features of reality at the same time that it is to claim that the ladder cannot be directed to those features; hence, the pretense.

What Diamond argues for, on the other hand, is a genuine throwing away of the ladder. She – and Wittgenstein, on her reading – does not chicken out. She really throws out the ladder; the ontology is shown to be based on the confusion of taking the language of "features of reality" seriously.[126] It is not that traditional ontological, philosophical vocabulary is the wrong way to reach a determined goal; rather, it is simply nonsense, "plain nonsense, which we

---

[123] See P. M. S. Hacker, *Insight and Illusion: Themes in the Philosophy of Wittgenstein* (Oxford: Oxford University Press, 1972); Hacker, *Wittgenstein* (New York: Routledge, 1999); D. F. Pears, *The False Prison: A Study of the Development of Wittgenstein's Philosophy*, 2 vols. (Oxford: Oxford University Press, 1987–88).

[124] See Cora Diamond, "Throwing Away the Ladder" in *The Realistic Spirit*, 179–204.

[125] Diamond, "Throwing Away the Ladder" in *The Realistic Spirit*, 181–94.

[126] Diamond, "Throwing Away the Ladder" in *The Realistic Spirit*, 181.

are not in the end to think of as corresponding to an ineffable truth."[127] To chicken out is to think that there really is something there; we just cannot talk about it. To proceed genuinely is to realize that philosophical language looks like it points to or picks out reality, but it does not. Diamond calls this process one of showing us that philosophy traditionally is the "illusion of perspective" and not the correct perspective that we cannot put into words.[128] In short, as Diamond reads him, Wittgenstein, in the *Tractatus*, is quite radical about philosophy and what it accomplishes.[129] He holds no metaphysical doctrine, although he certainly has views about what philosophy can accomplish, that is, what from which philosophy can liberate or "redeem" us and how it does so.

Diamond believes that metaphysical claims about features of reality are plain nonsense. They are not, as the orthodox would have it, a kind of deep nonsense that somehow points to something that is shown but cannot be spoken of or described. To use an example from Frege, the sentences "There are objects" and "Objects exist" are simply nonsense. It is not just that we cannot say this about something; it is that such nonsense discredits the very issue of there being such realities. Talk about such realities is nonsense; metaphysical inquiry points us in the wrong direction altogether. Plato is not mistaken because he believes that we can say things about Forms; he is wrong to think that language and thought point at all to some metaphysical reality. Wittgenstein, on Diamond's reading, does not think that the world is made of facts but we cannot talk about them; what he believes is that it is wrong to think that an analysis of language in any way leaves us with a true picture of reality. Such an analysis shows us that metaphysical language is simply nonsense and points us toward nothing about the world.[130] We cannot say "there are objects" or "there are facts" or "there are forms," not because there are such things but we cannot express them directly, descriptively, and so forth, but rather because there is nothing such sentences say or try to say; there is no "inexpressible *content*."[131] As Matthew Ostrow summarizes Diamond's view:

> . . . refusing to countenance the possibility of any sort of meaningful gesture toward the ineffable, she bites the bullet on Wittgenstein's behalf and proclaims that as far as the *Tractatus* is concerned, its own statements really are nonsense, plain and simple. There is no Tractarian counterpart to the Kantian *Ding an sich*, no deep features of reality that are somehow made manifest in Wittgenstein's utterances.[132]

---

[127] Diamond, "Throwing Away the Ladder" in *The Realistic Spirit*, 181.

[128] Diamond, "Throwing Away the Ladder" in *The Realistic Spirit*, 196.

[129] Cf. James Conant, "The Method of the *Tractatus*" in Erich H. Reck (ed.), *From Frege to Wittgenstein*, 420–24.

[130] See Diamond, "Throwing Away the Ladder" in *The Realistic Spirit*, 197.

[131] Diamond, "Throwing Away the Ladder" in *The Realistic Spirit*, 197–98; on Diamond's reading, see Ostrow, *Wittgenstein's Tractatus*, 5–8.

[132] Ostrow, Wittgenstein's Tractatus, 5.

Diamond's interpretation, then, does a number of things for us. It helps us to see how philosophy might function in a number of different ways. There are traditional Western metaphysics and a philosophical type of clarification that shows us what cannot be said but still is so, in a sense, and can be pointed to. But there is also a liberating philosophy that exposes the way traditional metaphysics is wholly confused and mistaken. Diamond's reading also shows us that talk about features of reality might be thought to be a misguided way of getting at what really is so or alternatively simply nonsense, that leads us to take metaphysical outcomes seriously when we should not. Finally, it leads us to realize that what Wittgenstein says our language shows can either be *something about reality* or *something about* the way traditional philosophy distorts or misguides us in our thinking. All of this will enable us to ask, more clearly, how we should understand what Levinas says about language and the face and what he means when he uses language to designate the face and responsibility.

Let me return to Moore for a moment. He thinks that there is ineffable knowledge and "effable" knowledge. That is, there is knowledge that we cannot put into words. He thinks of this as a kind of practical knowledge but particularly concerning how we are as selves or persons. Moore takes this to be a variation on the Frege-Wittgenstein point: There are things that can only be shown but not said. He applies this to Derrida's *différance*. I want to let this pass, although I have my doubts, and turn to Levinas. Can we apply the same analysis to Levinas? Can we say that language about the face shows the face but cannot say it or speak about it, describe it, and so forth? Or does Diamond's view of nonsense and of philosophy suit Levinas better?

Before we try to answer this question, let me call attention to one further feature of readings of Wittgenstein's *Tractatus* and the notion of nonsense. It concerns Wittgenstein's seeming injunction that the point of the work is not to get us to think or say things correctly as much as it is to get us to act in a certain way or at least to live, with a better understanding of how to live. Two famous texts point in this direction. The first is the statement at the end of the *Tractatus* (7): "Whereof one cannot speak, thereof one must be silent." Mathew Ostrow interprets this to mean that Wittgenstein takes his claims to be fulfilled by what we do, not by what we say, and that this means ceasing to philosophize.[133] One might connect this practical outcome with Wittgenstein's comment, in a letter to Ludwig von Picker, that the real point of the *Tractatus* is ethical.[134] As he says, the work seeks "to draw limits to the sphere of the ethical from the inside." The ethical, I take it, is not what he has written but the part of the work that is "*not* written"; it involves what one does, how one lives and

---

[133] Ostrow, *Wittgenstein's Tractatus*, 14.
[134] Ostrow, *Wittgenstein's Tractatus*, 16–17 and n. 37; cf. Hacker, *Insight and Illusion*, 82–83.

acts.[135] Might there be a similarity between how Wittgenstein takes his own purposes to be ethical and how Levinas takes the point of his philosophy to be ethical? Is it possible that Levinas's ethical commitments are not simply formal, as Wittgenstein's might be thought to be, but also substantive – concerned with justice and responsibility?

ETHICS AND THE LIMITS OF LANGUAGE

Let us now return to Levinas. In *Otherwise Than Being*, he seeks to avoid the terminology of ontology when talking about and referring to the encounter with the face of the other person. Philosophical language and everyday, natural discourse are both immersed in this terminology of ontology. We say that things exist, have properties, are related one to another, appear one way or another, and so forth. We refer to things, describe them, and talk about them. Just as in *Totality and Infinity*, these linguistic and cognitive dealings with things occur within the domain of totality; things, people, and events are present to us as agents and observers. We experience and think about them. They come formed, shaped, structured, and classified. Levinas's project, in part, is to show how we have experiences like these that expose or call attention to what lies outside the limits of totality. He talks about insomnia and fatigue, for example, and our experience of the other person's suffering. What lies beyond totality, whether it is the "there is" or "evil" or "the face of the other" or "*illeity*," cannot then be referred to or described by everyday or philosophical language in a nonfigurative, direct, literal way. In a sense, albeit not a literal one, these transcendent entities do exist for Levinas. They are there, so to speak, and the names we use to designate them and to talk about them do point to something or call attention to something. Of course, it is also true that these things are not things at all. The face is not a feature or characteristic; it is not grasped perceptually or cognitively. We have called it a dimension or aspect of all social life or interaction. Alternatively, we might say that it is a mode of relationship. But my point here is simply that it is about how things are; it is not utter nonsense to talk in these terms. Nor is it utter nonsense to call the self's relation to the other, via the other's face, "responsibility," "hostage," "obsession," "substitution," and "persecution."

This is all familiar by now, but it is helpful to recall it, for it seems to suggest that Levinas's philosophical discourse about the face-to-face, as of all *others*, might best be understood along the lines of the standard or traditional reading of Wittgenstein in the *Tractatus*, as Moore and Priest suggest about Derrida. This conclusion may be correct, but at the same time we should not be too quick.

[135] Wittgenstein, "Letters to Ludwig von Picker" in *Wittgenstein: Sources and Perspectives*, ed. C. G. Lucknardt (Ithaca, NY: Cornell University Press, 1879), 95.

Cora Diamond and James Conant may be right about Wittgenstein, nonsense, his deflationary conception of philosophy, and his metaphysical "reluctance," and what they say may also help us to clarify Levinas.

In a critique of the Diamond-Conant interpretation, Hacker says that it is a "*Leitmotiv*" of the *Tractatus* "that there are things that cannot be put into words, but which *make themselves manifest*."[136] What a logical analysis does is *show* these things or truths, "the logical form of reality."[137] He calls these "ineffable truths about reality," some metaphysical, others ethical. They are what language and thought, when logically understood, cannot express but can nonetheless show or direct our attention to.[138] Hence, philosophy shows us what can be expressed and what cannot and also "*why* the essence of the world and the nature of the sublime – of absolute value – are inexpressible."[139] This is what he and others, on several occasions, called the "mystical" teaching of the work.[140]

This account shares several features with Levinas's talk about the face and responsibility. First, the face is something that cannot be said but can be shown – that is, our attention can be directed to it. To be sure, for Levinas, philosophy does not do this through a logical analysis of language. Rather, it contrasts the face with other ways of experiencing the other person and characterizing her, acting toward her and relating to her, and it analyzes concrete experiences that point beyond themselves to what is genuinely other, beyond the bounds of our concepts and categories. In one way, the job of philosophy is to help make us aware of a regularly ignored way of relating to other persons, but it is also to expose how the other person is manifest to each of us in a way ordinary language cannot express. Second, the face is a locus of "absolute value," of what makes life meaningful and significant. Just as for Wittgenstein such a locus of value is inexpressible and yet determinative of how we should live, so is the face and responsibility for Levinas. Finally, just as the logical form of language, which shows how reality is structured, makes thought and language possible, so the face makes social life possible.

There is something, however, that distinguishes Levinas's discourse about the face-to-face, and this is where Conant and Diamond are helpful. Levinas's philosophical strategy for exposing the face, as an act of ethical command and obedience, is to use terms that are sharply contrasted with traditional philosophical vocabulary and that are picturesque and dramatic. They are metaphorical, exaggerated, and hyperbolic. In this respect, Levinas's terminology is akin to

[136] Peter Hacker, in *The New Wittgenstein*, 353.
[137] Peter Hacker, in *The New Wittgenstein*, 353.
[138] Cf. Hacker, in *The New Wittgenstein*, 368, 370, 371–82.
[139] Hacker, in *The New Wittgenstein*, 382.
[140] See Hacker, in *The New Wittgenstein*, 372–74.

traditional terms applied to the divine or the transcendent. Indeed, some are
drawn from that venue: "holy," "saintly," "pious," "glory," and more. Others
are intended to capture an extreme sense of passivity and imposition, which
Levinas seeks to emphasize: "obsession," "trauma," "persecution," "accusation," and "hostage." This is not at all Wittgenstein's strategy, on the traditional
reading of the *Tractatus*, for his interest is in the way the logical form of language
shows something about the nature of reality and what lies beyond thought and
language. To Levinas, the other is most significantly ethical, not quasi-scientific
or metaphysical in the traditional sense. It is a matter of calling attention to
a very particular fact and *responding to that fact responsibly*; it is not a matter of
directing our thoughts to a general form or structure. That is, the point of
Levinas's thinking and writing about the face is to alter our actions and our way
of life.

For neither Wittgenstein nor Levinas, however, does the locus of absolute
value for human life lie in some other world. It is a dimension of this life that
ordinary language and thought, so embedded in a visual, scientific, exploratory
frame of mind, hide from view. The transcendent is not, for either, mystical
in any conventional sense, not the realm of isolated, extraordinary experience.
Rather, it is embedded in our experience and in our lives, even if language is
unable to articulate it in normal ways.

Suppose, then, that we take the distinction between what can be said and
what cannot be said but only shown from Wittgenstein's *Tractatus*, as it is read by
Peter Geach, G. E. M. Anscombe, P. M. S. Hacker, and others, and apply it to
Levinas's philosophical attention to the face-to-face encounter. If we do, then
we might ask how Levinas's work *shows* but does not say this dimension or aspect
of human social existence. For it is clear that in *Time and the Other, Totality and
Infinity*, and the essays of the 1950s and early 1960s, he does so and that from the
mid-1960s through *Otherwise Than Being* and thereafter, he continues to do so,
albeit in new and different ways. The first thing to say is that Levinas employs a
variety of strategies to point to and disclose this "unsuspected *horizon*" of human
experience.[141] He uses "quasi-phenomenological" description; he examines
limit-experiences and compares them; he employs imaginative, dramatic terms
and expressions; he appropriates religious, political, and legal vocabulary and
uses it in novel ways; he uses what de Boer calls exaggeration and contradiction –
he has a particular affection for hyperbole, as he puts it; and he draws telling
comparisons – for example, with the so-called invincibility of skepticism. The
second is that the comparisons are not intended to clarify what the face is or
how it "appears" or "reveals" the other person's need and suffering. Rather,

[141] The expression is from Levinas, "Signature" in *Difficult Freedom*, 243.

the comparison is meant to help us see how the relation of being-for-the-other is always present, so to speak, and thus how it is different from our ordinary existence and yet is always present within it. That is, no matter how our culture and society hide it, indeed no matter how much language and thought themselves cannot *touch* it, still the relation is there. It is a permanent, if undesignatable or "oblique," feature of all human social existence.

Finally, for Levinas what lies beyond the limits of ordinary language and everyday thought is ethics and religion. What it means, that is, concerns how we live and ought to live. The face-to-face is the venue of ultimate importance and point to our lives. It is not a matter of living with greater clarity of mind. Rather, it is about living with greater sensitivity to the needs of others, with an appreciation for how we should acknowledge others, accept them, and act in their behalf. Grasping what lies hidden at the horizons of our lived experience is to grasp what generosity and justice mean and to care for others before we seek to understand them. Like the Russian woman in Grossman's *Life and Fate*, it is to give the other a piece of bread before or even in conflict with what we think or feel about him. This is ethics of a powerful and determinative kind; it is central to our lives, as ordinary as it is extraordinary, and yet beyond the limits of thought and language.

11

Judaism, Ethics, and Religion

Throughout his career, Levinas understood Western culture and society as a combination of two worlds, the biblical and the Greek – what others have called Hebraism and Hellenism or Athens and Jerusalem. Levinas, of course, has his own special way of interpreting this trope, as we shall see, and his own way of envisioning it in order to estimate the value of Jews and Judaism for Western culture (and world culture). In part, it is a philosopher's perspective on that culture and the themes and tendencies that constitute it. At the same time, it is a Jew's perspective on what Jewish life means, both to Jews and to others. In this chapter, I want to look at this conglomerate of issues. We will cover a number of themes, for Levinas's relationship to Judaism is multifaceted.[1]

One theme is the historical reality of the Jewish people as a persecuted, suffering group, the target of anti-Jewish and anti-semitic attacks.[2] In this regard, the Jews are a kind of historical barometer. The level of suffering they have endured is an indication of the degree to which others have neglected or opposed their responsibility to justice and goodness. Jews and their situation, then, reflect the character of Western culture. This is one of their roles: to demonstrate the ethical character of European and Western society.[3]

---

[1] For a basic overview, see Cohen, *Elevations*, 126–32. See also Peperzak, *Beyond*, Ch. 3 and especially Wright, *The Twilight of Jewish Philosophy*.

[2] Antisemitism as a central feature of Western culture and history has been a theme for various thinkers – for example, Arendt, Adorno, and Horkheimer. One might argue that it is characteristic of post-Enlightenment and post-Hegelian historicisms that vilify technology and urbanization and the rise of fascism and totalitarianism as the mechanisms and outcomes of xenophobia and intolerance, of nationalism and assault on the other.

[3] See Steven Smith's *Spinoza, Liberalism, and the Question of Jewish Identity* (New Haven, CT: Yale University Press, 1997); see also Hilary Putnam, "Levinas and Judaism" in *The Cambridge Companion to Levinas*, 34: All people are victims of antisemitism.

Connected to this is a second theme: the special relationship of Jews and Judaism to the Holocaust and Nazism. Levinas famously said that his life and career were "dominated by the presentiment and the memory of the Nazi horror."[4] In Chapter 1 we canvassed evidence for this claim, but we saved for this chapter a more extensive and deeper analysis of what it means or might mean and especially of the sense in which Levinas's work might be understood as a response to the atrocities of Auschwitz and the twentieth century.[5]

A third theme concerns Levinas's interpretation of Jewish learning and the relation between study of texts – primarily the Talmud – and the central ethical teaching of responsibility before the face of the other. Levinas emphasizes the tenacity and perspicacity with which the Bible and the Talmud teach the primacy of ethics, justice, and generosity. We shall discuss his Talmudic teachings, his writings about Jewish life, and how he conceives the teaching of the ethical as Judaism's central mission. This is part – indeed, a large part – of what Levinas means when he says that Jews should teach the Greek West to speak Hebrew.[6] Levinas's interpretations of the Jewish people as a persecuted minority, of the Holocaust, and of ethics as the central Jewish teaching are all then related to a fourth theme: his understanding of Zionism and the State of Israel. Levinas wrote several essays on this topic in the postwar period and then again in the 1970s and early 1980s.[7]

The major twentieth-century Jewish thinkers of interest to philosophers are Hermann Cohen, Franz Rosenzweig, Martin Buber, Emil Fackenheim, and Joseph Soloveitchik. There has recently also been significant attention paid to Gershom Scholem, Walter Benjamin, Hannah Arendt, and Jacques Derrida. It will be useful to view Levinas alongside these figures, in order to place some of his Jewish commitments in the context of other Jewish thinking about revelation, ethics, politics, law, ritual, covenant, messianism, and similar themes.

Levinas's ethical view, the central and primordial character of responsibility to and for the other person, concerns all human existence insofar as it is social

---

[4] Levinas, "Signature" in *Difficult Freedom*, 291.
[5] This will lead us to Levinas's essays "Transcendence and Evil" and "Useless Suffering," his consideration of suffering, and his views about the so-called "end of theodicy." Of special interest will be recent work on these issues by Susan Neiman in *Evil in Modern Thought*; Richard J. Bernstein in *Radical Evil*; and Richard A. Cohen in *Ethics, Exegesis and Philosophy*, Ch. 8. See also the chapter on these themes in Joshua Shaw's dissertation "Putting Ethics First: Reconsidering Emmanuel Levinas's Ethical Metaphysics.
[6] In addition to the work of Robert Gibbs and Richard Cohen, we shall look at *The Twilight of Jewish Philosophy* by Tamra Wright. A relatively early account can be found in Susan Handelman, *Fragments of Redemption* (Bloomington: Indiana University Press, 1991).
[7] Howard Caygill has recently discussed this literature in *Levinas and the Political*, and we shall want to see how Levinas's Zionist thinking is related both to his moral and political ideas and to his conception of Jewish destiny.

or interpersonal. It is, that is, universal, and if such an ethical view is the core of Jewish existence and teaching, then in a sense Jewish existence, too, is universal. To teach Greek culture to speak Hebrew is to remind everyone – if all people are by extension members of "Greek" culture – of something they already are but of which they are unaware. It is to see a special historical role for Jews and the Jewish tradition, but to see such a role – as it was for Rosenzweig – as restricted to history. It dissolves in eternity. We will want to think about this tension, so prominent a feature of all Jewish life in the modern world, the tension between universality and particularity, from Levinas's point of view.[8]

ATHENS AND JERUSALEM

As we saw in Chapter 1, Levinas was fond of referring, in the 1980s, to the epic novel of Vasily Grossman, largely in interviews, but also occasionally in popular essays. One of these, published in 1986, is called "The Bible and the Greeks."[9] In that essay, he describes European, Western culture as a unity of "the Bible and the Greeks," where "Greek," he says, is "the manner in which the universality of the West is expressed." Greek, that is, is the root of our ordinary, everyday language, of our scientific, theoretical, and overall cultural discourse. It is Levinas's word for an attitude or posture that underlies our thought, talk, and action. Greek is the language of totality, grounded in the correlations of subject and object, of self and world, actor and action, knower and known. The Bible teaches a different lesson; it is the source of another dimension of our lives, not Greek in character. It is the lesson of ethics and responsibility, as we have explored in earlier chapters. Hence, because all our language is Greek, the latter "intends to translate – ever anew – the Bible itself," which teaches about a "justice hidden behind justice … more faithful to its original imperative in the face of the other." This framework is the context for Levinas's primary goal in the essay, to note a crisis in this European culture, a moment of threat and urgency, and to ask if the crisis can be endured and overcome. He puts it this way:

The history of modern Europe is the permanent temptation of an ideological rationalism, and of experiments carried out through the rigor of deduction, administration, and violence. A philosophy of history, a dialectic leading to peace among men – is such a thing possible after the Gulag and Auschwitz?[10]

Rationalism, on Levinas's reading, is beset with the possibility and the risk of rigorous, organized oppression, dehumanization, and destruction. After these

[8] This is a central theme of Levinas's essay on Mendelssohn, "Moses Mendelssohn's Thought" in *In the Time of the Nations*, 136–45.
[9] Levinas, "The Bible and the Greeks" in *In the Time of the Nations*, 133–35.
[10] "The Bible and the Greeks" in *In the Time of the Nations*, 135.

have been realized in Stalinism and Hitlerism, however, can we hope for recovery? Can peace arise after such horrors and such violence?

Levinas calls on Grossman's testimony or affirmation and associates it with the teaching he finds at the core of the Bible:

The testimony of a fundamental book of our time such as Vasily Grossman's *Life and Fate*, in which all the systematic safeguards of justice are invalidated and the human dehumanized, sees hope only in the goodness of one person toward another, the "little kindness" I have called mercy, the *rahamim* of the Bible. An invincible goodness, even under Stalin, even under Hitler. It validates no government, but rather bears witness, in the mode of being of our Europe, to a new awareness of a strange (or very old) mode of spirituality or a piety without promises, which would not render human responsibility – always my responsibility – a senseless notion. A spirituality whose future is unknown."[11]

Levinas is referring to the incident of the Russian woman inexplicably handing the piece of bread to the hated German soldier and Ikonnikov's commitment to the resilience of isolated, senseless acts of kindness. He identifies such acts with what the Bible calls *rahamim* (mercy) and claims that even Stalinism and the Holocaust cannot destroy the possibility of such acts. They are outside moral systems and political ideologies; they are not their product, nor do they "vindicate" them. They are not the results of motives we have every right to expect to be operating in the situation in question. Rather, the reality of such acts *testify* to an old – permanent – feature of human existence, what he calls a "strange spirituality." It is this spirituality, this piety, Levinas believes, that is all we can hope for, exactly what we can and should cultivate, and it comprises the central biblical – that is, Jewish – teaching. When he says, moreover, that its future is unknown, what he means is that the chances of its realization, of individuals and societies now coming to shape their lives in tune with it, are beyond our calculation and certainly beyond our confidence. The twentieth century signals a massive suppression of such piety, of this sense of responsibility, and no one can tell if it is not only "invincible" but also resilient.[12] Can we reasonably envision the emergence of a world committed to generosity, justice, and goodness in the wake of Stalinism and Hitlerism and subsequent atrocities and genocidal acts?

Levinas's point, in "The Bible and the Greeks," is not simply that the biblical teaching and the Greek world differ and yet collaborate in Europe, in Western culture, and that the horrors of the twentieth century make one dubious about

---

[11] Levinas, "The Bible and the Greeks" in *In the Time of the Nations*, 135.
[12] One might contrast the optimism of Martin Buber in "Dialogue Between Heaven and Earth" in Buber, *On Judaism* (New York: Schocken, 1967), 214–25. More akin to Levinas's uncertainty is that of Eliezer Berkovits in *Faith after Auschwitz* (New York: Ktav, 1973).

the possibility of the biblical teaching becoming dominant or even effective. Levinas's little story is more Oedipal than that. As we have seen, he argues that the Greek world grows out of the biblical. The Bible teaches "the possibility of a responsibility for the alterity of the other person, for the stranger without domicile, . . . for the material conditions of one who is hungry or thirsty, for the nakedness of the defenseless mortal."[13] It is the teaching of request and commandment, taught, for example, in the story of Genesis 24, as the rabbis read it, with the waters of Rebekah's well rising "in the service of mercy."[14] And out of this world of engagement with the face of the suffering other arises the Greek world, via the third party, the need for assessment, judgment, calculation, deliberation, knowledge, science, the state, and political authority. "The unique beings recognized by love . . . must be brought into the community, the world."[15] The connection is a derivation of a kind, as we have said, the Bible a kind of condition for the Greek, a kind of parent. Levinas here focuses on its linguistic dimension: "Greek is Europe's inevitable discourse, recommended by the Bible itself," and hence, as a kind of "metalanguage," "which intends to translate – ever anew – the Bible itself."[16] And translation is a form of violence, of oppression, perhaps even repression.

The current crisis, then, is not just a tension between two aspects of one civilization. It reveals the suppression of the parent by the child's passions and drives, the willful assault of the child on the parent's hopes. Europe has become obsessed with definition, precision, universality, structure, and violence; it resists but still remains open to the ancient biblical spirituality, its sense of kindness and mercy. Body has come to dominate soul. Indeed, the lineage is precise: "a dehumanized humanity, surrounding institutions that were nonetheless the outgrowth of an initial revolutionary generosity and concern for the rights of man. . . ."[17] Hitlerism is the legacy of romanticism and even Rousseau; Stalinism arose out of Marxism and its democratic, humanitarian roots. Levinas sees hope in Grossman's message, but he muses: how much hope, how deep, how resilient?

AN AUSTERE HUMANISM

This short, late piece expresses a good deal about Levinas's understanding of the role and content of Jewish life and Judaism. But it is only a short, late expression. To appreciate properly Levinas's views on Judaism, we need first to look back

[13] "The Bible and the Greeks" in *In the Time of the Nations*, 133.
[14] "The Bible and the Greeks" in *In the Time of the Nations*, 133–34.
[15] "The Bible and the Greeks" in *In the Time of the Nations*, 134.
[16] "The Bible and the Greeks" in *In the Time of the Nations*, 134.
[17] "Beyond Memory" in *In the Time of the Nations*, 89; cf. 90.

at some of his early writings, from the postwar years, especially those collected in 1963 in *Difficult Freedom*.

After the Second World War, while representing the Zionist World Congress in Buenos Aires, Zvi Kolitz, a young journalist, was invited to contribute an article to the Yom Kippur edition (September 25, 1946) of a local Yiddish newspaper, *Di Yiddishe Tsaytung*. He composed a fictional piece, in the form of a letter left in the rubble after the Warsaw Ghetto uprising, "Yosl Rakover Talks to God."[18] Transmitted anonymously, the story surfaced in Tel Aviv, then Germany and France, and was taken by some to be a genuine document: the impassioned religious testimony of a victim of the revolt. In 1955, it appeared in a French translation in a Zionist journal in Paris. Levinas gave a radio talk about the story on April 25, 1955, and it has become justifiably famous.[19] It is called "Loving the Torah More Than God," a phrase that he appropriates from Yosl Rakover's prayer to describe Judaism as what he calls an "austere humanism."[20]

Levinas presents the letter as "a text that is both beautiful and true," one that offers, he says, a "Jewish science." What is the content of this clear and true picture of Judaism? What is Judaism's "austere humanism"? Levinas begins by noticing that "the suffering of the innocents" in the ghetto – and presumably also in the death camps – led many to deny God, to atheism. The problem of evil, theodicy, engaged in the face of such suffering, often leads to rejection. But, he notices, it does so because the conception of God that it refutes is "childish," a God of rewards and punishments. An empty heaven testifies to a childish mythology. Yossel is keener than this. His Judaism is adult, not childish. He does not reject God, but he does take His burdens upon himself. Yossel claims that God hid His face. Levinas takes this claim to be a true one. It says that the world has been turned over to savagery, the time has come when the just suffer at the hands of the wicked, and there is no help. This image of God hiding His face, of *hester panim*, is not, Levinas says, "a theological abstraction or a poetic image." Rather, it is an accurate description of a time of utter destitution and failure. "It is the moment in which the just individual can find no help. No institution will protect him."[21] The good person suffers. The only hope is that others will respond to that suffering and stretch out a hand.

---

[18] For the story, see Zvi Kolitz, *Yosl Rakover Talks to God*, translated and edited by Paul Badde (New York: Pantheon, 1999), 48–54. This recent edition includes Levinas's essay on the piece.

[19] Levinas, "Loving the Torah More Than God" in *Difficult Freedom*, 142–45.

[20] "Loving the Torah More Than God" in *Difficult Freedom*, 145. The phrase does not appear in all versions of the text – for instance, it is missing in the English translation that was published in Albert Friedlander (ed.), *Out of the Whirlwind* (New York: Union of American Hebrew Congregations, 1968).

[21] "Loving the Torah More Than God" in *Difficult Freedom*, 143.

Moreover, the God who hides is Yossel's God, the God of the Jews, who are those who suffer, whose existence and whose teachings – whose Torah – call for morality and conscience.[22] The suffering of the just person in behalf of a justice that struggles to realize itself "is physically lived out as Judaism." Judaism is not a confession, not an exclusive ideology. It is one way of living a life of suffering that teaches others what justice requires of all.

How can one believe such a thing or commit to such a fate? Levinas's answer is that it involves not a leap of faith but rather an education in Torah. In short, one learns to be a Jew by learning the teachings of the Bible. Levinas quotes Yossel: "I love him, but I love even more his Torah...." One *learns* what suffering means and what justice or responsibility requires; one *learns* what Judaism is and appropriates it. The God who hides becomes *my* God, he says. "God is real and concrete not through incarnation but through Law." This is an adult view of God and Judaism, not a child's view; it is a "complete and austere humanism," for it means that the "adoration" of God is learned through the Torah and expressed through human kindness and generosity.[23]

Already in 1955, then, Levinas has in hand the two major components of his conception of Judaism: that the suffering of the Jews is a plea for help and responsible concern, for justice, and that the primacy of ethics is the central teaching of the Torah. There is, that is, a conjunction of Jewish fate and Jewish soul; what the Jew teaches through his face, he also teaches with his mouth. A year later, in 1956, writing about the dilemmas of Jewish identity and the struggle of diaspora Jews for a "content" for their Judaism, Levinas calls it a "Jewish humanism."[24]

The core of that humanism is the law that is taught by "the great texts of rabbinic Judaism, which are inseparable from the Bible." What these texts teach or, as Levinas puts it, "expose" is not rules or dogmas but rather "an entire world, ... a literature and a civilization."[25] Moreover, it is a world brought to life by "monotheism," the "vision of God [as] a moral act," or, as he says here – as later in *Totality and Infinity* – "this optics is an ethics."[26] This monotheism, with these texts and their teaching about the primacy of goodness and response to the face of the other, is, he says, a "humanism," a "civilization built on justice."[27] Once, we might suppose, this task was called "election" or "chosenness"; Levinas calls it a "rare privilege" to promote "as one of the highest

[22] "Loving the Torah More Than God" in *Difficult Freedom*, 144–45.
[23] "Loving the Torah More Than God" in *Difficult Freedom*, 145.
[24] Levinas, "For a Jewish Humanism" in *Difficult Freedom*, 273–76, esp. 273.
[25] "For a Jewish Humanism" in *Difficult Freedom*, 274; cf. "Judaism" in *Difficult Freedom*, 24–26.
[26] "For a Jewish Humanism" in *Difficult Freedom*, 274–75; cf. TI, 23.
[27] "For a Jewish Humanism" in *Difficult Freedom*, 275.

virtues the knowledge of its own sources," precisely because the content of that knowledge is ethics, justice, and responsibility. The Jewish people, that is, are chosen to teach, to explore their own textual resources in order to "expose" their own universalism. This is the sole purpose of diaspora Judaism.[28]

The most comprehensive of Levinas's early essays on Judaism, I think, was first delivered as a talk on education in 1957. It uses a motif we have already seen: the distinction between a childish and an adult religion, a distinction that has Kantian resonances. Indeed, its title employs the latter expression: "A Religion for Adults."[29] Like the other essays we have discussed, this one was written at the same time that Levinas was at work on *Totality and Infinity*. In the two works, he approaches the same goal from two points of view and shows how the same primary feature of human life is revealed through Judaism and through a philosophical exploration.

There is no need for us to consider every feature of this essay; rather, we should focus on the understanding it presents of Judaism, its character, and its role. Levinas does call attention to the destruction of European Jewry from 1933 to 1945, which he calls the experience of "total dereliction," of "Passion."[30] Thus, the Jewish people "found itself at the heart of the religious history of the world" even while it "remains on the margins of the world political history, of which it has had the moral privilege to be the victim."[31] Levinas affirms, here, too, that Jewish suffering reveals the depths and the extent of abandonment by others, occasional episodes of heroism notwithstanding, including some that Levinas himself here recalls.[32]

But Levinas then turns to his major theme: Judaism's "basic theses on man," or what he calls its "philosophical anthropology."[33] It is the teaching of the Bible and, in all their particularity and apparent parochialism, of the rabbinic texts. Levinas calls it "a link between man and the saintliness of God," but he makes a point of distinguishing the latter from God as a numenal or spiritual being.[34] He goes so far as to call such a numenal or sacred God "violent," an idol; and the Judaism of Abraham, freed of such mythology, an "atheism" – that is, a nontheism.[35] The Judaism he is preparing for the reader is disenchanted, demystified, what we have seen to be ethical, responsible, just – an

---

[28] For these themes, see also Levinas, "Assimilation Today," 257; cf. "How Is Judaism Possible?," 250–54; and "Israel and Universalism," 175–76, all in *Difficult Freedom*.

[29] Levinas, "A Religion for Adults" in *Difficult Freedom*, 11–23.

[30] "A Religion for Adults" in *Difficult Freedom*, 11, 12.

[31] "A Religion for Adults" in *Difficult Freedom*, 12, 13.

[32] "A Religion for Adults" in *Difficult Freedom*, 12.

[33] "A Religion for Adults" in *Difficult Freedom*, 12–13.

[34] "A Religion for Adults" in *Difficult Freedom*, 14.

[35] "A Religion for Adults" in *Difficult Freedom*, 15.

"austere humanism." The core of this Judaism and the central teaching of Torah, Bible, and Talmud is the experience of the "presence of God through one's relation to man"; "through my relation to the Other, I am in touch with God." The other person is "situated in a dimension of height, in the ideal, the Divine."[36] Once again, Levinas tells us that "ethics is an optic," which here means that "ethics is not the corollary of the vision of God, it is that very vision."[37] This teaching is clearly manifest in Judaism's texts. It is what Maimonides means when, according to Levinas, he argues that the positive meaning of negative attributes should be read as imperatives: "God is merciful" means "Be merciful like Him."[38] Indeed, the coincidence of social justice with the relationship with the Divine is "the entire spirit of the Jewish Bible."[39]

Levinas acknowledges that this teaching is an "austere doctrine." It is demanding, exceedingly so, but it does not lead to despair.[40] What it expects is education and effort, and what it hopes for is an "aspiration to a just society... [through] religious action," a state of mind that Levinas says is "perhaps... [what] we normally call Jewish messianism." That is, Judaism accepts a severe teaching in a spirit of hope and opportunity, not of frustration and despair.

The centrality of ethics "allows us to understand the meaning of Jewish universalism."[41] Levinas explicitly argues that the traditional doctrine of election, the core of Judaism's particularism, is shown to incorporate a kind of universalism. Election is constituted by responsibility, and Levinas's notion of the face-to-face clarifies that while this responsibility for justice and generosity is universal, at the same time it is what the Jewish doctrine of election means. Each person has a moral duty to each and every other, for each of us is "elected" or "summoned" by each and every other. Judaism teaches the centrality of such duty. It is not unique to Jews, nor is Judaism its only advocate. But it is the core of Judaism and of Jewish particularity, so that when Jews speak of chosenness, what they mean is not some unique dispensation that comes from God but rather their ethical responsibility to others.[42] The notion of the Jewish people being singled out and chosen by God is a "mythical" representation or image, as it were, of the ethical fact that each of us elects and calls to responsibility every

---

[36] "A Religion for Adults" in *Difficult Freedom*, 16, 17.
[37] "A Religion for Adults" in *Difficult Freedom*, 17.
[38] "A Religion for Adults" in *Difficult Freedom*, 17.
[39] "A Religion for Adults" in *Difficult Freedom*, 19.
[40] "A Religion for Adults" in *Difficult Freedom*, 20–21.
[41] "A Religion for Adults" in *Difficult Freedom*, 21.
[42] "A Religion for Adults" in *Difficult Freedom*, 21–22.

one of us. "Moral awareness," for the Jew, is "an awareness of being chosen." Levinas calls it a "particularism that conditions universality."[43] "Israel," as it were, is a moral notion – not a historical, national, or racial one, and this is part of its nature as landless, wandering, diasporic.[44] For Levinas, as for Abraham Joshua Heschel, Judaism is an inhabitant of time and not space, and time means not history but "conscience," the call of justice, the hope and responsibility for a just society.

Why is this Judaism – ethical, universal, messianic, particular – a "religion for adults?" First, Judaism is taken up with responsibility and justice, obligations that one must learn to understand, acknowledge, and accept for oneself. Children feel intensely their own needs; their desires are firm and full. Such desires dominate the child's world. In many ways, to outgrow childhood is to come to acknowledge others as independently important and to appreciate one's responsibility for them. It is to become educated, to learn the sense of obligation and concern, directed toward others, that is associated with adulthood. Second, Levinas is precise about calling this a religion for adults. It is not a religion of myth or fairy tale; it is not framed in terms of a patriarchal divinity, of rules and law, of rewards and punishments. Kant called such a religion "statutory" and suggested that it is demeaning and oppressive.[45] Levinas's religion is otherwise; it does not mystify the notion of the divine; it realizes that the language of God arises for us when we are aware of our responsibility to others and of the demands of justice. It treats such language not literally but indirectly or figuratively, as an expression of conscience, of our ethical sensibility. Such a religion is mature and not childish.

Furthermore, adulthood must leave behind the child, her pleasures, her naïveté, innocence, and selfishness. In short, adults must resign themselves to what they have lost. They have learned to accept what they no longer have. Adult hopes are not childish ones; they are real and realistic. Judaism sees the past as gone and the future as genuine but neither too idealized nor wholly up to others. It is up to us, if we respond as we must and as we ought, with generosity and a sense of justice and concern. But this kind of Judaism only has

---

[43] "A Religion for Adults" in *Difficult Freedom*, 22.

[44] "A Religion for Adults" in *Difficult Freedom*, 22–23.

[45] In *Religion Within the Limits of Reason Alone* (New York: Harper, 1960), Kant claimed that Judaism was such a religion, that its legalism, otherworldly rewards, and heteronomy were characteristic of it and separated it dramatically and radically from the genuine history of moral development, the aim of which was a moral, rational faith. See also *Religion Within the Boundaries of Mere Reason*, trans. George di Giovanni, in Kant, *Religion and Rational Theology*, ed. Allen W. Wood (Cambridge: Cambridge University Press, 1996).

346 Judaism, Ethics, and Religion

hope because it realizes that the past, childhood, is gone, not to be recovered or reenacted, but mourned, genuinely and not mistakenly.[46]

Finally, Levinas's Judaism does not misconstrue, as a child might, the notion of election and the relation between Judaism's particularity and its universality. He has at least two mistakes in mind. One is to take election as a matter of privilege, when its real core is responsibility and thus a sense of burden or demand. The other mistake is to take its responsibility only instrumentally, as if its particularity is its unique contribution to a universal goal, even if that goal is morality or the ideal moral community. Levinas rejects all of this.[47] Election is not a means to a universal goal; it is responsibility and therefore is itself universal. Jewish suffering and Talmudic teaching do call attention to the Jewish responsibility for others. But Jewish distinctiveness is a *historical* fact and *not* an *ethical or religious* one. Levinas is decisive about this. Ethics is not uniquely Jewish, of course; nor are its texts a unique resource for teaching goodness. Jews, as all persons, are each responsible to each and every other person, "elected" by the face of suffering and the need of the other. In a sense, then, the only justification for Jewish distinctiveness is the historical "accident" that its teachings are an especially valuable resource for educating all humanity to an "austere humanism." At the same time, that distinctiveness is historically confirmed, as it were, by the suffering and persecution of the Jewish people.

Unlike Mordecai Kaplan, then, Levinas does not condemn chosenness altogether as an anachronism. Nor does he treat it as a decisive religious or theological fact grounded in divine will, a view shared by Joseph Soloveitchik in his own way, Michael Wyschogrod, and Emil Fackenheim.[48] In a way, Levinas's view is akin to Spinoza's, that chosenness is an historical-political fact and not a theological-moral one.[49] The central difference between the two, with regard to chosenness, is that for Spinoza it only exists as a metaphor for the political and military success of the Jewish state, whereas for Levinas it is an ethical fact that, while shared by all, historically realizes itself in the life of the Jewish people as their central rabbinic teaching and their chief historical credential: suffering.

---

[46] See Espen Hammer, *Stanley Cavell*, 173. Cavell discusses this sense of maturity and growth, of education of the self to greater awareness and understanding of oneself and others, in many places – for example, in *Conditions Handsome and Unhandsome, Pursuits of Happiness, Cities of Words*, and *Contesting Tears*. It is a central theme of what he calls "Emersonian or moral perfectionism."

[47] See Levinas, "Israel and Universalism" in *Difficult Freedom*, 176–77.

[48] See Joseph Soloveitchik, *The Lonely Man of Faith* (New York: Doubleday, 1992); Michael Wyschogrod, *The Body of Faith* (Minneapolis: Seabury Press, 1983); and Emil L. Fackenheim, *What Is Judaism?* and *Quest for Past and Future* (Bloomington: Indiana University Press, 1968).

[49] See Spinoza, *A Theologico-Political Treatise* (Cambridge, MA: Hackett Publishing, 2001), Ch. 5.

Levinas, in other words, does not try to defend Jewish particularity as much as he tries to understand it. The people and its texts exist. We are nonetheless all elected by the other to the demands of ethical responsibility. What, then, does the particularity of the Jewish people mean? This is the question Levinas seeks to answer.

ETHICS AND PRAYER

From these early essays, we thus can gain a basic picture of Judaism, Israel, and the Jewish people. Much remains to be said, however. Several themes demand our attention: Levinas's treatment of suffering, evil, the Holocaust, and the problem of theodicy; his understanding of revelation, autonomy, and law; his understanding of messianism, eschatology, and prophecy; and his discussion of Zionism. As we turn to his essays and writings, especially from the 1970s and 1980s, Levinas's basic picture is retained, modified, and enriched. It also, in a very unique fashion, unites the universalist tendencies of modern, liberal Judaism with a traditional commitment to the centrality of the Talmudic texts and tradition.

To begin, we ought to wonder how Levinas can accommodate the ceremonial or ritual laws of Judaism into his ethically centered picture. Earlier, we discussed the charge made against Levinas that the kind of life he seems to be requiring is exceedingly narrow, even one-sided. In this regard, one might easily prefer an Aristotelian ideal, which is concerned with and respects the fullness of life over Levinas's demanding and apparently restricted one. There is an analogue regarding his conception of Jewish life. Just as we might ask if Levinas sees any independent or even special virtue in enjoying a symphony or a film, or producing either, so we might inquire whether he takes Jewish ritual conduct, worship, or prayer to be important or valuable, except perhaps instrumentally and derivatively. To be sure, not all modern forms of Judaism have, at all times, emphasized Jewish ritual and prayer. Classical Reform certainly did not, and Kaplanian naturalism has done so, but only for contingent reasons. Traditional Jewish thought has always elevated the Law, or Halakhah, often without isolating ritual practices. Rosenzweig gave them a special role to play in the life of the "eternal people," while Buber opposed law and ritual as obstacles to moments of dialogue. Where, we might wonder, does Levinas stand on such matters?

Let me approach these themes by considering Levinas's reflections on *Nefesh Hahayyim* (*The Soul of Life*), a book written by the Lithuanian rabbi *Hayyim of Volozhin*, a disciple of the Vilna Gaon, and published in 1824. In the late 1970s and 1980s, Levinas discusses this famous work of Eastern European Talmudic Judaism several times, and in his discussions the issue of prayer frequently arises.

The first of Levinas's essays, "'In the Image of God': According to Rabbi Hayyim Volozhiner" appeared in 1978, and we might best start with it.[50]

Nefesh HaHayyim was "the theoretical blue-print for the great nineteenth century Lithuanian Torah academies," as Norman Lamm puts it.[51] It was a theological work with kabbalistic roots that develops an ethical, metaphysical ground for the study of Torah.[52] It begins with a "kabbalistic anthropology" and eventually arrives at an account of man's *tikkun* (repair),[53] the commandments, and the Halakhah (Jewish Law);[54] hence, it incorporates the gist of R. Hayyim's "fundamental religious outlook"[55] and is a defense of the centrality of Torah to Judaism, the "supremacy of Halakhah and its study" as the "highest ideal."[56] According to the book, "the most sublime activity of the Jew is that of study – higher than performance of the commandments, than prayer, than pious contemplation, and so important as to maintain its significance independent of its motivation."[57] In Levinas's early paper on the book, he focuses on its anthropology, its view of the "humanity of man." Levinas calls it an "ultra-modern wisdom" presented "under rabbinic cover" and takes its burden to place responsibility for the course of the universe on man and on human responsibility for the other and for the entire world.[58] It is only through human action that God is associated with the world; everything depends upon him.[59] "Man, by acts in agreement with the Torah, *nourishes* the association of God with the world."[60] Levinas takes R. Hayyim to be saying that man is responsible for God's link to the universe and thus for the world and for others.[61]

What conclusions does Levinas draw from his reading? First, he concludes that for R. Hayyim being or existence is grounded in ethics; "the ethical meaning of human activity" causes all others to live or die; "the association of God with the worlds, or his distance from them – the being or non-being of the

[50] See Levinas, "Judaism and Kenosis" in *In the Time of the Nations*, 114–32; "'In the Image of God': According to Rabbi Hayyim Volozhiner" in *Beyond the Verse*, 151–67; "Prayer Without Demand" in *A Levinas Reader*, 227–34.

[51] Norman Lamm, *Torah Lishmah: The Study of Torah for Torah's Sake . . .* , 59.

[52] Lamm, *Torah Lishmah*, 59.

[53] Lamm, *Torah Lishmah*, 63.

[54] Lamm, *Torah Lishmah*, 64.

[55] Lamm, *Torah Lishmah*, 65.

[56] Lamm, *Torah Lishmah*, 68, 71, 72; see also Levinas, "Prayer Without Demand" in *A Levinas Reader*, 229.

[57] Lamm, *Torah Lishmah*, 72, 73; see also Ch. 3. See also Levinas, "'In the Image of God'" in *Beyond the Verse*, 153; "Judaism and Kenosis" in *In the Time of the Nations*, 120.

[58] "'In the Image of God'" in *Beyond the Verse*, 153, 154, 161–62.

[59] "Judaism and Kenosis" in *In the Time of the Nations*, 124.

[60] "Judaism and Kenosis" in *In the Time of the Nations*, 125.

[61] "Judaism and Kenosis" in *In the Time of the Nations*, 125; see also "'In the Image of God'" in *Beyond the Verse*, passim.

creature – depends on me."[62] This is how Levinas reads the notion "in His image" was man created: "Being *is*, through ethics and man."

Second, he pays special attention to R. Hayyim's analysis of prayer. It is clear that Levinas realizes that Judaism involves study, performance of commandments, interpreting texts, and even devising theological systems. And it also includes prayer and worship. But if ethics, the acting on one's responsibility to and for others, is central to Jewish life, what then is prayer, and what role does it play? In the *Nefesh HaHayyim*, Levinas discovers a unique view of prayer that he finds appealing. In "Judaism and Kenosis" (1985), Levinas comments that for R. Hayyim "at no time is prayer an entreaty for *oneself*; properly speaking, it is not an entreaty, but an *offering of oneself*, an outpouring of the soul."[63] It is, as a *berachah* (blessing), a "generous offering [of the self], for the purpose of associating God and the world," a pouring out of the soul and thus an act of love.[64] It is not a "demand addressed to God" but rather "the soul's delivering itself up to the heights, . . . rising upward like the smoke of sacrifices."[65] This interpretation is his first step, that prayer is not either a petition directed to God or a demand made of Him. But still, self-sacrifice and the notion of offering oneself to God as a device for bringing the world and God together, to secure the world's existence, are not sufficient. To Levinas, being must be grounded in ethics. How is prayer an ethical act?

Here is the second step of Levinas's reading: the world's, including our world, need for their being "man and man's prayer, which are *for the others*." Prayer "signifies . . . seeing to the salvation of others instead of – or before – saving oneself."[66] The offering of one's soul is toward God by being to the other person; prayer is an expression of this sacrifice for others, an acknowledgment of it. "True prayer, then, is never for oneself, never for one's own needs."[67]

But, Levinas asks, is this not surprising? Man suffers; he has needs. Can he not ask God to satisfy the needs and relieve the suffering?[68] The Talmud, he notes, permits such supplications but only for personal hardships that we suffer as part of the distress or persecutions of the entire people. The people of Israel is God's deputy, "the bearer and subject of Holy History." The "persecution of Israel" is the humiliation and profanation of God's purpose. Individual needs are insufficient to justify petitionary prayer, but personal suffering as part of

---

[62] "Judaism and Kenosis" in *In the Time of the Nations*, 126.
[63] "Judaism and Kenosis" in *In the Time of the Nations*, 128.
[64] "Judaism and Kenosis" in *In the Time of the Nations*, 128, 129.
[65] "Judaism and Kenosis" in *In the Time of the Nations*, 128 (order of text changed).
[66] "Judaism and Kenosis" in *In the Time of the Nations*, 129.
[67] "Judaism and Kenosis" in *In the Time of the Nations*, 129.
[68] "Judaism and Kenosis" in *In the Time of the Nations*, 129–30.

an attack on the people is sufficient. To pray is to call upon God to serve His own goals.[69] It is, as it were, to express one's sense of abandonment by others, the fact that Jews are being oppressed and that such persecution and oppression ought to cease.

However, what about prayer for personal hardships or suffering? "Is the human suffering of the individual condemned to silence?" Levinas asks.[70] It might look as if Levinas takes R. Hayyim to rule out such personal prayer altogether. But I do think that that is his point when he says that "according to Rabbi Hayyim of Volozhin, praying for relief from one's own misery is never the ultimate aim of a pious prayer – the prayer of the just."[71] On the one hand, the goal of *all* prayer is God's need for the just man to elevate the world to God. On the other hand, the *ultimate* purpose of the prayer of the one who suffers for his sin is "to relieve the suffering of God, who suffers in [man's] suffering." In praying for oneself, one prays for God; and in God's suffering, man's suffering and his sin are already assuaged. Hence, one does not ask for relief; one already accepts one's suffering as relieved in view of God's excessive suffering. What one prays for is that God's suffering will be relieved and with it that of all people.[72] The just man prays *to* God and also *for* Him, and this he does only by reaching out to the other person who suffers.[73]

Levinas seems to realize, in the teachings of R. Hayyim, an appreciation of the fact that "no life of study can dispense with either worship or ritual practices."[74] In the *Nefesh HaHayyim*, the kabbalistic architecture of the emanations of God culminate in human beings and their action. The whole edifice and thus God's presence in it, in other words, all of being, depend upon human action, or, as R. Hayyim puts it, "each man becomes responsible for the life and death of all the other worlds and men."[75] Hence, Levinas translates this cosmological picture into the language of his ethical metaphysics: "[T]he responsibility for others therefore comes to be for man the meaning of his self-identity. . . . [T]he being or non-being of the universe depends upon [man's] adherence to the Torah."[76] Ontology is inadequate to provide the significance or meaning of existence; for that, ethics is necessary. Ethics as responsibility for the other person is the "origin of all meaning."[77] This is the origin of justice, the ground of purpose and meaning, what brings significance to existence, or, in an older vocabulary,

[69] "Judaism and Kenosis" in *In the Time of the Nations*, 129–30; see also 130–31.
[70] "Judaism and Kenosis" in *In the Time of the Nations*, 130.
[71] "Judaism and Kenosis" in *In the Time of the Nations*, 130.
[72] "Judaism and Kenosis" in *In the Time of the Nations*, 130.
[73] See also "Prayer Without Demand" in *A Levinas Reader*, 229–30.
[74] "Prayer Without Demand" in *A Levinas Reader*, 228.
[75] "Prayer Without Demand" in *A Levinas Reader*, 230.
[76] "Prayer Without Demand" in *A Levinas Reader*, 230, 231.
[77] "Prayer Without Demand" in *A Levinas Reader*, 230, 231.

value to a world of fact.[78] It is also the universal foundation of the particularity and chosenness of the Jewish people, Levinas says.[79] Thus, he sees this kabbalistic cosmology as depicting a universe dependent upon the responsibility of each person for every other, a "reversal," as he puts it, of views that take nature or subjectivity to be its foundation. In such a system, what is prayer? It "never asks for anything for oneself; . . . it makes no demands at all, but is an elevation of the soul." But what does this mean? What concretely and practically is the prayer of the just man, "prayer which conforms . . . to Jewish piety"?[80]

First, as Levinas sees it, prayer is an act of offering or elevation, of donation. Through it, the soul gives itself to God, attaches itself to God by loosening its adherence to being.[81] But here Levinas seems to tie prayer as an act of utterance and worship to ethics. The worlds of emanation, the created worlds, must not simply *be*; they must be justified through human action in behalf of others. Prayer, the "service of the heart," he says, is essential; it refers to "repairing the ruins of creation," and, Levinas writes, "prayer means that, instead of seeking one's own salvation, one secures that of others."[82] Does Levinas mean that prayer *expresses* this priority of the other and one's commitment to the other's well-being – to feed the hungry, clothe the naked, and relieve the pain and suffering of the other person? Or does he mean that in a sense prayer is identical with this responsibility? Is prayer a sign for the priority of the ethical, or is prayer itself nothing but the ethical? I am confident that Levinas means the former. He does not recommend abandoning prayer or worship, the utterance of words of praise and petition, collective service, for ethical acts. Nor does he mean that the true prayer is not such utterance but rather acts of kindness and generosity. Rather he sees the real point of prayer to be the way it expresses the sense of generosity, benevolence, and justice that is central to human life. Prayer is an *affirmation* of one's commitment to living for others. Hence, Levinas does not expunge prayer from Jewish life. What he does say is that "true prayer . . . is never for oneself, never 'for one's needs,'" never a demand.[83] True prayer is uttered in the spirit of giving.

As in "Judaism and Kenosis," Levinas here, in "Prayer Without Demand," goes on to ask about the prayers of those who suffer. His response is twofold. On the one hand, he notes that the Talmud authorizes such prayers, but only when the individual's suffering is caused as part of the persecutions and the misery of the people as a whole. One can petition God, but only in behalf of

---

[78] One also sees this motif in the Jewish theological commitments of Soloveitchik and Berkovits, who, like Levinas, are indebted to Kant in this respect.

[79] "Prayer Without Demand" in *A Levinas Reader*, 231–32.

[80] "Prayer Without Demand" in *A Levinas Reader*, 232.

[81] "Prayer Without Demand" in *A Levinas Reader*, 232–33.

[82] "Prayer Without Demand" in *A Levinas Reader*, 233.

[83] "Prayer Without Demand" in *A Levinas Reader*, 233.

God's sacred mission invested in the people of Israel, the Jewish people. On the other hand, Levinas asks again: "[I]s our human suffering, then, condemned to silence? Does the Talmud's ruling about prayer for oneself absolutely exclude the claims of the unhappy 'I'?"[84] The *Nefesh HaHayyim* is clear: No prayer primarily concerned with one's own unhappiness can be considered pious. If the just person suffers, his prayers have a different point. His suffering is also God's suffering, for suffering is being abandoned by others and for this reason and in this way an indication of the fact that being lacks meaning and significance. Hence, when the just man prays out of his suffering, he is in essence "praying for the suffering of God who suffers through [His] human suffering."[85]

What does this mean? For Levinas, one's fundamental commitment ought to be the goodness of others, to help them, to feed and clothe them, to reduce their suffering and misery. When I suffer, this manifests the failure of this responsibility; it represents it and contributes to it. Hence, in theological terms, when each of us suffers, God suffers with us. "God's suffering" is a *representation* of the state of affairs that occurs when there is a failure of human responsibility, when the world lacks just institutions, when persecution and oppression are rampant. To pray for relief of my personal suffering, then, is not a narrow, restricted petition. It expresses my concern for all suffering persons, for justice and goodness everywhere, and my plea to others to relieve my pain and the pain of all, as well as my commitment to do my part in bringing about such justice and kindness.

In the end, then, Levinas can even find a place within Judaism for liturgy, worship, and personal prayer. The question that he asks is not whether the time devoted to prayer ought to be devoted to better purposes. Nor is he interested in expunging certain kinds of prayer in favor of others. Rather, Levinas seeks, through his reading of *Nefesh HaHayyim* and its kabbalistic mythology, to register his conviction that human ethical action in behalf of others is fundamental to human life and to God's purposes for the Jewish people and that the activity of prayer should be understood in these terms. Prayer may seem to be personal and petitionary, but in fact it should not be understood that way, neither by us nor by the individual Jew. It is expressive of the individual's commitment to justice and responsibility and to the task of all humankind to realize justice and reduce suffering. As a form of conduct and discourse, then, prayer is an act of acknowledgment, acceptance, and affirmation; it is also an expression of hope. As Norman Lamm interprets R. Hayyim's account, the proper attitude in prayer and worship is utter selflessness; "true prayer is completely theocentric."[86] What Lamm reads literally as a confirmation of theocentrism, however, Levinas reads

[84] "Prayer Without Demand" in *A Levinas Reader*, 234.
[85] "Prayer Without Demand" in *A Levinas Reader*, 234.
[86] Lamm, *Torah Lishmah*, 78–80.

as a commitment to ethics and an "austere humanism."[87] What his account does, then, is to expose an aspect or dimension of prayer that has been hidden from view. He exposes it by reading the *Nefesh HaHayyim* in a novel way, by reading behind its kabbalistic and theological vocabulary. In so doing, Levinas shows how the texts of Judaism not only disclose the true character of Jewish life but also how study of those texts can teach something – the centrality of the ethical – to Western culture.

THE HOLOCAUST AND THE END OF THEODICY

We have arrived at an important juncture in discussing Levinas's understanding of Judaism. A number of issues have emerged and require our attention. One is Levinas's approach to reading the texts of Judaism, his hermeneutics, which is centrally important insofar as these texts are resources for revealing the centrality of the ethical but do so only when read correctly and in a revealing way. Another issue is Levinas's view of revelation, a topic of signal importance to Buber, Rosenzweig, Scholem, Fackenheim, and others. To some of these thinkers, revelation is one locus of the divine–human relation; but given Levinas's understanding of theological discourse and language about "God" and the "divine," his understanding of revelation must differ. We need to explore what it is and what role it plays for him. Third, our account of prayer raises the more general question of Jewish ritual conduct in response to the commandments (*mitzvot*) and to Jewish law (Halakhah). As Edith Wyschogrod puts it, "[w]hat is the justification for Jewish ritual if ethical action is founded in the upsurge of the other and if such action is the way in which Judaism appears in the world? What, in short, accounts for the necessity of Jewish ritual *praxis*?"[88] In addition to issues such as these theoretical and philosophical ones, however, Levinas's understanding of Judaism also depends crucially upon his historical situation as a Jew living in the shadow of Auschwitz. For several reasons, I think, we ought to confront first Levinas's understanding of evil, suffering, and the Nazi Holocaust and his place among those who have produced philosophical and theological responses to those dark times.

There have been several recent discussions of Levinas, evil and the Holocaust. While Susan Neiman only mentions him in her book *Evil in Modern Thought*,

---

[87] For a different view, that prayer brings the Jew near to the ethical, see Wright, *The Twilight of Jewish Philosophy*, 128–33, esp. 133. Obviously, such an instrumental account is possible, but I have tried to explain why I think it and other alternatives are unsatisfactory as primary interpretations of Levinas's respect for Jewish prayer.

[88] Edith Wyschogrod, *Emmanuel Levinas*, 165; see also Wright, *The Twilight of Jewish Philosophy*, 118–23.

Richard Cohen devotes an entire chapter to Levinas and the Holocaust in *Ethics, Exegesis and Philosophy*, as does Richard Bernstein in *Radical Evil*.[89] There is also discussion in Tamra Wright's *The Twilight of Jewish Philosophy*. Neiman and Bernstein consider Levinas largely as a Western philosopher, among a group including such figures as Theodor Adorno, Hannah Arendt, Hans Jonas, Albert Camus, Giorgio Agamben, and Maurice Blanchot.[90] Cohen and Wright do discuss his philosophical approach, of course, but they are also interested in his relevance for Judaism and post-Holocaust Jewish life and thought. I will say something about both sides of Levinas's persona; indeed, I think that it is hard and perhaps impossible to avoid doing so. For our purposes, Levinas wrote three pieces of special importance regarding evil and the Holocaust: "Loving the Torah More Than God" (1955), "Transcendence and Evil" (1978), and "Useless Suffering" (1982).[91] We have said something already about his early response to the document "Yosl Rakover Speaks to God," with its doctrine of God's hiding His face (*hester panim*). As we now look at the recent discussion of him, our attention will primarily focus on the latter two essays.

Earlier, we saw that Levinas takes Stalinism and Hitlerian fascism to mark a crisis in European culture, a crisis that now includes as well the atrocities we associate with the genocidal acts in Iraq, Cambodia, Bosnia, Rwanda, and elsewhere during the late twentieth century. Both these regimes involved the oppression, persecution, and murder of millions of people; they engaged in horrific forms of torture and destruction. Stalinism was the outcome of Marxism and socialism and thereby, for Levinas, discredits the humanism invested in that tradition; it functions as a kind of historical *modus tollens*. Nazism realizes the worst nightmares of technological rationality and racist nationalism; the systematic murder machines – the killing squads and death camps – mark a watershed in European culture. Levinas returns to the horrors again and again, if only in passing; the trauma never goes away. Bernstein tries to argue that all of

---

[89] Neiman, *Evil in Modern Thought*, 238–39, 291; Cohen, *Ethics, Exegesis and Philosophy*, Ch. 8; Bernstein, *Radical Evil*, Ch. 6, and the revised version of Ch. 12 in *The Cambridge Companion to Levinas*. See also Joshua Shaw, *Putting Ethics First: Emmanuel Levinas on the Priority of Ethics* (unpublished doctoral dissertation, 2004), Ch. 4. Robert Eaglestone "argues that [Levinas's] philosophy, throughout and in every way, from particular words and sentences to his overall aims, is a response to the Holocaust" (*The Holocaust and the Postmodern*, 10) in Ch. 9, 249–78.

[90] Bernstein does talk about Judaism and Auschwitz, but his perspective is primarily philosophical and not theological.

[91] "Loving the Torah More Than God" can be found in several places but most conveniently in *Difficult Freedom*. "Transcendence and Evil," which is Levinas's review of Philippe Nemo's *Job and the Excess of Evil*, can be found in *Collected Philosophical Papers*, 175–86; in the English translation of Nemo's book, 165–82; and in *Of God Who Comes to Mind*, 122–34. "Useless Suffering" is translated in *Entre Nous*, 91–101; and also by Richard Cohen in Robert Bernasconi and David Wood (eds.), *The Provocation of Levinas*, 156–67.

Levinas's thought, his commitment to the primacy of the ethical, is a response to the Holocaust. While that may be at least partially true, what is certain is that for him the Holocaust viewed broadly plays a special role historically. The fact of such extreme atrocities and suffering tells us something about our world and how we should respond to it. It defines our historical and political situation. Cohen puts the question succinctly: "How can one affirm God, Israel's election, and ethics after the Holocaust?" Or, as Emil Fackenheim says, today we must take both God and Auschwitz seriously; we must confront the horrors honestly and expose ourselves and our thinking to it, and yet we must go on, as Jews and as human beings.

I think that it is useful to compare Levinas's thinking about suffering, evil, and the Holocaust with that of Fackenheim.[92] Levinas does cite and briefly discuss Fackenheim in "Useless Suffering," but their thinking differs in important ways, and the differences as well as the similarities can help us to understand Levinas more fully.

Fackenheim's strategy is this: the Nazi atrocities have taken place, and they have left us with fragmentary remains: reports, memories, evidence, and more. How do we respond to this mass of material and to the memories? How can we respond, and how ought we to respond? How do we go on? Fackenheim, as a philosopher and theologian, seeks to understand what took place, and this means to comprehend in some intellectually satisfying manner not only discrete episodes as historical events but also all the suffering – the horrific atrocities, the policies and practices, the totality of evil – that occurred in the years from (at least) 1933 to 1945. Philosophically and theologically, as a cognitive enterprise, Fackenheim seeks to cope with the Holocaust, for himself and for others like him, who respect the evil for what it was, the victims, and the requirements of thought. What this means is that the intellectual tries to understand and explain what happened and why. Fackenheim claims – in many places, using many different examples as illustrations – that historians, social scientists, psychologists, philosophers, and theologians all fail at this task and often recognize and admit that they do and that they should. No matter how hard intellectuals try and how deep their research, ultimately the Nazi atrocities contain inexplicable, incomprehensible features that are integral to the evil of the event and cannot be mastered to the intellectual's satisfaction – not responsibly and honestly so. If we take the theological word "theodicy" to stand for all such attempts to

---

[92] For selections from Fackenheim's writings relevant to the reasoning I shall set out, see Michael L. Morgan (ed.), *The Jewish Thought of Emil Fackenheim* (Detrait: Wayne State University Press, 1987). For discussion, see Michael L. Morgan, *Beyond Auschwitz: Post-Holocaust Jewish Thought in America* (New York: Oxford University Press, 2001), and "Fackenheim and the Holocaust: Setting the Record Straight," *Yad Vashem Studies* 32 (2004), 7–20.

incorporate and thereby explain the Holocaust and give it enough meaning to make it intelligible, then, Fackenheim argues the Holocaust defies theodicies. Also, among the episodes that Fackenheim uses to argue for this failure of theodicy are cases of innocent suffering, especially of infants; cases of horrific Nazi policies and practices; and cases of individual atrocity, including remarks and acts of particular perpetrators. In short, we cannot master the evil of this event in thought.

But to master the evil in thought is one thing; to respond to it in action is another. If the first is impossible, the second is unavoidable. Fackenheim argues that this necessity to respond is not a kind of factual or conceptual necessity; it is not just that we must always respond to any event that has taken place, consciously or not. Rather, the necessity is moral and religious; facing a "whole of horror," the only response is resistance. Trying to find an intellectually satisfying understanding or explanation is already a response; with its failure, going on to act in life is also a response, and a morally necessary one, a debt to the victims for some, a reaction to the evil for others, an act of faith and a response to God for still others, and for some simply a moral imperative, as yet with no determinate ground. Fackenheim argues, then, that the imperative – the obligation – is binding and that it is possible to perform, binding upon Jews, Christians, and others.

Beyond being an act of opposition to evil, what is the content of this obligation to respond? Fackenheim claims that the content must be articulated hermeneutically. For Jews, for example, the imperative requires a commitment to the survival of Judaism and the Jewish people, to resist all attacks on human dignity, and much more. In general, as I read him, Fackenheim elaborates the imperative, or this picture of post-Holocaust Jewish life, by showing how particular cases of traditional Jewish life and belief were challenged during the Holocaust years and, when invested with new meaning, might be recovered now with a revised post-Holocaust significance. Given the radical character of the evil of Auschwitz, every recovery must be fragmentary, he argues, to be honest to that evil, but it must also be a recovery, a mending or healing, to be faithful to the past and to avoid total despair about the future. Overall, then, reconstructing a genuine post-Holocaust Judaism is a hermeneutical task that for each particular practice or belief reaches into the pre-Holocaust past, takes the horrors and evils seriously, and seeks recovery by reinvesting old forms, perhaps modified, with new meanings.[93]

---

[93] Fackenheim's most explicit account of the hermeneutical character of this Jewish "mending" of the world, of recovery in its many senses, can be found in *To Mend the World: Foundations of Post-Holocaust Jewish Thought* (Bloomington: Indiana University Press, 1994), Ch. 4, Sections 8–15.

Fackenheim, then, can be seen as performing two tasks, and while they may seem to be carried out together and often are, they can usefully be distinguished. One is the task of seeking a general rule for responding to the evils of Auschwitz; here he argues against the satisfactory fulfillment of intellectual responses and then for an obligation of resistance that is morally binding – even if its grounds are indeterminate – and possible to be performed. The second task is to artic- ulate hermeneutically the many forms that the imperative takes, its ramified contents. If we now turn to Levinas and place his treatment of suffering, evil, and the Holocaust alongside Fackenheim's, we will see that there are interesting similarities but very deep differences between them. Of paramount importance will be the status of the encounter with the evil of Auschwitz and what that encounter means. Fackenheim takes the Nazi atrocities to be historically dis- tinctive and unprecedented, marking a historical epoch that changes the very character of life and thought – that challenges the continuity of our beliefs and principles and leaves us with a healing that is fragmentary at best. Fackenheim's thought is for this reason deeply historical. Levinas's thinking is also historical, to be sure, but in a very different way, for his conception of history is less linear or narrative and his commitment to ethics is deeply ahistorical.[94]

Let me begin looking at Levinas on these matters by asking what is meant by the widely cited claim that for him the Holocaust marks the "end of theodicy." Susan Neiman describes this view in these terms:

The claim that whatever was left of religious faith before Auschwitz could not survive it became famous in works of witnesses like Elie Wiesel's *Night*, or of theologians like Richard Rubenstein's *After Auschwitz*. . . . But unlike most con- temporary thinkers, Levinas did not restrict the word *theodicy* to justifications of God's goodness that were modeled by Leibniz. Rather, he drew as much on secular forms of theodicy. . . . Theodicy, in the narrow sense, allows the believer to maintain faith in God in face of the world's evils. Theodicy, in the broad sense, is any way of giving meaning to evil that helps us face despair. Theodicies place evils within structures that allow us to go on in the world. Ideally, they should reconcile us to past evils while providing direction in preventing future ones. Levinas claimed that the first task could not be maintained in good conscience after Auschwitz. He thus gave philosophical expression to an idea shared by many: the forms of evil that appeared in the twentieth century made demands modern consciousness could not meet.[95]

---

[94] For discussion of Fackenheim on these issues, see Michael L. Morgan, *Beyond Auschwitz*, and Morgan, "Emil Fackenheim, the Holocaust, and Philosophy" in Michael L. Morgan and Peter Eli Gordon (eds.), *The Cambridge Companion to Modern Jewish Philosophy* (Cambridge: Cambridge University Press, forthcoming).

[95] Neiman, *Evil in Modern Thought*, 239, 291.

Neiman takes Levinas to be using "theodicy" in a broad sense to refer to any intellectual way of placing and comprehending a past evil that also gives direction about how to prevent future ones. She takes him to be saying that we should abandon theodicies after Auschwitz. It – and other modern evils – are beyond our understanding.

Levinas's claim gives rise to a host of questions. What does Levinas think about theodicy: as the effort to place evils intellectually within structures or patterns, in order to allow us to go on in the world, and to give evils meaning so that we can face and cope with despair? Is Neiman right that Levinas's rejection is tied precisely to modern evils or perhaps even uniquely to Auschwitz? Cohen says that Levinas rejects theodicy, as Richard Rubenstein does.[96] But is Cohen right that Levinas's rejection of theodicies is *like* Rubenstein's response to them? Moreover, Cohen adds: "After the Holocaust, to be sure, [Levinas] rejects theodicy. . . . The negative lesson of the Holocaust, then, is precisely the end of theodicy."[97] But what does this mean? What does Levinas think about suffering and evil?[98] Why would theodicy be somehow unsatisfactory after Auschwitz but not before?

Levinas's general discussion of suffering and evil occurs in his review of Philippe Nemo's book *Job and the Excess of Evil*, titled "Transcendence and Evil."[99] In this essay, Levinas analyzes and describes three moments or features of evil and suffering; his aim is to clarify *all* suffering and evil. What we want to know is if he takes the evil of Auschwitz to be distinctive, if it, although not *all* evil, has brought about the "end of theodicy." Indeed, what does that expression mean?

Levinas prepares the reader to understand Nemo's phenomenology of evil by discussing the limitations of thought, the transcendence of the other, and the way the phenomenological method can be used to disclose "repressed or forgotten intentions" and thereby to make explicit or elucidate what is otherwise hidden from view.[100] We have interpreted this to mean that for Levinas there are aspects or dimensions of everyday experience that are outside our normal vocabulary and conceptions and that determine human social life in fundamental ways. There is, in particular, a dimension of our relationship with each and every other person, the face of the other, that is of this kind. Here he takes Nemo to have recognized how evil occurs in this way. Whether the suffering is

---

[96] Cohen, *Ethics, Exegesis and Philosophy*, 268.
[97] Cohen, *Ethics, Exegesis and Philosophy*, 268–69.
[98] Bernstein asks this question; see Bernstein, *Radical Evil*, 169.
[99] First published in 1978, reprinted in *Of God Who Comes to Mind* and in *Collected Philosophical Papers*.
[100] "Transcendence and Evil" in *Collected Philosophical Papers*, 177.

mine or the suffering of the other person, that suffering is beyond our normal vocabulary and understanding in some way and speaks to us. Nemo, and here Levinas, calls this "face" of evil its being an *excess*: "[E]vil is an excess in its very quiddity. . . . [S]uffering *qua* suffering is but a concrete and quasi-sensible manifestation of the non-integratable, the non-justifiable."[101] Levinas emphasizes that evil is the "non-integratability of the non-integratable." I think that what Levinas means is that what makes evil what it is – above and beyond its type, its duration, its features, and so forth – is the fact of its being unassimilable into ourselves, its being ours in a sense but utterly not ours in another. He calls it an "irreducible disturbance," insofar as its otherness or unassimilability cannot be reduced to any of its features, even to the fact that it is an unsettling opposition to us. Its nature is to be "not finding a place, the refusal of all accommodation with . . . , a counter-nature, a monstrosity, what is disturbing and foreign of itself."[102] There is, that is, something purely outside the self about evil and suffering, yet an outside, a dissonance, a disturbance that is also, of necessity, mine and aimed at me. It is something I suffer.

We are on the brink of the second moment of evil; but before we reach it, we must notice two features of Levinas's account. First, the evil or suffering that Nemo is exploring is Job's. That is, it is the pain and suffering that is beyond the self and yet afflicts it. It is not here the other person's suffering; it is mine – or anyone's. In *At the Mind's Limits*, the philosopher and journalist Jean Améry describes the torture he experienced in the Gurs concentration camp in France, where he was imprisoned by the Nazis. On the one hand, he describes the pain, the sensory intensity of it, excruciating and rupturing; on the other hand, he reflects on the sense of identification with one's body and the loss of confidence in sociability and the solidarity with others that torture brings about. But as one reads his account, so numbing and agonizing, one also has the sense of something totally alien to him utterly invading and overwhelming him without any sense of relief or distance and yet retaining its oppositeness, its otherness. Améry's pain is his and yet not him, almost beyond bearing.

Second, evil as excess, as the unintegratable otherness, is beyond theodicy, Levinas says. It is a dimension of evil or an aspect of suffering that cannot be justified or explained. What Job's friends offer does not touch this aspect of the suffering he is experiencing. This evilness of evil is "the resistance it opposes to theodicy."[103]

We must now turn to the second moment of evil: that it contains an "intention." That is, "evil reaches me as though it sought me out; evil strikes me as

---

[101] "Transcendence and Evil" in *Collected Philosophical Papers*, 180.

[102] "Transcendence and Evil" in *Collected Philosophical Papers*, 180.

[103] See "Transcendence and Evil" in *Collected Philosophical Papers*, 180–81.

though there were an aim behind the ill lot that pursues me, as though someone were set against me, as though there were malice, as though there were
someone." In feeling pain and suffering, Levinas says, I seem to be a target,
as if the suffering is "persecution" and I were elected or chosen to be persecuted, and in this experience of evil as targeted or aimed at me, I "awake to
myself."[104] Once again, we are here still dealing with the self's experience of
pain and suffering; while there is something intrinsically alien about that pain,
it does seem aimed at me. I cannot escape it; indeed, it finds me and possesses
me, as if its being mine is unavoidable for it. There is nothing free-floating or
indifferent about suffering. If I have it, then in a sense it is because it has, and
wants to have, me. And furthermore, given its primordial nature, this attachment to me is central to my having a sense of myself, here as the I that is
in pain.

But I do not simply receive the suffering; I am no inert receptacle or blank
tablet. In receiving it, I seek to repel it, to rid myself of it. I reject it, or better,
I react in horror to it. Evil is already the hatred of evil; "[E]vil strikes me in my
horror of evil." I accept it, and yet it is impossible for me to accept it.[105] My
reception is at the same moment a rejection.

This is enough to show that Levinas has read Nemo carefully and accepted the
core of his phenomenology of suffering. The kind of experience that is here
explicated is the experience of personal suffering or pain. Levinas takes the
analysis to be akin to his own earlier analyses of experiences, such as insomnia,
fatigue, and eros, where we find ourselves in touch with something other than
the contents of everyday experience[106] or, to be more precise, when we realize
that there are dimensions of our everyday experience and our relations with the
world around us that are normally hidden from our view. As I indicated, Améry
could describe his sensory and reflective experiences when undergoing torture,
but, Levinas would say, the pain and the suffering – as evil – have this threefold
character as well, even if they lie outside our normal conceptual framework and
our everyday vocabulary.

It is in this sense, then, that this suffering – as a kind of evil – is beyond
theodicy, is untouched by it. For theodicy is a matter of description and justification, of fitting evil into a structure or pattern that is part of our everyday or
theoretical way of thinking and talking about the world. Suffering as evil does

---

[104] "Transcendence and Evil" in *Collected Philosophical Papers*, 181–82.
[105] "Transcendence and Evil" in *Collected Philosophical Papers*, 183. One might compare Levinas's phenomenological account with Fackenheim's account of the response to the evil of
Auschwitz, as a horrified surprise and a surprised horror, in *To Mend the World*, esp. 233–40.
[106] Levinas is, in his earlier works, under the influence of Heidegger and Blanchot. These works
include "On Escape," *Existence and Existents, Time and the Other*, and *Totality and Infinity*.

take place in that world, and in one sense it can be described and explained, but in another – as elucidated by Nemo and here by Levinas – it cannot. In its "quiddity," evil lies beyond theodicy.

Given what we know of Levinas, this would be a disappointing place for him to conclude. On the one hand, it would be unsatisfying to discover that in a sense – and a rather weak one – all suffering marks the limits of theodicy. And on the other hand, it would be unsatisfying, too, if the only case of suffering that Levinas discussed in the essay is the self's own pain and suffering. Fortunately, however, Levinas takes a decisive further step. He remarks: "One is surprised that there never appears on the foreground [of this commentary on the book of Job] the problem of the relationship between the suffering of the self and the suffering which a self can experience over the suffering of the other man."[107] He even suggests that in the book of Job itself there is a "secret indication" of this further issue. Levinas points out that God's challenge to Job at 38:4, "Where were you when I founded the earth?," is a "denunciation" of Job that assumes as background his fraternal solidarity with all creation and his "responsibility for everything and for all."[108] With these comments, then, we draw near to what is clearly of central concern to Levinas himself.[109]

Levinas then claims that even Nemo himself has *hinted* at the theme at the core of Levinas's thinking: transcendence as it is revealed in the "face of the other man."[110] In a crucial passage, he ties Nemo's theme together with his own:

That in the evil that pursues me the evil suffered by the other man afflicts me, that it touches me, as though from the first the other was calling to me, putting into question my resting on myself and my *conatus essendi*, as though before lamenting over my evil here below, I had to answer for the other – is not this a breakthrough of the Good in the "intention" of which I am in my woe so exclusively aimed at? Is it not theophany, and revelation? The horror of the evil that aims at me becomes horror over the evil in the other man.[111]

Much of this is familiar. What seems unusual is the emphasis on the way each of us, in response to the claim of the other person, suffers over his suffering – the evil suffered by the other afflicts and touches me. Here is a real sense of the

[107] Levinas, "Transcendence and Evil" in *Collected Philosophical Papers*, 184.
[108] Levinas, "Transcendence and Evil" in *Collected Philosophical Papers*, 184.
[109] Cohen fails to see the difference between the two. See *Ethics, Exegesis and Philosophy*, 271–75, where he collapses them. Richard J. Bernstein also fails to note the distinction in *Radical Evil*, 174–80.
[110] "Transcendence and Evil" in *Collected Philosophical Papers*, 185.
[111] "Transcendence and Evil" in *Collected Philosophical Papers*, 185.

good that is deeper and fuller than my realization of a good other than the evil
that assails me. Here is a good made up of my responsibility for the other and
my obligation to assist him, help him, support him.

With this move, two important possibilities come into view. One is that
Levinas can give a more profound meaning to the "end of theodicy," for he
can take it to refer to not every case of suffering in and of itself but rather a
situation when the suffering of the other, to an extreme degree, is caused by
and not alleviated by most people – that is, when the persecuted and afflicted
are abandoned by the world. Another is that Levinas can now use the idea that
the response to suffering is to assist the other, to respond to the plea and call
directed to each of us by those in pain, to clarify how a post-Holocaust life
should be conducted. It is in "Useless Suffering" (1982) that Levinas carries out
this task.

In the opening section of this later essay, "Phenomenology," Levinas recovers
the main features of his earlier account and emphasizes its importance for his
own thinking.[112] The ethical problem of pain and suffering, "useless" by nature,
is what it means as a call to others for assistance, as a "demand for analgesia,"
"the original call for aid, for curative help, help from the other me."[113] Or,
as he says, beyond pure suffering appears the "interhuman."[114] But if this is
the ethical problem *par excellence*, it is, he said, "high-minded" to think that
as a civilization, bound to feed the hungry and heal the sick and reduce the
suffering of others, we are indeed succeeding. Rather, the situation is much
more "uncertain," at a point in modernity when we are "emerging at the end
of a century of unutterable suffering."[115] With this comment, Levinas is on the
brink of applying his analysis to the question of post-Holocaust life.

As in "Transcendence and Evil," Levinas calls attention to the "radical difference between *the suffering in the other*, where it is unforgivable to *me*, solicits
me and calls me, and *suffering in me*, my own experience of suffering, whose
constitutional or congenital uselessness can take on meaning, the only one of
which suffering is capable, in becoming a suffering for the suffering (inexorable
though it may be) of someone else." He calls this "the just suffering in me
for the unjustifiable suffering of the other," an "attention to the suffering of
the other" that is a "supreme ethical principle ... commanding the practical
discipline of vast human groups," both "despite [and] because of the cruelties
of our century."[116] Moreover, "the consciousness of this inescapable obligation

[112] Levinas, "Useless Suffering" in *Entre Nous*, 91–94.
[113] "Useless Suffering" in *Entre Nous*, 93.
[114] "Useless Suffering" in *Entre Nous*, 93–94.
[115] "Useless Suffering" in *Entre Nous*, 94.
[116] "Useless Suffering" in *Entre Nous*, 94.

brings us close to God in a more difficult, but also a more spiritual, way than does confidence in any kind of theodicy."

This is a provocative paragraph. Levinas shifts his focus from the experience of suffering to its impact on the self. He characterizes the self's attention and response to the other's suffering as itself an experience of suffering. Cohen emphasizes Levinas's claim that my suffering, which is intrinsically useless or pointless, can "take on meaning" only by "becoming a suffering for the suffering of someone else." Cohen treats this as something that the self *can do*; it can *make* its suffering *compassion* for the other.[117] The self can set aside theodicy, the attempt to explain or understand suffering by making it an object, by externalizing it. Levinas, according to Cohen, is here claiming that "any attempt to erase the suffering of the sufferer by inserting an explanatory distance between the sufferer and his/her suffering... is not only a sham and hence futile, it is immorality itself."[118] The proper and moral thing to do is to take responsibility for the other. Such a commitment is the hallmark of a post-Holocaust Jewish faith and of a genuine human response to the atrocities of the twentieth century.

Cohen's reading is based on all of Levinas's essays on these matters; we are in the midst of interpreting the essay "Useless Suffering." But his account raises several questions that we need to keep in mind as we continue. First, in what sense is our suffering something we confer with meaning by making it compassion for the suffering of the other? Or is Levinas saying that the only sense in which suffering has any meaning at all is when we see it as a response to the other? Or is it the case both that our suffering is meaningful in a sense and that we can make it so? Second, what is theodicy, the end of theodicy, and the way in which theodicy is an affront to suffering, a failure to cope with it rather than a responsible way of so doing? Third, what role do the Holocaust and the other atrocities of the twentieth century play in our approach to suffering and to theodicy? Is our situation, after these events, distinctive in any important way? Finally, what does the general issue of suffering mean for Judaism and the cruelties of the century? Is Judaism distinctive, and does a post-Holocaust Judaism differ from Judaism in the past?

Levinas turns to the idea of theodicy next. It involves finding meaning in the experience of pain and suffering by locating events in a large design or picture. Theodicy thereby seeks to give order to what is intrinsically absurd and meaningless. It is a "temptation," to find a place of intellectual satisfaction and a way of living in peace, even when there is pain and destitution. Theodicy is moreover an ancient tactic, and one that has taken many forms – religious consolation,

[117] Cohen, *Ethics, Exegesis and Philosophy*, 276–77; see also, "Useless Suffering" in *Entre Nous*, 100. On compassion, see Levinas, *Entre Nous*, 107.
[118] Cohen, *Ethics, Exegesis and Philosophy*, 277.

philosophical resignation, political hopes, and utopian expectations. It contrives justifications in order to bring peace of mind or to direct our future.

What makes our age – after the horrors of world wars, totalitarianisms, Hitlerism, Stalinism, Hiroshima, the Gulag, and the genocides of Auschwitz and Cambodia [Levinas mentions them all, at one time or another] – the "end of theodicy?"[119] His answer: "[P]erhaps the most revolutionary fact of our twentieth-century consciousness... is that of the destruction of balance between Western thought's explicit and implicit theodicy and the forms that suffering and its evil" took on in that century.[120] Here we have suffering inflicted deliberately with no rational limits under the aegis of politics divorced from ethics, "gratuitous human suffering in which evil appears in its diabolical horror," so that there is a manifest "disproportion between suffering and every theodicy." Auschwitz and "the Holocaust of the Jewish people under the reign of Hitler" are here the "paradigm." They show this imbalance, this disproportion or incommensurability between the amount and degree of suffering, on the one hand, and the capacity of explanatory frameworks to cope with it, on the other, "with a glaring, obvious clarity."[121] In short, for Levinas, the evil and horror of the atrocities of the century defy comprehension in thought.

It may be, as he claims, that all suffering is fundamentally meaningless and thus beyond theodicy. But what we have now, in the twentieth century, is a *crisis* in the "normal" way of coping with evil and suffering, for whatever success theodicies once had, even if limited, today is destroyed. Recent evils defy *all* theodicy through and through. They do not simply *limit* theodicy; they *destroy* it. Hence, the need for an ethical response, to act in order to relieve suffering, is *underscored*; it is highlighted and *dramatized*, for the old intellectual strategies are shown to be not merely insufficient; they are exposed as completely inappropriate and defective. It is not that recent atrocities are more deserving of attention and action in behalf of the suffering of the victims and of others. Rather, their character so cripples our capacity to become reconciled and to cope that our genuine and fundamental responsibilities are put in the most glaring light. Theodicy may once have cast a shadow over those responsibilities, hidden or camouflaged them. But the cloud or mist is lifted, and the demands placed upon us are dramatically evident in a vivid way.

Although Levinas is not extremely precise in this account, he does help us to begin to answer our questions. First, theodicy is one way we use to cope with

---

[119] "Useless Suffering" in *Entre Nous*, 97. One might add now the Iraqi assault on the Kurds; the Serbian atrocities against the Bosnians; Rwanda and the genocidal acts against the Tutsis; and the genocide in Darfur.

[120] "Useless Suffering" in *Entre Nous*, 97.

[121] "Useless Suffering" in *Entre Nous*, 97.

the evil of suffering; we seek to explain such occurrences and to satisfy our sense of anxiety by so doing. But the constellation of horrific events in the twentieth century is of such a kind that it thwarts all attempts at such explanation and disables our intellectual satisfaction. Second, we are always, in every relationship with others, responsible for aid, assistance, and kindness. The atrocities of the twentieth century do not alter this dimension of our interpersonal relations; they do not increase the demand, do not create it or elevate it. What they do is remove the temptation of theodicy whereby such responsibility has been hidden. They discredit one possible response by exposing its failures as a response, even on its own terms. By realizing that we no longer can or should be tempted by explanations or rely on them, our responsibility emerges from the shadows and becomes vividly manifest. We see or should see, more clearly than ever before, what our humanity requires of us.

Finally, then, the Holocaust does not uniquely expose our responsibility in this way. It is a paradigm of the dissonance between our intellectual aspirations and the reality of suffering and evil. Perhaps most of all, its horrors resist the comfort of theodicy and explanation. In responding, we respond to others in our world, but we realize the centrality of our obligation because of Auschwitz and the other atrocities it stands for, from the Stalinist purges to the slaughter of Bosnians, Cambodians, Kurds, and Tutsis. Insofar as we realize our obligations and responsibilities more vividly, moreover, we do in a sense give *our* suffering a meaning it did not previously have, but only in a sense. For in another sense, that responsibility is present for us as long as the face of the other calls us into question and makes demands of us, which is a deep and permanent feature of all human social life. What we choose to do is to acknowledge those demands first by not being tempted to theodicy and then by attending more vigorously and committedly than before to the obligations thereby disclosed. In this way, as Cohen claims, Levinas does charge us not to detach or distance ourselves from the suffering of others but rather to commit ourselves, to take upon ourselves compassionately, the task of alleviating it.[122] But our actions are not *directly* responses to Auschwitz, its victims, or the victims of other atrocities in the constellation of horrors.[123] We respond to the suffering of others *today*, in our own world, by recognizing that the suffering of those victims in the past disabled the capacity for theodicy, that this result makes dramatically prominent what our own deepest obligations are in the present, and that the extreme persecutions

---

[122] See Cohen, *Ethics, Exegesis and Philosophy*, 276–78.

[123] In a way, insofar as they are acknowledgment of the victims of those atrocities and thus a recognition of their place in our social lives, even though they are now dead. But in the most obvious way, as acts of reaching out to alleviate suffering and pain, our actions cannot in any way accomplish that for the victims themselves.

of the past century mark a period of abandonment that needs to be recognized and no longer allowed to continue.

RESPONDING TO SUFFERING

In "Useless Suffering," Levinas quotes and responds to the third chapter of Fackenheim's *God's Presence in History*. As we have seen, Levinas reads such theological texts for his own purpose, and this case is no different. In some ways, he reads Fackenheim correctly and accurately, but in other ways his reading reflects his own views more than Fackenheim's. Levinas's first point is one of agreement. Like Fackenheim, he also takes the horrors of Auschwitz – the torture, massacre, the "pain in its utter malignancy" – to mark the "end of theodicy.... [and to] reveal the unjustifiable character of suffering in the other."[124] Fackenheim is responding to his sense that Auschwitz marks a radical rupture in all systems of thought, that it is evil for evil's sake, something unexplainable and without meaning or purpose, not to be assimilated to philosophical accounts, theological justifications, or historical explanations. In Fackenheim's words, if Hegel were alive today, he would no longer be a Hegelian; even the most comprehensive philosophical system cannot comprehend the death camps of Nazism.[125]

However, Levinas adds something that is surely an exaggeration: "[T]he justification of the neighbor's pain is certainly the source of all immorality."[126] As we have seen, indulgence in theodicy may contribute to suffering and immorality; it may mislead people or serve as a mechanism to avoid active response. But it is certainly not its *source*, nor is it the only feature of our lives that occludes our sense of responsibility. Doubtless, Levinas overdramatizes for rhetorical purposes, but his point is at least partially true. And the outcome is a problem or challenge. The events of the twentieth century testify to the cruelties of which we are capable. In this situation, the "philosophical problem ... concerns the meaning that religiosity, but also the human morality of goodness, can continue to have after the end of theodicy."[127] Fackenheim asks this question in his own way: How can one take Auschwitz seriously and still go on? How can one expose one's thought to the Holocaust and heed nonetheless the imperative to

---

[124] "Useless Suffering" in *Entre Nous*, 98.
[125] Fackenheim's most developed account is in *To Mend the World*. See also Emil L. Fackenheim, "Would Hegel Today Be a Hegelian?" *Dialogue* 9 (1970), 222–26; and *The Religious Dimension in Hegel's Thought* (Bloomington: Indiana University Press, 1968). For discussion, see Michael L. Morgan, *Beyond Auschwitz*.
[126] "Useless Suffering," in *Entre Nous*, 99. Cf. Levinas's attacks on ideology and totalizing systems of thought.
[127] "Useless Suffering" in *Entre Nous*, 97.

respond? Once the extremity of evil is manifest and our strategies for coping or reconciling ourselves are disabled, what hope is there?

Levinas thus far has understood Fackenheim, by and large, correctly, and the question he asks is Fackenheim's as much as it is his own. It is his next step, as he cites Fackenheim's response to this situation, that leads him to translate Fackenheim and revise him in his own way. First, he paraphrases Fackenheim's commitment that "Auschwitz would paradoxically entail a revelation from the very God who nevertheless was silent at Auschwitz: a commandment of faithfulness." In order not to bring to completion the Nazi enterprise, to annihilate Israel and forget "the ethical message of the Bible, which Judaism bears," the Jews are obligated "to live and to remain Jews."[128] Details of this paraphrase are not completely right, but we can pass over them. This is surely the gist of Fackenheim's 614th commandment and its elaboration. But we know that for Levinas Jewish obligation, like everyone's, is centrally ethical and that the discourse of divine revelation signifies the command of the face of the other person and our responsibility to others. Hence, Levinas now rereads this account, focused on the Jewish people, in a universal way; moreover, he translates the talk of revelation into ethical terms:

The portion of humanity that, from Sarajevo to Cambodia, witnessed a host of cruelties in the course of a century in which Europe ... seemed to have fully explored its subject – the humanity that, during all these horrors, breathed – already or still – the smoke from the ovens of the "final solution" crematoria where theodicy abruptly appeared impossible – will it, in indifference, abandon the world to useless suffering, leaving it to the political fatality ... of blind forces that inflict misfortune on the weak and conquered, while sparing the conquerors, ... ? Or, ... must not humanity now, in a faith more difficult than before, in a faith without theodicy, continue to live out Sacred History ... that now demands even more from the resources of the *I* in each one of us, and from its suffering inspired by the suffering of the other, from its compassion ... which is no longer suffering "for nothing," and immediately has meaning.... [A]re we not all committed – like the Jewish people to their faithfulness – to the second term of this alternative? This is a new modality in the faith of today ... ; a modality most essential to the modernity that is dawning.[129]

After Auschwitz, then, and after the atrocities from World War I to Cambodia, how should we respond ethically? To do what we always should have been doing, in a situation in which it is more urgent and more "difficult": to be compassionate to others and to make primary in our personal and social lives

---

[128] "Useless Suffering" in *Entre Nous*, 97.
[129] "Useless Suffering" in *Entre Nous*, 99–100.

our obligation of responsibility to others, to relieve suffering and pain, to oppose persecution and oppression and injustice. For Levinas, this is what the recovery of Judaism means; it is what hearing and obeying God's command means. It is what opposing "the criminal enterprise of National Socialism" means.

The differences between Levinas and Fackenheim are significant. For Fackenheim, Auschwitz uniquely defies intellectual explanation or justification and calls for a response. For Levinas, Auschwitz, while paradigmatic of how all theodicy fails, is one of a constellation of atrocities and horrors that define our situation in the twentieth century. Moreover, while the Holocaust may expose the temptation of theodicy, human responsibility is a feature of all social existence. Second, Fackenheim takes all persons to be bound to respond by opposing the forces of evil and hatred, and for some, *Jews*, believers still, the ground of that obligation will be a divine command. For Levinas, the obligation is a permanent one that arises for each and every person always out of every particular social relationship and one that is binding and necessary for all, universally, for the same reason, as an essential feature of every social encounter and all social life.[130] Third, for Fackenheim the response of opposition to the evil of the perpetrators is religious and moral, hermeneutically understood with its particular content by each person as he or she seeks to appropriate the past, through the dark prism of Auschwitz, for the present. For Levinas, the response is thoroughly, or at least primarily, ethical, determined by the precise needs, the pain, the suffering of those who face us today; the obligation is universal even if the particular application is contextual and historically particular.[131] This "ultimate vocation of our people" is also "the ultimate vocation of and for humanity."

Levinas explicitly universalizes Fackenheim's account of authentic response to the radical evil of Auschwitz, but he does not deny that Auschwitz is exemplary of twentieth-century cruelties and horrors or that there *is* or *should be* a Jewish response. Indeed, he joins together the human response and the Jewish one; we have already suggested how. Bernstein takes Levinas's philosophy itself to be an example of such a response; he claims that Levinas's "entire philosophical project can best be understood as an *ethical* response to evil and the problem of evil that we must confront after the 'end of theodicy.'"[132] I think that this proposal, while not completely correct, does contain within it an element of truth.

---

[130] See Cohen, *Ethics, Exegesis and Philosophy*, 278, where Cohen quotes Levinas, "Scandal of Evil," 17.

[131] For a different interpretation and a thoughtful account of Levinas and Fackenheim, see Wright, *The Twilight of Jewish Philosophy*, 97–108.

[132] Bernstein, *Radical Evil*, 167. Cf. Robert Eaglestone, *The Holocaust and the Postmodern* (Oxford: Oxford University Press, 2004), Ch. 9.

First, Bernstein calls attention to Levinas's comment, in an interview in 1986, that "the reference to Auschwitz, where God let the Nazis do what they wanted" is an "explicitly Jewish moment in my thought" and that it raises "the essential problem ...: can we speak of an absolute commandment after Auschwitz? Can we speak of morality after the failure of morality?"[133] He notes that this is the problem of the meaning of religiosity and morality after the end of theodicy.[134] In fact, Bernstein should have realized that Levinas's first comment has more than one meaning. Levinas certainly does ask whether morality is possible once theodicy is no longer available, but he also seems to be asking whether morality as a response to human suffering and need is possible after the twentieth century, when the level of abandonment and indifference and worse, of oppression and cruelty, has been so extreme.[135] Furthermore, Levinas is asking about the obligation to be responsible for others. To be sure, his view – that such an obligation is a dimension of *all* human social life – does answer the historical question, but it is certainly not clear that it is a response to that question, except in a historical or personal sense. That is, the connection between the problem and Levinas's answer may be historical and biographical but not philosophical.

Second, Bernstein notes the fact that Levinas, in "Transcendence and Evil," follows Nemo in taking evil and suffering to breach totality and in this sense to resist theodicy.[136] But this is not what the "end of theodicy" means. Nor is it why the only response to evil and suffering that is the right one is the ethical response: to reach out to alleviate the suffering. Levinas says, as Cohen underlined, that the way to make my suffering meaningful is to become compassionate: to attend to and act in behalf of the other's suffering. It is because *that* is my fundamental responsibility and obligation that I can make my own suffering meaningful and significant. What the end of theodicy means is that I no longer should feel tempted to hide that responsibility or ignore it in favor of some form of justification. The sheer transcendence or meaningfulness of suffering does not call for the ethical response, unless it is the other's suffering, not my own. Indeed, Bernstein misses Levinas's point that the crucial step is to acknowledge and deal with not my suffering but rather the suffering of the other person.[137] He thinks

133 Bernstein, *Radical Evil*, 168; see also his "Evil and Theodicy," in *The Cambridge Companion to Levinas*, 254. Bernstein is quoting from "The Paradox of Morality," 176.
134 Bernstein, "Evil and Theodicy" in Critchley and Bernasconi (eds.), *The Cambridge Companion to Levinas*, 256.
135 Bernstein clearly sees that Auschwitz, for Levinas, is a paradigm of more general horrors; see "Evil and Theodicy" in Critchley and Bernasconi (eds.), *The Cambridge Companion to Levinas*, 256–57.
136 Bernstein, "Evil and Theodicy" in Critchley and Bernasconi (eds.), *The Cambridge Companion to Levinas*, 261.
137 Bernstein, "Evil and Theodicy" in Critchley and Bernasconi (eds.), *The Cambridge Companion to Levinas*, 262–63, 264; Bernstein takes the move for granted.

that we have obligations to others because we understand what suffering is, but this is not correct. For Levinas, we are responsible before we understand and before we suffer; the other's suffering confronts us first, so to speak.[138]

In one sense, then, Levinas's philosophy is a historical response to the horrors of Auschwitz. He responded to the suffering of its victims, and he responded as well to the failure of political ideologies and philosophical thinking to prevent that suffering. The Holocaust provoked Levinas to see things differently. But the central insight of his philosophical inquiry is that all human existence is first and foremost the responsibility to reach out to others around us. Hence, we are led to ask in what way his thinking can itself be understood as such an act of generosity and support. If Levinas's philosophy is in fact a response to the Holocaust, then it ought to be an act of kindness to others. But clearly, doing philosophy of any kind, as a mode of thinking, writing, and speaking, does not contribute *directly* to feeding the hungry or clothing the naked. How, indeed, can philosophy be an act of generosity to others? The answer is that it can be such an act not directly but *indirectly*. It can serve indirectly to facilitate such acts in others. It can, that is, open the eyes of those who might act generously by disclosing for them what is occluded by modern culture and life, by teaching them to understand their obligations to others and eliciting within them a drive to act on those obligations. Philosophy can teach us to respond to the face of the other person. Moreover, if Levinas is right, there are other, perhaps more effective, ways to teach the same lesson. One would be to interpret relevant literary works, such as the texts of the Jewish tradition, in such a way that this teaching is evident and then to expound those interpretations. This kind of literary interpretation of salient texts can become another way to contribute to a culture of responsibility and justice. For Levinas, who was a philosopher and a Jew, this, too, would be a way in which his life and his thought constitute a response to the Holocaust.

REVELATION IN JUDAISM

A central feature of Judaism is to cultivate justice and generosity, to care for the widow, the orphan, and the stranger.[139] This task is especially important,

---

[138] Bernstein, "Evil and Theodicy" in Critchley and Bernasconi (eds.), *The Cambridge Companion to Levinas*, 265.

[139] See, for example, discussion of these themes in Emil Fackenheim, *What Is Judaism?*, 167–80. Fackenheim cites, as biblical support, Deuteronomy 10:17–18 and Psalms 113:7–9. He takes caring for such figures as central to Jewish ethics: "[S]ince losers there are, and since God does love them, it is a *mitzve* [good deed] for us to love them as well, and to do what we can to relieve their condition. One might call this the mainspring of Jewish ethics. It is, at any rate, what gives it its special flavor" (169).

even if all the more difficult, after Auschwitz and the other atrocities of the twentieth century. Moreover, while the suffering of the Jewish people makes the challenge all the more urgent for it, that suffering is a witness to others of how radical has been the abandonment of others and the indifference. But there is more to Jewish life than acting in behalf of others and representing the depth and significance of that obligation. Levinas takes the textual tradition of Israel to teach the centrality of such a task and what it means, so that study, teaching, and education are integral to Jewish life and to the Jewish mission to European civilization and the West. And there is the life of the *mitzvot*, of ritual and commandment. Why and how are these activities central to the vocation of Jewish life and especially of post-Holocaust Judaism? Let me start by considering Levinas's important essay of 1977: "Revelation in the Jewish Tradition."

The concept of revelation has been widely discussed in twentieth-century Jewish thinking, both theological and philosophical.[140] For Buber and Rosenzweig, it meant the divine–human relationship, conceived as an event of divine presence to the human, an address or command that established for the human a link to a transcendent ground of meaning. Hence, from the human side, revelation was conceived by Buber, early in his career, as an ecstatic, mystical act or later as an encounter between an I and a divine Thou, always within a worldly I-Thou episode.[141] For others, including Gershom Scholem and Walter Benjamin, Buber's view was unacceptable precisely because it had an intuitive, irrational quality, in the tradition of Friedrich Jacobi and Søren Kierkegaard. For them, revelation was necessarily complemented by a tradition of reception and interpretation, by commentaries and the language of texts.[142] For Buber and certainly for Rosenzweig, revelation did generate response, and the response was conceived as human and free, but Scholem and Benjamin, and perhaps Rosenzweig, took the real core of revelation to be its textual reverberations rather than its intrinsic character as a concrete event. More traditional Jewish thinkers – Abraham Joshua Heschel and Joseph Soloveitchik for example – elevated that traditional content by treating it as the operative and preeminent mode of revelation, so that for them and many others what revelation meant was the oral and written Torah itself. In their eyes, the content of revelation, as

[140] See Morgan, *Interim Judaism*, Ch. 2.
[141] For an excellent, deep analysis of Buber on these themes, see Emil L. Fackenheim, "Buber's Concept of Revelation," in Schilpp and Friedman (eds.), *The Philosophy of Martin Buber* (La Salle, IL: Open Court, 1967), reprinted in Morgan (ed.), *The Jewish Thought of Emil Fackenheim* (Detroit: Wayne State University Press, 1987), and in Morgan (ed.), *Emil Fackenheim: Jewish Philosophers and Jewish Philosophy* (Bloomington: Indiana University Press, 1996).
[142] See Gershom Scholem, "Revelation and Tradition as Religious Categories in Judaism" in *The Messianic Idea in Judaism* (New York: Schocken, 1971); I discuss Scholem and Benjamin as well as Buber and Rosenzweig in *Interim Judaism*, Ch. 2.

well as its facticity, comes from the divine, and the vast hermeneutical enterprise, routed through human ingenuity and labor, is itself of divine origin; it
is inspired or prophetic.[143] For liberal theologians and philosophers, a central
issue was the role of human freedom or autonomy in the interpretation and
articulation of revelation; for traditionalists, God was the source and ground of
revelation in every way. In Abraham Joshua Heschel's beautiful formulation, the
Bible is not human theology; it is God's anthropology.[144]

Levinas, we should expect, comes to this theme out of an affinity with traditional and rabbinic Judaism and an attraction to the preeminence of Aggadic
and Halakhic textuality and the uniform status of the oral and written Torah,
embodied in the Bible and the Talmud. At the same time, Levinas takes theological language and concepts such as revelation not literally but rather as
expressions of our deep ethical sensibility. Hence, we might expect that for him
the Bible and Talmud are revealed, sacred documents because of their content
and central teaching, the human responsibility for others, and not because of
their source. For him, then, when we speak of God's revelation, on the one
hand, we might be taken to mean precisely the texts that teach that lesson and
on the other hand the revelation of the face itself, which is the *content* or the
reality of that teaching. As we turn to "Revelation in the Jewish Tradition,"
this is the world in which Levinas speaks, and these are our expectations for his
own place within it.

Levinas calls "the narratives and the message of Scripture" "the signs of
the Revelation that was received" and the Talmud "the other form of the
Revelation."[145] Reading, he suggests, is the way that Jews "inhabit" the "living
space" of Revelation. He distinguishes between the orthodox, who accept the
history of Divine "proximity" and Providence literally, and "modern Jews" (the
majority), for whom Revelation is a problem. How, he asks, can such modern
Jews understand the Revelation of an "exteriority" to human reason? What
new conception can they call upon? Before one inquires into the content of
Revelation, we need a clarification of its "ontological status or regime."[146]

But in fact, Levinas turns to its content first and the way its forms call
for interpretation and examination.[147] The revealed texts require that the student go "beyond the plain meaning" and penetrate "the strange or mysterious

---

[143] See Joseph Soloveitchik, *Halakhic Man* (Philadelphia: Jewish Publication Society of America,
1983), and Abraham Joshua Heschel, *Heavenly Torah* (New York: Continuum, 2005; originally
in Hebrew, 1962 and 1965).

[144] Abraham Joshua Heschel, *God in Search of Man*, 412: "[T]he Bible is God's anthropology rather
than man's theology."

[145] Levinas, "Revelation in the Jewish Tradition" in *Beyond the Verse*, 130.

[146] "Revelation in the Jewish Tradition" in *Beyond the Verse*, 130–31.

[147] "Revelation in the Jewish Tradition" in *Beyond the Verse*, 131.

ambiguity or polysemy authorized by the Hebrew syntax."[148] What emerges
is a "specifically Jewish exegesis of Scripture" that elucidates and evokes the
"innumerable meanings [hidden] in the Word of God."[149] This is "*Midrash*, or
search, or interrogation." The way, then, that the content employs the reader,
Levinas says, already gives us a hint about the *status* of Revelation: "its word
coming from elsewhere, from outside, and simultaneously dwelling in the person who receives it."[150] And here Levinas gives us what we expect, that the
Revelation is a call to the self from the outside, "calling to the unique within
me." The message of the Revelation, the voice, goes out to each who hears it
and is inflected through him, and they, these listeners or hearers, are many.[151]
Intrinsically, then, the content that calls out to the "freedom of this exegesis"
is directed to and refracted through multiplicity. But this fact leads to a serious question: "[H]ow is such a call to the diversity of people insured against
the arbitrary nature of subjectivism?"[152] Levinas answers that readings are not
isolated and whimsical; rather, they form parts of a unity, a historical tradition
of commentaries and readings that frame a kind of "historical continuity" to
which every serious and responsible reader must refer.[153]

The four central features of Jewish revelation are captured in two distinctions,
between oral law and written law and between Aggadah and Halakhah. But the
core idea about its content is that it is prescriptive or normative; it is *mitzvah* and
Halakhah.[154] Later, we shall return to the role of ritual and law in Judaism;[155]
here Levinas locates it at the heart of Revelation. It is what "gives unity to the
Jewish people."[156] And yet, as he notes, study of the Torah "is equal in religious
value to actually carrying them out," a remarkable albeit powerful judgment
indeed.[157] Alongside the law, moreover, are the "apologues and parables" of the
Aggadah that "constitute the metaphysics and philosophical anthropology of
Judaism."[158] These texts, some collected together, others interspersed throughout the Talmud, should be taken as contemporaneous in order to clarify and
characterize Judaism's system of thought.[159]

---

[148] "Revelation in the Jewish Tradition" in *Beyond the Verse*, 132.
[149] "Revelation in the Jewish Tradition" in *Beyond the Verse*, 132.
[150] "Revelation in the Jewish Tradition" in *Beyond the Verse*, 133.
[151] "Revelation in the Jewish Tradition" in *Beyond the Verse*, 133–34.
[152] "Revelation in the Jewish Tradition" in *Beyond the Verse*, 134.
[153] "Revelation in the Jewish Tradition" in *Beyond the Verse*, 135; see also 137: "[T]radition . . .
confers unity on the texts."
[154] "Revelation in the Jewish Tradition" in *Beyond the Verse*, 140.
[155] See "Revelation in the Jewish Tradition" in *Beyond the Verse*, 143.
[156] "Revelation in the Jewish Tradition" in *Beyond the Verse*, 143.
[157] "Revelation in the Jewish Tradition" in *Beyond the Verse*, 141.
[158] "Revelation in the Jewish Tradition" in *Beyond the Verse*, 141.
[159] Fackenheim also claims a preeminence for Midrash, conceived as a totality and a unity, and as
the expression of Judaism's native theology. See the first chapter of *Quest for Past and Future*

These comments inform us about the form or structure of the Revelation. What about its content?[160] Levinas tells us exactly what we would expect. Distrust myth and politics; they are unavoidable and useful, but do not count on them. The flaws of ideology were a central theme of Grossman's *Life and Fate* and one reason Levinas was so fond of citing the book. The central teaching of the Revelation is "to approach one's neighbor," to be concerned for the "lot of the widow and orphan, the stranger and poor," and to approach with hands full, with bread from one's own mouth.[161] "My very uniqueness lies in the responsibility for the other man."[162] This is what it means to obey God and thus to be free. The central teaching of Revelation is the primacy of the ethical, cultivated to be sure through the "yoke of the commandments" and the ritual law but nonetheless at the core of Jewish life.[163]

Levinas finally arrives at his major question: "[H]ow might a Jew 'explain' to himself the very fact of the Revelation in all its extraordinariness, which, if the Scriptures are taken literally, tradition presents to him as coming from outside the order of the world?"[164] Revelation, that is, is said to come from outside, to call us, to *command* us.[165] What does this mean? What is this call to vigilance, this disruption? It is a call to responsibility, a call that only makes sense as not only coming from the other but also directed at one who hears it. There is Revelation only if there is a person who calls and one who is called.[166] Such a hearer is also a student, a scholar, a man of reason. "He is taught and he teaches."[167] But Revelation, before it is reception, is command, and, as Levinas finally confirms, it comes from the outside only if such "a rupture or a breach in the closed order of totality, of the world, or of the self-sufficiency of its correlative, reason" is possible.[168] We have arrived, then, at a motif that we have discussed before: Levinas's critique of totality and his commitment to the infinite as the face of the other person. This breach of totality is not a "magical" or "miraculous" event; rather, it is a feature or dimension of everyday life that is ignored, neglected, or obscured by all of the concepts and language that constitute our everyday or theoretical ways of experiencing and understanding

(Bloomington, IN: Indiana University Press, 1968) and Ch. 1 of *God's Presence in History* (New York: New York University Press, 1970): "The Midrashic Framework."

[160] "Revelation in the Jewish Tradition" in *Beyond the Verse*, 142–43.

[161] "Revelation in the Jewish Tradition" in *Beyond the Verse*, 142.

[162] "Revelation in the Jewish Tradition" in *Beyond the Verse*, 142.

[163] This theme, stated so clearly in this essay, is present throughout Levinas's Talmudic lessons. See also "On the Jewish Reading of Scriptures" in *Beyond the Verse*, 101–15.

[164] "Revelation in the Jewish Tradition" in *Beyond the Verse*, 143.

[165] "Revelation in the Jewish Tradition" in *Beyond the Verse*, 144. The command comes first.

[166] "Revelation in the Jewish Tradition" in *Beyond the Verse*, 145.

[167] "Revelation in the Jewish Tradition" in *Beyond the Verse*, 145.

[168] "Revelation in the Jewish Tradition" in *Beyond the Verse*, 146.

the world we live in. It is the face that exposes the other's needs and suffering and that calls to us for response and acceptance. Just as Levinas had, as long ago as the 1950s and then in *Totality and Infinity*, argued that the idea of the infinite is the face of the other,[169] that the breach is an ethical one, so here, in this essay, Levinas claims that the "model of revelation" is ethical.[170] In a sense, the status of revelation is conferred by its content; it is not that revelation calls us to care for the other person. It just *is* the call of the other, whose command makes us responsible and thereby makes us who we are. That *is* Revelation.

Levinas asks whether Judaism in some way evokes the "'rationality' of a reason" unlike the "reason of the philosophical tradition."[171] He points to the prominence of the prescriptive and of obedience, the love of one's neighbor, the "taking upon oneself of the other's destiny."[172] This is an "infinite responsibility, a responsibility against my will, one that I have not chosen."[173] It is the "'Here I am' [*hineni*] of man welcoming his neighbor."[174] His conclusion, then, is that the "fact of Revelation" as a "relation with exteriority" is this encounter with the other's face. Such an encounter is "the model worthy of transcendence" so that he can say: "[T]he Bible is Revelation . . . as an ethical kerygma."[175] Revelation in Judaism just *is* our ethical responsibility to which the other person calls us. It is that dimension of all our life that is so often hidden from us, ignored or neglected, and yet is always there and available, the obligation to generosity and justice that is prior to all else.

Levinas wants this recognition and this obedience, moreover, to be a form of rationality, but not a philosophical or everyday form. It is rationality as a kind of coming to awareness or attentiveness, what he calls an "awakening."[176] Here we come to realize who we are by first grasping what we owe, a sobering up or awakening that puts us in touch with a feature of life too often neglected or occluded. The Bible and Talmud teach this lesson. Genuine life lives it. It is the content and the very fact of Revelation.

There is no naturalism here, no denial of Revelation. Nor, however, is this the picture of a traditional theism with its moments of divine epiphany and miraculous action. It saves the remarkable character of Revelation by seeing what lies hidden in and not above the interhuman, social world, and it sees the

---

[169] See "Revelation in the Jewish Tradition" in *Beyond the Verse*, 149.
[170] See "Revelation in the Jewish Tradition" in *Beyond the Verse*, 149.
[171] See "Revelation in the Jewish Tradition" in *Beyond the Verse*, 149; see also 148–50.
[172] See "Revelation in the Jewish Tradition" in *Beyond the Verse*, 149; see also 148–50.
[173] "Revelation in the Jewish Tradition" in *Beyond the Verse*, 147.
[174] "Revelation in the Jewish Tradition" in *Beyond the Verse*, 148.
[175] "Revelation in the Jewish Tradition" in *Beyond the Verse*, 148.
[176] "Revelation in the Jewish Tradition" in *Beyond the Verse*, 150. Elsewhere, he also calls it a "sobering up."

value in Jewish textuality: that it teaches this lesson when properly understood. The Cartesian idea of the *infinite* is the philosophical analogue of *Revelation* in Jewish tradition; ethics is the content and substance of both.

RITUAL AND THE LAW

Along the way to this conclusion, as I noted, Levinas comments that "the most characteristic aspect of Jewish difficult freedom lies perhaps in the ritual that governs all the acts of daily life, in the famous 'yoke of the Law.'" This might seem to be a strange thing for Levinas to say. As a descriptive statement about orthodox Judaism, it may be true. Surely, the detail and extent of the ritual law is indicative of a traditional Jewish life. But even if it is true, can Levinas think that it should be? Indeed, can he find a significant place for Jewish ritual at all? It would be odd to be so immersed in the Talmud only to dismiss or ignore its legal, ritual dimension completely. To be sure, Levinas himself focuses on the Aggadic (interpretive) portions of the text, but he commends its primarily Halakhic (legal) character, and Jewish law is, among other things, ritual and ceremonial observance. In Wyschogrod's words, "[W]hat is the justification for Jewish ritual if ethical action is founded in the upsurge of the other and if such action is the way in which Judaism appears in the world? What, in short, accounts for the necessity of Jewish ritual *praxis*?"[177]

Let me start with Wyschogrod's answer: "According to Levinas, the obedience to ritual law constitutes a discipline that tends toward justice. In obeying ritual law, the demand of the other is recognized; the other, in this case God, has a right to suppress the egoity of the separated self."[178] For the moment, suppose that this answer is clear and acceptable: Jewish ritual is valuable as a regimen for everyday life that is a "discipline" in behalf of justice. Still, "why is ritual law necessary?"[179] Wyschogrod has no answer; Levinas seems to have none.

Tamra Wright, in *The Twilight of Jewish Philosophy*, discusses Wyschogrod's two questions and her understanding of Levinas's account of Jewish ritual as a "severe discipline" that "tends toward justice."[180] Wyschogrod drew on Levinas's "A Religion for Adults" for her interpretation of Levinas's justification for the ritual law. There Levinas explains that the law demands effort, regularity, and amounts to training; it cultivates "a courage that is calmer, nobler and greater

---

[177] Wyschogrod, *Emmanuel Levinas*, 165. See Levinas, "The Name of God According to a Few Talmudic Passages" in *Beyond the Verse*, 123–24.
[178] Wyschogrod, *Emmanuel Levinas*, 165.
[179] Wyschogrod, *Emmanuel Levinas*, 166.
[180] Wright, *The Twilight of Jewish Philosophy*, 118–23.

than that of the warrior." In Judaism, goodness and legalism are in harmony, he says.[181] Wright accepts Wyschogrod's view and yet argues that the question of the law's necessity "loses its force" if we distinguish, as Levinas does, between recognizing one's ethical responsibility and acting on it or obeying the obligation to be just. It might seem that "ritual practice," Wright claims, "is needed not to enable us to hear [or recognize] the commandment, but to prepare us to respond to it in a positive fashion, acting in accordance with our responsibility."[182] She cites several comments that Levinas makes in the interview "The Paradox of Morality" where he distinguishes between the authority of the face and its force. Clearly, Levinas realizes that not all people, all the time, and with sufficient commitment, act in behalf of others. But Wright notes an ambiguity: Levinas admits that not all people "recognize" their responsibility to others, where "recognize" can mean both "are aware of" and "act on or obey." In the end, then, Wright's judgment regarding Jews, ritual, and the good is that "the commandment[183] which issues from the face can always be recognized, but is not always obeyed, and the discipline of Jewish law can help prepare us to obey the Other. Whether or not there are other ways of preparing to welcome the Other remains an open question." Indeed, one can easily suppose that there are and must be.

I am not convinced that separating the acknowledgment of the obligation to others, acceptance of them, from acting on one's responsibility toward them in fact is a wise strategy; in fact, it may be impossible. Outside of killing the other, all actions in relation to him or her involve some level of acknowledgment or acceptance, some responsiveness to the face. In fact, even killing the other, as an act, involves such acceptance. The more one is conscious of that fact and of the responsibilities one owes, the more one can act more fully in behalf of them. If Jewish ritual conduct disciplines or trains the Jew to greater attentiveness and greater sensitivity to others, it serves a useful purpose. Indeed, it may do so in an especially effective way. In short, it may train the Jew to see things more clearly and to be sufficiently disciplined to act in behalf of what he or she sees to be right and good. But while the law is thereby valuable for the Jew, it hardly is uniquely valuable for these purposes, and it certainly cannot be so for all people, non-Jews included.

In "Revelation in the Jewish Tradition," as I indicated, Levinas comments that Jewish ritual is "the most characteristic aspect of Jewish difficult freedom," and this might be taken as a descriptive point that what is most distinctive and manifest in Jewish life is ritual conduct. But, of course, this does not tell us

---

[181] Levinas, "A Religion for Adults" in *Difficult Freedom*, 18–19.
[182] Wright, *The Twilight of Jewish Philosophy*, 119–21, esp. 120.
[183] Wright, *The Twilight of Jewish Philosophy*, 121.

why, nor does it tell us how ritual functions or what it means and accomplishes. Levinas goes on: "[I]n ritual a distance is taken up *within* nature *in respect of nature*, and perhaps therefore it is precisely the waiting for the Most-High which is a relation to Him – or, if one prefers, a deference, a deference to the beyond which creates here the very concept of a beyond or a towards-God."[184] This is a difficult text, a perplexing and unclear one. Let me suggest a reading: Ritual in Judaism is explicitly a response to divine command. Thus, ritual acts constitute a kind of deference to God that serves to establish a sense of a beyond, which Levinas of course believes is in fact the relation to the face of the other person. Jewish ritual, then, is a step on the way to seeing such a relationship, to our receptivity to it. Such ritual acts, which help train Jews to acknowledge otherness and thus to recognize one's responsibility to others, do so by occurring in nature by setting up a "distance" between the Jew and God as other. Ritual acts, that is, are part of the mythology of theology; they deal with Jews and God, but what they accomplish is a first step in the process of education that leads to the acknowledgment of the face of the other person.

I would not want to claim that what Wyschogrod noticed and Wright elaborated should be replaced by this account. It is more likely that Levinas had a number of reasons for thinking Jewish ritual to be valuable and significant, all connected with the priority of the ethical but in different ways. What this interpretation adds, however, is the idea that ritual is not solely about motivation and obedience. It is also about awareness or recognition of the face as a commanding presence and in a very precise way. Operating within theological territory, ritual points beyond nature and totality, and in this way it prepares the Jew for an awareness of his or her ethical responsibilities. The dense life of ritual conduct may cultivate abilities that will ultimately serve ethical purposes; it may be a training for obedience. But it also encourages the Jew to acknowledge that which confronts her from outside nature, from beyond the everyday. That is, it trains her to see what lies hidden in concrete ordinary life, a dimension of responsibility, purpose, and meaning too often hidden from view.

Wyschogrod asked whether ritual law and obedience to it is *necessary* for Jewish life. I think that Levinas would not be happy with the word "necessary" or the way the question is framed. In an interview, he said that he could "accept the idea that the singular contributes to the universal." Even the pope, he said, recognized in Jewish existence "almost a character of necessity." But he then cautioned about the word "necessity." The point is that Jewish existence – its people, readings, and life – has a "permanent signification," that there is "a value to the survival of Judaism."[185] The same caution might be directed at the

---

[184] "Revelation in the Jewish Tradition" in *Beyond the Verse*, 143.
[185] Levinas, "Interview with Francois Poirié" in *Is It Righteous to Be?*, 69.

question of ritual in Jewish life. The issue is not whether it is necessary; rather, it is whether ritual is valuable and meaningful. Is it justified? Is there a point to it? And Levinas's answer is yes, for many reasons, insofar as it serves the greater purposes of human responsibility and justice.[186] Levinas, then, is not interested in justifying the necessity of Jewish survival or of the role of ritual in Jewish life, but he is concerned deeply about justifying the fact of Jewish existence and the fact of ritual. This is the task of finding meaning or value.

It should also be said that for Levinas the Bible and the Talmud, the chief texts of Judaism, not only include Aggadic passages that speak of God and man and that incorporate the philosophical framework of Judaism. They also primarily include Halakhic, or legal, texts that prescribe obligations. It would be altogether strange if these norms, which commanded obedience, were in fact ignored as norms and if obedience to them were not meaningful and valuable. Moreover, because the central teaching of the former is a universal ethics, an austere humanism, surely obedience to those ritual norms should also contribute, in some way or ways, to the same universal ethical conception of human life. Levinas certainly indicates that they do, even if his account of how ritual contributes is neither complete nor precise enough.

ETHICS AND EDUCATION

Judaism's most important role, however, is educational. If read properly, the Bible and the Talmud teach ethics and responsibility. What is Levinas's hermeneutical method, and what are its products?

The Bible, the Talmud, and other Jewish texts are not the sole resources for teachings about the interhuman and ethical responsibility. This obvious point is well worth underscoring. Levinas takes Shakespeare, Dostoyevsky, Pushkin, and many others to be valuable sources concerning the primacy of the ethical and the social.[187] Jewish and Hebrew texts may be exemplary and especially useful, but they are hardly unique. Like some fiction and poetry, religious texts can

---

[186] See Levinas, "In the Name of the Other" in *Is It Righteous to Be?*, 198: "I take worship seriously, because those venerable gestures maintain and exalt man's humanity"; see also 258.

[187] It is tempting to compare Levinas's engagement with Jewish texts as well as with Shakespeare, Dostoyevsky, and others, with Cavell's engagement with Shakespeare and Hollywood films. For the latter, see Anthony J. Cascardi, "'Disowning Knowledge': Cavell on Shakespeare" in Richard Eldridge (ed.), *Stanley Cavell*, 190–205, esp. 194: "...Cavell's work on Shakespeare shifts the ground of the analysis of tragedy [from action] to the questions of knowledge and doubt, which in turn point to the problems of acknowledgment and avoidance" and "the moral of skepticism." Similarly, one might say, Levinas's reading of the Talmud shifts the ground of the analysis from theology and law to what he calls the ethical, the primary responsibility of human social existence.

be shown to feature Levinas's ethical themes, and Jewish ones, on his reading, and teach these themes everywhere, with nuance and conviction, although they are but one among many such resources. Nonetheless, because these themes *pervade* the Bible and its commentaries and because they are the featured core, on his view, of that entire literary tradition, Levinas takes Hebrew language and literature to be virtually synonymous with awareness of the central ethical obligation to others.[188] Hence, as he often says, Jews have the responsibility to teach the Greek West to speak Hebrew. Jews, that is, must first learn what their own texts mean and then communicate that meaning to the world.[189]

The texts, preeminently the Bible and the Talmud, are not theological. Levinas is concerned primarily with the nonlegal, or Aggadic, passages, precisely those that thinkers like Fackenheim have taken to be theological.[190] For Levinas, however, even they are philosophical and not theoretical or ideological. Indeed, the legal passages also disclose, on careful reading, a philosophical core, the primacy of the ethical and responsibility.[191] And the task of the skilled interpreter is to unearth that core, to translate it into Greek and then to communicate it, on the model of the original Greek translations of the Bible, the Septuagint.[192] Earlier, we discussed how we must understand this effort at speaking about the face-to-face with a language not suited to it. Here, what I want to emphasize is that Hebrew, in order to be understood, must be translated. This is what study requires, both the exploration that discloses the core meaning of the texts and the communication of that teaching in everyday terms.[193] There is a project of discovery and disclosure that incorporates and involves a translation into Western language and thought.

Furthermore, the real outcome of this process and in fact the core that Jewish texts teach is not a new theory, even an ethical one, but rather ethical action itself. The product of exegesis, in other words, is not a new interpretation of these old texts, but rather a way of life that is aware of human responsibility and acts in behalf of others, that is responsive to the needs and suffering of others. Exegesis is a just life.[194]

---

[188] See Levinas, *Ethics and Infinity*, 117.

[189] See Putnam, "Levinas and Judaism" in Critchley and Bernasconi (eds), *The Cambridge Companion to Levinas*, 45–53; Jill Robbins, *Prodigal Son/Elder Brother*, Ch. 4. See also Cohen, Gibbs, and Handelman.

[190] See Cohen, *Ethics, Exegesis and Philosophy*, 217; Emil L. Fackenheim, *God's Presence in History* (New York: New York University Press; 1970), Ch. 1; and Morgan (ed.), *The Jewish Thought of Emil Fackenheim* (Detroit: Wayne State University Press, 1987).

[191] Robbins, *Prodigal Son/Elder Brother*, 105.

[192] Robbins, *Prodigal Son/Elder Brother*, 105; 115–16.

[193] See Robbins, *Prodigal Son/Elder Brother*, 125–29.

[194] I think that this is one of the central claims that Richard Cohen makes in *Ethics, Exegesis and Philosophy*.

In order to explore these themes, let me look at two essays by Levinas: "On the Jewish Reading of Scripture" (1979) and "From Ethics to Exegesis" (1985).[195] My goal is to understand what Levinas takes the method and role of such reading to be, especially what part it plays in Jewish life.

In "A Religion for Adults" (1957), Levinas calls the Bible in "its specifically Jewish physiognomy," by which he means the Bible as interpreted in the Talmud and generally in rabbinic commentaries, a "route" that leads from Jewish particularity to its universalism.[196] That universalism and its meaning is constituted by the "ethical relation," for, as he puts it, that relation is "not the corollary of the vision of God, it is that very vision."[197] Throughout the essay, Levinas uses biblical, Talmudic, and other rabbinic texts to express and articulate that central teaching. In "From Ethics to Exegesis" (1985), Levinas returns to the same theme. "The reality of Israel" – which we find in the material and historical content of Judaism's documents and practices – is a "formation and expression of the universal."[198] This universal is what he calls the ethical, responsibility toward the other, a "structure or modality" that is "hidden beneath consciousness" and is exposed by means of a phenomenology "attentive to the horizons of consciousness."[199] The Bible and Talmudic, rabbinic literature express this hidden structure theologically and narratively. Levinas calls these texts and interpretations a *"figure* in which a primordial mode of the human is revealed, in which, before any theology and outside any mythology, God comes to mind."[200] Alternatively, "the entire Torah, in its minute descriptions, is concentrated in the 'Thou shalt not kill' that the face of the other signifies...."[201] These texts, that is, express God's Torah in the *language of human beings*, that is, in theological and mythological terms. Exegesis or hermeneutics is the way that this secret, the teaching of the ethical, is revealed and "ever renewed."[202] Levinas uses metaphors of life, death, and reanimation: an old book, written in a dead language, whose teaching is to be "resuscitated, in order that its innumerable intentions may be reawakened." He calls such exegesis "a solicitation" and an "appeal" to the Talmud and rabbinic commentaries, in behalf of a sense of prophecy that precedes theology, a "difficult universality."[203]

[195] See also the Talmudic reading Levinas, "The Translation of the Scripture" in *In the Time of the Nations*, 35–54.
[196] Levinas, "A Religion for Adults" in *Difficult Freedom*, 13.
[197] "A Religion for Adults" in *Difficult Freedom*, 17.
[198] Levinas, "From Ethics to Exegesis" in *In the Time of the Nations*, 109.
[199] "From Ethics to Exegesis" in *In the Time of the Nations*, 109.
[200] "From Ethics to Exegesis" in *In the Time of the Nations*, 110.
[201] "From Ethics to Exegesis" in *In the Time of the Nations*, 111.
[202] "From Ethics to Exegesis" in *In the Time of the Nations*, 112.
[203] "From Ethics to Exegesis" in *In the Time of the Nations*, 112–13.

Levinas claims that the Bible and Talmud have always contained this central teaching. But I think that he would argue that Jewish readers have not always appreciated this fact or grasped this message. Nor have others heard it from Jewish readers. To hear the "prophetic word" is to hear, from within Judaism, "the wisdom of the commentary of the masters." But Jews and others in the West have read the texts differently, and the outcome is our century, with its horror and atrocities. Now, in an especially urgent way, we live in a time when the "past refuses to be forgotten – a past of world wars and the camps of the twentieth century: Concentration and Death. A past of the Passion of Israel under Adolf Hitler." In such a time, the prophetic word of the Bible and its commentaries needs to be heard. The task of exegesis, of a life of hearing the message of responsibility, is indeed urgent.[204]

Levinas's commitment to reading the Bible through the prism of rabbinic commentaries not only aligns him with traditional Jewish hermeneutics – a point emphasized, for example, by Susan Handelman; it also suggests a comparison with Gershom Scholem and a contrast with readers as diverse as Spinoza, on the one hand, and Martin Buber and Franz Rosenzweig, on the other.[205] For one thing, several of these readers see the biblical text and commentaries on it in terms of their relation to revelation. For Buber and Rosenzweig, for example, that revelation is an event of divine-human encounter that is pre-conceptual and preliteral, so that the Bible itself is the record or repository of the first Hebrew and Jewish literary responses to the formative revelatory events that established the history and destiny of the Jewish people. These texts incorporate the earliest articulations of the Jewish understanding of what a meaningful human life would be historically and what its character and goals should be. The aim of modern readers, then, should be to recover that pristine formulation and its content and to grasp what it means for Jewish life today. This recovery requires a reading that seeks to return to the text itself and its central teachings, which, for Buber and Rosenzweig, concern the shaping of genuine communities grounded in interpersonal love and concern. Buber privileges the biblical text and castigates the rabbinic commentaries, especially the tradition of Halakhic literature, as a later distortion of the original message. Hence, he calls for a return to the text itself in all its pristine purity, read in its original language. For very different reasons, Spinoza also denigrates rabbinic commentaries and calls for a return to the Bible itself, but his reading is not an attempt to disclose the original articulation of the meaning of a founding revelation. Rather, it is an effort to disclose the central, universal ethical teaching of the text by using

---

[204] "From Ethics to Exegesis" in *In the Time of the Nations*, 113.
[205] See Susan Handelman, *Fragments of Redemption* (Bloomington: Indiana University Press, 1991); Morgan, *Interim Judaism*, Ch. 2.

historical and scientific methods to distinguish this abiding moral message from the historical contexts and personal rhetorical features that incorporate it.

Scholem, on the other hand, rejects the Buberian commitment to a founding prelinguistic revelation and the attack of Buber and Spinoza on traditional rabbinic interpretations. For him, and for his friend Walter Benjamin, the revelation itself is linguistic, and the Torah is not a response to it as much as it is its unique literary form. The vast legacy of commentaries and readings that constitute Jewish textuality is the bridge, the mediation, between every contemporary reader and that original revealed, divine, unique linguistic revelation. To recover that origin requires reading it through the layers and perspectives of that tradition, whether normative and rabbinic or nonnormative and kabbalistic.[206]

Levinas's hermeneutics – its overall structure and its method – shares something with the readership of Buber, Rosenzweig, Spinoza, Scholem, and Benjamin. Of course, it also shares something with the method of traditional Talmudic interpretation.[207] Like them, he treats the Bible as basic and as the source of Jewish or Hebrew spirituality. But unlike Buber and Spinoza, he does not reject the vast textual tradition that stems from and reacts to the Bible; he respects it and studies it. As for Scholem, Benjamin, and the traditional readers, Levinas affirms the importance of rabbinic Judaism, "the oral tradition of exegesis which crystallized in the Talmud and its commentaries" that gives the Bible what he calls its "specifically Jewish physiognomy."[208] Without this tradition, the Bible is many books with many teachings. With it, the Bible pronounces and proclaims *one* message. In this regard, Levinas is most like Spinoza, whose momentous development of a historical reading of Scripture served to isolate and elevate the Bible's central ethical core, the obligation to act generously and justly, to love one's neighbor as oneself.[209] To be sure, Levinas casts his own reading of the Bible, the Talmud, and rabbinic Judaism as a teaching of ethics as a traditional Jewish reading and as what monotheism truly means. Ironically, it is a Spinozist content poured into an orthodox Jewish form, and it is bold, if not

---

[206] See Morgan, *Interim Judaism*, Ch. 2, and Scholem, "Revelation and Tradition as Religious Categories in Judaism" in *The Messianic Idea in Judaism*.

[207] Levinas often recalls his studies with the Talmudic genius Chouchani in the late 1940s and early 1950s; it is the method Chouchani taught him that Levinas employs in his Talmudic lessons. See Samuel Moyn, "Emmanuel Levinas's Talmudic Readings: Between Tradition and Invention," *Prooftexts* 23:3 (Fall 2003), 338–64.

[208] "A Religion for Adults" in *Difficult Freedom*, 13; see also *Is It Righteous to Be?*, 275. See Cohen, *Ethics, Exegesis and Philosophy*, 243. For an excellent treatment of the rabbinic tradition, see Jay Harris, *How Do We Know This?*

[209] See Spinoza, *Theological-Political Treatise*; see also J. Samuel Preus, *Spinoza and the Irrelevance of Biblical Authority* (Cambridge: Cambridge University Press, 2001). Cohen discusses Spinoza and compares him to Levinas in *Ethics, Exegesis and Philosophy*.

surprising, to hear Levinas call the primacy of the ethical the Bible's "prophetic" teaching.[210]

Unlike these readers, however, Levinas was not really a theorist. He showed no interest in hermeneutics as a study of methods of interpretation. We have no treatise from him, like Hans-Georg Gadamer's *Truth and Method*, nor essays like those of Buber and Rosenzweig.[211] Most of all, what we have – famously – is a series of readings, primarily of Talmudic texts and of other Jewish writings. In fact, Levinas invested a great deal of himself in these readings, in learning and refining a way of reading the Talmud and then in the actual readings themselves (there were 23), which cover a period of at least 30 years, from 1960 to 1989.[212] Others have written about these readings, especially the Talmudic lessons that he gave annually during these years, and there is no need to do so here or the space to discuss them properly.[213] But on two occasions, his readings shed important light on the role and character of such textual interpretations.

READING JEWISH TEXTS

In the 1979 essay "On the Jewish Reading of Scriptures," Levinas seeks "to illustrate, by examples, certain ways of reading" the Bible within traditional Jewish texts.[214] Here, Levinas elicits from traditional texts themselves insights about how to read those very texts and the Bible, of which they are themselves exegesis; thus results, as he calls it, an "exegesis of the exegesis," a reading of a "commentary of the Scriptures" that "can take us on the path towards transcendence," toward "the epiphany of God... involved in the human."[215] In the end, moreover, this reading requires "modern language" and reference to "the problems of today," to which these texts testify.[216] Let me say something here about this requirement.

---

[210] See *Is It Righteous to Be?*, 283–85; and OB, 140–52.

[211] See Hans Gadamer, *Truth and Method* (New York: Continuum, 2004); Martin Buber and Franz Rosenzweig, *Scripture and Translation* (Bloomington: Indiana University Press, 1994); see also Levinas, *Is It Righteous to Be?*, 161: "I have no rule for interpretation."

[212] Robert Gibbs gives a complete list of the published readings, from Levinas's annual presentations at the meetings of French Jewish intellectuals; in *Correlations in Rosenzweig*, 175. All but two have been translated into English. In addition, Levinas gave regular Talmudic lessons while he was director of the Ecole Normale Israélite Orientale, the school of the Alliance Israélite Universelle.

[213] For discussion, see the introduction to Levinas, *Nine Talmudic Lessons*; Robbins, *Prodigal Son/Elder Brother*; Wyschogrod, *Emmanuel Levinas*; Wright, *The Twilight of Jewish Philosophy*; and Handelman, *Fragments of Redemption*.

[214] "On the Jewish Reading of Scriptures" in *Beyond the Verse*, 101.

[215] "On the Jewish Reading of Scriptures" in *Beyond the Verse*, 101, 102, 112.

[216] "On the Jewish Reading of Scriptures" in *Beyond the Verse*, 102.

The text Levinas looks at is Tractate Makkoth of the Babylonian Talmud, page 23b.[217] The issue in the text is whether the flogging inflicted as a punishment by a court can affect the subject's atonement concerning his or her being excluded from eschatological rewards, which is a divine judgment. That is, can the result of a human act annul one of divine judgment?[218] Levinas says that his goal is to locate the "meaning" hidden behind and within the "antiquated language" of the text in its own "specific universe." To accomplish this goal requires raising "the anachronisms and local colour" like a curtain. He calls this concreteness and the way it hides generalities and meanings "the paradigmatic modality of Talmudic reflection."[219] Reading requires locating what is hidden behind that concreteness.

Levinas then reads the text and in the course of his reading shows how its meaning concerns the primacy of the face of the other and of responsibility, how it concerns "transcendence and height" and how it relates to the word "God."[220] Hence, as he puts it,

[T]he statement commented upon exceeds what it originally wants to say; that what it is capable of saying goes beyond what it wants to say; that it contains more than it contains; that perhaps an inexhaustible surplus of meaning remains locked in the syntactic structures of the sentence, in its word-groups, its actual words, phonemes and letters, in all this materiality of the saying which is potentially signifying all the time. Exegesis would come to free, in these signs, a bewitched significance that smoulders beneath the characters or coils up in all this literature of letters.[221]

Throughout this summation, the text in question is the Bible and the Talmudic comments, and the exegesis is the rabbinic exegesis of the Bible and Levinas's exegesis of the Talmud. But primarily, the text is the Bible and the exegesis is the Talmud and rabbinic commentaries.

Levinas asks: What makes the book divine, sacred? What is its "signature?" His answer concerns its "inspired" content, not its form. The divinity of the Bible derives from its inner meaning, from the meaning that "beckons" to a hearing that listens beyond the words, that "awakens" a genuine listening to the "meaning of meanings, to the face of the other man."[222] The Bible is sacred and has its special status because it disturbs our everyday, customary understanding

---

[217] This Talmudic passage is also discussed in Levinas, *New Talmudic Readings* (Pittsburgh: Duquesne University Press, 1999), 47–77; the lesson is from 1974.

[218] *New Talmudic Readings*, 47–77.

[219] "On the Jewish Reading of Scriptures" in *Beyond the Verse*, 103.

[220] "On the Jewish Reading of Scriptures" in *Beyond the Verse*, 103–7.

[221] "On the Jewish Reading of Scriptures" in *Beyond the Verse*, 109; see also 110–11.

[222] "On the Jewish Reading of Scriptures" in *Beyond the Verse*, 111.

and grips us with the call to a realization of our responsibility to others. Its message is its medium, or at least its significance. For others, from traditional Jewish readers to those like Buber and even Scholem, the Bible is sacred because it is revealed, or it is taken to be sacred because it is either taken to be revealed or taken to be an original response to revelation and is thus grounded in revelation. And in all these cases, revelation is an event of divine–human encounter or divine–human communication. For Levinas, the voice that speaks to the reader through the words of the Bible is the voice of suffering and responsibility; the Bible articulates the meaning of the other's face, and that is what makes it divine or why the reader should take it to be so. Even when the Bible does not use the word "God," as in the Book of Esther, there is this ethical awakening when the "ontological rest of being" is "torn and sobered up."[223] For Levinas, the status and authority of the text derives from its message and not from its origin.

The *right* reading of the Bible, then, responds to its call by listening and by hearing its message, to respond to the face. As Levinas would have it, Talmudic and rabbinic commentary, in *its* listening and responding, in *its* exegesis, confirms to today's reader the central meaning of the Bible. Indeed, we might say, each act of exegesis, when it reveals various modalities of that central ethical message, confirms, through an act of listening that is also an act of reading, the voice that speaks through the texts and to the reader.

But is this the right reading? Indeed, might this transcendence not just be the outcome of "man's interiority, his creativity or subconscious?"[224] This is an obvious criticism, what Levinas calls a "modern-day resistance." His own reading might just be his own subjective response to the text. Such a criticism goes to the heart of Levinas's worry about totality and idealism. He sees this: He paraphrases the question about whether his reading that takes the Bible and Talmud to disclose transcendence as a general question about ethics itself. He asks: "Is not ethics basically autonomous?" Let us be clear. Levinas is not asking about whether *any* reading can be said to be the right one;[225] rather, he is asking about whether *his* reading can be the right one. Does the *text itself* appreciate this objection, that there is *no transcendence*, and respond to it or anticipate it? Levinas thinks that it does. The text juxtaposes two views, one that reason is sufficient and the other that along with reason, divine judgment intervenes. According to one view, reason is solely human; according to the other, it is human and also divine. Yet, while tradition records that the latter is retained, the former rejected,

---

[223] "On the Jewish Reading of Scriptures" in *Beyond the Verse*, 112.

[224] "On the Jewish Reading of Scriptures" in *Beyond the Verse*, 113.

[225] Levinas may think that tradition supports his reading as the most likely one, but he has no argument for there being only *one* correct reading. See *Is It Righteous to Be?*, 164.

both are "written down." That is, as Levinas puts it, the text may appear to retain an ambiguity, and "would not the man of today [today's reader] recognize in this ambiguity the alternating movements of his own thought?"[226] Today's reader may take texts, the Bible and its commentaries, either with Levinas's openness to an ethical spirituality or with historians and philologists who seek to naturalize and demystify them. The text itself calls on us at least to alternate back and forth, to take it to be open to transcendence or to be closed to it. Its ambiguity would result in an "alternation" of perspectives that can be hesitant and incredulous but that also can be open – awaiting a hermeneutic, as he puts it.[227] The text does not guarantee that Levinas's reading is correct, but it does itself acknowledge its possibility and even encourage an openness for it. The Talmud, in this light, is not dogmatic. It underscores the possibility of its own receptivity.

This is a valuable conclusion, one that is all the more appealing because it is not dogmatic but rather open and even suggestive. Levinas realizes that our culture and our language are unavoidable features of our lives. The Bible and Talmud cannot call upon us to reject them totally, nor should they call upon us to read these texts reductively and narrowly. And once we realize that the ethical teaching he calls "transcendence" is unavoidable, we can see the case it makes for its significance and how the texts in their own way disclose that case. The alternating of readings matches the fact that in life both transcendence and totality are unavoidable; we ought to appreciate that our social life is grounded in responsibility, but also that it requires language, thought, argument, theory, institutions, principles, and policies. Philology is as necessary as the third party and the practices of justice.

TRANSLATING THE BIBLE AND THE TALMUD

We noted earlier that for Levinas our contemporary readers require a "modern language" that calls attention to the "problems of today."[228] He also noted that the Bible and Talmud couched their teachings in an ancient vocabulary and in concrete issues of a bygone culture. The point of these requirements is that transcendence is revealed in texts in language, and if Hebrew is more attuned to expose it, our modern language is surely not. For that we need translation, a translation of Hebrew into Greek – of the ancient texts into modern terms – and even more fundamentally of the grounds of the ethical into language itself.

---

[226] "On the Jewish Reading of Scriptures" in *Beyond the Verse*, 114.
[227] "On the Jewish Reading of Scriptures" in *Beyond the Verse*, 115.
[228] "On the Jewish Reading of Scriptures" in *Beyond the Verse*, 102.

Levinas's best account of this issue is the Talmudic lesson "The Translation of the Scripture."[229]

The lesson deals with passages from the Tractate Megillah (8b and 9a–9b), and its subject is the question "whether or not [Jewish religious] law authorizes the translation of the very verses in which it is framed, and thus the presentation of the Scriptures, the Hebrew text of the tradition, in a foreign language, without compromising their dignity and spiritual significance."[230] Levinas takes the Greek language to represent European and Western civilization, the domain of theory, of the everyday, and of the shapes of consciousness that life takes for us.[231] To learn from the Bible and its commentaries requires exploring it in our own terms, relating it to modern problems, and thus translating its stories, motifs, and figures into our language, what "Greek" stands for.

The lesson is about what the Talmud itself says about such a translation of Hebrew spirituality into Greek terms. Can it be done? Does it sacrifice the meaning of the original or distort it? The text refers to the legend about the origin of the Septuagint, the first Greek translation of the Pentateuch; Levinas claims that for all its fantastical character and "anecdotal value . . . [the story] contains a truth independent of its historical reality and is a teaching . . . [whose] truth is what interests us."[232]

Let me attend only to the central points that Levinas makes. First, the Talmud, as so often, records contending views. There are those who hold a "universalist stance, which recommends a 'translatable Judaism,' open to the language of the nations" without losing its sacred (ethical) character, and there are those who claim that "there is no universal meaning of Judaism separable from the traditional forms. An untranslatable Judaism."[233] Second, the text distinguishes between "cult and culture," as Levinas puts it, between the books and universal teaching of Judaism, on the one hand, and the "unalterable Judaism . . . of the synagogue" with its ceremony and ritual. The latter is untranslatable and internal; the former is "a Judaism open to modernity."[234] Third, there is something unique about the "exceptional relationship between biblical wisdom and Greek."[235] The Torah retains its sacred character when translated into Greek; there is a sense in which "rabbinic Judaism wishes to be a part of Europe."[236]

---

229 "The Translation of the Scripture" in *In the Time of the Nations*, 33–54; see also Gibbs, *Correlations in Rosenzweig and Levinas*, 164–67.

230 "The Translation of the Scripture" in *In the Time of the Nations*, 36.

231 See *Is It Righteous To Be?*, 161; Gibbs, *Correlations*, 156–57.

232 "The Translation of the Scripture" in *In the Time of the Nations*, 38.

233 "The Translation of the Scripture" in *In the Time of the Nations*, 40, 41.

234 "The Translation of the Scripture" in *In the Time of the Nations*, 44.

235 "The Translation of the Scripture" in *In the Time of the Nations*, 47.

236 "The Translation of the Scripture" in *In the Time of the Nations*, 48. The problem of translation is closely related to the relationship between totality or ontology and infinity or ethics. I have tried to show that for Levinas they are dimensions of one human life, so to speak. There

Levinas calls this an "assimilation into Europe," but only "up to a point," an "alliance between the Hebrew and the Greek Bible, [an] assimilation – that page 9b of the Megillah 'authorizes' by relating the miracle of the agreement of the seventy-two translators."[237]

Fifth, this assimilation, this alliance and translation, is limited. It exists but only "up to a point." The Talmud records, and Levinas discusses, 15 cases where the Septuagint, the Greek, "corrects" and does not strictly translate the Hebrew. The point of these corrections, Levinas claims, is to show that "there is a domain of the untranslatable at the heart of the Pentateuch itself." Why? In some cases, he argues, the corrections have historical or political reasons; they are intentional alterations to avoid confusion or misreading or worse. But in other cases, the corrections reveal what he calls "more subtle reflections." In certain texts, the literal meaning calls out for interpretation and gives rise to *midrash* and a tradition of interpretation. The written meaning is elaborated by a tradition of reading. Hence, translating the Torah into Greek can be a "trial" that exposes moments when the written text cannot or ought not be grasped without that tradition. It is a challenge to the biblical teaching to "welcome" Western philosophy and culture, while exalting its own "genius." Translation, that is, is not simple or easy; it marks a task: how to communicate to modern culture this ancient teaching and yet to maintain one's integrity, to know when "correction" is necessary or expedient and when it is impossible.[238]

Finally, "perhaps also [the Bible] *must* be translated into Greek."[239] Greek brings with it clarity. It brings method; it deciphers, demystifies, demythicizes, and depoeticizes. It is the heart of our academic discourse; it is conceptual and prosaic. And these functions, as Levinas hints, are necessary for the Bible and its ethical core. Without them, the message may remain hidden, elusive, and obscure. It may be a risk to translate the Bible; but without that risk, there is no hope of learning what it teaches and living by it.

In an earlier chapter, we discussed the objection that the face as trace – as the epiphany of what is beyond being, of the absolutely absent – is somehow beyond thought and expressibility. There is at least an analogue between that problem and the question of translating the Hebrew Bible into Greek discourse. Indeed, it may be that the problem is more than an analogue; it may be the original, founding case of such a translation question. In the case of the Bible, the Talmud, rabbinic commentaries, and other Jewish texts, there is a chain of

---

is no infinity without totality; infinity is the most fundamental dimension of ordinary life. Hence, the central teaching of the Bible, its Hebrew message, *must* be translated into Greek, the language of the everyday. We shall say more about these issues shortly.

[237] "The Translation of the Scripture" in *In the Time of the Nations*, 48–49.

[238] "The Translation of the Scripture" in *In the Time of the Nations*, 51–52; for Levinas's comments, see *Is It Righteous to Be?*, 274–75.

[239] "The Translation of the Scripture" in *In the Time of the Nations*, 52.

tradition, of exegesis and reinterpretation that is renewal and recovery. There is, as I mentioned earlier, a homogeneity or continuity that unites that tradition as an enunciation and elaboration of a core teaching. That continuity confirms the reading and increasingly the correctness of it.[240] But there are needs – social, political, and even internal and interpretive – for opening those texts and that tradition to the rest of life, to Greek language and Western culture. The risks are obvious. In this Talmudic lesson, Levinas spends more time on the benefits, which are as plentiful when they are internal as external. He affirms the particularity and the universality of Judaism. Translation is a bridge between them, a major one but not the only one. It is one vehicle for the educational role of Judaism in Western culture and today in modern culture. As we have pointed out, the suffering of the Jewish people, as a barometer of the failings of civilization, is one dimension of that educational role. A more positive dimension is the role of teacher, of educating others through the exegesis of the Bible and rabbinic texts, of preaching the word in the "language of humankind."[241] Indeed, when we ask ourselves how Levinas conceives his own role as a philosopher, as a Jew, and as an ethical agent, education about responsibility and justice is certainly of central importance.

INTERPRETING LEVINAS ON INTERPRETATION

Among discussions of Levinas as a reader of Jewish texts and the relation between Hebrew and Greek in his thinking in several works – for example, those by Wyschogrod, Wright, and Colin Davis – the most important, I think, are the chapters on Levinas in Robert Gibbs's *Correlations Between Rosenzweig and Levinas*, especially Chapter 7, and Chapter 7 in Cohen's book *Ethics, Exegesis and Philosophy*. For our purposes, concerning the role of interpretation, the character of translation, and the issues of correctness and objectivity, we will turn to Gibbs's account.

According to Gibbs, Levinas's attitudes toward Greek culture, language, and wisdom changed over the course of his career. I believe, however, that clearly by the time he gave the Talmudic lesson on translation and discussed exegesis in the essays we examined, he took the Greek language – everyday language in Western culture and the discourse of philosophy, of the academy, and of the intellect – to be somehow important. For us, it is the language of

---

[240] On this issue of objectivity, see Wright, *The Twilight of Jewish Philosophy*, 164–69; there are many readings of Scripture – *Is It Righteous to Be?*, 164; Cohen, *Ethics, Exegesis and Philosophy*, 257–58.
[241] See Wright, *The Twilight of Jewish Philosophy*, 141–69; she gives a reading of "The Translation of the Scripture" on pp. 149–56; see also Wyschogrod, *Emmanuel Levinas*, 168–71.

modernity, and translation into it is desirable and even necessary. Gibbs discusses translation in Chapter 7 and points out that it is a matter of modes of thought as well as terminology and vocabulary.[242] Moreover, Gibbs realizes that translating Hebrew into Greek is at the core of Levinas's entire philosophical enterprise. It is not something that goes on only in the Talmudic lessons and in the exegesis of Jewish texts; rather, it is what happens whenever Levinas examines, analyzes, exposes, and elucidates the face-to-face encounter and primordial interpersonal responsibility. I have underscored this point: All Levinas's philosophy, in a sense, is such a translation.[243] Gibbs, for example, calls attention to the biblical and Hebrew origins for Levinasian terms such as "holiness," "face," and even "*illeity*." At the present, however, for us, the most important part of Gibbs's account is his discussion of Levinas's "philosophical hermeneutics."[244]

Gibbs makes these points. First, "Hebrew" is the Bible, but only as it is read through the Midrash and rabbinic commentaries. We noted that this traditional belief, articulated theoretically by scholars like Scholem, is central to Levinas.[245] Furthermore, it is clear that these interpretations provide multiple readings, although it is clear, too, that all express in one way or another the same ethical core. Second, the style of the Talmudic and Midrashic texts is spare and clipped. It is not rhetorical, while Greek is.[246] Third, Levinas's own exegeses are in Greek – they use modern language, philosophical terms and figures, and references to history, scientific inquiry, and urgent contemporary issues.[247] But by and large, his readings are philosophical and not historical or philological or traditional, in any orthodox sense. They are akin to traditional reading, but whatever similarity there is in form is belied by their content. At the deepest level, they demythologize and demystify in favor of revealing his ethical humanism.[248] Fourth, he devotes himself to Aggadah and not Halakhah, for the latter is legal material that deals with conduct, whereas he is interested in the religious and ethical meaning of the Bible and these texts.[249] Indeed, as

---

[242] Gibbs, *Correlations*, 164–67.
[243] See Putnam, "Levinas and Judaism," in Critchley and Bernasconi (eds.), *The Cambridge Companion to Levinas*, 37–39, 43–45; cf. Gibbs, *Correlations*, 165–66.
[244] Gibbs, *Correlations*, 167–75.
[245] Gibbs, *Correlations*, 167.
[246] Gibbs, *Correlations*, 167–68. Obviously, "rhetorical" here must be taken in a rather narrow, specific sense, as a literary style of a certain sort, one that includes the use of literary figures and tropes of a standard type. This does seem a rather extraordinary claim, because rabbinic literature does use literary figures – for example, parable and analogy – even if it does not use such figures in the same way and to the same extent as Greek literature.
[247] Gibbs, *Correlations*, 168–69.
[248] Gibbs, *Correlations*, 168–70.
[249] Gibbs, *Correlations*, 170.

Gibbs points out, the universality of the Talmud's ethical message is central to its character.

To these points, Gibbs adds a comment on Levinas's claim, made in the lesson on translation, that Hebrew actually *requires* Greek translation. It requires it and calls for it. I have already noticed how and why Levinas says this, but it will be useful to see what Gibbs says and then to clarify what Levinas is really saying. Calling attention to a discussion of Aggadah and Halakhah in a lesson on Baba Kama 60a-b, given in 1975,[250] Gibbs notes how Levinas's introductory comment points out that the Talmud shows how Halakhah leads to Aggadah and then back – that is, how religion leads to philosophy or how Hebrew thought leads to Greek. That is, one cannot stay with Hebrew texts; they require conceptual elucidation and exploration. Gibbs says that the key to understanding the *necessity*, that Hebrew calls for Greek, is "that one must speak in conceptual language."[251] It is the key but not the whole key: Another part is that "the Sages themselves are pursuing universality." Gibbs then adds two further points: that Levinas takes Genesis 9:27 to mean that Hebrew needs the beauty and clarity of Greek or philosophical articulation and that translation into Greek, as the Septuagint shows, is a trial or test that "reveals the merit of the tradition."[252] Gibbs summarizes his discussion by claiming that to Jews Levinas argues that the Hebrew texts themselves require translation and to non-Jews that Western culture needs the translation to make up for the ethical sensitivity it lacks.

Gibbs's summary is helpful, but his account of why the Bible and Talmud require "translation" into modern terms is insufficiently deep. As we noted when we looked at the Talmudic lesson on translation, Levinas does say that the Bible seeks the clarity of philosophical formulation and that such translation is a trial or test that exposes the role that Midrash plays as it seeks to clarify problems in the text that translation into philosophical language simply corrects and cannot otherwise cope with. But none of this explains why the Hebrew text that teaches responsibility calls for and requires translation into everyday, modern, or Western terms. These points are suggestive but not in the end explanatory, as is the point that if we seek to speak about the ethical, we need to do so in conceptual vocabulary. But this last point, while not in itself adequate, is more helpful. The point needs further clarification.

"Greek" stands for theoretical discourse but also for the ordinary language of everyday life; it stands, that is, for all the ways that we normally articulate, describe, or express our everyday, interpersonal relations. By extension, it stands

---

[250] In Levinas, *Nine Talmudic Readings*, 182; see also Gibbs, *Correlations*, 171.
[251] Gibbs, *Correlations*, 172.
[252] Gibbs, *Correlations*, 172.

for the ways that our relationships are conducted. Moreover, we live in these articulable relations; and to the degree that we recognize our responsibility for the other person and seek to realize it, we do so through these relations and in everyday social acts. As we have so often argued, the ethical and the everyday are not alternative ways of relating to others, as if we could choose to live only in exclusively ethical relations. The problem we face is whether we are aware of our responsibilities and whether we live our relations with others as responsive to them, out of acknowledgment, acceptance, and respect. Hence, just as the face-to-face *requires* everyday life, so Hebrew, the mode of thought that identifies our responsibility, *requires* Greek, the mode of thought and discourse that gives responsibility its expression. In a sense, when it comes to our thought and discourse, Hebrew is the *content*, while Greek is the *form*. Neither can do without the other or does do without the other. This may not be exactly right, but it is close: It is at least true that there is no Hebrew without Greek, while no Greek is genuinely meaningful without Hebrew.

Gibbs concludes his discussion of translation with "two remaining questions."[253] One is whether Hebrew writings are necessary for Greek culture, whether "Judaism has something unique to offer."[254] Frankly, I think that Levinas is clear about this. The teaching of the Bible, the primacy of the ethical, is not *uniquely* taught by the Jewish tradition or present in Hebrew texts. One can learn it from Shakespeare, Pushkin, Dostoyevsky, and elsewhere – and even in Jewish texts, not all are biblical or Talmudic, for one finds the teaching in Grossman and in the *Nefesh HaHayyim* of Rabbi Hayyim of Volozhin. It is dominant, however, in the Bible and its exegetical tradition and is characteristic of it, so that historically the Hebrew and Jewish tradition has represented that teaching most profoundly and characteristically.

Gibbs's second question is whether Judaism has an "untranslatable core," or whether in the end Judaism's "particularist universality" cannot be overcome.[255] In the end, has Levinas "sold out" Jewish particularity, as Gibbs puts it? He takes the Talmud lesson on translation, particularly the section on the Septuagint and the 15 corrections, to show that there is something in the Bible that Greek cannot or will not translate. As Levinas says, these 15 corrections "signify that there is a domain of the untranslatable at the heart of the Pentateuch itself."[256] Gibbs takes this to be an issue about philosophy and Judaism, and he argues for their compatibility. They do not necessarily compromise each other, for Levinas: Philosophy can – indeed, must – accept the other, and Judaism "seeks

[253] Gibbs, *Correlations*, 173–75.
[254] Gibbs, *Correlations*, 173.
[255] Gibbs, *Correlations*, 173.
[256] "The Translation of the Scripture" in *In the Time of the Nations*, 50.

universality through its own particularity."[257] I agree that Levinas sees the two as mutually supporting and cooperative. But it is also important to remember what Levinas calls a "more subtle reflection" revealed by the corrections in the Septuagint. The *reason* that the Septuagint corrects the Bible is because the Bible, read in its own exegetical tradition, *threatens* the Greek world or is *challenged* by it. Translation is a "necessary trial" for the ethical teaching; it is a trial about the "possibility and necessity" of expressing the Torah in Greek, of translating the ethical teaching into philosophical or Western discourse and thus of finding a way to make our Western lives ethical. Translation tests the ability we have in our everyday lives of living justly in behalf of a basic generosity or concern for others. In short, the issue for Levinas is not about guarding or respecting Jewish particularity. In a sense, Judaism and the Hellenic West, Hebrew and Greek, are ineluctably tied together; they are two dimensions of human existence. They are one, just as are the saying and the said, the face-to-face and the social world of the third party. The challenge is not to respect the universality of Judaism while protecting its particularity; rather, the challenge is to find a way to use Greek to disclose the meaning of Hebrew. No translation can afford to misconstrue, nor can it succeed in making the original redundant or irrelevant. Gibbs has asked the wrong question and worried about the wrong things.[258]

Levinas helps us to see these limitations and the point of translation elsewhere, in a Talmudic lesson on Sanhedrin 99a and 99b. Discussing a *baraita* (non-Mishnaíc Tannaitic text) on Numbers 15:31 and the interdiction against those who "scorn the word of the Lord," Levinas comments:

What is the *meaning* of that notion of the heavenly origin of the Torah? In the *literal sense*, of course, it is a reference to the Sinai Revelation, at the divine origin of the text. There is no question here of putting that meaning aside. (italics mine)[259]

At one level, that is, we can express in our terms what this idea refers to, even if the terms are such that we cannot grasp or experience what they mean. The event is a myth, a story. What does "the heavenly origin of the Torah" invoke in our lives?

But if it is not possible to describe the *lived meaning* of such terms, one can inquire about the *experience* in which it is approached. This is not "spiritualizing" or "liberalizing" religious notions, it is the attempt to seek for them a *translation* that the properly religious surplus of truth already *presupposes*.... The Torah is transcendent and from heaven by its demands that clash, in the final analysis, with the pure

[257] Gibbs, *Correlations*, 174.
[258] See Wright, *The Twilight of Jewish Philosophy*, 158–69.
[259] Levinas, "Contempt for the Torah as Idolatry" in *In the Time of the Nations*, 61.

ontology of the world. The Torah demands, in opposition to the natural persever-
ance of each being in his or her own being (a fundamental ontological law), care
for the stranger, the widow and the orphan, a preoccupation with the other person.
(italics mine)[260]

Levinas proposes an interpretation – a translation – of the literal meaning into
an account of the *experience* that is assumed by the literal meaning of the text.
That experience is the demand of the other's face that calls upon us to extend
care and kindness even when that requires setting aside our natural desires and
interests. This is the *existential correlate*, as it were, of the textual reference to the
heavenly origin of the Torah. It is what the fact of Sinaitic Revelation means
in our lives. Translation into Greek may never capture completely the nature of
that demand, but it provides us with access to the "religious surplus of truth"
that cannot in principle be grasped as a "lived meaning" – that is, we cannot
know literally what "the revelation at Sinai" means – and cannot be literally
articulated in everyday discourse. This is the point of Jewish hermeneutics, of
reading and translating Hebrew texts and teaching their lessons.

ESCHATOLOGY, ETHICS, AND POLITICS

The ultimate goal of such reading and of Jewish life, indeed of all life, is to
feed the hungry and clothe the naked, to reduce suffering and practice justice.
Levinas sees this goal as akin to ethics and politics, to be sure, but his favored
expressions for it, as a goal, are religious and Jewish. He calls it "messianism"
and "prophetic eschatology." He also calls it "peace."[261]

Many of the biblical motifs and Hebraic vocabulary – from "election" and
even "face" to "glory," "holiness," and "prophecy" – that Levinas appropriates have many purposes, among them to signal the close association he sees
between ethics and human responsibility with all that we call "religious." In the
twentieth century and certainly from Weimar through the postwar period, as
philosophy and Western culture have become increasingly "disenchanted" and
secularized, this terminology and these motifs have taken on a very restricted
venue. To transport them into philosophical discourse was and remains a challenging, surprising, and even shocking accomplishment, and it is safe to think
that Levinas knew exactly how dramatic it was and what risks he ran in so
doing. On the one hand, he could easily have been misunderstood as abandoning philosophy altogether for some kind of parochial or even confessional
stance. On the other hand, he could have been simply dismissed as misguided

---

[260] Levinas, "Contempt for the Torah as Idolatry" in *In the Time of the Nations*, 61.
[261] See, for example, Levinas, TI, 22–26, 304–7; see also, 149–52.

396   Judaism, Ethics, and Religion

or anachronistic or both. We could take one of these attitudes and find many sympathetic readers, but I am inclined to be more charitable and to take Levinas to be saying something important about religious life, morality, everyday experience, and philosophy and to be seeking a new perspective on all of them. Levinas is no reductionist, no Spinoza or Kant or Hegel. But just as he feels that religion harbors something of importance, so he believes that philosophy needs religious resources to call attention to its most important teaching.[262]

Levinas's use of the expressions "eschatology" and "messianism," however, occurs in a more complex context. These terms, in the twentieth century and especially in German and continental thought, have not been so narrowly restricted to religious or theological venues. From the beginning of the century and certainly after World War I, they have been widely employed by philosophers, poets, social and cultural critics, literary theorists and critics, political thinkers, and historians. Levinas's work emerges out of modernist culture, and the discourse of messianism and redemption was a prominent feature of that culture. From Georg Simmel, Martin Buber, Rainer Maria Rilke, and Franz Kafka to Ernst Bloch, Walter Benjamin, Siegfried Kracauer, Theodor Adorno, Georg Lukács, and Franz Rosenzweig, reflection on the fragmentation and nihilism of Western civilization, on alienation and a crisis of values, was mixed with new ways of thinking about history, hope, and the messianic.[263] Levinas's appropriation of this vocabulary, then, was not idiosyncratic. As in the case of many others, moreover, his use and interpretation of the terms arose out of both philosophical reflection and Jewish sensibility.

We might be confused, as we approach Levinas on messianism, about what issues concerning this idea and this theme interest him. There are many questions that he, or we, might find difficult and worth exploring. What is the relationship between the messianic and history? Is there a messianism without teleology or some narrative view of history? How is the messianic related to human conduct, to divine action, or to both? What is the character of the messianic? What kind of a state or condition is it? Is the messianic an object of hope or a task to be accomplished? Do we live in a period after the "end of

---

[262] Hermann Cohen, more than a century ago, claimed that a neo-Kantian ethics required the biblical idea of "messianism" without which it would not be complete. Fackenheim argues for the contribution Judaism can make to philosophy in Encounters Between Judaism and Modern Philosophy (New York: Basic Books, 1973) and To Mend the World 3rd ed. (Bloomington: Indiana University Press, 1994).

[263] For discussion of these features of Weimar culture and their impact throughout the twentieth century, see Morgan, Interim Judaism; Anson Rabinbach, In the Shadow of Catastrophe (Berkeley: University of California Press, 1997); Michael Löwy, Redemption and Utopia (Stanford, CA: Stanford University Press, 1992).

messianism" and the "demise of eschatology?" What is the nature of "messianic peace?" What is the relationship between time and the messianic?[264]

In the important essay "Beyond Being, Ontology and Eschatology in the Philosophy of Emmanuel Levinas," Theodore de Boer discusses the relation among war, peace, and messianism in terms of Levinas's critique of totality.[265] In *Totality and Infinity*, de Boer points out, Levinas "opposes the 'eschatology of Messianic peace' to the 'ontology of war,'" and in so doing he "posits an antithesis between the Jewish prophetic tradition and the whole of Western philosophy, which he considers dominated by the concept of totality." The key to the contrast, de Boer notes, is the "ontological pluralism" that is manifest in the relation of the person to the other in terms of "responsibility, goodness, hospitality, and humility." That is, in the tradition of totality, "when the Other is reduced to the Same, Messianic peace turns into the peace of empire, . . . that is, into a peace resulting from the death or subjection of the other."[266] It might be more correct to say that within Western life and thought the dichotomy of war and peace concerns subjugation and coordination, oppression and accommodation. It conceives of these pairs as modes of the basic domination of the other by the same. Messianic peace, on the other hand, as the recognition and realization of responsibility, is more fundamental and more determinative of who we are and what social life ought to be. In short, the vocabulary of messianism calls attention to the ethical as a hope, as an ideal to be realized, and as a standard for our lives, according to which our struggles to achieve historical peace and to avoid conflict can be understood and evaluated.

This suggests, moreover, that Levinas's messianism is not necessarily associated (and perhaps not at all) with a linear or teleological account of history. In his fragments on the concept of history, Walter Benjamin articulated an episodic, discontinuous conception of the messianic and associated it with traditional Jewish messianism, albeit according to his own, somewhat eccentric interpretation. As I suggested, Levinas might usefully be viewed as part of that tradition of messianic reflection that developed before and after World War I. Some of these figures were religious anarchists, some socialists, some antipolitical, others political through and through. Their thinking was regularly tied to some narrative about the decline of Western civilization and a crisis of values, and each in his or her own way proposed a solution, through revolution, art, religion, or some

---

[264] In the last section of this chapter, I will turn to Levinas's discussion of Zionism and, in terms of it, his views on messianism and the political. For now, however, I focus on issues that are relatively independent of his account of Zionism and politics.

[265] Theodore de Boer, "Beyond Being, Ontology and Eschatology in the Philosophy of Emmanuel Levinas" in *The Rationality of Transcendence*, 33–55.

[266] De Boer, "Beyond Being . . ." in *The Rationality of Transcendence*, 33–34.

combination of them or proposed that the times were apocalyptic and beyond redemption. Benjamin, in current discussion, is a core member of the tradition, along with Bloch, Lukács, Rosenzweig, and a host of others – Buber, Scholem, Spengler, Heidegger, and Landauer among them.[267] Many, but not all, were secular or religious Jews, whose thinking achieved a synergy of traditional Jewish messianic ideas with post-Hegelian and neo-Romantic idealism and who challenged the ideal of *Bildung*, of bourgeois progress and optimism, and of the alignment of Judaism with this German idealism.[268]

In an outstanding essay on this "new Jewish sensibility," Anson Rabinbach characterizes it as a "modern Jewish messianism: radical, uncompromising, and comprised of an esoteric intellectualism that is as uncomfortable with the Enlightenment as it is enamored of apocalyptic visions – whether revolutionary or purely redemptive in the spiritual sense."[269] The central feature of this view was a novel view of messianism, which, according to Rabinbach, "demanded a complete repudiation of the world as it is, placing its hope in a future whose realization can only be brought about by the destruction of the old order." It was a vision that was "apocalyptic, catastrophic, utopian, and pessimistic."[270] It was about recognizing the fragmentation and alienation of society and envisioning a recovery of its wholeness only through destruction, about a new view of European culture and politics.[271]

Drawing on Gershom Scholem's account in his magisterial essay "Toward an Understanding of the Messianic Idea in Judaism," Rabinbach characterizes "four different dimensions to Jewish messianism."[272] First is the "restorative aspect" that includes a utopian vision of a past to be recovered, that is opposed to any idea of reform or progress and invokes the reclaiming of esoteric (secret) knowledge.[273] Second is a "*redemptive* utopian aspect" that points to a unity beyond history and includes a "decisive and total break with the past."[274] The prominence of a public, disruptive event, a caesura, is an "*apocalyptic* element."

[267] See Löwy, *Redemption and Utopia*; Richard Wolin, *The Frankfurt School Revisited* (New York: Routledge, 2006).
[268] See Rabinbach, *In the Shadow of Catastrophe*, 27–28.
[269] Rabinbach, "Between Apocalypse and Enlightenment: Benjamin, Bloch, and Modern German-Jewish Messianism" *In the Shadow of Catastrophe*, 27–65, esp. 28 (originally in *New German Critique* 34 (Winter 1985)).
[270] Rabinbach, *In the Shadow of Catastrophe*, 29, 30.
[271] Rabinbach, *In the Shadow of Catastrophe*, 29.
[272] Gershom Scholem, "Toward an Understanding of the Messianic Idea in Judaism" in *The Messianic Idea in Judaism* (New York: Schocken, 1971), 1–36; cf. Moshe Idel *Messianic Mystics* (New Haven, CT: Yale University Press, 2000).
[273] Rabinbach, *In the Shadow of Catastrophe*, 31.
[274] Rabinbach, *In the Shadow of Catastrophe*, 32.

It calls for a leap from present to future and for a "catastrophic upheaval" as the "precondition for the full restitution of the messianic period."[275] Finally, there is the fact that "determined action or profane events" are irrelevant and therefore that messianism has a "profound *ethical ambivalence*."[276] In the essay that follows, Rabinbach explores the messianic thinking of Bloch, Benjamin, and a number of others, and he concludes that Benjamin, for one, formulates a view that is apocalyptic, that rejects normal politics and "historical activism" in favor of an esoteric, redemptive intellectualism, and that is genuinely anarchic and radically utopian.[277]

Rabinbach is right that for Benjamin the redemption of Western culture from fascism will involve a destructive leap and a rupture and furthermore that it will not be the result of historical and political activism. Rather, it will require episodic revelations of the cause and character of urgencies and danger and subsequent response to such "knowledge." That knowledge is got by genuine historical inquiry, that of the literary critic, who "establishes a conception of the present as the 'time of the now' which is shot through with chips of Messianic time."[278] And that redemption occurs to make that present instant – *any* present – messianic, "for every second of time was the strait gate through which the Messiah might enter."

For Levinas, prophetic eschatology and messianism are similarly redemptive and episodic or momentary.[279] They are the ethical as it occurs at any moment in acts of responsibility, of kindness and generosity (or ethical acts that are as pure as one could imagine, given the situation).[280] And they are the ethical when it transforms social practice and political policy into justice. Levinas is not apocalyptic, nor is he intellectualist, but he is redemptive and utopian. In some ways, moreover, like Benjamin, he conceives of the messianic as outside the historical and the political, if we take them to be constructed according to traditional narratives. But in other ways, Levinas does not reject social and political institutions as much as he fears their corruption and appreciates the extraordinary failures of Western civilization, particularly in the twentieth century. He does not despair; he retains some hope, but only if individuals can understand their

[275] Rabinbach, *In the Shadow of Catastrophe*, 32–33.
[276] Rabinbach, *In the Shadow of Catastrophe*, 33–34.
[277] See Rabinbach, *In the Shadow of Catastrophe*, 62–65.
[278] Walter Benjamin, "Theses on the Philosophy of History" in Benjamin, *Illuminations* (New York: Harcourt Brace & World, 1968), 265, 266; see also the recent translation of "On the Concept of History," in *Walter Benjamin, Selected Writings, Volume 4, 1938–1940* (Cambridge, MA: Belknap Press, 2003), 397.
[279] See Bernasconi, "Different Styles of Eschatology," 7ff.
[280] One thinks of the action of the Russian woman, described by Grossman in *Life and Fate*.

infinite responsibilities and if they can learn to live by them.[281] In his valuable essay "Different Styles of Eschatology: Derrida's Take on Levinas's Political
Messianism," Robert Bernasconi calls attention to this nonteleological way in
which Levinas takes the messianic to interrupt history: "Messianic eschatology
is not a doctrine of last things. . . . The 'beyond history' is . . . that which interrupts history. . . . Eschatology in Levinas is not a question of the future, but a
disturbance or interruption of the present."[282] Messianic peace and prophetic
eschatology are not teleological themes.[283] But they do involve human acts –
acts of kindness and justice.

Bernasconi is particularly interested in Derrida's comments on eschatology
and messianism in Levinas. Strictly speaking, as he shows, Levinas is not happy
with the expression "eschatology," because it suggests so strongly a teleological
philosophy of history.[284] This is especially clear in the passages from *Totality and
Infinity*, including those I just cited, and in comments from Levinas's interview
with Richard Kearney.[285] The first feature of Levinas's messianic thinking or
ethics, then, is its episodic character: It is a matter of transforming moments
(or periods) of history through responsible, generous, caring actions. In this
respect, Levinas's messianism is akin to Benjamin's.

Bernasconi, however, then turns to a further issue: the relation between
Levinas's messianism and politics. If Levinas is like Benjamin in rejecting a
linear eschatology, he nonetheless differs in other respects. I do not see him as
apocalyptic; we may now live in a time of crisis, in the shadow of a century of
atrocities and horrors, but this is history, for Levinas, not a necessary feature of a
redemptive situation. However, the major difference between the two, I think,
concerns politics – the nexus of economic, social, and organizational structures
and institutions that make up our public lives. Here Levinas is guarded but more
sanguine than Benjamin, who is decidedly negative.[286] In order to discuss this
subject – the relation between political action and messianic ethics – we need
to turn to our last topic: Levinas's Zionism, for arguably it is in this concrete
situation, concerning Israel and Zionism, that the issue emerges in the most
vivid manner.

---

[281] There are times when Levinas has hopes of this kind for Marxism; see Simon Critchley, "Persecution Before Exploitation: A Non-Jewish Israel?," *Parallax* 8:3 (July–Sep. 2002),
71–77.

[282] Bernasconi, "Different Styles of Eschatology," 7.

[283] See TI, 22–23, and "Revelation in the Jewish Tradition" in *Beyond the Verse*, 143.

[284] Literally, it is a "doctrine of last things."

[285] See TI, 21–23, 241–44; Kearney interview, in Cohen (ed.), *Face to Face with Levinas*, 30;
Caygill, *Levinas and the Political*, 97–98.

[286] Benjamin is negative about the importance of political action for messianism in the fragment
on theology and politics and arguably later, in the 1930s, as well.

LEVINAS'S ZIONISM

Howard Caygill discusses Levinas's views about the State of Israel in *Levinas and the Political*, but his interest is the way Levinas's writings engage with traditional problems in political theory and political science.[287] There are a number of perspectives one might take on Levinas's Zionist writings, in terms of their place within the tradition of Zionist thought within Judaism, their relationship to Western views of Judaism and politics, their relation to thinking about political institutions and ethical theory, and what they say that is related to traditional Jewish thinking about messianism and the Land of Israel. I do not want to conduct a full-scale inquiry here into Levinas's Zionist thinking in terms of these and other venues. Rather, I want to ask two questions: How does Levinas see the relationship between Jewish universalism with its central focus on the ethical and justice, on the one hand, and the State of Israel, on the other? And, is there any connection between his conception of the ethical as messianic, as prophetic eschatology, and the Jewish state? In "Different Styles of Eschatology," Bernasconi discusses these issues in the light of Levinas's three essays on Zionism collected in *Beyond the Verse*.[288]

In his early writings, Levinas clearly claims that the State of Israel, to live up to the ideals of the state, should be religious, and this means that it must be committed to the "difficult and erudite work of justice." The land and the state are the venue and opportunity for the Jewish people to carry out its work: the "execution of justice." As Levinas puts it, the genuinely religious Jews are "those who seek to have a State *in order to have justice*" (my italics).[289] Levinas accepts the functional role of the political, of government, but sees it as requiring an ethical character. For Jews, then, the State of Israel is like a sculptor's marble or clay, to be shaped in a way that exemplifies justice and generosity. The material itself is of no intrinsic value. It becomes valuable as the setting and opportunity for people to realize a society of justice and goodness.

But if the state is a necessary venue for the practice of justice, it is not an unproblematic one, and Levinas is very clear about the dangers. The State of Israel could lapse into a nationalist program and take on the character of power politics. All states run this danger, and Israel, after the Holocaust, motivated by practical, political concerns as much as – and perhaps even more than – religious and moral ones, is surely not immune from such a lapse.[290] Ideally, the

---

[287] Caygill, *Levinas and the Political*, 159–98.
[288] Bernasconi, "Different Styles of Eschatology" in *Research in Phenomenology*, 12–16; Caygill, *Levinas and the Political*, 170–98.
[289] Levinas, "The State of Israel and the Religion of Israel" in *Difficult Freedom*, 216–20; cf. Caygill, *Levinas and the Political*, 160–61.
[290] Caygill, *Levinas and the Political*, 162–66.

State of Israel was "the heir to the vocation of protecting 'Israel's ethics' that was previously undertaken by the reading of the Torah."[291] But the pressures, external and internal, on a modern state endangered this project; the state of Israel could easily "betray . . . its religious vocation to Israel. The risk that now emerges is . . . the destruction of Israel by the actions of the state of Israel."[292]

As Caygill argues, this danger of corruption is explored in the essay "From the Rise of Nihilism to the Carnal Jew."[293] The risk is one of reducing Israel entirely "to political categories," forgetting the "eschatological dream" and sliding into "nihilism." For Levinas, the risk, that is, concerns "assimilation," becoming a state like others, without a sense of conscience. He calls this the difference between the Universal Israel – spiritual, ethical, seeking the truth of justice – and an Israel of Fact, that for all its reality risks abandoning its prophetic vocation.[294] Once again, Levinas takes the State of Israel as an opportunity and not an end in itself and as an opportunity it can fail. It is at risk. Political practices can serve to realize justice, or they can ignore or impede it. As Caygill underlines, the core of Israel's opportunity is that it be "worthy of an ultimate sacrifice." Levinas then says: "The State of Israel, in this sense, constitutes the greatest event in modern Judaism."[295]

Caygill takes Levinas to mean that Israel bears the responsibility to sacrifice, but I am not sure that he has understood Levinas correctly. Levinas takes Israel's vocation, its destiny, to be its universalism. That is, Israel is like each and every nation; it is *chosen*. "Each nation worthy of the name is chosen" and has an "ability to carry out the common task. . . . Each nation must behave as though it alone had to answer for all."[296] Levinas calls this a limitation of "political sovereignty" in behalf of "moral sovereignty." This means being willing to die for an idea, and that is what the ideas of abnegation and sacrifice mean to Levinas. The State of Israel is "the greatest event in modern Judaism" because it is the Jewish people's opportunity, as a people, to die for a principle, for justice. To Levinas, secular Jews, who have abandoned Judaism and its texts, do not see this opportunity or this task. Of course, not all nonsecular Jews see it either. If the State, then, is modern Judaism's "greatest event," it is not because it gives Jews a chance to engage in power politics or to become imperialists or to fight for their own physical survival. It is because it gives Jews a chance

---

[291] *Beyond the Verse,* 9; see Caygill, *Levinas and the Political,* 164.

[292] Caygill, *Levinas and the Political,* 164.

[293] Caygill, *Levinas and the Political,* 164–66; see "From the Rise of Nihilism to the Carnal Jew" in *Difficult Freedom,* 221–25.

[294] "From the Rise of Nihilism to the Carnal Jew" in *Difficult Freedom,* 223–24.

[295] "From the Rise of Nihilism to the Carnal Jew" in *Difficult Freedom,* 225; cf. "The State of Caesar and the State of David," in *Beyond the Verse,* 187.

[296] "From the Rise of Nihilism to the Carnal Jew" in *Difficult Freedom,* 224.

to live socially and politically in accord with what responsibility and justice require, to live an ethical life as a society. In a twist, at the end of the essay, and in perhaps an incautious way, Levinas calls this responsibility for the other person Israel's – that is, the Jewish people's – "invisible universality," its "carnal essence," and "its innate predisposition to involuntary sacrifice, its exposure to persecution."[297] Its essence, that is, is to recognize its obligations to others, to realize concretely its "original responsibility." Its worldly persecutions are an emblem of its primordial persecution, which we know, for him, is its original ethical obligation and responsibility to and for others.

The Jewish State could become a total corruption of the ethical ideal. Becoming a political state is certainly a threat and could itself become an object of veneration and ultimate respect. Clearly, Levinas opposes all such situations as distortions. But because social life and thus politics are necessary features of our lives, no matter how fully we must accommodate, still the genuine political goal ought to be to increase justice. This is true for all people and all states. It is especially true for the State of Israel insofar as the Jewish people's tradition carries the ethical message as the central feature of the Bible, the Talmud, and their commentaries as well. Caygill claims that this is one of the central lessons of Levinas's comments on the "messianic dream" in his Talmudic lessons, to illuminate "the State of Israel as bearing witness to the promise of a new kind of state."[298] He makes the nice point that investing in the political and pinning one's hopes to it might be a matter of making alliances with assassins – and thus of being "duped by morality."[299] But Levinas seems to realize that it is nonetheless worth the risk and even *necessary* to accept it. What is called for is vigilance.[300]

Politics is politics, but messianism is ethics. In "Space Is Not One-Dimensional" (1968), reflecting on French Jewish response to the Six Day War, Levinas says that what brings the "Reign of the Messiah closer" is not the fact of Israel being a state "but because the men [sic] who inhabit it try to resist the temptations of politics ... [and] because this state ... embraces the teaching of the prophets."[301] Allegiance to Israel, then, by French Jews – and by implication others as well – is allegiance to this prophetic, ethical, universal vocation and not to another political entity.[302] It is not a matter of dual loyalty. Indeed, this is even true of those who care about Israel's Arab enemies. What

---

[297] "From the Rise of Nihilism to the Carnal Jew" in *Difficult Freedom*, 225; cf. "Space Is Not One-Dimensional" in *Difficult Freedom*, 263.

[298] Caygill, *Levinas and the Political*, 167.

[299] Caygill, *Levinas and the Political*, 168.

[300] Caygill, *Levinas and the Political*, 170–72.

[301] Levinas, "Space is Not One-Dimensional" in *Difficult Freedom*, 263–64.

[302] Levinas, "Space is Not One-Dimensional" in *Difficult Freedom*, 264.

holds for French Jews and for us all, the need to care most about justice and the other, holds, too, he says, for "you too, my Muslim friend, my unhated enemy of the Six-Day War!"[303] We will return to this theme of friends and enemies, but not until we have considered further the risks and dangers politics poses for the realization of ethics in political and social life.[304]

Levinas published *Beyond the Verse* in 1982. In the Foreword, he notes that the last three pieces, called collectively "Zionisms," deal explicitly with the relation between politics and ethics and with the conflict between Israelis and Arabs.[305] I want to look at the essays first with regard to the larger themes, the relation between politics and religion or ethics, the necessity of the political, and the risks of political corruption. "The State of Caesar and the State of David" was written in 1971, and, as Caygill notes, it summarizes Levinas's thinking of the 1960s.[306] Levinas begins by discussing texts that acknowledge the need for the state. But, he says, "the State of Caesar, despite its participation in the pure essence of the State, is also the place of corruption *par excellence* and, perhaps, the ultimate refuge of idolatry."[307] Levinas does not spell out these corruptions in concrete, analytic terms. This is neither his style, nor would such enumeration lend itself to the textual and interpretive tactics of the essays. We can nonetheless look for hints.

For example, Levinas recognizes that according to certain Talmudic scholars the form of the pagan state involves various features that are in tension with the messianic ideal: The state is jealous of its sovereignty; constantly seeks hegemony; is imperialist, totalitarian, and conquering; can be oppressive; and is attached to a realist egoism.[308] It seeks adoration and fidelity. Furthermore, the state is grounded in a contradiction; it "subordinat[es] some men to others in order to liberate them."[309] Thus, Levinas recognizes that all forms of

---

[303] Levinas, "Space is Not One-Dimensional" in *Difficult Freedom*, 264.

[304] Critics might well take this to be apologetic and even disingenuous. But Levinas is a universalist, as we have seen, and one who takes the ethical as determinative for how one ought to live. Social, political, and economic institutions are necessary, but they do not deserve our most fundamental allegiance. Levinas's point here seems to be that loyalty to France is not in conflict with loyalty to Israel insofar as both should be vehicles to the same ultimate goal, the most just society possible. Indeed, as long as there is evidence that a given nation's heritage aspires to just and benevolent treatment of all people, both within and without its domain, it deserves our allegiance. Without that evidence, one would be hard put to claim that the nation in question aspires to such a goal. It might represent a commitment to power and domination for its own sake.

[305] Levinas, Foreward, in *Beyond the Verse*, xv.

[306] Caygill, *Levinas and the Political*, 170.

[307] "The State of Caesar and the State of David" in *Beyond the Verse*, 183.

[308] "The State of Caesar and the State of David" in *Beyond the Verse*, 184.

[309] "The State of Caesar and the State of David" in *Beyond the Verse*, 184.

government, even those grounded in a social contract, involve subordination of some by others and run the risk of oppression, domination, and persecution. "By serving the state, one serves repression; by serving repression, one becomes a member of the police force."[310] Domination and conflict are endemic to political life. If they can be mitigated or reduced, then the state and the lives of its citizens are bettered, but the risk is always present that they will not be mitigated. In social networks, justice can never be perfect, but it can be the plumb line for institutions, policies, and practices. When it is not, division and enmity dominate. Still, in public life politics is required to organize and distribute, to protect and control, to act in behalf of goodness and to facilitate acts of kindness and concern. Levinas notes that one does not save oneself by rejecting the political altogether, for the tension between freedom and exploitation is something "against which the very person who refuses the political order is not protected, since in abstaining from all collaboration with the ruling power, he makes himself party to the obscure powers that the State represses."[311]

At the end of the essay, Levinas calls attention to comments of Dan Avni-Segré, an Italian Jew teaching in Haifa, which he had heard at the Ninth Colloquium of French Jewish intellectuals. Segré had discussed the infancy of Jewish politics in Israel and the hopes for the future; he had spoken of a "monotheistic politics" as the "culmination of Zionism" – a task "beyond the concern to ensure a refuge for those who are persecuted."[312] This messianic ideal of what for Levinas would be a just state marks out a place between corrupt power politics and a facile and careless moralism.[313] In 1971, it was one way of talking about what messianism could bring to politics in the Jewish state.

I do not think that Levinas's conception of messianism and politics is unique to Judaism and the State of Israel. Messianism involves all those commitments that are concerned with our responsibilities to others; it is about realizing ethics in our lives. Politics is about the institutions of organized social life that enable us to live together and with one another. Politics should have a messianic vision; it should be guided by ethical conscience and by the hope that its institutions and its citizens will live just lives. Messianism and politics are both unavoidable features of all of our lives.

In the life of the Jewish people and in Zionism, these ideas operate in a specific way. For Levinas, the Bible and the Talmud often reflect on the engagement of the political and the messianic, and, after the Nazi destruction and with the

---

[310] "The State of Caesar and the State of David" in *Beyond the Verse*, 184.
[311] "The State of Caesar and the State of David" in *Beyond the Verse*, 184.
[312] "The State of Caesar and the State of David" in *Beyond the Verse*, 187.
[313] "The State of Caesar and the State of David" in *Beyond the Verse*, 184.

establishment of the modern State of Israel, these issues have a precise, concrete reference. Israel is not a unique state in many ways, but it does arise with a great weight of historical specificity. Its challenges are not its alone.[314] But they are emblematic of what modern states ought to confront and meet. On Levinas's reading, the Jewish people carries a special burden to enact its persecution through just institutions and, in the State of Israel, to embody them. Israel is the name of this people's return into history and, at the same time, of the political and messianic opportunities for us all.

For these reasons, the concrete problems that face Israel are of signal importance, and it is necessary to see how Levinas grapples with them. Here the central issue is how Levinas deals with engagement with the face of one's enemy, and this means how Israel ought to deal with its Arab neighbors in general and the Palestinians in particular. As Caygill puts it, "[I]f the State of Israel ignores human rights, then this means that through a brutal irony of history the prophetic mission of Israel becomes endangered by its own adoption of the form of the state."[315] The two major texts in which this challenge is most markedly faced, if at all, are "Politics After!" (1979) and the radio interview "Ethics and Politics" (1982).

Caygill argues that in these texts Levinas's judgment of the Palestinians and Arab nationalism is ambivalent.[316] At one point, commenting on "Politics After!", Caygill says that we have every right "to expect a more nuanced sense of historical development from Levinas, and a more explicit acknowledgment of the possibility that the past and present of the State of Israel is capable of ruining the promises of the future."[317] That is, Levinas may take politics to be necessary for ethical messianism and Israel to be historically devoted to creating a just social and political order, but no state is immune from corruption or failure, Israel included. Can Levinas recognize such a possibility? Even if the Holocaust recommends a special role for Jewish self-defense in Israel, surely, by Levinas's own very high standards, self-defense cannot be a blanket justification for all political practices, even repressive and horrific ones. As Caygill accurately points out, the issue came to a head for Levinas with the massacre of Palestinian refugees – men, women, and children – at the camps at Sabra and Shatila in September 1982.[318] In a radio conversation with Shlomo Malka and Alain Finkelkraut, less than two weeks after the events, Levinas was called upon

[314] See the reference to "the society of Western countries, which remain faithful, after the horrors of Hitler, to the nostalgic longing for the Just City and a merciful justice," in *In the Time of the Nations*, 8.
[315] Caygill, *Levinas and the Political*, 174, 186–94.
[316] Caygill, *Levinas and the Political*, 186.
[317] Caygill, *Levinas and the Political*, 190.
[318] See Caygill, *Levinas and the Political*, 190–94; cf. "Ethics and Politics" in *A Levinas Reader*, 289–97.

to say something about responsibility, and, to say the least, he was evasive. One wonders if there is significance even in this evasiveness.[319]

Levinas considers explicitly, in the Foreword to *Beyond the Verse* (1982), the question whether our passions and ideas are not at risk "in the purely political sense" if they are divorced "from their prophetic and ethical depths."[320] And, as I read him, he charges the Jewish people not to evade its responsibilities and moral conscience by claiming its status as chosen. It must, and thus Israel must, face the question: "Can we understand the suffering of others?"[321] Levinas notes that we cannot tolerate any weighing up of sufferings. Sufferings do not have discrete measures. Still, the Holocaust is a benchmark, a radical break – and the outcome of "a millenial history of outrages and tears, of permanent insecurity and of the shedding of real, warm blood." Levinas calls *this* "the concrete cause and real *raison d'être* of Zionism," not, he says, domination and persecution. That is, Zionism is a movement to acknowledge Jewish suffering and reduce it. It is politics constituted to reach out to the afflicted, to the hurt, to the abandoned; it is about helping Jews and not oppressing others. What, however, will that require? What must be done for the State of Israel, in its situation, to protect Jews from suffering and to secure itself?

Levinas says that Zionism is not about what Israel's neighbors do or ought to do; it is about "the necessity for the Jewish people, in peace with its neighbors, not to continue being a minority in its political structure."[322] This is not, Levinas adds, just a matter of "historical necessity" or what we might call political expediency in order to guarantee Jewish survival. It is about recognizing that ethics as responsibility applies "*to me*, to the individual and the person that I am,"[323] but it cannot mean that in order to be ethical I must be willing to martyr myself. That is, I should not exclude from the parameters of my ethical responsibility those others who are close to me, my kind, my family: "Those near to me are also my neighbors."[324] Some might take this to be callous, but others might take this response to be extreme. We should recall Bernard Williams's famous remark that a man whose wife is drowning and yet who deliberates about whether to save her or another person is guilty of having one thought too many.[325] Levinas is clear that in the context of society, where we are responsible for everyone, judgments are a necessary accommodation, and to

---

[319] In tune with this critical spirit, Simon Critchley gives a brief sketch of the political problems that face Levinas; see his editor's introduction to *Parallax* 24, 1–3.

[320] Foreward in *Beyond the Verse*, xv.

[321] Foreward in *Beyond the Verse*, xvi.

[322] Foreward in *Beyond the Verse*, xvii.

[323] Foreward in *Beyond the Verse*, xvii.

[324] Foreward in *Beyond the Verse*, xvii.

[325] Bernard Williams, "Persons, Character and Morality" in Williams, *Moral Luck* (Cambridge: Cambridge University Press, 1981), 18.

accommodate in favor of those close to you is, depending upon the situation, beyond reproach.[326] Without details, Levinas's comment, and the suggestion that Palestinians may need to remain a minority and may not deferentially have *their* suffering reduced, may be difficult to appreciate fully. But the overall point is, I think, clear: that modern Zionism should remain ethical to the degree that it can, remembering its role for Jews in the aftermath of a history of enormous suffering and persecution and especially of the Holocaust.

Let me turn to "Politics After!," which is an overview of Zionism and a specific response to Anwar Sadat's peace initiative of 1977.[327] Levinas in this essay explicitly raises the problem that the conflict between Jews and Arabs is grounded in the fact that the State of Israel was created on land, claimed by the Jewish people, yet "lived on for centuries by those who call themselves Palestinians, who are surrounded on all parts and over vast expanses by the great Arab people of which they are a part."[328] This is not, he claims, simply a "political" problem; there are moral and psychological features that need to be considered. Jews should "wish and hope for a reconciliation between Jews and Arabs" and should "foresee it, above and beyond becoming peaceful neighbors, as a fraternal community."[329] Levinas, that is, sets a lofty moral goal, and he takes Sadat's trip to Jerusalem in November 1977 as a momentous step on the way to realizing it. It is momentous because, for Levinas, it involved Sadat's recognizing the ethical character of antisemitism and of one's responsibility to the other. It was a realization of what is necessary for "social living itself"[330] and in its own way an acknowledgment of all that Hitler and the death camps meant for ethical, social life. Zionism is an ethical and not a narrowly political movement, and thus the reconciliation of Jews and Arabs in the land is an ethical matter, rooted in the universalism of Zionism and its ethical core.[331]

In political terms, Zionism and the establishment of the modern Jewish state on a land already occupied may seem like nationalist imperialism, callous and belligerent. But Levinas takes its import to be ethical, to express an attempt to realize in fact a political-ethical society in behalf of all. It is not a matter of "an armed and dominating State . . . [pitted] against the unarmed Palestinian people whose existence Israel does not recognize." Rather, it is about Israel, "the most fragile, the most vulnerable thing in the world, in the midst of its neighbors, undisputed nations, rich in natural allies, and surrounded by their lands."[332] This

---

[326] For a different critical attitude, see Caygill, *Levinas and the Political*, 189–90.
[327] See Caygill, *Levinas and the Political*, 190.
[328] Levinas, "Politics After!" in *Beyond the Verse*, 188.
[329] "Politics After!" in *Beyond the Verse*, 189.
[330] "Politics After!" in *Beyond the Verse*, 190.
[331] "Politics After!" in *Beyond the Verse*, 191–92.
[332] "Politics After!" in *Beyond the Verse*, 193.

is what makes Sadat's visit such an "exceptional transhistorical event. . . . For a moment, political standards and clichés were forgotten. . . . Cautiousness and precautions were forgotten. . . ."[333] No one knows if Sadat saw Israel clearly in its moral role. Levinas surely does not know; he wonders what Sadat sensed in Zionism, whether he grasped the opportunities and heard the "prophetic promises," whether he was aware that Israel could not live its vocation without a state and a land and yet "a State which will have to incarnate the prophetic moral code and the idea of its peace."[334] Nonetheless, regardless of his intentions, Sadat provided an opportunity: "the suggestion that peace is a concept which goes beyond purely political thought." The peace Levinas has in mind, of course, is not merely the cessation of war; rather, it is the realization of a fundamental cooperation, of fraternity, and mutual acceptance and concern.

In this essay, then, Levinas does not raise the question of what Israel should do vis à vis its Arab neighbors and its Palestinian refugees, at least not in any explicit way. He assumes that every Israeli Jew should want reconciliation and peace with both groups. What he does, instead of asking what *should* have been done, is to characterize what Sadat *has achieved*. He sees the event of Sadat's visit and the peace as an offer, as an act of acceptance, of recognition, and by implication he urges that Israel act in kind, that it reach out to secure the offer and help advance the opportunity. He makes no specific reference to what this might involve or what it might mean for dealing with the Palestinian problem as a political one. But he does imply that such an act must elicit a response and that no genuine one, out of the heritage of Zionism, should degrade the act into an exclusively political one and fail to appreciate its ethical importance.

Levinas's thinking about the State of Israel is complex. Like many others, he sees Zionism and the state in terms of the long history of Jewish suffering and persecution and in the shadow of Hitler and the Nazi destruction. At the same time, he takes Zionism to be grounded in a prophetic vision of a desire to realize a just and humane society and to organize and conduct politics to express what justice requires. Furthermore, he is realistic about the historical situation of the land, the State of Israel, and the Arab world. There is a need, he realizes, to create a "fraternal community" with Israel's neighbors, but at the same time – to respond to Israel's ethical calling and to its millenial suffering – the Jewish people cannot, in his eyes, risk its majority control over Israel's future and its promise. The conflict with the Palestinians may be intractable; it certainly can expect no easy solutions. Just as, in a sense, all are responsible for the horrors and atrocities of the twentieth century, so Jews and Israelis are responsible for the pain and suffering of their Palestinian neighbors. But as we have seen, no

---

[333] "Politics After!" in *Beyond the Verse*, 193.
[334] "Politics After!" in *Beyond the Verse*, 193–94.

one can act on *all* one's responsibilities; justice is *always* a matter of degree and accommodation. Yet, particular concrete events may shape and alter the balance. In his most explicit public encounter with such events, the radio conversation after the massacres at Sabra and Shatila, Levinas says as much as he ever does about these matters.[335]

First, Levinas reminds us that our primordial responsibility for aid to the other person is not about — not generated by — particular acts. It is about how we are related to the other fundamentally and permanently, "an original responsibility of man for the other person."[336] This responsibility exists whether one is guilty or not. Furthermore, to be Jewish is to be "attentive" to this responsibility: One is personally implicated, he says, each time someone is guilty. Second, the dominant and Israeli reaction was to have felt and expressed responsibility in this case, regarding the massacres; it was a moral response. Real innocence is not absolution; it is "an exalted state of responsibility."[337] The Holocaust does not absolve; it "in no way justifies closing our ears to the voice of men." But responsibility for others does not mean that defense is impossible; defense, to protect those close to us, is "a politics that is ethically necessary."[338]

Clearly, this is background. Levinas here claims that ethics is fundamental but that politics, self-defense, and concern for oneself and one's neighbors are not only possible but even necessary. But, as Finkelkraut then points out, the question arises about conflict between the two. What about an apparent confrontation between ethics and "political necessities" or *raison d'état*?[339] Or, to put it more precisely: In recent times, have not political necessities, or the pleas in their behalf, taken priority? Have we not become obsessed with politics, too willing to accommodate or compromise our moral conscience to political necessity? In this case, the *we* are Jews and Israelis, concerning the affairs of the state.

---

[335] To be sure, it may not be enough. Levinas, as we shall see, does not make a clear and precise judgment about who is right and who is wrong, especially about whether Israel is guilty for the massacres and what should be done in response to that guilt. Given who Levinas is and the circumstances at the time of the interview, if Levinas was evasive or irresponsible, can he be forgiven? By whom? If Levinas's treatment of Israel and the problem of Palestinian rights seems to many to be morally irresponsible, his statements about Asia and Asian cultures have been judged by at least one commentator to be virtually "insane." See C. Fred Alford, "Levinas and Political Theory," *Political Theory* 32:2 (April 2004), 159–61, where Alford cites Levinas's essay on the conflict between the Soviet Union and China as evidence of Levinas's complete lack of understanding toward the cultures of Asia: "Le Débat Russo-Chinois et la Dialectique" in *Les Imprévus de l'Histoire* (Montpellier, France: Fata Morgana, 1994), 171–72. The essay is now translated in Levinas, "Dialectics and the Sino-Soviet Quarrel" in *Unforseen History*, trans. Nidra Poller (Champaign: University of Illinois Press, 2004), 107–9.

[336] "Ethics and Politics" in *A Levinas Reader*, 290.

[337] "Ethics and Politics" in *A Levinas Reader*, 291.

[338] "Ethics and Politics" in *A Levinas Reader*, 292: "Alongside *ethics*, there is a place for *politics*."

[339] "Ethics and Politics" in *A Levinas Reader*, 292.

To this, Levinas argues that the "Zionist idea . . . is a political idea" that has an ethical justification, to "put an end to the arbitrariness which marked the Jewish condition, and to all the spilt blood which for centuries has flowed with impunity across the world."[340] For Levinas, this means "a political unity with a Jewish majority," what he calls the "essence of Zionism," "a State with an army and arms, an army which can have a deterrent and if necessary a defensive significance." And, as we have heard before, he justifies this morally, because "my people and my kin are still my neighbours."[341] But – and now Levinas faces the critical issue: "There is also an ethical limit to this ethically necessary political existence. But what is this limit?"[342] The issue, of course, is a historical and not a philosophical one; it involves in this case, with these events, a people with an ethical tradition and an ethical conscience. What needs to occur is for events that should not have happened to affect "the concrete consciousness of those who suffer and struggle."[343] Levinas's point, I take it, is that here philosophy is not relevant, although it is Levinas's judgment to make, about what has been done and what now should be done, because it is everyone's judgment to make.

Levinas is explicit: Sabra and Shatila are "the place where everything is interrupted, where everything is disrupted, where everyone's moral responsibility comes into play."[344] He then says, enigmatically, "Everyone's responsibility." I do not think that Levinas means directly that the massacres at Sabra and Shatila were everyone's responsibility in the sense that everyone brought them about or that everyone was equally a perpetrator. What I think he means is that, in his eyes, these events register on or interrupt, as he says, everyone's moral responsibility, everyone's conscience, everyone's ethical sensibility. The events matter ethically to us all, and thus they are significant for everyone near and far.

Then, when asked directly whether for the Israeli the Palestinian is not "above all" the other, Levinas demurs. His answer is that the other is the neighbor and that this can mean your kin. "If your neighbor attacks another neighbor," he says, "or treats him unjustly, what can you do?"[345] In such a situation, at least one must try to determine who is right and who is wrong. But for Levinas, the central point is that these events "disturb" and challenge everyone. In particular, they threaten the Jewish soul and, as he goes on to note, Jewish books, the books that carry the central ethical teaching of Judaism and mean more to Israel than

---

[340] "Ethics and Politics" in *A Levinas Reader*, 292.
[341] "Ethics and Politics" in *A Levinas Reader*, 292.
[342] "Ethics and Politics" in *A Levinas Reader*, 293.
[343] "Ethics and Politics" in *A Levinas Reader*, 293.
[344] "Ethics and Politics" in *A Levinas Reader*, 293.
[345] "Ethics and Politics" in *A Levinas Reader*, 294.

the land. Levinas ends the conversation by affirming this point, recalling a passage from the Talmud, that "a person is more holy than a land, even a holy land." This comment may be indirect and muted, but it expresses, to my ears, distress and worry in the midst of a deep fidelity. Levinas clearly understands Zionism as a movement to rectify a heritage of suffering, and yet, the massacres at Sabra and Shatila have registered in him a worry that the mission of Israel is in jeopardy. Perhaps he is reluctant to express more concern because there is too much he does not know or because his worries are too deep. Nonetheless, he does not hide his anxiety as much as he lives with it, as he recommends we all do – and indeed must.[346]

ETHICAL MESSIANISM

The messianic occurs, at concrete moments, when a person or an institution enacts the ethical and lives with others in justice and with responsibility. This kind of messianism, beyond war and peace, is a central theme of Levinas's thought and of his conception of Judaism. The two are intimately entwined for him – and increasingly so, as the years go by. More and more, especially in essays, talks, and interviews, he recalls Talmudic teachings to express the centrality of responsibility and its nuances. But at the same time that he calls on his Jewish heritage to illuminate his ethical vision, so his understanding of responsibility determines his reading of Jewish life, ritual, books, and politics. Prophetic eschatology, Zionism, the Bible and Talmud, all mingle in a way that calls for a deep rethinking and modification of Western philosophy and European culture.

Commentators regularly refer to this conglomerate as Levinas's effort to teach the Greek West to speak Hebrew or to remind Greek philosophy and culture of the teachings of the Bible. However one interprets these metaphors, they signify – all of them – the fact that Western culture, with all the trappings of philosophy, literature, science, and art, both hides and yet is grounded in an ethical sensibility that is biblical in character, as Levinas sees it. That biblical heritage is vital to our living full human lives, but it is not sufficient on its own. Western culture, with its Greek roots, is necessary for life, but it, too, is inadequate, bereft of the understanding of social interaction and responsibility to others without which the risks of domination, persecution, violence, and suffering are very high indeed. In Levinas's vocabulary, terms like "assimilation" and "universalism," while reminiscent of the Enlightenment, carry a different meaning, similar to that of earlier rationalists and modern thinkers but unique

---

[346] For a much more negative appraisal of Levinas's responses in the radio conversation, see Caygill, *Levinas and the Political*, 192–94.

nonetheless. They are the hallmark of his vision of the Jewish people, historically distinctive and yet with a universal soul, a prophetic soul, whose central vision is a life of kindness and justice for one and all.

Throughout this book, I have argued that the face-to-face and human responsibility for the other, primordial and determinative, are features – if often occluded – of all our social interaction; they are what is fundamental to all social life. Levinas himself declares that this contemporaneity, that is also a diachrony, is a central theme of *Otherwise Than Being*. In the essay "Essence and Disinterestedness" (later revised as the first chapter), after distinguishing between the saying and the said, Levinas asks: "Can this *saying* and this *unsaying* be assembled, can they be at the same time?"[347] That is, when we realize that ethics is a feature or dimension of all ontology, of all human existence, is this not a betrayal of the special character of the ethical? Is there not here a risk of idealism or naturalism? Or, in his terms, does not this "simultaneity" reduce the *other* to *being*, ethics to ontology?[348]

The same problem arises for Levinas's understanding of Judaism, the Bible, the Talmud, and Jewish life. When we realize that Judaism is simultaneous with, if often hidden or distorted by, Western culture and civilization, is it also betrayed? Is it *necessarily* betrayed? Is the translation not itself a distortion? Of course, Levinas does not think so. In the case of responsibility, what prevents such necessary betrayal is diachrony, that the face is always a trace of an absolute absence, of *illeity*. One might say the same about Judaism and its central teaching: It is always present in our lives as a "trace" of an absent revelation. Sinai is not a historical event in the life of the Jewish people as much as it is a symbol of what is primordial for all human life. Indeed, it is more than a symbol; it is the way of life of Jews and thereby a reality within Western life and society. In this way, as I have claimed, terms such as "Hebrew," "Greek," "Jew," "Israel," and "Zionism" ultimately are metaphors for Levinas, signifying fundamental features of the human condition, and the Jewish people is, as it were, a living metaphor.

To be sure, like eros, femininity, paternity, and others, they are contested. They have their own connotations that upset at the same time that they illuminate and resonate. But Levinas's affinity for the way concreteness and particularity exist alongside universality and abstractness is something he does not avoid. Nor does he elude what is difficult. But what he does say – especially his comments on Zionism – often seems disturbing. Nonetheless, there is reason to respect his candor and his reticence, for the specific situations in question are not uncomplicated.

---

[347] Levinas, "Essence and Disinterestedness" in *Basic Philosophical Writings*, 114.
[348] Levinas, "Essence and Disinterestedness" in *Basic Philosophical Writings*, 114.

Indirectly, the State of Israel, then, is not exclusively a Jewish concern, in Levinas's eyes, nor indeed is Judaism – its books and central teaching – an exclusively Jewish matter. Judaism and the Jewish people are one historical manifestation of a central truth about humanity: "Judaism is valid not because of the 'happy end' of its history, but because of the faithfulness of this history to the teachings of the Torah." Judaism is not about a divine promise, whether fulfilled or not, whether renounced or not. The history that matters is one of commitment to ethics and to a real messianism. It is "a history which cannot get through our time, nor testify to its truth without taking on, somewhere, political conditions. That is why the State of Israel is important today to the Torah of Israel and to its meaning for all men."[349] And what is important to Israel's teaching is important to all humankind in fact. For all its brute particularity, its life, its suffering, the Jewish people are the soul of humanity, and their essence is universalism. And to the degree that their messianic, ethical purpose requires a political reality, to that degree too is that political reality of importance to all humankind. To some, this may seem narrow, parochial, and even self-serving, but to Levinas it is noble and elevating. Nor should we forget that in his own eyes Jews are not the only Jews, nor is Israel the only Jewish state. All people are Jews, and all states are Israel, but no less than all Jews speak Greek and live in the Greek West.[350]

[349] Levinas, "Dialogue on Thinking-of-the-Other" in *Entre Nous*, 206.
[350] Here I am alluding to a comment, frequently cited, of Bernard Malamud, that all people are Jews, only they don't know it.

CONCLUSION

Levinas and the Primacy of the Ethical

Kant, Kierkegaard, and Derrida

One can summarize Levinas's central thought this way: He combines Kant's commitment to the primacy of morality with Kierkegaard's faith in God. What does this summary mean? For Levinas seems to acknowledge no transcendent God, nor is his commitment to morality akin to Kant's recognition of the moral law. One way in which Levinas is viewed as preserving a Kantian spirit concerns the priority of the ethical. But if we look at Levinas carefully, we see that his commitment to the primacy of the ethical is different from Kant's. Moreover, their difference is significant.

Arguably, Kant, like Plato, Socrates, and others, takes ethics to be primary precisely because ethical virtues and rules are of a higher status than other qualities that we have and norms or principles that we employ. Quite commonly, we interpret all three of these figures, for example, as arguing for the priority of moral considerations when compared to personal advantage or self-interest. Among other things, this is what makes *akrasia*, or moral weakness of will, such an interesting issue for them. For Kant, as for Plato, we can say that moral considerations generally outweigh prudential ones; desires for personal advantage should be given less weight than moral goals and interests. The idea is that what is right or good should matter more to us than enjoying a movie, having a pleasant and fulfilling meal, or taking a long hike. This kind of preeminence or worth, attributed to the ethical, involves separating the domain of the ethical from other domains of human activity and interest and ascribing more value to the moral domain than to the others.[1] When moral obligations conflict with

---

[1] I mentioned this issue of the primacy of the ethical or the authority of moral reasons in Chapter 9, when I introduced Putnam's charge against Levinas, that his singlemindedness is too narrow a conception to deal adequately with what one might call a "eudaimonistic" conception of human well-being. In his collection of essays, R. Jay Wallace acknowledges this problem several times and says some very suggestive things about it, especially with regard to Joseph Raz's pluralism,

other kinds of duties, they ought to be preferred; they ought to carry more weight. There may be – for Kant – moral dilemmas. But for conflicts between the moral and the nonmoral, no dilemmas are serious.[2]

Like many commentators – Buber, for example, and later Fackenheim, to mention two prominent Jewish ones – Levinas takes Kierkegaard, in *Fear and Trembling*, to be making the anti-Kantian point that in conflicts between the ethical and the religious, the religious always should take priority. This priority is the priority of faith, and it takes the shape of the teleological suspension of the ethical. Levinas – in a conventional way – takes Kierkegaard to be advocating this priority, but his interpretation certainly has been contested and ought to be.[3] For our purposes, the point that is significant is that Levinas objects to this conclusion, that when the divine call and ethical obligation conflict, the former should take priority. Kant, of course, in *The Conflict of Faculties*, does so as well, but certainly for different reasons.[4] It may be that Kierkegaard, on this reading, admits a certain anguish in the conflict that faces Abraham, but for Levinas the anguish is mitigated to some extent by his trust in God, that all will be returned to him and that Isaac will be saved. But once again, as in the case of Kant, the conflict only arises because the ethical is segregated and set in opposition to something else – here, faith – and must contest with it for preeminence.

This assumption is not one that Levinas makes. Indeed, his view about the ethical and its primacy rejects it completely. He may read Kierkegaard conventionally – as an anti-Kantian Kantian, as Fackenheim puts it, but his objection to Kierkegaard is not that he gives faith too much credit and ethics too little. In a sense, it is that at best the dilemma, if tragic, is religious and that the anguish, if real, is nonetheless softened. For Levinas, that is, ethics is not

---

Harry Frankfurt's consideration of things we care about, and T. M. Scanlon's contractualism. See Wallace, *Normativity and the Will*, 130–43, 206–11, 307–21.

[2] For a discussion of the distinction between resolvable and irresolvable moral dilemmas, see Rosalind Hursthouse, *On Virtue Ethics*, Ch. 2 and 3. Cf. Dancy, *Moral Reasons*, 109–26, esp. 123–25. See also Bernard Williams, "Ethical Consistency" in *Problems of the Self: Philosophical Papers, 1956–1972* (Cambridge: Cambridge University Press, 1976). Some irresolvable moral dilemmas, according to Hursthouse, are very serious or "terrible," and these she calls "tragic dilemmas" (71–77). For Levinas, ethical dilemmas are endemic to social life; presumably, some are more serious, more gripping and painful, than others. Hursthouse argues that in order to understand best our moral judgment and moral decisions in such tragic situations, it is best to treat the notions of character and virtue as primary, rather than to focus on moral rules or action-guiding principles. There is reason to think that Levinas might think this suggestion marks an advance in moral sensitivity, but not a sufficiently deep one, unless it is enriched with an appreciation of the fundamentally social dimension and responsibility of such character.

[3] For Levinas's account of Kierkegaard, see "Kierkegaard: Existence and Ethics" in *Proper Names*, 66–74. See John Lippitt, *Kierkegaard and Fear and Trembling* (New York: Routledge, 2003).

[4] Buber and Fackenheim are not in full agreement with Kierkegaard either. Buber takes the divine-human encounter to occur within, and not beyond, interhuman dialogue, while Fackenheim understands faith to be embedded in history and not an escape from it.

primary because it is a separate but preeminent domain of duties or virtues or whatever. Nor is the dilemma, if tragic, an extra-moral one, or the anguish, strain, and sense of compromise mitigated.

The point here, if simple to articulate, is telling. Throughout this book, we have shown that for Levinas each of us is called to compassion and concern for the other, for each and every other person, all the time, in every way. At the same time, we are always with the third party; we always live among other people, some near and some far, in a vastly complex social world. And because our social lives are always complex and varied and our interactions – near and far – multiple, we always are faced with dilemmas, always involving compromises and accommodations, and always – to one degree or other, tragic and ethical. No interpersonal act or situation can avoid the need to make decisions, compare and evaluate, and compromise and accommodate. Hence, because the ethical is comprehensive and infinite, all our lives are filled with negotiating moral dilemmas.[5] Ethics is primary not because it is a restricted but preeminent domain – of rules or virtues or ideals. It is primary because it is unrestricted and present everywhere, and while determinative and defining, it situates us in the midst of permanent moral dilemmas that we can never fully resolve but that always challenge us nonetheless.

In this sense, all life is tragic to one degree or other. While this places us in a permanent position of strain and frustration, it is not a futile situation. For the burden, infinite and compelling, that falls upon us and that we should so keenly sense, is not a contrivance or a rule, externally formulated and imposed. It is intrinsic to our very existence with one another; it is what makes life valuable and significant, what makes responsibility necessary and nobility possible. What gives rise to our sense of obligation to others is the *face* – it is the way we experience or should experience the other's need for us, how the other's dependency and even suffering reaches out to us and calls each of us to help, to alleviate, and to care. We are addressed by each person's unique humanity. All our lives are unavoidably embedded in this network of call and address, summons and response. If this fills us with anguish and frustration, it also fills us with a sense of worth and purpose; it fills us with the Good.

The presence and character of moral dilemmas are a test for moral thinking. There is a rich literature on the phenomenon of moral dilemmas.[6] We can learn a good deal from it about conflicts of obligations, rights, and more. But what

---

[5] If the duty for beneficence is universal, facts are such that it is always limited in one way or another. Moral dilemmas are a permanent feature of ethical life – in fact, of all life.

[6] There are important papers collected in Christopher W. Gowans (ed.), *Moral Dilemmas* (Oxford: Oxford University Press, 1987); H. E. Mason (ed.), *Moral Dilemmas and Moral Theory* (Oxford: Oxford University Press, 1996); Peter Baumann and Monika Betzler (eds.), *Practical Conflicts: New Philosophical Essays* (Cambridge: Cambridge University Press, 2004). See also Hursthouse, Dancy, and Williams, cited in note 2.

we learn, while it may help us to learn how one might confront particular types of situations to which the presence of the third party gives rise, will not test Levinas's central insight. For him, the multiple types of such dilemmas, even the classifying of them at all, are a by-product of moral theories and normative accounts that are ways of coping with the social condition we live in unavoidably. The presence of moral dilemmas, ways of characterizing them, and solutions to them – these are not challenges to his ethical insight but rather part of the process of coping with it and living with our realization of it.

I have noted that for Levinas, being in the grip of moral dilemmas, all of which are tragic to one degree or another, is a permanent feature of our social existence. Levinas does not read Kierkegaard's *Fear and Trembling* as a eulogy to such a view. Rather, he takes Kierkegaard to be characterizing Abraham as a paradigmatic knight of faith who suspends the ethical in favor of a higher *telos*, his submission to God. It is striking to find, then, a view like Levinas's own ascribed to Kierkegaard, but we find just such an attribution in Jacques Derrida's interpretation of Kierkegaard in *The Gift of Death*.[7] According to Derrida, Abraham's anguish and terror in the face of his dilemma is not extraordinary or unusual. Rather it "illustrates . . . the most common and everyday experience of responsibility." Derrida's explanation of why this is so sounds very much like our earlier account of Levinas: Because my responsibility is to each and every other and because there are always third parties – social life is complex and plural: "I cannot respond to the call, the request, the obligation, or even the love of another without sacrificing the other other, the other others."[8] We always must make choices, compromise, and accommodate. Mt. Moriah is "our habitat every second of every day."[9] Giving to one person always involves sacrificing others, and at every moment, with every choice and action, I am always engaging in such a movement, always sacrificing or abandoning one person for another.

As a reading of Levinas, this is correct – or at least partially so. But it is surprising, as I suggested, to find it proposed as a reading of Kierkegaard. Moreover, as an interpretation of Levinas's reading of Kierkegaard, it is certainly not correct.[10] Levinas would agree that "the highest expression of the ethical is in terms of what binds us to our own and to our fellows," but he would deny that this is Kierkegaard's view.[11] Derrida encourages us to think that for Abraham, as

---

[7] See Jacques Derrida, *The Gift of Death*, 53–81. For discussion, brief but clear, see Lippitt, *Kierkegaard and Fear and Trembling*, 158–59.
[8] Derrida, *The Gift of Death*, 68.
[9] Derrida, *The Gift of Death*, 69.
[10] Lippitt gives reasons against it, in *Kierkegaard and Fear and Trembling*, 159.
[11] Derrida, *The Gift of Death*, 59.

Kierkegaard understands him, ethics or the ethical order, the domain of moral theories and everyday morality (à la Kant and Hegel), is paradoxical: "[T]he generality of ethics incites to irresponsibility."[12] What Derrida means is that ethics subverts the absoluteness of responsibility; it makes pure or uncondi- tional responsibility impossible. But, as I have argued, Levinas takes the social as unavoidable; it is our lot to have to live with many other people and thus with mitigated responsibility. We should always recognize the weight of responsibil- ity, even if − and while − we realize that pure responsibility is impossible. But that is not a paradox; it is life, our situation as human beings in a social world.[13] Too much ethics, in the sense of an overindulgence in moral principles and such, may be a "temptation" that will "end up making us irresponsible," but some ethics in this sense is our lot and our calling.[14]

Furthermore, Derrida says that we always sacrifice but that we cannot justify our choice. What is involved are clashes of orders of responsibility; Derrida calls this "sacrificial war," and he says that we "can never justify this sacrifice." "Whether I want to or not, I can never justify the fact that I prefer or sacrifice any one (any other) to the other."[15] Hence, Derrida seems to deny all justification: we cannot justify the religious order against the ethical, the theological against the political, and so forth. Moreover, in any particular case, we cannot justify why we choose to help one person rather than another, to save one child or feed one hungry person rather than to save or feed another.[16] But surely, Levinas would not accept such an extreme, antirationalist conclusion. For him, the complexity of the social is precisely what gives rise to comparison, judgment, assessment, thought, rationality, and discourse. We are not left with silence; we are led to speech and reason.[17] This is one reason why our ordinary ethical lives are not represented well by Abraham, who notoriously does not speak and is (virtually) silent. If Derrida − among others − is right about Abraham's silence, then his Levinasian reading cannot be right for Kierkegaard.

Derrida seems to want to surprise or shock us by pointing out how "para- doxical" our ethical lives are. Levinas believes that our lives are immersed in moral dilemmas and that we should feel the burden of being called to assist others − beyond our capabilities or resources. But this should not lead us to "anguish" or "terror," especially not because it always involves compromise and sacrifice. We should not feel an extraordinary strain or frustration because

---

[12] Derrida, *The Gift of Death*, 61.
[13] Derrida calls this dilemma or situation "paradox, scandal and aporia" in *The Gift of Death*, 68.
[14] Derrida, *The Gift of Death*, 61–62.
[15] Derrida, *The Gift of Death*, 70.
[16] Derrida, *The Gift of Death*, 70.
[17] We have discussed these matters in earlier chapters, and will do so in the Appendix. For Derrida, see *The Gift of Death*, 57–81 *passim*.

our lives are always torn in many directions, because we cannot act as we would like. We should feel the need for all of us to do what we can and ought, so that the aid given to all and the efforts to alleviate suffering, can be maximal. What we know no one of us can achieve to any high degree, we also know can be accomplished more fully and better when all are invested in meeting the challenges we face. Even if I cannot care for many alone or do much on my own, we all, working together, can accomplish a great deal. We can collectively do much to reduce suffering, to feed the hungry, to clothe the naked, and to provide others with decent, humane lives.

Kant, Kierkegaard, and Derrida – Levinas would find all somehow too weak in either their appreciation for the preeminence of ethics or their rejection of its preeminence. For him, ethics is an expression for the very social nature of our living with others in the world. When he calls it "religion" and use expressions like "glory," "holiness," and such, he casts over that social and intersubjective fact an aura of sublimity and authority that we reserve for all that is highest in worth. Ultimately, then, that preeminence and priority is nothing more than the face with which we confront one another – with all that it reveals and demands – but also nothing less. Such is Levinas's "austere humanism."

APPENDIX

Facing Reasons

THE FACE AS A REASON TO ACT

Levinas regularly claims that the "epiphany of the face" or our engagement with the face of the other person – our being hostage to the other, accused by the other, traumatized by the other, summoned, called, and so forth – all that gives rise to substitution and responsibility – is radically particular. It is an asymmetrical relation between each self and each and every other person, but it is uniquely particular in its character. The I is a particular I, and the other is a particular other person – and of course also each and every particular other person. But what is particular from one point of view is general from another. In a sense, for each of us in our social lives, all pain and suffering, all human existence impinges on us, calls us into question. Each of us primordially is a target of all human suffering and all human need. That is what is primary for each of us, what each of us is, first and foremost. We are responsible infinitely and boundlessly. As we live, then, we do not begin as selfish magnets; rather, we begin as unlimited selflessness and proceed, as we must, to compromise that selflessness, that hostageship. Each of us, like Leibniz's individual substances or monads, mirrors or expresses the world, but whereas for Leibniz that expression is representational and appetitive, for Levinas it is responsible and responsive. If this is so, however, then at every instant, for every I–Other relationship, I am summoned or called to respond by the face of infinite others, each one destitute, suffering, in need, and in pain. Hence, whatever pain or suffering there is in the world is a reason for me and for everyone to respond – to reach out, to be generous and just, to give to each and every other person from what I have.[1]

---

[1] Do I have to be aware of the other's claim upon me in order for it to be a reason for me to respond? No. But for it to be a motivating reason for me, I do. See Jonathan Dancy, *Practical Reality*, 57. Levinas distinguishes between the utterly particular face-to-face relationship that is a fact about the self's social existence vis à vis each and every other person and the various

One might read Levinas, then, as a moral theorist for whom our primary moral reasons are what Thomas Nagel famously called "objective" or "agent-neutral" reasons. In such terms, every particular face, given what it presents to each I, is an agent-neutral reason to act for every person. I would like to think about this placement or interpretation of Levinas's central insight, that it has a certain similarity to what Nagel means by an agent-neutral reason, or that its manifestations in everyday life – as in the case of eros or as in particular episodes that Levinas likes to recall[2] – can helpfully be described in terms of Nagel's notion. My goal is not to classify Levinas's primordial responsibility, nor is it to reduce it to Nagel's terms. Rather, it is to use Nagel's idea and responses to him by Christine Korsgaard and Stephen Darwall to help us understand better the character and status of the face-to-face relation as an ethical or normative one and how it fits into an understanding of human action and everyday life.[3] What I will do, then, is give an account of Nagel's view and his arguments and explain how Korsgaard and Darwall respond to Nagel. I will ask, as I proceed, how Levinas might respond. My interest is not simply to ask which position is closest to Levinas's own; rather, it is to place him into their conversation, so to speak, and thereby to identify what features of the views that emerge most helpfully assist us in understanding the ethical significance of the face of the other person and what Levinas means by infinite responsibility to the other. The chief subject of this appendix, then, is the sense in which Levinas is and is not a moral theorist.

Nagel's terminology of agent-neutral and agent-relative, or objective and subjective, reasons is part of a larger project concerning human rationality, especially rationality with respect to action. In Levinas's terms, rationality regarding thought and action is a feature of human situatedness in the world and therefore of fundamental ontology. It is the kind of inquiry that he would associate with Heidegger's inquiry into human *Dasein* in *Being and Time*. Hence, because his own structure of the epiphany of the face and responsibility for others is beyond

---

ways in which I acknowledge or come to the aid of particular other persons in the course of my daily life. My everyday acts of kindness or neglect can be motivated by my responsibility to the other person to one degree or other. My primordial responsibility to all others is not a matter of degree.

2 For example, those from Grossman's novel *Life and Fate*, especially the expression of pain in the nape of the neck and the German officer's horror at his work of finding and uncovering the bodies of dead Russians.

3 The features of agent relativity that Nagel introduces amount to constraints on the universality of utilitarianism. There is a certain kinship between Levinas's understanding of the ethical and utilitarianism. The constraints that Nagel discusses, then, tell us something about how, on a Levinasian view, the complexities of everyday life and our interpersonal relations influence the ways we must make sacrifices *in ordinary life* as we try to carry out our responsibilities to others.

ontology and essence, it might seem patently mistaken to characterize the face and its role in terms of an account of reasons for action. Up to a point, of course, I would agree. No such attempt at clarification can be literally accurate and without shortcomings or distortions. But I am inclined to think, for several reasons, that it might be helpful and elucidatory. One reason is that Levinas himself explores everyday, ordinary occurrences as locations where our primordial responsibility expresses itself manifestly. When it does, it takes on everyday or ordinary features and becomes susceptible to description or even analysis. Indeed, Levinas himself in *Time and the Other* and *Totality and Infinity* carries out a phenomenological analysis of *eros* in just this spirit and precisely in order to reveal indirectly something about the face-to-face that underlies it or that is expressed through it. Increasingly during his career Levinas either looks at carefully or merely cites in passing episodes that are particularly vivid, genuine cases of everyday acts of kindness or generosity in order to depict what he has in mind, to call attention to its centrality for all we do, or to give evidence for it. These are sufficient reasons by themselves for us to feel comfortable using an analysis of rational action to help us understand better what kind of a role the engagement with the face of the other person plays.

Furthermore, especially after the essay "Essence and Disinterestedness" and *Otherwise Than Being*, Levinas emphasized what he called the simultaneity of the saying and the said or of ethics and politics. In this book I have focused on this unity as fundamental for understanding Levinas as a philosopher, whose goal is to clarify the ethical foundations of ordinary, social life. Some social forms, interpersonal relationships, or institutions and practices tend to obscure and distort the face-to-face, and Levinas is himself moved by the way twentieth-century society has effectively achieved these ends. But at the same time, other relationships and attitudes serve to invoke and enhance responsible, ethical life, and by noticing and examining these cases and types, we stand to learn something about the ethical dimension they express. Now it may be, of course, that by focusing on an analysis in terms of reasons and rationality, we are playing into the hands of the enemy, but we should not be so quick to judge. For it might be that some forms of rationality express something important about our relationship to other persons even while rationality also serves us as individuals. Rationality need not always be self-interested and instrumental.[4] It may incorporate at some level the kind of universality that Levinas invokes, albeit in a different way. This is yet to be seen. If reason is associated with respect for persons, it is one way to tie rationality and freedom to an altruistic sensibility. This is not Levinas's way, of course, but it might be that the role of reasons in

---

[4] Contra Jean Hampton, for example, who argues that it is; see Hampton, *The Authority of Reason* (Cambridge: Cambridge University Press, 1998).

rational action can help us to see the primacy of the other in a new light, if not exactly what Levinas has in mind, at least closer than we might first think.

NAGEL ON AGENT–NEUTRAL REASONS

In *The View from Nowhere*, Thomas Nagel considers the distinction between agent-neutral and agent-relative reasons; he discusses it again in *The Last Word*. In these two works, he renamed and reworked the distinction between objective and subjective reasons that he had introduced in *The Possibility of Altruism*.[5] There he had argued that "the only acceptable reasons are objective ones."[6] Basically, it is this argument that he later, as a result of criticism, abandons, although he continues to think that moral reasons are agent-neutral and yet that there is no general argument about reasons that can get us from things being agent-relative to their being agent-neutral reasons.[7] Nagel's account has been discussed by Korsgaard, Darwall, and others.

There are reasons for believing and reasons for acting. Here I am concerned with the latter, and thus with the justification of actions, why a person takes an action to be the right one to perform. Justification is not explanation. Explanations give accounts of why actions are performed, causal accounts in terms of motives, drives, desires, and such psychological states. Justifications concern the rationality of those actions and why the actions mean something of significance or why they matter to the agent and, on balance, seemed like the best ones, the right ones, to perform. Reasons contribute to this justification, either for the agent, trying to determine for herself what is right to do, what one ought to do, or to someone other than the agent, trying to judge whether the agent's action was in fact the right one for her to have performed.[8] In Sellars's terms – appropriated, for example, by John McDowell – there is a space of reasons and a space of causes; justification concerns the former, explanation the latter.

Clearly, the face of the other person is not simply a cause of my responding; it engages me, summons me, calls me into question, puts me in a certain position, and, in its suffering and destitution, makes me responsible. Is it, or the need or suffering it bespeaks, in some sense, a reason for my being responsible? And is my being responsible a reason for my acting? Strictly speaking, of course, the face and the suffering (or need) of the other person, the call for acknowledgment, acceptance, recognition, and aid, all are not reasons of any kind. They are

---

[5] See Thomas Nagel, *The Possibility of Altruism* (Princeton, NJ: Princeton University Press, 1970); *The View from Nowhere* (Oxford: Oxford University Press, 1986); and *The Last Word* (Oxford: Oxford University Press, 2003).

[6] Nagel, *The Possibility of Altruism*, 96.

[7] Nagel, *The View from Nowhere*, 159; see also N. Sturgeon, "Altruism, Solipsism, and the Objectivity of Reason," *Philosophical Review* 83 (1974), 374–402.

[8] See Nagel, *The View from Nowhere*, 142.

neither reasons nor explanations but ground both, if only in a metaphorical sense. They make both possible and meaningful. But there does seem to be a kinship between a certain kind of reason – objective or agent-neutral ones – and the status and role of the face in terms of the self's responsibility and actions, and that is what I want to explore. Is one person's need or pain everyone's responsibility?

As Nagel points out, reasons can be general in several ways. They can be general in *scope*, applying to everyone – for example, the imperative not to steal or not to kill. In both cases, we ought not to do something to anyone; we ought not to steal from anyone and we ought not to kill anyone. In this sense, a reason can be either general or restricted. In addition, norms and reasons can be considered in terms of their relation to the agent; they can be reasons for a particular person or for all persons. The moral principle about not killing applies to everyone; no one should kill. But my being hungry is a reason for me to eat something, not for everyone to eat something. In *The View from Nowhere*, Nagel appropriates Derek Parfit's distinction between reasons that are agent-relative and reasons that are agent-neutral for the purpose of marking this latter difference.[9]

One might think that the face-to-face constitutes a reason for the agent to act that is *particular* and *restricted* in both these ways. That is, it would appear that the other person's need, destitution or suffering, is a reason for me exclusively to respond in kindness to that particular other person. One might think, that is, that if the face is a reason, it is restricted and agent-relative. But this conclusion might be too hasty. If it is a reason at all, then the face is a reason in each and every face-to-face relation, and because each person has such a relation with every other person and each person is an other to every self, in fact the needs and the suffering of each person are reasons why each and every person is responsible, and furthermore, as Levinas often says, each of us is responsible to and for every other all the time. Therefore, pain and suffering turn out to be a completely general reason for response, for acts to alleviate them, to aid and acknowledge and support, for everyone's suffering and for every agent. That is, the obligation to relieve suffering is completely general in both regards; it is everyone's obligation, and it applies to everyone's suffering. This also applies of course to the obligation to acknowledge and accept the other person, that is, the norm that regulates all social relationships and social actions.

It is possible to consider suffering and pain from the point of view of the person who has them and from the point of view of another person who can and should relieve them. For many reasons, this dual perspective is the way Levinas discusses pain and suffering – indeed, all social life. For him, the social

---

[9] See Nagel, *The View from Nowhere*, 152–53 and n. 4. Parfit makes the distinction in *Reasons and Persons* (Oxford: Oxford University Press, 1984), 143.

arises first, so to speak, in face-to-face, first- and second-person, interactive encounters. But once we see that he takes such encounters to involve the need of the other person for my acknowledgment, acceptance, and more, which is called for by the presence of the other person, then we can see that from a detached perspective what Levinas is saying is that social life – especially pain and suffering – is in and of itself a reason for social acceptance and generosity (and by implication, justice). The fact of each person's living with and in terms of particular other people is a reason for each and every person to care about every other person. Moreover, because living in society is the human condition, our social life is essentially one of unlimited, unrestricted responsibility that is, as Levinas puts it, accommodated and qualified given our limited capacities and resources and the extent of our responsibilities.

Nagel says that "it is not easy to follow the objectifying impulse without distorting individual life and personal relations."[10] In a sense, Levinas would say the same, but for different reasons. For Nagel, the issue is to find objective principles that are "reasonable," that is, to look at our lives as they are lived from inside and to control them "reasonably" from outside. Nagel really is concerned about "distortion." Levinas also, in a sense, is interested in what we have available from the inside, but only because we ought to respond to what obliges us, summons us, from the outside, and this is so demanding that it always involves accommodation on our part, from the inside. What calls upon us from the outside, so to speak, is not an abstraction or generalization; it is particular and then a sum of all particular demands.

Nagel takes pleasure and pain to be a simple case. Let me focus on pain and suffering. Suppose we begin by accepting the idea that they "provide at least agent-relative reasons for . . . avoidance."[11] Nagel now asks the question that really interests him: Do pain and suffering have only agent-relative value, or do they provide an agent-neutral reason to act as well?[12] *Is it the case not only that each of us has a reason to relieve his or her own suffering but also that we have a reason to remove the suffering of others?*[13] Is suffering as a reason relative or neutral?[14] For Nagel, any answer will start by affirming that pain and suffering

---

[10] Nagel, *The View from Nowhere*, 155.

[11] Nagel, *The View from Nowhere*, 158.

[12] Nagel, *The View from Nowhere*, 158–59.

[13] Nagel begins with the agent's own pain or suffering. He takes it to be basic that the agent's pain or suffering is a reason for her to alleviate it, avoid it, and so forth. His question is whether the agent's suffering can be another person's reason to alleviate it. In a sense, Levinas begins with the other person's pain or suffering; he claims that at a basic level, the most basic level, it is a reason for the agent, the self whom the other person addresses or calls, summons, or "faces," to alleviate or relieve it. One might argue that for Levinas, the other's claim on me is prior to my own interest in myself. We shall see if this is a profitable way to view the difference between Nagel and Levinas.

[14] Nagel, *The View from Nowhere*, 159.

are relative to me and then arguing why they ought to be reasons for others (indeed, for all others) – that they are neutral. In *The Possibility of Altruism*, he had argued for all cases, not just this one, that no reason could be just agent-relative, but in fact all agent-relative reasons "were really subsumable under neutral ones."[15]

In *The View from Nowhere*, he thinks that that is true of this case but not generally.[16] His basic idea is that assuming this neutrality makes more sense of our social lives, for it means that I am reasonable not only to want to have my own suffering reduced but to expect others to think so, too, about my suffering. Not only do I want relief; you should want my relief too.[17] Nagel puts it this way: "The pain, though it comes attached to a person and his individual perspective, is just as clearly hateful to the objective self as to the subjective individual."[18] Pain and suffering are bad, no matter who has them. Nagel says that the "evaluative authority of the sufferer" is what confers value on the suffering as agent-relative. Levinas would not say this, but both would agree that the suffering is an agent-neutral reason for everyone.[19] Levinas might point out that human life is intrinsically valuable and that when it is threatened or maligned, when people lack what they need or are in pain, something should be done, and the burden falls upon us all. And Nagel might agree. But they would reach this objectivity, as it were, from different starting points: Nagel takes it as fundamental that the person in pain wants to relieve or remove it; Levinas takes it as even more fundamental that our brute sociability means that the other person's pain and suffering and bare existence matter to each of us and burden us with responsibility. In a sense, we ought to want to remove the other's pain before my own, or, perhaps more plainly, my own pain means something *ethical* to me only because the other person's pain already makes a claim upon me.

For Nagel, then, some reasons are agent-neutral.[20] He points out that consequentialists think that all are,[21] but he does not agree. All values, he says, are not impersonal. We are like each other in some ways but not in all. Nagel calls

---

[15] Nagel, *The Possibility of Altruism*, 159.

[16] Nagel, *The View from Nowhere*, 159–62.

[17] Nagel, *The View from Nowhere*, 160.

[18] Nagel, *The View from Nowhere*, 160.

[19] Nagel, *The View from Nowhere*, 161.

[20] Dancy, in *Moral Reasons*, Ch. 9–13, argues against such objectivity and for the agent-relativity of all reasons. Dancy notes that consequentialists like Shelly Kagan argue that all reasons are agent-neutral; see 190–92 and the references to Kagan, *The Limits of Morality* (Oxford: Oxford University Press, 1989), 356–85. But Dancy objects that Kagan does not deal effectively with the special considerations that arise in relationships of love and friendship (191). In a sense, Levinas takes our responsibility to others to be our primary reason for acting toward them in various ways, and he views that responsibility as utterly particular and utterly agent-neutral at once.

[21] Nagel, *The View from Nowhere*, 162–63. For consequentialists, all goods are everyone's concern.

this the conflict "between objective reasons and subjective inclinations."[22] It is, he says, "the central problem of ethics: how the lives, interests, and welfare of others make claims on us and how these claims, of various forms, are to be reconciled with the aim of living our own lives."[23] Nagel's strategy for examining this problem is to start with the agent neutrality of pleasure and pain and in general with the idea that there are such agent-neutral reasons for what people should or may do. He then proposes three types of reasons that are relative and investigates how they challenge or qualify these agent-neutral reasons. He calls them "reasons of autonomy," "deontological reasons," and "reasons of obligation." His aim, he says, "is to explain what it is that eludes justification in neutral terms,"[24] that is, how much that we value for ourselves, in a relative way, can and cannot be incorporated into an ethical system of objective, or agent-neutral, reasons. What remains unincorporated or unassimilated can then be viewed as reasonable qualifications or accommodations in our ethical system or principles. Nagel notes that consequentialists like R. M. Hare and T. M. Scanlon have sought to modify utilitarianism to incorporate many such exceptions; Nagel's project is somewhat different, an alternative account.[25]

Before I look at some examples of what Nagel does, it is worth noting how his project might be helpful in understanding something about Levinas's ethical thinking. What Nagel does is this: He starts with the idea that pleasure and pain are agent-relative; they matter to the person who is in pain or who suffers. He then argues that they are also agent-neutral; no matter who has them, they should matter to everyone. But, he asks, what agent-relative reasons might be resistant to such a move? That is, if we then assume that all reasons can work like pleasure and pain, where might we be wrong? How much that we value resists being treated as agent-neutral? In effect, how much of what is valuable to us forces us to qualify or mitigate the generality of our objective obligations? Is everything that could count as a reason for us to do something just like pleasure and pain – easily generalizable and objectified?

Now, clearly Levinas and Nagel have different starting points. Nagel begins with the individual agent: free, with desires, interests, values, and reasons. Levinas begins with the responsible self: called into question, hostage to the other, obsessed, and so forth. That is, Levinas begins with what he takes to be the most fundamental feature of our sociability: our being exposed to the claims of the other person upon us. But Nagel then asks what considerations that the individual has, in everyday life, might resist being neutralized and therefore might

---

[22] Nagel, *The View from Nowhere*, 163.
[23] Nagel, *The View from Nowhere*, 164.
[24] Nagel, *The View from Nowhere*, 165–66.
[25] See Nagel, *The View from Nowhere*, 166.

qualify how the agent acts on his or her principles. For Levinas, in a sense, each of us has an infinite number of unbounded obligations to each and every other person, but when we find ourselves in the actual social world, in a precise historical situation, we must qualify and assess how to act on that responsibility. It might very well be that it is precisely reasons like those that Nagel discusses that influence such assessment. That is, we might learn something about how Levinas thinks *the ethical* becomes moral and political conduct by examining how and why Nagel thinks our relative values resist neutrality. Nagel, that is, might help us to understand what Levinas's ethics means, what it comes to, when it occurs in the actual everyday world, when it manifests itself in ethical principles, in political and social life, and in personal decisions.[26]

Nagel starts with what he calls "reasons of autonomy."[27] Suppose I have a personal goal or desire: to climb a mountain, to visit a famous museum, or to learn to play the clarinet. Nagel notes that no matter how much I may want these things and am willing to sacrifice to accomplish them, there is no reason for others in general to care or to sacrifice in my behalf or to assist me. Why not?[28] We might ask: Why should everyone value something – say, the relief of pain and suffering? The answer is that pain is bad no matter who has it or what they feel about it. But these goals or interests are only valuable because someone wants them; otherwise, they are of no value at all. They are, as Nagel puts it, "optional." They depend upon someone having an interest in them, having them as a goal or aim or project.[29] They *derive* value rather than *have it intrinsically*. For Levinas, of course, in a sense this is exactly wrong; that is, everything of interest to anyone is intrinsically valuable to everyone, because everyone is responsible for and to everyone. Hence, at the level of moral principles, Nagel – along with T. M. Scanlon, John Rawls, and others – wonders whether any individual projects and interests are valuable at all, while Levinas wonders what might lead (or justify) us in particular social and ethical encounters to detach ourselves from another person's goals and so forth – that is, to consider them disposable or not binding or conditional. One ought, in principle, to treat all needs, interests, and values impartially, even though particular situations and conditions always make it necessary for us to qualify our obligations to responsibility and thus to treat them differentially.

---

[26] Of special interest, for example, will be what Nagel calls "deontological reasons," which restrict what we take ourselves to be permitted to do, and what he calls "reasons of obligation," which modify what we ought to do by introducing matters of relationship, membership, solidarity, and such.

[27] Nagel, *The View from Nowhere*, 166–71.

[28] See T. Scanlon, "Preference and Urgency," *Journal of Philosophy* (1975), 659–60; see also Rawls, *A Theory of Justice*, 173–75.

[29] Nagel, *The View from Nowhere*, 168.

Furthermore, for Levinas as for Nagel, one ought to treat *every person* impartially. As Nagel puts it, "No one is more important than anyone else,"[30] but in our everyday lives what this means is that we ought to deal with people in a way that is somewhere between taking all to be equally unimportant and taking all to be equally important.[31] Still, he wonders whether we should not be wholly "impartial between ourselves and others"[32] or whether such impartiality is limited. Famously, Bernard Williams noted that deliberating about whether to save one's wife or a complete stranger, when both are drowning and one can save only one, is to have "one thought too many." Does Nagel agree? He seems to.[33] That is, Nagel seems to acknowledge some place for "partiality toward oneself and one's personal cares and attachments." For Levinas, who explicitly agrees with the reality of partiality, the issue is grounded in the fact that all acts in behalf of others must be assessed in terms of other needs, one's resources, and such inevitable limitations. In short, for him partiality is a necessity to some degree or other. Not so for Nagel, because the scope of agent-neutral values is limited to begin with. He must explain why in some cases one is justified in preferring one's own interests and those of others close to us. The issue concerning neutrality and relativity concerns who the obligation falls upon; the issue concerning partiality and impartiality concerns those to whom the obligation is owed. For Levinas, both are in principle (or fundamentally) unlimited to begin with, so to speak, but in fact qualified, in all historically particular situations, and the question of partiality, as for Nagel, depends upon particular features of each situation and the comparative weight of the reasons or values involved. As Levinas sometimes puts it, the other does not mean only the stranger; it can be someone close to me whose needs, in a given situation, are more demanding than my own or than those of someone who is distant from me.[34]

Nagel finally turns to what he calls "deontological reasons."[35] These are agent-relative, because they apply only to particular agents, but they depend "not on the aims or projects of the agent but on the claims of others."[36] Nagel helpfully lists many of the most common of these constraints, from the obligations created by promises and agreements to the prohibitions against violating individual rights – not to be killed, injured, tortured, robbed, and so forth.[37] This may strike us as strange; surely a prohibition against cruelty, torture, murder, and robbery is an agent-neutral one. Nagel may have some restrictions in mind for

---

[30] Nagel, *The View from Nowhere*, 171.
[31] Nagel, *The View from Nowhere*, 171.
[32] Nagel, *The View from Nowhere*, 172.
[33] See Nagel, *The View from Nowhere*, 173.
[34] See Nagel, *The View from Nowhere*, 173.
[35] Nagel, *The View from Nowhere*, 165, 175–88.
[36] Nagel, *The View from Nowhere*, 175.
[37] Nagel, *The View from Nowhere*, 176; cf. 185.

such values, but his point makes better sense with regard to promises, contracts, and other arrangements that establish responsibilities for specific individuals.[38] His point is that there are times when such obligations or prohibitions conflict with some impersonal value, and yet, he wonders, how could these values be agent-relative and not wholly general? I think that Nagel's answer points to something that Levinas also thinks is important. That something is perspective. Agent-neutral reasons apply to everyone and thus do not reflect any particular point of view on the demand, need, or condition that deserves respect and attention. The crucial feature of deontological reasons is that they are tied to perspective, to the particular point of view of the person whom they target. The point of these reasons is that a particular agent has reason not to do what in general we all have reason to do.[39] In general, lives might be saved if one person dies, but if I am the one called upon to kill that person, it is something I ought not do.[40] Why not? Is this a relic of some atavism about individual agency? Nagel asks whether the issue concerns the relation between intention and evil.[41] Here, he says, the point is that to aim at evil is to adjust other things to accomplish it, but evil should repel and disgust us. To intend evil, Nagel says, is to swim against the normative stream, to engage in a kind of "moral dislocation."[42] What might seem right from a detached point of view will seem utterly unintelligible from a particular, personal point of view.[43] Nagel puts it this way: "Each of us is not only an objective self but a particular person with a particular perspective; we act in the world from that perspective. . . . So our choices are not merely choices of states of the world, but of actions."[44]

Nagel's special concern is the reason why rights-based theories – for example, Kantian ethics – would constrain consequentialist calculations of overall goodness. He starts, as we can see, by looking at the agent and asking why a particular agent should have reason not to do what, from an impersonal standpoint, would be desirable, and he ends by locating the justification in a matter of the agent's character and identity. Levinas, too, is fully aware that the demands of the face-to-face are somehow grounded in the utter particularity of the I and the other. Like Nagel, Levinas would agree that committing atrocities or cruelties to protect people is morally repugnant. But he also is especially cognizant of the role of the particular other person who is a potential victim of such cruelty. Nor does Nagel ignore the victim.[45]

[38] Nagel, *The View from Nowhere*, 177.
[39] Nagel, *The View from Nowhere*, 180.
[40] Nagel, *The View from Nowhere*, 180–81.
[41] Nagel, *The View from Nowhere*, 181.
[42] Nagel, *The View from Nowhere*, 182.
[43] Nagel, *The View from Nowhere*, 183.
[44] Nagel, *The View from Nowhere*, 183.
[45] Nagel, *The View from Nowhere*, 183–85.

Levinas would put it this way: It is true that the one person I might kill
to save others has a claim upon me not to kill her, but so, too, do the others
have a claim on me not to ignore their needs and their lives. Nagel makes a
similar point. He notes that according to a consequentialist view, those whom
I might save by killing one person "would have the right to object if I *didn't*
kill him to save them."[46] Nagel intervenes, objecting that this shows the flaw in
considering impersonal reasons alone. It surely seems right that the one person
at risk of my killing him can object in a way that the others cannot, but Nagel
has a hard time explaining why, calling upon the fact that he owns the life
that I am *aiming* to destroy.[47] Levinas seems better off: To him, all the possible
victims make a claim on me, and the only considerations against my killing
one to save the others concern *how* I might fail that responsibility, what my
precise relationship is to him, what resources I have available, and so forth. For
Nagel, "the key to understanding any of these moral intuitions is the distinction
between the internal viewpoint of the agent or victim and an external, objective
viewpoint that both agent and victim can also adopt."[48] In fact, the choice of
what point of view to take in the situations we have been discussing – how to
look at the reasons that apply – is central to ethics. As he puts it, "When we ask
ourselves how to live, the complexity of what we are makes a unified answer
difficult. . . . A fully agent-neutral morality is not a plausible human goal."[49]
The issue is how much we remain committed to our personal goals, projects,
and interests and how much detachment from our particular perspective is
appropriate.

What Nagel says about this tension is a compelling way of framing the
challenges that face us in developing moral principles, a theory of morality, and
making moral choices. For Nagel, the first-person perspective is natural and
basic; the detached perspective is natural but derivative. Detachment is an object
of aspiration, but for us, as historically situated agents, it is never fully attainable.[50]
Structurally, Levinas seems to acknowledge something similar. In our moral lives
in society, considering and acting in moral situations and responding to moral
principles, we *begin*, as it were, with unlimited responsibility to and for everyone,
but many factors relevant to our personal situation qualify and influence our
actual principles and choices. Nagel seems inclined to think that we should aspire
to greater objectivity and neutrality but not total objectivity. We do not want

[46] Nagel, *The View from Nowhere*, 184.
[47] Nagel, *The View from Nowhere*, 184.
[48] Nagel, *The View from Nowhere*, 185.
[49] Nagel, *The View from Nowhere*, 185; cf. 185–88.
[50] This idea that detachment, or an impersonal point of view, is an object of aspiration for individ-
    uals immersed in concrete situations in the world is common to such figures as Plato, Spinoza,
    Leibniz, and Kant.

to suppress our personal inclinations and interests altogether.[51] Levinas would agree. We may be responsible *prior to* everything else, but we are not responsible *instead of* everything else. One way of taking Nagel here is to read his account as an attempt to find a middle road between consequentialist and deontological moral thinking. He takes consequentialist ethics to be paradigmatically agent-neutral, for it is in fact neutral about whose goodness is in question and also about who is obligated to maximize that goodness. Levinas might be taken to accept the propriety of such a middle road as well. For him, no matter who we are as individuals, we are related to an unlimited society of others, near and far; their goodness is up to us, and yet we can only act within precise, narrow boundaries. We *should not* forget the demands placed upon us; nor *can* we ignore our existential limitations. No principles, no choices, no actions can operate without both these demands and these constraints.

For Nagel, a life without any detachment and without any agent-neutral reasons would hardly be human. It would be a life of desires, inclinations, and drives, but a life without reasons and thus without any objectivity. Levinas's sense of objectivity is grounded in the unique particularity of our interpersonal relations, but also in the generality of the claim that others make on all of us. Furthermore, it is grounded in the *substance* of that claim, on the destitution, suffering, need, and even the life of the other, whose very presence calls on me to accept, acknowledge, and support the other person alongside myself. Hence, when Levinas imagines a world that is inattentive to such responsibility, it is a world where people are abandoned or sacrificed or killed by others. Indeed, he sees the twentieth century, with its oppression, domination, and atrocities, as a period of such wholesale abandonment. It may be a matter of emphasis rather than one of real difference, whether one sees the horrors of genocide and totalitarianism, for example, as a total capitulation to rampant desire and power or as an unqualified – or virtually unqualified – abandonment of responsibility.

Nagel summarizes the discussion in *The View from Nowhere* in a few pages of *The Last Word*.[52] There he poses as a critical choice regarding morality the choice about admitting agent-neutral reasons into one's motivational repertoire. Of course, he takes this to be a matter of how "one is going to value oneself and one's own interests."[53] On the one hand, we value ourselves – our goals, projects, desires, and interests – "from our own point of view" and, on the other, "from the impersonal standpoint that assigns to us no unique status apart from anyone else."[54] Nagel rejects the wholly agent-relative or egoistic alternative as "highly

[51] Nagel, *The View from Nowhere*, 187–88.
[52] Nagel, *The Last Word*, 120–22.
[53] Nagel, *The Last Word*, 120.
[54] Nagel, *The Last Word*, 121.

unreasonable and difficult to honestly accept."⁵⁵ It is interesting, moreover, that he argues from the basis of the agent's interests but admits that the point applies as well to other persons. Not only does it sound strange and is it hard to imagine that we but no one else should care about our dying of hunger or suffering from pain; it also is hard to believe that other people should care about their own lives and well-being but that no one else should.⁵⁶ What we need, given such considerations, is a "system of reasons," a moral system, that assigns to persons both subjective and objective worth. Nagel argues that no single way of doing this "is clearly the right one," and he uses utilitarian and contractualist theories to show their inadequacies.⁵⁷ As he puts it, these two theories differ over how best to meet the requirement of "impartial interpersonal concern."⁵⁸ In what cases and exactly how should we all be obligated to care equally for everyone else? This sounds, then, very much like a question that Levinas, too, would address to us about our everyday moral lives. Once we acknowledge our infinite responsibility to and for others, how do we live by such a standard? Is there any systematic way to help us in making the accommodations that social life makes necessary?

KORSGAARD'S CRITIQUE OF NAGEL

To this point, I have been looking at Nagel's discussion of moral theory and morality in terms of his distinction between agent-relative (subjective) and agent-neutral (objective) reasons. I have also noted the way in which he associates this distinction with that of the personal point of view of the agent and the detached, or impersonal, point of view and the claims that these two perspectives make on us as agents. Moreover, I have suggested that these distinctions can usefully help us to think about what Levinas might say about our everyday moral lives, regarding principles, theories, and choices that we are called upon to determine. But before we go too far in this direction, we should consider more carefully Nagel's distinctions, and to help us do that I want to discuss two prominent critiques of Nagel, one by Christine Korsgaard, the other by Stephen Darwall.⁵⁹

⁵⁵ Nagel, *The Last Word*, 122.
⁵⁶ See Nagel, *The Last Word*, 122.
⁵⁷ Nagel, *The Last Word*, 122–25.
⁵⁸ Nagel, *The Last Word*, 124.
⁵⁹ Christine M. Korsgaard, "The Reasons We Can Share: An Attack on the Distinction Between Agent-Relative and Agent-Neutral Values," *Social Philosophy and Policy* 10:1 (1993), 24–51; reprinted in Korsgaard, *Creating the Kingdom of Ends*, 275–310. Stephen L. Darwall, *Impartial Reason*, Part III, 117–67.

What is striking about Korsgaard's essay is how Levinasian it is. At a deep level, it is about the sources of moral normativity, about what makes moral reasons moral.[60] And ultimately her criticism is that such reasons do not originate from objective realities or from personal desires or interests but rather from our personal interactions or our intersubjective encounters. An important result of realizing this, moreover, is that all deontological reasons are objective, impersonal, and agent-neutral. These certainly sound like Levinasian conclusions, and to a degree, I think, there is a similarity between Levinas and Korsgaard. But the agreement only goes so far, as I shall try to clarify. In order to get to this point, I will first look at Korsgaard's critique of Nagel in more detail.

Korsgaard frames her essay as a defense of what she takes to be a deep Rawlsian insight: that morality is grounded in an interpersonal situation about "how we should relate to one another," in which the task of a group of people is "to find the reasons they can share."[61] Let me accept this characterization of her central insight for the moment and go on to her consideration of whether there are both agent-relative and agent-neutral reasons and values. Korsgaard's strategy is first to explain the distinction and then to consider Nagel's arguments about "reasons of autonomy" and "reasons of obligation." Nagel tries to show that some reasons of these kinds cannot be made agent-neutral; they cannot be reasons or values for everyone. His paradigm situation is one where such reasons act as constraints on consequentialism, but presumably the issue is much larger. It is whether there *are* agent-relative reasons or values, why there must be reasons of both kinds, and if so, why. Korsgaard argues that the distinction distorts the real ground of moral value. She treats Nagel's discussion of autonomous and obligatory reasons, as he characterizes them, as a defense of agent-relative reasons – that is, as a defense of the idea that the value of some projects, actions, and so forth is grounded in the individual self, by itself.

Korsgaard notes that in *The Possibility of Altruism* Nagel argued that what is good-for-x must also be good-absolutely.[62] Basically, Nagel starts with personal desires or interests and argues that we take these desires or interests as values or to be reasons not only from our first-person point of view but also when we view ourselves from a third-person, or objective, perspective. They have "normative force" for me and then for anyone who considers me from a detached point of view.[63] Korsgaard then notes an ambiguity in the idea that this argument

[60] See Korsgaard, "The Reasons We Can Share" in *Creating the Kingdom of Ends, passim*, esp. 303 n. 6.
[61] Korsgaard, "The Reasons We Can Share" in *Creating the Kingdom of Ends*, 275; Rawls, *A Theory of Justice*, 139–42; Cf. Scanlon.
[62] Korsgaard, "The Reasons We Can Share" in *Creating the Kingdom of Ends*, 277.
[63] Korsgaard, "The Reasons We Can Share" in *Creating the Kingdom of Ends*, 277; cf. Nagel, *The Possibility of Altruism*, 82–85. It is of course not necessarily a compelling argument.

proves that all values that are good-for-x are also good-absolutely. This latter phrase could mean "good independently of all agents" or "good for anyone," and good-for-x could mean "good because x desires (values) it" or "good and x values it." That is, "good-absolutely" could be good not because I or anyone values it but because it is intrinsically or objectively good. Or, alternatively, "good-absolutely" could mean not "good because I value (or desire) it" but because anyone would value it. Korsgaard also notes that these two senses of "good-absolutely" are related differently to my desiring or valuing the good. In the first case, I value it because the goal or state or action is intrinsically good; in the latter, anyone would value it because I – and every I, or all of us – value it. Nagel, in fact, if Korsgaard is right, is not consistent about which kind of objective reason or good-absolutely he has in mind, in both *The Possibility of Altruism* and *The View from Nowhere.*[64] Korsgaard herself takes values or reasons to be grounded in what she calls our "intersubjectivity," or "how we should relate to one another," and she holds that this situation can have different ranges or domains and thus yield different outcomes. It is a view, she says, that has the advantages of avoiding "ontological or metaphysical commitments" and of explaining our moral convictions.[65]

Korsgaard now turns to Nagel's arguments in *The View from Nowhere* that "an individual may have agent-relative or subjective reasons which have a legitimate normative force for her, but which have no normative force for others."[66] She believes – quite rightly, I think – that Nagel was moved to this view by a criticism of utilitarianism, associated with Bernard Williams and Samuel Scheffler, that a moral theory ought to make room for individuality, for the attachments and projects that make us who we are.[67] First, Korsgaard considers what Nagel calls "reasons of autonomy" and what she dubs "idiosyncratic projects" or "ambitions."[68] Nagel argues that such "ambitions give those who have them reasons to do things, but do not give others reasons to help or to care whether these things get done," but she asks "why the normative force of ambitions is limited in this way."[69]

Korsgaard makes some important distinctions about ambitions that she gets from Nagel. Some values we locate or discover, and they are external to or outside of us; others we confer or determine by our desires, likes, or interests. Of the latter, some we confer individually, others collectively.[70] Take an ambition

[64] Korsgaard, "The Reasons We Can Share" in *Creating the Kingdom of Ends*, 278–82, esp. 279–81.
[65] Korsgaard, "The Reasons We Can Share" in *Creating the Kingdom of Ends*, 305 n. 17.
[66] Korsgaard, "The Reasons We Can Share" in *Creating the Kingdom of Ends*, 282.
[67] Korsgaard, "The Reasons We Can Share" in *Creating the Kingdom of Ends*, 282.
[68] Korsgaard, "The Reasons We Can Share" in *Creating the Kingdom of Ends*, 284–91.
[69] Korsgaard, "The Reasons We Can Share" in *Creating the Kingdom of Ends*, 284–91.
[70] Korsgaard, "The Reasons We Can Share" in *Creating the Kingdom of Ends*, 284–85.

that I have, based on a desire in me, to try to arrange my schedule so that I can go to the movies to see Wong Kar-wai's new film, *2046*. Korsgaard points out that in some situations that desire is unmotivated, but in others it is motivated, in the sense that I may have good and perhaps complex reasons for wanting to do so.[71] By refining our understanding of ambitions, then, Korsgaard puts us in a better position to ask whether they are as agent-relative as Nagel claims. This amounts to asking whether this is so for ambitions that arise from collective interests and more importantly when they are motivated at least in part by reasons that matter to others as well as to the agent in question. In the latter case, which she examines in some detail, I may *desire* some end and also *value* the end for general reasons. Korsgaard gives the example of wanting to write a book that will be required reading, which means, on her understanding, that I believe that someone should write a good book that will be required reading and that I want to be that someone.[72] Such an ambition, then, has both an agent-neutral component and an agent-relative one. Others can value the one, while rejecting the other. Korsgaard even suggests that where there is no agent-neutral component, the ambition is unreasonable altogether, "just a stupid piece of vanity."[73]

But as Korsgaard notes, this analysis leaves unclear the *status* of the reasons that motivate my ambition. If they are objective, then everyone should (or might) be moved by them, but surely there are ambitions where my reasons for having them are not objective in any metaphysical sense but are nonetheless plausible and compelling. Suppose I want to visit Glasgow in order to investigate local archives, to come to understand the local Jewish community, and to determine if my paternal ancestors did in fact live there at one time. This want is not simply whimsical or stupid or vain, nor are these reasons intrinsically valuable and important to everyone. Yet, they might ultimately convince others to help and assist me in achieving my goals, she says.[74] If I am a human being with reasonable, interesting goals and interests, it makes sense for others to share or to try to share them.[75] The ground for such sharing is the fact of intersubjectivity, as Korsgaard puts it, that involves a mutual respect for the humanity of the other person.[76] It *may* be the case, then, that certain ambitions are valuable for everyone when the reasons for having them are shared in this way, out of a sense of common humanity and mutual respect. In Korsgaard's view, then,

---

[71] Korsgaard, "The Reasons We Can Share" in *Creating the Kingdom of Ends*, 286.

[72] Korsgaard, "The Reasons We Can Share" in *Creating the Kingdom of Ends*, 288.

[73] Korsgaard, "The Reasons We Can Share" in *Creating the Kingdom of Ends*, 289, although it is not clear that she would make the general point.

[74] Korsgaard, "The Reasons We Can Share" in *Creating the Kingdom of Ends*, 289–90.

[75] Korsgaard, "The Reasons We Can Share" in *Creating the Kingdom of Ends*, 290.

[76] Korsgaard, "The Reasons We Can Share" in *Creating the Kingdom of Ends*, 290.

"reasons springing from ambitions are agent-neutral. But they spring from our respect for one another, rather than from our respect for one another's ends."[77] She seems to draw three conclusions from her analysis thus far: first, that the reasons that spring from an agent's ambitions may but need not be reasons for others to help me; second, that these reasons and ambitions are ultimately grounded in the agent's personal relationships; and finally, that these relationships and all human interaction are grounded in "our respect for one another's humanity."[78]

Korsgaard goes on to claim that the same analysis applies to Nagel's "deontological reasons."[79] Nagel argues that these prohibitions against harm, lying, breaking promises, and so forth are agent-relative and not, as we might think, agent-neutral.[80] The central idea in Nagel's argument for this claim is that to perform these actions – for example, to hurt someone or to lie to him or her – is "to aim directly at evil for your victim" and this means, as Nozick puts it, to treat your victim as a means.[81] And this is a "badness for you," Nagel argues. But Korsgaard disagrees: "Surely when you violate a deontological restriction, it is bad for your victim as well as for you."[82] This means that the reason not to hurt me and to lie to me is a reason not only for the agent to stop but also for me to act as well, for me, the victim, to complain or to resist or whatever.[83] Surely, as Korsgaard puts it, what the agent does is not "none of [the victim's] business." Why? Because the reasons or values that arise from these situations are tied to the fact that they are intersubjective, interpersonal relationships, between agent and other. In fact, she claims, the "agent-neutral reasons are *created* in personal interaction"[84] by the structure of universality and recognition or the call to mutual respect that is integral to such interactions. "We acknowledge the force of deontological reasons" precisely because "we regard one another as *persons*." As persons, we share in each other's ends, and we realize that we must treat the other person as end and not means, in ways to which they would consent.[85]

If we step back from the details of Korsgaard's critique of Nagel, we can see that she is not ultimately skeptical about the distinction between agent-relative and agent-neutral reasons and values. She does not doubt that there is

[77] Korsgaard, "The Reasons We Can Share" in *Creating the Kingdom of Ends*, 290.
[78] Korsgaard, "The Reasons We Can Share" in *Creating the Kingdom of Ends*, 299.
[79] Korsgaard, "The Reasons We Can Share" in *Creating the Kingdom of Ends*, 291–99.
[80] See Korsgaard, "The Reasons We Can Share" in *Creating the Kingdom of Ends*, 291ff.
[81] Korsgaard, "The Reasons We Can Share" in *Creating the Kingdom of Ends*, 294–95; cf. Robert Nozick, *Anarchy, State, and Utopia* (New York: Basic Books, 1977), 30.
[82] Korsgaard, "The Reasons We Can Share" in *Creating the Kingdom of Ends*, 297.
[83] Korsgaard, "The Reasons We Can Share" in *Creating the Kingdom of Ends*, 298.
[84] Korsgaard, "The Reasons We Can Share" in *Creating the Kingdom of Ends*, 298–99.
[85] Korsgaard, "The Reasons We Can Share" in *Creating the Kingdom of Ends*, 299.

a distinction of some kind being made. Furthermore, I do not take her to be denying that there are ambitions – desires, interests, or projects – that really are agent-relative. She may not think much of them; many may be stupid and vain. But there may be such ambitions. Her fundamental disagreement with Nagel is not about these matters. Rather, she explores these issues in order to expose a deeper, more fundamental difference, a disagreement about the sources or grounds of normativity. Nagel, as Korsgaard reads him, seems to accept certain features or impulses of consequentialism, but only up to a point. She does not. What grounds values, reasons, and norms is not our desires nor what we produce or some metaphysical reality. For her, the ground of moral norms is our intersubjectivity, and it is here that her account seems most Levinasian in spirit and thus here where we must be the most careful about interpreting what Korsgaard means.

Earlier, we noted that to compare Nagel on agent-neutral reasons and Levinas, it is important to keep in mind that we are talking about reasons, principles, moral theories, and their application. In the case of what Nagel calls "autonomous reasons," "deontological reasons," or "reasons of obligation," he asks how they function as constraints on consequentialism. But my point here is that the character and impact of these reasons or values is at the level of moral theorizing and everyday choice. It is about our decisions and policies or moral programs. Levinas generally focuses on the face-to-face relation and on personal responsibility to the other person at the level of the *grounds* of human experience, choices, and plans and not at those of experiences and plans themselves. We can project a pure moral program for Levinas, however, and we did so, claiming that ideally the needs and suffering of persons is a general objective reason for everyone to assist everyone in all cases, all the time. Then, just as Nagel asks what agent-relative reasons cannot be made agent-neutral, we can ask what factors in everyday life lead to a Levinasian qualification or accommodation of this unrestricted, completely general obligation. In the light of this account, we can see the point and the target of Korsgaard's basic disagreement with Nagel. She, like Levinas, would disagree with Nagel about what gives rise to our moral reasons to begin with, about what she calls the sources of normativity, of the values that are agent-neutral, of the reasons that are norms for everyone's choices and actions. Nagel seems to think that this source is the person as a free agent with desires and interests. For Korsgaard, it is our personal interactions, our intersubjectivity. As I mentioned earlier, this certainly *sounds* like Levinas. I want now to consider if it really is.

Throughout "The Reasons We Can Share," Korsgaard emphasizes this point, but the best place to start is a passage at the essay's conclusion: She says that "*all* neutral reasons for action arise from . . . the category of personal relations," which Korsgaard claims is the arena or domain that Nagel took to generate special obligations, to friends, family, and neighbors.[86] As Korsgaard sees it, such personal relations give rise to deontological reasons, to ambitions insofar as we are called upon to share "in each other's ends," and to special obligations to those who need our help.[87] In a Postscript to the reprinted version of the essay, she elaborates this point by saying that "*having* decent human relationships...is the primary concern of morality,"[88] and she sees this as a Kantian and Rawlsian position.[89] Her final formulation about the role of these *decent* human relationships is this:

A reason [is]...a normative claim, exerting authority over other people and yourself....To say that you have a reason is to say something *relational*, something which implies the existence of another, at least another self. It announces that you have a claim on that other or [it] acknowledges her claim on you. For normative claims...are claims we make on ourselves and each other.

The acknowledgment that another is a person is...something that stands behind the very possibility of reasons.[90]

What makes a human relationship *decent*? The answer is that decent human relationships involve people interacting in such a way that they acknowledge and respect the humanity in each other. As Korsgaard puts it with regard to ambitions and the way that we might share each other's interests and goals: "The Intersubjectivist sees the other as human, and *therefore* shares or tries to share the other's ends.... We should promote the ends of others not because we recognize the value of those *ends*, but rather out of respect for the humanity of those who have them."[91]

Here, then, is a key to Korsgaard's intersubjectivism. Our humanity – say, as rational or autonomous beings – does not directly give rise to moral reasons. But it is integral to the type of human relationship that does. As human beings, each of us makes a claim on the other person, or the other person makes a claim on each of us, and such claims of person on person are what give rise to reasons (norms, values) for action.[92] The other person appeals to me for help or aid; she calls upon me to share her ends or interests; she makes a claim upon me not to harm or injure her. And she does all of these things, has such effects on me, because she is a person and I am, and because I should

---

[86] Korsgaard, "The Reasons We Can Share" in *Creating the Kingdom of Ends*, 299.

[87] Korsgaard, "The Reasons We Can Share" in *Creating the Kingdom of Ends*, 299.

[88] Korsgaard, "The Reasons We Can Share" in *Creating the Kingdom of Ends*, 310 n. 46.

[89] Korsgaard, "The Reasons We Can Share" in *Creating the Kingdom of Ends*, 300–1; cf. 275–76, 281, 290.

[90] Korsgaard, "The Reasons We Can Share" in *Creating the Kingdom of Ends*, 301.

[91] Korsgaard, "The Reasons We Can Share" in *Creating the Kingdom of Ends*, 290.

[92] For development of this account, see Korsgaard, *The Sources of Normativity*, 132–45.

treat her as a person, as someone who is rational and autonomous, capable of consenting, respecting me, and caring for me, and deserving of my care and respect. Korsgaard suggests that by itself one's humanity does not give rise to reasons, but my relation to another's humanity does, and her relation to my humanity as well. Clearly, the claim that is integral to our *interpersonal relation* and the *humanity of each of us* go together, and it is worth considering how close or how tight that connection is, and whether there is any order of priority between the two.

Korsgaard says that "it is the status of humanity, as the source of normative claims, that is the source of all value. The argument, in other words, has brought us back to Kant."[93] It would take us too far afield to fill out the way in which this claim is Kantian. But in this essay, as in *The Sources of Normativity*, she makes this much clear: that our sense of ourselves as rational and reflective agents is what constitutes our moral identity and our valuing our humanity.[94] I do not think that Korsgaard thinks that we are alone, however, or that we establish this moral identity or humanity, in isolation. If it is fundamental to who we are, it is nonetheless fundamental only insofar as we are related to others, whose humanity we value and who value ours. This is the fact of intersubjectivity as real, factual personal interaction and relationships. In "The Reasons We Can Share," she does not say much about why and how this personal relationship begins with my valuing my own humanity as a rational, moral agent and then coming to value yours, and vice versa. In *The Sources of Normativity*, she says more. But for our purposes, the important point is that the interaction, intersubjectivity, or relationship is reciprocal and symmetrical. It works from self-valuing to other-valuing, even if in the end it is reasonable to say that each agent values the humanity of the other person for itself. Her argument is that private reasons remain private; what fixes the reciprocity of persons obligating one another are "reasons [that] are not private, but public in their very essence,"[95] and the way that the Intersubjectivist, and not the Objective Realist does that is to show how "the public character of reasons is indeed created by the reciprocal exchange, the sharing, of the reasons of individuals."[96] Now the argument Korsgaard uses, which she gets from Nagel, claims that when the other person calls you to stop hurting her, you take her pain to be a reason for you to stop, by imagining that you are she, which requires you to see what the two of you share, your common humanity.[97] Ultimately,

---

[93] Korsgaard, "The Reasons We Can Share" in *Creating the Kingdom of Ends*, 299.

[94] Cf. Korsgaard, *The Sources of Normativity*, 129.

[95] Korsgaard, *The Sources of Normativity*, 134–35.

[96] Korsgaard, *The Sources of Normativity*, 135; cf. 136ff.

[97] Korsgaard, *The Sources of Normativity*, 142–43.

then, even though moral reasons become objective or neutral for both people, the source of those reasons' authority is the tie to the humanity of each, prior to their being shared by both.

At one level, then, Korsgaard's account looks intersubjective or relational, but at another level it looks to be grounded in the subject, for the argument begins with the establishment of the subject's rational, reflective stance toward his own desires, interests, and impulses, and thus the subject's sense of his own humanity. The argument then situates that subject over against another person and seeks to show, by a universalization strategy, why the subject takes the other person's interests, ends, feelings, and such to be reasons for him to do something. The key step, moreover, is the recognition that the universalization strategy, sharing the other's reasons, only makes sense if the subject takes the other to be a moral person like himself. Hence, reasons are objective because I see you as another person like myself. For Korsgaard, then, the objectivity of values and reasons rests first on the subject's recognition of his own humanity or moral identity, second on the subject's acknowledgment of that same humanity in the other person, and finally the other person's expression of a need, interest, or end as making a claim on the subject.

Now that we have clarified what is involved in Korsgaard's claim about the intersubjective basis of neutral reasons, we can see how her account differs from one that Levinas might give. To begin with, Korsgaard takes values or reasons to arise for people in intersubjective situations, and this means that they arise out of personal relations. But it is clear that she and Levinas do not agree about what these interpersonal encounters involve and how reasons arise from them. An indication of the differences that separate them is her description, early in "The Reasons We Can Share," of what she calls "the primal scene of morality." Contrasting Rawls with others such as Nagel, Korsgaard says that "the primal scene of morality . . . is not one in which we do something to you or you do something to me, but one in which we do something together."[98] She then glosses this last phrase by describing it this way: "The subject matter of morality is . . . how we should relate to one another," and she credits Rawls with having "grasped this point" by framing the "original position" as one in which "a group of people must make a decision together" and thereby "find the reasons they can share."[99]

What does all of this mean? Morality is a matter of identifying and acknowledging reasons or normative claims that have authority for all people. The context in which this process of identification and endorsement goes on is one where people collaborate in order to make decisions about what reasons to

[98] Korsgaard, "The Reasons We Can Share" in *Creating the Kingdom of Ends*, 275.
[99] Korsgaard, "The Reasons We Can Share" in *Creating the Kingdom of Ends*, 275.

share – what norms to accept as reasons for acting toward one another in common ways. The chief strategy that each participant uses is to imagine herself as the other person; to imagine what it would be like to have certain goals and to need help to attain them or to imagine what it would be like to be the object of harm or injury, of lies or broken promises; or to imagine oneself as the agent's friend, child, or spouse. In all such cases, Korsgaard believes, one *can* imagine oneself in the other's place only if one values oneself as a rational moral agent and takes the other person to be valuable for the same reason. In such situations, people share norms as reasons because these are the reasons that respect the humanity of all those parties in conversation with one another.[100]

How different this is from Levinas. For him, the basic interpersonal encounter is the utterly particular one between two persons, where the other person summons the self to respond, makes a claim on the self, and calls the self into question. The self, then, is obligated or responsible *prior to* being self-conscious, reflective, free, or rational. In Levinas's terms, the subject is accused or obsessed, subjected to the other, face-to-face, hostage, and substitution. This terminology, much of it developed in the period leading up to the publication of *Otherwise Than Being*, emphasizes the passivity of the self, its basic responsibility to the other, and its sense of subjection. To put Levinas's point somewhat paradoxically, the other's need or suffering, present as the face of the other, is a reason for the self to respond and act, prior to the self's capacity to value it as a reason. Alternatively, we might say, the other's existence and condition is the ground of the self's responsibility as a compelling reason before it is an autonomous reason.

This distinguishes Levinas's "primal scene" from both Korsgaard's and from those – Nagel, consequentialists, and others – for whom that scene is interpersonal but agent-oriented. For Korsgaard, the "primal scene" is one in which people deliberate together about what values or norms to share. For others, it is a situation in which "one does something *to* or *for* someone else."[101] For Levinas, it is the situation of being called into question or summoned by the other person to be responsible and responsive, to acknowledge her, to accept her, and to extend a helping hand to her. In a sense, it is about being obligated to do something to or for the other person, prior to thinking about whether what to do is something we can all agree to do and even to determining what

---

[100] See Korsgaard, "The Dependence of Value on Humanity" in Joseph Raz, *The Practice of Value* (Oxford: Oxford University Press, 2003), 73: "It is not because of our shared values that we should accord consideration to one another but *because of our shared capacity for conferring value*" (my italics).

[101] Korsgaard, "The Reasons We Can Share" in *Creating the Kingdom of Ends*, 274. The "primal scene" is also social or interpersonal for O'Neill, Habermas, and Scanlon, but the character of the interpersonal relationship differs.

that action should be. If values, reasons, and norms are part of our everyday moral lives together, then the summoning or subjection Levinas calls attention to is not itself a reason for action. It is, more accurately, the relationship or the aspect of our interpersonal relations generally that gives rise to the norms of responsibility and justice that do become reasons for us to act. Like Korsgaard, then, Levinas is indeed interested in the intersubjective source of normativity, but he finds it – so to speak – not in our rational, reflective abilities and therefore not in our humanity or moral identity, as Korsgaard calls it, but rather in the fact of our social relationship with each and every other, of our being called by each and every particular person to live with and for her. Moreover, there is no question to be asked: Why does the other person turn to the self and call it to attention, pleading for acknowledgment and acceptance? This posture just *is* what standing before a self signifies; it just *is* what it means to live with others, and the burden it places just *is* what it means.

Set within the context of this encounter between Korsgaard and Nagel, then, Levinas's ethical thinking – the ethical dimension of his thinking, which is the core of his thinking and his life – is distinguishable in three important ways. First, Levinas differs concerning the ground of ethical life. Here Levinas is unlike Nagel and Korsgaard in two ways. On the one hand, Nagel's understanding of ethics involves the interplay of two factors: our personal desires and interests and our rational capabilities, with the latter viewed as a mechanism for constraining and refashioning the former. This is what the interplay between the first person and third person, between objectivity and subjectivity, are all about. Ethics arises with rational principles that sometimes limit our desires and impulses and with reasons for qualifying such principles when personal commitments override them. This is what goes on when we consider the role of connections and special obligations, the significance of individual projects and ends, and the claims that persons make on us concerning their rights and our obligations. But all of this ultimately points to the locus of value as the individual's desires and rationality. For Korsgaard, ethics arises specifically when people deliberate together about what to do and why; this situation may be actual or imagined, but it is the "primal scene" for morality. To be sure, the crucial fact about this scene is that both persons involved, you and I, are rational and free beings. We are able to decide about norms or reasons to share because we are rational – that is, capable of detached reflection and commitment – and because what norms or reasons to adhere to is up to us. Moreover, the criterion for which norms to adhere to and which to treat as personal and not sharable is self-respect and respect for the other, both of which are grounded in our rationality and freedom. For Nagel and Korsgaard, then, at the deepest level, ethics is grounded in the rational and free humanity of the individual. Ethical norms, however, arise for Nagel in situations where individuals consider what to do and for Korsgaard in situations where persons deliberate together about what norms and reasons to share.

Levinas differs in both respects. For him, each of us seeks to determine what to do and what principles to accept *whenever* we are related to others in a social world, and because this means that whenever we act, it refers to *all situations*. Each and every one of us, that is, is always determining what to do and why, both within the context of our situations and their histories and current features and within the context of the unique relation each of us has to each and every other person. That relation – what Levinas calls the face-to-face – carries within it an unlimited, unqualified obligation to respond with acknowledgment, approval, acceptance, assistance, and generosity. It is that nexus, with its determinative character, that for Levinas grounds all everyday ethics and politics. If, for Nagel and Korsgaard, I should respond to your hunger by offering you food or work or money, it is because all people as rational, free beings deserve our respect and aid. For Levinas, my response to your need is grounded in your claim on me and my responsibility to you and also is qualified by my situation: my resources, other obligations, limitations, and more. There is never a question of why the other person should matter to me; in a sense, the other person matters to me first of all, prior to anything else mattering to me and indeed even prior to my mattering to myself. For Nagel and Korsgaard, I matter to myself as rational and free (and as a being with desires and interests) before you matter to me, you matter only because in these respects you and I are alike. For Levinas, you matter to me first of all, in virtue of your facing me in our social world, and other things then do and indeed I matter to myself, only because of my obligation, my responsibility to you.

Second, then, Levinas differs because the situation, or primal scene, that gives rise to ethics, for him, is each and every encounter or relation between two unique persons. The *sheer presence of the other* makes a claim on me, calls me into question, puts me on the spot. This scene is ubiquitous. It does not nullify Rawls's and Korsgaard's scene of interpersonal deliberation. Nor does it take it to be privileged in any way. Rather, Levinas might see this deliberative situation as one way that moral systems, principles, and policies – and political ones too – are identified or can be taken to be identified. But such a situation is not actually significant, nor does it reveal in an especially perspicuous way how objective values or norms arise and what makes them objective.

Finally, Levinas, were he to use the terminology, would not mean the same thing by "objectivity." For Nagel and Korsgaard, norms or reasons are objective in several ways and for various reasons. They are objective if they apply to everyone, if they are binding or if they count for everyone, if they arise independently of my personal desires or interests, and if they are in force whether I am aware of them or not. For Levinas, I think, responsibility and the justice that derives from it are objective because they are binding unqualifiedly on all, for all, because of the human social condition itself, independent of any features the parties possess. To be sure, how this primordial responsibility to others manifests itself depends upon the contingencies of all social, historical situations, but the force or obligatoriness of my very existence among others comes from this fact, as it were, and this fact alone – not the "fact of reason" but rather the "fact of the interpersonal, face-to-face relation." It is this that Levinas calls by so many names that seem surprising, even eccentric, from "religion" and "sociality" to "accusation," "trauma," "enigma," "substitution," and "obsession."

DARWALL AND INTERSUBJECTIVE VALUE

Like Korsgaard, Stephen Darwall develops a view about "intersubjective value" based on a critical encounter with Nagel.[102] Like Nagel and Korsgaard, Darwall takes his start from an agent's personal preferences, desires, interests, and impulses. He does notice that some preferences or values are impersonal even if they are for the agent, in the sense that they are desires for some objective state of affairs to occur – not for a particular agent's experiencing, enjoying, or causing it, but just for it to occur.[103] Darwall takes such impersonal preferences or values to be especially important for our moral lives.[104] He calls this "a conception of value that is not relativized to ourselves as individuals."

Such values are not natural, grounded in desires, nor are they objective in some ontological sense. Darwall refers to them as "intersubjective values" and distinguishes two aspects of their intersubjectivity. First, they are valued for anyone in a particular valuing community and thus are not private or personal. Second, they are the expression of a kind of intersubjective agreement by members of that community.[105] The results are facts or states of affairs that can serve as "*shared objective reasons* to act":[106] "If something has intersubjective value relative to a community therefore, there are objective reasons for *any* member of the community to promote it."[107] But such values and reasons are not, for Darwall, tied to rationality in general, the way they are for Korsgaard. They are, as he emphasizes, relative to valuing communities and what it is that the values of those communities are grounded in.[108] That is, for Darwall a

---

102 Darwall, *Impartial Reason*, Part III.
103 See Darwall, *Impartial Reason*, 132–37.
104 Darwall, *Impartial Reason*, 139.
105 Darwall, *Impartial Reason*, 140–41.
106 Darwall, *Impartial Reason*, 144.
107 Darwall, *Impartial Reason*, 144.
108 See Darwall, *Impartial Reason*, 144–45; cf. Korsgaard, "The Reasons We Can Share" in *Creating the Kingdom of Ends*, 281–82.

value is intersubjective when all the members of a valuing community *value* a particular state of affairs and when their attitudes are "impersonally based," as he calls it.[109] Furthermore, the idea of such intersubjective values is tied to being able to view one's life as meaningful[110] and to having the attitudes of self-respect, self-esteem, and self-concern.[111] These features make sense only if our values are intersubjective and impersonal. It is not necessary for us to examine Darwall's argument for these connections; the critical point is that he claims that they exist.[112] In short, moral reasons must be impersonal, objective, and intersubjective.

What is it that makes values intersubjective for Darwall? I think that Darwall is clear that for values to be intersubjective is for them to be shared by the members of a valuing community because they are impersonal and not in any way dependent "on seeing things from a personal point of view."[113] Pain, misery, and suffering are impersonal in this way; if we agree to care about them, we do so regardless of who endures them and "independently of the person's relation to us."[114] The key that makes these values intersubjective is the impersonal point of view that is *intersubjective*. Darwall characterizes this point of view as one "that is available to all within a relevant group of valuing beings" or "a perspective common to a community of valuing beings."[115] A value is intersubjective, that is, if it is available to *any* person in the community because he could see it as impersonal, if he considered it carefully enough. If such values can be motivating reasons, they can be operative norms for how to act. They are sharable and general for members of the relevant community or group. Like Korsgaard, Darwall takes them to be relative to a group and sharable by the members of the group, as if they were the outcome of a group agreement. They express what is (or could be) important or compelling for *any* member of the group. Yet they are about how one member ought to act toward another.

But the burden of value does not arise when people encounter each other. Rather, it arises when they *consider together* how to act toward one another. These values or norms, that is, are the outcome of *deliberation* and *reflection* and not of engagement. They are the results of what we think about all of us and not of what each means to each and every other. In a sense, intersubjective values are general ones, cognitively derived from a view about what we are. For Levinas, this is ontological and derivative, not primordial and determinative.

---

[109] See Darwall, *Impartial Reason*, 147.
[110] See Darwall, *Impartial Reason*, 164–66.
[111] Darwall, *Impartial Reason*, 148.
[112] See Darwall, *Impartial Reason*, 146–67.
[113] Darwall, *Impartial Reason*, 138.
[114] Darwall, *Impartial Reason*, 139–140.
[115] Darwall, *Impartial Reason*, 140.

For him, ethics as moral principles arises from a normative or deontological foundation and not from a theoretical or cognitive one.

I have claimed that we should treat Nagel, Korsgaard, and Darwall as if they were dealing with two problems, first that of framing the character and range of a theory of moral norms or principles and second that of pointing out the metaphysical foundation of that theory. In a sense, all three begin with naturalist assumptions about human beings as agents with interests, wants, and desires and with rational abilities. Nagel conceives of moral agents as trying to coordinate the personal and impersonal, subjective and objective, points of view, and this means trying to determine which interests and reasons are personally relative and which are agent-neutral. Korsgaard takes the range of objective reasons to be broader than Nagel does but also not necessarily universal in scope. Although Darwall has less respect for formal and noninstrumental rationality, he looks more like Korsgaard than Nagel.

PLACING LEVINAS

Levinas, I have contended, can also be approached from these two perspectives, as someone concerned primarily to identify the metaphysical grounds of moral and political life and then to characterize what a theory of moral norms and political policies would look like. These two projects, one might argue, come together in the most explicit way in *Otherwise Than Being*. They are part of what it means to distinguish the saying from the said and then to show how they necessarily occur together. Before I turn to some passages in that book, however, it will be useful to see how Levinas can be viewed this way, as dealing with these two tasks, by turning first to an interview with Levinas conducted by R. Fornet and A. Gomez on October 3 and 8, 1982 and published in 1983.[116]

Korsgaard distinguishes between Objective Realism and Intersubjectivism as *interpretations* of agent-neutral values.[117] This is what I called earlier the meta-physical ground of moral theory and what role I have in mind – at least functionally – for Levinas's face-to-face and all it signifies. As I indicated earlier, one might see Levinas as accepting the idea that in social life each person's needs, misery, and suffering make a claim on each and every other person and hence could be understood as agent-neutral or objective values. Hence, the face-to-face relation grounds everyday moral thinking and ethical life; it is not an alternative to it as many portray it, as much as it is, in this sense, its source and ground. To the degree that such need and suffering is determinative of all ethical life (and all social life overall), it represents a type of Intersubjectivism,

[116] "Philosophy, Justice, and Love" in *Entre Nous*, 103–21; also translated in *Is It Righteous To Be?*
[117] Korsgaard, "The Reasons We Can Share" in *Creating the Kingdom of Ends*, 278–82.

but one that is very different from that of Korsgaard and Darwall. I think that this understanding of Levinas, however, is not explicit in Levinas's writings. Perhaps the best we can do to support it is to show how the basic picture of this twofold task is present in his thought.

In the 1982 interview, Levinas gives a sketch of how the face leads to justice, as a moral and political value. Levinas calls the face of the other person "the beginning of intelligibility" and what brings to us "the order of meaning which seems to me primary."[118] It is the ground of ethics but not yet of theory or philosophy. For theory, one needs the third party, so that one must approach and respond to the other *and* to this third party. This approach and responsibility he calls "taking upon oneself . . . the fate of the other."[119] If one's social world were limited to *one* such other, that would be it: I would have obligations to her, period. But – and Levinas is very clear about this – "I don't live in a world in which there is but one 'first comer'; there is always a third party in the world: he or she is also my other, my fellow."[120] I take this to mean that Levinas's project is to take the fact of our social lives as given, as the way things are. We live among and together with a host of people; we interact with many people all the time. Indeed, even if we ignore people nearby and are unaware of many who live a distance from us, we still live with them, and we are always interacting with them; we are *related to them* insofar as they and we live in the same social world and they make claims on us and each other, no matter how direct or indirect our relations are.[121] The face-to-face is a fact of every person-to-person relation, and the plurality of them is a direct consequence of the plurality of persons in the world.

Whenever I act, then, whether I do so with deliberation and with reflection, whether I seek to determine norms or principles for acting or just to decide what to do here and now, I am always – or I should always be – engaging in some kind of comparison or judgment, some weighing of responsibilities. In Levinas's terms, I must always calculate "which of the two takes precedence."[122] Levinas calls this "equity" and "justice" in this late period, and he sees it as the origin of theory and philosophy. My point is that this evaluating is what must go on whenever we act, always, for all of us, when we are trying to determine which option to take or which kind of action is best to take in similar circumstances. This means that Levinas recognizes very clearly that our lives are social and

---

[118] "Philosophy, Justice, and Love" in *Entre Nous*, 103.
[119] "Philosophy, Justice, and Love" in *Entre Nous*, 103.
[120] "Philosophy, Justice, and Love" in *Entre Nous*, 104; see also 105.
[121] For a recent discussion of these issues from an analytic point of view, see the essays in Deen K. Chatterjee (ed.), *The Ethics of Assistance: Morality and the Distant Needy* (Cambridge: Cambridge University Press, 2004).
[122] "Philosophy, Justice, and Love" in *Entre Nous*, 104; cf. 106–7.

interactive, that we are always comparing demands made upon us, and that we always compromise. This is what justice is all about. But these decisions are what we mean by practical choices and choices about moral and political principles. The face and all it reveals compels us to take each and every other person seriously and thus to engage in ethical deliberation and moral theorizing about principles. Levinas explicitly says that the face leads inexorably to justice and politics, but it is clear that it leads to ethics and moral thinking as well.[123] "Leads," however, does not mean temporally, for these two – justice and charity (or love, as he says here) – occur together: "They can seem alien when they are presented as successive stages; in reality, they are inseparable and simultaneous, unless one is on a desert island, without humanity, without a third."[124]

Against this background, Levinas is able to discuss the legitimacy and character of political institutions and of the state, and my suggestion is that we read what he says as also applicable to moral theories, to norms and principles. *Prima facie*, "If there were no order of Justice, there would be no limit to my responsibility."[125] But with such limits comes judgment, principles, "institutions and the state." This is the world of citizens – in the kingdom of morality and in the world of politics. For Levinas, moreover, not only is moral, social, and political life grounded in the face-to-face; it is also measurable by it. Legitimacy and illegitimacy of particular political and moral arrangements, or institutions, can be measured against this relation as a standard.[126] For example, as Levinas puts it, "a state in which the interpersonal relationship is impossible, in which it is directed in advance by the determinism proper to the state, is a totalitarian state."[127] Totalitarian regimes are "limits" on the very notion of a state. It is as if Levinas is arguing that because states are regimes of justice, responsive to the demands of generosity and kindness, regimes that exclude such things cannot be "legitimate" states.

At one end of the political spectrum, then, is the totalitarian state – virtually an oxymoron – and at the other end is "the ethical state" of the Bible.[128] We have suffered the first and need to remember what it was: the total abandonment of

---

[123] See "Philosophy, Justice, and Love" in *Entre Nous*, 105, 107: "[J]ustice itself is born of charity."
[124] "Philosophy, Justice, and Love" in *Entre Nous*, 107. One might take a statement like this one, that justice and charity are inseparable and simultaneous, to be Levinas's way of putting the central thesis of this book, that the encounter with the face of the other is constitutive of all social life and is contemporary with everyday life, theorizing about it, and so forth. I have tried to show how important an insight this is for understanding Levinas's thinking and its implications.
[125] "Philosophy, Justice, and Love" in *Entre Nous*, 105.
[126] "Philosophy, Justice, and Love" in *Entre Nous*, 105; cf. 108.
[127] "Philosophy, Justice, and Love" in *Entre Nous*, 105; cf. 108.
[128] "Philosophy, Justice, and Love" in *Entre Nous*, 106.

life to suffering and atrocity, torture and humiliation. The other state is a political ideal, as much as we can hope for and aim at. But even it is a compromise with structure, organization, and thus violence.[129] As Levinas puts it, ontology brings with it the determinism of being, and there is no way to avoid ontology. It hides or obscures the face of the other, to one degree or other. But to what degree?

At the end of this interview, Levinas discusses the idea of the just state, and he reflects on Marxism. He affirms "a possible harmony between ethics and the state,"[130] where "ethics" means the unlimited responsibility that is essential to our social existence, and "the state" is whatever moral norms and political principles and institutions we find it necessary to construct. Clearly, the two are both necessary: "Charity is impossible without justice, and . . . justice is warped without charity."[131] We have seen what this means: We live with many others, so that the obligation to be generous and kind must be institutionalized as justice; at the same time, such institutions must be grounded in and expressive of that responsibility that is manifest as generous and kind acts in behalf of others. All of this suggests that totalitarianism is a necessary risk, while the ethical state of the Bible is a necessary hope, an aspiration. Similar risks and hopes mark the spectrum of moral systems. Moreover, these judgments about necessity and possibility are reflected in Levinas's assessment that while Stalinism was a totalitarian excess and a horror, it was not genuine to Marxism itself, which is not "just conquest" but contains a "recognition of the other."[132] In his reading, Marxism at its core contains a kind of messianism, a humanism, a recognition of concern for the other.[133] Again and again, Levinas harnesses Stalinism to Hitlerism and opposes both to ideals like Marxism that, to him, express this kind of messianic aspiration.

LEVINAS AND CONTEMPORARY ETHICS

In *Otherwise Than Being*, these themes, concerning the interconnection between the primordially ethical and the political, are developed in a more technical

---

[129] "Philosophy, Justice, and Love" in *Entre Nous*, 106, 114. Levinas discusses the necessity of this compromise in the Talmudic lesson "Judaism and Revolution" in *Nine Talmudic Lessons*, 110. Commenting on a passage in Tractate Baba Metsia, 83a–83b, and a story about a conversation between Rabbi Eleazar ben Rabbi Simeon and a government office or policeman, Levinas distinguishes between a policeman, who belongs to the governmental machinery and simply carries out its orders, and a genuine revolutionary politics that understands the Good and the sources of Evil. He points out the necessity of serving both the Absolute and the state – of uniting ethics and politics.

[130] "Philosophy, Justice, and Love" in *Entre Nous*, 120.

[131] "Philosophy, Justice, and Love" in *Entre Nous*, 121.

[132] "Philosophy, Justice, and Love" in *Entre Nous*, 119–20.

[133] "Philosophy, Justice, and Love" in *Entre Nous*, 120.

way,[134] but this is not the place to examine what he says in detail. What I want to do is to try to show how the distinction and the account we have just set out are developed in this major work, so that we can see clearly how Levinas's thinking can be viewed alongside that of Nagel, Korsgaard, and Darwall.

Like politics, moral theory and moral systems are about institutions and principles. When Levinas says that "it is on the basis of proximity that being takes on its just meaning,"[135] he is claiming that the face-to-face *gives rise to* theory and judgment and accounts for their significance.[136] Alternatively, he claims that the obligation that grounds the ethical character of social life and all the "apparatus" of being – including moral rules and political institutions – are "assembled." They occur at the same time; they are simultaneous and are interrelated.[137] And yet the responsibility to others is the standard for such theorizing and practices.[138] Justice takes shape as the manifestation of responsibility in everyday social life; states and moral systems are just, to one degree or another, insofar as they express responsibility and interpersonal concern. Totalitarianisms fail utterly in this respect, while other regimes do better.

If we want to know how well moral and political systems do, perhaps the best hint that Levinas gives is the language he uses to clarify how the third party affects the self's relation to the other and how it affects the self's unlimited responsibility. First of all, even in the self's encounter with one particular other, while her responsibility is unlimited, her capacity to act out that responsibility is in fact limited. Each of us has abilities and resources that are finite in number and degree; in each case, there is only so much that one *can* do, no matter how much one recognizes one is responsible for. There are limits to how much one knows, to how near and far people are from us; there is only so much one can sacrifice, only so much one can share. Moreover, the multiple responsibilities conflict with one another and require coordination or even elimination. To be sure, there are things one must refrain from doing absolutely – doing physical harm, stealing, and killing, for example – but when it comes to acts of generosity and charity, even with regard to a single person, one cannot do all that one should or even all that one wants.

If we begin with this recognition – that when it comes to prohibitions and negations, the self can act in an unqualified way and never perform certain acts – we can see that this applies equally to all others just as it applies to a single,

[134] OB, 16, 156–62, 169–71.
[135] OB, 16.
[136] See OB, 157, where he discusses the "latent birth" of thinking, etc., in responsibility.
[137] OB, 7; cf. 157: "[J]ustice is necessary."
[138] OB, 16.

particular other person.[139] But in the case of positive, so-called virtuous acts, acts of kindness and charity (what Kant and others called "imperfect duties"), just as our resources are limited in the case of one other person, they are also limited when there are many others. Indeed, the limitations on the self's capacities are now complicated and multiplied. Even if I am primordially responsible to the other person in every way, for everything, I cannot in fact sacrifice all I have for her – or, perhaps more accurately, I am justified in not giving all I have to her, at the cost of my own life and well-being. Levinas shows every indication of accepting this kind of limitation. Hence, when I am confronted not with one other person alone but rather with many – indeed, with myriad others – the question of *how much* is increased and now complicated by the question of *to whom* I am able to act generously and with kindness. Levinas does not discuss with any precision how these questions arise or how they are addressed. What he provides are only clues, largely through the terminology he uses to identify how judgment, thought, and so forth arise from the face-to-face.

In Chapter 1 of *Otherwise Than Being*, for example, Levinas says that "the relationship between the neighbor and the third party cannot be indifferent to me when I approach. There must be a justice between incomparable ones. There must then be a comparison between incomparables and a synopsis. . . ."[140] Each and every other person is my neighbor, calls to me and summons me. But at the same time, they encounter each other, and they call to me from different points of view. In one sense, because my responsibility to each is unlimited, they are incomparable. But in another sense, I must compare them to determine what I should do for each, given my different relationships to each, the differences in their situations and needs, their relations to one another, and my resources and capacities. These conditions, I think, are what Levinas has in mind when he says that we must "be *with another* for or against a third party, with the other and the third party against oneself, in justice."[141] He calls this a "justice [that] takes form" out of comparing, assembling, and conceiving what one can and should do in our social, moral, and political lives.[142]

In Chapter 5, Levinas gives a fuller account.[143] He sketches – as I would put it – a genetic narrative of how thought, knowledge, and ultimately philosophy arise out of proximity or the face-to-face. "We then [in order to answer the

---

[139] In Chapter 3, we discussed the content of the face and Levinas's way of articulating the claim it makes upon the self, as if it were to say, "Thou shalt not kill" – that each face demands of us first and foremost that we not negate it, that we accept and acknowledge the other.

[140] OB, 16.

[141] OB, 16.

[142] OB, 16.

[143] OB, 156–61.

questions: "Why know? Why philosophy?"] have to follow in signification or proximity or saying the latent birth of cognition and essence, of the said, the latent birth of a question, in responsibility.... Proximity can remain the signification of the very knowing in which it shows itself."[144] I take this to be a rhetorical strategy, to expose those factors that situate the face-to-face and all it signifies alongside our everyday thought and experience. Or better yet, it situates the latter in the former; Levinas shows what the point of speaking, judging, thinking, and such activities really is and what it must answer to. As we have seen, the critical factor is the third party: "The responsibility for the other... is troubled and becomes a problem when a third party enters."[145] About this "new" presence, Levinas says a number of things. First, the third party is a neighbor to me and to my "original" neighbor. She does not simply stand alongside my neighbor. All of us are engaged in interpersonal encounters with one another. Second, my responsibility to each is affected by how they are related to one another and by what they have done *to* or *for* one another. Third, once there are such third parties, or additional others, all such relations are now, for me, both direct and mediated. "The other and the third party, my neighbors, contemporaries of one another, put distance between me and the other and the third party."[146] Fourth, the third party creates a situation in which my responsibility is limited and generates the question of justice – "comparison, coexistence, contemporaneousness, assembling, order, thematization, ... and the intelligibility of a system, and thence also a copresence on an equal footing as before a court of justice."[147] As we have already noted, once there are many others, they all make claims on me and on each and every self, "as before a court of justice." What I – and every self – does depends upon various relationships, the level of need, the acts in question, and our resources.[148]

This new situation, however, does not nullify or destroy the proximity or responsibility from which it arises and to which it answers. That dimension of the social relationship persists, remains firm, and continues to make its demands. Justice and all that is associated with it – life and thought – are modifications of the face-to-face and not replacements for it. They are modes of social and ethical life. They are, as it were, the ways that the face-to-face is lived in society; moral principles and political institutions, then, are among such modifications. They are *expressions* of the interpersonal demand that is responsibility, proximity,

---

[144] OB, 157.

[145] OB, 157.

[146] OB, 157.

[147] OB, 157.

[148] The text focuses on thought, theory, and philosophy, not on morality and politics. But my point is that the implications for these domains are clear.

hostage, and substitution.[149] And this means, of course, that they can be good or bad expressions, that is, they will be just to one degree or another. Levinas expresses this continuity by denying that responsibility is "constrained to a calculus by the 'force of things'" and by affirming that all these others – the third parties – still "obsess me" and that "this obsession cries out for justice."[150] That is, we compare, weigh, assess, and thereby construct principles and institutions of justice as a *result of* our fundamental responsibility or *because of* it. Another way Levinas puts it is to say that the "equality" implied by justice originates in a primordial "inequality." Before others are neighbors, they are faces.[151] Moral, social, and political institutions are not grounded in procedures for the efficient regulation of "human masses"; they are not Hobbesian mechanisms for "harmonizing antagonistic forces."[152] Rather, they arise out of and seek to express, as best they can, our fundamental responsibility to one another. "Justice, society, the State and its institutions, exchanges and work are comprehensible out of proximity."[153] Moreover, "the contemporaneousness of the multiple is tied about the diachrony of the two."

What does this involve? Levinas continues to drop clues and give us some hints, but without any sustained analysis. For example, he says that "justice remains justice only, in a society where there is no distinction between those close and those far off, but in which there also remains the impossibility of passing by the closest. The equality of all is borne by my inequality, the surplus of my duties over my rights. The forgetting of self moves justice."[154] It makes a difference whether one takes the "egalitarian and just State" to be grounded in a Hobbesian individualism or alternatively in "the irreducible responsibility of the one for all, and if it can do without friendships and faces."[155] These passages are not wholly without ambiguity, but let me suggest the following reading: When is a moral and political system really just? One requirement is impartiality, an equal respect for all persons and an equal protection of the rights of everyone. But this requirement is not sufficient for justice. A Hobbesian or Lockean

---

[149] See OB, 158.
[150] OB, 158; cf. 158–59, where he opposes "giving the self over to calculus."
[151] OB, 158: "The relationship with the third party is an incessant correction of the assymetry [sic] of proximity in which the face is looked at. There is weighing, thought, objectification, and thus a decree in which my anarchic relationship with *illeity* is betrayed, but in which it is conveyed before us. There is betrayal of my anarchic relation with *illeity*, but also a new relationship with it. . . . "
[152] OB, 159; see also "Philosophy, Justice, and Love" in *Entre Nous*, 105. Levinas often contrasts his view with the Hobbesian account. For example, see "Peace and Proximity" in *Alterity and Transcendence*, 144.
[153] OB, 159.
[154] OB, 159; see also 160–61.
[155] OB, 159–60.

state – legislative, judicial, and protectionist – may be just in the sense that it protects all equally, shows no favoritism, and is unbiased. Such a state may have laws
to protect rights, police those regulations, and try offenses, but it may have limited welfare agencies, no publicly funded education, no universal health care, and
so forth. It would be just, then, but it is not *just* in the sense that Levinas wants,
such that it expresses the extent and depth of each person's responsibility to each
and every other, that is, the surplus of duties or obligations over rights, the special burden of those who suffer in front of us, and the requirements and bonds
and allegiances to one's friends and family. He calls this "the spirit in society."[156]

Throughout these pages, Levinas uses the language of derivation and development, but my suggestion is that we interpret his analysis as structural and
relational, not as temporal and genetic. Furthermore, he shifts from talking
about the derivation of consciousness, thought, and even philosophy and science to discussing the emergence of law, politics, and the state. He calls all
of this "justice." My interest here is to take his remarks and hints as a way of
thinking about the domain of morality – moral deliberation, decision making,
reflection on moral principles, and the performance of moral actions. If we
call this the domain of moral systems, we do so in a very broad way. I do not
think that Levinas would favor any particular moral system – say, some form of
Kantian morality or of consequentialism, insofar as it is a system. If he acknowledges the value of norms, systems, or principles, it is as devices that facilitate
our approach to complex, demanding, concrete situations, where many factors
influence our deliberation and decisions. Norms or principles about what is
morally right to do are, for him, rules of thumb or helpful devices, in a sense –
obligatory but not absolutely so, binding but only as guidance and with care.
Where Levinas cites examples of morally complex situations, he always takes
them to be singularly demanding and worthy of careful, precise, contextual
reflection and consideration. Rules may give us guidance about how situations
might generally be approached, but our actual judgment or decision requires
more than their simple application. Rules introduce the kinds of factors that
are relevant, but not necessarily all of them. Nor do they prescribe exactly how
those factors might best be weighed or understood. In particular situations,
outcomes require a very specific process of deliberation and assessment.

SOME CONCRETE CASES

As I have argued, some of Levinas's terms help us to see what factors are relevant:
the closeness or distance of the other persons to us; their relations to one another;
what they have done to or for one another; what resources we have available;

---

[156] OB, 160; see also 161.

our connectedness to others, as friends, family, or colleagues; and the greater significance of our duties and responsibilities over our rights, interests, projects, privileges, and status. In one way or another, these factors arise as significant precisely insofar as they involve some kind of qualification of or attention to our primordial relation to the face of the other and the other's needs and suffering – that is, our responsibility. In this way, Levinas's moral thinking is grounded in the intersubjective or interpersonal.

But his understanding of that relationship is very different from the one we saw in Korsgaard or Darwall. Still, once at the level of deliberation about what to do and what reasons we have – the normative claims on us – it is interesting that Levinas's thinking reflects a similar set of concerns as Nagel's and Korsgaard's. Recall that Nagel wondered how far we could or should go in treating as agent-neutral three kinds of values or reasons: what Korsgaard called ambitions, what Nagel called deontological reasons, and what he called obligations – reasons based on personal connections or relationships. Nagel and Korsgaard did not agree on the degree to which such reasons should be considered agent-neutral, objective, and impersonal; they did not agree, therefore, on their respective moral weight. But they did agree that all three have some weight. What can we say – even given the little we have to go on – about Levinas's view of these three and similar considerations?

Let us call to mind some specific cases, to help us as we try to determine what Levinas might think about these factors, the values or reasons they introduce, and thus their moral weight, as I have called it. Remember, for example, the incident described by Vassily Grossman in *Life and Fate*, where an enraged Russian woman, infuriated by seeing a captured German officer pulling a young girl's body from the wreckage of a building, rushes toward him with a rock in her hand but, at the last instant, drops the rock and offers him a piece of bread. Her act is wholly surprising, completely dissonant with her anger, a "tiny act of kindness," totally uncalled for and spontaneous without apparent justification. Surely, Levinas is not recommending decisions and actions without deliberation, but he is praising the impulse to generosity that can, on occasion, virtually push aside normal responses.

Famously, in his conversation with Alain Finkelkraut and Shlomo Malka after the massacres in Sabra and Shatila in 1982, Levinas – perhaps enigmatically – responds to Malka's question about the role of the Palestinians for Israelis by pointing out that the other, who is the neighbor, can be one's kin. But when one neighbor attacks another, one must seek to determine who is right and who is wrong, who is just and who is unjust. He ends by saying "there are people who are wrong."[57] Howard Caygill, commenting on this response as

[57] "Ethics and Politics" in *A Levinas Reader*, 294.

well as other comments about Arabs and Palestinians, takes Levinas here to be unclear but largely evasive, apologetic, or insensitive.[158] Even more, Levinas seems to reduce one's decision and response to a matter of knowledge, even if it is unclear who has wronged whom. My point would be that the situation shows how Levinas urges us to take each case in all its particularity, to be aware of and sensitive to who one's neighbor is, what has been done, and what one's relationship is. To be sure, he may seem to be avoiding a judgment,[159] but at the same time he is claiming that a number of factors count against general or agent-neutral assessment and that his own views about the face of the other cannot be applied mechanically to each and every situation, without consideration and qualification.

In addition to particular cases like these – one fictional and one historical – Levinas discusses the actuality of the ethical in moral and political life in his Talmudic commentaries. Take, for example, his earliest lesson, on the topic of forgiveness, given in 1963.[160] The mention of Heidegger and references to the issue of the forgiveness of Germans point to the Eichmann trial and the questions of German guilt raised by it.[161] Clearly, the Talmudic lesson is Levinas's opportunity to clarify how one makes a decision about forgiving those who have committed acts of harm or offense and to reflect on guilt, repentance, and forgiveness and their interrelations. I am not interested here in a detailed reading of the commentary but rather in looking at what Levinas tells us about guilt, responsibility, and forgiveness in the course of it.

Levinas points out that his comments, focused on a few passages from Tractate Yoma of the Talmud (85a–85b, 87a–87b), while about forgiveness, certainly do

---

[158] See Caygill, *Levinas and the Political*, 186–94, esp. 190–93.

[159] I am not sure that he is avoiding a judgment. He comments that hundreds of thousands of Israelis made it clear, immediately after the massacres, by their demonstrations in the streets of Tel Aviv, that they were appalled at the events and took their own military to be culpable. Levinas acknowledges their judgment and seems to accept its authority, so to speak. But instead of focusing on it, he turns to the assumption that Malka seems to be making, that the other is paradigmatically one's enemy, and his response is that one should not forget that one's family and kin are also the other. One's responsibility to them is no less, because they and you have close connections, than one's responsibility to strangers and enemies. Being opposed to someone or distant from them does not by itself make them more appropriate or more demanding as objects of one's generosity, concern, and love.

[160] *Nine Talmudic Readings*, 12–29.

[161] See *Nine Talmudic Readings*, 20, 25; cf. 28–29. On the question Does an S.S. man have a face? see "The Other, Utopia, and Justice" in *Entre Nous*, 231. I am not sure that the theme is a direct response to the Eichmann trial. There may also have been events going on in France at the time, that also raised the issue of guilt and forgiveness, regarding Nazism and complicity. Alternatively, Levinas and his French colleagues might have in mind the Auschwitz trials in Frankfurt. I once asked Simon Critchley about the context, and he knew of no specific trials in France at the time.

not give a comprehensive picture of "what the Jewish tradition thinks about forgiveness."[162] The texts are not concrete or practical, nor are they simply abstract and conceptual. They are not theological either. Rather, these texts deal with information of value for the living of human life.[163] In particular, they are relevant to moral experience, especially the experience of forgiveness.[164] In general terms, what sorts of things do we learn about forgiveness from them?

Forgiveness is a kind of cleansing, of wiping the slate clean, or of rectification. Sometimes, in the case of certain transgressions or actions or failures, seeking that cleansing or rectification may be sufficient warrant for it to take place; in some cases, it is not. A response is sought and, for that reconciliation, is required. The harm, injury, or transgression is forgiven only if the other person performs that response. But this distinction might seem to make the latter more demanding, when another is wronged, whereas in fact the Talmud might want us to think otherwise, that it is more important to be cleansed before God than to be forgiven by one's victim; that is, the recovery of one's "moral conscience" and one's sense of personal wholeness is what is really difficult.[165] Levinas calls this a "total mobilization of oneself," a "healing of the self by the self," and "the effort the moral conscience makes to reestablish itself as moral conscience."[166] He associates this with the idea of *teshuvah* or return, an effort that seeks the state of being forgiven, of recovering one's moral groundedness. This is a process of moral recovery, one that, Levinas notes, is a "progress toward [the self's] own interiority and toward solitude," and in order to make this effort and carry out this progress, "one must rely on the objective order of the community."[167] In other words, forgiveness and guilt are about integrity of the self and the reestablishment of moral conscience, the self's coherence around a sense of orientation to what is morally required. It is about seeking to "reconquer the integrity that no one can reconquer for [the 'damaged' moral conscience]."[168] Sometimes, this itself is what one aims at exclusively, but at other times it requires as a prior stage the seeking of forgiveness from the injured party. But this end, this "inner rebirth," also has a "communal basis."

---

[162] *Nine Talmudic Readings*, 14.
[163] *Nine Talmudic Readings*, 14.
[164] *Nine Talmudic Readings*, 14–15.
[165] See *Nine Talmudic Readings*, 16–17.
[166] *Nine Talmudic Readings*, 17. Cavell, in his writings about moral or Emersonian perfectionism, as well as on the films he calls the comedies of remarriage, speaks about a person's coming to find him- or herself again or learning to be who he or she is, a trope found in Emerson and a host of other philosophers. Levinas's discussion of repentance and forgiveness as the self's healing of itself, of its finding its conscience once again, recalls these Cavellian thoughts.
[167] *Nine Talmudic Readings*, 17.
[168] *Nine Talmudic Readings*, 17.

We next turn to the request for forgiveness itself. From Levinas's exegesis of the Talmudic debate, we can extract a number of points. First, forgiveness requires that the guilty party "recognize his fault" and seek forgiveness from the person harmed or offended; the victim must be asked and be open to receiving the petition.[169] Moreover, even if there is a principle involved, if the guilty party has transgressed a rule or norm, still, in order for there to be reconciliation or cleansing, "the offended individual must always be appeased, approached, and consoled individually."[170] In fact, "the harmony with God, with the Universal, with the Principle" is an internal matter for the individual that requires the interpersonal "dialectic of forgiveness."[171] It is not an abstract or formal matter; it cannot be conferred by a court or a government or a judgment. That is, recovering wholeness or integrity, rebuilding one's moral conscience, is a process carried out between the agent of harm and his or her victim. It is the recognition once again of one's responsibility to the other when that state has been disturbed or destroyed.

Levinas's exegesis, then, turns to this dialectic of forgiveness and to how the Talmud reveals features of it. Sometimes, he notes, it is the victim who realizes what the offender or agent needs, and he seeks "to provoke a crisis of conscience" in the agent "about the forgiveness that the offender does not concern himself with."[172] But will this "excessive moral sensitivity" work, or will it provoke the unjust agent? Levinas takes the Talmud to be wary of such a dangerous game.[173] People are not all the same; they do not "form one humanity," that is, some have greater moral sensitivity than others or are more occupied with other matters: work, enjoyment, whatever. There is a "purity which can kill, in a mankind as yet unequally evolved." When a victim's concern is so enormous that it expresses itself in a "premature confidence in the humanity of the Other," it can result in catastrophe. This can easily occur when the victim encourages the guilty party to seek reconciliation.

What about "an offense between intellectuals?" Could such an act be unforgivable?[174] When a person has done wrong and asked for forgiveness, "the offended party can grant forgiveness when the offender has become conscious of the wrong he has done."[175] This implies, however, that "the offender is [not] capable of measuring the extent of his wrongdoing." People may not realize what they have done and for this reason may not "have the capacity to ask for

---

[169] *Nine Talmudic Readings*, 19, 20.
[170] *Nine Talmudic Readings*, 20.
[171] *Nine Talmudic Readings*, 22.
[172] *Nine Talmudic Readings*, 22.
[173] *Nine Talmudic Readings*, 23.
[174] *Nine Talmudic Readings*, 23.
[175] *Nine Talmudic Readings*, 25.

forgiveness." As Levinas puts it, "how is one to forgive if the offender, unaware of his deeper thoughts, cannot ask for forgiveness?"[176] Indeed, Levinas suggests a paradox, that forgiveness may be impossible precisely when it is asked for. For it has two conditions: "the good will of the offended party and the full awareness of the offender." But what if the "aggressiveness of the offender is . . . his very unconsciousness," his lack of awareness or attention? It is not clear whether Levinas means the offender's aggressiveness in performing the offense or in asking for forgiveness, but in either case the idea is that the offender is *essentially* unaware of his secret ambitions, of his unconscious motives and desires. Therefore, he cannot ask for forgiveness in all honesty, with transparency.

Then, however, Levinas reverses himself. Perhaps the Talmud is really suggesting that while "one can, if pressed to the limit, forgive the one who has spoken unconsciously," can one forgive the one "who is fully aware and destined for a great fate?" Levinas applies this suggestion, with its implied context the question of German guilt and forgiveness, to the case that so powerfully affects him, the case of Heidegger:

One can forgive many Germans, but there are some Germans it is difficult to forgive. It is difficult to forgive Heidegger. If [in the Talmud] Hanina could not forgive the just and humane Rab because he was also the brilliant Rab, it is even less possible to forgive Heidegger. Here I am brought back to the present, to the new attempts to clear Heidegger, to take away his responsibility – unceasing attempts which, it must be admitted, are at the origin of this colloquium.[177]

There is more to Levinas's lesson in 1963, but let me stop here, so that we can take stock of what he has accomplished and how. This lesson is an example of an exegetical technique whereby Levinas reads and interprets the Talmudic text as revealing various considerations relevant to a type of moral situation and how decisions might go in that kind of situation. He does not reveal a theory about such situations, here – for example, a theory about forgiveness. Nor does he frame or sketch an analysis of guilt and forgiveness. Rather, he recognizes a contemporary situation that calls for moral reflection and judgment and explores a Talmudic text to see what it discloses as significant considerations relevant to reflection and action in such a context. What is it important to think about when an agent has harmed or offended another and the question of forgiveness arises? Must the offender do something first – ask, console, compensate, seek reconciliation? How should the victim respond? What attitude should he have toward his offender? What about the offender's state of mind, knowledge, attitude, and self-awareness? What can the victim rightfully expect? Is revenge or retaliation

[176] *Nine Talmudic Readings*, 25.
[177] *Nine Talmudic Readings*, 25.

appropriate? Is it better not to seek it? Is it more right to forgive one who should have known better or not to forgive or "clear" such a person? These questions and issues do not configure a theory about guilt, forgiveness, and mercy, but they are relevant matters to consider. Much more, in any given situation, might be and perhaps should be said. Much more might and should be said about German guilt and how to respond to it. For Levinas, it might be that in this case there were crimes that are unforgivable, as Hannah Arendt called the acts of the perpetrators.[178] But to claim that there are such crimes is to arrive at a certain place after careful, complex moral reflection and exploration. It is not simply a matter of defining what forgiveness requires and judging that in the case of Nazi crimes and totalitarian domination some condition went unsatisfied. Particular situations may share features, but they are complex, and what distinguishes them, in various ways, may require different types of evaluation. More importantly, what Levinas calls "moral conscience" includes a conviction that each situation involves individuals in direct relationships and that moral reflection, decision making, and judgments are deeply personal, interpersonal, particular activities. Abstract or universal rules, norms, and policies give us guidance, but their role is always within very particular interpersonal moral engagements; their role is not to assimilate or ignore such particular episodes but to contribute to them and to the interpersonal relationships that take place within them.[179]

I think that we can use Levinas's notion of moral conscience to clarify the way that our primordial responsibility serves as a standard for our moral and political lives as they occur in the everyday. In a 1982 interview that we referred to earlier, Levinas makes it clear that responsibility and obligation to the other person precede all "deliberation" in everyday life. That is, in particular interpersonal encounters and, I believe, in considering principles for social life and for political, institutional practice, there is the possibility of "awakening" (or sobering up) to the other and of not doing so. "Evil," he says, is the "order of being," while acknowledging the other is the "penetration of the human into being," and there are no guarantees in our social, moral, and political lives that the good will triumph. Indeed, at times it may be that evil is overwhelming and "the human is completely extinguished," when the "ideal of holiness" is defied or ignored. When that happens, there is cruelty, oppression, war, violence, neglect, injustice, and atrocity. Levinas's own experience leads him to the grim acknowledgment that "most of the time, things happen that way." He has

[178] See Arendt, *The Origins of Totalitarianism*, 459.
[179] Similar remarks are not unique to Levinas. They also could be made, I believe, about the moral epistemology of many contemporary moral philosophers, including Martha Nussbaum, David Wiggins, John McDowell, Jonathan Dancy, David McNaughton, Sabina Lovibund, Rosalind Hursthouse, and Stanley Cavell.

"no illusions" and is not optimistic about the "political order," that is, about social, interpersonal, and political life generally.[180]

Levinas calls the twentieth century, as a time of evil, a domain of "bad conscience," the heir of Enlightenment and of religious wars, imperialism and colonialism, exploitation, world wars, genocides, the Holocaust, terrorism, poverty, and totalitarian domination.[181] The crisis of modern society and the malaise of culture express a shock with this outcome, a "horror" of killing and anxiety about suffering.[182] Internal to the modern situation is a "horrified surprise" at what has occurred and what has been allowed, and in that horror is revealed a sense of responsibility toward others, a holy ideal.[183] It is an acknowledgment of the face, which, Levinas claims, is not a "repudiation of politics" but rather a way to "the ethics of that state."[184] The voices that call for the recovery of such an ethical ideal, Levinas calls "prophetic voices." They "will recall, to the judgments of the judges and statesmen, the human face dissimulated beneath the identities of citizens."[185]

[These prophetic voices] are sometimes heard in the ones that rise up from the interstices of politics and that, independently of official authority, defend the "rights of man"; sometimes in the songs of the poets, sometimes simply in the press or in the public forum of the liberal states, in which freedom of expression is ranked as the first freedom and justice is always a revision of justice and the expectation of a better justice.[186]

Justice is required by charity, Levinas says, but at the same time charity – kindness, concern, responsibility – is the ideal of justice.[187] What he says about politics applies as well to moral principles and systems: "Legislation [is] always unfinished, always resumed, ... open to the better. It attests to an ethical excellence and its origin in kindness from which, however, it is distanced – always a bit less perhaps – by the necessary calculations imposed by a multiple sociality. ... "[188] This recognition of failure is "a bad conscience of justice, ... [which]

---

[180] "Philosophy, Justice, and Love," in *Entre Nous*, 114; cf. "Diachrony and Representation" in *Entre Nous*, 175.

[181] "Uniqueness" in *Entre Nous*, 191.

[182] "Uniqueness" in *Entre Nous*, 192.

[183] I take the expression "horrified surprise" from Emil Fackenheim, who uses it in his book *To Mend the World* to characterize the way that thought encounters the Nazi evil, as a whole that includes all its parts and yet is greater than those parts – the evil of the agents and of the crimes committed against its victims.

[184] "Uniqueness" in *Entre Nous*, 195.

[185] "Uniqueness" in *Entre Nous*, 196.

[186] "Uniqueness" in *Entre Nous*, 196.

[187] "The Other, Utopia, and Justice" in *Entre Nous*, 229.

[188] "The Other, Utopia, and Justice" in *Entre Nous*, 230.

knows it is not as just as the kindness that instigates it is good."[189] Bad conscience, then, is a realization of limitation, of failing to measure up to the ideal of infinite responsibility. But because such failure or shortcoming is a permanent feature of our lives, so is this bad conscience; it is transparency about what it means for us to live in the human condition, to live imperfectly but responsibly with others.

Recovering a moral conscience or good conscience, then, is not a personal matter alone. It is a part of a cultural, social, and historical process. Each of us, as we seek to express or recover such a conscience, is influenced by our culture and our world, and similarly the latter are affected by the efforts of individuals. Infusing being or nature with a sensitivity to the human is both an individual and a collective enterprise. And it is also a moral as well as a political one. Rules, principles, norms, values and reasons enter the process of recovery in several ways and for various purposes.

I have tried to show how recent philosophical debate concerning agent-relative and agent-neutral reasons helps us to see the relevance of Levinas's insight to contemporary moral philosophy. He is clearly an objectivist (or realist) and an intersubjectivist. But for him, the needs, pain, suffering, and destitution of each person are both agent-neutral and agent-relative simultaneously in terms of the rational claims they make on each and every one of us, as agents and as selves. Moreover, while the human condition thus understood has a *prima facie* force and is determinative, it can and perhaps must be qualified in ways that no single principle or rule can articulate. Moral life is a matter of negotiation and deliberation, and any relevant norms are at best guides for generic cases and not strictly binding.

CONCLUSION

I have placed Levinas's ethical insight and its implications for moral and political life into a setting of debate and discussion in recent Anglo-American moral philosophy. That setting concerns reasons, especially moral reasons, for action.[190] A reason is some feature, condition, or state of affairs that means something to someone with regard to how that person should act. It is a consideration or value that an agent takes to be relevant to what she should do. The debate has several dimensions and raises several issues about such reasons or values: Are moral reasons always binding for everyone? Or are some of them only binding for some of us? What makes them binding at all? Where does their weight or force come from? These are some of the issues raised in the works of Nagel,

---

[189] "The Other, Utopia, and Justice" in *Entre Nous*, 230.
[190] See Dancy, *Practical Reality* and *Moral Reasons*.

Korsgaard, and Darwall that I have introduced here and discussed briefly. I have tried to show that we can learn something about Levinas's thinking by placing his thought in this setting. But some may doubt this outcome and be skeptical about this whole project.

I do not think that we can or should ask whether the face, as Levinas characterizes it, or what the face presents – the other's needs, demands, claims, poverty, suffering, and so on – is a reason, in the sense discussed above. There is a very clear way in which the face is not a reason. Reasons are values or meanings that can be described in everyday terms. They help us understand why someone chooses to act in a certain way or why she should. All of this is cognitive, propositional, and linguistic, in one way or another. Reasons are conceptually articulated states of affairs or properties. For Levinas, on the other hand, the face is about how one particular person confronts another person, prior to thought, understanding, and language. It is about the human social condition at the most fundamental level. At this level, the face provides a quasi-meaning or, at best, a quasi-reason – that is, the other person's existence, need, pain, claim, or summons is meaning-like but not a meaning, reason-like but not a reason.

But, as we have seen, the face-to-face does not occur by itself or in an isolated and discrete way. It is, rather, one aspect or dimension, the deepest or most determinative aspect, of a complex of social relations that always exist for each of us. Within the vast complex network of social relations we live in, there is a dimension of each particular relation, the face-to-face, that has the normative force Levinas seeks to identify and describe. What the face-to-face does is to make a claim on each of us, but only in this multifaceted way, so that each unbounded responsibility we owe is in fact always qualified and compromised by the various – indeed infinite – relationships that simultaneously occur for each of us all the time. In ordinary experience, then, the face penetrates through or is expressed in deliberations, choices, and actions that are outcomes of various attitudes, feelings, and reasons, that move us and that we consider. Levinas, I think, calls this whole range of experience "politics." It includes deliberation, choice, and action in everyday moral, social, and political contexts. Levinas's attention, through much of his career, is on the face-to-face itself, what it means, and why it is so important for understanding human existence. With *Otherwise Than Being* and increasingly thereafter, he calls attention to how everyday life arises out of or emerges from the face-to-face and how the latter is an ethical ideal for human social life. I have tried to show how the debate about objective, or agent-neutral, reasons can help us to see the importance of this aspect of Levinas's project, by treating the needs and suffering of other persons, the ethical force of which is conveyed in the epiphany of the face, as akin to reasons, in the sense of that term used by Nagel, Korsgaard, and Darwall. And as they – especially Korsgaard and Darwall – try to show how agent-neutral or moral values are grounded intersubjectively, so, I claim, Levinas shows how moral and political life is rooted in the face-to-face and what it reveals. In this sense, for Levinas, our lives are deeply social and interpersonal.

To those who are skeptical, then, about what I have done, I answer that I have not tried to reduce or compress Levinas into an alien world. I have not, I think, distorted what he says. Rather I have tried to translate him into another set of terms while remaining true to his primary interests and true to the spirit of his work. I believe that Levinas and the others are in fact talking about a common subject and that he provides an approach to that subject – human existence and its social and ethical character – that is rich and distinctive. To show that this is so has been my goal.

Bibliography

Alford, C. Fred. "Levinas and Political Theory." *Political Theory* 32:2 (2004), 146–71.

Alford, C. Fred. *Levinas, the Frankfurt School and Psychoanalysis*. Middletown, CT: Wesleyan University Press, 2002.

Allen, R. E. (ed.). *Studies in Plato's Metaphysics*. London: Routledge & Kegan Paul, 1965.

Atterton, Peter, and Matthew Calarco. *On Levinas*. Belmont, CA: Wadsworth, 2005.

Baron, Marcia. *Kantian Ethics Almost Without Apology*. Ithaca, NY: Cornell University Press, 1995.

Bauman, Zygmunt. *Postmodern Ethics*. Oxford: Blackwell Publishers, 1993.

Bernasconi, Robert. "Different Styles of Eschatology: Derrida's Take on Levinas's Political Messianism." *Research in Phenomenology* 28 (1998), 3–19.

Bernasconi, Robert. "Rereading *Totality and Infinity*." In Charles Scott and Arleen Dallery (eds.), *The Question of the Other: Essays in Contemporary Continental Philosophy*. Albany, NY: SUNY Press, 1989, pp. 23–24, 225–26.

Bernasconi, Robert. "The Silent Anarchic World of the Evil Genius." In John C. Sallis, Giuseppina Moneta, and Jacques Tamianianx (eds.), *The Collegium Phaenomenologicum: The First Ten Years*. Boston: Kluwer, 1988, pp. 257–72.

Bernasconi, Robert. "The Trace of Levinas in Derrida." In David Wood and Robert Bernasconi (eds.), *Derrida and Différance*. Evanston, IL: Northwestern University Press, 1988, pp. 13–29.

Bernasconi, Robert, and David Wood (eds.). *The Provocation of Levinas: Rethinking the Other*. London: Routledge, 1988.

Bernasconi, Robert, and Simon Critchley (eds.). *Re-Reading Levinas*. Bloomington: Indiana University Press, 1991.

Bernstein, Richard J. "Evil and the Temptation of Theodicy." In Simon Critchley and Robert Bernasconi (eds.), *The Cambridge Companion to Levinas*. Cambridge: Cambridge University Press, 2002, pp. 252–67.

Bernstein, Richard J. *Radical Evil: A Philosophical Interrogation*. Cambridge: Polity Press, 2002.

Blanchot, Maurice. *The Infinite Conversation*. Minneapolis, MN: University of Minnesota Press, 1992.

Blanchot, Maurice. *The Writing of the Disaster*. Lincoln: University of Nebraska Press, 1986.

Bloechl, Jeffrey (ed.). *The Face of the Other and the Trace of God*. New York: Fordham University Press, 2000.

Bloechl, Jeffrey. *Liturgy and the Neighbor: Emannuel Levinas and the Religion of Responsibility*. Pittsburgh: Duquesne University Press, 2000.

Blum, Roland Paul. "Emmanuel Levinas' Theory of Commitment." *Philosophy and Phenomenological Research* 44:2 (1983), 145–68.

Carr, David. *The Paradox of Subjectivity: The Self in the Transcendental Tradition*. Oxford: Oxford University Press, 1999.

Cassam, Quassim. "Self-Directed Transcendental Arguments." In Robert Stern (ed.), *Transcendental Arguments: Problems and Projects*. Oxford: Oxford University Press, 1999, pp. 83–110.

Cavell, Stanley. *Cities of Words*. Cambridge, MA: Harvard University Press, 2004.

Cavell, Stanley. *The Claim of Reason*. Oxford: Oxford University Press, 1979.

Cavell, Stanley. *Conditions Handsome and Unhandsome*. Chicago: University of Chicago Press, 1990.

Cavell, Stanley. *Contesting Tears: The Hollywood Melodrama of the Unknown Woman*. Chicago: University of Chicago Press, 1996.

Cavell, Stanley. *Must We Mean What We Say?* Cambridge: Cambridge University Press, 1969.

Cavell, Stanley. *Philosophy the Day after Tomorrow*. Cambridge, MA: Harvard University Press, 2005.

Cavell, Stanley. *Pursuits of Happiness: The Hollywood Comedy of Remarriage*. Cambridge, MA: Harvard University Press, 1981.

Caygill, Howard. *Levinas and the Political*. London: Routledge, 2002.

Chalier, Catherine. *What Ought I to Do? Morality in Kant and Levinas*. Trans. Jane Marie Todd. Ithaca, NY: Cornell University Press, 2002.

Chanter, Tina (ed.). *Feminist Interpretations of Emmanuel Levinas*. University Park: Pennsylvania State University Press, 2001.

Chanter, Tina. *Time, Death, and the Feminine: Levinas with Heidegger*. Stanford, CA: Stanford University Press, 2001.

Chatterjee, Deen K. *The Ethics of Assistance: Morality and the Distant Needy*. Cambridge: Cambridge University Press, 2004.

Christman, John. *Social and Political Philosophy*. London: Routledge, 2002.

Cohen, Richard A. *Elevations: The Height of the Good in Rosenzweig and Levinas*. Chicago: University of Chicago Press, 1994.

Cohen, Richard A. *Ethics, Exegesis and Philosophy: Interpretation after Levinas*. Cambridge: Cambridge University Press, 2001.

Cohen, Richard A. (ed.). *Face to Face with Levinas*. Albany, NY: SUNY Press, 1986.

Cohen, Richard A. "What Good Is the Holocaust? On Suffering and Evil." In Richard A. Cohen, *Ethics, Exegesis and Philosophy*, pp. 266–82.

Conant, James. "The Method of the *Tractatus*." In Erich H. Reck (ed.), *From Frege to Wittgenstein: Perspectives on Early Analytic Philosophy*. Oxford: Oxford University Press, 2002, pp. 374–462.

Crary, Alice, and Rupert Read (eds.). *The New Wittgenstein*. London: Routledge, 2000.

Crary, Alice, and Sanford Shieh (eds.). *Reading Cavell*. London: Routledge, 2006.

Critchley, Simon. *The Ethics of Deconstruction: Derrida and Levinas*. 2nd ed. West Lafayette, IN: Purdue University Press, 1999.

Critchley, Simon. *Ethics, Politics, Subjectivity: Essays on Derrida, Levinas and Contemporary French Thought*. London: Verso, 1999.

Critchley, Simon. "Five Problems in Levinas's View of Politics and the Sketch of a Solution to Them." *Political Theory* 32:2 (2004), 172–185.

Critchley, Simon. *Very Little ... Almost Nothing: Death, Philosophy, Literature*. London: Routledge, 1997.

Critchley, Simon, and Robert Bernasconi (eds.). *The Cambridge Companion to Levinas*. Cambridge: Cambridge University Press, 2002.

Cullity, Garrett. *The Moral Demands of Affluence*. Oxford: Oxford University Press, 2004.

Dancy, Jonathan. *Moral Reasons*. Oxford: Blackwell Publishers, 1993.

Dancy, Jonathan. *Practical Reality*. Oxford: Oxford University Press, 2000.

Darwall, Stephen L. *Impartial Reason*. Ithaca, NY: Cornell University Press, 1983.

Davidson, Donald. "Reply to Føllesdal." In Lewis Edwin Hahn (ed.), *The Philosophy of Donald Davidson*. Chicago: Open Court Press, 1999, pp. 729–32.

Davidson, Donald. *Subjective, Intersubjective, Objective*. Oxford: Oxford University Press, 2001.

DeBoer, Theodore. *The Rationality of Transcendence: Studies in the Philosophy of Emmanuel Levinas*. Amsterdam: J. C. Giehen, 1997.

Derrida, Jacques. *Adieu to Emmanuel Levinas*. Stanford, CA: Stanford University Press, 1999.

Derrida, Jacques. *The Gift of Death*. Chicago: University of Chicago Press, 1995.

Diamond, Cora. "Ethics, Imagination and the Method of Wittgenstein's *Tractatus*." In Alice Crary and Rupert Read (eds.), *The New Wittgenstein*. London: Routledge, 2000, pp. 149–73.

Diamond, Cora. *The Realistic Spirit*. Cambridge, MA: MIT Press, 1991, 1995.

Drabinski, John. "The Possibility of an Ethical Politics: From Peace to Liturgy." *Philosophy and Social Criticism* 26:4 (2000), 49–73.

Drabinski, John. *Sensibility and Singularity: The Problem of Phenomenology in Levinas*. Albany, NY: SUNY Press, 2001.

Dreyfus, Herbert L. *Being-in-the-World: A Commentary on Heidegger's "Being and Time," Division I*. Cambridge, MA: MIT Press, 1991.

Dudiak, Jeffrey. *The Intrigue of Ethics: A Reading of the Idea of Discourse in the Thought of Emmanuel Levinas*. New York: Fordham University Press, 2001.

Eaglestone, Robert. *Ethical Criticism: Reading after Levinas*. Edinburgh: Edinburgh University Press, 1997.

Eaglestone, Robert. *The Holocaust and the Postmodern*. Oxford: Oxford University Press, 2004.

Ehrenburg, Ilya, and Vasily Grossman. *The Complete Black Book of Russian Jewry*. Trans. and ed. David Patterson. New Brunswick, NJ: Transaction Publishers, 2002.

Eldridge, Richard (ed.). *Stanley Cavell*. Cambridge: Cambridge University Press, 2003.

Evnine, Simon. *Donald Davidson*. Palo Alto, CA: Stanford University Press, 1991.

Fackenheim, Emil L. *To Mend the World: Foundations of Post-Holocaust Jewish Thought*. 3rd ed. Bloomington: Indiana University Press, 1994.

Fackenheim, Emil L. *What Is Judaism?* New York: Summit Books, 1987.

Føllesdal, Dagfinn. "Triangulation." In Lewis Edwin Hahn (ed.), *The Philosophy of Donald Davidson*. Chicago: Open Court Press, 1999, pp. 719–28.

Franks, Paul W. *All or Nothing: Systematicity, Transcendental Arguments, and Skepticism in German Idealism*. Cambridge, MA: Harvard University Press, 2005.

Franks, Paul. "Transcendental Arguments, Reason, and Skepticism: Contemporary Debates and the Origins of Post-Kantianism." In Robert Stern (ed.), *Transcendental Arguments: Problems and Projects*. Oxford: Oxford University Press, 1999, pp. 111–46.

Fryer, David Ross. *The Intervention of the Other: Ethical Subjectivity in Levinas and Lacan*. New York: Other Press, 2004.

Garrard, John, and Carol Garrard. *The Bones of Berdichev: The Life and Fate of Vasily Grossman*. New York: Free Press, 1996.

Gibbs, Robert. *Correlations in Rosenzweig and Levinas*. Princeton, NJ: Princeton University Press, 1992.

Glendinning, Simon (ed.). *Arguing with Derrida*. Oxford: Blackwell Publishing, 2001.

Goodman, Russell B. (ed.). *Contending with Cavell*. Oxford: Oxford University Press, 2005.

Grossman, Vasily. *Forever Flowing*. Trans. Thomas P. Whitney. New York: Harper & Row, 1972.

Grossman, Vasily. *Life and Fate*. Trans. Robert Chandler. New York: Harper & Row, 1985.

Guignon, Charles (ed.). *The Cambridge Companion to Heidegger*. Cambridge: Cambridge University Press, 1993.

Hahn, Lewis Edwin (ed.). *The Philosophy of Donald Davidson*. Chicago: Open Court Press, 1999.

Hammer, Espen. *Stanley Cavell: Skepticism, Subjectivity, and the Ordinary*. Cambridge: Polity Press, 2002.

Hand, Seán (ed.). *Facing the Other: The Ethics of Emmanuel Levinas*. Richmond, Surrey, England: Curzon, 1996.

Harris, Jay M. *How Do We Know This? Midrash and the Fragmentation of Modern Judaism*. Albany, NY: SUNY Press, 1995.

Hart, Kevin. *The Trespass of the Sign: Deconstruction, Theology, and Philosophy*. Cambridge: Cambridge University Press, 1989.

Harvey, Sylvia. *May '68 and Film Culture*. London: BFI Publishing, 1978, 1980.

Hendley, Steven. *From Communicative Action to the Face of the Other: Levinas and Habermas on Language, Obligation, and Community*. Lanham, MD: Lexington Books, 2000.

Herzog, Annabel. "Is Liberalism 'All We Need'? Levinas's Politics of Surplus." *Political Theory* 30:2 (2002), 204–27.

Heschel, Abraham Joshua. *God in Search of Man*. New York: Farrar, Straus and Cudahy, 1955.

Hill, Leslie. "'Distrust of Poetry': Levinas, Blanchot, Celan." *MLN* 120 (2005), 986–1008.

Hooker, Brad, and Margaret Little (eds.). *Moral Particularism*. Oxford: Oxford University Press, 2000.

Hudson, Stephen D. *Human Character and Morality: Reflections from the History of Ideas*. London: Routledge & Kegan Paul, 1986.

Hursthouse, Rosalind. *On Virtue Ethics*. Oxford: Oxford University Press, 1999.

Hursthouse, Rosalind, Gavin Lawrence, and Warren Quinn (eds.). *Virtues and Reasons: Philippa Foot and Moral Theory*. Oxford: Oxford University Press, 1995.

Hutchens, B. C. *Levinas: A Guide for the Perplexed*. New York and London: Continuum, 2004.

Jankélévitch, Vladimir. *Forgiveness*. Trans. Andrew Kelley. Chicago: University of Chicago Press, 2005.

Katsiaficas, George. *The Imagination of the New Left: A Global Analysis of 1968*. Boston: South End Press, 1987.

Klagge, James C. (ed.). *Wittgenstein: Biography and Philosophy*. Cambridge: Cambridge University Press, 2001.

Kleinberg, Ethan. *Generation Existential: Heidegger's Philosophy in France, 1927–1961*. Ithaca, NY: Cornell University Press, 2005.

Korsgaard, Christine M. *Creating the Kingdom of Ends*. Cambridge: Cambridge University Press, 1996.

Korsgaard, Christine M. "The Reasons We Can Share: An Attack on the Distinction Between Agent-Relative and Agent-Neutral Values." In Christine M. Korsgaard, *Creating the Kingdom of Ends*. Cambridge: Cambridge University Press, pp. 275–310.

Korsgaard, Christine M. *The Sources of Normativity*. Cambridge: Cambridge University Press, 1996.

Kosky, Jeffrey L. *Levinas and the Philosophy of Religion*. Bloomington: Indiana University Press, 2001.

Lamm, Norman. *Torah Lishmah: The Study of Torah for Torah's Sake in the Work of Rabbi Hayyim of Volozhin and His Contemporaries*. New York: KTAV and Yeshiva University Press, 1989.

Lear, Jonathan. "The Disappearing 'We.'" *Proceedings of the Aristotelian Society* 58 (1984), 219–42.

Lear, Jonathan. "Transcendental Anthropology." In Philip Petit and John McDowell (eds.), *Subject, Thought, and Context*. Oxford: Oxford University Press, 1986, pp. 267–98.

Levinas, Emmanuel. *Alterity and Transcendence*. New York: Columbia University Press, 1999.

Levinas, Emmanuel. "As If Consenting to Horror." *Critical Inquiry* 15 (Winter 1989), pp. 485–88.

Levinas, Emmanuel. *Basic Philosophical Writings*. Adriaan T. Peperzak, Simon Critchley, and Robert Bernasconi (eds.). Bloomington: Indiana University Press, 1996.

Levinas, Emmanuel. *Beyond the Verse: Talmudic Readings and Lectures*. Bloomington: Indiana University Press, 1994.

Levinas, Emmanuel. *Collected Philosophical Papers*. Trans. Alphonso Lingis. Pittsburgh: Duquesne University Press, 1998.

Levinas, Emmanuel. *Difficult Freedom*. Trans. Seán Hand. Baltimore: Johns Hopkins University Press, 1990.

Levinas, Emmanuel. *Discovering Existence with Husserl*. Trans. Richard A. Cohen and Michael B. Smith. Evanston, IL: Northwestern University Press, 1998.

Levinas, Emmanuel. *Entre Nous: Thinking-of-the-Other*. Trans. Michael B. Smith and Barbara Harshav. New York: Columbia University Press, 1998.

Levinas, Emmanuel. *Ethics and Infinity: Conversations with Philippe Nemo*. Pittsburgh: Duquesne University Press, 1985.

Levinas, Emmanuel. *Existence and Existents*. Pittsburgh: Duquesne University Press, 2001.

Levinas, Emmanuel. *God, Death, and Time*. Stanford, CA: Stanford University Press, 2000.

Levinas, Emmanuel. *Humanism of the Other*. Urbana: University of Illinois Press, 2003.

Levinas, Emmanuel. *In the Time of the Nations*. Bloomington: Indiana University Press, 1994.

Levinas, Emmanuel. *The Levinas Reader*. Seán, Hand (ed.). Oxford: Basil Blackwell, 1989.

Levinas, Emmanuel. "The Meaning of Religious Practice." Trans. Peter Atterton, Matthew Calarco, and Joelle Hansel. *Modern Judaism* 25:3 (2005), 285–89. [Orig. 1937].

Levinas, Emmanuel. *Nine Talmudic Readings*. Trans. Annette Aronowicz. Bloomington: Indiana University Press, 1990.

Levinas, Emmanuel. *Of God Who Comes to Mind*. Stanford, CA: Stanford University Press, 1998.

Levinas, Emmanuel. *On Escape*. Stanford, CA: Stanford University Press, 2003.

Levinas, Emmanuel. *Otherwise Than Being*. Pittsburgh: Duquesne University Press, 1998.

Levinas, Emmanuel. *Outside the Subject*. Stanford, CA: Stanford University Press, 1993.

Levinas, Emmanuel. *Proper Names*. Stanford, CA: Stanford University Press, 1996.

Levinas, Emmanuel. "Reflections on the Philosophy of Hitlerism." *Critical Inquiry* 17 (Autumn 1990), 63–71.

Levinas, Emmanuel. *The Theory of Intuition in Husserl's Phenomenology*. Evanston, IL: Northwestern University Press, 1973.

Levinas, Emmanuel. *Time and the Other*. Trans. Richard A. Cohen. Pittsburgh: Duquesne University Press, 1987.

Levinas, Emmanuel. *Totality and Infinity*. Pittsburgh: Duquesne University Press, 1969.

Levinas, Emmanuel. *Unforeseen History*. Urbana: University of Illinois Press, 2004.

Levinas, Emmanuel. "Useless Suffering." Trans. Richard A. Cohen. In Robert Bernasconi and D. Woods (eds.), *The Provocation of Levinas*. London: Routledge, 1988, pp. 156–67.

Llewelyn, John. *Emmanuel Levinas: The Genealogy of Ethics*. London: Routledge, 1995.

Løgstrup, Knud E. *The Ethical Demand*. Philadelphia: Fortress Press, 1971; South Bend, IN: Notre Dame University Press, 1997.

Lovibond, Sabina. *Ethical Formation*. Cambridge, MA: Harvard University Press, 2002.

Manning, Robert John Sheffler. *Interpreting Otherwise Than Heidegger: Emmanuel Levinas's Ethics as First Philosophy*. Pittsburgh: Dusquene University Press, 1993.

Marwick, Arthur. *The Sixties*. Oxford: Oxford University Press, 1998.

McCarthy, Timothy G., and Sean C. Stidd (eds.). *Wittgenstein in America*. Oxford: Oxford University Press, 2001.

McDowell, John. *Mind, Value, and Reality*. Cambridge, MA: Harvard University Press, 1998.

McDowell, John. *Mind and World*. Cambridge, MA: Harvard University Press, 1994.

McGinn, Marie. *Wittgenstein and the Philosophical Investigations*. London: Routledge, 1997.

McNaughton, David. *Moral Vision: An Introduction to Ethics*. Oxford: Blackwell, 1988.

Miller, Alexander. *An Introduction to Contemporary Metaethics*. Cambridge: Polity Press, 2003.

Miller, Alexander, and Crispin Wright (eds.). *Rule-Following and Meaning*. Montreal: McGill-Queen's University Press, 2002.

Moore, A. W. *Points of View*. Oxford: Oxford University Press, 1997.

Morgan, Michael L. *Beyond Auschwitz: Post-Holocaust Jewish Thought in America*. Oxford: Oxford University Press, 2001.

Morgan, Michael L. *Dilemmas in Modern Jewish Thought: The Dialectics of Revelation and History*. Bloomington: Indiana University Press, 1992.

Morgan, Michael L. (ed.). *Jewish Philosophers and Jewish Philosophy: Essays by Emil Fackenheim*. Bloomington: Indiana University Press, 1996.

Morgan, Michael L. (ed.). *The Jewish Thought of Emil Fackenheim*. Detroit: Wayne State University Press, 1987.

Morgan, Michael L., and Peter Eli Gordon (eds.). *The Cambridge Companion to Modern Jewish Philosophy*. Cambridge: Cambridge University Press, 2007.

Mouffe, Chantal (ed.). *Deconstruction and Pragmatism*. London: Routledge, 1996.

Moyn, Samuel. *Origins of the Other: Emmanuel Levinas Between Revelation and Ethics*. Ithaca, NY: Cornell University Press, 2005.

Mulhall, Stephen. *On Being in the World*. London: Routledge, 1990.

Mulhall, Stephen. *Stanley Cavell: Philosophy's Recounting of the Ordinary*. Oxford: Oxford University Press, 1994.

Murphy, Liam B. *Moral Demands in Nonideal Theory*. Oxford: Oxford University Press, 2000.

Nagel, Thomas. "Davidson's New Cogito." In Lewis Edwin Hahn (ed.). *The Philosophy of Donald Davidson*. Chicago: Open Court Press, 1999, pp. 195–206.

Nagel, Thomas. *The Last Word*. Oxford: Oxford University Press, 1997.

Nagel, Thomas. *The Possibility of Altruism*. Princeton, NJ: Princeton University Press, 1970.

Nagel, Thomas. *The View from Nowhere*. Oxford: Oxford University Press, 1986.

Neiman, Susan. *Evil in Modern Thought*. Princeton, NJ: Princeton University Press, 2002.

Nemo, Philippe. *Job and the Excess of Evil*. Pittsburgh: Duquesne University Press, 1998.

Neuhouser, Fred. *Foundations of Hegel's Social Theory*. Cambridge, MA: Harvard University Press, 2000.

New, Melvyn, with Robert Bernasconi and Richard A. Cohen (eds.). *In Proximity: Emmanuel Levinas and the 18th Century*. Lubbock: Texas Tech University Press, 2001.

Nietzsche, Friedrich. *Untimely Meditations*. Cambridge: Cambridge University Press, 1983.

Okrent, Mark. *Heidegger's Pragmatism*. Ithaca, NY: Cornell University Press, 1988.

O'Neill, Onora. *Bounds of Justice*. Cambridge: Cambridge University Press, 2000.

O'Neill, Onora. *Constructions of Reason*. Cambridge: Cambridge University Press, 1989.

O'Neill, Onora. *Towards Justice and Virtue*. Cambridge: Cambridge University Press, 1996.

Ostrow, Matthew B. *Wittgenstein's Tractatus*. Cambridge: Cambridge University Press, 2002.

Peperzak, Adriaan. *Beyond: The Philosophy of Emmanuel Levinas*. Evanston, IL: Northwestern University Press, 1997.

Peperzak, Adriaan (ed.). *Ethics as First Philosophy: The Significance of Emmanuel Levinas for Philosophy, Literature and Religion*. London: Routledge, 1995.

Peperzak, Adriaan. *To the Other: An Introduction to the Philosophy of Emmanuel Levinas*. West Lafayette, IN: Purdue University Press, 1993.

Plant, Bob. "Ethics Without Exit: Levinas and Murdoch." *Philosophy and Literature* 27 (2003), 456–70.

Plant, Bob. *Wittgenstein and Levinas: Ethical and Religious Thought*. London: Routledge, 2005.

Polt, Richard. *Heidegger: An Introduction*. Ithaca, NY: Cornell University Press, 1999.

Priest, Graham. *Beyond the Limits of Thought*. Cambridge: Cambridge University Press, 1995.

Purcell, Michael. *Levinas and Theology*. Cambridge: Cambridge University Press, 2006.

Rawls, John. *A Theory of Justice*. Cambridge, MA: Harvard University Press, 1971.

Raz, Joseph. *The Morality of Freedom*. Oxford: Oxford University Press, 1986.

Reinhard, Kenneth. "Kant with Sade, Lacan with Levinas." *MLN* 110:4 (1995), pp. 785–808.

Renaut, Alain. *The Era of the Individual: A Contribution to a History of Subjectivity*. Princeton, NJ: Princeton University Press, 1997.

Robbins, Jill. *Altered Reading: Levinas and Literature*. Chicago: University of Chicago Press, 1999.

Robbins, Jill (ed.). *Is It Righteous to Be? Interviews with Emmanuel Levinas*. Stanford, CA: Stanford University Press, 2001.

Robbins, Jill. *Prodigal Son/Elder Brother*. Chicago: University of Chicago Press, 1991.

Sandford, Stella. *The Metaphysics of Love: Gender and Transcendence in Levinas*. London: Athlone Press, 2000.

Scanlon, T. M. *What We Owe to Each Other*. Cambridge, MA: Harvard University Press, 1998.

Schnapp, Alain, and Pierre Vidal-Naquet. *The French Student Uprising, November 1967–June 1968: An Analytical Record.* Boston: Beacon Press, 1971.

Sher, George. *Beyond Neutrality: Perfectionism and Politics.* Cambridge: Cambridge University Press, 1997.

Simmons, William Paul. "The Third: Levinas' Theoretical Move from An-archical Ethics to the Realm of Justice and Politics." *Philosophy and Social Criticism* 25:6 (1999), 83–104.

Smith, Nicholas (ed.). *Reading McDowell: On Mind and World.* London: Routledge, 2002.

Smith, Nicholas H. *Charles Taylor: Meaning, Morals and Modernity.* Cambridge: Polity Press, 2002.

Smith, Steven G. *The Argument to the Other: Reason Beyond Reason in the Thought of Karl Barth and Emmanuel Levinas.* Chico, CA: Scholars Press, 1983.

Sokolowski, Robert. *Introduction to Phenomenology.* Cambridge: Cambridge University Press, 2000.

Stern, Robert. "On Kant's Response to Hume: The Second Analogy as Transcendental Argument." In Robert Stern (ed.), *Transcendental Arguments: Problems and Projects.* Oxford: Oxford University Press, 1999, pp. 47–66.

Stern, Robert (ed.). *Transcendental Arguments: Problems and Projects.* Oxford: Oxford University Press, 1999.

Taylor, Charles. *A Catholic Modernity?* James L. Heft (ed.). Oxford: Oxford University Press, 1999.

Taylor, Charles. *The Ethics of Authenticity.* Cambridge, MA: Harvard University Press, 1992.

Taylor, Charles. *Hegel.* Cambridge: Cambridge University Press, 1975.

Taylor, Charles. *Human Agency and Language: Philosophical Papers I.* Cambridge: Cambridge University Press, 1985.

Taylor, Charles. *Modern Social Imaginaries.* Durham, NC: Duke University Press, 2004.

Taylor, Charles. "Self-Interpreting Animals." In Charles Taylor, *Human Agency and Language, Philosophical Papers I.* Cambridge: Cambridge University Press, 1985, pp. 45–76.

Taylor, Charles. *Sources of the Self.* Cambridge, MA: Harvard University Press, 1989.

Taylor, Charles. *Varieties of Religion Today: William James Revisted.* Cambridge, MA: Harvard University Press, 2002.

Thomson, Judith Jarvis. *Goodness and Advice.* Amy Gutmann (ed.). Princeton, NJ: Princeton University Press, 2001.

Thomson, Judith Jarvis. *The Realm of Rights.* Cambridge, MA: Harvard University Press, 1990.

Toumayan, Alain P. *Encountering the Other: The Artwork and the Problem of Difference in Blanchot and Levinas.* Pittsburgh: Duquesne University Press, 2004.

Walker, Ralph C. S. "Induction and Transcendental Arguments." In Robert Stern (ed.), *Transcendental Arguments: Problems and Projects.* Oxford: Oxford University Press, 1999, pp. 13–30.

Wallace, R. Jay. *Normativity and the Will.* Cambridge: Cambridge University Press, 2006.

Wallace, R. Jay. *Responsibility and the Moral Sentiments.* Cambridge, MA: Harvard University Press, 1996.

Williams, Bernard. *Ethics and the Limits of Philosophy.* Cambridge, MA: Harvard University Press, 1985.

Williams, Bernard. "Persons, Character and Morality." In Bernard Williams, *Moral Luck.* Cambridge: Cambridge University Press, 1981, pp. 1–19.

Wolf, Susan. "Moral Saints." *Journal of Philosophy* 79:8 (Aug. 1982), 419–39. Reprinted in Robert B. Kruschwitz and Robert C. Roberts (eds.), *The Virtues: Contemporary Essays on Moral Character*. Belmont, CA: Wadsworth, 1987, pp. 137–52.

Wood, David, and Robert Bernasconi (eds.). *Derrida and Différence*. Evanston, IL: Northwestern University Press, 1988.

Wright, Tamra. *The Twilight of Jewish Philosophy: Emmanuel Levinas' Ethical Hermeneutics*. Amsterdam: Harwood Academic Publishers, 1999.

Wyschogrod, Edith. *Emmanuel Levinas: The Problem of Ethical Metaphysics*. The Hague: Martinus Nijhoff, 1974.

Index

Abraham, 186n35, 202, 261–262, 343, 416, 418–419
absence, absent, 130–131, 189–191, 193, 198, 198n71, 199, 201, 203, 206, 389, 413
accusation, 82, 82n73, 83–84, 132, 143, 155, 157, 173, 183, 202, 206, 304; *see also* persecution
acknowledgment, 71, 179–180, 182, 292, 295, 352, 424
   Cavell and, 72, 76–79, 76n50, 283n208, 316n61, 379n187
   of the other, 19, 27n84, 61, 66, 72, 75, 97n30, 98–99, 105, 119, 122–124, 128, 131, 133, 140, 377, 444–445, 462
Adorno, Theodor, 13, 31, 246n61, 264, 336n2, 354, 396
Agamben, Giorgio, 354
Aggadah, Aggadic, 372–373, 376, 379–380, 391–392; *see also* Midrash
alienation, 204, 396, 398
alterity, 42, 62–63, 76n50, 91,153–154, 171, 211, 259, 288, 305, 340; *see also* other
Althusser, Louis Pierre, 147
altruism, 255
Améry, Jean, 33, 359–360
anarchy, anarchic, 47, 54, 82, 157, 199, 309–310, 455n151; *see also* face
Anaxagoras, 144
Anscombe, G. E. M., xiin1, 93n17, 105n60, 334

anti-Semitism, 13, 16, 16n53, 30–31, 82n73, 336n2, 336n3, 408
anxiety, 195–196, 295
Arabs, 20, 32, 403, 406, 458
   Israeli conflict, 30–32, 34, 404, 408–409
Arendt, Hannah, 10n35, 11n41, 13, 31, 151n28, 246n61, 336n2, 337, 354
   forgiveness and, 34–35, 462
Aristotle, 54, 56, 87, 101, 112n75, 144, 146, 168, 175n5, 234, 261, 280, 290, 296
   desire and, 92, 92n15
   the divine and, 175
   McDowell's indebtedness to, 248n66, 250, 252, 259
   virtue and, 249
art, 295, 295n246, 296, 397
Asia, 410n335
asymmetrical, 154, 181, 183, 192, 421, 455n151; *see also* face
atheism, 180, 341, 343
   Western philosophy as, 90
Athens and Jerusalem, 336
Augustine, 56, 144, 205n94
Auschwitz, *see* Holocaust
Austin, J. L., 127, 323–324
authenticity, 196, 226, 230, 274n168, 290, 292
autonomy, 24, 89–90, 270, 275, 277; *see also* freedom
   Kant and, 64
   reasons of, 428–429, 435–436

477

autonomy (*cont.*)
  revelation and, 372
  the self and, 146–147
autrui, 65–66, 68, 81–82, 119–120; *see also*
    other
Avni-Segré, Dan, 405
awakening, 199–200, 375, 386, 462
Ayer, A. J., 175n6

Bakhurst, David, 117n9
Barbie, Klaus, 14, 34, 34n105
Barth, Karl, 57, 176, 179n12, 197, 205n94
Bauman, Zygmunt, 228, 233, 235
Begin, Menachem, 20
being, 47, 84, 151, 153, 195, 452, 462
  beyond, 188, 200, 308, 314, 327
  encounter with face as prior to, 47
  grounded in ethics, 348–349
  Heidegger and, 147
  impossibility of retreating from,
    211
  language and, 304
  Plotinus and, 189
being-in-the-world, 102, 104, 129
Beirut, West, 20
Beiser, Frederick A., 92n16, 146
benevolence, 112, 142, 204–206, 267, 286,
    351; *see also* goodness
  speech and discourse as an act of,
    201–202
  O'Neill and, 241
  world grounded in, 32
beneficence theory, 229n3
Benjamin, Walter, xiii, 86, 176, 217,
    217n27, 337, 371, 383, 396–400,
    400n286
Bennington, Geoffrey, 325
Bergson, Henri, xii, 39, 124
  time and, 208–209, 209n2, 210,
    212–213, 225
Berkeley, George, 87
Berkovits, Eliezer, 339n12
Bernasconi, Robert, 45–46, 45n17, 51,
    188n44, 292, 400–401
  on Levinas and Derrida, 321–323
  "Skepticism in the Face of Philosophy,"
    313, 316–318

Bernstein, Michael André, 12n43
Bernstein, Richard, 16n54, 354, 354n90,
    355, 361n109, 368–369, 369n135, 370
Bible, 111, 198, 337–340, 342–344, 367, 372,
    375, 379–389, 389n236, 390–394,
    403, 405, 412–413, 450–451
Blackburn, Simon, 229n2, 243n50
Blanchot, Maurice, xii, 14, 14n45, 39, 321,
    354
Bloch, Ernst, 396, 398–399
Boer, Theodore de, 45, 46n19, 50–51, 56,
    159, 334, 397
  The Rationality of Transcendence, 302–305,
    313–315
Book of Esther, 386
Bosnia, xii, 354, 364n119, 365
Bourdieu, Pierre, 147
Bouretz, Pierre, 63n3
Boyd, Richard, 229n2
Boyle, Robert, 284
Brandom, Robert, 85n2
Brink, David, 229n2
Broszat, Martin, 13
Buber, Martin, xii, 34, 46n20, 63, 124, 176,
    178, 182, 190, 232n15, 269, 290,
    339n12, 416, 416n4
  hermeneutics and, 382–384
  as Jewish thinker, 337
  law and, 347
  redemption, messianism, and, 396,
    398
  revelation and, 353, 371, 386
Buenos Aires, 341
Bultmann, Rudolf, 176

Calvinism, 98n35, 145
Cambodia, xii, 11, 17, 122, 354, 364–365,
    367
Camus, Albert, 354
caress, 129–130, 155
Carr, David, 149n20
Cassam, Quassim, 53–54
Cavell, Stanley, xii, xiin2, xiii–xiv, 12,
    12n42, 16n53, 45, 61, 248n67,
    276n182, 323, 462n179
  acknowledgment and, 72, 76–79,
    76n50, 283n208, 379n187

maturity and growth and, 346n46
    pain language and, 78n57
    perfectionism and, 268, 268n144,
        269–270, 270n151, 271–272,
        272n157, 273, 273n158, 274–276,
        276n181, 277, 277n184, 278–283,
        291n241, 292, 459n166
    skepticism and, 76, 76n50, 283n208,
        315n61, 320n77, 379n187
    Wittgenstein and, 76–78, 251, 269,
        272–274, 277
Caygill, Howard, 19n59, 20n61, 259, 288,
    337n7, 401–404, 406, 457
Chandler, Robert, 2–3
charity, 11, 20, 23, 27, 111, 233, 240, 450,
    450n124, 451–453, 463; *see also*
    generosity
    "regimes of," 9–10, 14, 24, 232
Christianity, 98n35, 145, 181
Chouchani, 383n207
Civil War, American, 16n53
Cohen, Hermann, 62n3, 102, 337, 396n262
Cohen, Richard, 14, 61n1, 181–182,
    194n64, 337n6, 380n194, 383n209,
    390
    on Levinas and the evil of the
        Holocaust, 354–355, 358, 361n109,
        363, 365, 369
    "What Good is the Holocaust? On
        Suffering and Evil," 16, 16n54
Cohn-Bendit, Daniel, 15
commandment, 73, 340, 348–349, 353, 369,
    371
    614th commandment, 367
commentary, 382–384, 386–388, 391, 403
    Levinas on *Baba Metsia*, 15, 451n129
communication, 43, 124–127, 130–132,
    135–136, 140, 164, 166
    art as, 295
    condition of, 119
    divine-human, 386
    face and, 119–120, 138, 159
    possibility of, 73–75, 133
communitarianism, 169, 230, 233, 288
community, 74, 103, 109, 214, 260, 310,
    316n61, 460
    ethics as ground of, 75

fraternal, 30
    Jewish, 437
    Judaism and, 346
    language and, 123n30, 133
    linguistic, 135–136, 141
    McDowell and, 162
    meaning and, 122
    O'Neill and, 237
    religious, 101
    value and, 446–447
Conant, James, 333
consciousness, 41, 106, 125–126, 151,
    182n25
    called into question, 121
    the *cogito* and, 149
    conscience as beyond, 94
    intentionality, phenomenology, and,
        48–50, 116–117, 150, 381
    irreducible to, 81
    naturalism and, 148
    internal time, 220, 226
consequentialism, 229, 289n235, 427,
    427n20, 428, 431–433, 435, 439, 443,
    456
constructivism, Rawlsian, 229, 229n2, 237,
    278
Cornell, Drucilla, 260
Crary, Alice, 277n184
creation, 102, 103n57, 221
Critchley, Simon, 19n59, 76n50, 146,
    149n17, 188n44, 268–269, 277–278,
    282, 292, 458n161
    The Ethics of Deconstruction, 260
Cullity, Garrett, 83n74, 289n235

Dancy, Jonathan, 117n9, 233, 233n18,
    427n20, 462n179
Darfur, 364n119
Darwall, Stephen, 289n235, 422, 424, 434,
    446–449, 452, 457, 465
Dasein (human existence), 104, 422
Davidson, Donald, xiii, 105n60, 116,
    328n121
    language and, 123n30, 138–141,
        161–162, 164
    meaning and, 124n31, 135n56
    the self and, 148, 162–167, 172

Davis, Colin, 390
death, 42n8, 155, 162,
    as other, 153, 153n38, 154, 211
    of the other, 26, 65–66, 153n38, 154,
        223–224, 227
    Rosenzweig and, 101
    the *there-is* and, 195–196
    time and, 211–212, 216, 218–219, 221,
        224, 226
deconstruction, 55n44, 260
Delbo, Charlotte, 67n21
democracy, 147, 274, 279
deontology, 278, 433
Derrida, Jacques, xii–xiii, xvii, 14, 19n59,
        60n50, 76n50, 147, 260, 337, 400
    critique of Levinas, 125
    debt to Levinas, 321–323
    ethics and, 230n5, 278, 283
    The Gift of Death, 418–420
    God, religion, theology, and, 175n6
    ineffability and, 323–328, 328n121, 329,
        331–332
    Levinas's response to, 187n43,
        187n44
    politics and, 294
    the self and, 160
    skepticism and, 55n44, 320
    "Violence and Metaphysics," 300–301,
        304–305
Descartes, René, 78, 90, 94, 99, 128,
        175n5, 188n47, 234, 261, 327
    God and, 48, 91, 199
    the self and, 144, 146, 149, 150n21, 157,
        160
Desdemona, 76n50
desire, 92, 92n15, 94, 103, 119, 126
    for the Good, 199–200
Deuteronomy, 370n139
diachrony, 187n43, 219, 222–225, 305, 307,
        309–311, 314, 317–320, 413, 455;
        see also illeity, God, trace
dialogue, 50, 55, 113, 302n7, 347, 416n4;
    see also Buber
Diamond, Cora, 329–331, 333
différance, 325–328, 331; *see also* Derrida
dignity, 24, 147, 264, 266, 356

Dilthey, Wilhelm, 124, 209–210
discourse, 69–70, 73–74, 93n18, 119,
        125–127, 131, 133–134, 136, 310;
    see also language, speech
    God and, 198, 201–202
    Greek and, 340
    skepticism and, 311, 313, 320
    theological, 185, 353
divine, 89–90, 178, 178n11, 181, 334, 344;
    see also God
    Aristotle and the, 175
    command, 179, 197, 197n70, 214, 368,
        378
    encounter with the, 193
    epiphany, 375
    judgment, 385
    love, 206
    providence, 175
    revelation and, 371–372
    the trace and, 190
    voluntarism, 179
    will, 346
domination, 10–11, 16, 27, 65, 69, 147,
        197, 235, 259n115, 262, 405, 407,
        433, 462–463
Dostoyevsky, Fyodor, 379, 379n187,
        393
Drabinski, John, 45n16, 45n17, 159
Dretske, Fred, 136
Dreyfus Affair, 16n53
Dummett, Michael, 124n31
duration, theory of, 209, 209n2
duty, 214, 216, 244, 249, 294, 297,
        298n254, 344, 416–417, 417n5,
        455–457; *see also* obligation
    imperfect, 453
Dworkin, Ronald, 267

Eaglestone, Robert, 354n89
ego, 121, 307; *see also* self
    confronted by the other, 82
    egology, 90
    transcendental, 88, 159
Egypt, 30
Ehrenberg, Rudolf, 213
Eichmann, Adolf, 34, 458, 458n161

election, 73, 79, 98, 98n35, 113, 185, 200,
214, 304, 342, 344, 346, 395
Emerson, Ralph Waldo, 16n53, 269–270,
272–274, 277, 279–280, 459n166
Empedocles, 144
empiricism, 116
England, 176
enigma, 85, 131, 202, 228n1, 302, 306,
308–309, 321; *see also* face
enjoyment, 41, 49, 65, 69, 72, 105–107,
129–130, 294–295, 460
the self and, 152–153, 156, 162
Enlightenment, xii, 117n9, 147, 336n2, 398,
412, 463
Epicurus, 211
epiphany, 180
divine, 375
of the face, 43, 47, 58, 68, 70, 72–74,
79–80, 92, 119–120, 122–123, 181,
218, 389, 421
of God, 188
of the infinite, 87
epistemology, 87, 96, 100
moral, 235, 248, 462n179
natural theology and, 203
naturalism and, 148
the self and, 144, 146, 160
epoché, 50
eros, 47n21, 63, 92, 92n14, 155, 211, 360,
413, 422–423
eschatology, 214–218, 227, 395–397,
399–401, 412; *see also* messianism
eternity, 210, 213, 216
ethics, 11, 19, 83, 96, 110, 159, 228n1, 261,
266, 269–270, 296, 299, 320n77,
335, 388n236, 419; *see also* morality
of deconstruction, 260
the face and, 46, 321, 445, 449–450
as first philosophy, 43, 228, 234, 270
as ground of being and existence, 348
as ground of language and community,
75, 108
Hellenistic, 92
Hermann Cohen and, 63n3
Hobbes and, 23, 23n69, 28
Israel and, 402, 404

Jewish, 370n139
Jewish life and, 349
Jewish texts and, 337–338, 342–343, 379,
383, 386
Kant and, 224n55, 64
Kantian, 229–230, 396n262, 431
Korsgaard and, 254–259, 444
Levinas and, 30, 64, 228, 231, 234,
242–243, 246, 259, 267–268, 298,
357, 416–417, 420, 429, 445, 448
McDowell and, 168, 248–254, 259
messianism and, 403, 405
Nagel and, 428, 432, 444
O'Neill and, 236–247, 259
as opposition to suffering, 18
as origin of all meaning, 350
origins of, 40
Platonic, 291
post-Holocaust, 16
prayer and, 347–353
primacy of, 100, 111
religion, God, and, 182n25, 188, 344,
395
revelation and, 376
Rorty and, 268
the self and, 146, 160, 162
sources of normativity in, 177, 190n53
the state, politics, and, xv, 9, 14, 18,
20–26, 108, 260, 286, 288–289, 293,
404, 423, 451, 451n129
Taylor and, 230, 263–268
time and, 208, 210
with system, 232
without system, 232
Wolf and, 298
eudaimonism, 171, 291
Europe, xii, 3, 9–10, 13, 26, 83n73,
231–232, 338–340, 367
evaluation, strong, 169–171, 263, 266; *see
also* Taylor
evil, 8, 112, 332, 431, 438, 451n129,
462–463; *see also* sin, suffering
Holocaust, suffering, and, 16–17, 34,
42n8, 353–362, 364–369, 463n183
as incomprehensible, 18–19
problem of, 341, 368

Evine, Simon, 164
exegesis, 373, 380–386, 390–391, 460; *see
　　also* hermeneutics, interpretation
existence, 40–42, 47, 153, 197, 211, 230,
　　247, 296, 370
　　economic, 104, 106
　　embodied character of human, 164,
　　　293
　　ethical dimension of human, 167, 466
　　of external world, 51
　　the face and human, 233, 278, 465
　　God's, 176, 184–185
　　God's 'presence' in human, 191, 193
　　as grounded in ethics, 348
　　hermeneutical accounts of, 210
　　human, 43n12, 50n25, 54, 56–57,
　　　95–96, 99–100, 105, 107–108, 119,
　　　149, 152, 154n43, 156, 168, 172, 177,
　　　234, 300
　　Jewish, 338, 378–379
　　meaning of, 190, 350
　　meaningful human, 201, 221, 224–226,
　　　290
　　natural, 105, 149, 224
　　of other minds, 51
　　philosophy justifying human, 307–308,
　　　310
　　possibility of meaningful, social human,
　　　159, 176
　　purpose of human, 157, 203
　　responsibility and human, 323, 337
　　social, 191, 267, 282, 288, 291, 293,
　　　296, 298, 335, 418, 421n1, 451
　　temporality of, 210–211, 213, 221,
　　　225–226
Exodus, 190, 190n53, 190n54, 197
experience, 47, 179, 205, 262, 264
　　conditions for, 52, 54, 321
　　death and, 211
　　description of, 101
　　différance and, 327
　　of eros, 47n21, 360
　　erotic, 153n38
　　of face of the other, 42, 45–48, 46n20,
　　　47n21, 395
　　of fatigue, 40, 47n20, 360

God and, 185, 190–191, 199
　　of insomnia, 40, 47n21, 153n39,
　　　360
　　language and, 187
　　of natural objects, 40
　　ordinary, everyday, 56, 87, 155n46, 159,
　　　167, 177, 199–200, 396, 454
　　possibility of, 51–53, 56, 58, 159, 328,
　　　439
　　religious, 176, 199, 202
　　sensory, 128
　　temporal character of, 209–210
　　of time, 213–214
　　time as the form of human, 220, 225
explanation, 424
exteriority, 47, 86–88, 104, 171, 220, 266,
　　372; *see also* Infinity
　　as irreducible to the same, 91

face, the, 20n60, 57, 59n46, 83n75, 84,
　　93n18, 105n60, 254, 256, 267,
　　283n208, 297, 327, 333–335, 358,
　　361, 413, 417, 421n1, 450n124,
　　453n139, 463
　　as beyond experience, thought,
　　　consciousness, language, 47, 300,
　　　300n1, 301–302, 321–322, 333
　　calling the self into question, 43, 67n21,
　　　72, 80–84, 93, 119, 124, 133, 154,
　　　228n1, 302, 365
　　compared with Rosenzweig's thought,
　　　100, 103
　　as concrete experience within ordinary
　　　life, 45–50, 46n20, 47n21, 86, 104,
　　　109, 187n43, 228
　　election and, 344
　　encounter, engagement with, xiv–xv, 11,
　　　19, 37–38, 38n117, 42, 61, 68, 70, 72,
　　　75, 78–79, 85–86, 92, 107, 115n1
　　epiphany of, 43, 47, 58, 68, 70, 72–74,
　　　79–80, 92, 119–120, 122–123, 181,
　　　218, 389, 421
　　eschatology, messianism, and, 214
　　ethics, moral theory, and, 46, 228, 233,
　　　321, 445, 449–450
　　future and, 212

the glory of the infinite and, 185–186,
191
height and, 180–183
human existence and, 233, 278, 465
illeity and, 189–194, 197, 200–203, 206,
309, 413
the infinite and, 48, 80, 92–94, 98, 104,
115, 115n1, 300, 374–375
intentionality and, 49n25, 66
as interlocutor, 119
Jewish texts and, 342, 381, 385–386, 391,
393
justice and, 22, 112, 237, 243, 286,
449–450, 454
language and, 74–75, 82, 93n18, 108,
133–138, 142, 159, 187, 300–302,
313–315, 320–323, 331
nakedness of, 4, 68, 70, 73–74, 80,
118n13, 124, 222
noema and, 58, 58n45
normativity (moral force) of, 55n42, 93,
190n53, 194, 197–198, 229n2, 246,
422, 465
of one's enemy, 406
outside of totality, 115, 115n1, 332
pacific opposition and, 69
as particular, 61, 86, 109, 243, 431
the past, diachrony, and, 219, 223, 305,
307–309, 319
persecution and, 15, 82–83
philosophy and, 370, 452–453
philosophy's task and, 305, 307–308, 310
as a plea, demand, command, summons,
5, 57, 69–70, 73–74, 79, 81–83,
97–98, 113, 119, 121–122, 124,
130–131, 395
politics, the state, and, 80, 86, 108,
194–195, 232, 232n15, 233, 243, 261,
286, 288, 445, 450
as pre-conceptual, 247, 253
as pre-ontological, 154n43
priority of, 58, 79, 82, 99, 253, 420
problem of supererogation and, 298n254
proximity and, 129–131, 243, 455n151
as a reason to act, 422–426, 431, 439,
443, 445–446, 448, 465–466

religion, theology, God, and, 64n10, 80,
174, 176, 178, 180–194, 197–203,
219
revelation and, 214, 367, 372, 374–375
ritual law and, 377–378
the self and, 149–150, 153–155, 157, 163,
165, 171–172
shame and, 93–94
the significance of, 66
skepticism and, 311–312, 315–317,
319–320
society and, 191, 288, 454
speech and, 134–135, 138, 178, 301–302,
304
as a standard, 121, 233
suffering expressed in, 5, 19, 57, 68n22,
75–76, 78–79, 85, 93, 106, 375
systematized rules and, 243–245
as a "thick" moral concept, 67
third party and, 24n73, 110, 137–138,
192, 340, 394
time and, 211–212, 214, 222
the trace and, 189–191, 193–194,
197–198, 203, 206–207, 307, 309,
389, 413
as transcendental condition for social
life, 45–46, 52–56, 73, 86, 313, 315,
321–322, 328, 333
two different interpretations of, 45–46,
45n17
as ultimate ground of meaning, 88
why Levinas uses the term, 68n22, 395
witness and, 185–187, 191
Fackenheim, Emil, xiii, 14, 18, 103n57,
337, 347, 353, 356n93, 370n139,
380, 396n262, 416, 416n4
Holocaust and, 355–357, 360n105,
366–368, 463n183
Midrash and, 373n159
fact-value distinction, 83–84, 197
faith, 198–199, 415–416, 418
moral, 64, 176
fascism, 230–231, 235, 336n2, 354, 399
Nazi, 23, 69, 122, 243, 259n115
fecundity, 113, 155, 155n48; *see also* paternity
Feinberg, Joel, 243n50

feminine, 63, 155
Ferry, Luc, 146–147
Fichte, J. G., 54, 56, 62n3, 70n32, 92n16, 261
Finkelkraut, Alain, 14, 20, 33, 406, 410, 457
Fish, Stanley, 117n9
Flew, Antony, 175n6
Føllesdal, Dagfinn, 138
Foot, Philippa, 249
forgiveness, 35–38, 458n161, 459, 459n166, 460
    of Germans, 33–37, 35n108, 458, 461–462
Fornet, R., 448
Foucault, Michel, 117n9, 144, 147
France, 15, 16n53, 20, 341, 359, 404n304, 458n161
Frankfurt, Harry, 416n1
Frankfurt School, 19
Franks, Paul, xi, 52–54, 64n12, 71n32
fraternity, 113, 244, 287, 310, 409
free will, 148, 151, 285, 287–288
freedom, 82, 97n31, 204, 245, 260, 270, 273, 275, 288n231, 423, 444, 463; see also autonomy
    condition for, 69
    death and, 153, 211
    of the existent, 151–152
    God and human, 193, 197, 198n71
    Nietzsche and, 281–282
    passivity of the self and, 155–157
    responsibility and, 105, 131–132, 173, 234, 287
    revelation and, 372–373
    rights and, 285, 288
    ritual, Jewish law, and, 376–377
    role of, in ethics, 64
    rules as impediments to, 243
    of the self, 80, 156, 158, 160–161, 163, 263, 283, 287
    shame and, 94
    the state and, 287, 405
    as theme of Life and Fate, 3, 10
    the there-is and, 196
Frege, Gottlob, 116, 124, 124n31, 321, 323, 325–331

Freud, Sigmund, 175
future, 209, 211–214, 216, 219–221, 224–226

Gadamer, Hans-Georg, 117n9, 124, 168, 384
Galilei, Galileo, 284
Garfield, Jay, 252n93
Gauthier, David, 229n2, 245–246
Geach, Peter, 334
generosity, 30, 74, 86, 93n18, 94, 132, 225–226, 228, 233–234, 246, 262, 278, 292, 335, 399, 452; see also benevolence, charity
    Anwar Sadat and, 31
    artistic creation as an act of, 295
    imperfect obligations and, 240
    Israel and, 401
    Jewish texts and, 337, 342, 394
    Judaism and, 370
    justice and, 244, 426
    Marxism and, 9, 231
    philosophy and, 370
    practical reason and, 239
    prayer and, 351
    as a response to the other, 6, 19, 92–93, 122, 124, 166, 190, 199, 201, 217, 286, 319, 345, 445
    revelation as event of, 95
    as selective and limited, 241, 245
    after Stalinism and Hitlerism, 339
    the state, politics and, 23–24, 27–28, 289, 450
Genesis, 186n35, 261, 340, 392; see also Bible
genocide, 18, 225, 433, 463
    Nazi, xii, 17
    Cambodia, 17
Germany, 15, 247, 341
Gert, Bernard, 243n50
Gewirth, Alan, 235, 243n50, 267
Gibbard, Alan, 235, 243n50
Gibbs, Robert, 337n6, 384n212, 390–394
gift, 105–107, 134; see also grace
    the other's face as a, 198–199
Glasgow, 437

glory, 184, 184n27, 185–188, 191, 197, 202, 228n1, 244, 259n115, 292, 304, 307, 334, 395, 420
God, 7–8, 99–100, 109, 176, 186n35, 187n43, 190n53, 261–262, 327–328, 343, 370n139; *see also* divine
  Buber and, 178, 290
  death of, 116, 118, 176, 184
  denial of, 341
  Descartes and, 48, 91, 199
  election and, 98n35
  forgiveness and, 459–460
  Herman Cohen and, 63n3
  the Holocaust and, 355, 367–369
  human action and, 348
  illeity and, 151n27
  Jewish texts and, 385–386
  judgment of, 217–218
  Kant and, 176, 180
  language of, 345
  law, ritual, and, 376, 378
  Levinas and, xvi, 48, 55n42, 87, 118, 122, 174, 176–207, 182n25, 197n70, 219, 259n115, 415
  the other and, 180–181, 191–193, 200–202, 344
  prayer and, 349–351
  revelation and, 372–374
  rights and, 284
  Rosenzweig, 95, 101–102, 201, 221
  the self and, 145
  Spinoza and, 175
  Taylor, 172, 177, 204–207
  theodicy and, 357, 363
  the third party and, 191–192
  via negativa and, 303
  of Western faiths, 87
  who hides, 341–342, 354
  word of, 224
Goebbels, Joseph, 34
Goffman, Erving, 255
Gomez, A., 448
good, the, 7–8, 67, 69, 91n12, 156, 188, 201, 272, 274, 299, 361–362, 417, 451n129

desire for, 199–200
  Taylor and, 101, 169–171, 177, 263–268
goodness, 30, 34, 84, 107, 200, 218, 228, 231, 246, 288, 339; *see also* benevolence
  acts of, 6–11, 17, 19, 23, 27, 32–33, 86, 112, 234–235
  aroused by the face, 73, 120
  as essence of humanity, 32
  grace of, 206
  height and, 181–182
  inability to systematize, 9, 18, 20
  Israel and, 401
  Jewish texts and, 342, 346
  justice tempered by, 37
  peace and, 27–28
  prayer and, 352
  the state, politics, and, 18, 286, 289
Gorky, Maxim, 2
grace, 214; *see also* gift
  an act of, 7, 206
  world grounded in, 32
Greek, 97n27, 110–111, 336–340, 380, 387–389, 389n236, 390–391, 391n246, 392–395, 412–414
Grice, H. P., 120, 124n31, 127
Grossman, Vasily, xv, 2–14, 18, 26–27, 32, 338, 340, 393
  Forever Flowing, 9n32, 10n38
  Life and Fate, xv, 2–13, 18–19, 26, 30–31, 46, 231, 235, 243, 319, 335, 339, 374, 422n2, 457
guilt, 63n3, 458n161, 459
  German, 34, 36, 458, 461–462
  over massacres at Sabra and Chatila, 21, 410n335
Gulag, 17, 338, 364

Habermas, Jürgen, 19, 233, 243, 246, 260, 267, 269, 277n183, 283, 443n101
Hacker, Peter, 329, 333–334
Hadot, Pierre, 274n168
Haifa, 405
Halakhah, Halakhic, 347–348, 353, 372–373, 376, 379, 382, 391–392
Hampton, Jean, 423n4

Handelman, Susan, 382
Hare, R. M., 428
Hayyim of Volozhin, 347–350, 352, 393
Hebrew, 198, 337–338, 383, 389n236,
        391–394, 412–413
    Bible, 389
    language, 380, 387
    literature, 380, 382
    syntax, 373
    texts, 379, 388, 395
Hegel, G. W. F., 43n12, 54, 56, 70n32, 95,
        101, 146, 162, 168, 175, 220, 366, 396
Heidegger, Martin, xii-xiii, 13, 39, 51n30,
        73, 88, 90, 96, 124, 129–130, 152,
        162, 246n61, 290, 328, 398
    death and, 195
    Derrida and, 322
    discussion of in "Is Ontology
        Fundamental?," 64
    Emersonian perfectionism and,
        272–273, 277
    forgiveness of, 36–37, 458, 461
    Levinas's critique of, 321
    "Meaning and Sense" and, 115
    Mitsein and, 154n43
    moral skepticism and, 55
    moral thinking and, 269
    Nazism and, 53, 147, 230
    ontology and, 100, 215
    phenomenological method and, 45
    revelation and, 102
    the self and, 146–147, 150, 160, 172
    time and, 208, 210, 220–221, 226
    trace as attack on metaphysics of, 323
    utilitarian character of language and, 304
height, 55n42, 68, 81, 97–99, 180–183, 185,
        189, 197, 259n115, 344, 385; *see also*
        face
Hellenism and Hebraism, 336
Herder, Johann Gottfried, 136
Heraclitus, 144
hermeneutics, hermeneutical, 119, 124,
        372; *see also* exegesis, interpretation
    accounts of human existence, 210
    Fackenheim and, 356, 356n93, 357, 368
    Levinas and, 353, 379, 381–384, 387,
        391, 393

Heschel, Abraham Joshua, 205n94, 345,
        371–372
heteronomy, 89–90, 345n45
Heydrich, Reinhard, 34
Hillgruber, Andreas, 13
Himmler, Heinrich, 34
hineni, 185, 186n35, 202, 261–262, 375
Hiroshima, xii, 17, 364
historicism, 169, 175, 336n2; *see also*
        relativism
    time and, 208, 210
history, 3, 117, 195, 217n27, 217n28, 220,
        225, 227, 338, 416n4
    American, 16n53
    anti-Semitism and, 336n2
    God and, 175
    the Holocaust and, 16–17
    Levinas and, xvi, 87, 208, 213–219, 226,
        357
    messianism and, 25, 29, 396–397, 400,
        413
    philosophy of, 338, 400
    role of Jewish people in, 15, 338, 382,
        406
    the self and, 162, 168
    time and, 208–209, 212–214
    of Western philosophy, xii, 175
Hitler, Adolf, 1–2, 10, 17, 25, 32, 34, 36,
        112, 122, 339, 364, 382, 408–409
Hitlerism, 17, 119n15, 262, 339–340, 364,
        451; *see also* Holocaust, Nazism
Hobbes, Thomas, 23–25, 40, 92, 105–106,
        132, 175n5, 237, 245–246, 261, 281,
        283, 286–288
    moral thinking and, 23, 23n69, 28, 269
    nature and, 196
    the self and, 145–146, 148, 150n21
Hobsbawm, Eric, xiin1
holiness, 176, 199, 201–202, 225, 228n1,
        259n115, 290, 391, 395, 420
holism, 162, 164, 166
Holocaust, 1, 9, 12–20, 16n54, 17n56, 25,
        38, 225, 354n90, 370, 463
    Arendt and, 34
    Charlotte Delbo and, 67n21
    Fackenheim and, 355–357, 360n105,
        366–368

Gurs, 359
Israel, Zionism, and, 401, 406–408, 410
Jankélévitch and, 35–36
Jewish responsibility to Germans
    during, 33
Jews, Judaism, and, 337
Levinas and, 353–355, 357–358, 362–370
meaninglessness of, 17
peace after, 338
philosophy and, 354n89
rahamim, 339
Treblinka, 2, 10
trials, 458n161
Honneth, Alex, 260
hope, 396–397, 399
Anwar Sadat and, 31
Ikonnikov as voice of, 9
Marxism and, 9–10
Horkheimer, Max, 31, 246n61, 264, 336n2
hospitality, 107
hostage, 82, 82n73, 83–84, 132, 143,
    155–159, 173, 183, 200, 202, 292,
    303, 321, 334, 421, 443
Hudson, Stephen D., 249n73
humanism, 90, 146–147, 354, 451
austere, 149n17, 341–344, 346, 379, 420
Jewish, 342
Levinas's, 148, 149n17
objective, 103
humanity, 75, 83, 111–113, 152, 245, 340,
    414, 460
Cavell and, 269
failure to respect, 147
goodness as essence of, 32
Korsgaard and, 254, 256–258, 437–438,
    440–444
meaning of, 85
Nazism and, 33
realization of, 30
vocation of and for, 368
Humboldt, Alexander von, 136
Hume, David, 25, 51, 83, 92
the self and, 146, 150
Hursthouse, Rosalind, 248n66, 249n73,
    416n2, 462n179
Husserl, Edmund, xii, 39, 45n16, 50, 88,
    96, 102, 124, 126, 128, 328

indebtedness to Kant, 51n30
intentionality and, 49, 78, 99
"Meaning and Sense" and, 115
phenomenological method and, 44–45
the self and, 150, 157–159, 172
skepticism and, 314
time and, 208, 210, 212, 219–220,
    225–226
transcendental philosophy and, 51–52

I-Thou relationship, 34, 46n20, 63, 190,
    371; *see also* Buber
Ibsen, Henrik, 273
idealism, 86, 97–100, 103, 121, 149, 215,
    386, 398
Davidson's, 165
death and, 211
epistemological, 95–96
German, 45, 51n30, 52, 54, 88, 146, 150,
    398
Rosenzweig's thought and, 102
time and, 212–213
transcendental, 17n56, 158, 308, 326
truth of, 41–42
identity, 160, 257, 267, 431
Jewish, 342
Korsgaard and, 254, 256, 441–442,
    444
Levinas and, 151, 156–157
modern, 204–205
Taylor and, 93–94, 162, 171, 263–265,
    267
ideology, 7–8, 10, 25n79, 187, 235; *see also*
    totality
failure of, 18, 20n60, 374
Levinas's opposition to, 19, 25, 31, 243,
    366n126
political, 231, 339, 370
idolatry, 29, 404
Ikonnikov-Morzh, 7–9, 13, 339
il y a, see there-is
illeity, 151n27, 187, 187n43, 188–194,
    198–203, 300, 301n2, 302, 309, 332,
    391, 413, 455n151; *see also* diachrony,
    God, trace
third person character of, 192
distinguished from the there-is, 195–197

Infinity (the Infinite), xvi, 47, 56, 104, 108,
   180, 200, 215, 243, 259n115, 261,
   308, 388n236
   as beyond totality, 131, 200, 225, 300
   as a breach of totality, 86–87, 108
   Descartes and, 48, 91, 199, 376
   diachrony and, 305
   eschatology and, 215–216
   the face and, 48, 80, 91–92, 98–99, 104,
      113, 115, 115n1, 194, 300, 374–375
   the glory of, 184–187, 244
   God as, 193, 197, 327
   philosophy's task and, 305
   the saying and, 190
   the self and, 156, 165
   the trace of, 191, 309
   witness of, 185, 185n35, 186
insomnia, 40–41, 47n21, 153n39, 321, 332,
   360
intentionality, 49n25, 52, 55, 58, 78–79,
   124
   consciousness and, 48–50, 150
   of the infinite, 91–92
   naturalism and, 148
   the other and, 97, 99, 102
   revelation and, 102
   sufficiency of, 103
interiority, 104; *see also* totality
interpretation, 11, 49, 370, 389–390; *see also*
   exegesis, hermeneutics
   Davidson and, 164
   Derrida's, of Levinas, 125
   of face, 45–46, 46n20, 48
   Levinas and Jewish textual, 384
   revelation and, 371–372
   self, 93, 93n20, 161, 169–170
intersubjectivism, 436–442, 444, 448–449,
   457, 464–466
intuitionism, 117n9, 247, 248n66
ipseity, 113, 150; *see also* ego
Iraq, 354
Isaac, 186n35
Isaiah, 202, 261–262
Israel, 345, 367, 371, 381–382, 400, 413;
   see also Zionism
   people, 21, 98n35, 198, 349, 352, 403

state, 20–22, 28–32, 247, 259, 337,
   401–403, 404n304, 405–409,
   410n335, 412, 414
Israeli Defense Forces (IDF), 20

Jacobi, F. H., 56, 371
James, William, 225
Jankélévitch, Vladimir, 13, 35–37
Jaspers, Karl, 176
Jerusalem, 30, 408
Jews, 15, 21, 195, 403–404, 413–414,
   414n350
   conflict with Arabs, 30–32, 404,
      408–409
   election and, 344–345
   Germans and, 32
   the Holocaust and, 16, 337, 367–368
   Jewish texts and, 382
   justice and, 37, 401–402
   Palestinians and, 31–32
   role of, in Levinas's thought, 16n53, 338
   suffering of, 342
   value of for Western culture, 336
Job, 359, 361
Jonas, Hans, 354
Joyce, James, 3
Judaism, xvi, 13, 98n35, 198, 344, 348,
   373n159, 375, 388, 393, 413–414
   adult, 341–342, 345–346
   as an "austere humanism," 149n17,
      341–344, 346
   diaspora, 342–343
   election and, 344, 346
   generosity and, 370
   the Holocaust and, 337, 354, 354n90,
      356, 363
   Israel and, 402
   Jewish texts and, 382, 411
   justice and, 342, 345, 370
   Kant and, 345n45
   metaphysics of, 373
   modern, liberal, 347
   orthodox, 376
   philosophy and, 396n262
   prayer and, 352
   recovery of, 368

responsibility and, 345
ritual and, 378–379
role of, in Levinas's thought, 340
study and, 349
value of for Western culture, 336, 353, 390
Zionism and, 401
justice, 14, 27–28, 33, 36–37, 67, 109, 142, 174, 225, 228, 233, 267, 269, 297, 335, 426, 444, 450n124, 451, 456, 463
after Stalinism and Hitlerism, 339
Cavell and, 76n50, 182–183, 270, 273–280
Derrida and, 260
diachrony and, 222, 310
the face and, 22, 112, 237, 243, 286, 449–450, 454
the Form of, 279–280n191
God and, 191–194
Israel and, 401–404, 410
Jewish texts and, 337–338, 343–344, 390
Judaism, Jews, and, 342, 345, 370, 401
law, ritual, and, 376, 379
love and, 23–26, 112n79
messianism and, 399–400, 412
O'Neill and, 236–240, 242, 245
origin of, 350
politics and, 286
prayer and, 351–352
principles of, 24, 110, 193, 237–238, 238n25, 239–240, 242, 245, 262, 272, 276–277
responsibility and, 107n66, 110, 112, 122, 237–238, 243–245, 444, 450, 452
rights and, 285
skepticism and, 311–312
Taylor and, 204–206
the third party and, 110–111, 138, 192, 218, 243, 285, 309, 387, 449, 453, 455
justification, 424, 428, 431

Kabbalah, kabbalistic, 348, 350–353, 383
Kafka, Franz, 396
Kagan, Shelly, 427n20

Kant, Immanuel, 24, 64n12, 88, 90, 92, 168n77, 250, 259, 275, 308, 328, 396, 432n50, 441
ethics and, 224n55, 245–246, 269
Husserl's indebtedness to, 51n30
imperfect duties and, 453
ineffability and, 323–324, 326
Judaism and, 345n45
Levinas and, 64n11, 68, 236, 415–416, 420
the self and, 146, 150–151, 160
rights and, 283–284, 287–288
skepticism and, 87
theology, religion, God, and, 64, 175–176, 180, 345
thing-in-itself and, 89
time and, 220
transcendental philosophy and, 45, 51–54, 71n32
Kantianism, 297
Kaplan, Mordecai, 346
Kar-wai, Wong, 437
Kearney, Richard, 14, 81, 400
Kerr, Fergus, 176n7
Kiarostami, Abbas, 79
Kierkegaard, Søren, 57, 90, 175, 178, 269, 290, 371, 415–416, 416n4, 418–420
Kittay, Eva, 238n25
Kleinberg, Nathan, 195
Kleist, Heinrich von, 273
knowledge, 111, 125, 305–307, 340, 379n187, 453, 458
challenge to synthesis of, 88
conditions of, 52
esoteric, 398–399
of external world, 51
of God, 180, 182n25
idealism and, 41–42
ineffable, 325, 331
intellectualist approaches to, 90
moral, 250, 252
ordinary, 56
of the other, 76
of other minds, 77
Rosenzweig and, 95–96
scientific, 87

knowledge (*cont.*)
    the self and, 143, 145–147, 160–161
    skepticism and, 311, 311n47, 312, 316,
        316n61, 317, 319
    Western philosophy and, 89
Kolitz, Zvi, 341
Korsgaard, Christine, xiii, 228n2, 233,
        245–246, 263–264, 452, 457
    Nagel, reasons for action, and, 422, 424,
        434–449, 465
    The Sources of Normativity, 254–259
Kracauer, Siegfried, 86, 396
Krymov, Nikolay, 4–5
Kurds, 364n119, 365

Lacan, Jacques, 147
Laclau, Ernesto, 19n59
Lamm, Norman, 348, 352
Landauer, Gustav, 398
language, 64, 70, 74, 113–114, 119, 125, 138,
        197, 310, 333; *see also* discourse,
        speech
    Cavell and, 77–78, 78n57
    Davidson and, 123n30, 138–141,
        161–162, 164
    everyday, ordinary, 137–138, 200–201,
        334, 392
    the face and, 74–75, 82, 93n18, 108,
        122, 133–138, 142, 159, 300–302,
        304, 313–315, 320–323, 331
    of God, 345
    limits of, xvi, 12, 20n60, 51, 300–301,
        321–322, 324, 326, 335
    McDowell and, 168
    meaning and, 115–117, 116n4, 124n31,
        125, 127–128
    the other and, 43, 127
    possibility, conditions of, 52, 73–75, 325,
        327–328
    proximity and, 130–132
    responsibility and, 133–134, 136, 138, 331
    skepticism, philosophy, and, 311–313,
        315–320
    theological, 178, 180–185, 187, 191,
        194–195, 198, 202, 205–206, 372
    third party and, 141–142, 192
    totality and, 300, 304

the trace and, 322
translation and, 380, 387–392
Wittgenstein and, 59, 329–331, 333–334
law, 198, 235, 239, 250, 379n187, 456
    ceremonial, ritual, 347, 376–377
    the face and, 69, 232
    God and, 342
    Jewish, 353, 376–377
    moral, 64, 415
    natural, 209
    oral, 373
    responsibility and, 110, 112, 244
    revealed, 179
    rights and, 284–288
    the state and, 24, 456
    written, 373
Lear, Jonathan, 58–60
Lebanon War, 20
Leibniz, Gottfried Wilhelm, 56, 88, 146,
        175n5, 357, 421, 432n50
Levinas, Emmanuel
    "Between Two Worlds," 100
    "The Bible and the Greeks," 338–340
    "Diachrony and Representation," 219,
        221–225
    "Essence and Disinterestedness," 413
    "Freedom and Command," 69–70
    "From Ethics to Exegesis," 381
    "From the Rise of Nihilism to the
        Carnal Jew," 402–403
    "God and Philosophy," 198–203
    "The I and the Totality," 137–138
    "On Jewish Reading of Scriptures,"
        384–387
    "Judaism and Kenosis," 349–350
    "Language and Proximity," 125–132
    "Loving the Torah More Than God,"
        341
    "Manner of Speaking," 305–306
    "Meaning and Sense," 115, 115n2,
        116–124, 188–190
    "Is Ontology Fundamental?," 63–65,
        66n17, 69
    Otherwise Than Being, 136–138, 155–158,
        183–188, 190–195, 243–245,
        310–311, 453–456
    "Peace and Proximity," 26

"Philosophy and the Idea of Infinity,"
   88–89, 94
"Politics After!" 30, 406, 408
"Prayer without Demand," 351–352
"The Prohibition Against
   Representation and 'The Rights of
   Man,'" 283–284
"A Religion for Adults," 182n25,
   343–345, 381
"Revelation in the Jewish Tradition,"
   371–376
"The Rights of Man and the Rights of
   Others," 284–287
"The Rights of the Other Man,"
   287–288
"Signature," 1
"Space is Not One-Demensional,"
   403–404
"The State of Caesar and the State of
   David," 29, 404–405
"Substitution," 81
Talmudic lesson on forgiveness, 35–38
Time and the Other, 40–43, 43n12,
   149–155, 210–212
Totality and Infinity, 43–44, 49n25,
   72–75, 88, 104–107, 113, 180–181,
   214–219
"The Trace of the Other," 190
"Transcendence and Height," 68,
   96–100
"The Translation of the Scripture,"
   388–389
"Useless Suffering," 17, 362
liberalism, 204, 272
life, 117
   democratic, 274–275
   the face and ordinary, everyday, 187n43
   forms of, 251, 253, 259–261
   the good, 18, 30, 265–266, 270,
      272–273, 293
   as grounded in responsibility, 387
   Jewish, 18, 337–338, 340, 347, 349, 351,
      353–354, 356, 371, 374, 376–379,
      381–382, 395, 412–413
   as meaningful, 53–55, 59, 96, 119, 123,
      159, 165, 191, 201, 216–217, 219,
      264, 382

moral, ethical, 204, 231, 234, 259,
   272–273, 275, 277n184, 278, 290,
   444, 448, 454, 458, 464, 466
ordinary, everyday human, xv, 9, 12–13,
   22, 32, 46–48, 50, 55, 59, 62–63,
   65–68, 70, 74–75, 78–79, 82, 83n75,
   84–86, 91–92, 97n27, 98–100,
   103–105, 107–109, 115–116, 120,
   122, 125, 131, 133, 140, 151–154, 160,
   165, 167, 172–173, 192, 200, 232,
   235, 310, 374, 392, 422, 422n3, 439,
   450n124, 462, 465
orienting of, 118–119, 183, 205, 210
political, 19n59, 25, 28, 135, 187n43,
   230, 234, 244, 262, 273, 275,
   284–285, 289, 310, 405, 429, 458
post-Holocaust, 362
reciprocal relations of social, 192
religious, 101, 177–178, 180, 197,
   202–203, 396
ritual law and, 378
social, 22, 54, 56, 62–63, 65, 75, 83n75,
   86, 107, 111, 113, 121, 123–124, 133,
   142, 150, 154, 159, 171, 192, 197,
   232, 234, 243–244, 246, 252,
   273–274, 277–279, 282, 284, 285,
   294–298, 309–310, 312, 320, 328,
   332, 358, 365, 368–369, 397,
   404–405, 408, 416n2, 418, 423,
   425–426, 429, 448, 450n124, 452,
   454, 462, 465
Llewellyn, John, 292
Locke, John, 24, 145, 175n5, 237, 269, 284
Logstrup, Knud, 228
Lovibond, Sabina, 248n66, 248n70,
   249n73, 462n179
love, 27, 92, 200–201, 205–206, 310, 383,
   427n20
   as eros, 63, 211
   justice and, 23–26, 112n79
   of the other, 5
   peace and, 25, 27, 286
   perfect, 134
   prayer and, 349
   revelation as an event of, 95
   Rosenzweig and, 214
   self, 290

Lukács, Georg, 176, 396, 398
Lutheranism, 145
Lyotard, Jean-François, 14

MacIntyre, Alasdair, xii, xiin1, 117n9,
    168n77, 175n6, 204
Mackie, John, 246
Maimonides, Moses, 182n25, 344
Malamud, Bernard, 414n350
Malka, Shlomo, 33, 406, 457, 458n159
Marcel, Gabriel, xii, 62n3, 190
Marion, Jean-Luc, 175n6
Marx, Karl, 147, 168, 175
Marxism, 9–10, 14–15, 25, 28, 230–232,
    340, 354, 451
McDowell, John, xii–xiv, 248n66, 248n67,
    424, 462n179
    ethics and, 230, 233n18, 248–254, 259
    rule following and, 249–253, 252n93
    the self and, 148, 162, 167–169, 172
    virtue and, 249–252, 252n90, 254
McNaughton, David, 80n60, 233n18,
    248n66, 462n179
meaning, 118–119, 124, 133, 160; *see also*
    sense, signification
    constitution of, 99
    crisis of, 118n13
    Davidson and, 124n31, 135n56, 140, 167
    Derrida and, 326–327
    the face and, 80, 115–116, 120–127, 131,
        142, 301
    of humanity, 85, 95–96
    language and, 115–117, 116n4, 124n31,
        125
    McDowell and, 168, 250
    noema and, 49
    phenomenology and, 44–45, 48,
        116–117
    revelation and, 95, 102
    theories of, 124–125
    the there-is and, 196
memory, 126, 223, 307, 313
Mendelssohn, Moses, 24n74, 287n227,
    338n8
Merleau-Ponty, Maurice, 115, 123–124
messianism, 25–26, 29–30, 208, 214,
    216–217, 217n28, 227, 344, 395–396,

    396n262, 397, 397n264, 398–400,
    400n286, 401, 403, 405–406,
    412–413, 451; *see also* eschatology
metaphysics, 89, 96, 98, 100, 160, 177, 221,
    230, 234, 304, 323
    Aristotelian, 259
    critique of, 175n6
    Derrida and, 305
    of Judaism, 373
    Levinas's (ethical), 18, 25, 28, 38–39, 43,
        86, 159, 247, 303, 314, 350
    natural theology and, 203
    of presence, 323
    traditional, 54, 87, 206, 328, 331
method, 93n17, 115
    historical, 208
    language and Levinas's, 302, 313
    phenomenological, 44–45, 48, 51n30,
        55, 124, 128, 155n46, 358
    scientific, 208
    transcendental, 44, 321
Midrash, 373, 373n159, 389, 391–392; *see
    also* Aggadah
Mill, J. S., 269
minds, problem of other, 76, 79, 315n61
Mitchell, Basil, 175n6
Mitsein (being-with), 154n43
mitzvot, 186n35, 198, 353, 371; *see also*
    commandment
modernism, xii, 12, 86, 176, 268n144
modernity, 172, 362, 388, 391
    crisis of, 1, 15, 18, 207
    failure of, 11
    Heidegger's attack on, 147
    malaise of, 204, 207
monotheism, 29, 342, 383
Montaigne, Michel de, 144
Moore, A. W., 324–329, 331–332
Moran, Richard, 162n62
moral
    agent, 43, 62n3, 176, 441, 448
    education, 249–250, 249n73
    psychology, 92
moral theory, xiii, xvi, 64, 92, 117n9, 179,
    190n53, 230, 233–236, 270, 278, 436,
    448, 450
    Aristotelian, 271–273

the face and, 228
Nagel and, 434
O'Neill and, 236
Rawls and, 276
self-interest and, 291
supererogation and, 298n254
Wolf and, 297–298
morality, 35, 53, 83n74, 98, 107, 187n43,
    215, 230, 235, 259n115, 366, 369, 415,
    419; *see also* ethics
God, Judaism, and, 342, 346
grounded in the face, 86, 121–122, 137
Korsgaard and, 254, 257–258, 435, 440,
    442, 444
Levinas and, 246, 396, 450, 456
McDowell and, 248, 250
Nagel and, 432–434
naturalism and, 148
the self and, 143–144
as self-forgetfulness, 152
Taylor and, 264
Wolf questioning preeminence of,
    297–298
Moscow, 4, 12–13, 27
Moses, 182n25, 190n53, 190n54,
    197–198
Mostovskoy, Mikhail, 7, 13
Moyn, Samuel, 179n12
Mt. Moriah, 186n35
murder, 65, 71, 71n33, 73, 81, 92, 134,
    218–219, 227–228, 293
Murdoch, Iris, 276n181
Murphy, Liam, 289n235
Musil, Robert, 3, 86
mysticism, 89
myth, 345, 374
of the given, 89, 117, 117n6
God as a, 180–182
of philosophy, 96
of *Timaeus*, 111–112
mythology, 18, 341, 343, 352, 378, 381

Nagel, Thomas, 229n2, 255, 422, 422n3,
    424–426, 426n13, 427–429, 429n26,
    430–446, 448, 452, 457, 464–465
nakedness, of the face, 4, 68, 70, 73–74, 81,
    93n19, 97, 118n13, 124, 222

nature, 107, 167, 172, 174, 196, 259n115,
    281, 328, 378
natural law, 28
naturalism, xii, 103, 146, 148, 196–197,
    203, 213, 248n27
Davidson and, 165
Kaplanian, 347
Korsgaard and, 256, 258
Nietzsche and, 281–282
revelation and, 375
of second nature, 162, 168–169, 172, 259
Nazism, Nazis, 1–3, 7, 10–11, 16, 30–31,
    33, 337, 354–357, 359, 366–367, 369,
    405, 409, 458n161; *see also* Hitlerism
Heidegger and, 147, 230
Nehamas, Alexander, 147
neighbor, 21, 33, 81, 83, 130–131, 184, 192,
    200–201, 287, 307, 374–375, 383,
    407, 451, 454
Neiman, Susan, 353–354, 357–358
Nemo, Philippe, 81, 358–361, 369
neo-Kantianism, 124, 176, 210
rise of, xii
Southwest school of, 209–210
neo-Platonism, 56, 188, 303
neutralism, 270–272
Newton, Isaac, 175n5, 284
Nietzsche, Friedrich, xii, 90, 117n9, 124,
    147, 175–176, 184, 272, 279n185,
    290
perfectionism and, 278–282
nihilism, xii, 53, 55, 117n9, 259n115, 396,
    402
noema, noesis, 49, 49n24, 49n25, 58, 93n17,
    99, 115
Nolte, Ernst, 13
nothingness, 195, 211
Novikov, Pyotr, 4–5
Nozick, Robert, 438
Numbers, 394
Nussbaum, Martha, 462n179

objectivity, xvi, 390, 432–433, 444–445
crisis of, xii
Davidson and, 164–165
moral, 118n9, 169
of values, xi

obligation, 5, 171, 181, 185, 189, 197,
    197n70, 200, 202, 214–215,
    223–226, 233–235, 238, 262, 267,
    283, 295–296, 417–418; *see also* duty
  Korsgaard and, 254–259
  limits of, 244
  moral, 416
  O'Neill and, 236, 239–240, 242,
    250–252
  to the other, 289, 291, 362, 370, 377,
    403, 425, 429, 462
  over-demandingness and, 289n235
  precise moral, 242
  primary, 229n3
  reasons of, 428, 429n26, 435, 439
  to respond to the Holocaust, 356,
    367–369
  rights and, 283
obsession, 81–83, 130, 132, 143, 155, 158,
    183, 304, 334
O'Neill, Onora, xiii, 168n77, 233, 235,
    240n34, 243–247, 259, 267,
    277n183, 443n101
  justice and, 236–240, 242, 245
  obligation and, 236, 239–240, 242,
    250–252
  rule following and, 252, 252n93
  Towards Justice and Virtue, 236–242
  virtue and, 236–237, 240–242, 245
ontology, 47, 84, 99, 108, 172, 198, 206,
    266, 301, 320n77, 332, 350, 388n236,
    422, 451
  encounter with face as prior to or
    beyond, 47, 56, 58
  the face and, 155n46
  Heideggerian, 100, 215, 306
  phenomenological, 50
  problem of supererogation and, 298n254
  the trace and, 322
  war and, 215, 397
  Wittgenstein and, 329
Ostrow, Matthew, 330–331
Othello, 76n50
other, 42, 47n21, 62, 90, 90n6, 179, 283,
    295, 302, 333, 393, 421, 426, 454;
    see also autrui, Infinity

  acknowledgment of, 19, 27n84, 61, 66,
    72, 75, 77, 98–99, 105, 119, 122–124,
    128, 131, 133, 140, 283n208, 315n61,
    335, 377, 422n1, 444–445, 462
  anti-Semitism and, 30
  as beyond language, thought, and
    consciousness, xvi, 8, 42n8, 87,
    301–303, 320
  as calling the self into question, 43, 68,
    72, 74, 97, 119, 132–134, 140–141,
    296
  death and, 153, 153n38, 211, 218, 224,
    321
  encounter, engagement with the face of,
    5, 11, 15, 43, 45–47, 46n21, 58, 61,
    65, 75, 79, 92, 107–108, 115n1, 149
  eschatology and, 215–217
  Fichte and, 70n32
  future and, 212, 214, 219
  glory of the infinite and, 185–186, 191
  God and, 180–181, 191–193, 200–202,
    344, 348
  the Good and, 200–201
  height and, 181–182
  as hunger, 74–75
  illeity and, 189, 192–194, 197, 309, 323
  as interlocutor, 119–120, 126
  Jewish, 20
  Jewish texts and, 340, 386
  Korsgaard and, 255
  Levinas's terminology surrounding the
    encounter with, 82n73
  murder and, 65–66
  neighbor as, 33, 111
  obligation to, 289, 291, 345, 362, 370,
    377, 403, 425, 429, 462
  O'Neill and, 236–237, 240–242
  as opposed to the same, 89
  Palestinian as, 33
  the past, diachrony, and, 223, 308
  persecution by, 82
  philosophy of, 50
  as plea, command, demand, summons,
    68–71, 81, 105, 113, 120, 141–142,
    228, 245, 283
  prayer and, 349, 351

priority of, 4, 54–55, 253, 291, 321
proximity and, 27, 128, 130, 138, 200, 244, 286
as reason for action, 440–445
recognition of, in Marxism, 9, 451
reduction to same, 89, 95, 397
as resistance to the self, 70
responsibility for, 7, 11, 22, 25–26, 27n84, 29, 38, 46, 71, 83n75, 98, 98n38, 113–114, 119, 122, 131, 140, 164, 245, 262, 278, 282, 296, 304, 345, 362–363, 369, 410, 418, 439, 462
revelation and, 375
rights of, 283–285, 287–288, 293
ritual law and, 377–378
the self and, 149–150, 153–155, 155n48, 156–158, 160, 163, 165, 171
as suffering, 153n39, 321
Taylor and, 264–267
the trace and, 189–193, 197, 309, 322–323
transcendence of, 358, 361
as transcendental condition for thought, speech, social life, 328
unique, unassimilable, irreducible, 27
value of concern for, 170–171, 196
welcoming, 43, 97, 134
witness, 191

Palestinians, 20, 31–33, 259, 406, 408–409, 410n335, 411, 457–458
Parfit, Derek, 229n2, 425, 425n9
Paris, 341
    1968 student revolt, 14, 15, 15n51
Parmenides, 88
particularism, moral, 80n60, 117n9, 233n18
particularity, 413, 433, 458
    death and, 101
    of face, 86, 109, 203
    Jewish, 338, 344–347, 351, 381, 393–394, 414
    of persons, 127, 228, 233, 284, 296
passivity, 165, 199, 222
    death and, 153, 211
    Levinas's use of terms capturing a sense of, 334

of self, 80, 82, 143, 154–158, 185, 303, 443
past, 209, 213, 219–227, 307–309, 313, 317, 322
paternity, 155, 155n48, 295, 413
peace, 27n84, 191, 202, 215, 230, 246, 287, 338–339, 395, 397, 409; *see also* war
    as function of the state, 25
    love and, 25, 27, 286
    political, 26, 31
    real, 26–27, 31
Pentateuch, 388–389, 393; *see also* Bible
Peperzak, Adriaan, 88n4, 134, 181
perfectionism, 272
    Aristotelian, 278
    Cavell and, 268, 268n144, 269–270, 270n151, 271–272, 272n157, 273, 273n158, 274–276, 276n181, 277, 277n184, 278–283
    Emersonian, xii, 268n144, 270n151, 272, 272n157, 273–276, 276n181, 278–279, 283, 291n241, 292, 459n166
    moral, 76n50, 268, 268n144, 269, 271–272, 272n157, 273, 273n158, 274n168, 275, 277–278
    political, 30, 271
    religious, 271–272
persecution, 13, 20n60, 82n73, 83–84, 155–157, 163, 183, 292, 321, 334, 360, 405; *see also* accusation
    as being confronted by the face, 15, 82, Jewish, 15–16, 18, 21, 30, 346, 349–350, 403, 406–408
    opposition to, 368
perspective, 431–432, 434–435
Phalangists, 20
phenomenology, 48–49, 50n26, 58–59, 100, 102, 115n11, 124, 304, 381
    of *Dasein*, 104
    of evil, 358
    Husserlian, 45, 55n43, 116, 210, 306
    of suffering, 360
    of time consciousness, 226
    transcendental, 44, 96
philology, 387

philosophy, 21, 85, 85n2, 86, 97n27,
    99–101, 103, 243, 392–393, 396, 453,
    456
  Anglo-American, analytic, xii-xvi, 39,
    124, 146, 148, 175n6, 176, 235–236,
    324, 464
  continental, 175n6
  end of, 19, 100
  German, 210
  God, religion, theology, and, 174–176,
    198–199, 202–203, 206
  Greek, 111, 412
  of history, 338
  the Holocaust and, 354, 370
  idealist trend in, 96
  Jewish, xiii
  Judaism and, 396n262
  Levinas, skepticism and, 304–306,
    306n26, 307–311, 311n47, 312–316,
    316n61, 317–320, 322, 333
  limits of, 323, 325
  of mind, 146, 204
  moral, 28, 204, 269–270, 276, 464
  motivation for, 55, 111
  natural, 145
  notions of meaning and sense and, 116
  notions of subjectivity and self and, 160
  ordinary-language, 176
  of the other, 50
  political, 160
  of religion, 175n6
  time and, 208
  transcendental, in relation to Levinas,
    xvi, 45, 51–59, 71n32, 73
  Western, xvi, 59, 76, 83, 88–90, 92n15,
    94–96, 100n42, 101, 102n51, 149,
    305, 323, 327, 397, 412
  Wittgenstein and, 59, 327–331, 333
Picker, Ludwig von, 331
Plant, Bob, 60n50
Plantinga, Alvin, 175n6
Plato, 56, 87–88, 90, 99, 147, 188, 188n47,
    276, 279–280n191, 296, 327, 330,
    415, 432n50
  desire and, 92, 92n15
  Parmenides, 305

  Republic, 10, 28, 57, 69, 91n12
  the self and, 144, 146
  Sophist, 89
  Symposium, 92n14
  Timaeus, 89, 111, 112n75
Platonism, 102, 144, 188, 202
  about meaning, 116, 122
Plotinus, 87, 99, 188, 188n47, 189–190, 327
pluralism, 397
  cultural, 118
  Levinas's, 259, 263, 266
  Taylor's, 169, 172, 263
Poirié, François, 109, 231
political theory, 270, 272, 276, 283, 401
politics, 9–10, 70, 96, 103, 109–111,
    112n79, 114, 215–216, 259n115, 261,
    292, 456; *see also* state
  Cavell and, 269
  cold war, 243
  conflict between Judaism and, 15
  Derrida, 294
  eschatology, messianism and, 395, 400,
    406
  ethics and, 14, 18, 20–30, 260, 286,
    288–289, 293, 404, 423, 451n129
  the face and, 80, 86, 108, 137, 194–195,
    232, 232n15, 445, 450
  failure of, 11, 17–18, 20
  Israel and, 401–407, 410
  justice and, 286
  Levinas and, 231, 236, 246, 285, 374, 465
  monotheistic, 29
  opposition to, 31, 243
  religion and, 195, 404
  the self and, 143–144
positivism, logical, 175n6, 176, 203
possession, 105–107
postmodernism, 12, 86, 117n9, 124, 149
prayer, 64, 187, 347, 349–353, 353n87
prerogatives, agent-relative (or
    agent-centered); *see* reason
presence, 131
  divine, 193–194
  of the face of other, 73, 78, 105–106,
    130, 132, 194, 261–262
  of God, 189, 191, 193, 202

present, 209, 211–213, 219–227, 307–309, 311, 313, 317, 322
Prichard, H. A., 291
Priest, Graham, 324–327, 329, 332
prophecy, 185, 187, 202, 220, 381, 395; *see also* witness
protention, 212, 219–220
proximity, 27, 30, 41, 81, 114, 125–133, 138, 156, 183, 192, 202, 244–245, 286, 302, 308, 452–455
   divine, 372
   the face and, 129–131, 243, 455n151
   prior to community, 310
   responsibility and, 128, 130, 200, 232
Psalms, 370n139
psychology, 178
psychological states, 76, 78, 106
Pufendorf, Samuel von, 284
Purcell, Michael, 107n66, 198n71
Pushkin, Alexander, 379, 393
Putnam, Hilary, xii–xiii, 76n50, 268–269, 277–278, 282, 296, 323
   criticism of Levinas's ethics, 290–293, 295, 297–298, 415n1

Quine, W. V., 116, 124n31

Rabinbach, Anson, 398–399
Railton, Peter, 229n2
Rakover, Yosl, 341
rationalism, 338
rationality, 64, 102, 104, 111, 145–147, 161, 163, 228, 259n115, 283, 287, 297
   action and, 422–424
   Darwall and, 446, 448
   Davidson and, 162–163, 165–166
   freedom and, 288
   Korsgaard and, 254, 257–258, 444, 446
   moral systems grounded in, 245
   Rawls and, 238
   of religious belief, 176
   revelation and, 375
   Taylor and, 264–265, 267
Rawls, John, 19, 22, 24, 40, 45, 193, 233, 235, 243, 245, 267, 281, 283, 286, 429, 445

   Cavell and, 272, 274–277, 280
   as a moral legislator, 269
   original position, 40, 237–238, 238n25, 442
Raz, Joseph, 229n2, 267, 415n1, 443n100
realism, 97–99, 102–103, 116
   epistemological, 95–96, 99
   metaphysical, 86
   moral, ethical, 99, 122, 228, 228n2, 249, 253, 258
reason, 88–89, 165, 167, 172, 204, 234, 243, 246, 259, 310, 319, 386, 419
   for action, 37, 249–250, 421, 421n1, 423–447, 464–465
   agent-neutral (objective), xvi, 422, 424–427, 427n20, 428, 430–431, 433–435, 437–439, 442, 445–446, 448, 457, 464–465
   agent-relative (subjective), 422, 424–427, 427n20, 428, 430–431, 434–439, 464
   of autonomy, 428–429, 435–436, 439
   deontological, 428, 429n26, 430–431, 435, 438–440, 457
   failure of, 17
   free will and, 287–288
   instrumental, 246n61
   Korsgaard and, 254–258, 264, 435–446
   limits of, 18
   of obligation, 428, 429n26, 435, 439, 457
   practical, 236–240, 240n34, 242, 246, 259, 263, 288
   Taylor and, 264, 267
Rebekah, 340
reciprocity, 62, 441
   I-Thou and, 63
redemption, 201, 396, 398–399
   Rosenzweig and, 102–103, 103n57, 201, 221, 396
reference, 115
relativism, xii, 115, 117n9, 169, 175; *see also* historicism
   cultural, 116
   moral, 259n115
   time and, 208, 210, 213

religion, 11, 19, 97n27, 101, 178, 191, 193,
    301, 307, 335, 397
  for adults, 343, 345
  critique of, 175n6
  as encounter with the face, 80
  eschatology and, 216
  as ethics, 84, 203, 292, 420
  Hermann Cohen and, 63n3
  Kant and, 64, 176, 345
  Levinas and, xv, 9, 64, 64n10, 174,
    176–177, 180–181, 187–188, 206,
    242, 296
  philosophy and, 174–176, 392
  politics and, 194, 404
  Rosenzweig and, 102
  the self and, 143–145
  Taylor and, 204–207
Renaut, Alain, 146–147, 149n20
representation, 219, 283, 310–311
responsibility, xiv, 30, 37, 47, 61n1, 74, 83,
    93n18, 94, 142, 155, 228n1, 231, 243,
    254, 256, 261, 289, 297, 323,
    361–362, 365, 370, 413, 418–419, 463
  election, 344, 346–347
  eschatology, messianism and, 216–217,
    217n28, 397, 399–400, 405, 412
  freedom and, 105, 131–132, 173, 234, 287
  fundamental social relationship of, 76,
    283
  the glory of the infinite and, 185–186,
    191
  God, religion, theology, and, 174, 180,
    183–184, 190, 192–194, 197–202,
    206, 290, 395
  height and, 181, 183
  illeity and, 189, 203
  inescapability of, 68, 98
  infinite, unlimited, xvi, 20n60, 68, 94,
    98, 112, 134, 192–193, 203, 229n3,
    244, 262, 289n235, 293–294, 296,
    375, 400, 422, 426, 432, 434,
    464–465
  Jewish existence and, 337–338
  Jewish texts and, 338–340, 343, 380–381,
    385–387, 390–393
  Judaism and, 345

  justice and, 107n66, 110, 112, 122,
    237–238, 243–245, 444, 450, 452
  language, 133–134, 136, 138, 140, 164,
    191, 331
  limits of, 243–245
  O'Neill, practical reason, and, 238–240,
    242
  the past, diachrony and, 220–227, 306,
    309–310, 314, 317, 319
  persecution and, 15, 403
  prayer and, 349–351
  as pre-ontological, 154n43
  problem of supererogation and, 298n254
  proximity and, 128, 130, 200, 232
  reasons for action and, 421–425, 427,
    427n20, 429, 432–433, 439, 443–446
  revelation and, 367, 372, 374–375
  ritual law and, 377–379
  the self, substitution, and, 92n15, 98,
    143, 156–160, 163, 165–166, 171–172
  sensibility as, 253, 257
  skepticism and, 311–312, 314–315,
    317–320
  speech and, 134, 140
  the state and, 24–25, 27, 285, 451, 456
  summoned to, 97
  surrounding the massacres at Sabra and
    Chatila, 20–21, 411
  systems grounded in, 245–247
  third party and, 452–455
  to acknowledge and accept other, 66,
    283n208
  to and for the other, 7, 11, 22, 25–26,
    27n84, 29, 38, 46, 57, 61, 71, 77,
    83n75, 98n38, 105–107, 113–114,
    119, 121–122, 131, 140, 228, 230, 235,
    262, 278, 363, 368, 410, 422n1, 462
  to one's enemies, 32–34, 38, 232
  universalism and, 259
  witness and, 186–187, 191
  Zionism, Israel, and, 30–31, 403, 410
retention, 220
revelation, 29, 87, 180, 284, 371, 382–383
  Benjamin and, 371, 386
  Buber and, 353, 371
  divine (God's), 73, 145, 181–182

Levinas and, 201, 214, 224, 353, 367, 372–376

of the other to the self, 58, 61, 74, 202, 245

Rosenzweig and, 95–96, 100, 102–103, 103n57, 179n12, 201, 213–214, 221, 353, 371

Scholem and, 371, 386

revolution, 15, 230, 397

Rickert, Heinrich, 124, 209

Ricoeur, Paul, 124

rights, 244, 253, 270, 284, 430, 455–457

human, 147, 284–287, 292–293, 340, 406

imperfect, 284, 286

natural, 283, 286

O'Neill and, 239–240

of the other, 283–285, 287–288, 293

perfect, 284, 286

rights-based theories, 431

Rilke, Rainer Maria, 396

ritual, 296, 353

Levinas and, 376–379

Robbins, Jill, 295n246

romanticism, 340

Cavell and, 76, 268n144

modernism and, 86

Rorty, Richard, 12, 19n59, 117n9, 230n5, 260–263, 263n125, 268, 276n181, 278, 283

limits of philosophy and, 323

Rosenstock-Huessy, Eugen, 103n57, 213

Rosenzweig, Franz, xi-xiii, 26n83, 39, 57, 59, 86, 124, 176, 178, 205, 205n94, 398

God and, 95, 101–102, 201

hermeneutics and, 382–384

historical role of the Jews and, 338

as Jewish philosopher, 337

law and, 347

Levinas and, 100, 100n42, 102n51

moral thinking and, 269

the old thinking and the new thinking, 90, 100

revelation and, 95–96, 100, 102–103, 103n57, 179n12, 201, 213–214, 221, 353

time, eschatology, history and, 208, 213, 217, 220–221, 396

totality and, 95, 95n22, 96, 101–103

Ross, W. D., 75n49, 248n66

Rothman, William, 268n144

Rousseau, Jean-Jacques, 24, 136, 275, 286, 340

Rowe, William, 175n6

Rubenstein, Richard, 357–358

rule following, 249–253

Russia, 10, 12, 247

Rwanda, xii, 122, 354, 364

Sabra and Chatila massacres, 20–21, 31, 33, 259, 406, 410–412, 457

sacred, the, 176–177, 180–181, 183, 206

sacrifice, 132, 171, 201, 402, 419

Sadat, Anwar, 30–31, 408–409

said, saying, 131, 134, 138, 155–156, 161, 185, 187, 187n43, 201–202, 222, 243, 394, 413, 423, 448; *see also* discourse, language

the infinite and, 190

as response to Derrida's critique, 301, 304–305

skepticism, philosophy, and, 308–312, 314–318, 320

saints, saintliness, 297

same, 42, 89, 97; *see also* self

imperialism of, 92, 96

the infinite as irreducible to, 91

put into question by the other, 68

reduction of other to, 89, 95–96, 397

Sandel, Michael, 230

Sanhedrin, 394

Sarajevo, 122, 367

Sartre, Jean-Paul, 62n3

Scanlon, T. M., 229n2, 237, 243n50, 267, 416n1, 428–429, 443n101

Scheffler, Samuel, 436

Schelling, F. W. J., 90, 178

Scholem, Gershom, 30n97, 337, 353, 371, 382–383, 386, 391, 398

Schopenhauer, Arthur, 124
Searle, John, 127
second nature, 162, 168–169, 172, 249, 259;
    see also McDowell
secularism, 204–205
self, xvi, 41–42, 209; *see also* ego
    Davidson and, 162–167, 172
    Fichte and, 71n32
    intentionality and, 49, 52
    Levinas's conception of, 80, 143,
        148–173
    McDowell and, 162, 167–169, 172
    modernity and, 144–149
    passivity of, 80, 82, 143, 154–158, 185,
        303, 443
    perfectionism and, 274–277, 277n184,
        279–283
    as responsibility, 92n15, 230, 233, 313,
        428
    substitution and, 82, 303
    Taylor and, 162, 169–173, 263–266
Sellars, Wilfrid, 89, 117n6, 424
sense, 118, 123, 133; *see also* meaning,
    signification
    Derrida and, 326
    the face and, 115, 119–121, 121n22,
        122–124, 142
    noema and, 49
sensibility, 107, 128–129, 247–248, 423
    Jewish, 396, 398
    modern, 205
    moral, ethical, 30, 169, 202, 249n73,
        251, 372, 411–412
    religious, 198
    as responsibility, 253, 257
Septuagint, 388–389, 392–394
Shakespeare, William, 379, 379n187,
    393
shame, 93, 93n19, 94, 97
Shaposhnikova, Alexandra, 4
Shaposhnikova, Yevgenia, 4–5, 46
Shaw, Joshua, 238n25
signification, 122, 125–127, 133, 220
    cultural, 119
    theological concepts and, 181
Simmel, Georg, 210n4, 396

sin, 350; *see also* evil
    doctrine of original, 296n247
Sinai, 5, 186n35, 394–395, 413
sincerity, 185
Singer, Peter, 83n74, 243n50, 267
singularity (ipseity), 126–127, 131
Six Day War, 259, 403–404
skepticism, xii, xvi, 99, 259n115
    Cavell and, 76, 76n50, 283n208, 315n61,
        320n77, 379n187
    Derrida and, 55n44
    examination of, 12
    Kant, 87
    Levinas and, 305–306, 306n26, 307,
        310–311, 311n47, 312–316, 316n61,
        317–320, 334
    moral, 53, 55
    motivation for, 55
    transcendental philosophy and, 51,
        53–54
Smith, Nicholas, 169–171, 204, 263n126,
    265–267
social contract, 40, 105, 405; *see also* Hobbes
socialism, 9–10, 14, 28, 354
sociality, 25, 27, 64, 70–71, 75, 238, 286,
    291, 293, 301; *see also* community
society, 40, 107–109, 112–114, 119, 132,
    172, 192–193, 215, 232n15, 398, 456
    diachrony and, 222
    the face and, 191, 288, 454
    justice in, 244, 286
    liberal, 272
    modern, 204, 246n61
    neutralism and, 271
    Nietzsche and, 280–281
Socrates, 92n15, 144, 415
Soloveitchik, Joseph, 205n94, 337, 346, 371
Soviet Union, xii, 2
speech, 43, 73, 125–127, 131, 137, 262, 419;
    see also discourse, language
    act, 131, 140, 314
    conditions of, 327–328
    Davidson and, 140
    face-to-face and, 134–135, 137, 178,
        301–302
    God and, 201–202

responsibility and, 133–134, 141
skepticism and, 311
totality and, 304
Spengler, Oswald, 398
Spinoza, Baruch, 41, 54, 56, 88, 175n5,
    261, 281, 383n209, 396, 432n50
  election and, 346
  God and, 175
  hermeneutics and, 382–383
  Nature and, 196
  the self and, 146, 148–150
Stalin, Joseph, 10, 339
Stalingrad, 6, 12–13
  Battle of, xv, 2–3
Stalinism, xii, 2, 7, 9–11, 14–17, 23, 25, 31,
    112, 122, 230–231, 235, 243, 259n115,
    262, 339–340, 354, 364, 451
state, 3, 10, 29, 112, 195, 204, 232, 245,
    288, 310, 340, 404–405, 450, 456;
    see also politics
  church and, 28, 195
  ethical, 23, 450–451
  ethics and, 23–25, 451, 451n129
  the face and, 232, 243, 286
  freedom and, 287
  Hobbesian, 23, 23n69, 40, 287, 455–456
  Jewish, 21–22, 29, 32, 346, 401, 403,
    405, 408, 414
  legitimacy of, 22–25, 23n67
  Levinasian, 23–24
  liberal, 272, 276, 286, 292–293, 463
  messianic, 29–30
  Moses Mendelssohn and, 24n74,
    287n227
  peace and, 26–28
  totalitarian, 23, 285, 450
state of nature, 40, 42, 105, 286–287
Strasbourg, 14n45
Strauss, Leo, 246n61
Strawson, P. F., 51
Stroud, Barry, 51
study, 296, 349–350, 371
  Halakhah, 348
  of Talmud in relation to responsibility
    and the face, 337
  of Torah, 348, 373

subject, *see* self
subjectivity, xvi, 82, 126, 143–173, 444
substance, 41, 151
substitution, 82, 132, 143, 155–159, 163, 173,
    183, 192, 201–202, 228n1, 244, 292,
    303–304, 421, 443
suffering, 42n8, 162, 211, 217n28, 300,
    301n2, 337n5, 341–342, 386; *see also*
    evil
  alleviation of, 204–207, 229n3, 233,
    241, 368, 420
  Cavell and, 77, 279
  David Bakhurst and, 118n9
  experienced as other, 153n39
  expressed in the face, 5, 19, 57, 68n22,
    75–76, 78–79, 85, 93, 106, 375
  God's, 350, 352
  Hermann Cohen and, 62n3
  the Holocaust, evil, and, 13, 16–17, 353,
    355, 358–370
  as incomprehensible, 18–19
  Jewish, 18, 21, 336, 342–343, 346, 371,
    390, 407–409
  of the other, 26, 115, 163, 182, 188,
    196, 198, 206, 214, 229n2, 230, 256,
    279–280, 285, 294, 299, 332, 334,
    340, 362–363, 427
  prayer and, 350–352
  as a reason for action, 421, 424–426,
    426n13, 427–428, 433, 439, 443,
    447–448, 464–465
  the twentieth century and, xv, 9, 11, 15,
    17
  work and, 153–154
Swinburne, Richard, 175n6

Talmud, 2n2, 29, 118n13, 337, 344, 349,
    351–352, 379n187, 380–393, 403,
    405, 412–413
  forgiveness and, 458–461
  revelation and, 372–373, 375
  ritual, law, and, 376
  Tractate Baba Kama, 392
  Tractate Makkoth, 385
  Tractate Megillah, 388–389
  Tractate Yoma, 458–459

Taylor, Charles, xii–xiv, 19, 124, 274n168,
      290
   ethics and, 230, 263–268
   the good and, 101, 169–171, 177
   as a moral perfectionist, 271
   philosophy and, 85n2
   religion, theology, God, and, 172, 177,
      204–207
   the self and, 148, 162, 169–173
   shame and, 93, 93n20, 94
Tel Aviv, 341, 458n159
temporality, 208, 212, 217, 220–223
   of human existence, 210–211, 213, 221,
      225–226
   of human experience, 210
   skepticism and, 311
tenderness, 129–130
testimony, 201–202
thematization, 81, 126, 184, 310
theodicy, 341
   end of, 13, 17–19, 337n5, 357–358,
      362–364, 366, 368–369
   the Holocaust, evil, and, 17, 355–369
   theology without, 225
there-is, 40, 151, 151n27, 153n39, 195–197,
      300, 301n2, 302, 321, 332
theology, 10, 151n27, 178, 187, 202, 307,
      372, 373n159, 378, 379n187,
      381
   critique of, 175n6
   natural, 198–199, 203, 328
   negative, 328
   philosophical, 89, 175n6
   philosophy and, 174–177
   traditional, 55n42, 180, 193
   without theodicy, 225
third party, 24n73, 113–114, 136–137,
      141–142, 244, 340, 394, 417–418;
      see also sociality
   justice and, 110–111, 138, 192, 218, 243,
      285, 309, 387, 449, 453, 455
   responsibility and, 452–455
Thoreau, Henry David, 16n53, 272
Tillich, Paul, 176, 182
time, 208–209
   Levinas and, xvi, 210–227
   objective, 212–213, 223, 225

Rosenzweig and, 213–214, 220–221
   subjective, 212–213, 223
Torah, 342, 344, 348, 350, 381, 383,
      388–389, 394–395, 414
   oral and written, 371–372
totalitarianism, 3, 10n35, 17, 243, 246n61,
      289, 336n2, 364, 433, 451–452;
      see also Hitlerism, Nazism, Stalinism
   Nazi, 12–13, 16, 38
   of the Same, 96
totality, xvi, 11, 20n60, 25, 27, 42, 65, 67,
      88, 149, 215, 235, 259n115, 269,
      373n159, 386
   beyond, transcends, outside of, or not
      included in, 53, 58, 119, 131, 153,
      200, 225, 300–301, 322, 332, 378
   bound to, 322–323
   breach, 80, 86–87, 108, 369, 374
   critique of, 113, 261, 374, 397
   Davidson's theory of the self as a, 165
   diachrony and, 305
   escape of, 3, 101
   as everyday, ordinary world, 48, 87, 104,
      112, 152
   features of the self as, 161
   Graham Priest and, 325–326
   Greek as language of, 338
   as idealism, 100
   language, speech, and, 300, 304
   partial truth of, 106
   phenomenology and, 115n1
   in relation to the infinite, 47, 56, 108,
      115n1, 388n236
   religion, theology, God, and, 177
   representation and, 283–284
   Rosenzweig and, 95, 101–103
   sufficiency of, 103
   unavoidability of, 108, 387
trace, 122, 131, 184, 184n31, 187–194,
      198–199, 201, 203, 207, 307, 309,
      320, 322–323, 325, 389, 413; *see also*
      diachrony, *illeity*
translation, 340, 380, 387–388, 388n236,
      389–395
triangulation, 138–139; *see also* Davidson
truth, 115, 125, 163–164
   ineffable, 325, 330, 333

language and, 139–141
  moral, 247–248, 250, 253
  skepticism and, 306, 316–318, 320n77
Tutsis, 364n119, 365

United States, 16n53, 82n73, 176
universalism, 412
  Israel's, 402
  Jewish, 343–344, 381, 401, 414
  Levinas's, 259
  moral, 230, 234
  of Zionism, 408
universality, 74, 79, 108, 125, 131, 233, 338,
    340, 413, 423, 438
  Jewish, 338, 345–346, 393–394
  of Talmud, 392
utilitarianism, xvi, 75n49, 229, 229n3, 278,
    297, 422n3, 428, 434, 436
  direct, 289n235
Urmson, J. O., 298n254
utopia, 25

value, 84, 118, 182, 229n2, 259, 267,
    333–334, 427, 429–431, 435–445,
    448, 457, 464–465
  challenge to, 176
  crisis of, 396–397
  of humanity, 254, 256
  intersubjective, 446–447
  moral, 228, 435, 449, 466
  objectivity of moral, xi, 51
  shame and, 93
  Taylor and, 169–172, 265–266
  the there-is and, 196
  Wolf, morality, and, 298
Vichy Regime, 35n108
violence, 9–10, 23, 27, 69, 81, 215, 230,
    315n61, 338–340, 451; *see also* war
virtue, 417
  of character, 249, 271
  McDowell and, 249–252, 252n90, 254
  O'Neill and, 236–237, 240–242, 245
vocative, 64
vulnerability, 245
  of the other, 58, 67, 75n49, 121, 123,
    193, 196, 222
  of the self, 156

Wallace, R. Jay, 228n2, 250n78, 289n235,
    415n1
Walzer, Michael, 19, 230
war, 24–29, 31, 69, 132, 134, 215–216, 230,
    245–246, 287, 397, 409; *see also*
    peace, violence
Warsaw Ghetto, 341; *see also* Holocaust
Weber, Max, 210n4
Western civilization, culture, xvi, 17, 338,
    396, 412–413
  anti-Semitism and, 336n2
  crisis of, 31, 38
  critique of, 86, 108
  decline of, 1, 397
  failure of, 18, 20n60, 399
  Israel and, 21
  Jewish texts and, 388–390, 392
  totality and, 300
  value of Jews, Judaism for, 336, 353,
    390
Wheeler, Samuel C., 328n121
White, Hayden, 117n9
Wiesel, Elie, 357
Wiggins, David, 233n18, 248, 462n179
Williams, Bernard, 12, 66–67, 67n20,
    162n62, 196n69, 234, 290, 323, 407,
    430, 436
Windelband, Wilhelm, 124, 209
wisdom, 249, 310
witness, 185, 185n35, 186–188, 191, 202,
    303n9; *see also* prophecy
Wittgenstein, Ludwig, xii, 12, 45, 58–60,
    60n50, 90, 93n17, 116, 116n4, 168,
    248n66, 321
  Cavell and, 76–78, 251, 269, 272–274,
    277
  ineffability, nonsense, and, 323–334
  McDowell's indebtedness to,
    259
  meaning and, 120, 124n31, 127
  pain and, 257
  private language argument, 133, 135,
    138–139, 255
  religion, theology, God, and, 176
  rule following and, 249–252,
    252n93
  the self and, 150

Wolf, Susan, 297–298
Wolterstorff, Nicholas, 175n6
Woolf, Virginia, 3
work, 49, 69, 150–151, 153–154, 162, 225–226, 460
World War I, xii, 367, 396–397
World War II, 2, 12, 33, 341
Wright, Tamra, 16n54, 45n17, 50–51, 337n6, 354, 376–378, 390

Wyschogrod, Edith, 25, 353, 376–378, 390
Wyschogrod, Michael, 205n94, 346

Xenocrates, 112n75

Zionism, 20, 397n264, 405; *see also* Israel
  Levinas and, 13, 20n61, 28–32, 337, 400–401, 407–409, 411–413
  Zionist World Congress, 341

LaVergne, TN USA
09 July 2010
188923LV00004B/1/P